Social Psychology

Second Edition

Sara Miller McCune founded SAGE Publishing in 1965 to support the dissemination of usable knowledge and educate a global community. SAGE publishes more than 1000 journals and over 600 new books each year, spanning a wide range of subject areas. Our growing selection of library products includes archives, data, case studies and video. SAGE remains majority owned by our founder and after her lifetime will become owned by a charitable trust that secures the company's continued independence.

Los Angeles | London | New Delhi | Singapore | Washington DC | Melbourne

Social Psychology
Second Edition

Thomas Heinzen
William Paterson University

Wind Goodfriend
Buena Vista University

⑤SAGE

Los Angeles | London | New Delhi
Singapore | Washington DC | Melbourne

$\circledS$SAGE

FOR INFORMATION:

SAGE Publications, Inc.
2455 Teller Road
Thousand Oaks, California 91320
E-mail: order@sagepub.com

SAGE Publications Ltd.
1 Oliver's Yard
55 City Road
London EC1Y 1SP
United Kingdom

SAGE Publications India Pvt. Ltd.
B 1/I 1 Mohan Cooperative Industrial Area
Mathura Road, New Delhi 110 044
India

SAGE Publications Asia-Pacific Pte. Ltd.
18 Cross Street #10-10/11/12
China Square Central
Singapore 048423

Acquisitions Editor: Lara Parra
Editorial Assistant: Elizabeth Cruz
Content Development Editor: Chelsea Neve
Production Editor: Andrew Olson
Copy Editor: Gillian Dickens
Typesetter: C&M Digitals (P) Ltd.
Proofreader: Barbara Coster
Indexer: Integra
Cover Designer: Gail Buschman
Marketing Manager: Katherine Hepburn

Printed in Canada

Library of Congress Cataloging-in-Publication Data

Names: Heinzen, Thomas E., author. | Goodfriend, Wind, author.

Title: Social psychology / Thomas Heinzen, William Paterson University, Wind Goodfriend, Buena Vista University.

Description: Second edition. | Thousand Oaks, California : SAGE, [2022] | Includes bibliographical references and index.

Identifiers: LCCN 2020032780 | ISBN 9781544393513 (paperback) | ISBN 9781071834961 | ISBN 9781544393483 (epub) | ISBN 9781544393490 (epub) | ISBN 9781544393506 (pdf)

Subjects: LCSH: Social psychology.

Classification: LCC HM1033 .H456 2022 | DDC 302—dc23
LC record available at https://lccn.loc.gov/2020032780

This book is printed on acid-free paper.

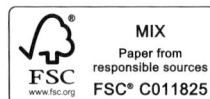

MIX
Paper from responsible sources
FSC
www.fsc.org
FSC® C011825

20 21 22 23 24 10 9 8 7 6 5 4 3 2 1

BRIEF CONTENTS

DETAILED CONTENTS

iStockPhoto/SerrNovik

FABRICE COFFRINI/AFP via Getty Images

iStockPhoto/stop123

Photo of Creation of Adam, fresco painted by Michelangelo (1475–1564), Sistine Chapel Ceiling (1508–1512) by Jörg Bittner Unna

CHAPTER 8. Group Processes   182

Don Bartlett/Los Angeles Times/Getty Images

Christopher Furlong/Getty Images News/Getty Images

CHAPTER 9. Stereotyping, Prejudice, and Discrimination 212

iStock/dimarik

Time & Life Pictures/The LIFE Picture Collection/Getty Images

APPLIED MINI-CHAPTERS

iStockPhoto/fizkes

iStockPhoto/SDI Productions

PREFACE

TO STUDENTS

We—Tom and Wind—*love* social psychology.

We've written this book with the sincere hope that you'll love it too, from the first page to the last. We want you to really enjoy your reading homework, to look forward to each chapter, and to want to keep the book as a reference. We know that's an ambitious goal, but we really think it can happen.

Here's what we have learned after many years of teaching: Social psychology will surprise you. Some insights will be pleasant; others will be disturbing. That is why how you experience your life after social psychology will be different, deeper, and probably better for you—and for everyone around you. You will gain the most if you dare to bring the honest questions hidden in the back of your mind out into the open in front of the class. Ask your professor, ask each other. Engaging in the material with a scientific curiosity is how we got hooked on social psychology ourselves.

Parts of this book were written with the hope that they will remind you of some important themes and questions to keep in mind. The features focus on three things:

1. The scientific, research-based story of social psychology. The feature called Spotlight on Research Methods reminds you of important methodology and statistical terms by highlighting an important, innovative, or controversial study in each chapter.

2. The social psychology all around you. The feature called Social Psychology in Popular Culture emphasizes concepts and theories from the book that can be seen in movies, TV shows, and songs. We hope that when you're relaxing with your favorite show, you can't help but think, "Hey, we just talked about that in my social psych class!"

3. How social psychology applies to you. Every chapter takes you through a What's My Score? feature, in which you can take a survey to see your own score on a variable developed by researchers. These surveys will help you see how various concepts relate to you, personally, and you'll also gain a better understanding of how the concept is studied by social psychologists. If you really get passionate about the field, you might use these surveys in your own research studies someday!

The bottom line is that we hope you really engage in every chapter and idea in the following pages. Social psychology isn't just a bunch of terms and theories—it's every interaction you have, every day, with every other person in your life. What could be more interesting than that?

TO INSTRUCTORS

Thank you for helping us.

We received so many suggestions from helpful reviewers and people who used the first edition of this book. We've incorporated as many of those suggestions as possible here in the second edition, because we saw the wisdom in each idea. We were proud that the first edition won the prize for the "Most Promising New Textbook of 2019" by the Textbook Authors Association. But we knew it could be better, and we couldn't have done that without your help.

Our Features

We sincerely want students to love social psychology as much as we do. To that end, we've included many features that hopefully appeal to modern students. For example, each chapter features a discussion of how concepts can be seen in popular culture. Students who vaguely recognize cultural differences in relationships can rely on our discussion of *Crazy Rich Asians* to better understand individualism versus collectivism, stereotypes, and more. The halo effect is emphasized through *Queer Eye*. Institutional discrimination is analyzed in *The Handmaid's Tale*. Conformity is examined through *The Marvelous Mrs. Maisel*. These features are fun ways to engage students in surprising, exciting ways.

We also create experiences through self-assessments (the What's My Score? feature) that introduce the depth of social psychology. Measuring their own need for cognition (Chapter 4) introduces a new way to experience self-reflection. Experiencing how the just world hypothesis is measured (Chapter 5) connects students to the impulse to blame the victim. Seeing how much their attitudes match those in a culture of honor (Chapter 11) helps them understand the concept and examine whether their beliefs are tied to aggressive tendencies. Again, each chapter provides a self-report scale to engage the students in an important concept. Experiencing social psychology is a deeper, more memorable way to learn.

Psychological literacy creates better citizens. We promote psychological literacy in several explicit ways when we encourage students to critically examine evidence and ask important questions about social phenomena. Every section of the book ends with a summary of main ideas, but—more important—we offer critical thinking questions. These can be used as discussion starters in class, or they can be the prompts for homework assignments given to students each week. Several are offered so that instructors or students can choose the questions of most interest to them.

Reminding students of the science behind social psychology is also an essential goal. Our Spotlight on Research Methods features, embedded in every chapter, remind students of important methodological and statistical terms. Students learn these in Chapter 2, but we don't want to isolate that chapter from the rest of the material. By using the terms repeatedly and explicitly highlighting them in the feature, we can scaffold learning and build a strong foundation of science.

The Mini-Chapters

Response to the inclusions of applied mini-chapters in the first edition was extremely enthusiastic! We're happy to share that these have been updated along with the main text. First, we've added two completely new ones, one on careers relevant to social psychology and realistic without a doctorate degree, and another on the fascinating relationship between pets and their humans. For those interested, there's a third new option on the social psychology of the military (for custom orders).

The mini-chapters also now follow a consistent format, with only two sections per mini. Just like the main chapters have new consistency with three sections, having a standard structure for the mini provides a predictable, accessible experience for students. And the content of the minis has been updated as well—there are a total of 242 new references, not counting those in the custom military mini.

A quick word on how to use the minis: Of course, it's up to you, but we encourage allowing students to be involved in which minis are addressed. Wind allows her class to vote on which chapters are covered at the end of the semester, and essay responses to the critical thinking questions are submitted for extra credit. Involving students in the choice of which to cover empowers them and gets them even more excited about the material. You could also allow each student to choose one mini and write an essay about how it could apply to their future career choice. Finally, you don't have to wait until the end of the semester; you might assign minis throughout the semester as a way for students to see various applications of earlier theories.

How you use the minis in your own class is flexible, but we hope they provide a fun and customizable experience to every instructor.

Changes in the Second Edition

Here's a bulleted list of some of the major changes you'll probably notice in the second edition, compared to the first:

- Every chapter has been revised to be in three sections, instead of varying from three to six. This way, students feel comfortable as they approach each chapter and know what to expect without feeling overwhelmed.

- Several of the popular culture features have been updated to focus on newer movies or TV series that students will know. *My Cousin Vinny, Remember the Titans,* and *Mean Girls* are gone, for example, and replaced by *Crazy Rich Asians, Mulan, The Handmaid's Tale,* and *The Marvelous Mrs. Maisel.*

- More research has been added on cultural differences and on advances from neuropsychology throughout the book.

- Language and examples have been updated throughout to be even more sensitive to diversity and to be gender inclusive. For example, when discussing a fictional or theoretical person, the pronoun "they" is always used (instead of "he" or "she") to avoid a false gender binary. Discussion of intersectionality now occurs several times as well, plus analysis of the social psychology of the #MeToo movement.

- Throughout, the glossary and marginal term definitions have been streamlined to be much shorter and accessible, but still accurate.

- Chapter 2 (Research Methods) now includes a hefty section on the importance of open science.

- Even more critical thinking and criticisms are discussed regarding the famous Zimbardo and Milgram studies in Chapter 7.

- In the main 12 chapters, well over 300 total new citations have been added. Of these, about two thirds were published in 2015 or later.

- Two brand-new mini-chapters have been added: "Social Psychology and Careers" and "Social Psychology of Humans and Their Pets." We hope these provide fun and important perspectives on aspects of social life to which almost every student can relate.

If you're looking for more detail, here's a chapter-by-chapter list of major changes.

Chapter 1

- Now in three major sections instead of four
- More discussion of intersectionality
- Updated list of people who have contributed to social psychology who are women and/or people of color
- List of "Big Questions" streamlined from 10 questions to 6
- Popular culture updates now include *Black Panther, Black Mirror,* and *The Handmaid's Tale*

Chapter 2

- Now in three major sections instead of four
- Popular culture updates now include *21 Jump Street* as an example of participant observation
- A large new section has been added on the open science movement

Chapter 3

- Now in three major sections instead of five
- Popular culture updates now include *Get Out* and *Crazy Rich Asians*
- Example of a circus ringmaster has been removed, to be more animal rights friendly
- Clarity in definitions and examples for self-perception theory, self-discrepancy theory, self-expansion theory, and positive illusions
- More balanced approach to the discussion of elevated self-esteem
- Provided more accurate discussion of the mark test in animals
- Forty-seven new references to update research

Chapter 4

- Now in three major sections instead of five
- Provided a trigger warning for the opening example about military conflict
- Changed photo of woman trying to open door, to avoid gender stereotypes
- Updated examples students reported as confusing
- Clarified explanation of mental accessibility
- Corrected example of representativeness heuristic
- Added more to the explanation of the planning fallacy, to discuss examples of students running out of time for assignments

Chapter 5

- Now in three major sections instead of five
- Clarified discussion of micro-expressions
- Added discussion of Weiner's three-step model of attributions
- Added examples of culturemes
- Popular culture updates now include a discussion of *Queer Eye* and the halo effect. Also changed Kevin Spacey example to Helena Bonham Carter
- Photo of Hillary Clinton and Trump updated to reflect more recent politicians
- Nineteen new references to update research

Chapter 6

- Now in three major sections instead of six
- In general, shortened the chapter to make it more approachable for students. Also rearranged concepts to flow better
- Lightened language regarding the famous Bob Kelly case to decrease possible student reactions to childhood sexual assault
- Popular culture updates now include a discussion of persuasion in *Moneyball*
- Seventeen new references to update research

Chapter 7

- Now in three major sections instead of four
- Changed opening photo to avoid unintended messaging about college parties
- Popular culture updates now include a discussion of conformity in *The Marvelous Mrs. Maisel*
- Emphasized current criticisms of the Stanford Prison Study (and changed from "Stanford Prison Experiment" to "Study")
- More discussion of alternative explanations for the results of Milgram's study
- Twenty-seven new references to update research

Chapter 8

- Now in three major sections instead of five
- Generally streamlined to make the chapter shorter and more accessible
- Removed reference to Sacajawea due to reviewer concerns
- Popular culture updates now discuss *The Avengers* instead of *Justice League*
- Added note of the failed replication of the Zajonc cockroach study
- Forty-seven new references to update research

Chapter 9

- Now in three major sections instead of five
- Popular culture updates removed *Remember the Titans* and *2 Broke Girls* and replaced them with *Mulan* and *The Handmaid's Tale*
- Added discussion of institutional discrimination
- Clarified the discussion of the Clark doll studies for accuracy
- Added paragraph questioning the validity of jigsaw classrooms
- Sixty-three new references to update research

Chapter 10

- Updated opening examples to discuss people working against anti-Semitic hate crimes in New York
- Shortened the chapter overall to make it more accessible to students
- Added discussions on neuropsychology and mirror neurons
- Added discussion of the social psychology of the #MeToo movement
- Added more on the dark triad
- Added a paragraph in the gender norms section regarding the false gender binary
- Thirty-five new references to update research

Chapter 11

- Now in three major sections instead of five
- Updated discussion on micro-aggressions

- Added the General Aggression Model
- Updated the discussion of the role of testosterone in aggression based on analysis provided by R. Sapolsky's book *Behave*
- Forty-four new references to update research

Chapter 12

- Now in three major sections instead of five
- Generally shorter chapter, due to reviewer suggestions it was too long
- Added Sternberg's triangular theory of love
- Expanded discussion on cross-cultural differences in relationships, specifically regarding arranged marriages and marriage motives
- Reduced discussion of both attachment theory and interdependence theory
- Updated popular culture chapter opening to discuss Beyoncé and Jay-Z instead of Jennifer Aniston and Brad Pitt. Also replaced symmetry example of Denzel Washington with George Clooney and Kim Kardashian

Teaching Resources

This text includes an array of instructor teaching materials designed to save you time and to help you keep students engaged. To learn more, visit sagepub.com or contact your SAGE representative at sagepub.com/findmyrep.

In Appreciation and Thanks

We thank reviewers for their detailed suggestions and corrections. We know we'll get better because (a) we enjoy getting better, and (b) reviewers will tell us how to get better. Good writing, like good science, grows through candid feedback. And for that, we have many people to thank.

The Textbook Author's Association has been a remarkable, unexpected resource. We encourage fellow teachers and future authors to use their many resources. Fortunately, there is a wealth of material about good writing. Two sources have been particularly helpful: *On Writing Well* by William Zinsser (1991) and the importance of storytelling in *Talks to Teachers on Psychology and to Students on Some of Life's Ideals* by William James (1899/1983).

Thank you also to the many people who adopted our first edition and offered excellent feedback on how to make it better. Specific thanks are due to a few people in particular who reached out personally. Major Drew Bond gave us a personal tour of West Point and gave us the idea to add a customizable mini-chapter on the military. Thanks to Brett Pelham, who corrected an example we used to have on heuristics. Amy Brown thoughtfully sent us a correction on one of our references.

To Lara, Chelsea, Jen, Katherine, all the reviewers, SAGE, Donna and Shawn, Carl Sagan, and the Amazing Randi.

SAGE Publishing wishes to thank the following reviewers for their input on the second edition:

Jeffery Gray, Charleston Southern University

Cicely K. Johnson, Brooklyn College

Maysa DeSousa, Springfield College

Lynise M Carr, Psychology Curriculum Specialist at Robert Morris University

Erin Dupuis, Loyola University New Orleans

Urvi Paralkar, Southern Illinois University Carbondale

Anthony E. Coy, University of South Florida Sarasota-Manatee

Renee Boburka, East Stroudsburg University

Elizabeth A. Melles, Northeastern State University

Edie McClellan, Midway University

Erin M. Myers, Western Carolina University

April K. Dye, Carson-Newman University

Cari Stevenson, Kankakee Community College

Maria Gritsch, California State University

Liz Wright, Northwest Vista College

Matt Diggs, Collin College

Amy Martin, Rockford University

Christopher A. Verwys, Rensselaer Polytechnic Institute

Kelly Henderson, Langston University

Caitlin M. Lapine, Touro College

Deana Julka, University of Portland

Donald W. Knox, Jr., Wayland Baptist University

We would also like to acknowledge the reviewers from the first edition:

Aaron J. Moss, Tulane University

Amanda ElBassiouny, Spring Hill College

Amy E. Sickel, Walden University

Beverly L. Stiles, Midwestern State University

Catherine A. Cottrell, New College of Florida

Corey Hunt, Grand Canyon University

Crystal M. Kreitler, Angelo State University

Daniel W. Barrett, Western Connecticut State University

Darin Challacombe, Fort Hays State University

David E. Oberleitner, University of Bridgeport

Emily A. Leskinen, Carthage College

Gregory D. Webster, University of Florida

James Cornwell, United States Military Academy

Jay L. Michaels, University of South Florida Sarasota-Manatee

John E. Myers, Northern Arizona University

Julee Poole, Kaplan University

Kristina Howansky, Rutgers University

Leah R. Warner, Ramapo College of New Jersey

Maya Aloni, Western Connecticut State University

xxiv   SOCIAL PSYCHOLOGY

Melissa Streeter, University of North Carolina Wilmington

Miranda E. Bobrowski, University at Buffalo, SUNY

Okori Uneke, Winston-Salem State University

Pamela Lemons, Salt Lake Community College

Patricia Schoenrade, William Jewell College

R. Shane Westfall, University of Nevada, Las Vegas

Rebekah A. Wanic, University of San Diego

Shayn Lloyd, Tallahassee Community College

Tammy Lowery Zacchilli, Saint Leo University

Wendy P. Heath, Rider University

Yvonne Wells, Suffolk University

ABOUT THE AUTHORS

Thomas Heinzen is Professor Emeritus of William Paterson University of New Jersey. He describes his career as "mostly fun" because of the diverse opportunities within social psychology. Most applications have revolved around the social psychology of creativity including

- Individual differences among the Johns Hopkins University Center for Talented Youth
- Program Assessment for the Rockefeller College of Public Affairs and Policy
- Agent Orange health statistics for the New York State Commission on Vietnam Veterans
- Technology assessment related to distance learning for Public Service Training Program
- Tractor rollovers for the New York Center for Health and Medicine
- Documentations of problem-solving among pre-retirement New York State bureaucrats
- Documentations of problem-solving among the frail elderly living in nursing homes
- Applications of game design to curriculum development

Professor Heinzen invested in students' lives by mentoring more than 60 student conference presentations. More recently, he created video games that teach critical thinking and the unwritten rules of college success.

He also has authored several books and published journal articles based on case studies, archival analyses, in-depth interviews, controlled experiments, and quasi-experimental designs. He has been elected a fellow of the Eastern Psychological Association (EPA), the American Psychological Association (APA, Division 1), and the Association for Psychological Science (APS).

Wind Goodfriend has been teaching psychology at Buena Vista University, a Midwestern liberal arts school for 15 years. Wind is a three-time Faculty of the Year award winner. She became Chair of Social Sciences in 2019. She also serves as the co-director of the gender studies program and volunteers as the chief research officer for the Institute for the Prevention of Relationship Violence. Wind has written 15 book chapters on psychology in pop culture, covering topics including *Game of Thrones, Wonder Woman, Doctor Who, Star Trek*, and more. She has developed a wide variety of undergraduate courses including special topics classes such as Psychology of Colonialism, Psychology in Popular Film, and Relationship Violence. She received her B.A. from Buena Vista University and both her Master's and Ph.D. in Social Psychology from Purdue University.

iStockPhoto/SerrNovik

1 An Introduction to Social Psychology

Core Questions

1.1 What is social psychology?

1.2 What are some big questions within social psychology?

1.3 How can social psychology make my life better now?

Learning Objectives

1.1 Explain social psychology's origin story and what social psychologists do now.

1.2 Analyze important questions about social thought and behavior.

1.3 Apply social psychological concepts to your own life and experiences.

- A man on the street is having a seizure, but no one else seems concerned. What would you do?

- Seven people, including you, around a table have been asked to say which of three lines matches the length of a fourth line. The correct answer is obvious: Line 2. But the first six people declare "Line 1." It's your turn to provide an answer. What would you do?

- You're being paid to participate in a scientific study about memory and learning. Your job is to press a switch that delivers electric shocks each time another participant makes a memory error. You're supposed to increase the shock level each time, but the highest levels are labeled "DANGER: SEVERE SHOCK." What would you do?

Social situations are powerful.

These scenes aren't from the popular reality television show *What Would You Do?* on ABC. They are real experiments in social psychology. So…what would you do? If you are like most people, you probably answered, "I would help the man having a seizure even if no one else appeared concerned," "I would report the correct line no matter what other people said," and "I would never administer dangerous electric shocks to an innocent person." Your beliefs about yourself would probably be noble, flattering, and self-esteem enhancing. But there is a good chance that you would be wrong. Why? You probably underestimated the power of the immediate social situation.

In controlled experiments, a high percentage did *not* help the man who had a seizure (Darley & Latané, 1968). Many people *did* cave in to peer pressure when reporting the length of the line (Asch, 1956). And a frightening number of people delivered the highest possible level of electric shock—even when the other person (an actor who was secretly not really harmed) screamed in pain that he had a heart condition (Milgram, 1963, 1974).

Get ready for an exciting—but sometimes disturbing—ride of self-discovery as you enter the fascinating world of social psychology.

WHAT IS SOCIAL PSYCHOLOGY?

>> **LO 1.1:** Explain social psychology's origin story and what social psychologists do now.

Someone is going to change your life.

That person could be a friend slipping away into substance abuse, a caring grandparent, a disappointing romantic partner, an inspiring teacher, a manipulative cult leader, or a frustrating coworker. Their influence may harm or help; they're all out there, waiting for someone just like you to cross their path.

Social psychology is the scientific study of how people influence each other's thoughts, feelings, and behaviors. Someone—and probably several people—will influence the curve of your life, just as you will influence others. Some social influences are obvious; a robber with a gun clearly wants to influence you to hand over your money.

Reuters/Claro Cortes

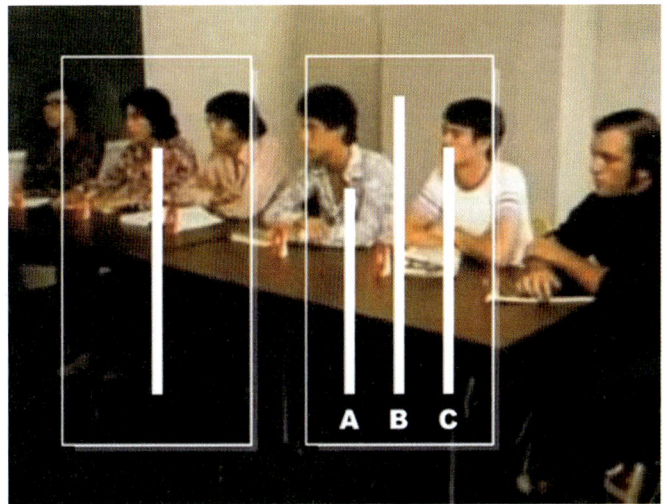
D-janous via Wikimedia Commons

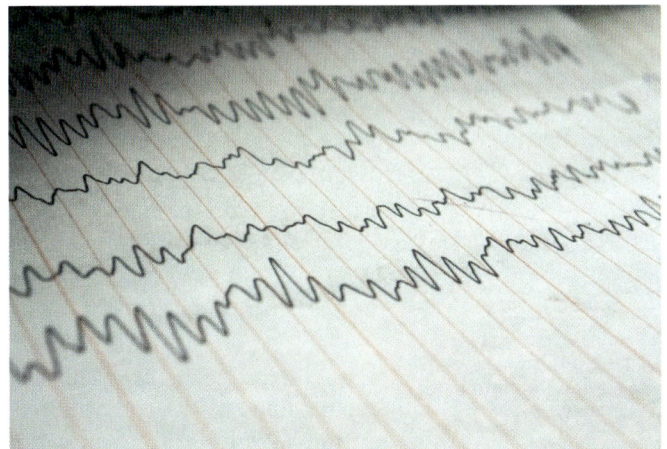
© istockphoto.com/VarvaraShu

Social psychology: The scientific study of how people influence each other's thoughts, feelings, and behaviors.

But many social influences are subtle; for example, advertisers try to influence you with earworms (melodies that get stuck in your head) and attractive models.

We can be influenced even when we are alone. We may change our clothes or choose what to post to Facebook because we worry about someone's opinion. One of our students persevered in college by imagining what it would mean to her own children if she were the first in her family to graduate from college. We also are subtly influenced by cultural expectations, social roles, and legal guidelines.

The Origins of Social Psychology

If you love high stakes—epic stories such *The Avengers* or *Game of Thrones*—then you might love social psychology.

The birthing pains of social psychology were epic, violent, and real: World Wars I and II. Sigmund Freud was so "shocked and shaken by the carnage of the Great War" that he perceived a "cosmic struggle" between two dueling psychological forces: life and death (see Batson, 2012, pp. 243–244). Freud tried to provide epic answers, most plainly in his book about *Civilization and Its Discontents*. But his answers were often speculative and based on private observations. The early social psychologists wanted more testable, scientific answers to the questions about humanity that arose during and because of the world wars.

Scientific Thinking About Social Problems

Let's go back even further in history. If there's a birthplace for scientific psychology, it's Germany about 150 years ago. In the late 1800s, Wilhelm Wundt started the first scientific laboratory there, specifically designed to apply the scientific method to human thought and experience. Wundt's persistent, pioneering research is why many consider him the "father of psychology." He was also the first person to call himself a psychologist.

Both Wundt and Freud (who was in nearby Austria at about the same time) were asking questions about personality, individual perceptions, and how culture affects thought. Over the next few decades, most Europeans who considered themselves psychologists were interested in explaining abnormal behavior (like Freud) or in basic thought processes like sensory perceptions or memory (like Wundt). Just a few years later, most psychologists in the United States studied nonhuman animals (usually pigeons and rats) because their behavior was easier to observe and measure. Not many scholars were studying everyday social interactions like conformity, prejudice, or heroism.

Weltrundschau zu Reclams Universum 1902

Wilhelm Wundt (1832–1920), now largely considered the "father of psychology."

Social Conflicts and Private Curiosity

Fast forward to those two horrifying world conflicts, which changed the trajectory of psychology forever. The unanticipated, industrial destruction of 16 million people in the first "Great War" startled even those who had organized the conflict. The failure to make peace at the Treaty of Versailles led directly to the deaths of 60 million more people only 20 years later during World War II. Clearly, humanity's self-knowledge had not kept up with its technological advances. It was a call to action within psychology: Researchers realized that studying rats in mazes or psychoanalysis wasn't enough. Social psychology emerged out of the emotional rubble produced by these two devastating world wars.

Those wars are now long behind us—but only in time. Their consequences continue to shape public policies and the story of social psychology. Modern social psychologists are worried about new conflicts rooted in old versions of authoritarianism. We also carry epic anxieties about global warming, environmental sustainability, mass incarceration, legalized torture, cyberbullying, media violence, systematic prejudice, and false confessions of guilt.

Before you get too depressed, know that many social psychologists also are motivated by the more positive side of humanity. Researchers today have labs that study attraction and meaningful sexuality and love, cooperation, why and when strangers will help each other, the motivation to stand up to harmful conformity, and more. The crisscrossing threads holding all these diverse topics together include (a) a focus on the individual and (b) science-based methods.

Technology also has helped social psychologists create thousands of small answers to a few big questions. For example, driving simulators enable us to safely study attempts at mental multitasking while driving. It's a precise, relatively small question, but it helps us understand how humans think. Likewise, software using online surveys captures the strength of beliefs or reactions to images on a computer screen, measured in milliseconds. It's another precise, relatively small applied question that helps us understand basic research about how attitudes can lead to prejudice and discrimination.

You can see the importance of this kind of work when you remember how much time people spend on social media, a world in which images appear on screens for only seconds as people scroll. Virtual reality is increasingly used to monitor how people respond to different social situations, such as practice job interviews, where technology can control social variables such as the sex or race of the person sitting across from you.

Modern social psychologists are trying, through applied and basic research, to equip individuals with the psychological tools they need to walk intelligently—even courageously—deeper into the 21st century.

Applied and basic research join forces in studies using driving simulators. As applied research, driving simulators help us understand the dangers of so-called multitasking (e.g., trying to drive while texting). As basic research, driving simulators help us understand how humans swiftly organize incoming sensations and perceptions from a social world.

Content Domains: Social Thinking, Social Influence, and Social Behavior

The content domains of social psychology are represented in Figure 1.1: social thinking, social influence, and social behavior. The circles in this Venn diagram overlap because we usually experience them as a blend. That is why the first three sections of this book explore each area separately but reunite them in a fourth section of mini-chapters. Each mini-chapter describes how social psychologists apply social psychology to particular social problems.

For example, the first section on social thinking examines how we define the self and make judgments about other people. The second section investigates three consequences of social influence: conformity, prejudice, and persuasion. The third section focuses on social behaviors such as helping, aggression, and romantic relationships. The mini-chapters at the end of the book explore how they intersect with economic decisions, environmental sustainability, criminal justice, and much more.

The Content Domains Represent Career Opportunities

There are at least three reasons why these content domains have turned social psychology into such a popular college course. First, social psychology satisfies some of our curiosity about everyday social interactions. Second, doing social psychology develops marketable skills (described in the mini-chapters). Third, social psychology helps you become a social problem solver. Satisfying curiosity, building marketable skills, and supporting social problem solving are impressive accomplishments for such a young

FIGURE 1.1

These three content domains within social psychology describe the thoughts and decisions people make about one another.

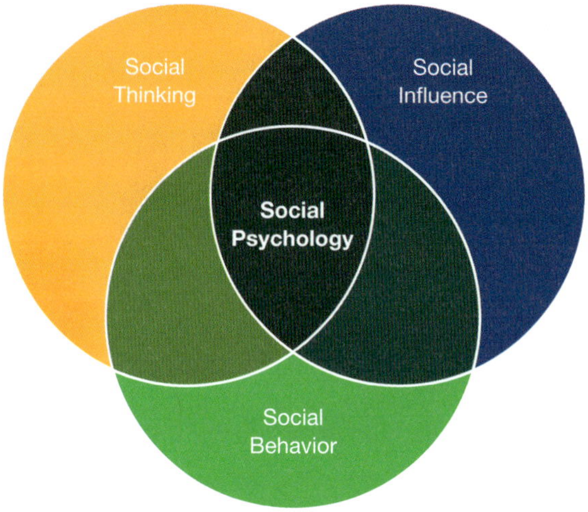

science. By "young," we mean that scientific social psychology is only about 100 years old, give or take a few decades (see Farr, 1996).

Professional organizations suggest a discipline's relevance. The American Psychological Association has a separate division for social and personality psychology. In addition, there are two additional, independent professional organizations: the Society for Personality and Social Psychology and the Society of Experimental Social Psychology. Their conferences are crowded, and there are dozens of textbooks just on social psychology (including this one!). About 185 schools in just the United States offer graduate degrees in social psychology. Perhaps this "young" discipline has finally reached its adolescence.

Social psychologists are active around the world, thanks in part to our ability to communicate and share ideas and data electronically. It is an exciting time to engage with social psychology, both personally and professionally. Who knows? You may want to explore the many career paths available to social psychologists. We will alert you to career opportunities in every chapter, but almost all of them can be categorized as social problem solving. If you hope to solve complex social problems, then you are going to need some strategies and methods that you can rely on.

Distinguishing Among Similar Academic Fields

Academic disciplines are distinguished by their methods and observations (see Table 1.1). What distinguishes social psychology from similar fields?

Sociologists usually explore large social behaviors at a group level, using surveys and demographic data. Anthropologists focus on how culture and behavior change over time with methods that rely on "thick" (detailed) observations, sometimes made from inside the culture. Clinical psychologists focus on mental illnesses or problematic thoughts and behaviors, often working with people predefined as being in a specific population of interest (e.g., people suffering from severe depression).

However, no single discipline has "methodology rights" to any one approach. When social psychology is at its best, it uses multiple methods of scientific approach to answer questions, including a blend of qualitative data (such as interviews with individual people) with quantitative data (such as experiments; see Brannen, 1995). You'll learn more about research methods in Chapter 2.

Sociology: The study of human society and social behavior at the group level.

Anthropology: The study of culture and human behavior over time.

Clinical or counseling psychology: A subfield of psychology that helps people who have maladaptive or problematic thoughts and behaviors.

TABLE 1.1

Different Ways of Asking and Answering Research Questions

	PREFERRED METHODS	FOCUS OF OBSERVATIONS	EXAMPLE: THE STUDY OF AGGRESSION
Sociologists	Surveys, demographic patterns of data	Group-level behaviors and social expectations	Group characteristics of aggressive behavior
Anthropologists	Detailed observations of people in a given culture	A discrete group of people over time	Cultural habits of aggression within a discrete setting
Clinical psychologists	Therapeutic interviews and tests	Individuals who have problematic thoughts or behaviors	Individual and interpersonal causes of aggression
Social psychologists	Controlled experiments and observations	Everyday people in individual or group settings	Experiments testing the causes and control of aggression

For example, almost all social sciences have tried to understand human aggression. (Understanding aggression can lead to psychology careers in policing, criminal justice, forensic psychology, and civil and marriage dispute mediation.) Table 1.1 describes how each discipline tends to rely on slightly different methods to make their distinctive observations.

- A sociologist is most likely to study aggression by creating or consulting demographic data regarding long-term patterns.

- A cultural anthropologist will usually make "thick," detailed observations of how children's aggressive behaviors are influenced by the culture of a particular town or village.

- A clinical psychologist may use interviews to understand aggression at a personal or small group level—and then test therapeutic interventions.

- A social psychologist is more likely to invent a way to (temporarily and safely!) manipulate aggression in an experiment, focusing on individual reactions to group or environmental pressures.

Of course, sociologists and anthropologists also conduct experiments, and psychologists can't get started without observing something! Multiple methods create a blend of research approaches that can increase or refine confidence in the validity of our observations and conclusions. For example, both Solomon Asch (who studied conformity in the line-matching experiments) and Stanley Milgram (who studied obedience in the electric shock experiments) included qualitative interviews with participants who did not conform that helped researchers understand how and why they were able to resist negative influences. Studies that explore healthy, adaptive behaviors are now called **positive psychology**, the scientific study of human strengths and virtues.

Social Psychology Is Personal: Kurt Lewin's Story

You probably would have liked Kurt Lewin (see Marrow, 1969), the man now considered the pioneer or "father of social psychology."

Lewin was known to miss an occasional class when he was teaching at the University of Iowa. The reason? He was deeply involved in listening to students at a local café. Perhaps Lewin fit the stereotype of the passionate but absentminded professor. His vision for psychology could be summed up in just two words: **action research**, the application of scientific principles to social problem solving.

Positive psychology: The scientific study of human strengths, virtues, positive emotions, and achievements.

Action research: The application of scientific principles to social problem solving in the real world.

Fine Art Images/Newscom

**Kurt Lewin (1890–1947),
whom some consider
the "father of social
psychology."**

It is difficult today to appreciate how deeply World War I shocked the world. The killing had become industrialized, but the dying was still personal. Kurt Lewin's brother died in the war; Kurt himself was wounded and awarded the Iron Cross. When the Nazis rose to power, Lewin urged his mother to flee with him to America, because they were Jewish and feared the consequences of increasing anti-Semitism. She refused, confident that Germany would honor a mother who had lost one son and claimed a second as a wounded war hero. Sadly, she was wrong: She disappeared, probably into one of the concentration camps.

As a Jewish World War II immigrant to the United States, Lewin studied the dynamics that allowed a Hitler to rise to power—and a Holocaust to happen. He was recognizing one of social psychology's central insights: the power of the situation. Lewin organized his insights into what became a simple but famous equation:

Lewin's equation: $B = f(P, E)$.

Lewin proposed that every person's behavior (B) is a function (f) of both P, the individual person, and E, their immediate environment (Lewin, 1936). In other words, our individual choices and actions are partially based on who we are—factors like our personality and how we were raised—and partially based on the immediate situation. Social psychologists still use those two criteria to predict behavior.

Kurt Lewin's warm, collaborative approach to teaching and learning probably would have astonished Wilhelm Wundt and Sigmund Freud. Lewin encouraged everyone to "express different (and differing) opinions [and] never imposed either discipline or loyalty on his students and colleagues" (Marrow, 1969, p. 27). British psychologist Eric Trist described Lewin as having "a sense of musical delight in ideas." Lewin once became so distracted during a conversation that Trist had to push him onto a moving train so he wouldn't miss it (Marrow, 1969, p. 69).

Lewin unfortunately died in 1947, only a few years after the end of World War II. However, the effects of war on Lewin's pioneering work are reflected in many of the chapter contents of this and every other social psychology textbook: aggression, prejudice, persuasion, and prosocial behavior. His work, as well as other research that followed in his footsteps, is also influential in the world of business and management. Lewin used scientific methods to apply those two factors, P and E, to socially relevant topics—and he inspired many others to follow his lead.

Social Psychologists Value Diversity

We routinely experience diversity as beautiful, even awe-inspiring.

Diversity is a field of wildflowers, each adding to the total view in a unique and essential way. Just as diversity often produces what we regard as beautiful, shutting the door on social diversity sometimes appears (from our present perspective) ugly and embarrassing. For psychology to be a complete study of human behavior, both the participants in our studies and the researchers designing them must come from diverse backgrounds.

Robert Guthrie (1976/2004) examined psychology's history of diversity—and the lack of it—in a book (colorfully!) titled *Even the Rat Was White*. And diversity is a richer, more complicated reality than calculating which ethnic or gender group people belong to. **Intersectionality theory** recognizes that our sense of self, our identity, is based on many "developmental and contextual antecedents of identity" (Clauss-Ehlers et al., 2019, p. 232), including self-definition.

**Intersectionality
theory:** The study of how multiple identity factors (such as race, gender, and socioeconomic status) combine to form how people are perceived and treated by others.

TABLE 1.2

Many important social psychologists have been women and/or people of color.

Mary Whiton Calkins

Mamie Phipps Clark and Kenneth Clark

Alice Eagly

Lisa Diamond

Claude Steele

Mahzarin Banaji

That means that people aren't perceived as a single social category; we're all a combination of our ethnicity, religion, social class, gender, and so on. Intersectionality theory studies how we're affected by the combination of all of these variables as we're simultaneously judged on all of them by others. A gay Black man will be treated differently than a heterosexual Asian woman—and both will be treated differently if they are wearing expensive, designer clothes. Exactly how all of these variables combine is the focus of intersectionality research.

The positive effects of diversity on social psychology are demonstrated by some of the pioneering scholars who are women, people of color, and people who are differently abled. They will continue to push social psychology beyond its original European American, heteronormative boundaries (see Table 1.2). Their stories also demonstrate how much is lost by ignoring the beauty of diversity. Consider just a few examples:

- Mary Whiton Calkins was born during the American Civil War. She fought hard to study psychology at Harvard—despite a formal policy blocking women from enrolling. She became the first female president of the American Psychological Association *and* of the American Philosophical Association. She published four books and over 100 research papers—and reset expectations about what women could achieve within psychology.

- One of Kurt Lewin's students, Beatrice Ann Wright, died as recently as 2018 (at the age of 100; see Wright, 1983). She is credited with establishing research on people who are differently abled through her book *Physical Disability—A Psychosocial Approach*. She applied Lewin's concept of interactions between the person and the environment to understand the experience of physical disabilities. She was honored with a lifetime achievement award by the American Psychological Association.

- Mamie Phipps Clark and Kenneth Clark were a married African American couple who played an important role in social justice. Mamie Clark's master's thesis started the basic research that influenced one of the most famous decisions by the Supreme Court. The case of *Brown v. Board of Education* (see Benjamin & Crouse, 2002) established a legal justification for the desegregation of public schools. She and her husband were the first African Americans to earn PhDs in Psychology from Columbia University. Their "doll studies" vividly demonstrated the harmful effects of internalized racism on children (you can search YouTube for the visual record of some of their interviews with children). Kenneth Clark became the first African American president of the American Psychological Association. This research is described in more detail in Chapter 9: Stereotyping, Prejudice, and Discrimination.

- One of the most famous field studies about group prejudice was conducted by Muzafer Sherif, who was born in Turkey in 1906. In the same year that William Golding (1954) published *Lord of the Flies*, Sherif, his wife Carolyn, and their research team brought young boys to a "summer camp" run by psychologists. They created situations that first produced group prejudices—and then other situations that reduced conflict and transformed those prejudices into a pleasant summer camp experience (see Chapter 9).

- Alice Eagly has also devoted her research to reducing prejudice, with a particular focus on sexism. Her theoretical model (described in Chapter 9) continues to inspire applied research. For example, social role theory is being used to engage more girls and women in STEM (science, technology, engineering, and math) careers.

- Lisa Diamond has devoted her career to lesbian, gay, bisexual, transsexual, and queer/questioning (LGBTQ) issues, including the fluidity of gender and sexual orientation. Her research emphasizes that people's gender and sexual identity can change over time and that these changes can be so powerful that they can happen to people even when they resist the changes because of socialized prejudice.

- Both Claude Steele and Mahzarin Banaji explore how culture and stereotypes affect people of color. Steele, an African American professor who served as the provost at the University of California, Berkeley, introduced the idea of stereotype threat. He designed clever experiments that helped explain how stereotypes and anxiety influenced students of color to perform worse on some college-level tests. Banaji is also interested in how stereotypes and prejudice can influence all of us without our awareness. She helped to develop one of the most controversial tests to measure prejudice in the field of social psychology (see Chapter 9).

Across its history, many social psychologists have been motivated by a desire to use science to help solve social problems. This enduring commitment led the field to a more inclusive, diverse, and yes—even a more beautiful understanding of the human experience.

THE MAIN IDEAS

- Social psychology is a subfield of psychology that scientifically studies how people influence each other's thoughts, feelings, and behaviors.

- Social psychology can be broken up into topics focused on social thinking, social influence, and social behavior, and each topic has concepts that can be applied to everyday people in the real world.

- Kurt Lewin is considered by many to be the "father of social psychology," and he believed individual behaviors are determined by both someone's personality and by the social situation or environment.

- Many other important social psychologists have been women, people of color, people who are differently abled, people of various sexual orientations, and other variables representing the valuable diversity in our world.

CRITICAL THINKING CHALLENGE

- If World War II and the Holocaust had never happened, would psychology be where it is today? Would social psychology exist or be as popular if the world hadn't been inspired to understand the events leading up to and ending that war? What other topics might be considered more important?

- Lewin suggested that behavior is determined by both personality and the given social situation or environment. Which do you think is more influential? When you consider your own behavior across a variety of situations (such as in class, at a religious event, or when you're hanging out with friends), is your behavior fairly consistent due to a strong personality, or do you change how you act to better fit in with what's expected, given the environment?

- Can you identify another field (not psychology) where major progress or innovative thinking came from scholars who represented diverse backgrounds? For example, what scientific, literary, or other important ideas would be missing without women, people of color, LGBTQ people, people who are differently abled, and so on?

WHAT ARE SOME BIG QUESTIONS WITHIN SOCIAL PSYCHOLOGY?

>> LO 1.2: **Analyze important questions about social thought and behavior.**

After the two world wars, social psychology stabilized into a core of basic and applied researchers with a big two-part mission: (1) to understand how our thoughts, feelings, and actions are influenced by other people and (2) to apply those insights to social problems. That big mission is made slightly more manageable by organizing the wide variety of topics in social psychology into the big questions listed in Figure 1.2.

These questions explore (1) nature and nurture, (2) how we explain why good people sometimes do bad things (and vice versa), (3) how humans think about social information, (4) why we live in groups, (5) why prejudice persists, and (6) whether science is the best way to learn about social behavior. These six questions convey the philosophical reach that, day by day, motivates many social psychologists. Individual studies may only examine a small, specific piece of the larger puzzle, but social psychologists are slowly putting those pieces together.

Big Question 1: Is Behavior Shaped More by Biological Factors ("Nature") or by Environmental Factors ("Nurture")?

Behavior is influenced by nature *and* nurture.

You will encounter the "nature versus nurture" debate whenever you try to explain behavior, but it seems especially salient for exceptional behavior. Were brilliant mechanics, exceptional athletes, sharp scholars, creative programmers, and creative

FIGURE 1.2

Social psychology's big questions motivate researchers and provide a framework for understanding what social psychologists do.

- Is Behavior Shaped More by Biological Factors ("Nature") or by Environmental Factors ("Nurture")?
- How Can We Explain Why Good People Do Bad Things—and Vice Versa?
- How Do Humans Think?
- Why Do Humans Live in Groups?
- Why Do Stereotypes and Prejudices Exist and Persist?
- Is Science the Best Way to Learn About Social Behavior?

artists born that way (nature) or did their experience and training shape what they became (nurture)? The nature-nurture debate applies to the ordinary rest of us, too.

I [Tom] was a solid "C" student in high school, with a few exceptions—but then I excelled in college and graduate school. Did the change occur because my brain and hormones had developed post-adolescence? Or was the change because of psychological motivation to move past the boring, unpleasant jobs from my earlier life?

Nature refers to influences from biology or physiology, such as genetics and hormones. They are often (but not always) beyond our control. On the other hand, **nurture** refers to influences that come from our life circumstances, experiences, and environment. Many psychologists describe the "nature" versus "nurture" debate as a **false dichotomy**, the presentation of two opposing and mutually exclusive options that disregard any alternative explanations.

In almost every case, *both* nature and nurture influence behavior—what psychologists call an **interaction**. For example, physically attractive people may be naturally beautiful. But a temporary bad complexion or a life-changing car crash could alter their good looks—and remove many of the advantages of being beautiful (see Chapter 5).

Kurt Lewin, the observant World War I trench soldier with "a musical delight in ideas," understood how nature and nurture interacted within social psychology. Behavior (B) is a function (*f*) of *both* the personality and biology (P) that you were born with (nature) and the environment (E) that you live in (nurture).

The Hall of Fame baseball player Roberto Clemente played for the Pittsburgh Pirates for 18 seasons. He died in 1972 in a plane crash during one of his many humanitarian missions throughout the Caribbean. Was Clemente born to be an exceptional humanitarian and athlete—or is there more to his story?

Louis Requena/MLB via Getty Images

Big Question 2: How Can We Explain Why Good People Do Bad Things—and Vice Versa?

You are complicated; we all are.

Two men walked into a busy convenience store in northern New Jersey, a state with strict gun laws. They each carried a large gun, prominently displayed. They bought breakfast sandwiches and coffee and made small talk with the cashier. They both wore

a T-shirt that declared: "I Carry Guns to Protect YOU From Bad People." After they left, a young woman, probably of high school age, spoke up. "How do I know," she asked the room, "whether they were good people or bad people?"

In social psychology, questions about who (or what) is good and bad are not reserved for preachers and extremist radio talk shows. Social psychologists explore what many call "good" and "evil" by creating controlled experiments that explore the situations that reliably produce prosocial behaviors that help others (Chapter 10) and aggressive behaviors that are intended to harm others (Chapter 11). The more pressing question social psychologists can answer is how we all justify our actions using our own personal perspectives, politics, culture, and social norms. It is how we explain our own complicated "goodness" and "badness" to the most important audience of all—to ourselves.

This big question is also a practical question. What would happen to a society without laws and social punishments? Would humans become pure altruists and create communities of self-sacrifice for the greater good (like honeybees)? Or would we become lonely sexual competitors willing to stab rivals through the neck (like hummingbirds)? Or are we both?

Movie antagonists are more interesting when the question of whether they are "good" or "bad" is complicated. In the blockbuster movie *Black Panther* the antagonist feels justified in taking over the country Wakanda because he was orphaned and abandoned by the royal family. In addition, he believes he can lead Wakanda toward a future in which they help other children in need. Are his motives really that bad?

Big Question 3: How Do Humans Think?

We all have two different ways of thinking.

You probably have some big decisions on your personal horizon. What are you going to do for a career after you graduate? Where will you live? Will you get married? What about children? For every major decision in your life, you'll have to weigh what your instincts or "gut" tells you to do right along with what your logical, thoughtful, practical mind tells you. This book covers a lot of decisions we make, including whether we hold prejudices, how we decide to commit to a relationship partner, and more. All of these decisions are interesting individually, but a larger system of understanding how we think in general is called social cognition (see Chapter 4).

The study of social cognition explains why decision-making humans rely on two thinking systems. One system is fast and intuitive; the other is slower and logical. You can apply some logic to your career decisions by estimating your job choices and future earnings at the Bureau of Labor Statistics (see https://www.bls.gov/mwe/). But some careers will just "feel right" and you will be tempted to "go with your gut." Is logic the way to go? On the other hand, can you really trust your intuition?

Big Question 4: Why Do Humans Live in Groups?

We are social animals.

Our social impulse may explain why we use solitary confinement (in prison) to punish people and use social events (like college graduation ceremonies) as rewards. An evolutionary perspective in psychology offers explanations in terms of how living in groups increases our chances of meeting, mating, and safely delivering our genes into the next generation. A functioning group improves our survival skills, teaches us how to share resources, and socializes us to help others. Groups also help us develop our self-identity, usually through comparisons of our own situation to the people we see around us (Chapter 3).

On the other hand, group decisions aren't always better. Group interactions may encourage a shift in group opinions that lead to more dangerous decisions, a mob

Nature: Influences on our thoughts and behaviors from biology or physiology, such as genetics and hormones.

Nurture: Influences on our thoughts and behaviors from our life circumstances, how we were raised, experiences, and our environment.

False dichotomy: A situation presented as two opposing and mutually exclusive options when there may really be additional options or a compromise.

Interactions: The combination of several influences on an outcome, such as the influence of both personality and environment on behavior.

Computers now allow even isolated people to connect to each other. Our motivation to stay connected to loved ones is part of our social nature.

© istockphoto.com/dimarik

mentality. Groups can also stumble into a conspiracy of silence that prevents the most thoughtful, skeptical members of a group from voicing their true opinions. In addition, when people submerge their individuality in groups, they may experience a feeling of anonymity and behave as if there are no consequences. Some group members might become lazy by coasting on the work of others. Chapter 8 focuses on how these group dynamics influence decisions and outcomes, in both positive and negative ways.

Cultural norms may be the most subtle yet powerful form of social influence at the group level. It is difficult to appreciate our own cultural assumptions until we spend time in a different culture, because they are so imbedded into how we grew up and see the world now. It would be a mistake to say that culture influences people in definite, predestined ways—but it would also be a mistake to deny the influence of culture at all. Social psychological research has explored important cultural differences across a wide variety of specific contexts, so we'll discuss those studies throughout the entire book.

Big Question 5: Why Do Stereotypes and Prejudices Exist and Persist?

You can understand why stereotyping has attracted so much attention from social psychologists. Figure 1.3 displays the psychological path from stereotyping to social conflict. People experiencing social injustice won't put up with it forever.

Many social psychologists oppose social injustice, and the obvious place to dispel it is at the beginning: stereotyping. There's only one problem: Humans can't stop stereotyping—and probably would not be happy if we could. It seems to be an automatic instinct. Chapter 4 describes why stereotyping evolved in the first place, and Chapter 9 describes the types and consequences of stereotyping. Theories about stereotyping allow us to ask more specific questions: Why is it a basic human tendency to group and label people into different categories? Do particular stereotypes pop up across different parts of the world and different cultures? Why does stereotyping persist?

Big Question 6: Is Science the Best Way to Learn About Social Behavior?

This is a good news/bad news question; we give you the bad news first.

Social psychologists felt terrible when some of us discovered what was called the **replication crisis**. Some of the classic studies we all thought were foundations of the field were brought into question when scientists who tried to re-do the studies found different results. Everything we thought we knew seemed to be turned upside

Replication crisis:
A recent concern in psychology that the results of some studies aren't found again when scientists try to repeat them.

FIGURE 1.3

The psychological path from stereotyping to social conflict.

Stereotyping ⟶ Prejudice ⟶ Discrimination ⟶ Social Injustice ⟶ Social Conflict

down as people both inside and outside of the field questioned the validity of social psychology's theories and conclusions. The crisis seemed to develop in three stages (see Earp & Trafinow, 2015).

First, a few years ago, some well-known social psychologists were caught cheating (by their students!). Those scientists had simply made up their data or manipulated it by doing things like only keeping results that confirmed their theories in efforts to make a name for themselves. It was outright fraud, but we won't name names; they are already embarrassed, and some of them got fired.

Second, an investigation revealed a research culture that rewarded original studies but offered few rewards for replicating someone else's research. That means that once a single study has found an interesting result, not that many people make sure the result is solid by trying to find it again (the very definition of replication).

Third, few replications suggest that our literature may be stocked with so many **false positives** (also called **Type I errors**) that we don't know what to believe. False positives happen when the analyses of the study imply a finding exists when it might not really be there or might be so weak that it's hard to tell if it really has much of an effect on actual behavior.

The good news is that there is a way to fix the problem. Science, as a tool of discovery, doesn't care about human vanity, ego, or greed. The answer to the replication crisis is twofold. First, people who conduct replications or "re-dos" of other people's work should be praised for their contribution to science. Second, scholars in the field need to change some of their practices to make their process more open and honest, such as being willing to share their raw data with the public (so that others can check their work). You'll read more about these fixes, called "open science," in Chapter 2.

And there is more good news. Most of the everyday work in social psychology is quantitative. However, there is a growing recognition that qualitative studies, especially case studies, have shaped psychology's story in fundamental ways (see Rolls, 2013). We'll highlight several of these throughout the book.

Social psychology—just like any field of study—is made up of humans, doing our best. We sometimes make mistakes, but we learn from them and make the next step of progress even better.

We focus your critical attention on the methods used by social psychologists in three ways. First, an entire chapter (Chapter 2) is devoted to helping you understand the research methods and statistical analyses most often used in social psychology. This chapter will serve as a foundation for your understanding. We reinforce that understanding with our second emphasis: In the later chapters, each time a methods or statistics terms is used, we put it in italics to help you notice it. We also mark methods discussions with an icon in the margin that looks like little gears turning, a reminder that our theories are based on scientific studies. Finally, each chapter highlights the detailed and clever methods used in one particular study. In all these ways, we hope to remind you of the science behind social psychology.

Do particular stereotypes pop up across different parts of the world and different cultures? Why does stereotyping persist?

False positives: An error in which scientists believe a finding exists when it really doesn't, because of weak or incorrect statistics.

Type I error: See *false positives.*

THE MAIN IDEAS

- One way to think about important topics in psychology is to consider the "big questions" asked by the field.

- This book provides evidence on both sides of these questions, but research is still needed to fully understand the complicated nature of human social experiences.

- Social psychology asks these questions because they are interesting from a philosophical or academic perspective but also because they actually affect people's everyday lives.

CRITICAL THINKING CHALLENGE

- Go back to each of the big questions asked in this section. Think about times in your own life when you've thought or behaved in a way that seems to confirm one side of the debate or the other. Now, try to identify a time in your life that confirms the *other* side of the question. Do you think your behaviors in general provide support for answers to these questions? What about when you think of other people's behaviors?

- Many popular books and movies focus on utopias (perfect societies) or dystopias (malfunctioning societies). Examples of dystopias are *Lord of the Flies*, *Black Mirror*, and *The Handmaid's Tale*. Why do people like this kind of story? Is it because it makes us feel good—our society is better by comparison—or because it serves as a warning, reminding us of what society could become?

- Which of the big questions posed here is the most interesting to you, personally, and why?

HOW CAN SOCIAL PSYCHOLOGY MAKE MY LIFE BETTER NOW?

>> **LO 1.3:** **Apply social psychological concepts to your own life and experiences.**

At the risk of sounding like a late-night television infomercial, "Would you like to study less, learn more, and earn higher grades?" Here's how to do it.

Any personal application of social psychology will make the information more interesting and memorable (Craik & Lockhart, 1972). For example, at the beginning of this chapter, we asked, "What would you do?" in different situations. Did you just read the words? That's not studying; that's reading. Studying social psychology is easier if you mentally engage by imagining what you would do if you (a) saw someone have a seizure, (b) experienced peer pressure in the line experiment, or (c) were ordered to deliver an electric shock. You've got a great imagination; use it. Here are three other tricks of the trade.

Apply Each Topic to Your Own Life

Use the Table of Contents.

The chapter titles will tell you which ones you can most easily apply to your life. For example, most of us are very interested in romantic attraction, sexuality, and dating partners. If that interests you, then pay special attention to Chapter 12. If you have been the victim—or the perpetrator—of stereotypes and prejudice, then you'll be excited about Chapter 9. You've been manipulated by peer pressure in some way, so take advantage of what you learn about social influence in Chapter 7. Our personal interests connect us to much bigger ideas, so use what you learn in Chapter 2 to develop your own hypotheses in every chapter.

You can be creative as you explore social psychology. For example, why do so many high school students in the cafeteria separate themselves into the same sorts of groups? Do you have a hypothesis? Do you know how you'd actually go out and test this hypothesis (ethically, of course)? If you find yourself quietly people-watching and then thinking, "I wonder why...," then you might be in line for a career connected to social psychology.

Use the Self-Report Scales to Compare Yourself to Others

Do you like quizzes about yourself on Facebook or BuzzFeed?

Those are fun, for sure—but they're not exactly scientific. Fill out the surveys and questionnaires you'll find in every chapter, starting with Chapter 2. You will probably enjoy the self-report scales in each chapter because (a) reading the items and jotting down the numbers will clarify the underlying concept, helping you learn and remember it, and (b) you will learn a little bit more about yourself. In Chapter 3, for example, you will experience one way that social psychologists measure self-esteem. Scoring each item will help you understand how researchers think—and the relative importance of self-esteem to your own life.

Critically Analyze Your Opinions After Each Section

Ask yourself difficult-to-answer questions.

Critical thinking requires deeper processing, which is its own reward. It's the ability to analyze, apply, and explore ideas in new and open-minded ways. And deep processing also makes it easier to remember information for an exam (Craik & Lockhart, 1972). We need the next generation of critical thinkers, you (!), to harness the science of social psychology in a variety of careers to fulfill its two great missions: (1) to understand how our thoughts, feelings, and actions are influenced by other people and (2) to apply those insights to social problems.

The social problems are out there, waiting for you.

Nobel Prize–winning physicist Richard Feynman once stated, "I would rather have questions that can't be answered than answers that can't be questioned." Science requires us to have healthy skepticism but to go beyond simply criticizing others by offering ways to create new knowledge and advances in our own field of study.

THE MAIN IDEAS

- Being able to personally relate to theoretical ideas and to critically analyze them also makes them easier to remember later.

- This book offers several opportunities for readers to apply concepts to themselves, including self-report scales to measure certain topics.

- Social psychology can only progress when new thinkers approach topics with scientific thinking and friendly skepticism.

CITICAL THINKING CHALLENGE

- Social psychology claims to provide insight into important topics that apply to real people's lives. However, most findings in the field are published in academic journals that only other scientists read. How can social psychologists do a better job of sharing their research with everyday people or with people or organizations that could use the research findings to actually improve the world?

Critical thinking:
The ability to analyze, apply, and explore ideas in new and open-minded ways.

- The beginning of this book discussed a reality show called *What Would You Do?* in which people are put into situations that are manipulated and then recorded without their knowledge to appear later on TV. What are the ethical implications of this type of program? Once people learn that they were essentially "tricked," do you think they can learn from the experience? Do you think that participants in social psychology research studies can do the same thing—learn from the experience?

- Again, look over the Table of Contents of this book. Do you think there are important topics that are missing? Are there aspects of the social experience that you think social psychology needs to address or spend more time studying?

CHAPTER SUMMARY

What Is Social Psychology?

Social psychology is the scientific study of how people influence each other's thoughts, feelings, and behaviors. It includes the study of

(1) social thinking, such as how we define the "self" and how we perceive the world;

(2) social influence, such as how we can persuade other people, why we conform, and the dynamics of stereotypes and prejudice; and

(3) social behavior, such as helping, aggression, and romantic relationships.

All these areas of social psychology can be applied to a variety of settings.

Social psychology also can be understood by comparing it to similar but different academic fields. It has some similarities, but also important differences, from fields such as sociology, anthropology, and clinical and/or counseling psychology. Social psychology studies "everyday" thoughts and behaviors throughout life, including both negative behaviors (such as discrimination or aggression) and positive behaviors (such as helping or cooperation).

One of social psychology's pioneers was the German World War I veteran Kurt Lewin, whom many people consider the "father of social psychology." Lewin was a Jewish man greatly influenced by both World Wars I and II. When he immigrated to the United States, he devoted his academic career to understanding social dynamics. Lewin famously suggested that each person's social behaviors are influenced by both personality and the social environment. Many other influential social psychologists followed in his footsteps. Some of these later social psychologists were women, people of color, or differently abled in some way that helps us recognize the inherent value of diversity.

What Are Some Big Questions Within Social Psychology?

Social psychologists use the scientific method to obtain many small answers to a few big questions. No single research study can find a single or simple answer to these questions, but each study helps us understand one more piece of the puzzle. Seven of the most important big questions in social psychology are as follows:

1. Are we shaped more by personal, biological factors ("nature") or by environmental factors ("nurture")?

2. How can we explain why good people do bad things—and vice versa?

3. How do humans think?

4. Why do humans live in groups?

5. Why do stereotypes and prejudices exist and persist?

6. Is science the best way to learn about social behavior?

How Can Social Psychology Make My Life Better Now?

You will enjoy and learn more from each chapter by imagining how you can apply it to your own life. To help, each chapter has a feature called What's My Score? Here, you can fill out a survey that measures where you fall on one of the variables discussed in that chapter. If you are honest on these surveys, it will help you gain insight into how the topics discussed might affect your choices and actions.

In addition, each section of every chapter ends with critical thinking questions. Your understanding will grow into permanent knowledge as you evaluate your opinion of different theories. Social psychology is the most fun when you start doing it, so try to design some way to test your own ideas. Perhaps you are the next famous social psychologist who will be included in books like this one.

CRITICAL THINKING, ANALYSIS, AND APPLICATION

- As we learn more and more about social psychology, will the field continue to grow in numbers, or will people stop studying it once we have more answers? Do you think spending your life as a social psychologist would be a worthwhile endeavor, or are there more important ways to spend your career?

- Consider the six big questions covered in this chapter and put them in order of importance. Which would you say is the most essential and urgent question that social psychologists should be studying, and which is less important? Justify your order of importance with historical or personal evidence.

- Do you think that every academic discipline, job, and career benefit from having diverse kinds of people involved? What are some of the advantages of providing opportunities for traditionally minority or marginalized people in any job or field of study?

- What aspects of your own social world do you think would benefit from further analysis by social psychologists? Which chapters of this book sound like the most interesting or intriguing? Which topics are you most excited to study?

FABRICE COFFRINI/AFP via Getty Images

2

Research Methods

Core Questions

2.1 How do social psychologists design studies?

2.2 How do experiments work in social psychology?

2.3 How can I recognize trustworthy research?

Learning Objectives

2.1 Describe the scientific method, methods of descriptive data collection, and correlations.

2.2 Understand the strengths and weaknesses of experiments and how their results are analyzed.

2.3 Explain why reliability, validity, random sampling, ethics, and open science signal good research.

Like all sciences, social psychology usually moves like snail: steady but slow. It is slow, in part, because what social psychologists study is usually often invisible—and therefore difficult to measure. For example, prejudice, persuasion, altruism, and romantic love are all scientific constructs, theoretical ideas that cannot be directly observed. Although the scientific process is slow, social psychology is growing fast. It is growing fast because so many students are attracted to Kurt Lewin's vision of an applied science.

Perhaps social psychology's popularity explains why so many passengers were carrying long plastic or cardboard tubes on a recent plane ride. The plane was full of people presenting at a conference sponsored by the Society for Personality and Social Psychology (SPSP), which happens at the end of every winter. The tubes contained rolled-up posters summarizing the most cutting-edge research in the field. This chapter describes how all those professional established scientists, graduate students, and even a few undergraduates created those studies—and it invites you to join us.

HOW DO SOCIAL PSYCHOLOGISTS DESIGN STUDIES?

>> LO 2.1:   Describe the scientific method, methods of descriptive data collection, and correlations.

The working world is full of designers.

We have fashion designers, graphic designers, architectural designers, cookware designers, landscape designers, and game designers. To become a clear-thinking social psychologist, you must become a research designer. Although there are guidelines, designing research is also an art that you can develop with experience—just like a fashion or a landscape designer.

The purpose of a research project often determines its design. The purpose of basic science is to increase understanding, create testable theories, and predict social behavior. Basic research strives to understand a given phenomenon more. The purpose of applied science is to translate those theories into applied problem solving or social action. Applied research is used to make the world better in some tangible way, like reducing aggression or increasing self-esteem.

Both are important. Basic research is important because, as social psychology's pioneer Kurt Lewin famously recognized, "There is nothing so practical as a good theory" (see Bedeian, 2016; Lewin, 1951, p. 169). Applied science is where theory wrestles with reality—but with the understanding that reality always wins. If a theory does not describe reality, then the theory has to change. Figure 2.1 displays the four phases of the scientific method used in both basic and applied research.

This section answers the core question "How do social psychologists design studies?" by

(1)   describing the scientific method,

(2)   comparing descriptive research designs, and

(3)   explaining correlations.

Apply the Scientific Method

The whole scientific method is greater than the sum of its parts.

The parts of the scientific method include hypothesis generation, types of designs, procedural techniques, and measurement tools that are slightly different in every science. But the whole of the scientific method is an attitude based on healthy skepticism, the belief that evidence is the most trustworthy way to know about something. Healthy skepticism also implies a stubborn, Galileo-like refusal to believe something just because an authority says so. When opinion meets data, the data win.

Constructs: Theoretical ideas that cannot be directly observed, such as attitudes, personality, attraction, or how we think.

Basic science: Research that increases understanding and theory within a field like psychology.

Applied science: Research that translates theory into applied problem solving or social action.

Scientific method: A systematic way of creating knowledge by observing, forming a hypothesis, testing a hypothesis, and interpreting the results.

FIGURE 2.1

The scientific method includes these basic elements.

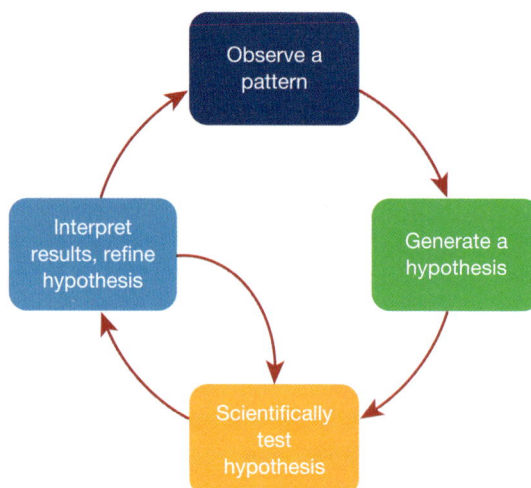

Most research stories cycle through the same four phases. This pattern of research, shown in Figure 2.1, is repeated with endless variations. You will grow accustomed to this rhythm: observation, hypothesis, testing, and interpretation of the results.

• *Phase 1: Observe a pattern of behavior.* Imagine that you are in a coffee shop quietly observing other customers. You notice that men frequently interrupt people during conversations—and that seems to be especially true when their conversation partner is a woman. Welcome aboard; you started the scientific journey when your curiosity prompted you to ask, "Is this a pattern?" (By the way, this exact observation was tested in coffee shops and drugstores back in 1975 by Zimmerman and West.) Phase 1 of the scientific method begins when we observe what we think is a reliable pattern of behavior. Of course, Phase 1 doesn't always start with literal observation in this way. It can also start with observation of studies already done on a topic, when you notice something that could be added to this line of research to enhance understanding.

• *Phase 2: Generate a hypothesis.* A formal **hypothesis** specifies what you believe will happen when you test your observations. It's an educated guess in the form of a statement. You might hypothesize that (1) men interrupt more than women do in general, and (2) men interrupt women more than they interrupt other men. Hypotheses are never stated as questions (such as, "Who interrupts more, men or women?"). They start as statements of what you think is going to happen, so that you can either reject the idea as wrong, gain support that you're right, or realize that the answer is more complicated than you originally thought.

• *Phase 3: Test the hypothesis.* You can do this in a wide variety of ways, which are described in the rest of this chapter. In this case, you'd probably use discreet observation techniques to watch people's behaviors in public places (like the coffee shop). But there are a lot of other options, and we'll cover those soon. And remember that a single study showing a pattern probably isn't enough to be really confident that your hypothesis was right; you need replication to build that confidence.

Hypothesis: A specific statement made by a researcher about the expected outcome of a study.

• *Phase 4: Interpret the results and refine your hypothesis.* If you found that your hypothesis was totally wrong, you might need to start all over at Phase 1. Or, you might realize that your hypothesis is true some of the time but not all of the time. In that case, you refine the hypothesis and test it again.

Imagine that we found support for the basic idea that, overall, men are indeed more likely than women to interrupt someone. Consider the following possible new, refined hypotheses:

- Women with more assertive personalities are more likely to interrupt others, compared to women with less assertive personalities.

- Men are less likely to interrupt women they find physically attractive, compared to women they don't find attractive.

- Men interrupt others more in friendly or informal settings, compared to formal settings such as at work.

- Men from cultures with more traditional gender roles are more likely to interrupt women than are men from more egalitarian cultures.

Any scientific data story can only unfold if our observations are as objective as possible, our hypotheses are specific, our tests are fair, and the results are properly interpreted. Any individual research study is a very small piece of a very big puzzle. Importantly, the methods and procedure chosen for any given study will have important implications for what conclusions can safely be drawn. Every completed study brings us a tiny bit closer to understanding the complicated world of social interaction.

Begin With a Descriptive Design

Many research projects begin with a descriptive design.

There are a lot of choices when it comes to choosing a way to gather data for a study, and we won't cover all of them here (it's not a research methods book). We'll start with three options that typically fall into the category of descriptive designs. **Descriptive designs** define, explain, and clarify patterns of people or events that happen without experimenter intervention.

The idea is that they would have happened anyway, and the researcher's study helps us describe those observations in a more detailed way. Imagine you are trying to understand how, when, and why some first-year college students drop out before their second year—and who is more likely to drop out compared to others. Here are three ways we could try to answer that question using descriptive designs.

Archival Data

Archival data are stored information that were originally gathered for a different purpose but can now be used to test hypotheses.

For example, most colleges and universities collect (and store) lots of information about their students. It includes application information (like high school GPA and hometowns), courses taken at that college, how long it took to graduate, what students majored in, and more. This is a lot of information, and patterns could be hypothesized and tested regarding whether certain types of students drop out more or less.

There are many sources of archival data. Newspapers may report quotations from people who witnessed important events like natural disasters—and those quotations could be analyzed. Census data might be used to track patterns such as how many people of a certain socioeconomic status are married, cohabiting, or live alone. Facebook profiles and posts are used by social psychologists to study how people reveal personal information about themselves. Police records contain data that can reveal patterns of reported domestic violence or other crimes.

Archival data are a rich source of information that might be waiting quietly for someone to analyze and reveal patterns of human behavior.

Naturalistic Observation

Another option is scientific surveillance.

Descriptive designs: Methods of gathering data that define, explain, and clarify patterns that happen without experimenter intervention.

Archival data: Stored information that was originally created for some other purpose that can later be used to test hypotheses, such as census or college records.

This descriptive design is usually called **naturalistic observation**, or watching people in their natural environments and recording their behaviors with a preset coding system, based on your hypothesis. By "natural," we don't mean in a cornfield or a forest but where the behavior normally occurs (such as a coffee shop). To find out what kinds of conversations college students have about dropping out, we might go to campus locations where we think we might overhear such conversations. This might be places like dorm lounges, academic success offices, free tutoring spots, or maybe even campus bars.

You may already notice that systems of data collection can sometimes overlap. If you decided to observe people's behaviors over several hours of videos that had to be created as security surveillance, you'd be using both naturalistic observation and archival data. You might also be using your critical thinking skills as you start to wonder about two important questions regarding naturalistic observation.

First, is naturalistic observation ethical? Video surveillance may have issues regarding the taped people's privacy (see Bhatia et al., 2019). For example, video surveillance is being developed in order to track unvaccinated individuals who, unknown to themselves, may be carrying a highly contagious, airborne disease into an international airport and then onto other countries.

Even without videos, observing people and using them for your own research purposes may be unethical because they haven't given consent to be part of your study. For this reason, companies, colleges, and universities always run their study ideas through an objective ethics committee before they engage in any research endeavors (this is described more later in the chapter). That said, most laws support the idea that if people are out in public, they are giving up their right to privacy.

A second question you might be thinking is, "If people realize they're being observed, wouldn't they change their behaviors?" If that thought occurred to you, then congratulations—that is a legitimate scientific concern. **Reactivity** occurs when people's behavior changes when they know that they're being watched. They might become more polite, or try to show off, or say nice things about their boss, or do anything else they think makes them look like better people. When that happens, your study will have problems because the behavior you're trying to observe is no longer natural and authentic.

One possible solution to this problem is **participant observation**, which is when researchers go undercover and pretend to be part of the natural environment so that no one notices them. They might pretend to be a substitute teacher in a school, a maintenance worker at a park, or a member of a cult. In this way, hopefully the patterns

Naturalistic observation: Watching and recording people's behaviors where they would have happened anyway, but for research purposes.

Reactivity: When people change their behavior because they realize they're being observed.

Participant observation: A technique used during naturalistic observation where scientists covertly disguise themselves as people belonging in an environment.

In the movie *21 Jump Street*, two young police officers go undercover pretending to be high school students, so they can bust a new drug that's hitting the community. In *Imperium*, Daniel Radcliffe's character works for the FBI and infiltrates a White supremacist group, pretending to be racist. If any of them had been social psychologists doing research with this undercover technique, it would have been called participant observation.

they observe and record will reflect genuine social interactions. The more authentic the behavior being observed, the better it is for research.

Descriptive Surveys

Sometimes the simplest way to collect data works best: Just ask.

Research surveys ask people to honestly report their thoughts, emotions, and behaviors. Often surveys include **self-report scales**, which ask people to respond to several items on a range (such as from 1 = *strongly disagree* to 7 = *strongly agree*). The researcher later sums or averages the responses to items and assigns that participant a score on a given variable. College administrators might ask current students to complete satisfaction scales as a way of trying to predict who might drop out versus make it all the way to graduation.

Creating a good survey is not as easy as it looks. Too few questions mean you won't get the information you desire. Too many questions mean participants will get bored, quit, or just make up information to get it over with. But when done well, there are many advantages to the survey method. Surveys

(a) are relatively inexpensive,

(b) can reach hundreds of people relatively quickly,

(c) can assess personal information in ways that may not be possible through naturalistic observations, and

(d) attract participants from anywhere in the world (especially if the survey is online). That's good because it means we can get a wide diversity of participants.

However, self-report surveys have a big problem: **social desirability**. This occurs when participants provide inaccurate information—they fudge their answers—in order to impress or please the researcher or simply because they don't want to admit something. For example, would you tell the truth if asked whether you've ever mistreated a romantic partner, cheated on a test, stolen something, or used illegal drugs? Do not despair! The What's My Score? feature describes one way to circumvent this problem when collecting data through surveys.

Self-report scale: A survey where participants give information about themselves by responding to several items along the same theme.

Social desirability: The tendency for participants to provide dishonest responses so that others have positive impressions of them or because they don't want to admit something.

WHAT'S MY SCORE?

⬙ Measuring Social Desirability

Social desirability damages the quality of self-report scales when participants answer in a way that they think makes them look good. One creative way around this problem is to include a measure of how willing participants are to be honest. Most people *have* done many of the bad behaviors listed in this scale. So, if research participants don't admit to any of them, then they are probably changing their answers on other parts of the survey to look good.

Instructions: Listed below are several statements concerning personal attitudes and traits. Please read each item and decide whether the statement is true or false as it pertains to you personally.

Circle "T" for true statements and "F" for false statements.

T F 1. Before voting, I thoroughly investigate the qualifications of all the candidates.

T F 2. I never hesitate to go out of my way to help someone in trouble.

T F 3. I sometimes feel resentful when I don't get my way.

T F 4. I am always careful about my manner of dress.

T F 5. My table manners at home are as good as when I eat out in a restaurant.

(Continued)

(Continued)

T F 6. I like to gossip at times.

T F 7. I can remember playing sick to get out of something.

T F 8. There have been occasions when I took advantage of someone.

T F 9. I'm always willing to admit it when I make a mistake.

T F 10. There have been occasions when I felt like smashing things.

T F 11. I am always courteous, even to people who are disagreeable.

T F 12. At times I have really insisted on having things my own way.

Scoring: Give yourself 1 point if you said TRUE for Items 1, 2, 4, 5, 9, or 11. Then, give yourself 1 point if you said FALSE for Items 3, 6, 7, 8, 10, or 12. The more points you have, the more you are trying to manage your impression—in other words, you have a higher score on social desirability.

Source: Crowne and Marlowe (1960).

Understand Correlational Analyses

For many students (including your authors), the **correlational analysis** was a door-opening experience into the surprisingly pleasant world of statistics.

A correlation starts with two pieces of information from each participant. Each piece of information is a number that represents where that person falls on a range, or continuum, for two variables of interest. For example, you can ask people (1) how many hours they study each week and (2) their grade point average (GPA). The obvious hypothesis: More studying is associated with higher grades.

Figure 2.2 tells a beautifully nuanced yet easy-to-understand story. The pattern of dots flows upward and to the right, so the general theme is that more hours spent studying each week is associated with higher grades. And each individual dot is also

Correlational analysis: A statistic testing if two continuous variables are systematically associated with each other.

FIGURE 2.2

In this graph, each dot represents one person. For each person, study hours per week fall on the *x*-axis, and grade point average (GPA) falls on the *y*-axis. By looking at the general pattern, we can determine whether the two variables are correlated.

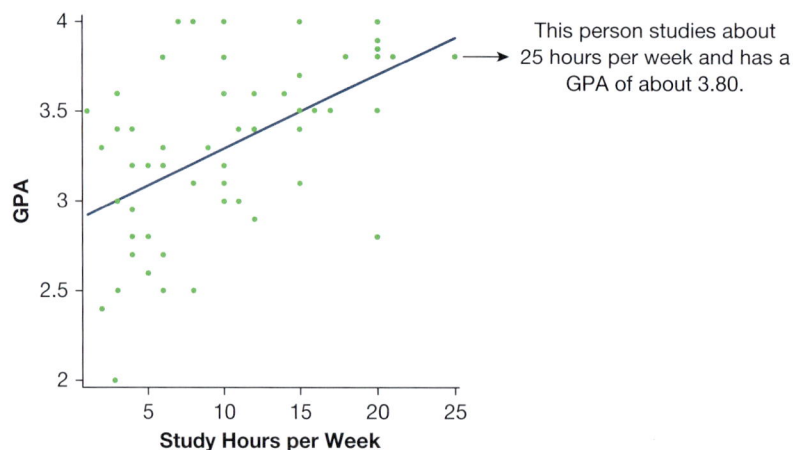

This person studies about 25 hours per week and has a GPA of about 3.80.

a personal story. People in the upper left get high grades without studying very much; people in the lower right get low grades but study a great deal.

Correlations in which both variables move in the same direction are called "positive" correlations. Here, as studying goes up, grades go up—or as studying goes down, grades go down. So studying and grades have a positive correlation. If the two variables move in opposite directions—as one goes up, the other goes down—it's called a "negative" correlation. You might hypothesize a negative correlation between partying and grades: More partying means lower grades.

Correlations will always be represented as a number that ranges from –1.00 to +1.00. You already know what the sign (positive or negative) means. The number represents how closely each dot on the graph follows the pattern, or how close the dots are to the line. If they are all *exactly* on the line, then the association between the two variables is perfect, and the number will be 1.00 (either positive or negative). As the number gets closer to zero (from either direction), the dots start to spread out. That means there's more variation, and the association isn't as strong.

How to think about correlation numbers and graphs is summarized for you in Figure 2.3.

Caution! Correlation does not imply causation.

While it is *possible* that some correlations show causal relationships, be careful. The correlation could be caused by a third variable. In the case of a student who spends many hours studying and has a very good GPA, both of these outcomes might have been caused by the student's (1) motivation to do well, (2) level of pressure from parents, (3) amount of enjoyment of class subjects, or (dare we hope) (4) the skill and engagement of a fine professor.

FIGURE 2.3

Correlations always range from –1.00 to +1.00. The sign (positive or negative) indicates whether the two variables move in the same direction or in opposite directions. The number (from 0.0 to 1.0) tells you how well each data point fits onto a general pattern. If a correlation is zero, it means there is no pattern or association between the two variables.

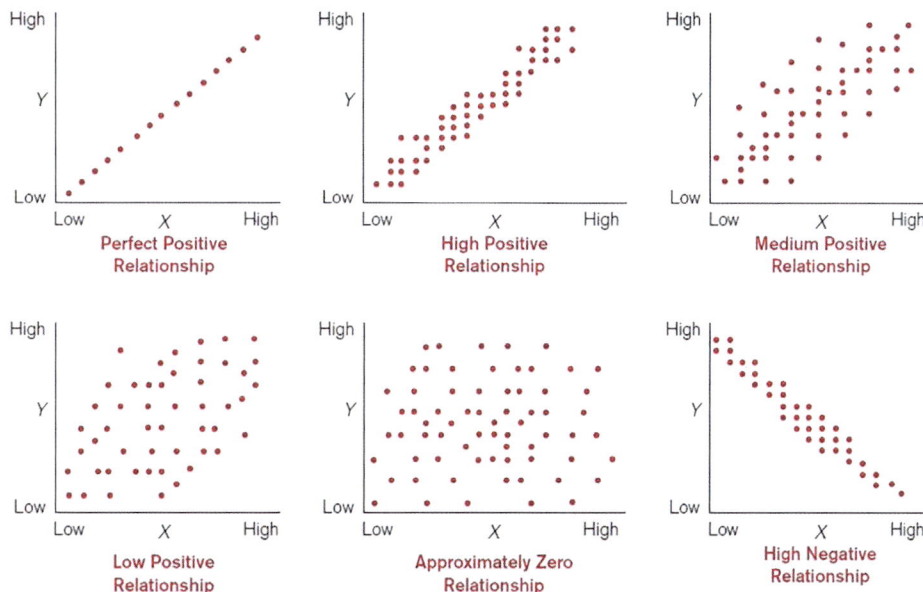

▶ Correlation and Causation in *Harry Potter*

Pictorial Press Ltd / Alamy Stock Photo

Most people are familiar with the Harry Potter series of books and movies, in which a young boy discovers he's a wizard and attends a boarding school to learn

spells. In the sixth book, *Harry Potter and the Half-Blood Prince* (Rowling, 2005), Harry first gets the chance to learn the magical power of "apparition," or the ability to disappear and reappear in a different location. Harry's first apparition lesson is an example of his awareness that correlation does not imply causation.

Harry describes his apparition teacher's appearance and how that appearance might be linked to the ability to disappear:

> He was oddly colorless, with transparent eyelashes, wispy hair, and an insubstantial air, as though a single gust of wind might blow him away. Harry wondered whether constant disappearances and reappearances had somehow diminished his substance, or whether his frail build was ideal for anyone wishing to vanish. (p. 382)

Harry doesn't know whether having a wispy appearance caused his teacher to have a greater apparition ability—or whether his talent at apparition has caused him to appear wispy. While Harry suspects there's a correlation or association between the two things, he knows that without more information, he can't know which is the cause and which is the effect. It's also possible that the association is merely a coincidence or that both are caused by something else. Without logical research designs, the secrets of apparition may remain unknown to Muggles (nonmagical folks) and wizards alike.

A weird example about ice cream will help you understand the "third variable" problem. There is usually a correlation between amount of ice cream sold per year in any given city and the number of people in that city who drown that year. Is ice cream consumption causing drowning or vice versa? Probably not. It's more likely that a third variable explains the correlation: heat. Towns that have hotter temperatures (such as Miami, Florida, and Austin, Texas) probably sell more ice cream. In addition, more people swim in these towns, also due to the heat (which unfortunately sometimes leads to more drownings). So, while it might look like the two variables of ice cream and drownings are related, both are actually caused by something else.

Even if there is a causal relationship, we might not know which is the cause and which is the effect. Think about the controversial idea that watching violence on TV causes children to act more violently in real life. The correlation seems to be real, but the causal relationship may go in the other direction. Maybe children inclined to be violent already are attracted to TV violence. Simple correlations are only clues. But they are a provocative way to begin engaging with research designed to solve social problems.

THE MAIN IDEAS

- The scientific method, which is used by social psychologists who conduct research, includes (1) observing a pattern, (2) generating a hypothesis, (3) scientifically testing the hypothesis, and (4) interpreting results so that the hypothesis can be refined and tested again.

- Three ways to gather descriptive data are (1) archival data, (2) naturalistic observation, and (3) surveys.

- Correlations test whether two continuous variables (or variables that have scores along a range) are associated with each other in a systematic way.

CRITICAL THINKING CHALLENGE

- Think about the classrooms you've been inside recently. Consider the physical aspects of the room (such as size, type of desks, color, art on the walls, and so on). Then consider how people choose to sit in the room during classes (such as whether they prefer the front or back row, how much they spread out, what kinds of people tend to sit together, and so on). Generate three hypotheses about how either the physical environment or the social environment shapes learning.

- Imagine that you want to do a study on how companies support leadership within their organizations. First, describe how you might conduct the study using archival data; then, how you'd do it with naturalistic observation. Finally, describe how you would conduct the study differently if you decided to give people who work there a survey. What kinds of questions would you ask? How would you get people to fill it out honestly?

- Describe two positive correlations you think are true in your own life, and identify two negative correlations you see in your own life. Then, choose one of those correlations and discuss whether you think there is a causal relationship between the two variables or whether a third variable drives what appears to be an association.

HOW DO EXPERIMENTS WORK IN SOCIAL PSYCHOLOGY?

>> LO 2.2: **Understand the strengths and weaknesses of experiments and how their results are analyzed.**

If the most famous book about experimental designs were going for a big audience in the self-help market, then it might be called *How to Think Clearly*. However, the helpful book written by Donald Campbell and Julian Stanley (1966) had a less dramatic title: *Experimental and Quasi-Experimental Designs for Research*.

The original target market for this groundbreaking book was the unruly world of education research. Campbell and Stanley (1966, p. 2) wanted to calm things down and remind researchers that experimentation takes time, replications, and multiple methods. They organized the world of experimental research design into three categories:

(1) preexperimental designs,

(2) quasi-experiments, and

(3) true experiments.

Preexperimental Designs

Main strength: everyone is treated equally. Main weakness: no comparison group.

The simplest experimental design is called a **preexperiment**. Here, a single group of people is tested to see if some kind of experience or treatment had an effect. Imagine a college is interested in making sure new students succeed, especially in their first year. The faculty design a class all incoming students have to take that's called something like "Freshman Seminar" or "University Success." The college requires *every* new student to take this class, then tracks that group's success through outcomes like their GPA at the end of the semester.

You can see that with preexperiments, because everyone is treated exactly the same, we avoid ethical concerns that might come up in research designs in which different groups are formed. For example, if the college required half of the incoming students to take the class and told the other half of students they weren't allowed to take the class, one of the groups might be at a disadvantage. This problem becomes even more clear when we think of research in areas like mental health interventions. If we design a new therapy to decrease anxiety, giving it to everyone who suffers from anxiety sounds the most fair.

But the problem with preexperiments also then becomes clear: Once we see results, can we really know any changes were because of the treatment? If grades in that year's incoming class are particularly good, how do we know they weren't just smarter than last year's class? And if anxiety decreases, was it the therapy—or something else that happened, like a change in the culture? We can be more confident that an experience or treatment has the effect we think it does when we use the next two research designs.

Quasi-Experiments

Main strength: enables comparison between groups. Main weakness: may not control alternative explanations.

Sometimes we want to compare groups that exist naturally. We might want to study people who have survived natural disasters (like tornadoes or hurricanes) compared to those who have never been in one. We might want to compare people who have served time in prison to those who haven't, people in the military versus civilians, athletes versus nonathletes, people who drink coffee versus those who don't . . . and so on.

Quasi-experiments compare outcomes between or among groups that are naturally occurring. For example, when comparing whether men or women are most likely to interrupt in a conversation, we use two groups (men and women) that existed regardless of our study. There are often extremely interesting questions that can only be asked through quasi-experiments, because people are already in their respective groups. We can now compare one group to another—which was impossible with preexperiments.

But here's the weakness: Even if we find a difference, we can't really be sure *why* that difference exists. In our interruption study, if one group interrupts more, is it because of genetics? Hormones? How boys versus girls are raised in our culture? Descriptive research (explained in the section above), preexperiments, and quasi-experiments all suffer from the same downfall: **confounding variables**.

Confounding variables are factors or issues that offer alternative explanations to why our results came out like they did, which limit our ability to ever say "Variable X caused changes in Variable Y." None of the methods of data collection described so far let us make claims about *causality*, because they all have confounding variables. The only way around confounding variables is a true experiment.

True Experiments

Main strength: controls (most) confounding variables. Main weakness: usually requires more time and effort.

Preexperiment: A research design in which a single group of people is tested to see whether a treatment has an effect.

Quasi-experiment: A research design where outcomes are compared across different groups that occur naturally.

Confounding variables: Alternative explanations for why results came out as they did, which limit a researcher's ability to claim a causal relationship between variables in a study.

The true experiment is the gold standard across all the sciences. That applies especially to social psychology because a **true experiment** compares two or more groups that are equal in every possible way except one (the variable we're testing in the study). The only way to make sure that the groups are equivalent to each other in every way *except* what we're studying is to use **random assignment**. Random assignment means that each person in the study has an equal chance of being put into any of the groups involved. We might flip a coin, draw names from a hat, or use a computer to assign people randomly to various experimental conditions.

Why does random assignment work—how does it eliminate confounding variables, or other explanations? With enough people in each group, random assignment creates a *statistical probability* that, on average, the people in each group are pretty similar to each other. If you have 100 people in your study and you know that half of them are men and half are women, then randomly assigning each person to be in either Group A or Group B of your study means there's a pretty good chance that Group A will consist of about 25 men and 25 women—and the same goes for Group B. Thus, random assignment creates roughly equal groups.

The idea is that in a true experiment with random assignment, the groups you're studying should be as equivalent as possible in every way *except* which group they're in. That way, if the two groups have different outcomes at the end of the study, the only possible reason must be the experimental manipulation—there's just no other explanation. Honestly, it is probably impossible to control every confounding variable. And random means just that—it's possible that random chance will lead the groups to be slightly different in other ways. But random assignment is the best technique we have, and it's why good *replications* are so important to any science.

Independent and Dependent Variables

True experiments have two types of variables (see Table 2.1).

The **independent variable** creates comparison groups, based on random assignment, that will have different experiences in the study. It's the variable that's being manipulated by the experimenters. For example, researchers might have one group of

True experiment: A research design comparing two or more groups that have been created with random assignment.

Random assignment: Placing participants into various conditions of a study using a chance method, to eliminate confounding variables by making the groups as equal to each other as possible.

Independent variable: A variable that is manipulated at the beginning of an experiment to determine its effect; it's how the groups are different from each other at the start of the study.

TABLE 2.1

Independent and Dependent Variables in Experiments

STUDY BASICS	INDEPENDENT VARIABLE	DEPENDENT VARIABLE
Students listen to either classical or rock music while they study, to see if music affects their memory on a test later.	Type of music (classical or rock)	Performance on the memory test
People write an essay about either death or puppies, then rate how much anger they feel.	Essay topic (death or puppies)	Level of anger
Children watch a commercial with dolls or with trucks, then are rated on how aggressively they play with clay and crayons.	Commercial topic (dolls or trucks)	Level of aggression
Sports fans see images of athletes wearing black jerseys or green jerseys and are asked to rate how well they expect each player to do that year.	Jersey color (black or green)	Expectations of players' performance

students listen to classical music and have the other group listen to rock music. So, the independent variable is *type of music*—it's the experimental manipulation that makes the groups different from each other at the very beginning of the study.

Of course, we also have to measure some kind of outcome, which is the **dependent variable**. Maybe while our two groups listen to either classical or rock music, everyone reads the same passage from a textbook. Then, we measure their memory on a test of the material: the dependent variable. In this case, we've hypothesized that *memory scores* are "dependent" on whether participants heard classical or rock music. In experiments, the independent variable is the *cause* being tested (here, type of music) and the dependent variable is the *effect* or outcome (here, memory test scores).

If the groups really were equivalent to each other in every way except the independent variable, any differences in the dependent variable must have been caused by which group they were in. This is how true experiments allow us to make causal inferences. Sometimes, studies include a neutral or baseline group as well that receives no treatment. For example, a study might include (a) a group of students who listen to rock music, (b) a group of students who listen to classical music, and (c) a group of students who listen to no music at all. In this case, that last group—the neutral group—is called a **control group**.

Analyzing Results in Experiments

Once you're done with the study and have your results, how do you know if the hypothesis was supported?

Comparing Two Groups: The *t*-Test Statistic

If your study only had two groups in it, you'll use a test called a *t*-test (see Figure 2.4).

The **t-test** statistic compares the mean and standard deviations of both groups to see if they're different from each other. You might find it interesting that this test was first created by a man named William Sealy Gossett, who used it to test whether different batches of Guinness beer tasted the same (Mankiewicz, 2000).

Dependent variable: The measured outcome at the end of an experiment that is affected by the independent variable.

Control group: A group of participants in a true experiment that serves as a neutral or baseline group that receives no treatment.

t-test: A statistical test that compared the mean and standard deviations of two groups, to see if they are different from each other.

FIGURE 2.4

One way social scientists look for patterns is by comparing average scores within different groups of participants. When we compare two groups, as here, we use a *t*-test. When we compare three or more groups, we do an analysis of variance, or "ANOVA."

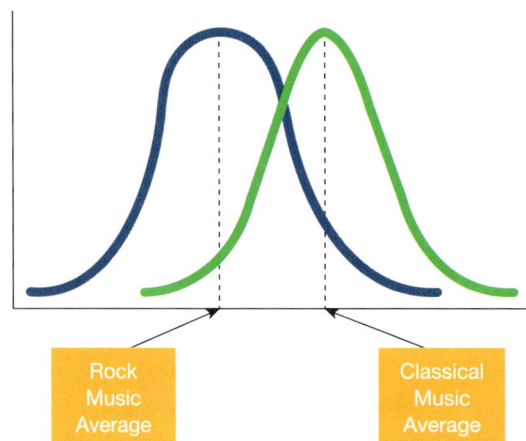

Rock Music Average

Classical Music Average

There were two critical components to Gossett's statistical invention: (1) the sampling had to be random, and (2) the sample had to be big enough to be representative of all casks of beer Guinness made in a given day. It would not be good for Guinness's business if the morning batch tasted different from the afternoon batch. Gossett's invention of the *t*-test statistic for comparing two groups (the morning vs. afternoon batches) ensured consistent quality in Guinness. When we use it for social psychology research, we usually want the groups to be *different* from each other, showing that our independent variable caused some change in the dependent variable. But we can still be grateful for how beer helped us reach our conclusions (thanks, beer!).

We have Guinness to thank for the statistic known as the *t*-test.

Comparing Three or More Groups: Analysis of Variance

What if you have three or more groups in your study?

Think back to one of our earlier examples: Comparing memory test scores for students who studied while listening to rock music, classical music, or no music at all (the control group). Or, what if Gossett wanted to compare Guinness taste samples from more than two groups of beer—say, one from each day of the week?

The principle for comparing multiple groups is the same as comparing two groups. For each group, we calculate the mean and the standard deviation, just like before. However, when we're comparing three or more groups, the test is called an **analysis of variance**, or "ANOVA" for short. For example, perhaps the classical music group in a three-group experiment does better than the rock group—and maybe they are both better than the control group with no music at all. ANOVA tests will tell you whether at least one of the groups is different from the others. Different types of comparison groups require different statistical tests, and once you know the theory behind them, they can be fun to learn.

THE MAIN IDEAS

- A preexperiment is a method in which a single group of people is tested to see whether some kind of treatment has an effect.

- A quasi-experiment tests for the effect of a treatment in groups that have formed naturally, such as men versus women, or people who do or don't like to drink coffee.

- A true experiment compares outcomes on two or more groups that have been created by the experimenter through random assignment to condition. True experiments are the only methodology that can lead researchers to make claims about cause-effect relationships between variables. The variable that's manipulated and makes groups different at the start of the study is the independent variable, and the measured outcome at the end is the dependent variable.

- Researchers can compare the means and standard deviations of their various experimental groups to see if they differ from each other at the end of a study. When two groups are compared, a *t*-test statistic is used; when there are three or more groups, an analysis of variance test is used.

CRITICAL THINKING CHALLENGE

- Earlier, we discussed challenges to naturalistic observation (reactivity) and to surveys (social desirability). What are some challenges to experimental research designs? How could scientists overcome these challenges?

Analysis of variance (ANOVA): A statistical test that compares the means and standard deviations of three or more groups, to see if they are different from each other.

- Imagine that you have a hypothesis that people who drink a lot of caffeine will experience heightened emotions over the course of a day. Explain how you might test your hypothesis using a preexperiment, a quasi-experiment, and a true experiment.

- True experiments are needed to test things like advances in medicine. If someone found a pill they think could cure cancer, a true experiment would require a study in which participants with cancer are randomly assigned to either a group that gets the pill or a control group of people who get a placebo. Neither can know whether they're getting the "real" pill or the placebo. What are the ethics of this kind of study, where people's lives might actually be in the balance?

HOW CAN I RECOGNIZE TRUSTWORTHY RESEARCH?

>> LO 2.3:   Explain why reliability, validity, random sampling, ethics, and open science signal good research.

You are asked to consume research many times each day.

Some of it is legitimate, but much of it is nothing more than "I read somewhere . . ." Research claims on TV or online about foods, drugs, and toothpaste are uncertain. Advertisements clearly have a conflict of interest in whether they're honest about the benefits of their products. Recognizing trustworthy friends, products, and research requires similar skills built from painful life experiences. You may not develop those skills until you've been burned a few times.

This section answers the core question "How can I recognize trustworthy research?" by describing

(1)   the meanings of reliability, validity, and random sampling;

(2)   the ethical guidelines that support social psychological research; and

(3)   the "open science" movement.

Reliability, Validity, and Random Sampling

Part of the appeal of digital textbooks is practical: Printed textbooks are heavy!

Sometimes, your arms and back hurt from lugging them around all day. So, you become curious about just how much those suckers weigh. You pile them on top of the scale at your local gym and it gives you a result: 36.8 pounds.

No wonder your back hurts! But then your friend tells you that the scale is often off by several pounds, which she knows because she sometimes compares what that scale tells her to the scale at her doctor's office on the same day. So you try again. This time the same scale tells you that the exact same pile of books weighs 33.2 pounds. Surprised, you take the books off and put them back on, and now it says 40.6 pounds! Clearly, you can't trust this scale because it is unreliable.

It doesn't matter if we are research psychologists, clinical psychologists, or just trying to have an intelligent conversation. If we run into the same problem weighing self-esteem instead of textbooks, then we don't really know what to believe about self-esteem.

If you use a scale like this one to weigh yourself, how confident are you that the result is correct or that it wouldn't change if you stepped off and back on?

Shutterstock/Andrey_Popov

Reliability is consistency of measurement, over time or over multiple testing occasions. It doesn't matter if it is a weight scale, an intelligence test, a train that does not keep to schedule, or a friend who may or may not show up on time: To be trustworthy, consistency is key.

A study must also be high in internal, construct, and external validity. High **internal validity** signals confidence that your results mean what you think they mean. For example, if you forgot to use random assignment in the music and memory study, then you have opened the door to self-selection and alternate explanations. Randomly assigning participants to different conditions reduces that threat to internal validity because it helps eliminate confounding variables. Another way to improve internal validity is to ensure **construct validity**, which is whether the tests, surveys, and so on chosen for the study really measure what we think they're measuring.

High **external validity** builds trust in your results if they apply to other people or settings. For example, many social psychology studies have used college students as participants. That's great—if you are a college student and the results apply to you. But those results might be limited in their **generalizability**, or how much they apply to people "in general." This problem is sometimes known by the acronym WEIRD because so many participants are Western, Educated, and from Industrialized, Rich, Democratic cultures. We know less about other kinds of people—the diversity in participants is sometimes lacking.

One of the best ways to increase generalizability—and thus external validity—is to use **random sampling** (not the same thing as random assignment). Random sampling means that the people in your study were randomly selected from the larger population of interest. If you want to know the opinions of students at your college or university, the easy approach would be asking for volunteers or surveying people who live in a certain dorm. But if you want data you can trust, random sampling would mean getting a list of every student and choosing the people in your study in some truly random way. Hopefully, that technique results in a sample of participants who represent the diversity of people across your entire population.

Ethics and Institutional Review Boards

"The therapists . . . they should be in prison right now, today."

It is distressingly easy to lose our moral compass. Bob Kelly had good reason to be critical of therapists during a presentation at the Duke University Law School. As owner of the Little Rascals daycare in Edenton, North Carolina, Bob (and six others) had been falsely accused of sexually abusing some 90 children. There was no physical evidence—none!

So, some of the most important "evidence" included reports from psychological therapists. Sentenced to 12 consecutive life sentences, Bob Kelly's conviction was overturned—but only after 6 years in prison. It was also unlikely that the therapists had lied. They had somehow lost sight of the ethical guidelines that guarded them and their profession. It seems they genuinely thought he was guilty, even though there was no evidence of that conclusion. We have a solemn responsibility to treat people with respect. That includes how we use unobtrusive methodologies like naturalistic observation and even archival studies when we examine people's life information.

Researchers (across the sciences) rely on **institutional review boards (IRBs)**, committees that consider the ethical implications of any study. *Before* any of us begin formal research that might affect participants and be published, we are obliged to submit our methods for review. Your local IRB committee is typically composed of representatives from different departments in a college, university, research institute, or corporation—and sometimes from a combination of such organizations.

Many committees include a lawyer and sometimes a member with no background in research at all, to represent the "average person's" perspective. The IRB committee will consider applications for every study your university might run, then decide in

Reliability: Consistency of measurement, over time or multiple testing occasions. A study is said to be reliable if similar results are found when the study is repeated.

Internal validity: The level of confidence researchers have that patterns of data are due to what is being tested, as opposed to flaws in how the experiment was designed.

Construct validity: The degree to which tests, surveys, and so on chosen for a study really measure what we think they're measuring.

External validity: The extent to which results of any single study could apply to other people or settings (see *generalizability*).

Generalizability: How much the results of a single study can apply to the general population (see *external validity*).

Random sampling: A sampling technique where a researcher randomly chooses people to participate from a larger population of interest.

Institutional review boards (IRBs): Committees of people who consider the ethical implications of any study before giving the researcher approval to begin formal research.

Ethical violations in the Tuskegee Syphilis Study helped establish the need for IRBs to prevent future violations of trust. Participants in this study of syphilis were not (a) told the purpose of the study, (b) given a chance to leave the study, or (c) treated with penicillin that might have cured them.

American Psychological Association (APA): A large organization of professional psychologists who provide scholarly publications, writing guidelines, and ethical standards for research.

The National Archives at Atlanta

advance if there is any potential serious harm involved. If there is possible danger, the study won't be approved.

The specific guidelines for psychology come from both our local IRB committees and the **American Psychological Association (APA)**, an organization of professionals in the field who have determined what the ethical standards of research should be. Note that the standards currently in effect from the APA were not always in place. Some of the studies you'll read about in this book were done before APA standards and IRB committees were standard—and thus, some of those studies have been harshly criticized for being harmful to the people who were in them. Protecting and respecting participants should be the highest priority for anyone conducting research. What are the guidelines?

The American Psychological Association lists several "rights" that they say all participants should have. Again, consider each of these as you read about studies in this book and consider whether you think the study was ethical. In addition, if you have the chance to participate in any studies yourself, it's important for you to know what your rights are—so that you can stop participating at any point if you are uncomfortable or

---

💡 Questions Your Institutional Review Board Might Ask

Institutional review boards (IRBs) are committees that review ethical considerations for any new study; you need to get IRB approval before you can move forward. To know more about this process, consider the questions below; they are the typical types of questions any researcher will need to answer before starting the research process. Researchers are required to type their answers and submit them to the IRB committee for review, along with copies of any materials such as surveys, videos, and so on.

- What is the purpose of your study, and what are the hypotheses?

- What kinds of participants do you plan to use? How many? How will you recruit them? Will they be compensated for their participation through something like money or extra credit?

- Are the participants from any kind of legally protected group, such as children, prisoners, people with disabilities, and so on?

- How will you get informed consent?

- What are the specific questions you will ask or experimental procedures you will use?

- Will there be any deception? If so, what is the justification for that deception?

- How will debriefing occur?

- What are the potential harms (physically, emotionally, or mentally) that participants might experience, short term or long term?

- Will you provide any resources if participants have questions or concerns?

- Are there any potential benefits participants might experience as a result of being in your study?

- How long will your study take? How will you ensure that the data collected will remain confidential and/or anonymous?

- Do you plan to present your results to the public, such as through a conference presentation or publication? If so, will the participants have access to these results themselves if they are interested?

Hopefully, you can see that IRB committees take their jobs very seriously—as they should. There also are career opportunities waiting for you if you are interested in protecting the rights of both human and nonhuman animals. These careers combine elements of law, philosophy, science, and psychology.

feel like you don't want to continue for any reason. Some of the participant rights identified by the APA are as follows:

- **Informed consent**: Participants should be told what they will be asked to do and whether there are any potential dangers or risks involved in the study before it begins.

- **Deception**: Participants should be told the truth about the purpose and nature of the study as much as possible. *Deception,* or hiding the true nature of the study, is only allowed when it is necessary because knowing the truth would change how the participants responded.

- **Right to withdraw**: Participants have the right to stop being in the study at any time, for any reason, or to skip questions on a survey if they are not comfortable answering them.

- **Debriefing**: After completing the study, all participants should be given additional details about the hypotheses of the study, allowed the opportunity to ask questions, and even see the results if they wish. This *debriefing* after the study is complete should definitely include an explanation of any deception that was involved (if deception occurred) so that participants have the right to withdraw their data if they are upset about the deception.

If you want to design your own study, you should consider all these criteria for the quality of good research. In addition, you'll have to get approval from your school's IRB committee as well before you begin. To learn more about the IRB approval process, see the Spotlight on Research Methods feature.

The "Open Science" Movement

Ethics are always important.

We've already discussed some ethical considerations, such as avoiding deception in studies whenever possible, making sure we get informed consent before participants start in a research project, and so on. The ethics of science are even broader, though, when we start to think about how studies happen from start to finish. What if a researcher misrepresented their results or decided to form hypotheses only after they knew how the study's results turned out? What if they refused to share their data with other people, who could confirm the findings?

Open science is a movement to make scientific research transparent, accessible, cooperative, reproducible, and honest. The aim of open science is to remove barriers for the creation of studies, sharing of data and results, and analysis of implications or conclusions. It's a way of saying to others, let's all do this together in an open, honest environment. Open science is also a reaction to the "replication crisis" discussed in Chapter 1. As scientists, social psychologists want to be honest and confident about our research conclusions.

There are several ways that open science encourages this kind of communication and exchange; a few are preregistration, results-blind peer review, and publication badges.

Preregistration

Imagine that a scientist does a study in which they're not really sure what they're looking for.

This is called exploratory research, and there's nothing wrong with it. But now imagine that after the results are analyzed, the scientist publishes the study and more or less pretends that they predicted the outcomes from the beginning. They look super smart! But it's not an honest approach.

Open science's solution is **preregistration**, a practice of specifying—in advance—your hypotheses, procedure, and statistical plan for analyses (see Nosek et al., 2017).

Informed consent: Participants' right to be told what a study will involve, including potential dangers, before the study starts.

Deception: Hiding the true nature of an experiment from a participant so they act more naturally.

Right to withdraw: The right participants have to stop being in a study at any time or to skip questions on a survey.

Debriefing: Additional details given to participants after participation in an experiment.

Open science: A movement to make science more transparent, cooperative, reproducible, and honest.

Preregistration: Specifying your hypothesis, procedure, and statistical plan for a study before collecting data.

This plan is made publicly available to anyone, so you are committing to everything in an open, transparent way before you begin your study. Several preregistration templates have been created to help people through this process, where researchers can post their plans on independent websites.

Preregistration is not without problems. For example, you might say that you're going to get 100 people for your study, but you can only get 75. Or you might assume that people will pay attention to instructions during your procedure, but some of them don't and they mess up what they are supposed to be doing. Or you might realize after you've collected data that you had a typo on your scale that changed what the question was asking. Scientists are certainly not perfect, and mistakes can be made. But all of these changes can simply be documented and explained. That way, readers of the research can understand exactly the process that occurred and why changes had to be made.

Typical questions you'll answer on a preregistration form are things like this:

- What are your hypotheses? If you're doing a quasi-experiment or experiment, what are the independent and dependent variables? If you're doing a correlation study, do you expect a positive or negative correlation?

- What exactly will the procedure be—what will participants do? What will be the order of procedural steps? How long with it take each person to do the study? How will you do random assignment (if relevant)?

- How will you recruit participants, and how many do you expect to find? Will anyone be excluded from data analysis—and if so, why?

- How will each of your variables be measured and calculated? What statistical tests will you use to analyze the results?

Results-Blind Peer Review

Every academic field has professional journals, where researchers publish their results.

Most of these journals are what we call "peer-review" journals. That means that before any article is accepted for publication, it's sent out to other experts on that topic to see what they think. Those people, called reviewers, give the author(s) anonymous feedback about whether they think the article is worthy of being published. Sometimes the reviewers will make suggested changes that they want to see, and if those changes are made, the article will be published. Sometimes, however, the reviewers can simply say that they don't like the study and stop it from being published.

Until the open science movement, all of this reviewing happened after a study was completed and written up. That meant that the peer reviewers knew how the study turned out. The problem with this is that it can lead to biases in what is and isn't accepted for publication. Maybe the reviewers wouldn't like the results because they go against a theory they favor. A more common problem is that studies usually weren't published if their results didn't show statistically significant findings or results that matched their hypotheses.

These problems can largely be eliminated with a practice called **results-blind peer review**, which means that reviewers are asked about the importance of the study *before* they see the statistical outcomes, as shown in Figure 2.5. If they agree that the study has merit, they accept it for publication at this stage. Reviewers will also be asked for their feedback after the results are calculated—but now they comment on whether the study followed the preregistration plan and interpreted everything correctly.

That way, even if the results surprise everyone, the study still gets published. Chris Chambers, the chair of a committee at the Center for Open Science, stated the benefits of this process like this: "The incentives for authors change from producing the most beautiful story to producing the most accurate one" (Center for Open Science at https://cos.io/rr/). Just like a relationship partner, science is even more beautiful when it's accurate and honest.

Results-blind peer review: Asking experts to judge a potential study's value and quality before the data have been collected and analyzed.

When an article goes through the results-blind peer review process, outside experts give feedback about the quality and importance of an article before the data are actually collected. Then, they review a second time, focusing on whether the study followed the original design plan.

DEVELOP IDEA → DESIGN STUDY → COLLECT AND ANALYZE DATA → WRITE REPORT → PUBLISH REPORT

Stage 1 Peer Review ↑   Stage 2 Peer Review ↑

Publication Badges

Beyond the rewards of knowing you're doing good science, what incentives are there for people to engage in open science practices?

One reward is the use of **badges**, or visual icons that mark a study with signals that it has followed these procedures. You can see what the badges look like, at least for some journals, in Figure 2.6. If a study was preregistered, once it's published, the red badge will appear on the first page. If the authors have made their procedural materials available to everyone, they get the orange badge, and if they have posted their original, raw data spreadsheets online, they get the blue badge.

Over 50 journals now use the badge system, and early trends show that they really do increase the number of scientists who share their data publicly (Kidwell et al., 2016; Rowhani-Farid et al., 2017). The open science movement is likely going to increase in

Badges: Visual icons that can mark if a study used open science practices.

Professional journals are increasingly marking studies with these images, called badges, when they follow open science guidelines. These examples are from the Center for Open Science.

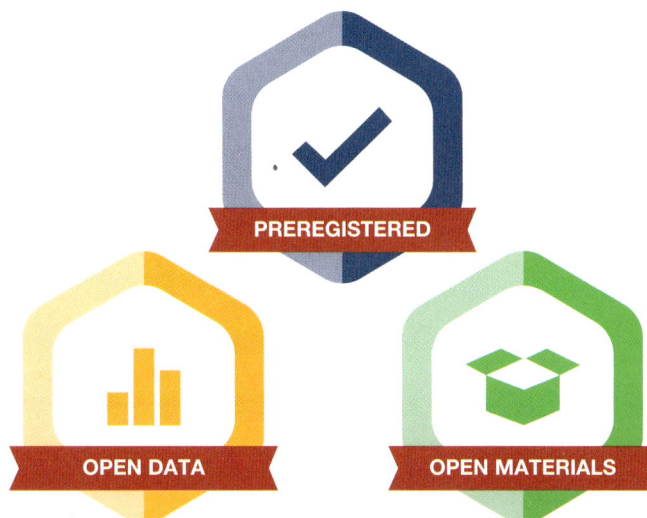

PREREGISTERED

OPEN DATA   OPEN MATERIALS

usage and popularity over the next several years, as many people see it as the only way to make the scientific process truly objective and transparent.

THE MAIN IDEAS

- Reliability, validity, and random sampling are all criteria regarding the quality of any given research study.

- Ethical considerations are also very important when evaluating research studies. The American Psychological Association lists several participant rights, such as informed consent and debriefing. In addition, any study must be approved by an IRB before it can be conducted.

- "Open science" is a movement to make research more transparent, cooperative, and honest. It involves preregistration, results-blind peer review, and badges indicating whether studies have used the process before publication.

CRITICAL THINKING CHALLENGE

- Imagine a study conducted in 1930, before the APA enacted ethical guidelines and before IRB committees were common. If that study were unethical but highly interesting in terms of the results, should textbooks still talk about the study and what we learned from it? Does continuing to talk about the study disrespect the participants, or does learning from it mean that at least we are attempting to get some good from the bad that already occurred?

- Different IRB committees have different levels of strictness regarding ethical thresholds. For example, one committee might be fine with a study that causes participants to temporarily be angry, sad, or aggressive—while another committee might consider the same study unethical. If you were to serve on an IRB committee, how would you decide what the threshold of danger or harm should be? What's the balance between possible risk of harm versus what could be learned from the study?

- Some professional journals charge for copies of their articles or require people to pay for subscriptions. Others offer their articles to readers for free, but they require that the scientists themselves pay to publish their work in the journal. What do you think is the best system for research to be available to other scientists or the general public, in terms of how it is funded? Should there be a new system, like a "science tax" that everyone pays but is used to make scientific progress available to everyone? Discuss how you think science should be funded and why.

CHAPTER SUMMARY

How Do Social Psychologists Design Studies?

Basic researchers advance theories, while applied researchers translate those theories into real-world settings or people. Both types of researchers use the scientific method, a systematic way of creating knowledge. Descriptive designs clarify patterns of data without experimenter intervention. Examples of descriptive designs are use of archival data, naturalistic observation, and self-report surveys. Each method has strengths and weaknesses. Descriptive data are often analyzed using correlation tests. Correlations tell whether two continuous variables have a system association with each other but cannot tell whether there is a causal relationship between those variables.

How Do Experiments Work in Social Psychology?

Preexperiments are studies in which a single group of people is tested to see if a treatment or experience has an effect. When scientists want to compare two or more groups to each other, they can use quasi-experiments or true experiments. Quasi-experiments compare naturally occurring groups to each other, while true experiments create groups using random assignment (participants are randomly put into one of the study's groups). The variable that makes groups different from each other at the start of a study is the independent variable, and scientists are testing whether that has an effect on the outcome of the study, which is called the dependent variable. To analyze results, a *t*-test is used when there are only two groups in a study, while an analysis of variance (ANOVA) tests for differences in three or more groups.

How Can I Recognize Trustworthy Research?

Reliability, validity, and random sampling are all important things to consider when trying to evaluate the quality of a research study. Reliability is whether the measures used are consistent. Internal validity is the extent to which results are interpreted in an accurate way, based on the setup of the study. External validity is the extent to which results could apply to other people or settings. Random sampling will hopefully result in a diverse variety of different kinds of people in the study. In addition, the ethics of any proposed study will be reviewed by a committee called an institutional review board (IRB). Examples of ethical considerations are whether a study includes informed consent, deception, and debriefing. Finally, the "open science" movement is a trend in psychology that encourages researchers to be honest, open, and transparent with their research from start to finish—for example, they might post spreadsheets of their data online so that other scientists can check the accuracy of their statistical analyses.

CRITICAL THINKING, ANALYSIS, AND APPLICATION

- Which of the research methods described in this chapter seem the most appealing to you? Why is that method appealing, and what issues or concerns do you have with the other methods?

- Find a news report that makes a claim that one variable causes another (for example, "Drug X leads to bad behavior," or "Access to birth control leads to risky sex," etc.). Is the causal relationship being suggested one that seems valid? Why or why not? How could this causal claim be scientifically tested?

- How many times does a study have to be replicated for researchers—or the general public—to be confident in the results? Even if a study is never replicated, does that mean that the data are useless? What other explanations could there be for results that seem to change (in other words, aren't replicated)? Is it possible that researchers simply haven't identified the exact reason why the pattern happened the first time, for example?

- Ideally, studies have generalizable samples of people who participate. But what if you want to generalize your findings to all of humanity? It's clearly impossible to use random sampling across everyone in the world, so most people just use participants who are nearby volunteers. What's the balance between convenience for the researcher and the need for a diverse, generalizable sample of participants? Are any studies truly high in external validity if they don't have true random sampling?

iStockPhoto/xavierarnau

3

The Social Self

Core Questions

3.1 How do we understand the "self"?

3.2 How do we know the self is social?

3.3 Are we honest about ourselves?

Learning Objectives

3.1 Explain how social psychology has defined self-awareness and the self-concept.

3.2 Analyze how our self-perceptions and group affiliations influence how we think, feel, and behave.

3.3 Describe the risks and rewards associated with positive self-illusions, moderate self-deceptions, and artificially boosting self-esteem.

Who are you if you have lost your memory?

Movies and shows about memory loss explore the mystery of who we are:

Homecoming (2018–present): A counselor chemically deletes soldiers' traumatic memories so they can quickly return to war.

Bladerunner 2049 (2017): A man tries to connect spotty memories from his childhood, only to realize they are not really his.

Get Out (2017): A White family systematically subdues the memories of Black people to control their bodies.

Finding Dory (2016): A friendly but forgetful blue tang fish searches for her long-lost parents.

Total Recall (1990/2012): A man in the future discovers his memory has been altered as he struggles to discover his true self and history. How much is true, and how much is a lie designed to cover up a covert spy operation?

HOW DO WE UNDERSTAND THE "SELF"?

>> LO 3.1:   Explain how social psychology has defined self-awareness and the self-concept.

The characters in these dramas had to imagine their self into existence.

We all imagine our self because the self is the story we tell ourselves about who we are. It is a "functional fiction" (Swann & Buhrmester, 2012), a made-up, pieced-together tale of uncertainties that has an audience of only one person but is influenced by all the people around us. The self-story may begin with the proverbial slap on a newborn baby's backside (or the more likely suction device up the baby's nose). Before that moment, we were part of someone else's body. Then, with a snip of the umbilical cord and a sudden breath of air, we became a separate, living creature.

But did we know it at that moment? The scientific challenge is to develop a reliable way (see Sedikides & Skowronski, 1997) of discovering how and when we develop the **self-awareness** (also called **self-recognition**) that we are a separate entity from other people and objects.

This section answers the core question "How do we understand the self?" by

(1) considering experimental research on self-awareness and

(2) discussing components of the self-concept.

Self-awareness: The understanding that we are a separate entity from other people and objects in our world.

Self-recognition: See *self-awareness*.

We Have Self-Awareness: The Mirror Self-Recognition Test

How we think about ourselves changes.

The creator of psychology's first textbook, William James (1890), wrote that the self "is the sum total of all that a person can call his [today we would say "their"] own," including

not only his body . . . but his clothes and his house . . . his reputation and works . . . his yacht and his bank-account. All these things give him the same emotions. If they wax and prosper, he feels triumphant; if they dwindle and die away, he feels cast down. (p. 292)

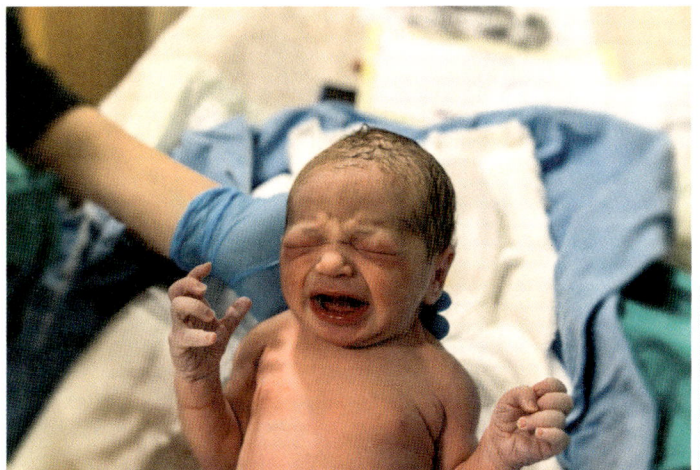

Is this the first moment of self-awareness?

Shutterstock/osonmez22

You might not have a yacht, but you get the point. Charles Darwin first explored self-awareness using *naturalistic observations* of William (born in 1839), the first of his 10 children. Darwin was a proud, new papa. He recorded in detail his child's talent for imitation and interpreted it as one early signal of self-awareness (Darwin, 1877).

Imitation as a signal of self-awareness continued to guide investigators across the next century (Anderson, 1984; Damon & Hart, 1988). One study documented 2- to 3-week-old infants imitating a mouth opening, a finger moving, or a tongue appearing between the lips (Meltzoff & Moore, 1977). By 1989, the same research team had documented imitation among infants who were less than 72 hours old (including a 42-minute-old infant!). However, imitation of others is not the only way people or animals signal self-awareness.

Darwin (1872) had also explored the self-awareness of orangutans with a creative experimental technique. He reported that

> many years ago, in the [London] Zoological Gardens, I placed a looking-glass on the floor between two young [orangutans]. . . . They approached close and protruded their lips towards the image, as if to kiss it, in exactly the same manner as they had previously done towards each other. (p. 142)

Those orangutans acted as if the creature in the mirror were another animal, not themselves. They did not seem to exhibit awareness that the mirror image was actually themselves.

Almost 100 years later, in 1968, Gordon Gallup created the **mirror self-recognition test** (also called the mark test). He first anesthetized some chimpanzees, macaques, and rhesus monkeys so they would be asleep. Then he marked each animal with a nonodorous, nonirritating red dye just above the eyebrow. The animals could not smell, feel, or see the red dye without the help of a mirror.

Like Darwin, Gallup wanted to know whether the waking animal would respond to their mirror image "as if their image represented another animal" (Gallup, 1968, p. 782). If the animal ignored the red dye, then it probably perceived that the creature in the mirror was some other animal. That "other" animal just happened to have a red splotch on its forehead. But if the waking animal touched the unusual red dye on its own face, then the animal was telling us, "That's me in the mirror": self-awareness.

Mirror self-recognition test: A mark is placed on an animal's forehead, and then the animal is placed in front of a mirror. Self-awareness is assumed if the animal touches the mark on its own forehead.

Self-concept: The personal summary of who we are, including our positive and negative qualities, relationships to others, group memberships, and beliefs.

In Gallup's first study, the four chimpanzees (but not the other primates) touched the strange red mark on their *own* foreheads after seeing it in the mirror. Eureka! Gallup had scientifically demonstrated self-awareness among chimpanzees. Note, however, an important caveat or limitation: The mark test only indicates awareness of a *physical* self. We don't know if these animals have a psychological sense of self.

Mirror self-recognition studies have now documented self-awareness among other great apes (Parker, 1991), Asian elephants (Plotnik et al., 2006), killer whales (Delfour & Marten, 2001), dolphins (Marino, 2002), and magpies (Prior et al., 2008). Again, some scholars question whether these animals really have self-awareness the same way that humans do (e.g., Suddendorf & Butler, 2013). In addition, while this list might surprise you, this physical sense of self-awareness is still extremely rare in the animal kingdom.

Michel Gunther/Science Source

Do nonhuman animals have a sense of self? A YouTube.com search for "animal self-recognition" results in videos of elephants, lions, chimpanzees, and others toying with their image in a mirror.

The Self Requires a Self-Concept

The **self-concept** is how we answer the question, "Who am I?"

Julian Finney / Getty Images Sport / Getty Images

One way to know how we're doing on a certain skill or trait is by comparing ourselves to people who are both better and worse, like a silver medalist might do. They're not as good as the gold medalist, but at least they're better than the bronze!

It includes our summary assessment of our positive and negative qualities, our relationships to others, our group memberships, our beliefs and opinions, and more. The self-concept is formed through **schemas**, mental structures and frameworks that help us summarize and organize how we perceive and experience the world. So, **self-schemas** are mental structures that help us summarize and organize our perceptions about self-relevant information (Markus, 1977). We use those summaries to build our self-concept (Hewitt & Genest, 1990). Self-schemas help create what Cervone (2004) calls "the architecture of personality."

Our self-concept and self-schemas are acquired in several ways, including comparing ourselves to others and influence from our group memberships and cultures.

Comparing the Self to Others: Social Comparison Theory

How would you know if you are shy?

Social comparison theory proposes that we make assessments about who we are by comparing how we think or act to those around us. We need them because concepts like "shy" are abstract and subjective (Festinger, 1954). Social comparisons inform us whether we are relatively shy, competitive, rich, anxious, athletic, or anything else (Bachman & O'Malley, 1986; Marsh et al., 2001). College students, for example, compare their body size and eating patterns to their peers (Tylka & Sabik, 2010) or images they see in the media such as advertisements (Bessenoff, 2006), which can affect their self-esteem.

There are two types of social comparisons we can make.

- *Upward Social Comparisons*. When we make an **upward social comparison**, we compare ourselves to someone who is better than us. While the comparison might be a little humbling or even depressing, it may help us improve. For example, most people who watch celebrity chefs or Instagram feeds enjoy getting tips on how to make their own food taste or look better.

- *Downward Social Comparisons*. When we make **downward social comparisons**, we compare ourselves to someone who is worse than we are. This might not help us improve, but it sure feels better. My cupcakes might not win any contests, sure, but they're better than what my 8-year-old son tried to make. Downward social comparisons boost our ego, help us get through rough times, and potentially remind us that we've made progress from where we started.

Schema: A mental structure or framework for organizing the world.

Self-schema: A mental structure that summarizes and organizes our perceptions about self-relevant information.

Social comparison theory: We make assessments about who we are by comparing how we think or act to those around us.

Upward social comparison: When we compare ourselves to someone who is better than us, often to improve on a particular skill.

Downward social comparison: When we compare ourselves to someone who is worse than us, often to feel better.

The different effects of upward and downward comparisons highlight the importance of how we process information (Suls & Wheeler, 2000). The W.I.D.E. guide to social comparisons identifies four factors that influence how social comparisons influence subjective information processing (see Figure 3.1):

- *Who.* We evaluate our abilities automatically (Gilbert et al., 1995) by comparing ourselves to *similar* others (Gibbons & Buunk, 1999). If you're an athlete, comparing yourself to people on your own team or from similar schools is the most useful. Comparing yourself to a professional athlete or to a middle school beginner isn't as helpful to know where you stand.

- *Interpretation.* How we interpret social comparisons influences our self-concept. Finding out you have a mild but chronic illness could be processed optimistically or pessimistically (Brandstätter, 2000; Michinov, 2007). You might think, "Thank goodness it's not more serious," or, "My entire life is about to change." Your interpretation will affect your outlook and your behaviors.

- *Direction.* The direction of our social comparison influences our self-concept. Comparing yourself to better athletes is an upward social comparison (that makes you feel worse), and comparing yourself to worse players is a downward social comparison (that makes you feel better). Downward social comparisons tend to enhance our self-concept (Burleson et al., 2005; Gibbons et al., 2002; Guimond et al., 2007; Major et al., 1993).

- *Esteem.* Protecting our self-esteem influences our self-concept. A losing athlete may say to their opponent, "You played extremely well today," implying that the opponent had to play their best to win (Alicke et al., 1997). We'll explore more psychological tricks that protect our self-esteem a little later in this chapter.

FIGURE 3.1

The W.I.D.E. guide suggests that social comparisons are made up of four factors.

W	I	D	E
Who	Interpretation	Direction	Esteem

Source: Adapted from Suls and Wheeler (2000).

Group Memberships and Culture: Social Identity Theory

Henri Tajfel was captured by German soldiers during World War II.

That's when his self-concept became more than a vague philosophical debate. Tajfel was a Polish-born Jew who had volunteered to join the French army. When the Germans asked him, "Who are you?" Tajfel faced a terrible dilemma: Should he admit he was Jewish? He did—but he also falsely presented himself as a French citizen, which probably saved his life. After surviving the war with other French prisoners, Tajfel became a social psychologist who proposed that the self is composed of two general categories:

1. personal characteristics (like serious, funny, grumpy, and tall) and

2. social role characteristics (like American, student at your school, and teams you're on).

Your self-concept is organized around what Tajfel called **social identity theory**, which proposes both a *personal identity* and a *social identity* (see Rivenburgh,

Social identity theory: Our self-concept is composed of two parts: a personal identity and a social identity, made up of our group memberships and culture.

The social self is influenced by cultural expectations and traditions that show up in surprising ways in controlled experiments.

2000; Sherif, 1966b; Tajfel, 1981, 1982; Tajfel & Turner, 1986). Your personal identity is restricted to just your individual traits, goals, and behaviors. In contrast, your social identity is made up of your group memberships and relationships to others.

Group Memberships. You are complicated; very.

Your groups are an extremely important part of your identity, although which groups matter the most at any given time can vary. If you're a member of an athletic team, school choir, theater group, or gaming club, it might become important when you're trying to decide how to spend your Saturday afternoon.

Here's another way you are complicated: Your self-esteem can go up or down depending on whether these groups are harmonious and successful (something familiar to all Cubs fans!). Being in one group might lead you to have stereotypes about the others. No matter what groups you're in, they affect how you view your self-concept.

Cultural Expectations. Culture is like the water fish swim in; we don't notice it until we leave it.

If you've gone to college in a part of the country (or the world!) that's not where you grew up, you might experience culture shock. But local cultures also carry silent expectations. For example, regional affiliations also influence how we perceive one another.

Within the United States, people from New England are often perceived as intelligent but snobbish, Midwesterners as hardworking but hicks, Southerners as hospitable but racist, and West Coasters as laid back but superficial (Berry et al., 2000). Probably you read that last sentence and were offended regarding the stereotype about your own region—but you also probably understood that the stereotype does exist, even when it's unfair (just like all stereotypes).

Bumping into another culture is a good way to learn about your own expectations. That's why some colleges and universities encourage students to travel abroad, or at least to spend time with some international students or organizations. Learning about other cultures can be a fascinating and fun experience—but cultural differences can also lead to misunderstanding and conflict.

Individualism and Collectivism. Japan is a highly collectivistic culture.

When Japanese workers get on an elevator, they arrange their positions in the elevator according to their social rank. And if it is out of order, then they all get out at the next floor, rearrange themselves, and reenter the elevator! Millions of Japanese people live in limited space, so conformity and order are necessary to make life manageable for all of them. But it is strange to most Americans who live in a country with seemingly endless borders.

One of the most fundamental but intriguing ways social psychology has studied cultural influences on the self-concept is by comparing "Eastern" or Asian cultures (such as Japan, China, Korea, and India) to "Western" cultures (such as the United States, Canada, and most countries in Europe). Cultural differences have been identified as aligning in two different directions, displayed in Figure 3.2.

FIGURE 3.2

Identity can be shaped by culture.

Personal Identity
(Western)

Social Identity
(Asian)

Autonomy
Individualism
Independence
Assertiveness

Relatedness
Collectivism
Interdependence
Self-Effacement

The pattern of research results seems to support that self-concept in many Western cultures is one of an **independent self**, meaning one that is focused on individual needs. Western cultures often emphasize personal successes, competitive spirits, and individual self-esteem (Hui & Triandis, 1986; Triandis et al., 1984). These cultures have been thus been labeled **individualistic**.

In contrast, many Eastern or Asian cultures lead to an **interdependent self**, or one that is focused on family or group needs. These cultures emphasize collective goals; values include working for the greater good of a family, company, or other such social group. These cultures have thus been labeled **collectivistic**, because of their emphasis on the larger social group.

Table 3.1 helps us understand how cultural norms influence how we think about the self (Markus & Kitayama, 1991). While the rugged, tough cowboy and the ambitious stockbroker are admired in the United States for their independence, they might be criticized in Japan for their selfishness. The conciliatory team player who is valued in Japan may be perceived as wimpy and nonassertive in the United States. The traits and behaviors, especially in group settings, that are valued in each culture are different—and each can seem rude to the other.

Independent self:
A self-concept largely based on internal, personal qualities (often found in Western cultures).

Individualistic: Term for cultures that emphasize the self, independence, and personal success.

Interdependent self:
A self-concept largely based on social qualities, group memberships, and relationships with others (often found in Eastern or Asian cultures).

Collectivistic: Term for cultures that emphasize the larger social group, interdependence, and family.

TABLE 3.1

Some Examples of How Culture Affects Views of the Self

	TO GUIDE GROUP BEHAVIOR	TO GET CHILDREN TO FINISH THEIR FOOD	TO IMPROVE WORKER PRODUCTIVITY
American culture recommends that . . .	. . . "the squeaky wheel gets the grease."	. . . children think of the starving children in Ethiopia and how lucky they are to be American.	. . . workers stand in front of a mirror and repeat: "I am beautiful."
Japanese culture recommends that . . .	. . . "the nail that stands up gets pounded down."	. . . children think about the farmer who worked so hard to produce the rice for you and how disappointed they will be if it is not eaten.	. . . workers hold a coworker's hand and repeat: "They are beautiful."

Source: Data from Markus and Kitayama (1991).

Marriage: The Laboratory of Clashing Cultures. Maybe . . . "two can live as cheaply as one."

But it is still not a great justification for getting married. Spending time with people from different cultures and really trying to appreciate their perspective can lead to wonderful outcomes. For example, when people from different cultures get married, overcoming cultural differences can lead to particularly good relationships and positive psychological outcomes for their children as well (Bagley et al., 2019). But it's not going to be easy because you can't identify all of the silent assumptions that each carries into the relationship.

Honestly, almost all newlyweds have to get over some assumptions about each other and married life. As Falicov (1995) observed, "Strictly speaking, we all intermarry, even if we marry the boy next door. . . . Even the fact that people marrying are of different genders can introduce considerable discrepancies in worldviews and experiences" (p. 231). For an example of how culture can affect romantic relationships and marriage, see the Social Psychology in Popular Culture feature.

SOCIAL PSYCHOLOGY IN POPULAR CULTURE

▶ Culture and Marriage Expectations in *Crazy Rich Asians*

Pictorial Press Ltd / Alamy Stock Photo

Rachel is a spunky, progressive professor at NYU. She was raised by a single mother in a lower-middle-class lifestyle.

Nick is also a professor at NYU, but he was born and raised in Singapore. He comes from one of the 10 richest families in all of Asia.

They're both ethnically Chinese, but in the best-selling book (Kwan, 2013) that became a popular movie

(Chu, 2018), *Crazy Rich Asians* explores whether Nick and Rachel can maintain their love for each other despite cultural differences. When Nick brings Rachel to Singapore to meet his family, it's clear they don't approve of her. They believe Rachel won't fit in with them, both because of her American values and her socioeconomic status.

Specifically, Nick's mother doesn't believe Rachel will be capable of putting the family's needs above her own; she assumes American women are inherently individualistic. Upon first meeting Rachel and learning about her professional career, Nick's mother comments, "Pursuing one's passion. How American." Later, Nick's mother continues by emphasizing her own collectivistic values: "I chose to help my husband run a business and to raise a family. For me it was a privilege. But for you, you might think it's old-fashioned. . . . All this doesn't just happen. It's because we know to put family first, instead of chasing one's passion."

The analysis of cultural differences based on both country of origin and family wealth is explored in a delightfully comedic, yet poignant way in this popular story.

THE MAIN IDEAS

- Self-awareness is the understanding that we are a separate entity from other people and objects in our world. One way that scientists have attempted to measure self-awareness is called the mirror self-recognition test.

- Our self-concept is the personal summary of who we believe we are, including both good and bad qualities. One way to know who we are is by comparing our self to those who are both better than us (upward social comparison) and worse than us (downward social comparison).

- Social identity theory describes the self as a mixture of personal and social identities. An example of our social identity is from our culture; "Western" cultures tend to lead to individualistic selves, whereas "Eastern" or Asian cultures often lead to collectivistic selves.

CRITICAL THINKING CHALLENGE

- Identify three activities you enjoy doing, such as sports, hobbies, and studying various subjects. Then, make one upward social comparison and one downward social comparison for each activity. As you identified one person who was better than you and one person who wasn't as advanced, what emotions resulted from each type of comparison?

- List three ways in which you typically perceive the world that you think might have been influenced by your regional, national, or specific social cultures (e.g., your religion, political party, etc.). One way to do this might be to think about how your perceptions might be different from the perceptions of people from different cultures.

- Discuss a time when you interacted with someone who seemed to have a very different cultural perspective than you. Explain how your interaction might have been affected by cultural assumptions or beliefs, in both good ways and challenging ways.

HOW DO WE KNOW THE SELF IS SOCIAL?

>> **LO 3.2:**   **Analyze how our self-perceptions and group affiliations influence how we think, feel, and behave.**

We humans are magnificent and in many different ways.

We invent, write poetry, create music together, and survive crises of our making. But we are also petty, deceitful, prone to violence, moody, and many other unattractive things. Like winning the lottery, the gift of self-awareness changes our lives in both good and bad ways. We can't *un*-win the lottery after we have won it, and we can't undo having self-awareness after it has occurred.

iStockPhoto/cyano66

Our "self" sometimes seems like an orchestra, made up of many moving parts and managed by a central conductor who makes music out of the chaos.

Like it or not, our social self is like an orchestra conductor for our complicated life. Our social self directs the emphasis for our attention and manages a story that brings coherence to the entertaining chaos all around us. We'll explore four theories about the social self and the corresponding evidence. They all lead to the same general conclusion: The self is social. How we think about our own traits and behaviors is constantly influenced by the people around us.

This section describes five explanations that emphasize the social nature of the self by

(1) emphasizing that we learn about ourselves through our behaviors (self-perception),

(2) describing how our personal goals are influenced by others (self-discrepancy),

(3) visualizing how we grow and improve through our social relationships (self-expansion),

(4) explaining how self-presentations influence behavior in different situations (self-presentation), and

(5) demonstrating how group identifications influence personal self-esteem (collective self-esteem).

Self-Perception Theory: Behaviors Tell Us Who We Are

A friend of mine [Wind's] met my parents a few years ago and was chatting politely with them.

She casually mentioned to my parents, "Wind really loves waffles!" I was surprised— I don't think I had ever talked to my friend about waffles, and I didn't really consider myself a big waffle fan. When I asked my friend about her statement, she said, "Every time we go to brunch, you always order waffles." I thought about it for a second, realized she was right, and discovered that yes, I guess I do love waffles!

We make inferences about other people's sense of self by observing their behaviors over time, just like my friend did with me. **Self-perception theory** proposes that we answer the question, "Who am I?" by observing our *own* behaviors and then making inferences (Bem, 1967; Bem & McConnell, 1970).

If you regularly volunteer at a local dog shelter, then you infer that you must be someone who cares about animals. If you love to travel and eat exotic foods, then you infer that you must be open to new experiences. If other people seem to think you're funny, you'll likely incorporate "good sense of humor" into your self-concept. One of the most straightforward ways to decide who you are is by simply observing what you do.

For example, you might think of yourself as "religious" or not, depending on how often you actually attend religious services or engage in holiday rituals (Salancik & Conway, 1975). Maybe you can learn things about yourself by analyzing which characters you choose when you play video games (Klimmt et al., 2009) or whether you feel loyalty to other online gamers during cooperative play (Teng, 2018). People who like to travel might slowly become supporters of tourism in their hometown or region, as their attitudes reflect their experiences (Woosnam et al., 2018). And seeing yourself take control and help others makes you more likely to think of yourself as a leader (Miscenko et al., 2017).

Self-Discrepancy Theory: Our Goals Are Influenced by Others

How complicated is your social self?

So far, we've assumed that we all have a fully formed, single self-concept. Psychologist Tory Higgins (1987, 2002) suggested that in reality, we all have *three* simultaneous selves. All three of them are shaped by how we think of ourselves in a social world and are influenced by the people we think might be judging us. Consider each and try to think about how they apply to yourself.

Actual, Ideal, and Ought Selves

Here's another way you are complicated: three selves!

The first self is the "actual" self, the person we think we are right now. It includes both our good and bad qualities, as well as the qualities we think other people see in us. The actual self is like a snapshot of our current life. This self can acknowledge our strengths and admit our weaknesses. It includes our personal traits, our group memberships, and everything we've discussed so far in terms of the self-concept.

But importantly, Higgins suggests we also have a second "ideal" self, the person we hope to become in the future. Our ideal self is the best version of our potential, adding positive or enhanced qualities, achieving our dreams, and eliminating any aspects of our current self we don't like. It's the person we strive to become, based on what *we* want, including our secret desires. If you could, for example, have any job in the world, or look a certain way, or live a particular lifestyle, what would it be? That's your ideal self.

Self-perception theory: The idea that we form our self-concept by observing our own behaviors and then infer our motivations, attitudes, values, and core traits.

Finally, there's one more: the "ought" self. We're all aware of what other people in our life want for us—you might know what your parents, relationship partner, or professors are hoping for you. That's the third self, the ought self. It's the person we think other people want for us or expect of us. It includes what our culture does and doesn't approve of. It influences what major we choose, how we dress, how we act when we're in public, and so on. We feel the eyes of judgment upon us and know that other people either like who we seem to be or don't.

When Selves Don't Align

You probably saw this coming.

So now, according to Higgins, we're juggling these three simultaneous selves that don't always match up. Any mismatch between our three selves creates a **self-discrepancy**. How do you feel when your actual self doesn't match your ideal self? Are these emotions different from those you experience when your actual self doesn't match your ought self?

When the actual self and ideal self don't match—in other words, when we don't live up to our own ideals or we fail to achieve our dreams—Higgins predicts that we'll experience "dejection-related emotions" such as disappointment, shame, embarrassment, and possibly even depression (Higgins, 1987).

On the other hand, when our actual self doesn't match our ought self, Higgins says we'll feel that we haven't lived up to others' expectations. That kind of failure produces "agitation-related emotions" such as guilt, fear, self-contempt, and anxiety. Of course, the ideal situation would be that all three selves (actual, ideal, and ought) are exactly in alignment, with perfect overlap.

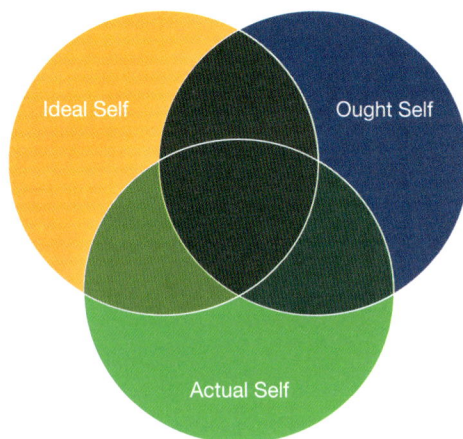

FIGURE 3.3

Three selves might exist for each of us, according to self-discrepancy theory.

As you can see in Figure 3.3, this would be like a Venn diagram of three circles. Each time the selves get closer together, the circles overlap more until only a single, perfect circle remains because they are all the same self. How likely do you think this is to achieve? Can you see discrepancies between your actual, ideal, and ought selves?

Research has revealed interesting examples of self-discrepancy. If you live in the United States, it's clear what your ought self should be in terms of your body shape: Women should be thin with large breasts, and men should be tall and muscular. If you feel the pressure of discrepancy between your actual self and ought self in terms of body size and shape, it might lead you to diet and exercise (which might be healthy), but it will also likely lead to depression and potentially more extreme behaviors like plastic surgery (Heron & Smyth, 2013; Vartanian, 2012). Immigrants and ethnic minorities might feel anxiety if they don't believe they fit into the ought self that's emphasized by acculturation (Levinson & Rodebaugh, 2013).

People who don't live up to their own ideal self of being popular and relaxed in social settings might experience social phobias (Johns & Peters, 2012). There are many ways in which self-discrepancy can lead to problems. On the other hand, working toward self alignment can also result in great feelings of achievement.

Self-Expansion Theory: We Grow Through Our Relationships

Can our self-concept include other people?

Several psychologists over the years have proposed that we have a basic motivation to realize our greatest potential. **Self-expansion theory** is the idea that one way we grow and improve is by including close others into our definition of our self-concept (Aron & Aron, 1996; Aron et al., 2001). The theory says that we all have a basic

Self-discrepancy: When a mismatch exists between an individual's actual, ideal, and ought selves.

Self-expansion theory: The idea that we can include close relationships as a way to grow and improve our self-concept.

motivation to grow our sense of self, to expand in our resources, talents, knowledge, and social networks. We want to be smarter, stronger, richer, more popular, and better at what we try to do. If we psychologically bond with others and feel that these individuals now become part of who we are, then their strengths, resources, knowledge, and skills can help us grow and have new opportunities.

One way to expand the self is to form an intimate relationship with another person who pushes us toward improvement and self-exploration. On a pragmatic level, for example, sharing expenses with someone (like rent or a mortgage) helps us achieve financial stability. When a friend or partner can teach us new skills (like how to cook, golf, or balance a checkbook), we expand in our talents and abilities. And an ideal romantic partner also helps us expand spiritually, philosophically, and intellectually by engaging our minds in new and interesting ways.

Psychologically including others in our self-concept is measured by the **Inclusion of the Other in the Self (IOS) Scale**. This measurement tool presents people with a series of seven Venn diagrams with increasing overlap between "self" and "other" (see Figure 3.4; Aron et al., 1992). Participants simply choose the pair of circles that they feel accurately indicates how much their self-concept now includes the other person. That might mean a sense of similarity, feelings of closeness, or thinking about how the decisions you make about your life will affect the other person.

FIGURE 3.4

Inclusion of the Other in the Self (IOS) Scale. When you think about someone else who's important to you, which set of circles best represents your relationship with them?

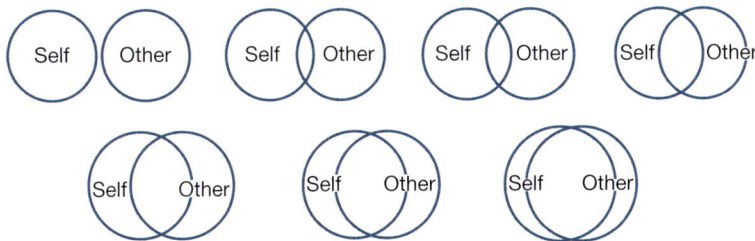

Source: Aron et al. (1992).

The IOS Scale is most commonly used in research on romantic partners, such as spouses (e.g., Agnew et al., 1998). Note that some people have questioned the content validity of the scale, though, as the instructions are fairly vague and might be interpreted in different ways by different participants (Agnew et al., 2004).

That said, we might be especially attracted to people, or most compatible, when they offer us a way to improve our self-concept and feel like the best version of our selves when we're together. The scale also been used in other contexts. Thinking of yourself as a leader may be helped if you include people you admire as leaders into your self-concept—heroes you can look up to (Dansereau et al., 2013). People join fan clubs or wear T-shirts of certain bands to feel like famous and admired stars are part of their identity (Lee et al., 2019). And generally being more open to including others into your self-concept helps reduce prejudice and promote positive interactions with people who might, at first, seem different from you (Dys-Steenbergen et al., 2016).

Self-Presentation Theory: We Adapt to Fit Into the Situation

Faking it.

Besides actually changing and improving who we are, there's another way to navigate our social world: We can fake it—and it seems to be a pretty popular way to live.

Inclusion of the Other in the Self (IOS) Scale: A scale used to measure psychological inclusion of others in the self-concept with a series of progressively overlapping circles.

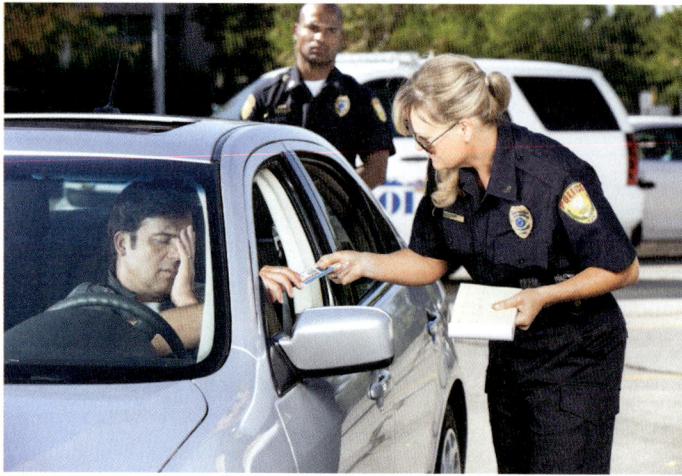

© istockphoto.com/avid_creative

Can a smiling face mask your real feelings when pulled over by police? If so, you're good at impression management.

For example, we use social media (Facebook, Snapchat, Instagram, etc.) to present a selection of the best parts of ourselves and our lives.

It's not just losing 10 pounds on a dating site. We also fill our pages with photos of us happy and smiling. We add clever quips about current events, successes, popular people and topics, and so on. This carefully curated selection of flattering aspects of our self-concept is a social performance (see Goffman, 1959). Shakespeare, of course, figured it out in *As You Like It* when he wrote, "All the world's a stage/ And all the men and women merely players."

You have probably noticed that people, including yourself, perform in slightly different ways for different audiences: family, friends, peers, supervisors, professors, and store clerks. You present yourself as funny and fashionable on a first date. On a job interview, you're professional and intelligent. At a funeral, you're somber and quiet.

Self-presentation theory is the idea that we change how we present ourselves in various situations to create a certain image of who we are (Baumeister & Hutton, 1987). We are motivated to fit in and please our audience, because of our basic drives to be accepted in a social world. Sometimes this tendency is called **impression management**, when we consciously and strategically engage in behaviors that we hope others will notice and appreciate.

Impression Management Techniques

To be frank, impression management is social manipulation. What are some specific techniques?

- *Ingratiation:* Flattery works. Ingratiation is engaging in behaviors specifically designed to flatter someone and influence them. One of the most important times ingratiation might work to your advantage is during a job interview (Stevens & Kristof, 1995). Specifically, you can compliment and praise your interviewer—a technique called other-enhancement—and you can pretend to agree with everything they say, a technique called opinion conformity.

- *Self-enhancement:* Making statements about how your accomplishments are better or more frequent than they really are is one path to self-promotion. You might also take credit for work or ideas that weren't really your own, which has been called entitlement by some researchers.

- *Conspicuous consumption:* Wearing a Rolex, driving a sports car, and displaying trendy fashion logos are examples of conspicuous consumption, the purchasing of products specifically chosen to show off how successful you are. There are many professions where conspicuous consumption is considered part of the job: You need to display your wealth so that potential clients can see how awesome you are at selling houses, choosing stocks, or managing other clients! And most of us probably think about how our use of products might attract potential mates; the stereotype of women liking men who drive expensive cars is well known. Note, however, that conspicuous consumption can backfire; for example, most women decode such displays of wealth as a sign that men are looking for uncommitted sexual partners (Sundie et al., 2011).

Self-Monitoring Lets Us Become Social Chameleons

Some people act the same way no matter what.

How much we choose to engage in impression management behaviors varies quite a bit. Some people don't do it—no matter what the situation is, they are consistent in

Self-presentation theory: The idea that we present ourselves strategically to make an impression on others.

Impression management: Consciously engaging in behaviors we hope will lead to desired outcomes and others liking us.

how they act. They are always shy, sarcastic, confident, bitter, anxious, or whatever else they are. Either they are bad at impression management, or they choose not to try. When people are generally consistent in their behaviors across situations, social psychologists say they are low in a concept called **self-monitoring** (Snyder, 1974). They don't "monitor" the situation or how they act because they don't feel they have to.

In contrast, people who are high in self-monitoring easily change how they act in different settings. They assess the situation and modify their behavior to fit in—like social chameleons (Kilduff & Day, 1994). In a cooperative environment, they cooperate; in a competitive environment, they compete. High self-monitors may gravitate to certain public careers such as sales, politics, and acting; they tend to be more motivated by social status (Flynn et al., 2006). Those careers require people who can read an audience and adjust their pitch.

Whether you're a low or high self-monitor has a variety of interesting social connections. College students who are high self-monitors are generally more liked by their peers, and groups with high self-monitoring members often report better group cohesion (Qiongjing & Zhixue, 2018). High self-monitors are often chosen as group leaders (e.g., Eby et al., 2003). But be careful—people who change how they act can appear inauthentic, untrustworthy, and self-serving (Kleinbaum et al., 2015; Ogunfowora et al., 2013; Pillow et al., 2017). In sales, it can lead to unethical practices designed to deceive customers (Yang et al., 2019).

It's reasonable that people who can easily and comfortably fit in with anyone will be more popular and may advance more quickly in their workplaces. However, sometimes people who are high in self-monitoring can seem inauthentic to others. If they are always changing how they act, others will wonder, who is the "real" person? At an extreme, high self-monitors might purposely hide who they really are (a classic example is the serial killer Ted Bundy!).

Do you think that you are a high or a low self-monitor—and is that working well for you?

Collective Self-Esteem: Groups Influence How We Feel About Ourselves

Our self-concept includes our group memberships (self-identity theory).

How we feel about our groups influences how we feel about ourselves. **Collective self-esteem** is our evaluation of the worth of our social groups (Tajfel, 1981, p. 255). You can experience collective self-esteem about the reputation of your college or university, religious and political affiliations, your nationality (e.g., during the Olympics), and more. They all influence how we feel about ourselves.

Sports fans among the students at Ohio State University (OSU) helped Professor Robert Cialdini understand collective self-esteem. Cialdini's *naturalistic observations* directed his attention to students who said, "*We* won," after a school victory, but "*They* lost," following a defeat. Ohio State students were also more likely to wear clothing displaying their school colors following a victory compared to a defeat (Cialdini et al., 1976).

Cialdini called the group's enhanced collective self-esteem following a team victory **basking in reflected glory (BIRGing)**. He concluded that group members are more likely to brag about OSU when the team won but to distance themselves when they lost. They don't have to be on the team—rooting for their team is enough.

But why does identifying with a sports team mean so much to so many people? Explanations keep coming back to evolutionary psychology. Our ancestors survived by building alliances and coalitions (Wann & James, 2018). Groups make us stronger and more secure.

Kruger et al. (2018) offered evidence for this group-based evolutionary explanation by demonstrating how much we want allies, especially in hostile territory. They observed reactions as fans wearing prominent team gear discovered each other in different settings. Imagine a Red Sox fan finding another Red Sox fan in Boston versus a Red Sox fan finding another Red Sox fan at Yankee Stadium.

Self-monitoring: Individuals' ability to strategically notice and adjust their own behavior in different situations.

Collective self-esteem: Our evaluation of the worth of our social groups.

Basking in reflected glory (BIRGing): A method of self-enhancement that involves affiliating with an in-group when that group has been successful.

Their expressions of group loyalty and identification were stronger in "enemy" territory. In addition, identifying with some team, sometimes by adopting superstitious behaviors, makes uncontrollable events (to the fan) feel controllable (Kay et al., 2010). And when "your" team wins, it feels wonderful—even if you were thousands of miles away.

Hero Images/Hero Images/Getty Images

Students are more likely to wear their school colors after a big athletic win. We make our group identity more obvious to others when our group does well.

THE MAIN IDEAS

- Self-perception theory proposes that we form our self-concept by observing our own behaviors, then make assumptions about our internal values, attitudes, and so on.

- Self-discrepancy theory suggests that instead of a single self, we all have three selves: (1) the actual self (who we are right now), (2) the ideal self (who we'd like to become), and (3) the ought self (who others expect us to be). When these three selves don't match, we have negative emotional reactions.

- Self-expansion theory is the idea that we all want to grow and improve, and one way to do that is to cognitively include other people into our self-concept.

- We can also change how we present our selves to others. This can happen through specific impression management techniques, according to self-presentation theory. In addition, people vary in how much they monitor the social situation and adapt to it through their behaviors, an idea called self-monitoring.

- Collective self-esteem is our evaluation of the social groups in which we are members. One example is how we view sports teams; when our favorite team does well, we tend to show our affiliation with that team. This tendency is called Basking in Reflected Glory.

CRITICAL THINKING CHALLENGE

- Think of at least two times when you realized something about your self-concept by observing your behaviors. Why did you not have this self-insight before you noticed your own behaviors?

- Make a list of traits that make up your actual self, then one for your ideal self, and finally one for your ought self. Mark the traits that match across lists, and mark the traits that don't match. How do you feel about the traits that don't match? Are the emotions you experience in alignment with what self-discrepancy theory hypothesized you would feel?

- Identify a time when you strategically changed how you presented yourself to gain popularity, to fit in, or to get a specific advantage (such as a job offer, audition for a play, etc.). Think about how that example of high self-monitoring worked out—was it entirely negative, entirely positive, or a mixture of both? Were you able to sustain that impression management over the long term?

- Beyond sports, there are many social groups created for people with similar self-interests, such as *Star Trek* conventions or religious retreats. What is the function of this sort of social gathering in terms of how it strengthens self-reflection and social aspects of the self? How do these types of groups exemplify BIRGing?

ARE WE HONEST ABOUT OURSELVES?

>> **LO 3.3:** **Describe the risks and rewards associated with positive self-illusions, moderate self-deceptions, and artificially boosting self-esteem.**

The story we tell ourselves about ourselves is a compelling one.

Of course it is; it's about *our* version of events (Silvia & Gendolla, 2001). But what if our beautiful self-story is, well, a lie—or at least an enhancement? Psychologist Steven Pinker compares our storytelling selves to political spin-doctors who are always looking for ways to make their candidates look good (Pinker, 2002). Like some real politicians, we create self-concepts that smell a little bit too good to be true. Why not? If I am the screenwriter, producer, director, and final-cut editor of my self-story, I can make the story come out any way that I want. Does that make our self-concept fiction or nonfiction?

We answer the core question "Are we honest about ourselves?" by

(1) describing optimal margin theory,

(2) reviewing some self-serving cognitive biases, and

(3) describing the risks and rewards of boosting self-esteem.

Positive Illusions Can Be Beneficial: Optimal Margin Theory

Let's be blunt about it: Sometimes we lie to ourselves.

For example, when our romantic partner asks, "Do these clothes make me look fat?" most partners understand that the desired responses are probably, "No," or, "You look great, but your black top might look even better." Is there anything wrong with believing that we are a little bit more attractive, caring, intelligent, or insightful than we really are? Roy Baumeister (1989) developed **optimal margin theory**, which suggests possible benefits of a slight to moderate range of healthy distortions of reality. A little bit of self-deception might be a good thing; too much distortion can cause problems.

Instead of the "cold, hard truth," we appear to benefit from **positive illusions** that rely on unrealistic optimism and an inflated self-concept. For example, drivers know that a potential car accident is around every corner, but positive illusions help us manage such chronic stress by maintaining an illusion of more control over our driving fate than we really have (Kruger et al., 2009; Taylor et al., 2000). These kinds of positive illusions are correlated with less anxiety (Brockner, 1984), better coping with stress and setbacks (Steele, 1988), lower levels of depression (Tennen & Herzberger, 1987), and general life satisfaction (Myers & Diener, 1995).

Shelley Taylor and her colleagues assert that we use three types of positive illusions that promote our mental health. We

1. cling to the belief we can control our own lives more than we can (control),

2. believe in an unrealistically optimistic view of the future (optimism), and

3. discover meaning in critical life events, such as bereavement (meaning).

Optimal margin theory: Slight distortions of reality can improve psychological well-being.

Positive illusions: Unrealistic optimism about the future and an inflated view of one's self-concept.

Age can just be a number—how old you feel is subjective.

Even though they are deceptions, positive illusions about the self-concept promote mental health and the ability to care for others, be happy, and engage in productive work (Taylor & Brown, 1988). One way we exaggerate our self-concept is when we believe we have a rich, complicated set of personality traits that enable us to succeed across many situations (Sande et al., 1988). The researchers called this flattering view of the self the multifaceted self (p. 13)—in short, we believe we're complex, flexible people with a huge toolkit of skills ready to go at a moment's notice (when, in fact, most of us might just be good at a few things).

Another common positive illusion among older people is **subjective age**, or how old we *feel* (compared to our actual, chronological age). One research team tested 800 French retirees between ages 60 and 95 (Gana et al., 2004). They wanted to find out (a) whether self-deception about subjective age was harmful or helpful and (b) whether the possible benefits of self-deception stopped when people deceived themselves too much. Would they go too far?

The French retirees enjoying positive illusions about their subjective age "reported more satisfaction with daily pursuits (leisure time), higher self-worth, and less boredom proneness" (Gana et al., 2004, p. 63). However, the people in this sample may not have gone over the edge into unhealthy self-deception. The 85-year-olds, for example, may have thought of themselves as closer to 70 but probably did not think of themselves as 15-year-olds.

But too much self-deception can be harmful. Viewing yourself as unusually lucky won't make you a good gambler more likely to win the lottery! The belief that we can control chance events can lead to huge financial mistakes (Flyvbjerg et al., 2003; Lovallo & Kahneman, 2003). Similarly, overly optimistic or confident people have gone bankrupt trying to control the stock market or start up a new business (Sommer, 2015). And there are potential disasters for people who unrealistically believe they won't suffer from diseases like cancer and thus don't engage in preventative medicine (Mehrotra et al., 2007).

Self-Serving Cognitive Biases: Small Lies We Can Live With

So positive illusions have both good and bad effects.

It's the same "sometimes good, sometimes bad" story for cognitive distortions called **self-serving cognitive biases**, unrealistic beliefs about our self-concept. This

Subjective age: How old individuals feel, instead of their chronological age.

Self-serving cognitive biases: Mental distortions that enhance our self-concept, making us seem better than we really are.

includes bias about our traits, why we succeed, why we fail, and even whether we pay attention to feedback about ourselves. These unrealistic beliefs about our self are little lies we can live with.

Biased View of Our Own Traits

Try this 30-second exercise.

Table 3.2 shows how a hypothetical person might think about their three best and worst traits and how common those traits are in general society. Look at the example in the first set of rows, then try to complete the second set for yourself. After listing your three best and worst traits, estimate from 0 to 100 the percentage of students at your college or university who also possess this trait. If you want to experience this insight into yourself, then fill in the blank table below before you read the next section.

TABLE 3.2

What Are Your Best and Worst Traits?

MY THREE BEST TRAITS ARE	WHAT % OF MY PEERS SHARE THIS TRAIT?	MY THREE WORST TRAITS ARE	WHAT % OF MY PEERS SHARE THIS TRAIT?
Loyal to friends	50%	Disorganized	55%
Hard working	40%	Manipulative	65%
Stand up to bullies	30%	Short-tempered	70%

MY THREE BEST TRAITS ARE	WHAT % OF MY PEERS SHARE THIS TRAIT?	MY THREE WORST TRAITS ARE	WHAT % OF MY PEERS SHARE THIS TRAIT?

Now, look at the percentage columns you estimated. Are the percentages under "worst traits" higher than the percentages under "best traits," on average? Marks (1984) found that students tend to *underestimate* how many of their peers shared their positive traits and *overestimate* how many people shared their negative traits. Why would this tendency count as a self-serving bias?

If people show this pattern, they're framing their "best" qualities as rare—and that makes them special (see Goethals et al., 1991; Suls & Wan, 1987). Simultaneously, if our "worst" qualities are common, then they're not that big of a deal—everyone has this problem, so who cares? Sure, we might have some flaws, but they are common and particularly troublesome. This is sometimes called the **better than average effect**: Mathematically, we can't *all* be better than average . . . but most of us think we are.

Biased Explanations of Our Successes and Failures

Here's another habit of self-deception.

This one exposes a self-serving cognitive bias about how we explain our successes and failures. For example, did you get an A on a recent test? Your explanation is probably self-serving: You must have studied hard, or you enjoy great natural intelligence. When we succeed, we tend to credit our natural ability, hard work, or some other flattering explanation. But when we fail a test, we avoid the blame. We were sick, stayed up late helping a friend, or the test was unfair. In short, we come up with an excuse

Better than average effect: A form of cognitive bias in which people believe they are better than a typical person, even though statistically it's impossible for everyone to be "better than average."

Sometimes, our view of our self isn't quite accurate. But is that a bad thing?

for the failure that allows us to maintain a comforting, positive self-concept (Miller & Ross, 1975).

Biased Views of Feedback About the Self

A third self-serving cognitive bias is to view feedback in a skewed manner.

Many people enjoy taking little quizzes about themselves on websites like Buzzfeed, for example. If you like the feedback, then you might think, "Hey, that was a great quiz! Really insightful." But if you dislike the feedback, then you think that the questions were flawed (Baumeister, 1998; Pyszczynski et al., 1985). The quiz was designed poorly, the questions were written in a confusing way, or the concept was silly in the first place. By only taking in positive feedback and explaining away negative feedback, we can keep boosting our self-concept despite evidence to the contrary.

As usual, more research is needed. But several independent studies with different methodologies and researchers seem to be telling a similar story. Optimal margin theory might be right: A little bit of self-deception is common, and moderate levels can help maintain a positive self-concept. Would you like to learn how we use positive illusions in relationships? Read the Spotlight on Research Methods feature on "Positive Illusions in Dating Relationships."

SPOTLIGHT ON RESEARCH METHODS

Positive Illusions in Dating Relationships

One of this book's authors [Wind] focused my graduate school research on positive illusions in romantic couples (Goodfriend, 2005; Goodfriend et al., 2017). I measured positive cognitive biases within relationships in two different ways. First, I asked college students to list the five "best" and five "worst" aspects of their current partner. After making these lists (which everyone could easily do), the participants then considered each of these 10 traits and rated how common or rare they are in general society. As expected, people said their partner's best traits were rare—making them special and "a keeper"—but their worst traits were common and therefore no big deal. In short, the participants showed bias by thinking their partner was "better than average."

In a second study, I asked people to consider six hypothetical positive things their partner might do—such as giving them a surprise gift—and six hypothetical negative behaviors, such as betraying a secret of theirs to a third person. Each hypothetical behavior was presented as the first half of a sentence,

and participants were asked to write in the second half of the sentence to explain *why* their partner might have done this.

I found that when people were in happy, committed relationships, they wrote that positive behaviors must have been done because their partner was a good person or because they were in love. But, when trying to explain negative behaviors, they wrote that there must have been strange circumstances that required this behavior to protect each other. That trend didn't reach statistical significance for people in unhappy relationships.

In other words, in happy couples, positive behaviors had "dispositional" attributions, while negative behaviors had "situational" attributions. When in love, we give our partners the benefit of the doubt and provide excuses for their bad behavior. My data suggest that the insight attributed to philosopher Francis Bacon 400 years ago is probably still true of modern romantic relationships: "We prefer to believe what we prefer to be true."

Boosting Self-Esteem Is a Two-Edged Sword

Remember the elephant.

Bosson et al. (2000) compare the definition of self-esteem to the classic story of six blind men trying to describe an elephant. One feels its trunk and says an elephant is like a large snake; another feels its side and concludes that an elephant is like a wall. A third feels its tail and reports that an elephant is like a broom. Each of the blind men offers a different description because it is based on their private experience of touching the elephant.

Self-esteem can be similarly complex. Individual studies on this abstract concept might each explore just one small part of the larger whole. In this final section of the chapter, we'll understand the risks and rewards associated with boosting self-esteem by

- discussing how to define and measure self-esteem,
- describing how collective self-esteem depends on our social groups, and
- analyzing potential dangers of artificially boosting self-esteem.

Defining and Measuring Self-Esteem

Let's start with a simple definition.

Self-esteem is our subjective, personal evaluation of our self-concept. It's whether you like yourself—do you think your self-concept is a good one, such that you have a lot of positive things to offer the world? If so, you have a positive self-esteem.

Echo and Narcissus, John William Waterhouse 1903

In Greek mythology, Narcissus fell so deeply in love with his own image that he continued to stare at his reflection until he died. The personality disorder called narcissism is not the same thing as self-esteem, a subjective assessment of one's own self-worth.

What Self-Esteem Is Not

Think of barnacles on a boat.

Unfortunately, the public's understanding of self-esteem often includes many related constructs that, like barnacles on a boat, have attached themselves to the construct of self-esteem—and taken a free ride into our social thinking. Let's start scraping off some of those barnacles by clarifying what self-esteem is *not* (Baumeister et al., 1996; Crocker & Major, 1989, 2003; Greenwald et al., 2002).

- Self-esteem is separate from **narcissism**, an excessive self-love based on unwarranted belief in one's specialness relative to others (Neff & Vonk, 2009). Self-esteem focuses on whether we regard ourselves as a person of worth; narcissism focuses on whether we regard ourselves as *more* worthy than others (Donnellan et al., 2005; Vater et al., 2018).

- Self-esteem is also distinct from **self-efficacy**, the degree to which you believe that you are capable of completing a specific task or achieving a particular goal. Self-efficacy seems to be a good thing, at least most of the time.

Self-esteem: Our subjective, personal evaluation of our self-concept; whether we're happy with who we are.

Narcissism: Excessive self-love based on the belief that one is better than others.

Self-efficacy: Confidence in your ability to complete a specific task or achieve a particular goal.

Self-efficacy contributes to self-esteem (Begue, 2005), helps people cope with failure in the workplace (Newton et al., 2008), and encourages resilience in the face of chronic diseases such as diabetes (Yi et al., 2008).

- Self-esteem is not the same thing as **self-compassion**, an orientation to care for oneself in times of failure or suffering (Leary et al., 2007). Self-compassion makes us feel good because we treat ourselves with kindness. Instead of using self-serving biases to maintain a positive self-concept, self-compassion encourages recognition of faults but the acknowledgment that we can always improve (Neff, 2011; Neff & McGehee, 2010; MacBeth & Gumley, 2012).

Self-esteem is our subjective, personal evaluation of our self-concept—a private evaluation of our own worth. It is based on positive illusions and self-serving biases about our strengths and weaknesses, and it has a lot of implications about how we think about our social world.

What Self-Esteem Is

Self-esteem is however we measure self-esteem.

There are several different ways to measure or *operationalize* self-esteem—they are all different parts of the elephant. However, the most widely used measure is Morris Rosenberg's (1965) 10-item, self-report measure. Created over 50 years ago, its initial purpose was to investigate the adolescent self-image. But this short scale proved to be so useful that it has endured for several decades and hundreds of applications. It has clarified many of the connections between self-esteem and related psychological constructs (Brummett et al., 2007; Hair et al., 2007; Penkal & Kurdek, 2007).

Try it for yourself in the What's My Score? feature. (Filling it out will make it easier for you to understand what comes next.) As we discussed in Chapter 2 (Research Methods), the idea of any direct or *self-report* measure is simple: We ask; you tell. The critical assumption is that you are able and willing to provide a consistent (*reliable*) and accurate (*valid*) response to each item.

Notice, however, that some statements indicate high self-esteem and others (such as Question 2) indicate low self-esteem. Researchers often use this technique, called *reverse scoring,* to encourage careful reading of each item by discouraging participants from thoughtlessly writing the same response to every question. Read the scoring instructions to make sure you come up with the correct result.

Self-compassion:
An orientation to care for yourself in times of failure or suffering.

WHAT'S MY SCORE?

Rosenberg's (1965) Self-Esteem Scale

Instructions: Below is a list of statements dealing with your general feelings about yourself. If you strongly agree, circle SA. If you agree with the statement, circle A. If you disagree, circle D. If you strongly disagree, circle SD.

1. On the whole, I am satisfied with myself. SA A D SD

2. At times, I think I am no good at all. SA A D SD

3. I feel that I have a number of good qualities. SA A D SD

4. I am able to do things as well as most other people. SA A D SD

5. I feel I do not have much to be proud of. SA A D SD

6. I certainly feel useless at times. SA A D SD

7. I feel that I'm a person of worth, at least on an equal plane with others. SA A D SD

8. I wish I could have more respect for myself. SA A D SD

9. All in all, I am inclined to feel that I am a failure. SA A D SD

10. I take a positive attitude toward myself. SA A D SD

Scoring Instructions: Assign the following scores to your answers by writing the appropriate number on the blank next to each item. Then, add your scores up:

For Items 1, 3, 4, 7, 10: SA = 3, A = 2, D = 1, SD = 0.

For Items 2, 5, 6, 8, 9: SA = 0, A = 1, D = 2, SD = 3.

Higher scores indicate higher levels of self-reported self-esteem.

Source: Rosenberg, M. (1965). *Society and the adolescent self-image*. Princeton, NJ: Princeton University Press.

Boosting Self-Esteem Has a Dark Side

On the surface, the case for boosting self-esteem makes sense.

Low self-esteem is associated with many social problems, from overusing a cell phone, child abuse, school failure, teenage pregnancy, lack of empathy for those in need, crime, welfare dependency, substance abuse, aggression, antisocial behavior, depression, envy of others, delinquency, and suicide—among others. It is a long list with thousands of studies (e.g., Bianchi & Phillips, 2005; Donnellan et al., 2005; Ellison et al., 2007; Mecca et al., 1989; Phillips et al., 2006; Sa et al., 2019; Sharma & Agarwala, 2014; Swann et al., 2007; Vrabel et al., 2018).

However, you have reasons to be skeptical. The vast majority of these studies have been correlational. So we can't say that low self-esteem causes these negative outcomes. That said, helping people have a healthy self-esteem seems like a worthy endeavor. But is it?

Self-Esteem Is Popular

Self-esteem is so popular that boosting self-esteem has become a small industry.

Twenge (2006) discovered that among elementary schools, *self-esteem* is often listed in mission statements, often *before* reading, writing, and arithmetic. Look it up online. Your old elementary school probably has a mission statement similar to these:

istockphoto.com/asiseeit

Should children receive trophies just for participating or only for winning?

- Cannon Elementary School, Spartanburg, South Carolina: "We are committed to building self-esteem, enhancing creativity and individuality."

- The Margaret Gioiosa School, Staten Island, New York City, New York: "We believe that a child's self-esteem directly affects his/her achievement."

- Oak Park Elementary, Laurel, Mississippi: "To provide a safe and positive learning environment, promoting high self-esteem and parental involvement."

- Green Lake School, Seattle, Washington: "In pursuing its mission, Green Lake School adheres to these values: Building self-esteem ..."

- Grant Foreman Elementary School, Muskogee, Oklahoma: "The mission of Grant Foreman Elementary School will be achieved when all exiting sixth grade students possess: A healthy sense of self-esteem ..."

High self-esteem is almost universally considered a good thing. But remember that sometimes, people confuse self-esteem with narcissism. Occasionally, attempts to make sure people feel good about themselves can backfire so that instead of just liking themselves, they think they are "more deserving" or even "more pure" than others (see Baumeister et al., 2003). Believing that you're wonderful might also stop you from thinking you have any room for improvement—and there are some experiments that show this problem.

Will Boosting Self-Esteem Make Surgeons in Training Better Surgeons?

If you are about to go into a risky surgery, what kind of surgeon do you choose?

(a)   A surgeon with high self-esteem but low skills?

(b)   A surgeon with low self-esteem but high skills?

(c)   A surgeon with moderate self-esteem and moderate skills?

The teaching physicians at the Southern Illinois University School of Medicine were worried about whether their chronically high-achieving medical students were, well, teachable. So, they arranged for "an academic surgeon, who was seen by (medical) students as being an expert" (Boehler et al., 2006, p. 747) to provide either positive (self-esteem building) or negative (critical, specific, and instructional) feedback to the students. The medical students were learning an important skill: how to tie two-handed surgical knots.

The surgeon gave one group self-esteem boosting feedback: "Great job," "You're making progress," and "Outstanding." It was the kind of praise that high-achieving medical students had probably received most of their lives from teachers. The comparison group of students was given feedback based on their deficiencies, things they were doing wrong as they were learning how to tie surgical knots.

In other words, the *independent variable* was type of feedback: esteem-boosting praise versus specific skill-building guidance. The *dependent variable* became the quality of the surgical knots they were tying by the end of training.

How do you fairly evaluate the quality of two-handed surgical knots? The method used in this kind of situation is called *consensual assessment*. In this case, "three faculty evaluators observed and scored blinded videotapes of each performance" and made sure that there was "agreement among expert ratings of performance."

Figure 3.5 tells a sobering but also an amusing research story. It's sobering because the group of medical students that had been criticized tied better surgical knots than the group receiving esteem-boosting praise. Specific, negative feedback was more helpful at building their knot-tying skills than esteem-building platitudes.

But it's also an amusing research story. The self-esteem group (who tied poorer surgical knots) gave higher teacher ratings. Think about that the next time you rate your professors. Are you rating their effectiveness as teachers or whether they made you feel good about yourself—at the expense of authentically pushing you to be better?

Will Boosting Self-Esteem Make Weak Students Stronger?

Here's another "funny," counterintuitive study about boosting self-esteem.

This one involved psychology students who were earning grades of D and F (Forsyth et al., 2007). Their professors sent some of them self-esteem boosting email messages such as, "Studies suggest that students who have high self-esteem not only get better grades, but they remain self-confident and assured. . . . Bottom line: Hold your head—and your self-esteem—high." They were so startled by the results that the authors subtitled their paper, "An Intervention That Backfired."

Here's what happened: The self-esteem boosting messages were effective—but only at boosting self-esteem. More than two thirds (70%) of the participants recorded the highest possible self-esteem scores that the scale would allow after the comforting emails. But Figure 3.6 tells us that their academic performance actually got *worse* relative to the control group that didn't get the reassuring emails.

Promoting self-esteem backfired efforts to raise academic achievement! The struggling students' scores fell dramatically, from 57% to 38%. The group that did not receive those messages stayed the same.

Boosting self-esteem can backfire when (1) it's not necessarily deserved or (2) when the message is that you're somehow better than others. Instead of higher grades, boosting self-esteem seems to produce a cloud of negative behaviors: making excuses, self-sabotage, blaming others, arguing, scheming, and cheating (see Baumeister

FIGURE 3.5

Boosting self-esteem in surgeons might not lead to positive medical consequences.

Do Compliments Make Better Surgeons?

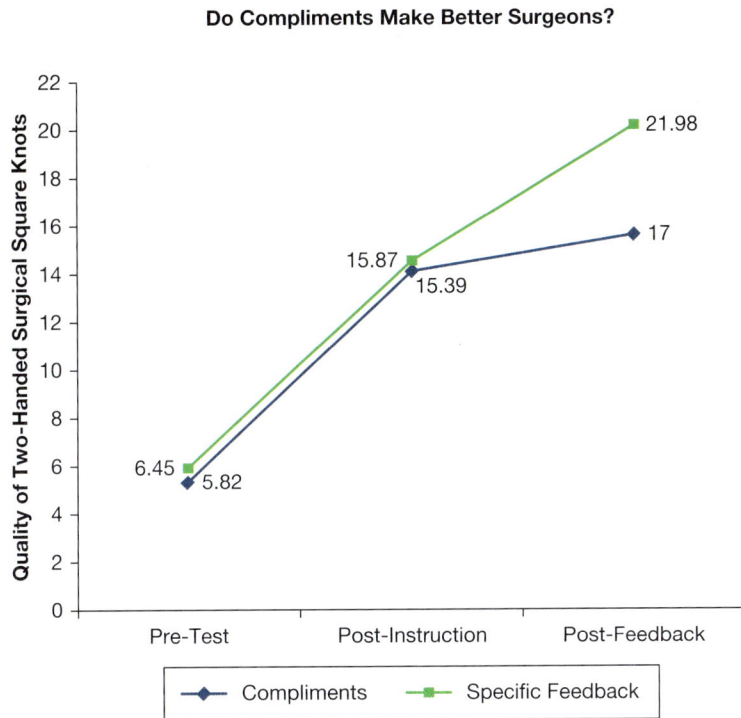

Quality of Two-Handed Surgical Square Knots

- 21.98
- 17
- 15.87
- 15.39
- 6.45
- 5.82

Pre-Test   Post-Instruction   Post-Feedback

◆ Compliments   ■ Specific Feedback

Source: Data from Boehler et al. (2006).

FIGURE 3.6

Can too much self-esteem lead to poor academic results?

The Effects of Boosting the Self-Esteem of D/F Students

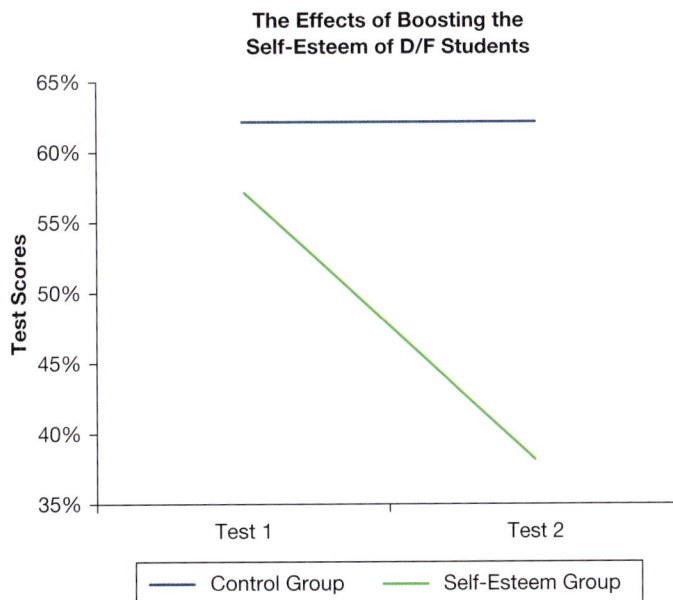

Test Scores

65% 60% 55% 50% 45% 40% 35%

Test 1   Test 2

Control Group   Self-Esteem Group

Source: Data from Lawrence et al. (2007).

et al., 2003; Crocker & Nuer, 2003). Bullies have high self-esteem (Karatzias et al., 2002). People with fragile but high self-esteem

1. are more reluctant to take intelligent risks

2. make fewer mistakes from which to learn

3. substitute competitive social comparisons for cooperative social supports

4. decrease their academic performance

5. avoid helpful feedback

6. increase levels of intergroup prejudice

7. increase bullying and aggression toward others

What's the take-home message? Healthy, high self-esteem is associated with a huge list of positive traits and experiences. Helping your friends, partner, and family members feel good about themselves is worthwhile. But it's also important to give honest feedback when people can improve and to make sure that we don't feel *better* than others in global, narcissistic ways. A little humility, coupled with confidence and self-care, can go a long way toward building a healthy, resilient, socially productive self.

THE MAIN IDEAS

- Self-esteem is our subjective evaluation of our self-concept. It's not the same as narcissism, self-efficacy, or self-compassion. Optimal margin theory says slight distortions of reality (positive illusions) can improve psychological well-being.

- We engage in many forms of self-serving cognitive bias, such as believing that our positive traits are rare (while negative traits are common), taking credit for successes but not failures, and believing only positive feedback about the self.

- Despite many attempts to boost self-esteem, some research studies show that elevating self-esteem can lead to negative effects (such as decreased academic performance).

CRITICAL THINKING CHALLENGE

- Identify at least one time when you realized you had an elevated view of your own talents or traits (a time you realized you had a positive illusion about yourself). Looking back on this now, was it good or bad for you to maintain this illusion? How did it affect you in both positive and negative ways?

- How important is having self-esteem to you? Based on the research reviewed above, should elementary and middle schools focus on increasing students' self-esteem? Why or why not?

- This section included Rosenberg's very popular self-esteem scale. When you consider use of this scale in research, do you think people's answers are variable depending on what they have recently experienced? In other words, could people's answers be more about their current mood than about their self-esteem in any stable, reliable sense? How could researchers measure self-esteem in a way that wouldn't be subject to daily or even hourly fluctuations based on what someone is currently experiencing or thinking about?

CHAPTER SUMMARY

How Do We Understand the "Self"?

The self is an abstract and subjective psychological construct—and therefore difficult both to define and to measure. We start with self-awareness, the understanding that we are a separate entity from other people and objects. A second step toward understanding the self focuses on the self-concept: a personal summary of who we believe we are. Social comparison theory says we assess our subjective traits by comparing our self to others. Social identity theory suggests that the self-concept is made up of both personal, individual characteristics (such as our personality traits) and social role characteristics, which include our relationships and group memberships. In this way, our self-concept is affected by social influences such as culture.

How Do We Know the Self Is Social?

Four theories help explain why the self is social. The first, self-perception theory, proposes that we form an impression of our self the same way we form impressions about others: by observing our own behaviors. Second, self-discrepancy theory concludes that we actually have three self-concepts. Our actual self is our perception of who we are right now, while our ideal self is the person we'd like to be, and our ought self is the self-concept we have that reflects what we think other people in our social world expect of us. When these three selves are different, we have negative emotional reactions. A third explanation, self-expansion theory, suggests that we all want to grow and improve over time, and one way to do this is through our social relationships. Finally, self-presentation theory proposes that we act differently to different audiences to gain social influence (also called impression management). People who often look around to assess the current situation to change their self-presentation are called high self-monitors. On the other hand, people who act consistently regardless of the current situation are called low self-monitors. Collective self-esteem is our evaluation of the worth of the various social groups to which we belong. Collective self-esteem is easy to see in sports fans, who are more likely to publicize their chosen affiliations when their team is doing well compared to when it's not. This tendency is called Basking in Reflected Glory.

Are We Honest About Ourselves?

Optimal margin theory is the idea that it can be healthy to maintain a small to moderate distortion of reality when it comes to our self-concept. In other words, maintaining some positive illusions about how wonderful we are may be beneficial. For example, some older individuals seem to be happier when their subjective age (how old they feel) is younger than their actual age. Self-serving cognitive biases help us maintain positive illusions about ourselves. One bias is that our positive qualities are rare (and therefore special), whereas our negative qualities are common (and therefore not particularly stigmatizing). Another mental bias leads us to attribute successes to something internal about ourselves (such as talent or effort) but attribute failures to something about the situation—so we can take credit for success but avoid blame for failure. A third cognitive bias questions negative feedback about the self but automatically accepts positive feedback. Despite the popularity of movements to increase self-esteem, several studies have shown that boosting self-esteem can sometimes lead to negative effects, such as lower academic performance.

CRITICAL THINKING, ANALYSIS, AND APPLICATION

- Do you think it's possible for any individual to really achieve full matching between his or her actual, ideal, and ought selves? Would this full matching be a good thing or a bad thing, and why?

- Consider the advantages and disadvantages to presenting different versions of yourself in different settings. Is this simply having social intelligence, or is it being less than authentic? Is the success and popularity that may follow from high self-monitoring worth changing who you appear to be? Or is your changing self always authentic—and you're simply choosing different aspects of yourself to be highlighted, like when stores choose to display certain products in more prominent locations? If you knew that a certain friend, politician, or romantic partner was very high in self-monitoring, could you truly trust that person and feel you knew who they "really" are?

- You've probably heard the phrase, "Ignorance is bliss." Would you rather have an extremely positive view of yourself, even if it were completely wrong, or have an accurate view of yourself that showed all of your flaws in glaring detail? On a scale of 0 to 100, how much "positive illusion" do you think would be the ideal amount, with 0 indicating none (potentially unhappy accuracy) and 100 being complete (happy but inaccurate perceptions)?

- What is your personal opinion about cultural or educational programs designed to enhance the next generation's self-esteem? Are the benefits from this type of program going to outweigh the potential drawbacks, such as inflated narcissism or a sense of entitlement?

MARWAN NAAMANI/AFP via Getty Images

4

Social Cognition

Core Questions

4.1 How do we think?

4.2 Why are there flaws in our mental machinery?

4.3 Where does intuition come from—and can we trust it?

Learning Objectives

4.1 Explain how our two thinking systems are mental structures that interact with culture.

4.2 Describe how and why dual processing creates unavoidable trade-offs in thinking.

4.3 Discuss how intuition uses and misuses mental accessibility that comes from priming, experience, and heuristics.

Trigger warning: This is a story about death during military conflict.

Sgt. First Class Edward Tierney was leading a nine-person patrol in Mosul, Iraq. A car was parked on the sidewalk, facing the traffic. The windows were rolled up. Two kindergarten-aged boys stared out the back window, their faces close together.

The nearest soldier said to Tierney, "Permission to approach, sir, to give them some water."

"No!" Tierney replied and ordered his men to pull back. Something seemed wrong. A bomb exploded, killing the two boys, and sending shrapnel across the face of the nearest soldier. Tierney's intuition could not save the two boys. But it probably prevented an even greater tragedy (see Carey, 2009). Sgt. Tierney later reported experiencing "that danger feeling" and an urge to move back before he logically knew why.

It doesn't matter whether you call it "going with your gut," "a hunch," or intuition because it all refers to the same idea: knowing something without knowing how you know. It can be a mysterious, life-saving experience—when it works, as it did for Sgt. Tierney. But our hunches also can lead to disaster. Sometimes, we are better off relying on logic, a way of knowing based on reasoned, thoughtful analysis of the objective situation.

Intuition and logic are the basic elements of social cognition, how humans process social information. We can understand the unavoidable trade-offs between intuition and logic through three core questions and learning objectives, beginning with "How do we think?"

HOW DO WE THINK?

>> **LO 4.1:** Explain how our two thinking systems are mental structures that interact with culture.

The combination of intuition and logic helps answer a difficult philosophical question: What, if anything, is so special about humans?

Every species, of course, is special in some way. But we humans do not run faster or grow more fur to protect against the cold. We are not larger or stronger than many species, and we are not better at seeing, hearing, smelling, or hiding.

However, there is one thing humans do exceptionally well: think. Our distinctiveness is not that we think—it is *how* we think. The dynamic combination of logic and intuition empowers us to quickly synthesize enormous amounts of information. This section answers the core question "How do we think?" by (1) summarizing dual processing, (2) describing how our two thinking systems interact, (3) identifying cultural influences on thinking systems, and (4) describing how memory structures facilitate thinking.

Dual Processing: We Use Both Intuition and Logic

You have just been surprised by a job offer!

But it requires you to move to a new country, and you only have 24 hours to decide. You recognize that it is a serious offer, so you need to figure out how to respond—and fast! Will you use logic, intuition, or both? Complex decisions usually make use of dual processing: thinking that combines logic and intuition (Bargh & Williams, 2006; DeNeys, 2006; Kahneman, 2003; Schneider & Shiffrin, 1977; Sherman et al., 2014; Simon, 1990). These two contrasting types of thinking have been described in many ways: "System 1 versus System 2," "quick versus slow," "implicit versus explicit." For this chapter, we most often will use the terms "intuition" and "logic" to summarize the descriptions in Figure 4.1.

Intuition is knowing something automatically without knowing how you know—it's like a gut feeling. Intuition requires minimal cognitive effort because it helps us sense and react to threats in the environment, which require immediate decision making. If your automatic reaction to the job offer is "No! Absolutely not!" then your intuition was

Social cognition: The study of how we process social information using a combination of logic and intuition.

Dual processing: The ability to process information using both intuition and logic.

Intuition: The ability to know something quickly and automatically; a "gut feeling" that takes little mental effort.

FIGURE 4.1

Two thinking systems: intuition and logic.

System 1	System 2
← Intuition	Logic →
Emotional	Analytical
Associative	Rule-Directed
Automatic	Controlled
Effortless	Effortful
Implicit	Explicit
Intuitive	Reasoned
Quick	Slow

Logic: The ability to use reason, think systematically, and carefully consider evidence when making a decision.

at the ready, even if you did not previously know how you felt about it. Sgt. Tierney's intuition enabled him to make a lightning-quick decision that saved lives.

Logic, by comparison, is knowing by thinking slowly and systematically. Logic requires mental effort and careful, purposeful reasoning. If you went home and started reasoning about the pros and cons of the job offer, then logic was adding its voice to this important decision. We humans have busy brains.

This sudden job offer has made your brain *very* busy. Something remarkable must be going on in there because the weight of the human brain represents about only 2% of our total body weight but consumes about 20% of our energy resources (Dunbar, 1998). Logical thinking requires more energy than intuition, so intuition is our energy-conserving default mode. Logic lingers in the background, stepping in only when needed (Kahneman, 2003, 2011; Stanovich & West, 2000, 2002).

For example, we all have probably been the star of a small comedy scene when we try to push our way through a PULL door (or vice versa). Our brain is on intuitive autopilot as we face this trivial decision. If we successfully pull open a PULL door (or push open a PUSH door), then we don't pause to congratulate our intuition or start singing, "We are the champions!" We just keep going.

But watch what often happens when someone tries to push open a PULL door. Most people push, push, push and rattle the door until their logical thinking breaks through with the logical thought, "Hey! What you're doing isn't working. Try something else." That brief consultation with logic changes your behavior: You pull open the PULL door. We need both intuition and logic to navigate our daily decisions (see Norman, 2013).

Figure 4.1 summarizes the strengths and weaknesses of our two thinking systems (Alter et al., 2007; Gilbert, 1991; Kahneman & Frederick, 2005; Lieberman, 2000). Quick decision making (intuition) makes our lives much easier and may even save our lives—just ask Sgt. Tierney. That's good. But it also risks sometimes making a

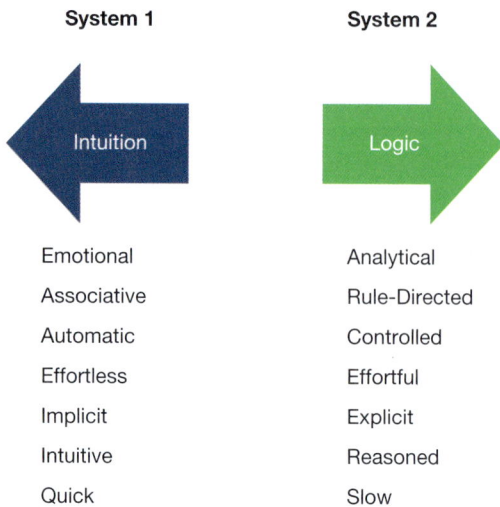

CBS Photo Archive/CBS/Getty images

Sheldon Cooper and Mr. Spock: Classic characters who are guided by logic instead of emotion or intuition.

hurried, catastrophic decision without considering the consequences. That's bad—and sometimes very bad.

On the other hand, relying on slow, analytical logic helps us understand what is happening from an objective point of view. That's good. But it also risks taking too long or missing opportunities through indecision. That's bad—and sometimes very bad. Our mental life is a constant trade-off between intuition and logic.

Our Two Thinking Systems Interact

If you drive a car, do you remember learning how to drive?

There were many demands on your attention: the sensitivity of the foot pedals, the movements of other drivers, road signs, traffic lights, pedestrians, and much more. But over time, your driving became almost automatic. Our "autopilot" mode of driving is fine for familiar routes with little traffic. But driving in a new city with several lanes of traffic, unfamiliar signs, and road construction requires strategic interactions between automatic thinking and mental effort.

Daniel Kahneman (2011) won the Nobel Prize for his research (with Amos Tversky) on intuitive versus logical decision making. These two thinking systems often interact like beautiful, well-trained dance partners. Intuition usually takes the lead because there are limits to our cognitive load, the amount of information that we can process or think about at one time.

Driving also demonstrates how smoothly our two thinking systems switch back and forth, a process also called cognitive load shifting (Abel et al., 1990; Alain et al., 2004; Jansma et al., 2001; Schneider & Pichora-Fuller, 2001; Velanova et al., 2007). You may be able to drive almost mindlessly, relying on intuition, until you notice another car weaving dangerously up ahead of you. Then, logic springs into action and tells you, "Concentrate! This could be dangerous! Observe, evaluate, and figure out how to avoid that dangerous driver!"

Discover whether you prefer logic or intuition in the What's My Score? feature, "Measuring Need for Cognition." Scores are neither good nor bad because some tasks are better suited for intuition, others for logical thinking (Furley et al., 2015). For example, in American football, kicking the ball for an extra point or field goal relies on a well-rehearsed intuition. However, running a complicated play among several players requires more logical thinking. As great teams practice the complicated play, the analytical gradually becomes automatic and intuitive (like driving a car). Some people simply feel more comfortable relying on logic, or they enjoy complex thinking in their leisure time (like playing chess or watching documentaries). Those people will tend to get higher scores on the measure provided.

Social Thinking Is Shaped by Culture—and Vice Versa

Most people from the United States don't even think about how to ride an elevator.

In Japan, however, there are strict rules of elevator etiquette. Several websites offer Westerners advice about how to navigate Japanese rules for entering, positioning, and

This frustrated man may need to use logic instead of intuition to realize why the door isn't opening.

Daniel Kahneman (right) won the Nobel Prize and the Medal of Freedom for his research on how our two thinking systems work together to make everyday decisions.

Cognitive load: The amount of information and thinking we can handle at one time.

Cognitive load shifting: When we can smoothly shift back and forth between intuition and logic, as needed.

exiting an elevator. The following additional category describes your possible duties as captain of the elevator:

1. If you enter the elevator first, congratulations! You just received authority over all the buttons!

2. To fulfill your task, stand in front of the control panel, and push the door open button for everyone else who is getting on. As special service, help communication between passengers and vehicle by asking on which floor everyone is getting off.

3. Quickly push (and hold) the close door button as soon as everyone is on board until the doors are safely shut. You wouldn't want to make anyone wait.

4. Pushing the buttons and holding the door lets you practice your reaction speed at every floor you arrive at. A crowd pushing out, a single person rushing in just as the doors are about to close—you can handle them all.

5. On your floor, again hold the door so everyone can get out. You see everyone out safely before you leave. The closest person now will take over your spot and hold the door for you and incoming passengers.

Japanese children absorb these (and hundreds of other courtesies) as they participate in Japanese culture. Another example is where to sit at a large table. In Chinese culture, which chair you choose as you walk into a dinner with a large table matters and indicates your status. Specifically, usually the chair facing the entrance is the seat of honor—although it matters what the shape of the table is.

In some cultures, then, things like elevator and seating etiquette are emphasized more or less explicitly, and people have to learn the "rules" so they don't make a rude mistake. For a fun example of seating in the culture of corporate boardrooms, check out the website https://www.scienceofpeople.com/seating-psychology/ for a test of where to sit when you meet with the boss!

WHAT'S MY SCORE?

🔥 Measuring Need for Cognition

Different people enjoy using the logical, thoughtful part of their brain to different degrees. In your free time, do you think it's fun to complete crossword puzzles, watch documentaries, solve logic problems, and engage in political debates? If so, you might be high in a personality trait called *need for cognition*.

Instructions: To measure your own "need for cognition," write a number next to each statement below using this scale:

1	2	3	4	5
Extremely uncharacteristic of me		Uncertain		Extremely characteristic of me

___ 1. I prefer complex to simple problems.

___ 2. I like to have the responsibility of handling a situation that requires a lot of thinking.

___ 3. Thinking is not my idea of fun.

___ 4. I would rather do something that requires little thought than something that is sure to challenge my thinking abilities.

___ 5. I try to anticipate and avoid situations where there is a likely chance I will have to think in depth about something.

___ 6. I find satisfaction in deliberating hard and for long hours.

___ 7. I only think as hard as I have to.

___ 8. I prefer to think about small daily projects to long-term ones.

___ 9. I like tasks that require little thought once I've learned them.

___ 10. The idea of relying on thought to make my way to the top appeals to me.

___ 11. I really enjoy a task that involves coming up with new solutions to problems.

___ 12. Learning new ways to think doesn't excite me very much.

___ 13. I prefer my life to be filled with puzzles I must solve.

___ 14. The notion of thinking abstractly is appealing to me.

___ 15. I would prefer a task that is intellectual, difficult, and important to one that is somewhat important but does not require much thought.

___ 16. I feel relief rather than satisfaction after completing a task that requires a lot of mental effort.

___ 17. It's enough for me that something gets the job done; I don't care how or why it works.

___ 18. I usually end up deliberating about issues even when they do not affect me personally.

Scoring Instructions: Some of the items need to be "reverse scored," which means that you cross off what you wrote and write a different number instead. For only Items 3, 4, 5, 7, 8, 9, 12, 16, and 17, flip the scale. So, if you wrote a 1, cross it off and write a 5 instead. If you wrote a 2, substitute a 4 instead. If you wrote a 3, it stays the same because it's in the middle of the scale, but a 4 becomes a 2 and a 5 becomes a 1.

After you reverse-score only the items indicated (half of the items should have stayed the same), add up your numbers. Higher scores mean you are higher in "need for cognition," and you prefer to rely on logic. Scores can range from 18 to 90.

Source: Cacioppo et al. (1984).

SPOTLIGHT ON RESEARCH METHODS

Culture Influences How We Think

© istockphoto.com/Diane Labombarbe

If you saw a pile of pens that were mostly the same but had one unique pen, would you choose the unique one?

Strange but telling cultural differences showed up in a *field experiment* in the San Francisco airport. Researchers offered European Americans or East Asians a gift choice from five free pens—four of which were of the same color, with the fifth being unique. Given this choice, would you pick the unique pen or one of the four matching pens?

The surprising thing was that people from the two cultural groups tended to make different choices that suggested individualistic or collectivistic social thinking (Kim & Markus, 1999). Specifically, 74% of European Americans preferred the pen that was a different color, but 76% of East Asians chose a pen that was the same color.

The researchers were careful to control *confounding variables*, co-occurring events that provide alternative explanations for their results. For example, the pens were the same quality and design, they came from the same company, and all used black ink. Across different participants, the researchers also changed the color of the pen that was different, to make sure one color wasn't simply more attractive.

Autobiographical memories help explain such odd little differences (Wang et al., 2015). European Americans (from individualistic cultures) are taught that uniqueness and nonconformity are valued; they usually chose the pen that was different. East Asians (from collectivistic cultures) are taught not to stand out from the group and always to put group needs first; they usually chose a pen that was like most of the others.

Another example of differences between cultures can be seen in Table 4.1, which highlights differences in family memory sharing (Wang, 2006, p. 185):

(Continued)

(Continued)

TABLE 4.1

Mother's Questions, Child's Answers

EURO-AMERICAN MOTHER (M) AND CHILD (C)
M: Tell me about the craft fair. Mommy and Daddy went to the craft fair. What did we go there for, do you remember?
C: Yeah. Christmas time.
M: It was Christmas time, we were getting some Christmas presents. Did you want to be there?
C: No.

CHINESE MOTHER AND CHILD
M: What story did Teacher Lin tell you at school?
C: "Qui Shao-yun." He didn't move even when his body was on fire.
M: The teacher taught you to follow the rules, right?
C: Um.

Source: Adapted from Wang (2006).

Notice how the European American mother encouraged her child to speak up ("Tell me about the craft fair. . . . What did we go there for, do you remember?"). She specifically encouraged her child's individualism ("Did you want to be there?"). This child responded with a blunt but independent "no." By contrast, the Chinese mother emphasized authority and following rules ("What story did Teacher Lin tell you at school. . . . The teacher taught you to follow the rules, right?"). These two children were absorbing very different cultural expectations. Memory researcher and Nobel Prize winner Eric Kandel (2006) has pointed out that "we are who we are because of what we learn and what we remember" (p. 10).

Memory Structures Facilitate Social Thinking

Here's an old problem with a new name: TMI (Too Much Information).

Our ancestors had the TMI problem. As farmers and hunters, they worried about crops, herds, weather, and making sure their children had the necessary survival skills. It was a lot to juggle without the technological supports many of us take for granted. Today, we experience information assaults from the digital world (cookies, popups, online product placements), traditional advertising (television, billboards, and jingles), and novel approaches (tattoos, supermarket floors, and jetways).

Fortunately, our adaptive brains developed a way to deal with the TMI problem: memory structures. **Memory structures** (sometimes called **mental structures**) are cognitive frameworks that help us organize and interpret social information. They include schemas, scripts, and stereotypes.

Schemas: The Brain's Spam Filter

Schemas are like your brain's spam filter.

Schemas are memory structures that automatically interpret, categorize, and prioritize incoming information (Bartlett, 1932; Johnston, 2001). Several other words describe

Memory structures: Cognitive frameworks that help us organize and interpret social information. They include schemas, scripts, and stereotypes.

Mental structures: See *memory structures.*

concepts similar to schemas: "templates," "worldviews," "viewpoints," and "archetypes." A child will have a schema for "dog" that is something like "has four legs and a tail." They will refine that schema when they learn about horses. An individual's schema for a politician could be either "public servant" or "selfish and money-grubbing"—or both. We hear the word "politician" and feel like we know something about that individual.

The schema memory structure explains why we don't have to relearn how to read every time we open a book. Instead, a schema maintains our ability to remember the shapes of letters, the sounds they correspond to, the meaning of the sounds, and their grammatical arrangements. Our memory structures are so firmly developed that it would be impossible for us to look at a book and *not* read the words. There are other types of memory structures: scripts and stereotypes. They each allow us to process large amounts of information at astonishing speed—exactly what we humans seem to do better than other animals.

Scripts: Mental Expectations About What Happens Next

Scripts tell us what comes next.

A **script** is a memory structure that shapes expectations about how specific social events will occur. For example, your cultural script for a marriage proposal tells you that the photographs shown here are out of order. Knowing how to propose properly (within a particular culture) can shape marital expectations. A *survey* of over 2,100 college students at the Universities of Iowa and Alaska found that participants, regardless of their sex or age, predicted a stronger marriage if the couple had conformed to a more traditional proposal script (Schweingruber et al., 2008). Scripts automate many social behaviors and help us navigate a complex social world.

Scripts govern other romantic behaviors we often think of as spontaneous. For example, a widely shared script about consensual sex begins with kissing and then proceeds in a predictable sequence to touching particular parts of the body (see Gagnon & Simon, 1987; Laumann et al., 1994). The traditional sexual script includes a "nearly universal sexual double standard that gives men greater sexual freedom" (Blanc, 2001, p. 190).

Going off-script—like deciding to spend several minutes licking your partner's inner knee—might cause surprise and potentially negative reactions. Scripts help us cruise through uncertain social situations, but they also can be harmful. For example, a misogynistic marriage script (e.g., the man is the "king of his castle") can lead to abusive relationships (Johnson, 2007).

Script: A memory structure that shapes expectations for how particular social events will occur.

Your mental script for how to get married tells you that these photographs are out of order.

The good news is that Dworkin and O'Sullivan (2005) found that harmful sexist scripts may be changing. College men across diverse ethnic backgrounds now generally prefer more egalitarian sexual and relationship scripts (Masters et al., 2013). However, traditional scripts still seem to shape people's general expectations.

Goodfriend (2012) *surveyed* 89 college students in the Midwest regarding two things: (1) whether they would consider engaging in nontraditional sexual behaviors and (2) their perceptions of whether these behaviors were socially acceptable. You can see the results in Table 4.2. All mean scores (or averages) were based on a scale of 1 (*definitely not acceptable or worth consideration*) to 7 (*definitely acceptable or worth consideration*).

Fewer people were willing to consider less traditional behavior, but there were some exceptions, and some interesting gender differences emerged (for example, men are more likely to consider plural marriage; women are more likely to consider bisexuality). While scripts guide our expected behaviors, there are always people who will decide not to follow "the rules."

Stereotypes Ignore Individual Differences Within Groups. Schemas help us organize overwhelming amounts of information into manageable chunks.

Scripts accomplish that goal by telling us what to expect in familiar social situations. Now we explore how **stereotypes** help us organize information by assuming that everyone in a certain group has the same characteristics.

Stereotype: A memory structure that assumes everyone in a particular group shares the same characteristics.

TABLE 4.2

Men's and Women's Views on Possible Sexual Paths, on a Range From 1 (*Not Acceptable*) to 7 (*Definitely Acceptable*)

	MEN'S AVERAGE	WOMEN'S AVERAGE
Marriage with one person for life		
I would personally consider.	6.47	6.65
Does society accept?	6.18	6.29
Premarital sex		
I would personally consider.	5.58	5.35
Does society accept?	4.95	5.12
Casually dating several people		
I would personally consider.	4.87	5.51
Does society accept?	4.42	5.29
Single and sexually active for life		
I would personally consider.	3.79	3.00
Does society accept?	3.71	3.33
Bisexuality		
I would personally consider.	2.42	3.37
Does society accept?	3.29	3.47
Group marriage or polygamy		
I would personally consider.	2.31	1.27
Does society accept?	2.08	1.84
Prostitution		
I would personally consider.	1.92	1.29
Does society accept?	1.95	2.06

Source: Adapted from Goodfriend (2012).

You may not behave according to the stereotype, but others will view you through the lens of their stereotypes. Your group membership as fraternity brother, older college student, garage band member, social justice activist, or athlete will trigger a stereotype that will make it slightly easier for others to think about you.

Psychology majors, for example, often have to deal with others' expectations that you are psychoanalyzing them. It's their stereotype, but it's your problem—if you care what they think of you. Of course, some aspects of a stereotype may be true for *some* members of a particular group. But it's still a logical mistake to assume that everyone in a group is the same as everyone else. We'll talk more about these assumptions, and the harm they can cause, in depth within Chapter 9. Like other mental shortcuts, stereotypes help us process huge amounts of information—but also may lead to errors in judgment.

THE MAIN IDEAS

- Social cognition is the study of how people combine intuition and logic to process social information. Intuition is automatic, fast, emotional, and effortless, while logic is controlled, slower, systematic, and analytical.

- There are limits to your cognitive load, the amount of information that our thinking systems can process at one time. Our default thinking process is intuition, and logic is used when needed.

- Social thinking is shaped by cultural influences, such as collectivism versus individualism.

- Schemas, scripts, and stereotypes all serve as memory structures that allow us to organize social information quickly and shape our behavior. But, they can also lead to incorrect assumptions and errors.

CRITICAL THINKING CHALLENGE

- We used metaphors and examples (mostly borrowed from other researchers) to describe the relation between intuition and logic, including driving, dancing, and sports. What other metaphors could describe the combination of automatic behavior or thought and controlled, systematic thought serving as a monitor and stepping in when needed? What other specific examples can you identify that show dual processing in your own life?

- Think of the popular fairytales of *Snow White and the Seven Dwarfs* and *The Little Mermaid*. Identify elements of each story that encourage an independent self (individualism) or an interdependent self (collectivism). This example becomes even more interesting when you consider the original versions from the Grimm Brothers and from Hans Christian Andersen.

- Identify three of groups in which you are a member (e.g., people in the marching band, people in your major, groups like your age, religion, or socioeconomic status) and corresponding stereotypes about your own groups. Do you fit these stereotypes or not? Can you think of other members of your group that either do or don't fit those stereotypes?

WHY ARE THERE FLAWS IN OUR MENTAL MACHINERY?

>> LO 4.2: Describe how and why dual processing creates unavoidable trade-offs in thinking.

Why do our big brains make mistakes in the first place?

Even after years of practice, people still make mistakes. There seem to be two underlying explanations for our chronic mental errors: information overload (TMI) and

KAREN BLEIER/AFP via Getty Images

Our brains don't like to process too much information at any given time.

wishing. The TMI problem isn't going away—instant information is constantly at our fingertips. And people will probably keep on wishing for what we want. The wooden *Pinocchio* will never turn into a real boy, and neither beasts nor frogs will ever turn into princes. Yet we seem wired to yearn for feel-good stories where magic fixes our problems.

This section explains why there are flaws in our thinking systems by

(1) understanding the problem of information overload and

(2) demonstrating how magical thinking can lead to serious social problems.

Information Overload Leads to Mental Errors

The brain developed an efficient but imperfect solution to the TMI problem: We throw most things out and organize what remains.

We Are Cognitive Misers

Let's be blunt about it: Sometimes we don't like to think more than we have to.

An economic "miser" hates spending money unless absolutely necessary. Likewise, a cognitive "miser" avoids effortful thinking. A **cognitive miser** takes mental shortcuts to minimize the cognitive load (Hansen, 1980; Taylor, 1981). It sounds like a lazy way to think, and it is—although "economical" or "efficient" might be a more precise word than "lazy." Under most circumstances, the brain searches for the shortest, quickest way to solve a problem, partly because logical brainwork (like studying for an exam!) requires effort.

For example, Daniel Kahneman (2011) noticed that people will stop walking if you ask them to calculate a difficult arithmetic problem in their heads. Multiply 2 × 4 and you will keep walking. But try calculating 23 × 278 in your head—you will stop walking. Even a leisurely stroll feels like effort to a brain that is being asked to do too much—so we stop and do one thing at a time. It's why we sometimes turn down the car radio when we're searching for a street address. We like to concentrate on one thing at a time.

For the same reasons, we prefer to stick to decisions once we've made them. Reconsidering options requires more effort. Making difficult decisions is such a relief that we don't want to do it again; our miserly mental habits just say no.

We Satisfice Because Perfection Isn't Worth the Price

The brain has a general strategy for the TMI problem.

Satisficing is making decisions based on criteria that are "good enough" under the circumstances (see Nisbett et al., 1983). When you buy a car, you won't read every review of every system and subsystem about every car you might purchase; you satisfice. You pick a couple of things that matter to you and focus on those.

When shopping for shampoo, you won't test every single product available at the megamart; you satisfice. If it's on sale or has a cute koala on it, you grab it and move on with your day. Some students juggle their academic lives by studying just hard enough to achieve a "good enough" grade; they satisfice. Satisficing is honored in

Cognitive miser: The tendency for humans to take mental shortcuts to minimize cognitive load.

Satisficing: Making "good enough" decisions to avoid cognitive overload.

the old saying, "Cs get degrees." Satisficing enables you to move on to the next thing demanding your attention.

We satisfice when making both minor and major decisions. We satisfice when buying consumer products (Park & Hastak, 1994; Simon, 1955); we also satisfice when choosing a college major or a career (Starbuck, 1963). We make some errors by satisficing, but we do it anyway because perfection isn't worth the price (Haselton & Funder, 2006; Simon, 1956).

Of course, some people don't like to satisfice—they enjoy thinking through all the options, or they worry about making the wrong decision. The scale in the next What's My Score? feature indicates whether you generally tend to be a satisficer or the opposite—a **maximizer**—when making everyday decisions.

Satisficers seem to be happier than maximizers (Snyder & Miene, 1994). Trying to gather all available information for every decision is associated with lower levels of happiness, optimism, life satisfaction, and self-esteem—and with higher levels of depression, perfectionism, and regret (Polman, 2010; Schwartz et al., 2002; Sparks et al., 2012). Perhaps that is why another Nobel Prize winner, Herbert Simon, suggested that satisficing directs many, and perhaps all, of our mental shortcuts (Simon, 1956).

Maximizer: Engaging in high cognitive load when making decisions by exhaustively examining every option.

WHAT'S MY SCORE?

The Maximization Scale

Instructions: Use the following scale to indicate your level of agreement with each statement, then add up all of your answers. The higher your score, the more you tend to maximize rather than satisfice (scores can range from 6 to 42):

1	2	3	4	5	6	7
Completely disagree						Completely agree

1. ___ When I am in the car listening to the radio, I often check other stations to see if something better is playing, even if I am relatively satisfied with what I'm listening to.

2. ___ No matter how satisfied I am with my job, it's only right for me to be on the lookout for better opportunities.

3. ___ I often find it difficult to shop for a gift for a friend.

4. ___ Choosing a show to watch is really difficult. I'm always struggling to pick the best one.

5. ___ No matter what I do, I have the highest standards for myself.

6. ___ I never settle for second best.

Source: Adapted from Nenkov, Morrin, Ward, Schwartz, and Hulland (2008).

Wishing: Magical Thinking Encourages Mental Errors

Joan Didion (2005) titled her book *The Year of Magical Thinking*.

Joan Didion described how her brain refused to accept the death of her husband of 40 years, fellow writer John Gregory Dunne. Her thoughts replayed thousands of little things that she might have done to prevent his heart attack. "If only" thinking, she slowly realized during the year after his death, must eventually yield to acceptance. She knew that it was illogical to give in to **magical thinking**, beliefs or perceptions that do not hold up to reality. It's thinking about a world that doesn't actually exist. But in her grief, she could not stop thinking, "If only . . ."

Joan Didion's logic-defying magical thinking shows up in experiments with other people. If you were in line for a free concert ticket and the person in front of you got the last one, then you probably will be more disappointed than if you were at the back of the line. It's easier to imagine that "if only" you had changed one little thing in your schedule and arrived 30 seconds earlier, then you would have been going to the concert (Boninger et al., 1994; Bouts et al., 1992; Kahneman & Tversky, 1982; Roese, 1997).

Magical thinking: Beliefs or perceptions that do not hold up to reality, such as counterfactual thinking, optimistic bias, and the planning fallacy.

The same kind of "if only" thinking leads Olympic athletes who finish in third place to feel happier than second-place competitors. Why? Second place encourages the magical thinking, "If only I had done one little thing differently, I could have won gold." On the other hand, the bronze medalist reasons that if circumstances had been just a little different, they might not have received any medal at all! They can think, "At least I got a medal!" Emotionally, third place might provide a better experience than second place because it leads to happiness and relief rather than frustration and regret.

Counterfactual Thinking: Upward and Downward

Counterfactual thinking is imagining what might have been.

It means thinking of alternative realities where differences in the past led to a different future (Davis & Lehman, 1995; Davis et al., 1995; Davis et al., 1996; Dunning & Madey, 1995; Dunning & Parpal, 1989; Einhorn & Hogarth, 1986). What if you had been born to different parents, chose a different college, or even had a different breakfast? How would the world be different now? Counterfactual thinking occurred in a group of tourists who somehow survived the terrible tsunami that took 280,000 lives across Southeast Asia on December 26, 2004.

Teigen and Jensen (2011) *interviewed* 85 surviving tourists, both parents and children. Most survivors comforted themselves, as much as they could, with **downward counterfactuals**. They imagined outcomes that were even worse than reality. "Only a matter of 1 [minute], one way or the other," reported one interviewee, "and everything would have been different [we might have died]." Such downward counterfactuals can be comforting, like a silver lining to tragedy: *At least we survived.*

By contrast, **upward counterfactuals** are imagined outcomes that are better than reality. *If only* something had (or hadn't) happened, things would have been different! One interviewee stated, "They could have issued a warning," when imagining what might have led to a better outcome. While downward counterfactuals are "at least" thoughts that lead to positive emotions, upward counterfactuals are "if only" thoughts that lead to negative emotions. "If only" thoughts can haunt you as you ruminate over tragedy. So why do we do it?

Counterfactual thinking: The tendency to imagine alternative facts or events that would have led to a different future; imagining "what might have been."

Downward counterfactuals: Imagined outcomes that are worse than reality; they can be comforting after things go wrong.

Upward counterfactuals: Imagined outcomes that are better than reality; they can help us learn from mistakes.

The 2004 tsunami as it hit Thailand.

"If only . . ." upward counterfactual thinking upset some college students (Leach & Patall, 2013) who imagined how they might have earned a better grade: "If only I had studied more . . ." In cases like these, upward counterfactuals might be helpful if (1) you have some control over the situation, like how you choose to study, and (2) if a similar situation will happen again. In this case, you can learn from the past and potentially make a different decision next time. Yes, you failed this exam—but you can do better on the next one. In short, upward counterfactual thinking can help us learn from mistakes.

For more on counterfactual thinking—and *Spider-Man*—see the Social Psychology in Popular Culture feature. We are complicated people, so counterfactuals can have both positive and negative consequences.

The Optimistic Bias

To-do lists suggest another common form of magical thinking.

If you keep a to-do list, how often do you actually check off every single item? I [Wind] keep an electronic sticky note on my computer desktop, on which I make a list at the beginning of each week of everything I need to get done. Although I have never, ever completed the entire list in a week, I have been making the list regularly for 7 years. My continued behavior demonstrates the **optimistic bias**, an unrealistic expectation that things will turn out well.

Apparently, I'm not the only one with an optimistic bias. Weinstein (1980) gave more than 250 college students a strange task: Think about 42 positive and negative events that you might experience in the future. First, think about how likely each event is to happen to you. Then, guess how likely each event is to happen to the "average" student at your college.

Positive events included liking your job after graduation, owning your own home, and having a respectable starting salary. Negative events included having a drinking problem, attempting suicide, and getting divorced shortly after marrying. The optimistic bias was shown in two different ways in this study. First, participants believed they were significantly more likely to experience the positive events than the negative events. Second, they also assumed that the positive events were more likely to happen to them than to the average student.

There's only one problem: It is not possible for everyone to be above average. Some of these students must have been deceiving themselves about how nicely their lives were going to turn out after graduation. However, remember what we learned in Chapter 3: A *little* self-deception is not necessarily a bad thing! Having hopes and dreams about your future might help you stay motivated through hard times and have big dreams.

Optimistic bias: The unrealistic expectation that things will turn out well.

SOCIAL PSYCHOLOGY IN POPULAR CULTURE

▶ Counterfactual Thinking in *Spider-Man*

Even people who aren't big comic book fans could probably tell you that Spider-Man got his superpowers when Peter Parker, a teenager, was bitten by a scientifically altered spider. But when any fictional character suddenly has special, superhuman abilities, what determines whether that character will be a superhero or a supervillain?

For Peter Parker, his choice to use his powers for good may be due to his use of upward counterfactual thinking. In most versions of the Spider-Man origin story, Peter doesn't immediately decide to take the hero route. For example, in one film version (Arad et al., 2012, starring Andrew Garfield), a few days after being bitten, Peter simply stands by as a man robs

(Continued)

(Continued)

Moviestore collection Ltd/Alamy Stock Photo

a convenience store—even though he could easily stop the crime. Unfortunately, the man then shoots Peter's beloved Uncle Ben. Peter's regret over his inaction causes him to start hunting criminals. Upward counterfactual thinking appears to haunt (and motivate) Peter as he imagines that Uncle Ben would still be alive "if only" Peter had done something.

The second half of the film continues this theme. The main antagonist is an evil scientist who morphs into a gigantic lizard only because Peter supplied him with an essential formula to alter his DNA. When several people attempt to tell Peter that it's not his job to stop the man-lizard, he tells them that it is his responsibility because it's his fault. Essentially, Peter is engaging in the upward counterfactual thought, "If only I hadn't provided him the formula he needed, none of this would have happened."

Thus, upward counterfactuals appear to have made Spider-Man choose a superhero's path because of his regret and wish for a better outcome in both situations. It's clear that upward counterfactuals and "if only" thinking have shaped Peter's interpretation of Uncle Ben's parting advice, the famous words of co-creator Stan Lee: "With great power comes great responsibility."

Students also tend to be overly optimistic about their test performance (Gilovich et al., 1993), and they are not alone in their optimism. Teens underestimate their likelihood of eventually becoming the victim of dating violence (Chapin & Coleman, 2012) or sexual assault (Untied & Dulaney, 2015). Potential blood donors overestimate their probability of actually making a donation (Koehler & Poon, 2006). Students who steal music instead of paying for it underestimate their chances of getting caught (Nandedkar & Midha, 2012).

The optimistic bias applies to romantic relationships as well. Many people make extravagant promises but don't follow through (Peetz & Kammrath, 2011). The people making these romantic commitments may sincerely mean what they say in the moment, but sometimes it's just the optimistic bias talking.

The Planning Fallacy

The optimistic bias can morph into a big problem.

The **planning fallacy** is unjustified confidence that one's own project, unlike similar projects, will proceed as planned (see Kahneman & Tversky, 1979). The first stadium with a retractable roof, announced for the Montreal Olympics in 1976, was not completed until 1989—and at a cost greater than the cost of the entire 1976 Olympics (Buehler et al., 1994). Australia's Sydney Opera House was estimated at $7 million but cost $102 million and 10 extra years. Boston's "Big Dig," a 3.5-mile tunnel, was estimated to cost $2.8 billion but came in at $22 billion—and with questionable structural outcomes.

Planning fallacy: The unjustified confidence that one's own project, unlike similar projects, will proceed as planned.

The Sydney Opera House and Boston's "Big Dig" project, both of which took much more money and time to create than originally planned. Were the architects and construction workers suffering from the planning fallacy?

Our optimistic bias can inspire big ideas so appealing that we gloss over crucial details. We recognize our optimism as a bias only when our plans start costing us scarce resources such as money and time (see Alter et al., 2010). As predicted by Baumeister's (1989) optimal margin theory of self-deception (described in Chapter 3), a little optimism can be helpful, but too much can be harmful.

But how much self-deception is too much when you are estimating major public works development projects that shape national agendas? History (and Albert Hirschman in 1967—and again in a 2015 republication) suggests that a reckless optimism is sometimes supported by a "Hiding Hand [that] is certainly not God, but it is pretty benevolent and works in mysterious ways" (see Flyvbjer & Sunstein, 2016). In other words, sometimes the planning fallacy leads to problems in a project's completion, but invisible ("hiding") forces save the day anyway.

How might this Benevolent Hiding Hand produce these social psychological non-miracles? According to the article,

> The planners' neglect of bad surprises is countered by a much happier surprise, which involves the sheer power of human creativity. Planners do not merely overestimate the likelihood of success and underestimate costs; they also underestimate potential responses to failure. (p. 1005)

Planning problems can therefore be saved by human creativity and ingenuity, when solutions to problems come from talented team members. However, Flybjerg and Sunstein estimated that the Benevolent Hiding Hand appears to succeed in only 20% of major development projects—so don't count on it.

Even more troublesome is that its evil twin also exists. This one is called the Malevolent Hiding Hand, which blinds planners to potential problems and high costs while simultaneously making planners overestimate how wonderful a project will be when it's done. The authors estimate that the Malevolent Hiding Hand holds sway in about 80% of development projects.

Another important piece of the planning fallacy that might hit home for readers of this book is that people often severely underestimate how long it will take to accomplish something. You might go into a study session assuming you can review all of your notes for an exam or write a research paper in just a couple of hours, only to find that the task is much more complicated than you thought. Keep the planning fallacy in mind next time you think about when you should start working on an important project or paper.

THE MAIN IDEAS

- Two mental mistakes that are fairly common are (1) errors due to cognitive overload and (2) wishful or "magical" thinking.

- People are generally cognitive misers, meaning we prefer mental shortcuts when possible. Doing the minimal needed amount of thought is called satisficing; the opposite is called maximizing.

- Magical thinking or wishful thinking is imagining other possible outcomes. Downward counterfactuals, for example, are "at least" thoughts that imagine a worse outcome, while upward counterfactuals are "if only" thoughts that imagine a better outcome. The optimistic bias and planning fallacy are other examples of magical thinking.

CRITICAL THINKING CHALLENGE

- Describe decisions in which it is more adaptive to maximize and other decisions in which it is more adaptive to satisfice. Which you do generally prefer, and why?

- Think of examples from your own life that illustrate different types of magical thinking: counterfactual thinking, optimistic bias, and the planning fallacy.

- If tragedy strikes you, do you tend to use more upward counterfactual thinking or downward counterfactual thinking? Which one leads you to feel better about what happened?

WHERE DOES INTUITION COME FROM—AND CAN WE TRUST IT?

>> **LO 4.3:** **Discuss how intuition uses and misuses mental accessibility that comes from priming, experience, and heuristics.**

The idea of intuitive knowing is exciting. But *why?*

1. Intuition tickles our vanity. It's pretty cool to think that *we* might be gifted in some mysterious way, almost like psychic powers.

2. Intuitive knowing would be useful. Finding lost children, buried treasures, and correct test answers would be a pretty handy (and highly marketable) skill.

3. Intuition leads to significant creativity in the arts and the sciences.

4. We need our intuition for minor and major life decisions.

The experience of intuition is sometimes exciting, even life-saving.

But at this point, the cognitive reality behind intuition seems downright ordinary. Sometimes it makes you wonder: Are scientists just out to spoil the fun?

Well, yes, depending on how you define "fun."

Scientists, however, find their fun by forming their beliefs around the **principle of parsimony**. We prefer the simplest possible explanation that explains the largest set of events or ideas. Parsimony also means "cheap"—so you can think of scientists as intellectual bargain hunters. We want an elegant theory without having to pay for it with exotic assumptions or magical beliefs. Relying on the simplest, evidence-based explanation is also called "Occam's razor" (Wind's favorite term) and "the principle of least astonishment" (Tom's favorite).

A parsimonious scientific explanation for intuition begins with the simple recognition that intuition requires **mental accessibility**. Mental accessibility is the ease with

Principle of parsimony: The tendency for individuals, especially scientists, to prefer the simplest answer that explains the most evidence.

Mental accessibility: The ease with which an idea comes to mind.

which an idea comes to mind. Sgt. Tierney had to be able to access the whispers of knowledge that led to him making the right call, despite many other legitimate, competing claims for his attention (Chapman & Johnson, 2002; Epley, 2004; Epley et al., 2004; Epley & Gilovich, 2001, 2004; Gilbert & Gill, 2000; Shedler & Manis, 1986; Strack & Mussweiler, 1997). So how does an idea become more or less likely to occur to us?

Figure 4.2 displays how three silent sources of intuition (priming, experience, and heuristics) influence what information comes most easily to mind. This section answers the core question "Where does intuition come from—and can we trust it?" by

(1) documenting how mental accessibility comes from priming, experience, and heuristics;

(2) reporting an experiment that demonstrated how even parallel, coordinated conclusions from heuristics can also be wrong; and

(3) concluding that we would be wise to respect—but not blindly trust—our intuition.

FIGURE 4.2

Three sources of intuition: priming, experience, and heuristics.

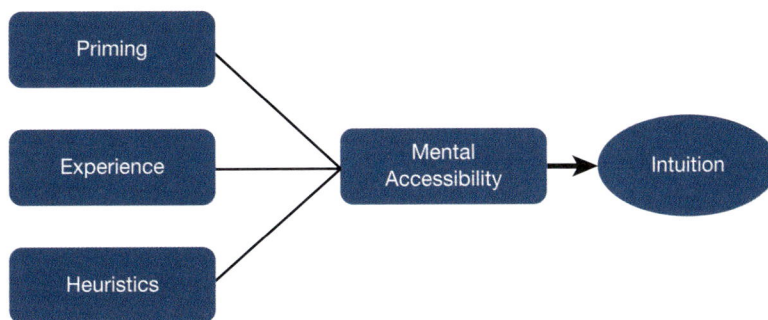

Priming Increases Mental Accessibility

Let's play a word association game: If I say "boxers," what comes to mind?

You might associate "boxers" with a kind of underwear. Or, a certain breed of dog might come to mind instead. A third option might be the image of famous boxers in the ring, like Muhammad Ali, Mike Tyson, or (maybe) Rocky Balboa. Each of these concepts—underwear, dogs, and fighters—branches off into new sets of concepts, all associated with each other. Which set of words comes to mind first might tell us a little about how you think, your personal interests, or your life experience.

Your entire collection of mental associations is called a **semantic network**, mental concepts that are connected to one another by common characteristics in your mind. Each person's semantic network will be unique. **Priming** refers to the initial activation of a concept (such as "boxers") that subsequently flashes across our semantic network, allowing other ideas to come more easily to mind (Cameron et al., 2012).

The word "priming" is like a metaphor for priming a wall before you paint it or priming an engine before you start it. Priming an idea once makes it more accessible to you later, and priming one idea can also make other, related ideas more likely to come to mind as well. In that way, priming increases mental accessibility—and intuition.

Priming is a hot issue in society. For example, parents worry that aggressive video games prime (make it easier for) children to be aggressive. With so many school shootings in the United States, it is difficult for parents not to be worried. Similarly, increased sexual images in advertising, movies, and TV shows might prime sexual urges.

Semantic network: A collection of mental concepts that are connected by common characteristics.

Priming: Initial activation of a concept within a semantic network that allows related ideas to come more easily to mind.

While some people say that they tune out advertising or mass media, it's hard to deny that they might influence culture and society. One interesting example of how priming and semantic networks might affect crucial decisions in the world of police officers is explored in the Spotlight on Research Methods feature.

SPOTLIGHT ON RESEARCH METHODS

How Priming Can Test For Racism

Your mental network of related concepts is both personal and social.

A famous research study used priming to test for the kind of racism that can subtly influence our behavior (Correll et al., 2002). They tested the strength of the associations between the concepts of "African American" and "weapons." Will some people connect these ideas within their semantic network?

This particular study demonstrates applied social psychology because it was inspired by a series of tragedies: police officers who fatally shot innocent suspects. The most fair-minded police officer might unexpectedly be confronted with a difficult situation. They must make a split-second decision about whether a particular person is dangerous—and waiting too long can be a deadly error. For example, they might have to quickly assess what's in someone's hand—is it a gun, a knife, a wallet, or simply a cell phone? Certainly, intuition will be important.

As if playing a video game, participants in the study watched as a bus stop, a convenience store, a park, and other scenes flashed by. One of these scenes included either a White or an African American man who was holding something in his hand. Participants had to push one computer button to "shoot" the man if he was holding a weapon (such as a knife or gun) and a different button to "not shoot" the man if he was holding something else (such as a wallet or a cell phone).

The *hypothesis* was that for at least some of the participants, the concepts of "African American" and "weapons" would have a strong association in their semantic network. Thus, when an African American person popped up on the screen, priming the concept of "African American" would also prime

"weapons" among people with higher levels of racist impulses.

In *theory,* those participants would be more likely to mistakenly "shoot" the African American targets—even when they were innocent (in other words, holding a wallet or cell phone). And that is exactly what happened when college students participated. They were more likely to "shoot" the African Americans on the screen, compared to the White people on the screen, regardless of what people were actually holding.

In this case, priming led to errors based on stereotypes. While priming does increase mental accessibility of concepts, sometimes that mental accessibility takes us into a semantic network of associations that leads to a tragedy.

The good news of this potentially controversial study was that when the researchers tried to *replicate* the findings with actual police officers from Chicago, they didn't find the same results. In fact, the police officers were less likely to make mistakes in either direction; they currently "shot" people on the screen holding weapons (regardless of what race those people were) and correctly did not shoot people on the screen holding other things (again, regardless of the race of the people on the screen).

This finding might surprise you, given the recent news coverage about shootings by police officers. When people are shot without good cause, it's absolutely a tragedy. And the experimental findings of this study are not much comfort to the families who have suffered from incidents like these. That said, one story of a mistaken shooting is more likely to make the news than 100 stories of correct decisions—so the media might not be particularly fair to police who use their intuition to make the right call.

Experience Improves Mental Accessibility

Experience may be intuition's best teacher.

For example, college students' brief observations of a teacher (totaling only 30 seconds!) at the start of a semester were fairly good predictors of student ratings of the teacher at the end of the semester (Ambady & Rosenthal, 1993; Babad et al., 2004). Why are students so good at sizing up teachers? Well, some scholars argue

Do you get strong impressions of your teachers or professors within minutes of the first day of class?

that students' immediate first impressions are biased evaluations based on things like the race, sex, age, and physical attractiveness of the professor. And there's probably something to that idea, as these biases are themes throughout this entire book. But, another view is that students really are experts in observing and evaluating teachers. Consequently, they have gotten very good at intuiting in the first few seconds how they will feel about the teacher and the class by the end of the year.

Personal experience also seems to explain two more feats of intuition. First, both gay men and lesbians are more likely than heterosexual people to intuitively detect someone's sexual orientation in still photographs and even in 1-second videos—a phenomenon jokingly referred to as "Gaydar" (Ambady et al., 1999). The participants in this study could not say what they saw, but they saw it—because they had seen it many times before.

Second, African American judges were more accurate than White judges at detecting subtle forms of nonverbal racial bias (Curhan & Pentland, 2007). They, too, could not say what they saw, but they saw it—because they had seen it many times before. Experience had sharpened their intuition. A surgeon who had trained many other surgeons across a long career summed up the importance of experience at refining intuition. "Good judgment comes from experience," he reported, "and experience comes from bad judgment."

Heuristics Facilitate Mental Accessibility

In a stress-free, no-hurry world, there is an easy way to solve problems: algorithms.

But we don't live in that world. An **algorithm** is a systematic way of searching for an answer that will eventually lead to a solution—if there is one. For driving direction problems, computerized programs use algorithms such as the fastest route, the shortest distance, or the avoid-all-tolls algorithm. For psychological problems, digital databases (such as PsycINFO) provide algorithms that access answers from every (available) book, journal article, and conference presentation. Algorithms search every possible answer before picking the "best" one.

However, algorithmic problem solving is often impractical. If you lost your keys somewhere in your house, an algorithm approach would be to start in the attic (or basement) and search every square inch until you found them. You'd succeed—eventually.

Algorithm: A systematic, logical, but sometimes slow method of searching for a solution to a problem or question.

But you can probably take a problem-solving shortcut by looking in the most likely spots first. The human brain, cognitive miser that it is, looks for mental shortcuts when making decisions: **heuristics**.

Algorithms rely on systematic logic; heuristics rely on intuitive probabilities. There are many heuristics, but we will introduce you to just three of these mental shortcuts: anchoring and adjustment, availability, and representativeness.

The Anchoring and Adjustment Heuristic

The **anchoring and adjustment heuristic** occurs when we make guesses about a numeric answer but are influenced by a starting point.

It makes sense that we do this—we have to start somewhere. But sometimes our guesses can be misled by a starting point that bogs us down. For example, choose either (a) or (b) below as the best answer to the following question. Then indicate your own most precise estimate.

"On average, how many full-time college students *in the entire United States* drop out before graduation?"

(a) ___ More than 200 students

or

(b) ___ Fewer than 200 students

Now indicate your own most precise estimate here: _____

Your most honest answer is probably, "I have no idea how many students drop out of college each year, but it's probably much higher than 200." You may be able to think of 5 or even 10 at your own school. So, being a cognitive miser, you grab at the ridiculous hint we floated in front of your brain: 200. You might end up with a guess around 10,000. But what if we had hinted at a different number: 25 million?

Again, your most honest answer to this question is probably, "I have no idea, but it's probably much lower than 25 million." In the first question, your estimate would be anchored by 200; in the second question, your answer would be anchored by 25 million. This time, your guess might have ended up somewhere around 100,000 or maybe even 1 million (Kahneman & Frederick, 2005; Mussweiler & Strack, 2001; Nisbett & Wilson, 1977; Trope & Gaunt, 2000; Tversky & Kahneman, 1974).

Your estimates would be *anchored* by what was mentally accessible (either 200 or 25 million) and then *adjusted* upward from 200 or downward from 25 million. The metaphor of the "anchor" is that our brains are like a boat. When we start at a certain place (in this case, a given number), we can only float so far from that starting point in any given direction. When faced with an uncertain reality, we will use almost any information as an estimate (Cervone & Peake, 1986; Marrow, 2002; Wilson et al., 1996).

There is some fine print to the anchoring and adjustment heuristic (see Bruza et al., 2011; Epley & Gilovich, 2006; Epley et al., 2004). Most of us

- tend to stop adjusting as we approach reality,
- are politely reluctant to challenge someone else's crazy estimate, and
- are more likely to challenge someone else's estimate if the topic is personally important or we possess expertise.

The anchoring and adjustment heuristic is another indicator that much of our thinking is guided by the principle of satisficing—being satisfied with a "good enough" answer to a question.

Heuristic: Any mental shortcut that makes it easier to solve difficult problems. While fast, these shortcuts can sometimes lead to mistakes.

Anchoring and adjustment heuristic: Our tendency to be influenced by a starting point when making numerical guesses about something, even if the starting point is unreliable.

The Availability Heuristic

Fame, for some reason, is a powerful social influence—even when you're only famous for being famous.

The Flintstones was a famous animated television show that reflected social expectations in the 1960s. The show helped sell millions of cigarettes. In one commercial (available on YouTube), Fred Flintstone and his pal Barney Rubble wanted a cigarette break as they observed their hardworking wives mowing their lawns and beating rugs.

Fred: "They sure work hard, don't they, Barney?"

Barney: "Yeah. I hate to see them work so hard."

Fred: "Yeah, me too. Uh . . . let's go around back where we can't see them."

The availability heuristic helps explain why modern advertisers continue to rely on famous athletes, actors, television shows, and personalities. The **availability heuristic** is our tendency to overestimate the frequency or importance of something based on how easily it comes to mind (Tversky & Kahneman, 1973).

Fame works because it gets our attention. Fame helps explain why we believe that Hollywood couples are more likely to have ugly divorces. We're much more likely to notice and remember news stories about ugly celebrity divorces, compared to happily married couples—and news outlets are much more likely to run divorce stories.

Let's jump from the 1960s to the 2020s—the availability heuristic persists. For example, regulars on Facebook tend to think that their friends are happier than they are (Chou & Edge, 2012). Why? Probably the available posts usually provide only positive, even boastful status updates—and neglect any embarrassing details. The "available" information in our memory is that our friends are happy and popular, doing fantastic things all the time.

Unfortunately, the availability heuristic sometimes also leads to mental miscalculations, such as believing that our Facebook friends lead almost perfect lives (Dougherty et al., 1999; Nisbett & Ross, 1980; Rothman & Hardin, 1997; Schwarz, 1998; Taylor & Fiske, 1978; Travis et al., 1989). We're much less likely to publicly share our embarrassing moments or our failures.

Availability heuristic: Our tendency to overestimate the frequency of something based on how easily it comes to mind.

Representativeness heuristic: Our tendency to make decisions based on what appears to be "typical," even when that goes against statistical likelihood.

The Representativeness Heuristic

All of our mental shortcuts come with trade-offs.

For example, when you need a store clerk, you probably would not ask everyone you see, "Do you work here?" That would be rude as well as waste your time. You are more likely to substitute a shortcut heuristic.

The shortcut is to look for someone wearing a uniform or a nametag (Kahneman & Frederick, 2005; Shepperd & Koch, 2005). Looking for the typical store clerk demonstrates the **representativeness heuristic**, a problem-solving approach based on the "typical" case. It is much easier than approaching every single other person in the store (the algorithm approach).

iStockPhoto./IPGGutenbergUKLtd

Certain cues tell us whether someone in a store probably works there—when we rely on these cues, we are using the representativeness heuristic.

Here comes the trade-off: Some shoppers may also be dressed as if they could be store clerks. And some store clerks may appear to be ordinary customers. You have to balance the slightly embarrassing risk of going up to the wrong person against the potentially efficient reward of finding a clerk quickly.

The example below, adapted from Swinkels (2003, p. 122), demonstrates how tightly mental errors are attached to the representativeness heuristic:

Rudy is a bit on the peculiar side. He has unusual tastes in movies and art, he is married to a performer, and he has tattoos. In his spare time Rudy takes yoga classes and likes to collect old vinyl records. An outgoing person, he's known to act on a dare more than once. Which occupation is Rudy most likely to have?

(a)   Farmer
(b)   Librarian
(c)   Trapeze artist
(d)   Surgeon
(e)   Lawyer

Here's the wrong answer: trapeze artist. People tend to pick that option because Rudy's behavior is typical of—or representative of—someone like a circus performer. But the total number of trapeze artists in the world is extremely small. Statistically speaking, he's much more likely to have any of the other options, which are so much more common. But this logical answer just doesn't *feel* as right as the one our intuition wants us to pick.

Parallel Heuristics Can Be Wrong

This next experiment is disturbing.

Our mental shortcuts are rapid, are automatic, and can operate simultaneously— even when they all reach the wrong conclusion. Yikes! It's extra persuasive when multiple mental shortcuts produce the same false intuition. For example, read the following memories from people who claimed to have observed a *live, televised* version of the tragic terrorist bus bombing at London's Tavistock Square on July 7, 2005 (from Ost et al., 2008, p. 82). Spoiler alert: There was no live, televised, or recorded version of the bus bombing.

Participant 9. *Bus had just stopped to let people off when two women got on and a man. He placed the bag by his side, the woman sat down and the doors closed, as the bus left there was the explosion and everyone started to scream while a leg was on the floor.*

Participant 13. *The event was shown after a brief report. The bus had stopped at a traffic light. There was a bright light and a loud bang and the top of the bus flew off and lots of screaming and then everything seemed still.*

Participant 24. *Bus moving normally, then explosion, debris everywhere, chaos.*

Participant 131. *The bus was moving slowly in traffic and then the back of the bus exploded. A lot of debris everywhere and people panicking.*

Participant 158. *Bus appears to turn into Tavistock Square and people stand to get off and there is a flash and then nothing.*

These all sound convincing, but they cannot be true.

To find out what was going on, Ost and colleagues (2008) recruited participants in Great Britain (where media coverage was extensive and repeated) and in Sweden (where there was less overall coverage). They first asked all participants the same question: "How well do you remember the television coverage of the London bombings?"

Then, as usually happens in an *experiment*, they *randomly assigned* the participants to one of three conditions by asking them whether they remembered seeing on television (1) the real aftermath of the explosion, (2) a computerized reconstruction of the explosion, or (3) closed-circuit, *live* television footage of the actual event.

The 2005 London bombing was devastating to many people—but sometimes inaccurately remembered.

The last two conditions weren't possible; they just never happened. There had never been any computerized reconstruction on television, and there were no closed-circuit television broadcasts of the actual event, only its aftermath. This experiment was asking a more disturbing question: Why might these participants sincerely believe something that could not be true?

The answer is in Figure 4.3. A higher percentage in the U.K. sample reported seeing what could not be true—the nonexistent closed-circuit televised event *and* the nonexistent televised reconstruction (Ost et al., 2008). Increased media exposure afterward

FIGURE 4.3

Heuristics can produce false memories.

% Reporting How They Saw Television Coverage of the London Bombing

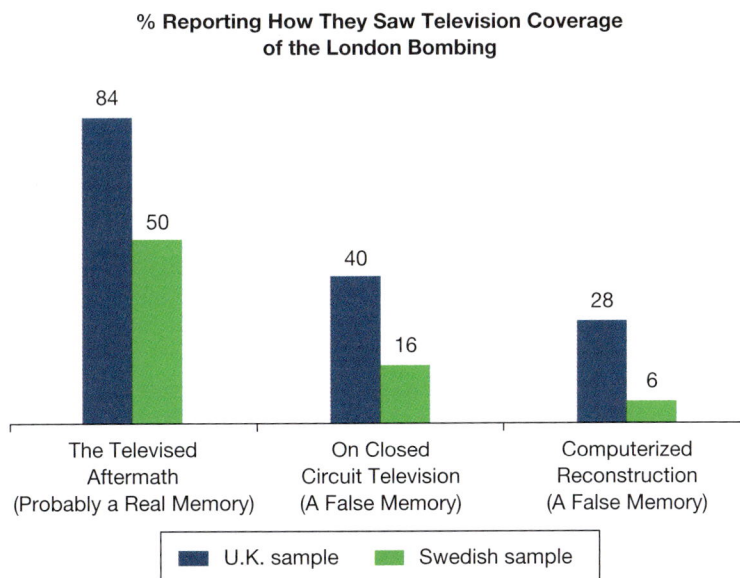

	U.K. sample	Swedish sample
The Televised Aftermath (Probably a Real Memory)	84	50
On Closed Circuit Television (A False Memory)	40	16
Computerized Reconstruction (A False Memory)	28	6

Source: Adapted from Ost et al. (2008).

had encouraged them to create intuitively appealing—but entirely false—memories of this tragic event (Fiske et al., 1982; Nisbett & Ross, 1980; Shedler & Manis, 1986; Taylor & Thompson, 1982).

At least three heuristics worked in parallel to mutually reinforce this false belief:

1. Media repetitions probably *anchored* people's imaginations so tightly that witnessing the event on television began to feel like an authentic memory.

2. It was a vivid, easy-to-imagine, and famous tragedy (*availability*).

3. Participants' stories followed what they thought would be typical or *representative* of an exploding bus.

All that social thinking told the same false story. The false details came so easily to mind that it was easy for U.K. citizens to believe that they really had witnessed this tragedy on television. But their intuitions were wrong. They sincerely believed something that could not be true.

Time out for a personal question.

Are you now wondering whether some of your beliefs or memories might not be true? We hope so. Healthy skepticism is healthy because it plants humanity in honest uncertainty rather than confident superstitions.

We Can Respect—but Not Trust—Our Intuitions

That's enough beating up on intuition; there is much more to the story.

It would be just as wrong to conclude that we should *never* trust our intuition as it is to believe that we can *always* trust our intuition. We can't live without a sophisticated intuition. Intuition helps us predict how other drivers are likely to behave, whether walking down an alley is safe, and what our romantic partner might be thinking: important stuff! Intuition saved Sgt. Tierney's life.

We need our intuition. And sometimes our intuition is wonderfully insightful. So, the intelligent middle ground is to respect but not blindly trust our intuitions. Our intuition will probably grow stronger if we can understand *why* and *how* it goes astray. Let's end the chapter with three biases that we've probably all experienced.

The Confirmation Bias: A Dangerous Way to Think

You love Professor X's classes. But your friend hates them.

As the class progresses, you notice all the things you expected to see: Professor X is helpful, funny, and super smart. But your friend notices all the things *they* expected to see, too: Professor X is somewhat crude, sometimes gets political, and gets weirdly angry when people in class use their cell phones. Both of you think that your expectations have been met.

Our intuitive thinking habits often take a fork in the road due to **confirmation bias**, the tendency to look only for evidence that confirms what we already believe—and to ignore contradicting evidence. If you think the U.S. president is going a great job, you notice and remember all of their successes. But if you're critical and think the other candidate should have won, you notice all the things they do wrong. Confirmation bias is a well-worn path to impossible beliefs.

- Persistent gamblers pay attention to their wins and explain away their losses (Gilovich, 1983).

- People who expressed an early hypothesis about a crime were more likely to be biased later (O'Brien, 2009).

- Psychiatrists tended to stick with their original diagnostic hunches—despite contradicting information (Mendel et al., 2011).

These mental failures harm more than individuals. There may have been other justifications for America's longest war, Operation Iraqi Freedom. But weapons of mass

Confirmation bias: Our tendency to notice and remember only evidence that confirms our beliefs and expectations.

destruction (WMDs) was not one of them (see Johnston, 2005; Straus et al., 2011), even though that's what the government and military kept expecting to find. Nickerson (1998) believes that the confirmation bias is the leading cause of "disputes, altercations, and misunderstandings that occur among individuals, groups, and nations" (p. 175).

There appear to be several reasons why confirmation is such a pervasive and an insidious mental failing. Confirmation bias can work with *any* belief system, takes advantage of what we want to believe, and feels reassuring. Perhaps this bias is why the world seems so divided on so many issues— because both sides keep finding more and more reasons to confirm the belief that their side is right . . . which means the other side must be wrong. Confirmation bias is, in other words, the opposite of having an open mind.

As physicist Neil deGrasse Tyson says, "The good thing about science is that it's true whether or not you believe in it."

The Hindsight Bias: A Self-Deceiving Way to Think

Our social thinking also gets tripped up by the **hindsight bias**, the backward-looking way we convince ourselves "we knew it all along."

This false belief convinces us that we could have predicted an outcome—but only after we know what happened. The hindsight bias may be just as subtle and dangerous as the confirmation bias because it creates an illusion of understanding that makes it difficult to learn from the past (Fischhoff, 1975, 2002, 2007). I [Tom] experience "I knew it all along" every time when my wife writes in the answer to a crossword puzzle that I instantly recognize—but only after she wrote it in. Apparently until then, I didn't actually know it!

Like other mental trade-offs, the hindsight bias can lead our intuition astray over minor matters, like the crossword puzzle. But it is equally dangerous over major matters. For example, some people believe that they should have been able to predict the terror attacks now famously called 9/11 (see Bernstein et al., 2011).

In hindsight, we feel as if we can "connect the dots" that led to the terror attacks on September 11, 2001. However, there was a similar attack 8 years earlier, on February 26, 1993. A yellow Ryder van, carrying 1,200 pounds of explosives, was parked near critical supports beneath the World Trade Center. The explosion was meant to tip the North Tower into the South Tower. Six people died from that explosion.

Despite this attack, everyone was shocked and surprised at the second, more successful attack. At the time, people did not predict what was going to happen in the future. It only seemed obvious after the fact. The subtle danger of the hindsight bias is that it gives an illusion of understanding and being able to predict the future when we really aren't good at it at all—but telling ourselves that we "knew" it is strangely comforting.

The Negativity Bias: Bad Is More Memorable Than Good

Ask your professors if they remember the worst student evaluation they ever got.

Professors who have been teaching a while have gotten dozens, if not hundreds, of evaluations. Well-liked and respected professors will probably remember a few specific positive comments—but it's the bad ones that really stick in memory. Like the famous line from Julia Roberts in the movie *Pretty Woman*, "The bad stuff is easier to believe. You ever notice that?" The **negativity bias** is our tendency to pay greater attention to negative information, perhaps because of survival instincts.

For example, unpleasant odors are perceived as more intense and evoke stronger emotional reactions than pleasant odors (Royet et al., 2003)—bad odors might be poison! It's easier to find an angry face hidden among happy faces than a happy face

Hindsight bias: Our tendency to believe we could have predicted the outcome of a past event, but only after we already know what happened; the false belief that we "knew it all along."

Negativity bias: Our tendency to notice and remember negative information better than positive information.

Are those dark clouds really a tornado heading our way? The negativity bias exists because we may only get to be wrong once about real threats.

hidden among sad faces (Hansen & Hansen, 1988)—an angry face is more likely to attack us. "Better safe than sorry" seems to be the guiding motto of the negativity bias (Fiedler et al., 2009; Öhman & Mineka, 2001). Bad things are more threatening, so we have to pay attention to them.

Our negativity bias can be both good and bad. It's good when it keeps us alive—but it can be exhausting! Figure 4.4, for example, reminds us that people living in tornado alley within the United States know that dark clouds and high winds sometimes predict devastating tornados. You may only get to be wrong once about a tornado; people with a greater negativity bias will be more likely to find shelter.

On the other hand, a farmer will have trouble getting crops in if they run for cover at the sight of every dark cloud. The "key organizing principle" for managing our negativity bias seems to be to "minimize danger and maximize reward . . . at each point in time" (Williams et al., 2009, p. 804). Or, as social psychologists keep reminding us, our behavior and thought processes depend on the situation. Paying attention to bad things might help us survive and maybe even learn from the past—but it can also be a bit depressing. Paying attention to the good stuff is a nice way to occasionally let ourselves engage in some comforting self-care.

FIGURE 4.4

Tornado alley and the negativity bias.

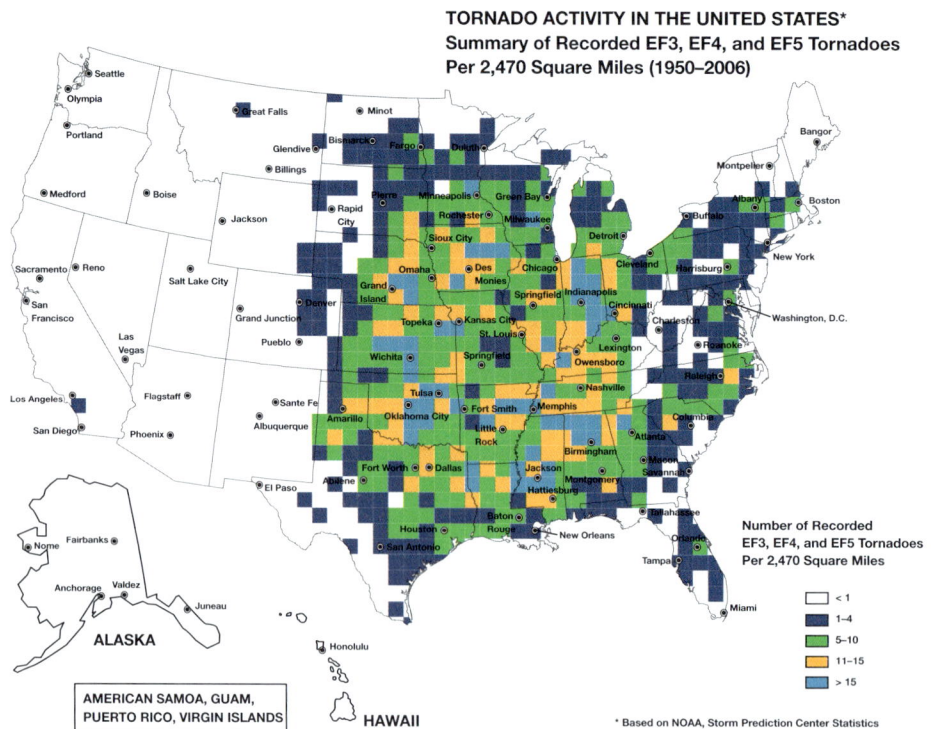

TORNADO ACTIVITY IN THE UNITED STATES*
Summary of Recorded EF3, EF4, and EF5 Tornadoes Per 2,470 Square Miles (1950–2006)

Number of Recorded EF3, EF4, and EF5 Tornadoes Per 2,470 Square Miles

- < 1
- 1–4
- 5–10
- 11–15
- > 15

* Based on NOAA, Storm Prediction Center Statistics

Source: United States Federal Emergency Management Agency.

THE MAIN IDEAS

- An algorithm is a systematic, logical approach to problem solving; a heuristic is an intuitive, mental shortcut approach to problem solving. Three examples of heuristics are anchoring and adjustment, availability, and representativeness.

- Heuristics operate automatically and simultaneously (in parallel) as we make decisions and solve problems.

- Three cognitive biases that occur due to faulty intuition are the confirmation bias, the hindsight bias, and the negativity bias.

CRITICAL THINKING CHALLENGE

- The belief that "going with your first choice" (or trusting intuition) when taking a multiple-choice test is not helpful (Lilienfeld et al., 2011). Instead, thinking more about a particular problem and considering all of the possible answers carefully increases the probability of getting it right (an algorithm approach). Why do you think that this psychological myth is so popular?

- Explain a time when you solved a problem or made a decision using a systematic, slow, but accurate algorithm approach. Then, explain a time when you made a decision using a heuristic. Discuss whether you generally prefer one method or the other and why.

- Try to think of five specific examples of times when someone gave you a compliment or praised you. Now, try to think of five specific examples of a time when you got negative feedback (an insult, criticism, etc.). Analyze how you feel about each set of memories, in terms of how easily they each came to mind and how vivid they are. Does the negativity bias seem to be in effect, or not? Why?

CHAPTER SUMMARY

How Do We Think?

Social cognition is the study of how people combine intuition and logic to process social information. These two systems of thinking combine and work together, and our ability to use both is called dual processing. Intuition is emotional, automatic, effortless, implicit, and fast. Logic, on the other hand, is analytical, systematic, effortful, explicit, and slow. Generally, our default is to use intuition, but we can quickly shift into logical thinking when needed. Each system of thought has advantages and disadvantages. Social cognition is also influenced by our culture. For example, "Western" cultures tend to emphasize individuality (with some exceptions), whereas "Eastern" or some Asian cultures tend to emphasize collective thinking and values.

We have three types of memory or mental structures that help us organize and interpret social information: schemas, scripts, and stereotypes. A schema is a memory structure that labels and organizes incoming information. Scripts guide our expectations for common, specific types of events. Finally, stereotypes assume that everyone from a certain group is the same. Stereotypes are discussed in depth in Chapter 9.

Why Are There Flaws in Our Mental Machinery?

We sometimes make mental mistakes for two reasons. The first is due to information overload; we can't process too much information at any given time. We are also cognitive misers, meaning that most people only think as much as needed (and not more). The general tendency to think to a minimum level is called satisficing; the opposite is called maximizing.

The second common reason for mental mistakes is called magical thinking, which refers to wishful thinking about alternatives to reality. Downward counterfactual thinking, for example, is when people imagine another outcome that's worse than what really happened as a way to comfort themselves (at least . . .). On the other hand, upward counterfactual thinking is when we imagine outcomes better than what really happened (if only . . .). Optimistic bias is an unrealistic expectation that things will turn out well. Finally, the planning fallacy is when people believe a project will go as planned and not need any additional time, money, and so forth to be completed.

Where Does Intuition Come From—and Can We Trust It?

While intuitive decisions sometimes seem mysterious or "psychic," the principle of parsimony suggests that intuition comes from mental accessibility. Accessibility is increased by priming, experience, and heuristics. Priming is mental activation of a concept and related concepts. More experience with any subject helps it comes to mind as well. Finally, heuristics are mental shortcuts that become a type of intuition. Three specific types of heuristics are anchor and adjust, availability, and representativeness. These heuristics all work in parallel and can be very persuasive when they point toward a common answer.

While intuition doesn't always lead to errors, it does influence our tendency to use biased thought processing. For example, the confirmation bias occurs when we search for evidence that confirms what we already believe. The hindsight bias is when we think we "knew something all along," even though we would not have guessed an outcome beforehand. A third example of biased intuition is the negativity bias, which leads us to focus on, notice, and remember negative information more than positive information.

CRITICAL THINKING, ANALYSIS, AND APPLICATION

- According to dual processing theory, humans are good at switching back and forth between intuition and logic, as needed. Do you think any other species have this ability? If so, provide specific examples to illustrate your point of view.

- On a scale of 0 to 100, how much balance do you like to have between easy but frequently mistaken thought versus difficult but accurate thought? If 0 means "super easy but often filled with mistakes" and 100 means "super difficult but always leading to the correct decision," where do you fall on this continuum? What would be the consequences if everyone in the world thought the same way that you have chosen?

- This chapter identified many examples of errors in social cognition thought processes. Choose the three errors, biases, or mistakes that you think are common in your own life and describe them. If you can identify these as frequent errors, does that mean you can change them? Do you want to change them?

- Now that you know more about social cognition, can you use your knowledge of other people's common mental mistakes to get them to do what you want? How could you use knowledge from this chapter to get people to like you, buy a product, vote for you, and so on?

Pictures Ltd./Corbis via Getty Images

5 Person Perception

Core Questions

5.1 What happens during and after forming first impressions?

5.2 How do we explain other people's behavior?

5.3 Why do we misjudge one another?

Learning Objectives

5.1 Explain how we form first impressions with nonverbal signals and how those impressions translate into self-fulfilling prophecies.

5.2 Analyze how we guess why people behave as they do through attributions.

5.3 Evaluate why we make flawed attributions.

Can walking through someone's dorm room or personal study area provide you with an accurate impression of that person's personality?

Yes. Samuel Gosling and his colleagues (2002) from the University of Texas in Austin found that independent observers could use someone's personal space to predict their scores on personality assessments. Look around your own room. What personality impressions do your clothes, objects, photographs, and the like make on others? Think back to when you were younger. Did you decorate your room with images or objects that had a special significance to you—that reflected who you were at the time? Taking this idea even further, Gillath and colleagues (2012) used even *less* information to predict what people might be like: pictures of people's shoes!

When you meet someone new, do you purposely try to make a certain kind of impression with how you dress, whether you smile, and if you have a firm handshake? And what about the flip side? Do you quickly form impressions of other people based on the same criteria? Forming impressions of other people requires that we put meaning on social information when we see other people, a process called person perception.

WHAT HAPPENS DURING AND AFTER FORMING FIRST IMPRESSIONS?

>> **LO 5.1:** **Explain how we form first impressions with nonverbal signals and how those impressions translate into self-fulfilling prophecies.**

You may not want to use a smiley face if you are applying for a job online.

Your future employer will get the wrong idea. A "smiley face" (in a work setting) tends to decrease perceptions of competence (Glikson et al., 2018). But we should not be surprised when the message sent is not the message received. **Person perceptions** are how we perceive others, based on our first impressions and how we interpret their behavior afterward (perhaps in biased ways). These perceptions are partially based on assumptions and stereotypes (Bruner & Tagiuri, 1954; Schneider, 1973) and therefore might be wrong.

This section answers the core question "What happens during and after forming first impressions?" by

(1) acknowledging two kinds of nonverbal signals we use to form first impressions (facial expressions and culturemes),

(2) analyzing the halo effect, and

(3) interpreting self-fulfilling prophecies.

Interpreting Nonverbal Signals

While a smiley face can be misinterpreted, it seems that we're extremely good at reading someone else's actual face.

When someone makes a first impression on us, we often look at their face. Are they smiling? Do they appear angry? Does your intuition tell you they are trustworthy? Two interesting questions have been addressed by social psychologists regarding how facial expressions affect our first impressions: (1) whether we can immediately detect other people's emotions and (2) whether we can tell when someone is lying. Both questions relate to the study of **nonverbal communication**, or how we signal information to others through our body language, tone of voice, and facial expressions.

The Universality Hypothesis of Facial Emotions

Are emotions expressed the same way around the world? Are facial expressions learned, or are they automatic instincts?

Consider two interesting studies. First, Friedman (1964) noticed that a blind, breast-fed baby smiled in response to her mother's voice. Much more recently, Matsumoto

Person perceptions: How we perceive others, based on first impressions and (possibly biased) interpretations of their behavior later.

Nonverbal communication: The many ways we signal information to others through body language, tone of voice, and facial expressions.

These photos show the six "universal" emotions through facial expressions that some research indicates can be understood regardless of culture. Can you identify which face is afraid, disgusted, surprised, angry, sad, and happy?

(2009) analyzed photographs of emotional expressions at the 2004 judo competition at the Olympic Games and Paralympic Games (held immediately after the Olympics). He compared the facial expressions of athletes who had been born blind, had lost their sight at some point, or were sighted. Faces of the athletes expressed the full range of emotions—happiness, regret, and deep sadness—and they showed striking similarity regardless of whether they were blind.

The **universality hypothesis** is the idea that facial expression of emotion is the same for everyone, regardless of culture, gender, or any other variable, because the look on our face when we feel something is an automatic biological instinct. Blind people using the same facial expressions as sighted people is one piece of evidence in support of the hypothesis, especially when displayed by infants who haven't been exposed much to things like different cultures. But to really test the hypothesis, researchers had to get a passport.

Paul Ekman and Walter Friesen (1971) traveled to several different cultures and showed people photographs of people expressing six basic emotions: fear, disgust, surprise, anger, sadness, and happiness. No matter where they went, people could easily pick out which photo went with each emotion. One reason for the cross-cultural agreement could have been because of learning and communication around the world through art and travel. So to test whether the universality hypothesis was really valid, they tested the South Fore people of New Guinea, a geographically isolated, preliterate tribe with no previous contact with "Western" civilization.

They first conveyed to the South Fore people short, emotional stories. Then they asked them to match the story to pictures of Americans—a culture they had never been exposed to—portraying various emotions. The South Fore people understood American emotional expressions—more evidence for the universality hypothesis.

Since then, others have done *replication studies* also supporting the universality hypothesis and extending it to include pride, shame, and embarrassment (Ekman et al., 1991; Harrigan & O'Connell, 1996; Keltner & Shiota, 2003). Some studies have questioned parts of the universality hypothesis (e.g., Gendron et al., 2014; Jack et al., 2012). However, in general, the universality hypothesis has been supported by multiple, independent researchers using a variety of creative methods.

This is an important conclusion: We all seem to share the same core emotional experiences—whether we grew up among the isolated South Fore people of New Guinea or were raised in the middle of crowded New York City.

Universality hypothesis:
The idea that nonverbal facial expressions are universal, regardless of culture.

Detecting Deception

And yet, we lie.

Despite our fundamental emotional similarity, we humans often lie to each other. One study asked people to carry small notebooks with them at all times for an entire week. Their task was to record every lie or deception they used in social interactions, no matter how big or small (DePaulo et al., 1996). Out of 77 college students and 70 community members (with an age range between 18 and 71 years), the students reported telling two lies every day and the community members reported one per day.

Deceptions occur in about 14% of emails, 27% of face-to-face interactions, and 37% of phone calls (Hancock et al., 2004; see also Hancock, 2007). Recently, mass media outlets have been accused of lying in the form of "fake news," undermining the credibility of the entire news and journalism ecosystem (see Reis et al., 2019). While we all have different ways we try to determine what information is valid or deceptive, when it comes to one-on-one interactions with others, we usually have to try to read a lie in someone's face.

In the photos shown here of presidential candidates, do you think one smile is phony and the other authentic (or maybe both are fake)? A **Duchenne smile** (named for the French neurologist Guillaume Duchenne de Boulogne) is a genuine, sincere smile. It uses the muscles that surround the eyes to pull up the cheeks, produce crow's feet wrinkles, and slightly lower the eyebrows. The ability to distinguish between genuine and fake smiles may be present even in 10-month-old infants (Fox & Davidson, 1988), going back to what we just covered on the universality hypothesis.

Sometimes we can also tell when someone's smile is fake. Facial indicators of lying were first identified in psychology research by slowing down a film of psychiatric patients lying about whether they were taking their medications (Ekman & Friesen, 1969; Ekman & O'Sullivan, 2006). Their faces were acting up in ways beyond their control.

Duchenne smile:
A genuine, sincere smile.

Can you tell if either presidential candidate is smiling sincerely?

The researchers discovered an expression they called **duping delight**, the facial smirk that appears right after people think that they have gotten away with a lie (see also Ekman & Frank, 1993). Duping delight is an example of a **micro-expression**, an involuntary flash of emotional honesty on someone's face. This occurs whenever concealed emotions are betrayed by automatic muscle responses, also called "reliable" muscles (Ekman & Friesen, 1974; Ekman & O'Sullivan, 2006).

Micro-expressions happen even though we don't want them to. In a job interview study, women displayed more false smiles (and did not interview as well) when the interview included three inappropriate sexually related questions (Woodzicka & LaFrance, 2005). The women were trying to be polite in the job interview situation, but their faces communicated their felt emotions. Similarly, the faked smiles of women hearing sexist jokes flashed more disgust than amusement (LaFrance & Woodzicka, 1998).

One study of high-stakes lying relied on *naturalistic observations:* televised footage of real people pleading for the return of missing relatives (ten Brinke & Porter, 2012). Later, half of the people were convicted of killing the person who was missing (based on overwhelming scientific evidence). They had tried to lie, but "failed attempts to simulate sadness and leakage of happiness revealed deceptive pleaders' covert emotions" (p. 469). These high-stakes liars tended to use fewer and more tentative words in their speeches.

Our ability to detect whether someone is lying varies. For example, when we're reminded of times when we've been socially excluded, we're temporarily better at distinguishing between fake and real smiles (Bernstein et al., 2010). Men appear to be more influenced by smiling than women, especially when a woman is smiling (Mehu et al., 2008). Japanese people tend to observe the upper half of the face, around the eyes, for indicators that communicate trust. In contrast, Americans focus on the lower half, around the mouth (Rule et al., 2010).

But generally speaking, we're not as good at detecting deception as we'd like to be. For one thing, when confronted with ambiguous facial expressions, we tend to assume the emotion being expressed is negative instead of positive (maybe because of the negativity bias we discussed in Chapter 4; Neta & Tong, 2016; Tottenham et al., 2013). For another, we tend to be overconfident in our ability to detect lies in others (Ekman et al., 1999; Porter et al., 2012).

Finally, there are lots of reasons why people lie. Ekman and O'Sullivan (2006) proposed a continuum of intentions when lying (see Figure 5.1). On one end of continuum is denial, where we're lying even to ourselves! In the middle is "white lies," where we might deceive to be polite or to avoid hurting someone's feelings (I love your new haircut!).

FIGURE 5.1

Continuum of intention to deceive.

1. Denial, Repression, Dissociation (unconscious rejection of reality)

2. Non-Conscious Self-Deceptions, Flawed Self-Assessment (unconscious lying to the self)

3. Positive Illusions, Self-Aggrandizement, Distortions (biased cognitions)

4. Factitious Disorders, Repetition to Belief (e.g., convincing yourself you are sick)

5. White Lies, Social Courtesies, Flattery, False Compliments (socially acceptable deception)

6. Malingering (pretending to be sick for convenience)

7. Deceptions of Kindness (e.g., doctors pretending to care more than they really do)

8. Deliberate High-Stakes Lying, Blatant Whoppers (purposeful lying to control others)

Source: Adapted from Ekman and O'Sullivan (2006).

Duping delight: The facial smirk that appears when people think that they have gotten away with a lie.

Micro-expression: An involuntary flash of emotional honesty on someone's face.

On the far end is deliberate high-stakes lying, or "deliberate whoppers." Here, the liar is purposely trying to control or manipulate others. Our face is more likely to betray us when lies move along that continuum toward intentions to deceive. Successful deceptions, on the other hand, are more likely when we believe what we're saying or have good intentions.

Culteremes as Symbols

She was wearing swastika earrings.

The older woman sat next to me [Wind] on the long flight from the United States to India. It took me a couple of hours to talk to her, but I eventually introduced myself and asked her about the earrings. She told me that in her culture and religion (she was Hindu), swastikas meant good luck—and that it was only since Hitler that they were "corrupted" to become a symbol for the Nazis. I was surprised, but I was even more excited for my month in India, where I could learn more.

Culteremes are culture-specific symbols that communicate widely shared ideas or social impressions (Feyereisen, 2006; Poyatos, 2002a, 2002b). Like inside jokes, cultures are filled with nonverbal messages that outsiders cannot be expected to understand (Angell, 1909; Buchner, 1910; Ekman, 2006; Fridlund, 1994; Izard, 1990; Lindstrom, 2011). Religious traditions have symbols of their faith; professional societies and governments adopt official seals; corporations spend millions of dollars branding their products into our neural structures (Lindstrom, 2011). But we form impressions of others when we see them displaying culteremes, like a cross necklace or a rainbow flag.

The right-facing Nazi swastika (shown on the flags) conveys a different cultural message than the left-facing swastika (shown on the building) on this Buddhist temple in South Korea, where it means energy or good luck.

Some cultural symbols change meaning or acceptance over time. For example, as I learned on that flight, the swastika represents a very different cultureme to Hindus and a slightly different cultureme to Buddhists. The left-facing swastika has been used for 5,000 years in Hindu art and architecture as a symbol of good fortune. Ramesh Kallidai of the Hindu Forum in Britain pointed out that "just because Hitler misused the symbol . . . does not mean that its peaceful use should be banned any more than Americans should ban crosses because they have been abused by the Ku Klux Klan" (BBC News, 2008).

Culture and religion can change the meanings of symbols. Easter celebrations, for example, often include pastel colors, bunnies, and eggs. These symbols were borrowed from pagan celebrations of spring, fertility, and birth. What we think of as a Christmas tree was originally part of the celebration called Saturnalia, the Roman holiday worshipping Saturn. While many modern Christians believe an upside-down cross is connected with satanism, it was originally used as a symbol of humility and love for Jesus by Saint Peter. Table 5.1 provides additional examples of how culture and religion affect our interpretation of certain symbols (Fontana, 1993).

Cultureme: Culture-specific symbols that communicate widely shared ideas or social impressions.

TABLE 5.1

Culturemes and Symbols Vary by Religion and Culture

SYMBOL	MODERN CHRISTIANITY	ALTERNATIVE INTERPRETATION
(inverted cross)	Many Christians believe an inverted cross is a satanic symbol.	Originally, the inverted cross was a Christian symbol of humility. St. Peter is supposed to have requested an inverted cross for his own crucifixion because he saw himself as unworthy of the same death Jesus received.
(pentagram)	A common modern Christian interpretation of the five-pointed star, or pentagram, is again that it represents satanism or anti-Christianity.	In Judaism, the pentagram can represent the five books of the Torah. For Wiccans, it can symbolize five elements of life (spirit, fire, air, water, and earth).
(harp)	A harp can symbolize passage to Heaven for modern Christians, as angels are frequently depicted as playing the instrument.	In ancient Celtic cultures, the god of plenty Daghda played the harp to summon each of the four seasons. It is now a national symbol of Ireland, where it was invented.
(evergreen tree)	An evergreen tree is one of the most recognized symbols for Christmas celebrations.	Originally used to celebrate the winter solstice in Scandinavian pagan rituals, early Christians combined the holidays and many of the symbols used by the more ancient religion.

A cross can be a symbol of faith, forgiveness, and charity—or a symbol of racism and hatred.

Nathan Benn/Corbis Historical/Getty Images

Perhaps there are two interesting lessons here: (1) Even if you assume you know what a certain symbol means, you might be wrong, and (2) you'd better do some research before you get that tattoo!

First Impressions Create Expectations

It doesn't take much to form an impression of someone.

For example, if someone's shoes are neat and polished, then we also may expect self-control, neatness, and organization in other parts of the personality. If someone is wearing worn-out, hand-painted combat boots, then we expect something very different. As the previous section discussed, we assume things based on symbols they adopt. I [Wind] was waiting outside an elementary school one day to pick up my niece when I saw a man with a drawing of a growling pit bull tattooed on his neck. I wondered what kind of person he was as he lovingly hugged a little girl who ran up to him. Sometimes, a single trait we notice in someone affects our entire impression of them.

Halo Effects

Imagine you're in this experiment.

In a classic study, Asch (1946) and Kelley (1950) used a single word to influence how students perceived a guest speaker in their classroom. They first *randomly assigned* students to read identical descriptions of the individual—identical, that is, except for one word buried in the middle of a sentence describing the speaker: "cold" versus "warm":

> "People who know him consider him to be a rather cold person, industrious, critical, practical, and determined."

Or

> "People who know him consider him to be a rather warm person, industrious, critical, practical, and determined."

Of course, the participants in each group thought that they were all reading the same description. But when they listened to and then evaluated the speaker, their first impressions had been manipulated by the expectations created by those two little words that, in this experiment, functioned as the *independent variable:* "cold" versus "warm."

Who could have imagined that those particular four-letter words could be so powerful? "Cold" and "warm" produced what Kelley (1950, p. 435) called a **halo effect**, when an entire social perception of a person or object is constructed around a single central trait (Allport, 1937, 1966; Allport & Vernon, 1933; Cooper, 1981; Dennis et al., 1996; Downey & Christensen, 2006; Feely, 2002; Ian, 2007; Kelley, 1950; Remmers, 1934).

In a halo effect, a **central trait** (such as "cold" or "warm") produces a perceptual aura that creates a unified impression about the entire person or object. Participants' evaluation of the speaker—the *dependent variable*—differed according to that one dimension. People who read that the lecturer was "cold" formed an impression of someone who was judgmental and impatient—a generally negative description. People who read that the lecturer was "warm" decided he was a person of character and strength—a generally positive description. For example, the students in this experiment indicated the following:

A GUEST SPEAKER DESCRIBED AS "COLD" IS	A GUEST SPEAKER DESCRIBED AS "WARM" IS
"intolerant"	"unyielding in principle"
"would be angry if you disagree"	"not easily swayed"

Both groups heard the same speaker give the same talk at the same time. But the subtle manipulation created different expectations in each group—and their perceptions matched their expectations. Next we'll cover two specific kinds of halo effects, one in the world of marketing and one in person perception.

Advertising and Misleading Health Halos

Advertisers understand the power of halo effects.

Diabetes is a serious, accelerating (and very expensive) personal and public health problem in the United States, especially for men (Baker, 2018). Diabetes requires significant self-management to avoid developing it in the first place or to manage it if you are already diabetic. One obvious solution: healthy eating. But there's a problem: Companies that sell products might be more worried about making money than about actually helping consumers. Health halos are mental shortcuts (or heuristics, as you learned in Chapter 4) that consumers use as simplistic cues to categorize their world of food choices (Pham et al., 2019).

Companies might label a product as "healthy" to get people to buy it; consumers might assume that the food is natural or organic, that it's low calorie, or that it has helpful vitamins or nutrients. The problem is that some packages or labels for what are advertised as "health bars" create a deceptive health halo effect that harms rather than helps someone on a diet (see Fernan et al., 2018).

Halo effect: When an entire social perception of a person is constructed around a single trait.

Central trait: A major characteristic in a person or object that creates a unified impression about the entire person (a halo effect).

The ads seem helpful and highlight healthy nutrients such as fiber and iron. However, "the presence of a traffic light warning label [about] sugar and calorie content . . . did not counteract . . . perceived healthfulness." The label makes us assume the product is healthy (the health halo), and we don't stop to investigate the details.

It gets worse. Children aged 7 to 11 years old participated in a related study about the "health" packaging of food products. The children (with parental approval) were assigned to view one of three child-friendly commercials:

(1) health halo (unhealthy foods/drink ads labeled "healthy"),

(2) nutrient-poor (unhealthy) food/drink ads, and

(3) actually healthy food/drink ads.

Do you need a drum roll of suspense to guess which commercial children perceived as the healthiest? The winner . . . was the first condition. Just the label of healthy created an impression that the product was good for you, even when it wasn't. These were commercials that "depicted children engaging in sports and then going out for fast food to celebrate, or an ad for sugary cereals that also shows fruit and milk on the table" (Harris et al., 2018, pp. 1–2). We're making mistakes about what we consume because of first impressions and noticing a single aspect of a product—and the companies are doing it on purpose.

A Strange Expectation: What-Is-Beautiful-Is-Good

There's another mistake we make when forming first impressions: We're drawn to physical beauty.

The expectations produced by physical beauty breed a bright halo effect and with an unusual name: the **what-is-beautiful-is-good effect** (Dion et al., 1972). Men, women, working professionals, and college students are all similarly influenced by physical beauty. The *generalizability* of this particular halo effect helps explain the widely accepted association that physically beautiful people somehow possess good moral character.

How widespread is this crazy-sounding what-is-beautiful-is-good halo effect? Hang on—this might be discouraging.

Teachers rate physically attractive children as smarter (Clifford & Walster, 1973). Pretty people get higher starting salaries and more raises at work (Frieze et al., 1991). Physically attractive defendants in court are given lighter prison sentences (Gunnell & Ceci, 2010). People with attractive profile photos on Facebook are more likely to get friend requests from strangers (Wang et al., 2010). Physically attractive college students are more likely to be given scholarships (Agthe et al., 2010). Professors who are "hot" get better student evaluations at the end of the class (Riniolo et al., 2006).

And that's just the beginning of what is sometimes called the "beauty bias."

Presumably, being attractive has little to do with one's intelligence, ability to get work done, or likelihood of committing crimes. Nevertheless, most people perceive attractive individuals as "better" in general and thus give them the benefit of the doubt. The "what-is-beautiful-is-good" effect is one specific type of halo effect.

The beauty bias may have declined somewhat over time (Hosoda et al., 2003). In addition,

What-is-beautiful-is-good effect: When physical attractiveness creates a halo effect such that beautiful people are also perceived to have several other positive characteristics.

Emma McIntyre/Getty Images

The show *Queer Eye* highlights a team of five gay men who essentially give makeovers to men and women who want a better image. The show seems to highlight the what-is-beautiful-is-good effect, but some critics have also argued that it perpetuates stereotypes and expectations that all gay men are fashionable.

there are limits to the effect. Most people in the United States are familiar with the stereotype that some beautiful people, like cheerleaders or models, aren't particularly intelligent (although assuming either more *or* less intelligence based on beauty is equally bad). At least one study shows that beautiful female executives are seen as less trustworthy "femme fatales" (Sheppard & Johnson, 2019). Finally, being "too" attractive might lead to jealousy and discrimination, especially from same-sex evaluators (e.g., Agthe et al., 2010, 2011).

But in general, the halo surrounding physical beauty is so bright that it confers the same kind of social status as intelligence, charm, humor, and athletic ability. We do seem to judge a book by its cover.

Expectations Can Lead to Self-Fulfilling Prophecies

Our impressions and assumptions about others can change how we act toward them.

And sometimes, their reaction to our behavior makes our expectations come true. Consider the what-is-beautiful-is-good effect as an example. If we assume attractive people are intelligent, funny, trustworthy, and generally more likeable, we'll give them more opportunities (Feingold, 1992). We hire them, befriend them, and make them popular. Those opportunities give them the chance to practice their social skills and advance in their careers, making them more successful. Our belief that they are amazing comes true, because of how we treat them. This is an example of a **self-fulfilling prophecy**: When our expectations lead to behaviors, from ourselves and from others, that makes those expectations come true.

Self-Fulfilling Prophecies in the Workplace

Sociologist Robert Merton (1948) pioneered early research about self-fulfilling prophecies.

He described a case study of a bank failure to demonstrate how even a false belief can turn into a self-fulfilling prophecy. In 1932, bank manager Cartwright Millingville was feeling justly proud that his bank was flourishing in the midst of the Great Depression. One Wednesday morning, the men from the local steel plants were coming in too soon—payday wasn't until Saturday. But a nasty rumor had gotten started that the bank was insolvent. More and more customers started withdrawing their money—and by the end of the day, the bank *was* insolvent.

Rumor had become reality: a self-fulfilling prophecy. Things would have turned out differently if people had a different expectation.

Expectations also help explain the self-fulfilling prophecies that influenced the job performance of new cashiers in a French grocery store chain. The cashiers were people from ethnic minorities who had recently immigrated from North and Sub-Saharan Africa. When the cashiers were assigned to work with a manager who was biased against immigrants, they were more likely to be absent, to leave work early, to scan items more slowly, and to take more time between customers. However, on days when the same cashiers were working with unbiased managers, "minorities perform significantly better than do majority workers" (Glover et al., 2017, p. 1219).

The explanation for poor performance was not that the manager disliked immigrant cashiers. Instead, the manager was uncomfortable around immigrants, interacted with them less, and provided less guidance during their initial six-month contract. But those managerial beliefs and behaviors helped produce a self-fulling prophecy: Only about 30% to 40% of cashiers were offered another contract after six months.

Other workplace studies have documented how self-fulfilling prophecies shape the workplace. Managerial expectations covertly influence employee productivity (Eden, 1990). Likewise, higher expectations from your boss can lead to more productivity and to a better relationship in general (Whiteley et al., 2012). For college students, the "workplace" is basically your classrooms—and the next part of this chapter explores how student performance can be influenced by the expectations of teachers.

Self-fulfilling prophecy: Expectations that make themselves come true because they change our own behavior and how others react to us.

▶ Self-Fulfilling Prophecies in Hollywood Films

This 1890 painting of the Pygmalion myth by Jacques Brunel tells the story of how a wish becomes a reality.

Self-fulfilling prophecies are sometimes called the Pygmalion effect. In the Greek myth, the shy sculptor Pygmalion fell in love with his own sculpture of Galatea, the most beautiful woman he could imagine. He asked the goddess Aphrodite to breathe life into her. With the twisted humor characteristic of Greek gods, Aphrodite granted his request but did not allow Galatea to love him back. It was a self-fulfilling prophecy: Pygmalion wished his passion into existence.

Professor Henry Higgins also wished his passion into existence in dramatic presentations of George Bernard Shaw's play *Pygmalion* and the musical *My Fair Lady* (Warner & Cukor, 1964). The refined linguistic Professor Higgins transforms Eliza—a screeching, low-class flower seller—into a "proper" lady (McGovern, 2011). The professor believed that he could transform Eliza into a woman with high-class language and manners, and thus he made it so by how he treated her.

You can hear echoes of the Pygmalion myth in the Disney version of *Pinocchio* (Disney et al., 1940) when a poor toymaker's wish breathes life into a wooden boy. In the 1983 movie *Trading Places* (Russo & Landis, 1983) a Wall Street tycoon bets his friend that he can transform a street hustler into a successful stockbroker. In each story, someone's life was transformed by others' expectations. But are we only the sum of other people's expectations? Are other people's wishes and expectations shaping us, as if we were marble or wooden puppets?

J. K. Rowling set up this same conflict in the Harry Potter novels (Rowling, 1997, 1998, 1999, 2000, 2003, 2005, 2007). In the magical boarding school Hogwarts, students are assigned to a certain "house" within minutes of their arrival. Each house is associated with stereotypes and expectations: Gryffindor is for the brave, Ravenclaw is for the intelligent, Hufflepuff is for the loyal, and Slytherin is for the cunning and ambitious. Do the students have these central traits before they even hit puberty, or does living in each house create expectations that shape the people they become?

The Pygmalion myth lives a vibrant, diverse life in popular culture about wishes and expectations that sometimes create their own reality.

Self-Fulfilling Prophecies in the Classroom

If you believe in your pet rat, will it be smarter?

In a fascinating study, Rosenthal (1994; Rosenthal & Fode, 1963) taught a class in which students taught rats to run a maze. He told half of the students that their rats were genetically "maze bright" (bred to be good at mazes) and half of the students that their rats were "maze dull." By the end of the semester, the rats' maze-running abilities showed big differences based on their labels. But the catch of the study is that *all the rats were identical*. Rosenthal had completely made up the labels and randomly assigned them to the rats (and their corresponding students). What the student-experimenters *expected* to happen did happen.

You've probably been affected by whether your teachers believed in you. When Rosenthal began corresponding with Lenore Jacobsen, a school principal in San Francisco, the stage was set for one of psychology's most famous—and still controversial—experiments. Rosenthal and Jacobsen (1968) gave students in 18 different classrooms across six different grade levels a test with a fancy (but meaningless) name, the Harvard Test of Inflected Acquisition. They used the so-called test to give teachers *bogus feedback* about students in their classroom.

Let's be blunt: Bogus feedback is lying, but it is a lie with an experimental purpose. They told the teachers that about 20% of the students across six grade levels were *expected* to be "intellectual bloomers." These bloomers would "show surprising gains in intellectual competence during the next eight months of school" (Rosenthal, 2002). In reality, the students had been selected at random.

Figure 5.2 shows us some of the data from that study. It shows that, grade by grade, what the teachers expected to happen did happen. Pay particular attention to the students in first and second grades. Figure 5.3 summarizes the teacher-student interactions that created these self-fulfilling prophecies.

The label of "intellectual bloomer" created expectations. Teachers used glowing language to describe the "bloomer" group. They were perceived as more likely to

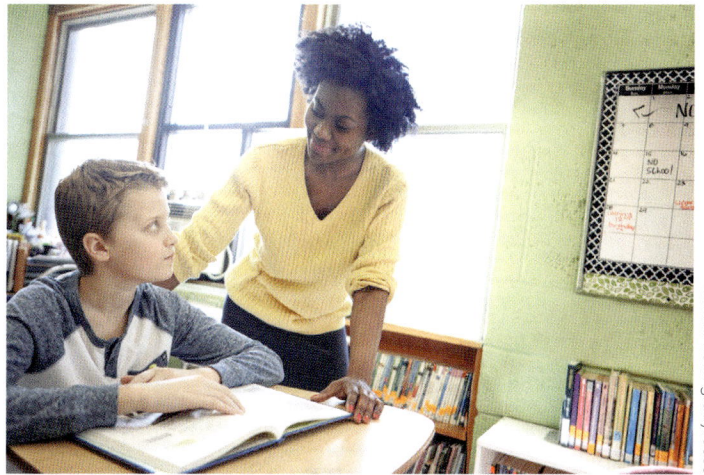

iStockPhoto/gradyreese

Have you ever had a teacher who expected you to behave well or expected you to behave badly? Did your actual behaviors come to match their expectations?

FIGURE 5.2

Students as bloomers.

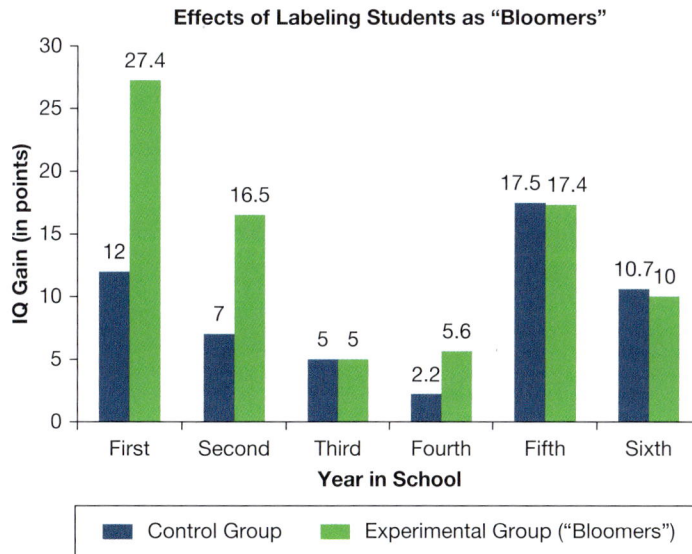

Effects of Labeling Students as "Bloomers"

Source: Rosenthal and Jacobson (1968).

FIGURE 5.3

How self-fulfilling prophecies become true in a classroom.

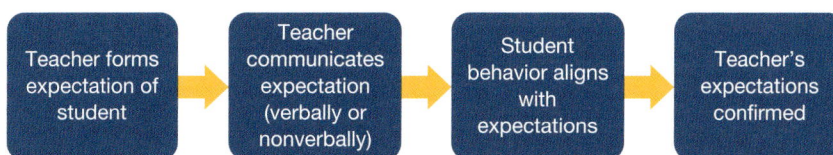

Teacher forms expectation of student → Teacher communicates expectation (verbally or nonverbally) → Student behavior aligns with expectations → Teacher's expectations confirmed

succeed, more interesting, more curious, more appealing, better adjusted, less in need of social approval, and even happier. In addition, some students who were *not* identified as intellectual bloomers also showed significant gains in IQ.

What effect did their *un*expected success have on their teachers? "The more children in the *control group* gained in IQ, the more *un*favorably they were judged by their teachers" (Rosenthal, 1994, p. 179). These students had violated their teachers' expectations—in a good way—but they were still judged unfavorably. It makes you wonder what in the world a kid has to do to shake off a bad reputation.

Replication and External Validity of Self-Fulfilling Prophecies

Rosenthal and Jacobsen's (1968) report triggered a controversy.

Their findings finally gave people someone to blame. If those darn elementary school teachers would only believe in their students, then all the other sociological, motivational, and family-related problems in education would magically melt away. Whenever there is an attention-getting finding from the world of research, you can count on the press to exaggerate the conclusions. Fortunately, chronically skeptical researchers scrutinized how the research was conducted and tried to *replicate* the findings—always a scientifically sound endeavor.

Hundreds of studies testing the reality of self-fulfilling prophecies have been conducted since those early experiments. In 2005, Jussim and Harber published a review of what we have learned about self-fulfilling prophecies since 1968:

1. Self-fulfilling prophecies do occur in the classroom, but they are only one of many influences on student achievement.

2. The effect of a self-fulfilling prophecy declines over time (which you can see in Figure 5.2).

3. Self-fulfilling prophecies can be especially influential on students who belong to groups that are already stigmatized (prelabeled in a negative way).

4. It is unclear whether self-fulfilling prophecies tend to do more harm than good. More research is needed.

5. Sometimes, what looks like a self-fulfilling prophecy is an accurate assessment made by a teacher.

In 2002, Rosenthal also reviewed the now sophisticated scientific literature that he had helped create almost 40 years earlier. By looking at the *meta-analyses,* Rosenthal confirmed that self-fulfilling prophecies can occur in classroom settings. He identified four ways in which teachers unknowingly communicate their expectations to students:

1. *Emotional climate,* through nonverbal cues that create a warmer social-emotional environment

2. *Expectations of effort,* by teaching more material and more difficult material

3. *Increased opportunities,* by giving students more opportunities to respond, including more time to respond

4. *Differential feedback,* by giving certain students more individualized feedback that allows them to assess their own progress

Self-fulfilling prophecies are not limited to physically attractive people, bank failures, maze-running lab rats, and teacher-student relationships. The process of a self-fulfilling prophecy appears to have *external validity;* that is, it applies across many situations.

*   Marijuana use. Children whose parents falsely assumed that they were already using marijuana were more likely to begin using marijuana. Students already using marijuana but whose parents said that they weren't were more likely to stop (Lamb & Crano, 2014).

- The courtroom. Judges' expectations can influence the directions they tell a jury in ways that can pave the way for verdicts of guilt or innocence (Blanck et al., 1990).

- Nursing homes. A caretaker's positive expectations can reduce depression in the residents (Learman et al., 1990).

- Romance. Positive illusions about your romantic partner can help that person rise to your optimistic expectations (Murray et al., 1996a, 1996b).

Here's a final example: the world of sports. Many people in Canada and Czechoslovakia are, to put it mildly, enthusiastic about hockey (Dubner & Levitt, 2006). The formal recruiting process begins with a strictly observed rule that a boy must have turned 10 by January 1. So, a boy born in late December could be playing against boys almost a year older. For early maturing boys, those extra months can represent the difference between a child's relatively frail body and a body maturing into a muscular adolescence.

When coaches and parents confuse physical maturation with athletic "talent," they are applying a label that can turn into a self-fulfilling prophecy (see Figure 5.4). Lots of good things flow toward these "gifted," "talented" so-called natural athletes: better coaching, more playing time, more encouragement, status, and higher levels of competition. So, boys born in January experience multiple layers of advantages:

- Greater physical, personal, and emotional maturity

- More attention from peers, fans, parents, and coaches

- More specific coaching of skills

- More competitive experiences

- Higher levels of competition

- Higher expectations from coaches, parents, peers, and themselves

For these young athletes, a rich network of reinforcers improves skills and raises expectations. Meanwhile, both advantaged and disadvantaged children experience the mysterious power of a self-fulfilling prophecy that began with nothing more remarkable than when they were conceived. Kids born in January have a brighter future ahead of them, at least in the world of hockey.

FIGURE 5.4

Number of births by month of two championship youth hockey teams.

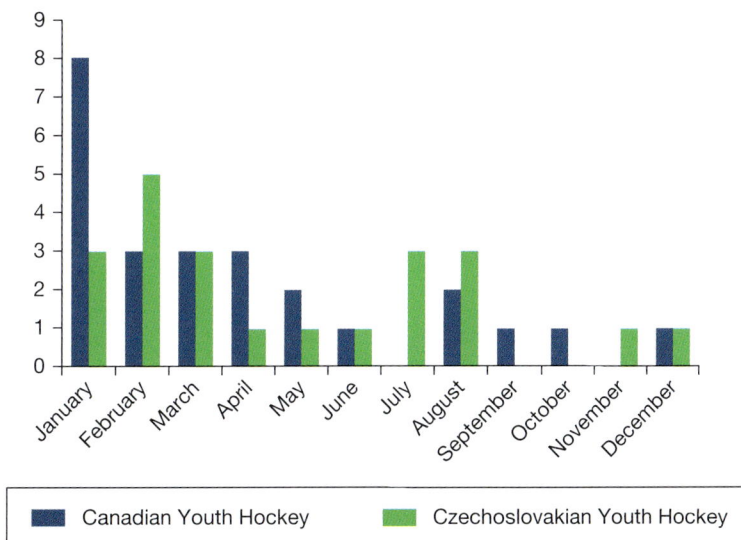

Source: Data from Dubner and Levitt (2006).

THE MAIN IDEAS

- The universality hypothesis is that some facial expressions of emotion are recognized in all humans, regardless of culture. While deception is hard to detect, micro-expressions betray our genuine feelings.

- Another form of nonverbal communication is culturemes, symbols that convey shared social impressions within a given culture.

- Perceptions of other people are influenced by first impressions. First impressions are sometimes based on a single trait that seems more important than others, such as physical attractiveness; this is called a halo effect.

- Expectations can be communicated in ways that become self-fulfilling prophecies (also called the Pygmalion effect). Self-fulfilling prophecies can lead to both positive and negative outcomes; research has replicated these effects across a wide variety of real-world settings, such as with children in classrooms.

CRITICAL THINKING CHALLENGE

- Think about the culturemes you use in your own life. Do you have tattoos, jewelry, or art in your home that displays symbols? Do others understand these symbols immediately, or is their meaning private? When you see others displaying a cultureme, do you immediately have assumptions about the type of people they might be or what their beliefs are?

- Why are "warm vs. cold" and physical attractiveness central traits when we're forming first impressions—what is it about these particular traits that seems so important?

- Think about how self-fulfilling prophecies have affected your own life in the classroom, on sports teams, at work, in social situations, or in your own goals and dreams for the future. What is one *positive* way that self-fulfilling prophecies may have pushed you toward something greater, and what is one *negative* way that self-fulfilling prophecies may have held you back?

HOW DO WE EXPLAIN OTHER PEOPLE'S BEHAVIOR?

>> LO 5.2:   Analyze how we guess why people behave as they do through attributions.

Understanding one another is hard work—and cultural differences don't make it any easier!

Fortunately, the human brain is relentlessly curious; unfortunately, like dipping our toes into cool water on a hot day, we often satisfy our curiosity with superficial explanations. Having *any* explanation for someone else's behavior sometimes seems to be more important to us than having an accurate explanation. So how do we try to explain other people's behavior to ourselves?

This section answers the core question "How do we explain other people's behavior?" by

(1) demonstrating our use of attributional thinking to explain behavior,

(2) distinguishing between internal and external attributions, and

(3) specifying how we use co-occurring events (called covariance) when trying to explain behavior.

Attribution Theory: We Guess the Cause of Behavior

Attribution theory views people as amateur scientists or detectives when trying to explain behavior. We look for clues and form hypotheses about others.

Our amateurish impulses are pretty good, however. We rely on reasoned, commonsense explanations (Heider, 1958; Kelley, 1955, 1973; Wegener & Petty, 1998). **Attributions** are how we answer the question "why?" It's our guess as to why someone did something. For example, when an attractive stranger smiles at you, your brain asks "why?" and starts generating explanations.

One self-serving explanation may be enough: "Because I am so darn good-looking." That first explanation may be so satisfying that you stop right there. But there are lots of other possible reasons for their smile (they are trying to manipulate you, they're a generally happy person and smile at everyone, and more). What attribution we ultimately land on depends on several factors.

Internal and External Attributions

Isolating possible causes is a scientific way of thinking.

Scientists, however, have to dig deeper than whatever explanations come most easily to mind. As a psychological scientist, you are expected to make attributions based on evidence—and to be especially skeptical of subjective impressions. To start, we tend to divide our attributions into two categories:

1. **Internal attributions** are dispositional, within-the-person explanations. They are factors under the person's control, personality, or conscious choices.

2. **External attributions** are situational, outside-the-person explanations. They are factors that lie outside of one's control such as getting sick, the weather, or luck.

We make internal and external attributions all the time, for our own outcomes. If we get an A on a test, we like to make internal attributions: We are so smart! We worked so hard! We are really good at this subject! All three causes are something about us, about our internal disposition. When we fail, we like to make external attributions: The test wasn't fair! I was sick! I was distracted! The cause for our failure was something about the situation.

An early model of attribution came from Weiner (1974, 1980, 1986). His idea was that attributions for other people's behaviors result from a three-stage process:

1. We observe someone else's behavior.

2. We assume they intended to act the way they did.

3. If it seems like the person was forced to act, our attribution is external (something about the situation). If it seems like the person acted this way freely, our attribution is internal (something about them).

Weiner focused his research on achievement. He thought that success or failure would come from ability and effort (internal attributions) and from task difficulty and luck (external attributions). Thinking that success comes from internal causes (like effort or skill) and failure is because of the situation helps us feel good—but it might not help us learn. Admitting to some responsibility for failure might motivate us to change things next time. There are other contexts in which internal versus external attributions affect how we see our social world.

Victim Blaming and Belief in a Just World

How do you explain why some people are overweight?

Attribution theory: The idea that we try to understand other people's behavior using commonsense explanations and clues.

Attributions: Our guesses for the cause of other people's actions or events around us.

Internal attributions: Explanations for someone's behavior that are about them, like their personality or conscious choices.

External attributions: Explanations for someone's behavior that are based on factors outside their control or about the circumstances, such as getting sick, the weather, or luck.

Other people's misfortunes can threaten our belief in a just, fair world. When you see victims of misfortune, do you assume they did something to deserve their fate?

External attributions about overweight people will rely on external, situational explanations such as stressful circumstances or genetic predispositions. Internal attributions about overweight people will rely on internal, dispositional explanations, such as a weak will, choosing not to exercise, or eating too much. Overreliance on internal attributions can lead to group prejudice (King et al., 2006), because it allows us to blame people for their group membership.

For example, prejudice toward those with a physical handicap is higher when observers attribute their handicap to some sort of internal moral failing (Goffman, 1963; Lerner & Miller, 1978). By the same twisted and unfortunate logic, some observers of rape victims will make internal attributions leading to the false beliefs that the victim was "asking for it" or somehow deserved to be assaulted. The same pattern is found in victims of domestic violence (Bargh, 1997; Bargh & Chartrand, 1999; Bargh et al., 1996; Crall & Goodfriend, 2016; Hafer et al., 2005; Strömwall et al., 2013; Valor-Segura et al., 2011).

Why do we tend to blame the victim (Lerner, 1965)? Internal attributions seem cruel when people have already suffered some terrible misfortune. Most of us don't want to be cruel, vicious, judgmental, or unkind. So why might we blame people for things they can't control?

The just world hypothesis asserts that people have a need to believe that they live in a world where people generally get what they deserve (Lerner & Simmons, 1966; see also Anderson et al., 1997; Gilbert & Hixon, 1991; Kleinke & Meyer, 1990; Murray et al., 2005). This comforts us because we feel like there's a systematic order to the world. Most important, belief in a just world helps us feel protected against bad things happening to ourselves. If we think that bad things happen to bad people, but good things happen to good people—and *I'm* a good person—then bad things won't happen to me.

We reveal our belief in a just world when we say things like, "What goes around comes around" or "Karma will catch up with them." Believing in a just world is associated with negative attitudes toward many kinds of people and ideas, such as being poor (Furnham & Gunter, 1984), having a disability, the effectiveness of charitable giving (Furnham, 1995), being abused by a relationship partner (Valor-Segura et al., 2011), having AIDS, and being a victim of rape (Furnham, 2003; Strömwall et al., 2013).

A strong belief in a just world even leads people to discount scientific facts about global warming (Feinberg & Willer, 2011). Why? The researchers explain that "the potentially dire consequences of global warming threaten deeply held beliefs that the world is just, orderly, and stable" (Feinberg & Willer, 2011, p. 34). We seem to turn off our logic and empathy if blaming people for their bad circumstances makes us feel safer or "better."

You can learn more about belief in a just world by taking the self-report scale in the What's My Score? feature. It's scary to think that the world is unpredictable. See the Spotlight on Research Methods feature to learn more about confronting scary realities in our social world.

Belief in a just, fair world is often associated with another individual difference called locus of control. Locus of control is a general belief about whether we're in control of our own future. People with an "internal" locus of control believe that they are in control. If they work hard, have self-discipline, and make good choices, they can achieve whatever they want in life. On the other hand, people with an "external" locus of control believe their future is out of their hands. What happens to them is ultimately up to fate, chance, powerful other people, political systems out of their control, or some higher power. Which sounds more like you?

Just world hypothesis: The idea that people need to believe in a fair world where people generally get what they deserve, which can lead to incorrect internal attributions for others' behaviors or outcomes.

Locus of control: Our belief about whether we can control our own future (internal locus) or that our future is up to luck, fate, or a higher power (external locus).

⬡ Measuring Belief in a Just World

Instructions: Next to each item, write how much you disagree or agree with it using this scale:

1	2	3	4	5	6
Strongly disagree					Strongly agree

___ 1. I've found that a person rarely deserves the reputation he or she has.

___ 2. Basically, the world is a just place.

___ 3. People who get "lucky breaks" have usually earned their good fortune.

___ 4. Careful drivers are just as likely to get hurt in traffic accidents as careless ones.

___ 5. It is common occurrence for the guilty person to get off free in American courts.

___ 6. Students almost always receive the grade they deserve in school.

___ 7. People who keep in shape have little chance of suffering a heart attack.

___ 8. The political candidate who sticks up for his or her principles rarely gets elected.

___ 9. It is rare for an innocent person to be wrongly sent to jail.

___ 10. In professional sports, many fouls and infractions never get called by the referee.

___ 11. By and large, people deserve what they get.

___ 12. When parents punish their children, it is almost always for good reasons.

___ 13. Good deeds often go unnoticed and unrewarded.

___ 14. Although evil people may hold political power for a while, in the general course of history good wins out.

___ 15. In almost any business or profession, people who do their job well will rise to the top.

___ 16. American parents tend to overlook the things most to be admired in their children.

___ 17. It is often impossible for a person to receive a fair trial in the USA.

___ 18. People who meet with misfortune have often brought it on themselves.

___ 19. Crime doesn't pay.

___ 20. Many people suffer through absolutely no fault of their own.

Scoring: Before adding the items together, first we have to "reverse score" some of them. So, for only Items 1, 3, 4, 5, 8, 10, 13, 16, 17, and 20, flip the scale. If you wrote a 1, cross it off and write a 6 instead. A 2 becomes a 5, a 3 becomes a 4, a 4 becomes a 3, a 5 becomes a 2, and a 6 becomes a 1.

Then, add up all of your responses. Higher scores mean a stronger belief in a just world; the possible range is 20 to 120.

Source: Rubin and Peplau (1975).

We Rely on Covariation to Explain Causality

Sometimes we become Sherlock Holmes detectives.

> Once you eliminate the impossible, whatever remains, no matter how improbable, must be the truth.
>
> —Sherlock Holmes, *written by Sir Arthur Conan Doyle*

When we guess as to why someone did something, we look for clues. We piece those clues together by asking, "What else was also going on just prior to or at the same time?" In scientific terms, we're looking for variables that *covary* or happen in *correlation* with the event. Kelley (1967) proposed a three-step or three-dimensional **covariation model of attribution** that he believed we use automatically when trying to understand why an event occurred.

Covariation model of attribution: Our attempts to find systematic explanations for why people act how they do.

Consensus: The dimension of Kelley's covariation model of attribution that refers to whether other people tend to act the same way toward a target person.

Consistency: The dimension of Kelley's covariation model of attribution that refers to whether the actor in the situation tends to act the same way toward everyone.

Distinctiveness: The dimension of Kelley's covariation model of attribution that refers to something unique about this situation that explains the actor's behavior toward a target.

Terror management theory: The idea that when we're reminded of our own eventual death, we embrace comforting beliefs.

Mortality salience: When researchers make the idea of death, especially an individual's own unavoidable death, more vivid.

Imagine that your professor starts yelling at another student, Carlos. Here, the professor is called the "actor" (because they are the ones who did an action) and the student is called the "target" (the recipient of the action). You will probably immediately wonder, "Why is this happening?" It could be something about the professor (the actor), something about Carlos (the target), or something unique about this particular situation. Our tendency is to look around for something else that happened at the same time. If Carlos just tried to cheat or use a cell phone in class when not allowed, we'll probably assume that was the cause of the professor's behavior.

According to Kelley's covariation model, we attempt to make attributions based on these three questions:

- **Consensus**: *Do other people act this way toward the target*? Do other teachers also yell at Carlos? If yes, then your attribution will lean toward the belief that Carlos probably deserves what he's getting. Our attribution will probably be about the target.

- **Consistency**: *Is this how the actor usually behaves*? Does the professor yell at every student? If yes, then your attribution will lean toward the belief that your professor is the cause of the situation. Carlos just happens to be the latest innocent victim.

- **Distinctiveness**: *Do the actor and target always act this way together*? Is this a rare event? If yes, you'll assume there's something unique going on here! It's probably only happening because of what Carlos just did—so we're more likely to make an external or situational attribution in this case.

As cognitive misers, we look for easy explanations, mental shortcuts (heuristics), stereotypes, and an intuition that sometimes lets us down. But we continue to show the tendencies described here because they often do work and because we find them comforting. We like to think we live in a systematic, logical, and fair world.

Experimentally Manipulating Thoughts of Death

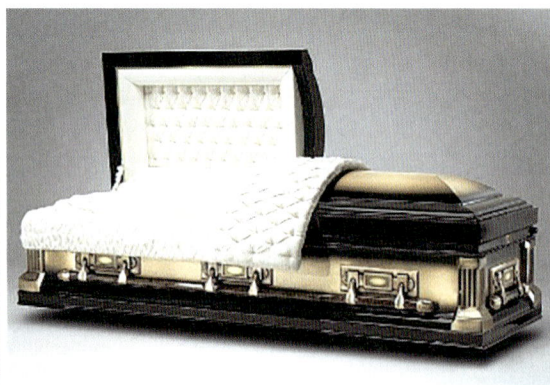

Shutterstock/Syda Productions

Terror management theory predicts that, when faced with our own eventual death, we will embrace comforting beliefs.

Creative researchers have tested this theory through grim manipulations called **mortality salience**: making

the idea of death more vivid. Vivid reminders of death are everywhere: seeing a funeral home, passing a hospital, hearing an ambulance, or buying life insurance.

One way to test the effects of mortality salience uses *random assignment* to create an *independent variable*: Half of the participants in a study are asked to write a response to the disturbing question, "What do you think happens to you as you physically die and once you are physically dead?" The other half write about what will happen to their bodies when they suffer a severe (but not life-threatening) injury or experience powerful dental pain.

Random assignment controls for most *confounding variables,* but researchers try to make the groups equivalent by making sure that both conditions are unpleasant physical experiences. That way, any differences in the outcome or *dependent variable* can't be due to thinking about pain or discomfort. People testing terror management theory want data based only on whether one group of participants had to confront death, while others didn't.

The results of several experiments tell the same general story. Participants who have to write about death—the "mortality salience" condition—assign more blame to people who have experienced something unfortunate compared to those who only had to write about a painful experience (thus, the dependent variable was amount of blame; Hirschberger, 2006). In other words, victim blaming goes up after we think about our own death.

We humans sure are weird! When the prospect of death and disaster is made real to us, belief in a just world leads most of us to have even *less* compassion for the innocent (Hirschberger et al., 2005). Similarly, people who write death essays recommend harsher penalties for prostitution, compared to people who write dental pain essays (Jonas et al., 2008). Israeli high school students who wrote death essays were more likely to say they were motivated to join the national military (Taubman-Ben-Ari & Findler, 2006).

When experiencing mortality salience, we seem to embrace any worldview that will bring us comfort. Perhaps we are telling ourselves, "At least my death *means* something."

THE MAIN IDEAS

- Attribution research explores how we automatically try to guess why people act the way they do, a process called making attributions.

- We often distinguish between internal attributions (a cause related to the person who did something) and external attributions (a cause related to the situation or environment).

- Our conclusions tend to be biased by factors such as our belief in a just world, which leads us to blame victims for their misfortunes.

- We rely on covariance to reach conclusions, including questions of consensus, consistency, and distinctiveness.

CRITICAL THINKING CHALLENGE

- People who believe in a just world are more likely to blame innocent victims if they believe the person "deserved" what happened. However, people who believe in a just world are also more likely to get upset if they think something unfair happened, such as when a friend gets fired. What variables might account for when people with this belief system decide that the victim of an event "deserved" it or not? How could you test for the influence of those variables in a research study?

- Think about each of the circumstances below. For each, analyze what's happening using the three steps of consensus, consistency, and distinctiveness. As you consider each situation and each step, how does your attribution change based on your conclusions for each step?

  o You see your classmate flirting with someone in the grocery store.

  o Your supervisor at work compliments you and suggests that you might be considered for a raise or promotion.

  o Your friend comes out of a movie theater crying.

- Consider terror management theory and how it might affect people who (1) survived a natural disaster, (2) lived through a war, or (3) witnessed a terrible event such as the terror attacks on 9/11. What kinds of behaviors might happen after these events that support the ideas within terror management theory?

WHY DO WE MISJUDGE ONE ANOTHER?

>> LO 5.3:   Evaluate why we make flawed attributions.

Once a perception takes root in our minds, it's like a stubborn weed that we can't seem to get rid of.

For example, we sometimes assume that actors who play good, pleasant characters must be nice in real life. Likewise, actors who play villains must be terrible people in real life (Tal-Or & Papirman, 2007). We know that they are just actors playing a role and yet it is difficult for us to separate the real person from the actor.

This section answers the core question "Why do we misjudge one another?" by

(1)   describing some of the consequences of misjudging others,

(2)   explaining how culture influences misperceptions, and

(3)   describing the self-serving nature of specific attribution biases.

Helena Bonham Carter often plays an evil lunatic, while Julia Roberts is known for playing sweet romantic leads. It is easy to assume their personalities in real life match those they play on the screen.

Mental Mistakes: From Small and Innocent to Big and Dangerous

We've already identified many persistent types of mental errors.

There are many more to come. Some of our mental errors may strike you as amusing when you recognize mistakes you've made when thinking about other people. These various misperceptions don't happen on purpose or because we're mean, bad people. That said, they can sometimes lead to major injustices.

For example, it may surprise you to learn that false confessions of crimes are not unusual. People may say they did something they didn't do because police put pressure on them, or they were trying to protect someone they loved who really did it, or they were genuinely confused, or they simply wanted a bit of fame. Sometimes, people who make false confessions later want to retract what they've said—but by then, it's probably too late.

Juries make attributions of guilt when confronted with a vivid, detailed, video-taped confession—even one that's later denied. A confession of guilt gives a jury almost everything their cognitive biases desire. To a juror, a confession makes sense only if the person is guilty (an internal attribution). A confession also means that the jury won't have to work very hard to reach a decision (they can be cognitive misers). In a trial, a videotaped confession also may be the first thing jurors learn from a prosecutor (first impressions).

This negative first impression lasts longer in memory than later positive information (the negativity bias). A confession makes it easy to judge everything else about the defendant as negative (the halo effect). As the trial goes on, the jury notices and remembers only evidence that supports what they already believe while disregarding contradictory evidence (the confirmation bias).

The resulting narrative overflows with convincing evidence that makes perfect sense to sincere jurors. You can understand, once again, why the strength of scientific psychology is based on humanity's hard-won virtue: healthy skepticism (Anderson et al., 1980).

The Fundamental Attribution Error

One flawed person perception is so common that its name includes "fundamental."

The **fundamental attribution error** occurs when we overestimate the influence of personality and underestimate the power of the situation. Imagine that the wait staff at a restaurant is particularly nice to you. On the way home, however, your bus driver is particularly gruff and cold. Most of us automatically assume that the waiter is a kind and friendly person, while the bus driver is mean and rude.

But we have forgotten to consider the power of the situation. The friendly waiter may be hoping to increase the tip. The unfriendly bus driver may be concerned about a dangerous traffic situation.

Attributing behavior to personality (internal or dispositional causes) rather than to situations (external causes) is deeply ingrained in our causal reasoning (Gilbert & Malone, 1995; Heider, 1958; Jones, 1979; Ross, 1977). One early experiment (Jones & Harris, 1967) involved two groups of students reading the same opinion essay that was highly critical of a political leader. The words were the same, but the participants in each group had heard different explanatory stories. Group 1 heard that the author had chosen to write that opinion. Group 2 heard that the author was required to write that opinion.

Like believing that an actor is a mean person because they played a mean role on stage or in a movie, knowing that a writer had been *required* to express an opinion did not seem to matter. Both groups of participants perceived the author as believing in whatever opinion was expressed. They simply ignored situational factors and made an internal attribution instead.

The fundamental attribution error isn't going away. Here are some more ways it influences our lives:

- Teachers who use ineffective methods are more likely to attribute student failure to their students than to themselves or their methods (Wieman & Welsh, 2016).

- People who see others post positive status updates on Facebook assume that their good fortunes are due to their personality instead of to passing circumstances (Chou & Edge, 2012).

- We tend to perceive that members of high-status groups must have earned their way and ignore inherited privileges (Nier et al., 2013). This matches the old folk saying, "A person was born on third base and thought they had hit a triple."

- Teenagers attribute bullying behaviors to the personality of either the bully or the victim rather than situational influences such as peer pressure, stress, or the school environment (Thornberg & Knutsen, 2011).

All of these examples show the fundamental attribution error because we assume people do things that reflect who they are. We forget to take the situation into account. Kurt Lewin, social psychology's pioneer, generated an enduring insight when he described how personality *and* environment both influenced behavior. The fundamental attribution error happens when we ignore half of his famous equation.

Fundamental attribution error: Our tendency to overestimate the influence of personality and underestimate the power of the situation when making attributions about other people's behaviors.

The Actor-Observer Attribution Bias

As usual with complicated humans, the fundamental attribution error comes with fine print.

We commit the fundamental attribution error when we think about what *other* people do. When we consider our own behavior, we remember the situation. The **actor-observer bias** is our tendency to think of personality (internal attributions) when explaining *other people's* behavior but think of external, situational causes when explaining *our own* behavior (Nisbett et al., 1973). A basketball player misses a game-winning jump shot. The fans reason that "he choked under pressure" (an internal, dispositional explanation). The player reasons that "the defender fouled me" (an external, situational explanation).

Gordon and Kaplar (2002) modified the game *Scruples* to teach students about the actor-observer bias. When asked, for example, whether they or someone else would provide an alibi for a friend having an affair, they had to choose a card stating "yes," "no," or "depends on the situation." Students often chose "depends on the situation" when the moral dilemma was happening to them. We are sensitive to the situational pressures we experience—and insensitive to what others are experiencing. Perhaps this is because we see ourselves in a wide variety of situations and how our behavior changes according to those circumstances. When we see other people, though, we often only see them in a single role and in a single setting.

Culture Influences Person Perceptions

Different cultural assumptions lead us to different explanations. For example, culture and the actor-observer bias team up to influence how we explain history. Subtle differences in how we use words can also lead to dangerous misunderstandings.

Explanations for Mass Murder Depend on Perspective

This is a grim topic, but an urgent question. How do we explain mass murder?

The actor-observer bias predicts that Germans and non-Germans are likely to generate different explanations for the Holocaust. People born inside Germany (even people born after World War II) are likely to reason, "You weren't there—you don't understand what it was like to live under Nazi rule." They take the situation into account. But the people born *outside* of Germany are more likely to think, "The world

Actor-observer bias: Our tendency to think of personality when explaining other people's behavior but remember the circumstances when explaining our own behavior.

Now in Amsterdam, people line up every day to visit the Anne Frank House, where she wrote her famous diary while hiding from the Nazi regime.

was watching you. You knew exactly what you were doing" (Doosje et al., 1998). They attribute what happened to the personality or wishes of the German people at the time.

The reality of German cruelty to Jews was vivid to people waiting in line to see the Anne Frank House Museum in Amsterdam, the Netherlands. That's where Doosje and Branscombe (2003) asked both non-Jewish Germans and non-German Jews waiting in the line to rate two simple statements:

- "I think the Germans mistreated the Jews because Germans are aggressive by nature." (A dispositional, internal attribution)

- "It is important to consider the behavior of the Germans toward the Jews in a historical context, rather than judge their acts in isolation." (A situational, external attribution)

Figure 5.5 portrays the *statistically significant* difference between the two groups in this *quasi-experimental study* ("quasi" because people were not randomly assigned to groups). While both groups acknowledged the historical context (the situation), the non-German Jewish people gave the internal attribution a higher rating, on average, than did the non-Jewish Germans. The Jewish people assigned more responsibility to the Germans who were "aggressive by nature," or to the national German personality.

FIGURE 5.5

Internal and external attributions for the Holocaust.

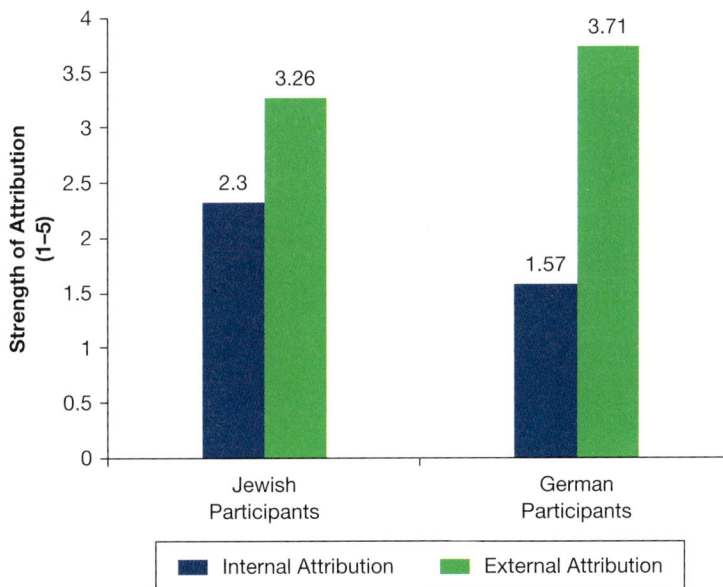

Source: Doosje and Branscombe (2003).

Cultural Explanations Embedded in Language

Table 5.2 demonstrates that even people who speak the same language can easily misunderstand one another.

When you add cognitive errors to cultural miscommunications, you have the opportunity for profound misperceptions of one another's motives. Cross-cultural research suggests that the fundamental attribution error may not be quite as fundamental as was once believed. Forgas (1998) found that simply being in a happy mood increases attributions to someone's personality. A bias is not very "fundamental" if it can be modified by a temporary change of mood (see Harvey & McGlynn, 1982; Harvey et al., 1981; Reeder, 1982).

TABLE 5.2

Cultural Miscommunications

PHRASE	MEANING IN AMERICAN ENGLISH	MEANING IN BRITISH ENGLISH
"Turn it up."	"Increase the volume."	"I don't believe you."
"How did you find the train?"	"How did you locate the train?"	"Did you enjoy the train trip?"
"Are you through?"	"Are you finished?"	"Did you make a phone connection?"
"I knocked her up this morning."	"I got her pregnant this morning."	"I knocked on her door this morning."
"May I have a rubber, please?"	"May I have a condom, please?"	"May I have an eraser, please?"

A more telling argument is that people in independent, self-reliant cultures are more likely to use dispositional explanations than people in collectivistic, relationship-oriented cultures (Norenzayan & Nisbett, 2000; Sampson, 1988; Smith & Bond, 1993). For example, in print and broadcast media stories, American Olympic athletes attributed their success to dispositional causes such as working hard, whereas Chinese Olympic athletes were more likely to say their success was due to national support (Hua & Tan, 2012).

Another comparison of American versus Chinese culture (Morris & Peng, 1994) analyzed how newspapers from each nation explained two very similar mass murders. Gang Lu was a Chinese physics student who had lost an award competition, appealed unsuccessfully, and was not able to find an academic job. He shot his advisor, the person who handled his appeal, fellow students and bystanders, and finally himself. Thomas McIlvane was an American postal worker who lost his job, appealed unsuccessfully, and was unable to find employment. He also shot his supervisor, the person who handled his appeal, coworkers and bystanders, and then himself.

Reporters from both English-language and Chinese-language newspapers sought to explain both of these tragedies. As Table 5.3 demonstrates, the English-language newspaper, the *New York Times,* emphasized personality traits (internal attributions).

TABLE 5.3

Newspaper Explanations of Mass Murders

	ABOUT MR. LU	ABOUT MR. MCILVANE
What the Chinese-language newspaper reported	"did not get along with his advisor" "rivalry with slain student" "isolation from Chinese community"	"gunman had been recently fired" "post office supervisor was his enemy" "followed the example of a recent mass slaying in Texas"
What the English-language newspaper reported	"very bad temper" "sinister edge to Mr. Lu's character" "darkly disturbed man" "whatever went wrong was internal"	"man was mentally unstable" "had a short fuse" "had repeatedly threatened violence"

When reporting about two crimes involving similar circumstances, a Chinese-language paper seems to emphasize the circumstances, while an English-language newspaper seems to emphasize personality traits.

The Chinese-language newspaper *World Journal* emphasized relational and situational explanations (external attributions).

We Make Self-Serving Attributions

We are all part of the problem.

The problem is that we all want to think of ourselves as intelligent, reasonable, popular people. When we make attributions in a biased way to maintain our self-esteem, we call that self-serving attributions. They explain outcomes in ways that advance or protect our personal interests. Let's talk about a couple of examples to finish out this chapter.

The False Consensus Bias

Here's an old story about stinky cheese.

A mischievous grandchild coats the mustache of his sleeping grandfather with a horrible-smelling cheese. The grandfather awakes and declares, "This room stinks!" He walks around the house and decides that "this whole house stinks!" He steps outside and discovers that "the entire world stinks!"

The false consensus effect occurs when we naively assume that our perspective is shared by others, that they see the world just as we do (Dawes, 1989; Dawes & Mulford, 1996; Nisbett & Kunda, 1985; Sherman et al., 1984). In developmental psychology, this idea is called egocentrism (Clement & Krueger, 2002; Hoch, 1987; Holmes, 1968, 1978). We assume our opinion is based on wise, thoughtful reflection—and that others are bound to reach the same conclusion! So we shake our heads with frustration when someone disagrees with us, because we honestly can't see how they can think what they do.

If you think the U.S. president is doing a great job, you see all the evidence of your opinion and probably talk to people who agree with you. It feels like people who don't like the current president must be some kind of weird minority. The problem is that people who don't think the president is doing well feel exactly the same way!

So, it is not surprising that students who admit to cheating believe that other students also cheated (Katz et al., 1931). Similarly, student athletes who use illicit performance-enhancing drugs overestimate how many other athletes do the same thing (Dunn et al., 2012). College men who admit to being perpetrators of sexual assault are significantly more likely to overestimate how many of their friends have done the same thing (Dardis et al., 2016). If we experience life in a certain way, then our stinky cheese bias, the false consensus bias, leads us to overestimate the number of people who experience their lives in the same way.

Of course, using our own experience is not an unreasonable way to estimate reality, especially if our private experience is the only evidence we have. But, like first impressions, the false consensus bias persists even when people are later provided with contradictory information. What has been called the truly false consensus effect occurs when we believe that others share our beliefs—even after we have objective, statistical information that contradicts that belief (Krueger & Clement, 1994; Krueger & Zeiger, 1993).

One student accidentally demonstrated how tightly the false consensus bias had wrapped itself around his thoughts. With unintended humor, the student declared, "I, like most people, do not generalize from myself to others" (Clement et al., 1997, p. 134).

The False Uniqueness Bias

Self-serving biases seem to turn up around every mental corner.

The last bias was based on assuming everyone was like us. This time, it's the false uniqueness bias. This bias requires a belief that we are more unique than others when it comes to socially desirable traits (Furnham & Dowsett, 1993). If our positive traits are rare, then we are special!

Do any of these findings apply to you? A false sense of uniqueness leads most store clerks to believe that they are tougher than most other store clerks at carding people

False-consensus effect: The overestimation of how many other people share our values, perceptions, and beliefs.

Truly false consensus effect: Overestimation that others share our beliefs, even after we have objective statistical information that contradicts that belief.

False uniqueness bias: The belief that we are more unique than others when it comes to socially desirable traits.

Ninety-nine percent of pet owners think their pet is uniquely intelligent. Do you think this is true of your dog, cat, or other pet family member?

when they try to buy cigarettes or alcohol (McCall & Nattrass, 2001). Most college students think that they are more constructive and less destructive in their romantic relationships than other college students (Van Lange et al., 1999). And most high school students think that they are more prosocial and helpful than other students (Iedema & Poppe, 1999; Monin & Norton, 2003).

It is easy to conclude that we are special when our bad traits are common, but our good traits are rare. We want to think of ourselves as unique, beautiful snowflakes. Here's the problem: Not even snowflakes are unique. In 1988, a scientist named Nancy Knight found two identical snowflakes in her microscope.

The Comic-Tragedy Behind Self-Serving Biases

Our private collection of self-serving biases can lead to comical conclusions.

For example, Nier (2004) discovered a self-serving glow of goodness so bright that it even shines on our pets. Almost all (99%) pet owners believe that their pets are above average in intelligence, and 18% of pet owners think that their pets are probably geniuses (Matheny & Miller, 2000). Similarly, 87% of Americans believe that they are more likely to go to Heaven than Mother Teresa or Oprah Winfrey (Stanglin & Gross, 1997).

However, the self-serving bias can shift from comedy to tragedy (Walther & Bazarova, 2007). Some hospitals maintain a self-serving organizational silence when faced with threats to patient safety (Henriksen & Dayton, 2006). The hospitals have a bias never to admit blame or to take responsibility because they are trying to protect their reputations. Similarly, many colleges and universities dread bad publicity about racial incidents, shootings on their campus, or sexual misconduct. Several news stories have come out regarding administrative cover-ups of these incidents.

In general, it is probably safer to admit our errors, endure the bad publicity, and correct mistakes—if our self-serving impulses allow us to acknowledge those mistakes in the first place. For college students, sometimes admitting that a bad grade *was* due to your own choices can help you improve the next time. For professors, maybe admitting that a class policy didn't work or that an exam question really was unfair is a way to help the next group of students in class. Self-serving biases can comfort us in the short term but can be damaging in the long term because we don't admit that we might have had something to do with the failure.

THE MAIN IDEAS

- When cognitive errors accumulate, they can lead to faulty social perceptions such as the fundamental attribution bias and the actor-observer bias.

- Cultural expectations make the fundamental attribution bias more likely to occur in independent cultures than in interdependent cultures. Problems can also occur when language means different things to different people.

- The false consensus bias occurs when we believe that others perceive the world in the same ways that we do; the false uniqueness bias occurs when we believe that we are more unique than others when it comes to socially desirable traits.

CRITICAL THINKING CHALLENGE

- Identify two times when you think a social misunderstanding occurred because two people came from different cultures. If you can't think of examples from your own life, choose examples from movies, TV shows, or books.

- When you share your opinion with others in social settings, such as discussing music or movie preferences with your friends, are you surprised when people disagree with you? If so, do you think this surprise is due to the false consensus error—or are there other possible explanations? Identify at least one context or opinion you have where you assume others agree with you, but it might be the false consensus bias at work.

- Consider times in your life when things didn't work out as you would have preferred, such as doing badly on a test or breaking up with a romantic partner. How much of this "failure" was due to your own faults or shortcomings, and how much was due to someone else or the situation? If you think that the majority of the blame lies somewhere else, are you making a self-serving and biased attribution?

CHAPTER SUMMARY

What Happens During and After Forming First Impressions?

Person perception is how we form impressions of other people. Nonverbal communication occurs through body language, tone of voice, facial expressions, and more. Some evidence indicates that at least six basic emotions are universally expressed through facial expressions, regardless of culture (fear, anger, disgust, surprise, sadness, and happiness.) Micro-expressions signal dishonesty in our faces, even when we try to control our facial expressions. A different type of nonverbal communication is a cultureme, which is a symbol used to convey meaning within a given culture. Culturemes, unlike facial expressions, are usually not understood by people from other cultures.

Sometimes particular traits will become more important than others; for example, how physically attractive people are affects our perception of them in general. When one trait affects how we view someone overall, it's called a halo effect. One specific type of halo effect is the what-is-beautiful-is-good effect, which is when physically attractive people are perceived as better in other ways as well (friendlier, more intelligent, etc.).

Sometimes, our impressions of others lead us to have expectations about their behaviors. When these expectations lead us to change our own behaviors, and our behavior affects the outcome of a social situation such that our expectation comes true, it's called a self-fulfilling prophecy. Self-fulfilling prophecies have been found in a variety of real-world settings such as classrooms, courtrooms, workplace settings, and even in the world of sports.

How Do We Explain Other People's Behavior?

When we guess at the cause behind an event or someone else's behavior, we make an attribution. When our attribution is based on something about a person's personality, motivation, or inner values, it's called an internal attribution (sometimes called a dispositional attribution). When our attribution is based on something about the situation or environmental circumstances, it's called an external attribution.

We often make attributions with the general belief that "good things happen to good people" and vice versa; this belief is called belief in a just world. Sometimes, this can lead to blaming innocent victims of misfortune. In general, believing that our fate is in our own hands is referred to as an internal locus of control. An external locus of control is when people believe that our fate is up to something outside of ourselves, such as fate, luck, or a powerful other person or supernatural being. Finally, our decisions and attributions can be biased when we are reminded of our own mortality, something that is studied within terror management theory.

One way that we attempt to make logical attributions about situations is by using Kelley's covariation model of attributions. Here, we ask ourselves three questions about the situation, including (1) consensus, (2) consistency, and (3) distinctiveness. Our answers to these three questions help us understand why something happened or why others acted like they did.

Why Do We Misjudge One Another?

Sometimes when we attempt to understand other people, we make mistakes. A very common mistake—so common that it's called the fundamental attribution error—is when we assume other people's actions are due to their personality and we forget to take the situation or circumstances into effect. While we do this when making attributions about other people, we don't make this mistake when explaining our own behavior. The difference in how we make assumptions about other people's behavior versus our own is called the actor-observer bias. In addition, while people from "independent" cultures tend to make the fundamental attribution error, people from "interdependent" or collectivistic cultures are less likely to do so.

We also tend to make attributions and assumptions about other people that protect our view of the self or our own interests. For example, the false consensus effect is the tendency to think that most other people agree with our personal opinions. The false uniqueness bias, on the other hand, is the perception that our good or positive qualities are fairly rare (and therefore we are special and above average). While these tendencies help us feel good about ourselves, they may prevent us from improving or confronting negative behaviors.

CRITICAL THINKING, ANALYSIS, AND APPLICATION

- Think about the self-fulfilling prophecies that different groups of people have to live with in your culture. For example, different races probably have different stereotypes and expectations about the types of adults they will become. How much of an influence do you think self-fulfilling prophecies have on the opportunities that different groups are given by society? How could educators, politicians, or other leaders use self-fulfilling prophecies to better the human condition?

- Some people are better than others at decoding nonverbal communication cues from others. For example, one symptom that's common in people on the autism spectrum is the lack of ability to understand subtle nonverbal cues such as when tone of voice indicates sarcasm. If you were speaking with someone you knew had trouble understanding nonverbal cues, how would you change your behaviors to communicate in other ways?

- Think of a time when you made an attribution about why someone did something—and it turned out later that you were wrong. What do you think happened to lead you to the wrong conclusion? What variables or aspects of the circumstance, the person, or your own frame of mind affected your ability to make a correct attribution—and can you control for these variables going into the future?

- Consider the way that news media (television, radio, etc.) cover stories about crimes, such as murders or terrorist attacks. Is the tendency for the reporters to assume the crimes occurred because the criminals were bad people—or do they think about other, external or situational explanations, such as oppression, religion, mental illness, and so on?

AP Photo/BOB JORDAN

6

Attitudes and Persuasion

Core Questions

6.1   What are attitudes and where do they come from?

6.2   Do attitudes predict behavior?

6.3   How do attitudes change?

Learning Objectives

6.1   Explain how attitudes are based on underlying beliefs that help predict behavior.

6.2   Describe difficulties in measuring attitudes and theories regarding whether they really predict human behavior.

6.3   Analyze how cognitive dissonance and paths to persuasion can change attitudes.

Was it a witch hunt for rumored child sex abusers?

Or did the employees of a small daycare center really commit these horrible crimes? The gossip was bad enough, especially in a town as small as Edenton, North Carolina. The group of accused daycare workers included owners Bob and Betsy Kelly, several of their employees at the Little Rascals daycare center, and a friend of Bob's who had never even visited the daycare.

Like rising floodwaters, powerful attitudes about child sex abuse swept away critical thinking, lifelong friendships, and even established legal standards. Many in Edenton made up their minds right away—and refused to change even after the moral panic subsided. They had come to believe that their own friends and neighbors, labeled the Edenton 7 by journalist Lew Powell, must be guilty of gross acts of child sexual abuse.

You may be tempted to think of the people in Edenton as evil or corrupt. But when I [Tom] became interested in this case, I went to Edenton and chatted with several residents, including some of the people involved. They were nice people, normal people. Most were courteous, interested, friendly to a stranger from "up north"—and still confused about what had happened in their little town a quarter of a century earlier. It was not a case for a clinical psychologist; it was and still is a casebook phenomenon for social psychology.

The legal case against Bob Kelly lasted 8 months. A jury found him guilty of 99 out of 100 charges. They punished him with 12 consecutive life sentences—one for each of the 12 alleged victims represented in court. Like the witch trials of Salem, it appeared that fear and panic had overcome logic. Only a few years later, all 99 convictions were reversed.

The attitudes that drove the Little Rascals case into the national spotlight help explain why famous researcher Gordon Allport (1935) declared that attitudes were social psychology's "most distinctive and indispensable concept."

WHAT ARE ATTITUDES AND WHERE DO THEY COME FROM?

>> **LO 6.1:** Explain how attitudes are based on underlying beliefs that help predict behavior.

Attitudes are inner evaluations or judgments of something or someone.

Those evaluations could be positive or negative (see Eagly & Chaiken, 2007). In Edenton, North Carolina, the judgments were negative and grew stronger with each arrest. People hated child abuse in general, and their attitude shifted toward demonizing seven people in particular.

Attitudes are an abstract and theoretical idea. But social psychologists' goals are practical: to discover how attitudes influence human behavior. Understanding the attitude-behavior connection is vital for political campaigns, military leaders, sales trainers, online advertisers, and multimillion-dollar marketing campaigns. For students, that means that there are many exciting career opportunities for people who become adept at identifying, measuring, and influencing attitudes.

This section answers the core question "What are attitudes and where do they come from?" by

(1) considering the complicated nature of attitudes and

(2) tracing attitudes to their beginnings as interactions between nature and nurture.

Attitudes: Inner evaluations or judgments toward something or someone, either positive or negative.

Attitudes Evaluate an Object

The "target" of an attitude is called an **attitude object**.

The attitude object could be a person, political policy, sports team, television series, song, painting, or even an abstract idea (see Petty & Cacioppo, 1996). Attitudes are based on beliefs, and they can quickly become complicated if we have mixed feelings about an attitude object.

Dual Attitudes: Opposing Evaluations Are Common

Dual attitudes are common—but sometimes uncomfortable.

During the historic Salem witch hunt, one of the accused was the town's previous minister, the Reverend George Burroughs. Standing before the gallows, Burroughs recited the Lord's Prayer perfectly—something that witches were not supposed to be able to do. Suddenly, the citizens of Salem were "of two minds"—but only one belief could win out. What should their attitude be? The Harvard-trained minister, Reverend Cotton Mather, reminded them that Burroughs had been found guilty. They hanged their former minister.

Dual attitudes are contrasting evaluations about a single attitude object. An addict will both love and hate their preferred drug. A teenager might love their parents yet also feel embarrassed and annoyed by them. A professional actor may love their career for its sublime artistic pleasures—yet hate it because of its instability and frequent rejection. How do we develop "love-hate" attitudes toward drugs, family members, careers, and everything else in our lives?

First, attitudes come from three different sources: affect (emotional, gut reactions to things), behavior (like habits), and cognition (thoughtful, logical reactions to things). Sometimes these three sources are called the ABCs of attitude formation, because of the first letter in each word (affect, behavior, cognition). The problem is that A, B, and C don't always come to the same conclusions (Smith & Nosek, 2011). For example, we may get an affective feeling (A) that we should not trust someone. Nevertheless, we may act (B) as if we trust the person because we can't logically explain (C) our feeling and we don't want to be rude.

Second, we might change our mind. The **model of dual attitudes** proposes that new attitudes override (rather than replace) old attitudes (Wilson et al., 2000). So if our attitude has changed over time, both attitudes are there—but the newer one is a little stronger. That might be why former lovers may fondly remember one another in the midst of a bitter breakup. The old beliefs and feelings do not disappear—they just fade within another complicating layer of beliefs.

There's a third explanation for why we sometimes have dual attitudes. Think about this: Would you eat a chocolate cockroach? **Implicit attitudes** are automatic, unconscious reactions toward an attitude object. We might not even realize we have them until a situation brings them out. On the other hand, **explicit attitudes** are the product of controlled, reasoned, conscious evaluations about an attitude object. It's the conclusion we come to after we really think about something.

Most people are aware that they love chocolate (an explicit attitude), an evaluation formed after experience and conscious enjoyment. But they may be relatively unaware of how much they dislike bugs until they visit a specialty chocolate store and suddenly see chocolate in the form of cockroaches or other "gross" things. Yech! Suddenly, the dual attitude is clear.

Univalenced Decisions Based on Attitudes

Even if you have a dual attitude, you usually have to make a single choice about what to do.

You can only vote for one candidate, you have to either accept or reject a marriage proposal, and you have to decide whether to eat the chocolate cockroach. (We suppose you could nibble it or break off a leg, but somehow that seems even more disgusting.).

Attitude object: The thing, person, place, or idea we evaluate when we form an attitude.

Dual attitudes: When we hold contrasting positive and negative evaluations about a single attitude object.

Model of dual attitudes: Proposes that new attitudes override, rather than replace, old attitudes. Both attitudes remain, with one stronger than the other.

Implicit attitudes: Automatic, unconscious evaluations and judgments that can sometimes be out of our awareness.

Explicit attitudes: Controlled, conscious, thoughtful evaluations and judgments we're aware of making.

Attitudes help us make **univalenced decisions**, a "yes or no," "good or bad" type of decision where a choice must be made, even if we have mixed feelings (a dual attitude). After all, attitudes are what Gordon Allport (1935) called a "predisposition or readiness for response." Our judgments often allow us to make a quick thumbs-up or thumbs-down heuristic decision (Priester & Petty, 1996).

Unfortunately, attitudes can sometimes lead to the wrong decision, because they can bias us (see Ajzen, 1991; Eagly & Chaiken, 1993; Thompson et al., 1995; Wilson et al., 2000). Chocolate should taste the same, no matter what shape it's in. And the prosecutors and jury (and many townspeople) in the Little Rascals case arrived at the same univalenced decision about their friends and neighbors: guilty.

They were wrong.

All of the charges were eventually overturned—but only after seven daycare workers were found guilty of over 400 counts of sexual assault, having intercourse in front of children, conspiracy, and much more. There was no physical evidence. Little Rascals had an open-door policy. Parents could pick up their children at any time. The charges were not plausible—but they were widely believed, because of strong premade attitudes and fear.

Barcroft Media/Barcroft Media/Getty Images

Many people have positive explicit attitudes toward eating chocolate, but when asked to eat a chocolate cockroach, you might have mixed feelings.

Attitudes Come From Both Nature and Nurture

Here's a question that can keep you busy for the rest of your life.

Do your attitudes come from nature (your inherited biology, genes, hormones, etc.) or from nurture (your social environment, how you were raised, and your life experiences)? Usually, the "nature versus nurture" question is a false dichotomy. This conclusion was emphasized by Kate Barlow (2019) when she declared that the "nature versus nurture debate is nonsense" (p. 68).

Nature did not win the debate. Nurture did not win the debate. The winner was the interaction, or what Barlow described as an "integrated genetic, social, developmental, and personality psychology." Her confidence was the product of thousands of twin

Univalenced decision: A decision based on an attitude about an attitude object that is either good or bad but not both.

BOB KELLY

AP Photo/WINDN

Bob Kelly, one of the owners of the Little Rascals daycare center. A 1997 story in *The New York Times* compared the case to the Salem witch trials.

Our tendency to adorn ourselves and publicly display group membership is probably a product of both genetic instinct (nature) and social conformity and norms (nurture).

studies that helped produce the field called **behavioral genetics**, the study of how nature and nurture interact. Let's examine contributions from each source.

Nature: Assortative Mating and Twin Studies

One way that nature and nurture interact is through **assortative mating**.

This process is how organisms that are similar tend to find and then mate with each other. For example, imagine that many years ago, a young couple, both in their 20s, fell in love after meeting in the bleachers at Wrigley Field while rooting for the Chicago Cubs baseball team. Why did they fall in love?

In terms of nature, they were both at an age when their bodies were biologically ready to mate and possibly have children together. In terms of nurture, they also have a lot in common. They live in the Chicago area, buy cheap tickets, and share enjoyment and loyalty toward the same sports team. Both nature and nurture worked together to help their interest blossom.

Another fascinating way to explore the importance of nature versus nurture is twin studies, especially with identical twins. For example, Klump et al. (2003) compared eating attitudes between 11-year-old twins and 17-year-old twins. The genetic influence for the younger twins was 0% but jumped to 54% among the older twins. In this case, the genetic influence on food attitudes and intake appeared to be activated in puberty, possibly due to changes in the hormone estradiol (Butera et al., 2010; Klump et al., 2010).

Twin studies can also give us insight into how genetic inheritance influences concepts as psychological as political attitudes (Kandler et al., 2012), parenting style (Wertz et al., 2019), and gambling (Davis et al., 2018). One indicator of the growth of applied behavior genetics—and corresponding career opportunities—is the development of twin registries (Odintsova et al., 2018). Those registries will also need psychology students who can recruit, maintain, and grow the population of twins willing to participate in social psychological studies.

Nurture: Social Learning and Conditioning

"Because I said so!"

Many new parents report the odd experience of saying things to their children that sound almost exactly in word and tone like what their parents once said to them. How we think and evaluate our world are certainly influenced by our life experiences. We will consider three separate possible sources of attitudes from nurture: social learning, classical conditioning, and operant conditioning.

Behavioral genetics: The study of how nature and nurture interact to form our attitudes and behaviors.

Assortative mating: The process when similar organisms tend to mate with each other (see *similarity-attraction hypothesis*).

Social learning theory: Proposed that we form attitudes by observing and imitating others.

Social Learning. **Social learning theory** proposes that we learn by observing others.

We form attitudes by observing others' attitudes and imitating them (Bandura, 1977; Perry & Bussey, 1979). One research team (Morgan et al., 2009), for example, found that people acquired positive attitudes toward organ donation after viewing four television shows (like *CSI: NY*) featuring characters in need of organ transplants. The effect was more pronounced if the viewers had experienced emotional involvement with the storyline.

Social learning also helps explain how attitudes that were once socially unacceptable become mainstream. When multiple U.S. presidents acknowledge using marijuana, it is difficult to justify incarcerating others for the same behavior. As the nation approves LGBTQ rights like legalized same-sex marriage, more and more people change their attitudes to align with what they perceive to be popular opinion. As we'll discuss in depth in the next chapter, we can shift our attitudes to fit in with others and follow what we think is a "normal," socially accepted line of thinking.

Classical Conditioning. The advertising industry often relies on sex.

Many copies incorporate sexuality into ads, even when the product is unrelated (like a hamburger or car; see Reichert, 2019). Why does sex sell? The companies hope that you will (a) pay attention and (b) learn to associate any positive feelings to their product. In other words, we have an automatic positive attitude toward sexual pleasure, and the company hopes we transfer that attitude to whatever they're selling.

This process is called classical conditioning: an automatic reaction to something after repeated pairing of a neutral stimulus to an unconditioned stimulus. The "unconditioned" stimulus is what causes our automatic reaction (a sexy model, for example). The "neutral" stimulus, in this case, is the product being sold (hamburger, car). Through repeated pairings, classical conditioning kicks in if we start to have an automatic and positive reaction to the neutral stimulus (in other words, it's no longer neutral; it's become a "conditioned" stimulus).

It doesn't have to be sex. For example, humor enhances a consumer's attitude both to the advertisement and to the brands shown (Chung & Zhao, 2003; Gelb & Zinkhan, 1986; Lee & Mason, 1999). Once the reward network in the brain has us laughing or at least amused, positive associations can take place—sometimes below the level of our awareness (Strick et al., 2009). We develop a positive attitude only because we have learned to associate that product with something we like.

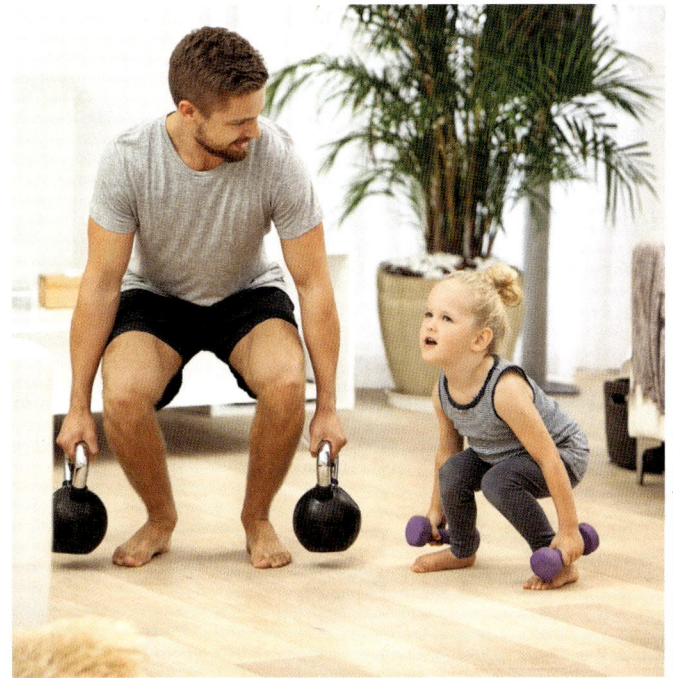

© istockphoto.com/SelectStock

Children often show a natural tendency to model the behaviors of their parents, which is one example of social learning theory.

Classical conditioning: A process when an automatic reaction or attitude to one thing is transferred to another after repeated pairings.

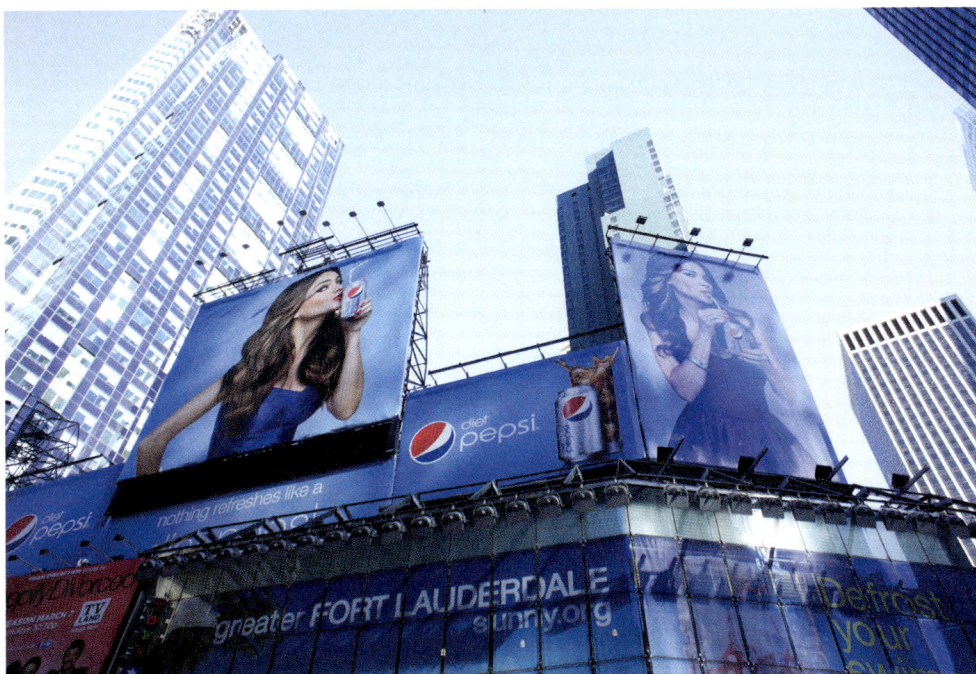

Richard Levine/Alamy Stock Photo

Operant Conditioning. Operant conditioning is the process of learning from past consequences.

If a past attitude or behavior led to a reward, it's likely to persist and become even stronger. On the other hand, attitudes and behaviors that led to negative consequences (punishments) are likely to decline. If people laugh at your jokes, then you are more likely to use humor and eventually develop a self-attitude that you are a good joke-teller. If you get compliments on your luxuriant hair, you'll have a positive attitude toward your shampoo brand.

Human interactions can be especially rewarding. Adolescents have a more positive attitude toward drinking alcohol when they believe drinking is rewarded by popularity and more party invitations (Goldstein et al., 2013). Attitudes learned from operant conditioning are particularly strong and persistent over time (Davies, 1982; Guenther & Alicke, 2008; Slusher & Anderson, 1989). Rewards in the past promise more rewards in the future. While our attitudes are formed from a wide variety of sources, it's important to understand their origins.

THE MAIN IDEAS

- Attitudes are inner evaluations or judgments of something or someone, either in a positive or negative direction. When we have a mixed evaluation, it's called a dual attitude.

- Implicit attitudes are automatic, unconscious reactions toward an attitude object, while explicit attitudes are controlled, conscious, reasoned evaluations. Even when we have dual attitudes or contradictory implicit and explicit attitudes, we often have to make a single, univalenced decision for our behavior.

- Attitudes are formed by both nature (biological influences like twin studies) and nurture (experiences formed through social learning, classical conditioning, and operant conditioning). The interaction of nature and nurture is the study of behavioral genetics.

CRITICAL THINKING CHALLENGE

- Name three attitude objects (a person, a place, and an idea) about which you have some version of a dual attitude, such as a love-hate attitude toward a person who both attracts and repels you. For each, identify why you have this dual attitude and whether the positive or negative evaluation seems stronger.

- Select any two of the following attitude objects and describe how both nature and nurture might influence its development: binge drinking, studying statistics, flying in an airplane, participating in extreme sports, and the desire to have children.

- Identify a product that you feel either positively or negatively toward not because of the product itself but because of an association you have with it. The association might be due to a commercial, a memory you have of using the product, and so on. Explain how classical conditioning led to your attitude toward the product.

DO ATTITUDES PREDICT BEHAVIOR?

>> **LO 6.2:** Describe difficulties in measuring attitudes and theories regarding whether they really predict human behavior.

Brenda Ambrose's child attended the Little Rascals daycare in Edenton, North Carolina.

But Brenda herself also worked there. She told *FRONTLINE*, "I still lie awake at night thinking how could they have done it with me in the room right across the hall?" Nevertheless, she sent her son to therapy and became convinced that he also must have been sexually molested by her coworkers.

Operant conditioning: A process when our attitudes or behaviors are strengthened by previous rewards or weakened by previous punishments.

Brenda was aware of the town's pervasive paranoia. She saw her longtime friends and neighbors develop negative attitudes without any regard for the evidence. Like the confused citizens of Salem who murdered their former minister, Brenda had complicated, contradictory, difficult-to-measure beliefs. Attitudes predicting behavior seem obvious: Of course we vote for the candidate we prefer, we buy products we like, and we date people we trust. But it turns out that decades of research in social psychology show that the connection between attitudes and actual behaviors is much more complicated (and fascinating!) than it first appears.

In this section we answer the core question "Do attitudes predict behavior?" by

(1) clarifying how both explicit and implicit attitudes are measured in research and

(2) explaining four theories regarding why attitudes might not always predict behaviors directly.

Measuring Explicit and Implicit Attitudes

The direct, explicit approach to measuring attitudes can be summed up in two words: "Just ask."

Remember that explicit attitudes are the ones we're aware of, ones that are available to our conscious minds and based on reasoned decisions. Usually, social psychology measures attitudes the simplest way possible: Ask people to fill out *self-report* measures like the ones throughout this book. This direct approach works great when people are (1) willing to tell the truth and (2) aware of what they think.

We already discussed the first criterion—honesty—in Chapter 2 when we covered *social desirability* issues in survey studies. One option is to measure honesty in reporting by including a social desirability scale (like the What's My Score? feature in that chapter). There's another, perhaps sneakier option: a bogus pipeline.

The Bogus Pipeline

A bogus pipeline is, simply put, a fake lie detector machine.

It's ironic: We're lying to our participants about whether we can tell if they're lying. It can look like anything that will convince them: a large machine with a bunch of wires that hook up to their hand, a helmet that straps onto their head with cords running to a computer, and so on. If we use a bogus pipeline, then ask people about their inner attitudes, we hope that they are more honest (to avoid looking like liars in front of us).

Does the bogus pipeline really work? Sometimes.

It seemed to work—on average—with some child molesters who told different stories when connected to a fake lie detector compared to a questionnaire (Gannon et al., 2007). However, the bogus pipeline did not seem to work in a study comparing what people told researchers about their use of alcohol and marijuana (Aguinis et al., 1995). Being hooked up to a bogus pipeline had more of an effect when college students were asked about romantic cheating than academic cheating (Fisher & Brunell, 2014). So it works . . . sometimes. And it only has a chance of working when people are aware of what the truth really is. What about when they're not?

The Implicit Association Test

What happens when people are reluctant to report the truth, or their attitudes are implicit—meaning people might not even be aware of them?

In those cases, a popular option for social psychologists is a creative method called the IAT, or Implicit Association Test. How does it work? The idea is that you might have subtle associations in your mind that pair concepts together in the form of implicit connections. For example, if you grew up in a culture that stereotyped women as being good at taking care of children, you might pair the concepts "woman" and "children" in your mind.

Bogus pipeline: A fake lie detector machine used to increase honest responses from study participants.

IAT: *See implicit association test.*

Implicit Association Test: An indirect way to measure attitudes or mental associations.

When your mental connections pair a concept with an evaluation, like "good," "safe," or "friendly," it becomes an implicit attitude. The idea behind the IAT is that we can measure those associations with sorting tasks on a computer. You're asked to sort words or images that appear on the screen into two categories (like male faces versus female faces).

The tasks get increasingly complicated when you have to sort images into two categories, switching back and forth. It measures implicit attitudes by scoring how many mistakes you make, plus *how quickly* you complete the sorting tasks. If it's easier for you to sort images when "women" and "children" are paired, compared to when "men" and "children" are paired, the assumption is that you have that association in your mental memory structures.

The best way to really understand how IAT tests work is by taking one yourself. The What's My Score? feature tells you how to experience the test online—and there are many different options of tests you can choose from (e.g., attitudes about people with different races, ages, body weights, religion, and more). Over thousands of participants, results from the IAT show that most people show at least small signs of unconscious stereotypes.

The IAT was developed by Tony Greenwald and colleagues (2002) to measure automatic, unconscious, implicit associations and attitudes. It might not be our "fault" if we have these associations; we might have picked them up from a biased culture (Bargh & Williams, 2006; Thaler & Sunstein, 2008). Just *having* a mental association doesn't mean you *agree* with it or act on it—it just means you're aware of a cultural stereotype or bias.

The IAT has been criticized because rapid mental associations do not necessarily predict actual prejudiced behavior (Blanton et al., 2009). In addition, several studies have questioned whether implicit associations lead to any meaningful outcomes beyond the difference of a few milliseconds on a strange computer task. There's also evidence that people within stereotyped groups often get IAT results that seem to show bias against their *own* group (e.g., Black participants who show negativity toward Black people in general). This form of internalized prejudice again appears to be the result of growing up in a racist culture, not necessarily actual, explicit negative beliefs or judgments.

That said, many social psychologists believe the IAT captures something important about our automatic beliefs (Jordan et al., 2005; Sheldon et al., 2007). IATs are used in thousands of studies, which a quick search on PsycINFO or GoogleScholar will show. Their controversial nature is still up for debate in many social psychology circles.

WHAT'S MY SCORE?

🜄 The Implicit Association Test (IAT)

It is best to experience the IAT for yourself. Just follow these instructions:

1. Search online for *Project Implicit* to be taken to Harvard's IAT.

2. Under "Project Implicit Social Attitudes", select your preferred language, then select "Go!".

3. Read the disclaimer, then select "I wish to proceed".

4. Choose any test that is of interest to you (you'll see several choices)! Follow the links and instructions you are given to complete the test. Note that after you are done, you'll get to compare your score to the thousands of other people who have taken the same test you did.

Using Attitudes to Predict Behavior

What's the use of studying attitudes if they don't predict behavior?

We can measure them all day long, using clever techniques like a bogus pipeline or an IAT. But if they aren't connected to what we actually *do*, what's the point? Social psychology went through a bit of a crisis when researchers started to point out that measured attitudes don't always match what people do—and it started with a famous study almost 100 years ago.

A Crisis of Confidence: The LaPiere Study

In 1934, racism against the Chinese was high.

Sociologist Robert LaPiere (1934) spent 2 years traveling across the United States with a young Chinese married couple. At that time, Chinese people suffered intense prejudice and discrimination, often in the form of being refused service at hotels and restaurants. While the prejudice was terrible, LaPiere used it to study the basic question: Would prejudiced attitudes predict prejudiced behavior?

Over that 2 years, the travelers stayed in 66 hotels and lodgings and ate in 184 restaurants. Thankfully, they were refused service only once. Six months later, LaPiere sent letters to the same hotels and restaurants asking them about their attitudes—and 92% of them explicitly stated that they would *not* serve Chinese people! These attitudes didn't match what had actually happened. What was going on?

LaPiere's study combined a *survey* with a *field study* in a way that made it feel like a *case study* of a discreet, 2-year experience. That's a powerful combination, but it was still far from a perfect study. Here are four possible problems with LaPiere's study:

1. The survey respondents may have provided only socially desirable responses. At the time, they may have thought refusing service is what LaPiere wanted to hear (after all, his name is French—not Chinese). Back then, the politically correct response was that they *would* discriminate.

2. The people answering the survey were not necessarily the same people who decided to let them into their hotel or restaurant.

3. The Chinese couple both spoke unaccented English and were accompanied by a respectable-looking White man, which may have influenced the decision.

4. The data were not collected at the same time as the behavior was observed. Maybe something happened in that 6 months to change people's attitudes.

5. Maybe the businesses regretted serving the Chinese couple for some reason and had changed their policy after LaPiere's visit with them.

While all of these possibilities exist, the evidence from LaPiere's study was certainly provocative: The general attitudes of the people managing all those hotels and restaurants did not align with their behaviors. When other researchers started testing the attitude-behavior link, they got similar evidence (a form of *replication*). When tested in *controlled experiments*, LaPiere's surprising findings turned out to be the rule, not the exception (see Dockery & Bedeian, 1989).

For example, students' attitudes toward cheating did *not* predict whether they actually cheated (Corey, 1937). Positive attitudes toward religion don't seem to predict actually going to a worship service or monetary contributions, either (Wicker, 1971). In 1969, Wicker reviewed the converging evidence about attitude-behavior research and found the average correlation between attitudes and behaviors was only 0.15! He suggested that for psychology research, "It may be desirable to abandon the attitude concept" (Wicker, 1971, p. 29).

The academic crisis in social psychology was slowly resolved. But it was resolved by something that the psychological therapists in Edenton did not have: unbiased data.

There were four main insights that helped rebalance social psychologists' understanding of how attitudes and behaviors are (or are not) linked:

1. The specificity principle

2. Self-perception theory

3. Impression management theory

4. The theory of planned behavior

Let's talk about each idea.

The Specificity Principle

The first solution to the attitude-behavior problem seems obvious now, but only in hindsight.

The **specificity principle** proposes that the attitude-behavior connection is stronger when attitude and behavior are measured at the same level of specificity. In other words, the more specifically you ask people questions (measure their attitudes), the better you'll be able to predict what they'll do. Maybe LaPiere's survey should have asked, "How likely are you to refuse service to a nice-looking, English-speaking Chinese couple accompanied by a professional-looking White man?"

A classic *longitudinal* study (Davidson & Jaccard, 1979) supporting the specificity principle was done in 1979, when birth control was first really available to regular people in the United States (before that, it was illegal or very hard to find; see Kennedy, 1970). The researchers asked 244 married women in the Midwest about their attitudes toward birth control, then followed up with them over the next 2 years to see whether they actually used various forms of it. The results are in Table 6.1. Notice that as the specificity of attitude measurement increases, so does the correlation between the attitude and participants' behavior. So one way to increase the attitude-behavior link was solved: Just ask better questions.

Self-Perception Theory:
Which Came First: The Attitude or the Behavior?

A second solution to the attitude-behavior problem is similar to the famous chicken or egg question: Which came first?

The assumption was always that attitudes came first and would predict behavior. You decide which candidate you like, then you vote. You decide what soap you like, then you buy it. But can you think of times when advice tells you to flip it? Have you heard the phrase, "Fake it 'til you make it"?

Specificity principle:
Proposes that the link between attitudes and behaviors is strong when the attitude and the behavior are measured at the same level of specificity.

TABLE 6.1

Correlations Between Four Attitudes and Increasingly Specific Behaviors

ATTITUDE OBJECT	CORRELATION WITH BEHAVIOR
1. Attitude toward birth control	.083
2. Attitude toward birth control pills	.323
3. Attitude toward using birth control pills	.525
4. Attitude toward using birth control pills during the next 2 years	.572

Source: Davidson and Jaccard (1979).

In Chapter 3, we introduced you to self-perception theory, the idea that we first observe our own behavior and then decide what kind of person we are. You might not have a particularly strong attitude toward your soap or shampoo brand—you might buy it simply because it's what you've always done or it's the brand your family bought when you were growing up. Maybe the action came first, and you formed the attitude second. Maybe you eat waffles a lot without really analyzing your attitude toward them.

The **facial feedback hypothesis** is one way to test the idea that behaviors can come first. It's the idea that if you move your face into a certain expression, the matching emotion will follow. Smile, and you'll be happy. This hypothesis has a long history, both in philosophy and in psychological science (see Coles et al., 2019). Figure 6.1 shows you two ways to hold a pen in your mouth:

1. with your teeth only (forcing your face into a smile) and

2. with your lips only (forcing a frown).

The first psychological experimenters in these now well-known studies (see Buck, 1980; Soussignan, 2002; Strack et al., 1988) created a *cover story* by implying that the study was about helping "physically impaired people who use their mouth to write or use the telephone" (p. 770). So, the *independent variable* was asking people to hold a pen in their mouth in ways that created two different conditions: a smile or a frown.

The *dependent variable* (the outcome variable that was measured) was how funny the participants rated cartoons they saw while holding pens in their mouths. So, which came first? Did a funny cartoon make people smile or did smiling first make the cartoon feel a little funnier?

You may be disappointed in the results, because the best summary of these many studies is "It depends." The most recent *meta-analysis* represented hundreds of facial feedback experiments. It was a careful, fine-grained analysis that subdivided those

Facial feedback hypothesis: The idea that emotions can happen after someone makes a corresponding facial expression.

FIGURE 6.1

Try holding a pen or pencil in your mouth as shown in the photos, which forces your face into a frown or smile. Do you feel happier when you are smiling?

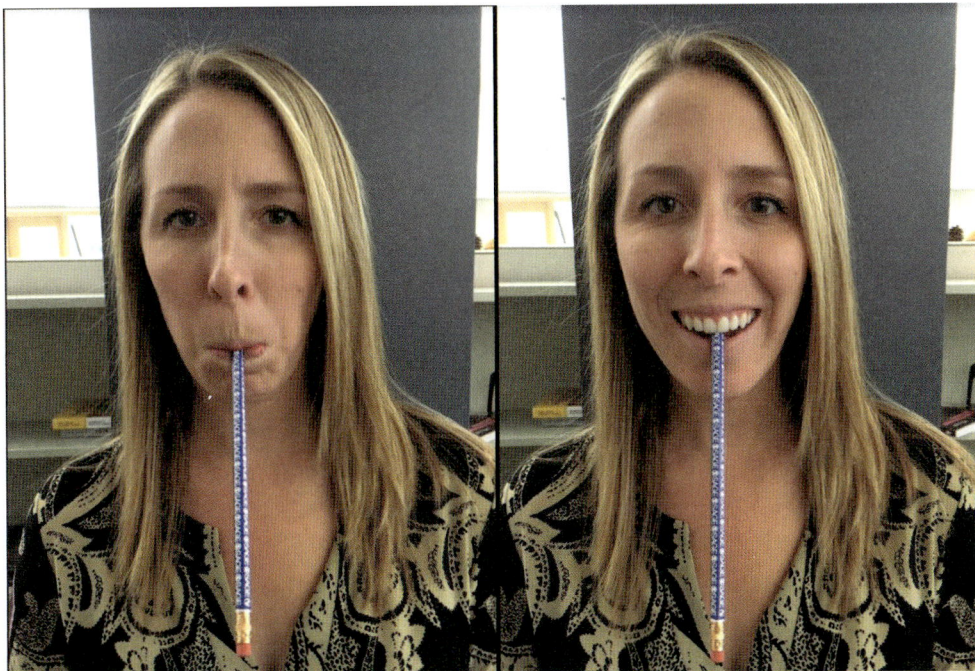

studies into categories such as whether participants were reporting an emotional experience (feeling amused) or judging whether the cartoon was funny.

The end of the story was that facial feedback is real—but the effects are small (Coles et al., 2019; Schnall & Laird, 2003; Wagenmakers et al., 2016). Smiling can help you feel better—a little bit, for a little while. Like most experiences in social psychology, we're complicated beings without simple solutions.

Impression Management

By this point in the history of social psychology, the weak connection between attitudes and behavior had a not very original name: the attitude-behavior problem.

In addition to the specificity principle and self-perception theory, this problem forced social psychologists into a third insight. Remember from Chapter 3 that impression management proposes that we modify our attitudes and behaviors in order to strategically influence how others perceive us (see Chapter 3; Steele, 1988). For example, you might pretend to agree with a first date or a professor, because you know it's a good strategy. So our behaviors might be better predicted by our read of the current situation than by our actual beliefs or attitudes.

Sometimes, expressed attitudes are short-term tactics designed to get us past a difficult moment (Gordon, 1996; Higgins et al., 2003; Jones & Pittman, 1982; Yukl & Tracey, 1992). Recall that we use techniques like ingratiation, self-enhancement, and conspicuous consumption to impress other people. We might do these things despite having hidden, internal attitudes that conflict with our outer behaviors—but we're doing it to manipulate others.

Note that this can come at a cost. According to **self-affirmation theory**, another option is trying to impress *ourselves,* to preserve our sense of worth (Sherman & Cohen, 2002). People who have been self-affirmed in experiments (for their positive social attitudes) tend to experience less stress (Creswell et al., 2005), better problem solving (Creswell et al., 2013), and higher satisfaction with their body types (Bucchianeri & Corning, 2012). So being authentic does have advantages.

These three explanations (slowly) helped social psychologists understand why general attitudes were not very good at predicting specific behaviors. A final theory helped explain that when it comes to predicting what people will do, we need to know more than just their attitudes.

The Theory of Planned Behavior

The **theory of planned behavior** brought confidence back to social psychologists' attitudes toward attitudes (see Ajzen & Fishbein, 1980; Fishbein & Cappella, 2006).

This theory proposes that attitudes are only one of three categories of belief—attitudes, subjective norms, and perceived control—that together predict behavioral intentions. These intentions, in turn, predict behavior (see Figure 6.2). In short, attitudes are one of the stars of the show—but it's an ensemble cast with three supporting actors. Figure 6.2 shows the entire vision of how we use three things to predict behavior within this theory.

Attitudes remain important—we measure them as specifically as possible, know that they might come after behaviors in some cases, and take impression management into account. There are two other factors in predicting behaviors. First are **subjective norms**, or our perception of what everyone else is doing. Even if you don't believe in using performance-enhancing drugs, if you think everyone else is doing it, you might start just because you want to "level the playing field." If you're in a class that's graded on a curve and you think others are cheating, you might consider cheating, too.

In addition to attitudes and subjective norms, your **perceived control** also influences your behavior. Perceived control is whether you think you're capable of doing what you want to do (Adler, 1930; Rotter, 1954, 1990). You might want to run a marathon but have realistic views of your physical limitations.

In a poignant example, Bettelheim (1943) linked at least a minimal sense of control as critical to surviving a concentration camp. Langer and Rodin demonstrated that feeling in control helped residents of a nursing home live longer, more active lives (see

Self-affirmation theory: Proposes that we try to impress ourselves to preserve our sense of worth and integrity.

Theory of planned behavior: Proposes that behaviors are best predicted by three factors: attitudes, subjective norms, and perceived control.

Subjective norms: Our perception of what other people are doing or what we think is "normal" or common in a given situation.

Perceived control: Our perception of whether we're capable of successfully accomplishing a given goal or behavior.

FIGURE 6.2

Bulimia scores before and after experiencing cognitive dissonance.

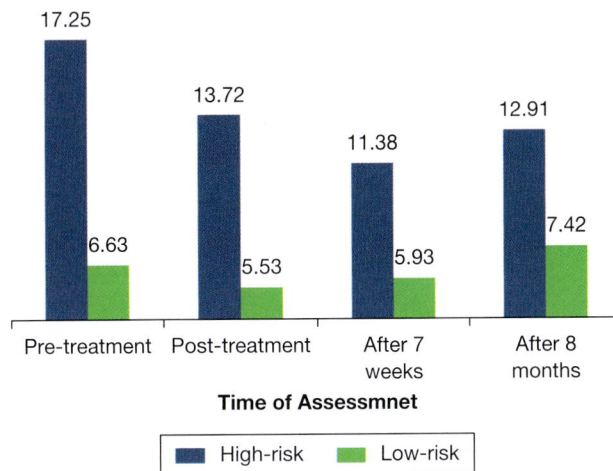

Source: Data from Becker et al. (2008).

Langer & Rodin, 1976; Rodin & Langer, 1977a, 1977b; Ubbiali et al., 2008). You're a lot less likely to cheat on an exam if you perceive that you'll get away with it (a high level of perceived control). In experiments, Seligman (1975) connected learned helplessness, or a sense that you can't control what happens to you, to clinical depression. Others have linked loss of control to increased rates of disease and death (Schmale & Iker, 1966).

When you have all three pieces of the puzzle, predicting behavior increases greatly. The theory of planned behavior suggests that all three factors make critical contributions to predicting human behavior: attitudes, subjective social norms, and perceived control. Armed with these new insights, social psychologists discovered that specific intentions were much better at predicting specific behaviors such as

- underage drinking (Lac et al., 2013),
- leaving abusive partners (Edwards et al., 2015),
- committing digital piracy (Yoon, 2011), and
- academic cheating by college students (DeVries & Ajzen, 1971).

What other places, occasions, or contexts do you think the theory would be useful in predicting behavior?

THE MAIN IDEAS

- There are two general strategies for measuring attitudes: a direct approach (for explicit attitudes) and an indirect approach (for implicit attitudes). When measuring explicit attitudes, participant honesty can be increased with techniques like a bogus pipeline (a fake lie detector). For implicit attitudes, the Implicit Association Test (IAT) may measure mental connections we have between ideas.

- Several studies showed that the link between someone's attitudes and their actual behaviors can be weak; a study by LaPiere is a classic example showing this. Social psychologists came up with four ways to explain the attitude-behavior connection: the specificity principle, self-perception theory, impression management theory, and the theory of planned behavior.

CRITICAL THINKING CHALLENGE

- What are the ethics of using a bogus pipeline? Should participants be "fooled" into thinking we can detect lies, to increase their honesty in other parts of a research study? What are the ethical and research implications of using techniques like this?

- Think of two reasons to *not* trust the results of an IAT. Now go one step further: How would *you* go about measuring attitudes toward something that people were reluctant to talk about or that they might not even be aware they have? In other words, what would be a better way to measure implicit attitudes?

- Think about a goal you have in life, such as (1) going to graduate school, (2) having a happy family, or (3) finding the perfect career. Choose one or two goals you have and explain how your behavioral intentions are explained by your attitude toward organ donation, your subjective norms, and your perceived control.

HOW DO ATTITUDES CHANGE?

>> **LO 6.3:** **Analyze how cognitive dissonance and paths to persuasion can change attitudes.**

Billions of dollars are poured into changing your attitudes.

Politicians want you to vote for them. Companies selling products want you to think your life will change after you buy their brand of shampoo, shoes, cars, and so on. Lawyers want you to hire them and, if you're on a jury, vote for their client. Nonprofits want you to listen to their public service announcements about smoking or the environment or not texting while driving.

So, do the campaigns work? Do our attitudes change (and therefore our behaviors)? The final section of this chapter answers the question "How do attitudes change?" by covering

(1) cognitive dissonance, or how we change our *own* minds;

(2) the structure of persuasive messages; and

(3) four specific persuasion techniques others use on us.

Cognitive Dissonance
Leads Us to Change Our Own Mind

How do terrorists sleep peacefully at night?

How do the Somali soldiers who assaulted women, buried them up to their necks, and then stoned them to death for refusing to marry them (Gettleman, 2011) eat breakfast the next day and live their "normal" lives? deWijze (2019) proposes naming some belief systems as "political evil" because they justify cruelty as normal. We can convince ourselves that our actions are justified—even moral—if we adjust our attitudes and beliefs accordingly.

Think about some historic examples of U.S. presidents who seemed to persuade themselves that what they were doing was right. Lyndon Johnson ignored evidence as he kept committing more American troops to a losing cause in Vietnam. President Richard Nixon created exotic justifications for illegal actions in the Watergate scandal. President Bill Clinton manufactured desperate explanations for lying about an affair in the White House. President George Bush created new justifications for invading Iraq even after failing to discover weapons of mass destruction.

Above, we said that self-affirmation theory is the idea that we try to preserve our sense of worth. Similarly, **self-justification** is the desire to defend our actions in a way that preserves (or enhances) our self-esteem and self-concept. We want to think

Self-justification:
The desire to explain our actions in a way that preserves or enhances a positive view of the self.

of ourselves as ethical, intelligent, good people. When that view comes into question, it causes **cognitive dissonance**, a state of psychological discomfort that occurs when we experience conflicting beliefs and behaviors (Festinger, 1957; Tavris & Aronson, 2007). When we feel cognitive dissonance, we often change our beliefs, perceptions, or attitudes in ways to reduce the anxiety. The Spotlight on Research Methods feature describes the methods used in one of the early experiments testing cognitive dissonance.

An Ingenious Method to Create Cognitive Dissonance

Leon Festinger's classic study on cognitive dissonance invented a clever methodology (Festinger & Carlsmith, 1959) that demonstrated how cognitive dissonance motivates attitude change.

- College students were asked to complete boring tasks. One had them spend 30 minutes turning 48 square pegs in quarter turns—and then start over again when they finished all 48. It was boring by design! Then, the experimenter asked them for a favor: Would they mind telling the next participant (who was actually a *confederate*, a researcher pretending to be a participant) that the task was super exciting and fun?

- Participants were told they would be paid for telling the lie, but here's where the experimental manipulation came in (the *independent variable*): Half were given $1 for telling the lie; the other half were given $20. (In 1950, $1 was comparable to $10 in 2020 and $20 was worth about $200.)

- After the participant lied, they were asked to report their true feelings about the task. How much fun was it really to turn those knobs?

Most people don't like to think of themselves as liars. But lying for $20? That was a great deal of money, especially in the 1950s. So telling a simple, harmless lie for a welcome $20 represented what Festinger and Carlsmith (1959) called *sufficient justification.* We are less likely to actually believe—or even pretend to believe—our little lie because that $20 gives us a ready explanation: Cognitive dissonance is low.

However, if you're willing to lie for only $1, what kind of person are you? Most of us wouldn't want to believe that we're willing to lie for just $1. To Festinger and Carlsmith (1959), the $1 lie represented *insufficient justification*—so, telling a lie for just $1 would generate high levels of cognitive dissonance.

It's overdramatic to say we've sold our soul to the devil for just $1, but that's the general idea—we've compromised our self-concept and gotten very little in exchange (see Bargh, 2018). But after we've done the deed, we would like to be rid of the dissonance. But how?

The simplest solution to our personal problem appeals to the cognitive miser in each of us: Just tell another lie. But this time, we need to lie to ourselves. Festinger and Carlsmith (1959) didn't call it a lie; they called it making it "easier for anyone . . . to persuade himself" (p. 206).

So, we tell ourselves that hey, it wasn't a lie, . . . turning those knobs was actually kind of fun! As predicted, the participants telling the lie for $1 were more likely to report that the boring task really was enjoyable, compared to those paid $20. Their higher levels of cognitive dissonance led to more attitude change.

When Prophecy Fails: A Case Study in Dissonance

When Leon Festinger (1957) introduced the theory of cognitive dissonance, he framed his theory around a question: Why did so many believers in doomsday cults become *more* committed to their beliefs when their leaders' prophecies failed?

There are many examples of failed prophecies of Jesus' return. Jesus did not return to Turkey (in the second century), to Germany (in 1533), to Jewish believers (in 1648), or to the United States (in 1844), even though "prophets" said that he would.

Cognitive dissonance: A state of psychological discomfort that occurs when we experience conflicting beliefs and behaviors.

AP Photo/Charles E. Knoblock

Dorothy Martin (identified as Marian Keech in Festinger's report) led a group who believed aliens would save them from a world-ending flood on December 21, 1954.

With each failed prophecy, some abandoned their beliefs. But many others became *more,* not less, committed to their positive attitudes toward their doomsday cults (Nichol, 1944). They created exotic explanations to resolve their dissonance, such as the prayers of the faithful had spared the world from disaster. Their belief saved the world!

Consider another example, this time about aliens. In the 1950s, one small group expected that a representative of the planet Clarion would arrive on a flying saucer to save them from a world-ending flood (Festinger et al., 1956/2008). This prophecy came from a woman named Dorothy Martin, a Chicago housewife. As the date for disaster drew closer (December 21, 1954), many followers increased their commitment. They left their jobs, dropped out of college, and left their unbelieving spouses. "I've cut every tie," declared one, "I've burned every bridge . . . I can't afford to doubt" (p. 170).

As the group huddled together on December 21, there was a knock on the door! But it was only some pranking teenagers. Midnight at Dorothy Martin's home came . . . and went: no floods, no flying saucers. The mental distress was terrific—until Dorothy Martin received the most joyous message of all from her alien friends: They had saved the world! The little group's sturdy faith, utter purity of purpose, and deep commitment to the truth had saved the world from destruction! The small group of enthusiastic believers started calling reporters to share the good news.

Let's assume that this group of people didn't really save the world from an alien flood—that their prophecy just didn't come true. At this point, they might have experienced some serious cognitive dissonance. They had given up their lives to be here, abandoned friends and relationships, and might have felt pretty silly. But instead of simply admitting all of that, many of them only further embraced their attitude that everything Dorothy Martin had said was true. Which would you choose: admit that your core beliefs were embarrassingly wrong—or create self-glorifying justifications for why you had been right all along?

Why does cognitive dissonance matter? Certainly, there are historical examples of people whose bad decisions snowball into colossal mistakes. We've already talked about hanging innocent people for witchcraft, sending innocent daycare workers to prison, or miscalculating the date of Jesus' return. Little lies we tell ourselves and build into a "mental trap" (Vohra & Singh, 2005) of self-justifications can grow bigger very quickly. For example, American soldiers who actually killed Iraqis were more likely to believe the war was beneficial to *both* countries, compared to soldiers who didn't have to kill people (Wayne et al., 2011; see Harmon-Jones et al., 2015). Soldiers have to resolve their cognitive dissonance by believing in their cause.

Cognitive dissonance does not have only grim, unpleasant consequences. It can also be used for problem-solving psychological intervention that motivate people to change their attitudes in positive ways. Public health researchers videotaped teenagers giving advice to other teenagers about how to increase their fruit and vegetable intake. Those teens then improved their own diets and self-concepts (Wilson et al., 2002).

Likewise, some sorority sisters experienced dissonance when they were required to publicly speak out against the thin ideal of female appearance. They reduced their bulimic behaviors. Moreover, Figure 6.3 suggests that for high-risk participants, cognitive dissonance continued to reduce their bulimia-related behaviors 8 months later (Becker et al., 2008).

In short, if you publicly endorse healthy habits, you'd experience cognitive dissonance if you didn't engage in those habits yourself. This is one reason that doctors

FIGURE 6.3

The six steps in McGuire's (1985) communication-persuasion process.

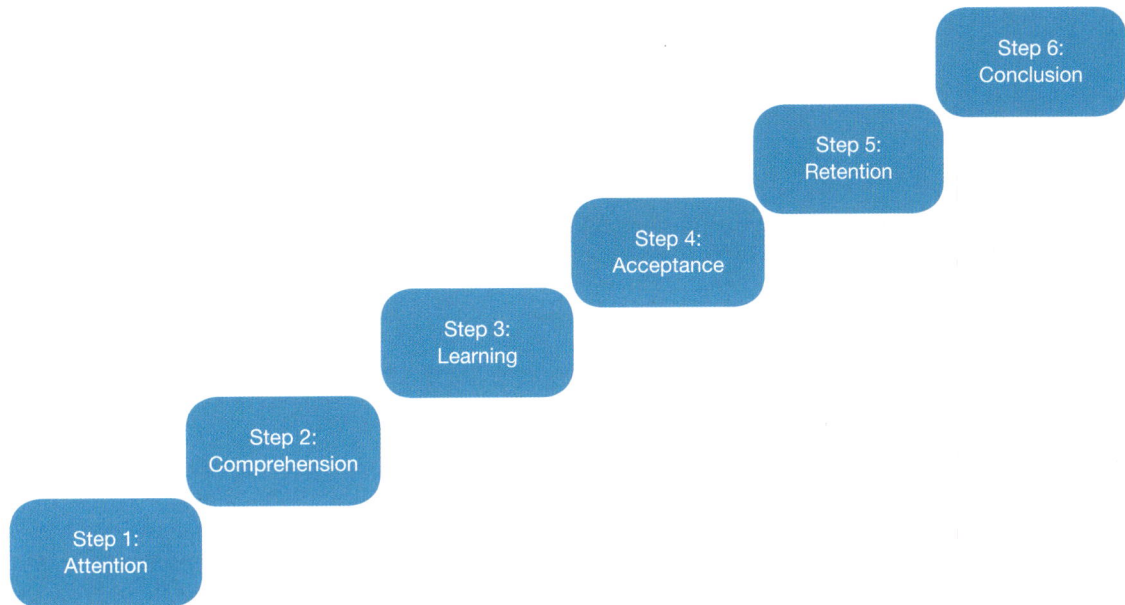

Source: Adapted from McGuire (1985).

and psychologists recommend that you publicly post things like New Year's resolutions regarding more exercise or stopping smoking: You're more motivated to follow through, to avoid embarrassment, and to reduce cognitive dissonance.

Individual and Cultural Differences in Dissonance

Why did some members of Dorothy Martin's alien doomsday cult abandon her when her prophecies failed? Why did others persist?

There are individual differences in how much dissonance we can stand before we abandon a treasured belief (Guild et al., 1977; Stone & Cooper, 2001). Extraverts can tolerate more dissonance than introverts (Matz et al., 2008)—and so can people with more symptoms of psychopathy (Murray et al., 2012). We are more likely to experience dissonance when we're worried about being perceived as a hypocrite (Aronson, 1999) or when our self-concept is threatened (Steele, 1988).

Cultural differences also influence cognitive dissonance created by lying. In one study (Mealy et al., 2007), Euro-Americans rated lying as more acceptable than Ecuadorians. However, people in both cultures rated lying to an outgroup as more acceptable than lying to their ingroup. We don't feel as bad when we lie to our "enemies." There is also a cultural difference in what is experienced as dissonant. *In*dependent-minded Americans experienced dissonance when their personal sense of competency was threatened. By contrast, *inter*dependent-minded Asians experienced more dissonance when they were threatened with group rejection (Kitayama et al., 2004).

The take-home message is that sometimes we change our beliefs and attitudes because we want to maintain a view of ourselves as reasonable people who make good decisions. When that view is threatened, we justify our actions and change our attitudes in ways that benefit us. In short, we sometimes persuade ourselves. But the last two sections of this chapter focus on when other people try to persuade us. How do others try to change our mind?

Paths to Persuasion: The Structure of Persuasive Messages Matters

Leaders of doomsday cults are not the only ones in the persuasion business.

Politicians, preachers, and prostitutes are all in the persuasion business. So are professors when they harp about critical thinking. Potential romantic partners also need to be persuaded about how wonderful you are. To be an ordinary, successful, social animal, we humans must be able to persuade and be persuaded.

Direct and Indirect Attempts: Are You Paying Attention?

Think about two commercials, both for the same new cell phone. Which would you find more persuasive?

> Commercial 1: Uses humor, fun music, and a famous well-liked actor
>
> Commercial 2: Explicitly explains the technology, new apps, and affordability of the phone

Both commercials can be very effective—and which one appeals to you more depends on a lot. The first approach is indirect and makes use of things like heuristics and emotional appeal. The second approach is direct and makes use of logic and common sense. If people are paying attention because they are highly motivated to get a new phone and want to know why this one is the best, the direct approach will work. If people are distracted, not motivated, or unable to understand the information about technology and apps, then the indirect approach is more effective (Petty & Cacioppo, 1986; see Monroe & Read, 2008).

The elaboration likelihood model (or ELM) proposes that there are two paths to persuasion (Petty & Cacioppo, 1986; see Monroe & Read, 2008). The first is a direct, explicit, or "central" route (which requires cognitive "elaboration" or thoughtful examination of the message). The second is an indirect, implicit, or "peripheral" route. The ELM says that the central route works best when an audience is high in both *ability* and *motivation* to pay attention to the message. If either ability or motivation is low, more persuasion will happen via the peripheral route.

A similar model, the heuristic-systematic model (or HSM; Chaiken, 1980; Chen & Chaiken, 1999), uses slightly different language but proposes essentially the same idea: There are two paths, one direct and one indirect. Which one to use depends on the audience (see Petty & Wegener, 1998).

Persuasion in the Courtroom, in Sports, and in Retail

Imagine you're on the jury for the Little Rascals case about accusations of child sex abuse at a daycare.

Two lawyers are trying to persuade you to see their side of the story. Some of your fellow jurors will rely on logical reasoning and physical evidence. They will be open to complicated explanations for motive and opportunity. These types of arguments follow the direct, elaborate, systematic, or central path to persuasion. They require the audience to both pay attention and understand the arguments. Theoretically, this kind of careful evaluation of reasonable doubt lies at the heart of the American judicial system.

However, the lawyers for the prosecution will probably promote indirect, highly emotional paths to persuasion. Innocent children should never be victimized! It is our responsibility as adults to protect our children. They will use emotional appeals that combine fear of the unknown suspect and empathy toward the victims. Each side may try to impress the jury by wearing expensive suits—and it also doesn't hurt if the lawyers and defendants are good looking. This type of evidence follows the (indirect) peripheral path to persuasion.

A real-life example of persuasion using the central or systematic route was highlighted in the film *Moneyball*, starring Brad Pitt; see the Social Psychology in Popular

Elaboration likelihood model: Proposes two paths to persuasion: a direct, explicit, "central" route and an indirect, implicit, "peripheral" route. Which works better depends on the audience's ability and motivation to pay attention.

Heuristic-systematic model: Proposes two paths to persuasion, called the "heuristic" (indirect) path and the "systematic" (direct) path.

Culture feature for more. While sports is a multibillion-dollar industry, even more money is spent every year on buying and selling of retail products.

Robert Cialdini (2001) described how the indirect, peripheral-heuristic path to persuasion worked when a retail storeowner was having difficulty selling turquoise jewelry to well-to-do vacationers. She had directed an employee to reprice the items at half off. But the employee misunderstood the message and doubled the price.

The surprising thing was that the tourists quickly bought out the previously difficult-to-sell jewelry at the much higher price. Why? The tourists were probably using a heuristic that simplified their decision making to "More expensive = Better quality" or "You get what you pay for." They quickly determined the jewelry was valuable and therefore had to have it.

The indirect path also makes use of celebrity endorsements. Why do we care what famous people think (Gakhal & Senior, 2008)? The **communication-persuasion matrix** (McGuire, 1985) helps explain by laying out six steps to persuasion. Figure 6.3 notes that Step 1 is just getting our attention—and famous people tend to do that. If we were already interested in the product, then we wouldn't need Step 1, the celebrity endorsement. We would use the central route to decide whether to buy the product (Kim & Na, 2007; Lee & Thorson, 2008). Celebrity endorsements are a way to drag potential buyers onto the peripheral-heuristic path toward a sale (Pieters et al., 2002).

Communication-persuasion matrix: Proposes six steps in the persuasion process—attention, comprehension, learning, acceptance, retention, and conclusion—which build on each other.

SOCIAL PSYCHOLOGY IN POPULAR CULTURE

▶ Persuasion in *Moneyball*

Pictorial Press Ltd / Alamy Stock Photo

"He's got a baseball body."

"Clean cut, good face." "Good jaw." "Ugly girlfriend."

In the year 2002, professional baseball scouts knew what they wanted—and they used tradition, stereotypes, and heuristics to guide them. The quotations above are from the sports film *Moneyball* (DeLuca et al., 2011). They represent some of the criteria the scouts used in selecting new players.

Oakland A's general manager Billy Beane (played by Brad Pitt) had a low budget, and he suspected his scouts weren't using the best strategy to find a winning team. So instead of relying on their stereotypes and

heuristics—a form of intuition—he put all his efforts into choosing players using statistics. *Moneyball* is the true story of Beane attempting to persuade the entire world of baseball that statistics were the way to win.

It was a hard sell, and at first no one believed in his strategy. In the film, a sports announcer voices his doubts: "This is not about statistics. This is about people." But when Beane's team started winning, people started changing their minds. Everyone involved had high ability and high motivation, so both the elaboration likelihood model and the heuristic-systematic model say they should have found logic and statistics persuasive. When the A's broke the record for longest streak of wins in baseball history, the critics finally believed in his unconventional strategy. Beane noted, "People are overlooked for a variety of biased reasons and perceived flaws. Age, appearance, personality."

He eventually succeeded in persuading fans, coaches, and team owners by focusing on logic and results: the central, direct route. In the end, his strategy took off and changed the entire world of professional baseball. One of the best lines in the movie is when Beane says, "Using stats the way we read them, we'll find value in players that nobody else can see." It's not a romantic strategy—but don't we all want to be seen for our true value?

Four Elements of Persuasion: The Message-Learning Approach

Hitler and his advisors were great at propaganda.

World War II resulted in at least 60 million deaths and a huge psychological imprint on multiple generations. One researcher, Carl Hovland, attempted to understand the persuasion processes that occurred so quickly and so effectively during the war. How did Nazi Germany—as well as other countries around the world—use propaganda posters and films to persuade the masses to believe in their cause and to get involved in the fight? Hovland's work produced the **message-learning approach** to persuasion (see Hovland et al., 1949; Hovland et al., 1953; Reis, 2019).

Hovland's straightforward approach, represented in Figure 6.4, reasoned that there were four elements to the persuasion process: the source, the message, the recipient, and the context (Hovland et al., 1953). An easy way to remember these elements is that they all answer the same general question: "Who (the source) said what (the message) to whom (the recipient) and how (the context)?" Consider each element of persuasion attempts in turn.

FIGURE 6.4

The message-learning approach to persuasion.

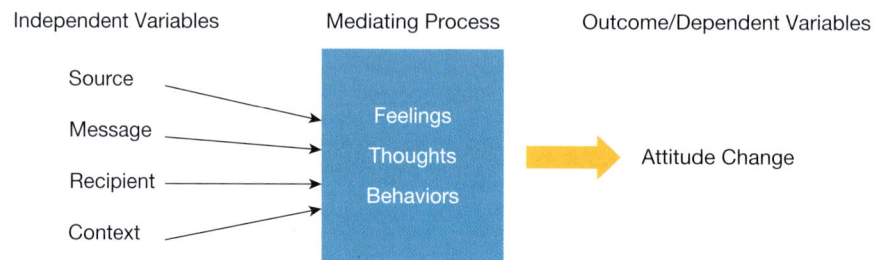

Source: Adapted from Petty and Wegener (1998).

Who: Source Variables. Source variables refer to who is giving the message. Several characteristics of the speaker can make the message more or less persuasive. For example:

- *Credibility:* Sources are considered more credible (and thus more persuasive) when they present a message that seems impartial (Eagly et al., 1978; Weber et al., 2012) and coming from an expert (Levenson et al., 1975).

- *Attractiveness:* Remember the what-is-beautiful-is-good effect (Chapter 5)? Beautiful speakers are perceived as more believable (Chaiken, 1980; Puckett et al., 1983), trustworthy, and educated on the subject (Praxmarer, 2011).

Said What: Message Variables. Message variables are the actual content of the message—what information was given? There seem to be two main factors here:

- *Personal importance:* We're more persuaded when the speaker explains how the issue matters to us, directly (e.g., Johnson & Eagly, 1989; Petty et al., 1992; Sherif et al., 1965; Zimbardo, 1960).

- *Framing:* Persuasion works better if you motivate parents by explaining how something like getting vaccinations positively affects the next generation or by focusing on positive aspects instead of negative aspects (Marsh et al., 2014).

Message-learning approach: Proposes that there are four elements to the persuasion process: the source (who is doing the persuading), the message (the persuasive information), the recipient (whom they are persuading), and the context (how they are persuading).

Source variables: Who creates and gives a persuasive message.

Message variables: The information provided in a persuasive message and how it is framed.

To Whom: Recipient Variables. Recipient variables are the audience, or the people receiving the message. Some critical recipient variables include the following:

- *Attitude strength:* If the audience has already made up their minds, persuasion will be much harder (Krosnick & Petty, 1995).

- *Intelligence:* Better-educated or smarter people are more likely to understand scientific evidence and focus on central messages instead of peripheral messages (Petty & Wegener, 1998; Rhodes & Wood, 1992).

- *Personality:* People who are high in openness to experience are more willing to consider new perspectives and possibly change their minds (see Gerber et al., 2013).

- *Self-esteem:* People with high self-esteem have the confidence to consider central-route arguments and use critical thinking to come to a reasoned conclusion, while people with low self-esteem can be more stubborn (Perloff & Brock, 1980).

- *Need for cognition:* Finally, people high in the need for cognition prefer the central route, as they enjoy deep thinking and analysis of messages (Cacioppo et al., 1996).

How: Context Variables. Finally, context variables refer to what's going on around the message. What are the situational circumstances happening when the message is being delivered? They include the following:

- *Distraction:* If there are a lot of distractions happening in the environment or in the recipient's mind, the message will be less persuasive and the audience will switch from the central path to the peripheral path (Festinger & Maccoby, 1964; Insko et al., 1974; Kiesler & Mathog, 1968).

- *Forewarning:* If you're specifically trying to *not* be persuaded by a message (see Petty & Cacioppo, 1979), you can resist it by generating counterarguments along the way (Cialdini et al., 1976; Leippe & Elkin, 1987; Tetlock, 1992).

- *Repetition:* There's a reason you keep seeing the same commercials over and over: Repetition helps build persuasion (see Gorn & Goldberg, 1980; Guo et al., 2019). It can be jingles that get stuck in your head, hundreds of signs in front yards with a candidate's name on them, or Internet device coordination so that the same user sees the same ads on their phone, computer, and tablet (see Aksu et al., 2018; Cecen, 2019).

Direct Persuasion Techniques: Straight-Up Manipulation Can Work

You already know about the two paths to persuasion (central route vs. peripheral route).

But there are also specific techniques that companies, politicians, and social persuaders use to gain your compliance. Knowing what these persuasion attempts look like can help inoculate you against their effectiveness. When you recognize them, you can wake up and say, "Aha! I can see what's going on here." Or, on the other hand, you can always use them yourself to persuade others.

The four specific techniques we'll cover in this last section are based on two overall psychological concepts: (1) commitment and consistency and (2) the norm of reciprocity.

Commitment and Consistency

Commitment and consistency go hand in hand.

Most of us want to present ourselves as logical, reliable, and "good" people, both to others and to ourselves. If we make a promise (especially a public one), we're

Recipient variables: The audience of a persuasive message.

Context variables: Situational aspects of how a message is received, such as repetition.

embarrassed if we don't keep it. Our preference for commitment and consistency leads us to be persuaded by two specific techniques.

The Lowball Technique.
Cialdini (2007) describes a technique he observed in salespeople at a car dealership.

The dealership would offer a fantastic deal, such as zero percent financing. Potential buyers would visit based on the offer and while there would engage in "ownership" behaviors such as test driving the car and discussing the car's benefits. Once the customer decided to purchase the car, however, the salesperson would suddenly discover a problem with the original incentive, such as the customer's low credit score. While some potential buyers would then leave, a surprising number bought the car anyway! Of course, the "scam" is that almost no one actually gets to cash in on the amazing original offer.

The lowball technique is offering a "deal" that changes after someone has decided to commit—and our need for consistency makes us move forward with the decision, even though the reason has changed. Cialdini (2007) explains this strange decision as customers being cognitively and emotionally committed to the purchase. It would be inconsistent to not purchase a product they've decided they want—even when the terms have changed.

Foot-in-the-Door Technique.
The foot-in-the-door technique occurs when agreeing to a small initial request makes us more likely to later agree to a much larger request.

It's like starting down a path that you just keep doing down. Charities often begin with asking you for a very small commitment, such as simply providing your email address or signing a petition. They might then follow this with progressively larger requests such as asking for donations of time or money. If you agreed to the first request, you must support this charity and believe in what it does—right? Failing to then agree to a later request may cause dissonance if you see your actions as inconsistent.

The name for this persuasion technique is a metaphor harking back to the old-fashioned door-to-door salesman, who might stick his foot in your door to avoid getting it shut in his face. If he can just get you to agree to a brief conversation about his fantastic product, you might then agree to invite him in. If you invite him in, then you might watch his demonstration and even purchase his product. The longer you continue on the path, the more likely you are to keep going because your behavior indicates that you must be interested.

Perhaps the most famous scientific study of the foot-in-the-door technique comes from residential California in the 1960s (Freedman & Fraser, 1966). Psychologists posing as volunteers walked around neighborhoods asking homeowners if they would be willing to display a small (3-inch square) sticker reading, "Be a Safe Driver." Almost everyone agreed to this tiny request. After all, isn't everyone in favor of safe driving? But Phase 2 of the study was the central test: When those same homeowners were approached 2 weeks later and asked if they would agree to a huge, ugly billboard in their yard reading, "Drive Carefully," would they say yes this time?

Freedman and Fraser (1966) found that if the request to display a billboard in the yard was the *first* thing they asked people (a control group), almost everyone refused. However, when they specifically went to the homes of people who had first agreed to post the tiny sticker 2 weeks earlier, fully 76% of these residents agreed to the billboard request. The researchers concluded that people who agreed to the initial, small request viewed themselves as agreeable, civic-minded citizens who cared about safe driving in their neighborhood. So refusing a request on the same issue later would be inconsistent with their view of themselves. Commitment and consistency led them to agree to actions that most other people saw as unreasonable.

The Norm of Reciprocity

Other techniques come from social norms.

One is the norm of reciprocity, which directs us to respond in kind to courtesies and concessions from others: You scratch my back; I scratch yours. We expect a fair exchange, and we feel guilty if we're the ones to break this social norm. Two specific

Lowball technique: A persuasion technique where people follow through with a decision even after the terms of a "deal" have changed.

Foot-in-the-door technique: A persuasion technique where people are more likely to agree to a big request if they've already said yes to a smaller one.

Norm of reciprocity: The idea that individuals respond in kind to courtesies and concessions from others, because we like things to be "fair."

persuasion techniques make use of the norm of reciprocity.

Door-in-the-Face Technique. The door-in-the-face technique occurs when we refuse a big request but later agree to a smaller request.

It's the opposite of foot-in-the-door, which starts small and gets progressively bigger due to commitment and consistency. Door-in-the-face starts big and then gets smaller—but the trick to this technique is that the eventual small request is what the asker wanted all along.

Imagine you want your friend to help you move a heavy chair. To get her to help, you might start by asking her if she is willing to *buy* you a new chair! She will probably (and reasonably) say no. You could then ask her to help you move all the furniture in your apartment—and she might say no again. But now, if you say, "Are you at least willing to help me move this one chair?" she is more likely to agree. You compromised (or at least, pretended to)—so she'll feel pressure to compromise as well, and you get what you wanted all along.

Cialdini and his research team first asked students to volunteer to chaperone a group of juvenile delinquents on a field trip to a zoo; 83% refused. But that was only the baseline comparison rate. Rates of acceptance *tripled* when they first asked students to do something much more demanding: to spend 2 hours per week for at least 2 years as counselors to juvenile delinquents (Cialdini et al., 1975). The field trip now seemed like small potatoes, by comparison. Asking for something big first—and then being turned down (a metaphorical door slammed in your face, which is where this technique gets its name)—makes it easier to engage the norm of reciprocity and gain compliance with a second, relatively smaller request.

Not-So-Free Samples. Free is never free.

The norm of reciprocity makes people more likely to fork over some money if they first have been given a small "gift." In addition to sampling the product, we feel guilty about getting something for nothing, especially when it comes from a smiling and friendly person. Charities use this technique when they send "free" stickers with your name and address printed on them in their mailed requests for donations. In many large, tourist cities, homeless people offer travelers help with directions, then ask for spare change. Survey companies will sometimes include a crisp $1 bill when they mail out their surveys, hoping people will feel guilty if they take the dollar without returning the survey. And if you've ever been to a big store like Costco, they're famous for their "free samples" of food.

We're happy to accept a free gift! But we often then feel at least a small obligation to return the favor. This is how companies can afford to give away so much free stuff—they end up making more profit through the psychology of persuasion.

"Free samples" are used by companies to make you feel guilty if you don't then buy something.

THE MAIN IDEAS

- Cognitive dissonance (incompatible thoughts, feelings, and behaviors) creates a discomfort that motivates us to change our attitudes, often through self-justification.

- Two ways (paths) influence us to change our attitudes: an attention-demanding central path and a heuristically guided peripheral path. In addition, there are four basic elements of a potentially persuasive communication: source, content, recipient, and context.

- The lowball technique and the foot-in-the-door technique are both persuasive because people feel good when they act consistently and with commitment to their decisions. In contrast, the door-in-the-face technique and "free samples" work because of the norm of reciprocity.

Door-in-the-face technique: A persuasion technique where people who refuse a large request are then more likely to agree to a later, smaller request.

CRITICAL THINKING CHALLENGE

- Identify three fictional villains who use self-justification to resolve cognitive dissonance they may feel regarding their evil deeds. In other words, how do these three villains avoid feeling guilty about their actions (and avoid feeling bad about themselves) by justifying what they do?

- Search YouTube for popular commercials (Superbowl commercials are usually good ones). For each product, describe whether the company is using the central route to persuade you (such as telling you how the product will improve your life) or the peripheral route (such as using attractive celebrities, fear, or humor).

- Imagine that you want to convince the professor of this class to offer you an extra credit assignment. How might you use all four of the techniques in this section to persuade them to do so? Describe how you'd use each one.

CHAPTER SUMMARY

What Are Attitudes, and Where Do They Come From?

Attitudes are an inner tendency to evaluate something (an attitude "object") either positively or negatively. We can have dual attitudes (mixed), but usually they lead us toward a univalenced decision (not mixed). Implicit attitudes are automatic, unconscious evaluations while explicit attitudes are thoughtful, reasoned evaluations. Attitudes are formed through both biological factors (such as genetics) and through our experiences (including social learning, classical conditioning, and operant conditioning).

Do Attitudes Predict Behavior?

While it seems obvious that attitudes should predict behavior, research shows that reality is complicated. First, it's sometimes difficult to measure attitudes. For explicit attitudes, one way to increase people's honesty in reporting is to use a fake lie detector called a bogus pipeline. For implicit attitudes, controversial techniques such as the Implicit Association Test (or IAT) measure reaction times in milliseconds and may reflect knowledge of cultural attitudes instead of individual beliefs or evaluations.

Four theories have helped explain whether attitudes really can predict behaviors. First, the specificity principle notes that behaviors are predicted best when attitudes are measured as specifically as possible. Next, self-perception theory states that sometimes, attitudes are formed *after* behaviors occur. Third, impression management is the idea that we sometimes pretend to have attitudes we don't, so that we can fit into our social surrounding. Finally, the theory of planned behavior suggests that while attitudes are needed to predict behavior, we also need to know someone's subjective social norms (whether they think other people are performing the same behavior) and their perceived control (whether they think they will be successful if they try the behavior).

How Do Attitudes Change?

Self-justification is the desire to explain our actions in a way that maintains a positive view of the self. One way that self-justification can drive attitude change is when we experience cognitive dissonance, which is anxiety or discomfort that occurs when we have to confront contradictory beliefs and/or behaviors.

In addition, attitudes can change because of external influence. When someone tries to persuade us, there are two general routes or paths they can take. One is direct, central, and based on providing factual information; this path is used when an audience has high ability and motivation to listen to the message. When audience ability or motivation is low, messages are more persuasive when they are indirect or peripheral, using things like humor, fear, or a celebrity endorsement. Either way, the message-learning approach to persuasion states that four aspects of persuasion attempts that matter are source variables (who's giving the message), message variables (what it actually says), recipient variables (who's listening), and context variables (the situational environment).

Finally, four specific persuasion techniques can be used on us. The lowball technique and foot-in-the-door technique are both based on the principle of "commitment and consistency." This is the idea that we like to appear consistent and to follow through with decisions. Alternatively, the door-in-the-face technique and "free samples" are based on the norm of reciprocity. This is the idea that we like things to be "fair" and feel obligated if someone else has already done us a favor or appeared to compromise.

CRITICAL THINKING, ANALYSIS, AND APPLICATION

- First, identify a personal attitude you have about (a) a particular politician, (b) a musical group you either love or hate, and (c) a social controversy of your choice (capital punishment, abortion, civil rights, etc.). For each of these three attitudes, try to identify (a) how you formed this attitude—the source of your opinion—and (b) whether your attitude seems to predict actual behavior.

- Almost every chapter in this book includes a self-report scale in which you answer questions about an attitude or opinion you have. As you take these scales, are you always completely honest? If not, why not? Do you find yourself potentially being dishonest because you want others to have a certain impression of you—or is it possible that you are even being dishonest with yourself? Would use of a bogus pipeline change your answers?

- Think about two specific times that you changed your mind after someone tried to persuade you. One incident should be a time when you were persuaded through the "central route," and one should be a time when you were persuaded through the "peripheral" route. Identify differences in how you were persuaded and whether the two different routes led to any discrepancies in the outcomes (e.g., different emotions about your changed opinion, differences in how long the change lasted).

- Is it ethical to use the persuasion techniques such as lowballing, foot-in-the-door, door-in-the-face, and free samples? Does the answer depend on what you are trying to get someone to do—such as vote for a politician versus live a healthier lifestyle? Defend your answer.

iStockPhoto/stop123

7

Social Influence

Conformity, Social Roles, and Obedience

Core Questions

7.1 What types of social influence exist?

7.2 What social forces compel conformity?

7.3 How are we influenced by social roles and obedience to authority?

Learning Objectives

7.1 Compare and contrast types of implicit versus explicit social influence.

7.2 Describe how informational and normative pressures to conform have persisted over generations and across cultures.

7.3 Analyze key experiments that demonstrate influence through social roles, obedience, and the power of the situation.

You are not alone if you recall middle school and high school as hard chapters in your life.

It is a time when social influence applies constant peer pressure (Brown, 1982) and popularity depends on knowing and conforming to unwritten rules. **Social influence** is when we change our thoughts, feelings, and behaviors because of pressure from our social world. Fortunately, as we grow older, our possible social roles expand far beyond the boundaries of high school stereotypes around sports, geekdom, or the arts.

Social roles continue to influence us as we age. Adults at social gatherings tend to ask, "What do you do for a living?" to identify individuals and form impressions. We feel the pressure of too many or conflicting social roles (Arthur & Lee, 2008). Our deeper commitments to certain roles (as parent, employee, lover, or friend) mature into social influences that stabilize society—we gradually become the gears that keep societies up and running. Sometimes, social influence is good: It might make us recycle or give to charity when we don't really want to. But history is also full of times when social influence went terribly wrong.

This chapter talks about both sides, and we highlight that a healthy society requires one more social role, a role that many are reluctant to play: the rebellious nonconformist (see Sunstein, 2019).

WHAT TYPES OF SOCIAL INFLUENCE EXIST?

>> LO 7.1: **Compare and contrast types of implicit versus explicit social influence.**

Mindless conformity, automatic social roles, and blind obedience can trick us into sleepwalking through our own lives. This section answers the core question "What types of social influence exist?" by

(1) distinguishing between implicit and explicit types of social influence,

(2) describing how social conformity can create a herd mentality, and

(3) documenting unusual cases of contagious conformity.

Two Categories of Social Influence

Social influence can be organized into two overlapping categories: implicit expectations and explicit expectations.

Implicit Expectations

Implicit expectations are the unwritten rules enforced by our social world. They are group norms that you learn by observing the world around you and sometimes when people give you compliments or tease you when you do (or don't) "fit in."

There are two types of implicit expectations. The first is **conformity**, voluntarily changing your behavior to imitate those around you. Twenty-five years from now, you will probably look at a current picture of yourself and wonder how you could have made such terrible fashion choices. You were simply wearing what everyone else was wearing. You learned the "rules" implicitly by observing others and by seeing the clothes advertised in ads and shops.

A second form of implicit social influence comes from **social roles**, expectations about how people are "supposed" to act based on their position. Social roles make up our stereotypes about people with different genders, careers, and even different hobbies. They are like characters we play, acting in given ways because it's what we're expected to do. Teachers wear different clothes and act differently than rock stars or ministers. We may not realize we have expectations for these social roles until they are violated (like an elderly Catholic nun in New York who wears a bikini and belts out Black Sabbath tunes).

Social influence: When our thoughts, feelings, and behaviors change because of pressure from our social world.

Implicit expectations: Unspoken rules enforced by group norms that influence our behavior.

Conformity: A type of implicit social influence when we voluntarily change our behavior to imitate those around us.

Social roles: A type of implicit social influence regarding how certain people are supposed to look.

FIGURE 7.1

Implicit expectations (conformity and social roles) plus explicit expectations (compliance and obedience). Sometimes, these four forms of social influence overlap.

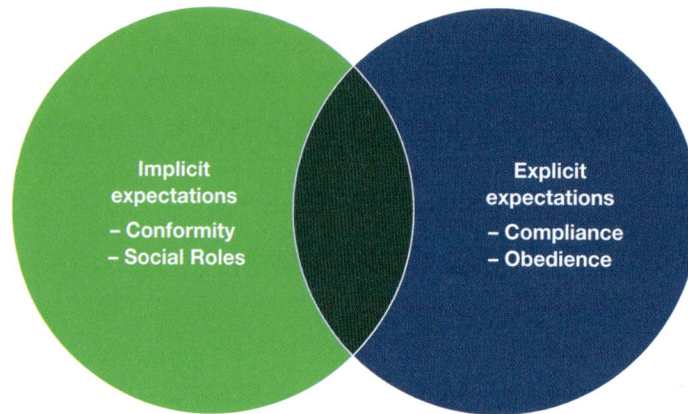

Explicit Expectations

Unlike implicit expectations, **explicit expectations** are clearly stated.

Some London curbs use explicit influence by painting "LOOK TO YOUR RIGHT!" as a reminder to non-British pedestrians about which side the cars are on. Museums mark off areas you're not allowed to enter, and fancy green spaces sometimes have signs like "Don't walk on the grass." There are also two forms of explicit expectations: compliance and obedience.

Compliance occurs when you behave in response to a direct or indirect *request*. Although they felt awkward doing it, healthy young graduate students asked people on a New York City subway to give up their seat. About two thirds of the subway riders complied (Milgram & Sabini, 1978)—just because someone asked. Compliance is a request, not a demand. There's not usually a punishment if you don't do it, but social norms make you feel at least some pressure to go along with these requests. When my partner [Wind's] got too close while inspecting a small display in the Minneapolis museum of contemporary art, one of the guards yelled, "STEP AWAY FROM THE ART!" She proceeded to follow us until we left the building, but we weren't "punished."

In contrast, **obedience** occurs when you change your behavior in response to an order from someone with power over you. It might be someone of higher status (like your boss) or someone who can directly punish you if you don't do it (like a mugger asking for your wallet). The expectation is stated clearly and often accompanied by an explicit consequence if you choose to disobey. In general, obedience can be considered a more extreme version of compliance.

As Figure 7.1 points out, there are times when implicit and explicit expectations can overlap. An unspoken (implicit) dress code at work might cross over to compliance if you're threatened with being fired unless you change clothes. A parent might have expectations for how you act that aren't direct requests, and the only "punishment" in not following their expectations is that they might tell you, "I'm not mad, I'm just disappointed." The social world is complex, and we often feel pressure to act on a variety of implicit and explicit levels.

Social Norms Can Create a Herd Mentality

Do you think of yourself as a nonconformist?

Our impulse to conform begins much earlier in life than you might imagine. Infants will imitate others when they are only 2 to 3 weeks old. Growing infants will automatically

Explicit expectations: Clearly and formally stated expectations for social behavior.

Compliance: A type of explicit social influence when we behave in response to a direct or indirect request.

Obedience: A type of explicit social influence when we behave in response to an order from someone with power over us.

August Landmesser defied social pressures to give the Nazi salute, probably because he had fallen in love with a Jewish woman, Irma Eckler. He was banned from the Nazi party after he and Eckler became engaged, and they were later denied a marriage license. If you want to learn more, several websites describe his quiet heroism in fighting against social pressures—with tragic consequences.

clap when others clap (see Meltzoff & Moore, 1977, 1989). Small children will whisper back when others whisper to them. Older children will automatically imitate one another's eating habits (Johnston, 2002).

As we grow older, we absorb these behaviors as **social norms** (also called **group norms**), the unwritten rules that indicate how people are expected to behave. They are, by definition, what's "normal." The practical rewards for social conformity are significant: They make us more popular and more likely to be appealing to potential romantic partners (Buss & Kenrick, 1998).

However, social norms can become dangerous. A **herd mentality** develops when humans blindly follow a group. At its worst, "going along to get along" encourages authoritarian leaders to require unquestioning unanimity. Nonconformists who go against the group can be courageous rebels—but they are often punished severely, like brave August Landmesser, who stood up against the Nazi regime in World War II.

In a herd of animals, each has to move in the same direction or they might get trampled. Can this be a metaphor for human tendencies to conform?

Conforming Is Contagious

It can be awkward to attend your first holiday meal with new in-laws.

No one tells you that Grandpa always sits in a particular chair or that the holiday meal, announced for 2 p.m., won't arrive at the table until 4:30. Your new relatives do not have to say anything to communicate their social norms. Instead, you observe that

Social norms: Implicit social rules about how people should behave.

Group norms: See *social norms.*

Herd mentality: The tendency to blindly follow the direction your group is moving toward.

at 2 p.m., the dining room table isn't set, the cooking is just getting started, no one sits in Grandpa's chair, and no one else seems surprised that the meal is so "late."

However, to their way of thinking—your new family's social norm—the meal is right on time. "Dinner is at 2 p.m." really means, "Come on over sometime in the afternoon; we'll start cooking." It probably didn't even occur to your new spouse to mention these social norms (see Gulati & Puranam, 2009). But next year, you will know better. Social norms communicate implicit yet specific guidance about social expectations.

A Harmless Social Contagion

This next study is like a mysterious highway traffic jam that develops when there is nothing to see.

Social contagion is the spontaneous distribution of ideas, attitudes, and behaviors among larger groups of people. One person on a busy New York City street stopped on the sidewalk and stared up at a sixth-floor window of a building (Milgram et al., 1969). That's all it took to start a small social contagion. Make no mistake: There was nothing special in the window—just some distant, difficult-to-see people looking back at them.

After only 60 seconds, the first person stopped staring and moved on. After pauses long enough to allow new sets of participants to enter the scene, groups of 1, 2, 3, 5, 10, or 15 *confederates* (members of the research team pretending to be among the participants) stopped and repeated the procedure while researchers discreetly made a movie of the crowds that formed and dissolved.

Like that mysterious traffic jam, the bigger the initial crowd, the more compelling it was for more people to join it. When a bunch of other people seem fascinated by something, we automatically look as well. Perhaps this is part of FoMO, or "Fear of Missing Out" (Przybylski et al., 2013).

Mass Psychogenic Illness: The Power of Mimicry

Looking up when there's nothing to see is pretty harmless—but social contagion can make people do weird things.

Mass psychogenic illness occurs when there are socially contagious physical symptoms with no physical cause. In the Middle Ages in Europe, rural areas sometimes had a problem called lycanthropy: Groups of villagers suddenly decided they were werewolves! Other superstitions, like belief in witch covens, hit their peak during this time when people in general were suffering from famine, depression, and the Black Death (Carson et al., 1996). People thought they had symptoms like headaches, marks on their body, and more.

Here's a more modern example: About 15 minutes after arriving at Warren County High School in Tennessee, a teacher noticed a "gasoline-like" smell in her classroom. This was followed by a headache, nausea, shortness of breath, and dizziness. The school was evacuated and 80 students and 19 staff members went to the emergency room with various symptoms, resulting in 38 hospitalizations (Jones et al., 2000).

The school reopened 5 days later, but the "epidemic" was not over; 71 more people went to the emergency room. Extensive testing could find no physical cause or evidence of toxic compounds. Researchers eventually noticed that the strange symptoms were communicated through "line of sight." Simply seeing someone whom you believed was ill could trigger hyperventilation. Rashes appeared to be caused by scratching rather than exposure. The Tennessee "outbreak" involved

- 18,000 person-days of lost labor

- 178 emergency room visits

- Eight ambulance trips

- 12 government agencies

- Eight laboratories

Social contagion: The spontaneous distribution of ideas, attitudes, and behaviors among larger groups of people.

Mass psychogenic illness: A form of social contagion where symptoms of an illness appear within a group but have no apparent physical cause.

- About $100,000 in direct medical expenses (in 1998 dollars)

- Thousands more dollars for laboratory tests and field studies

The Tanganyikan Laughter Epidemic

Is it possible to laugh too much?

An extreme version of social contagion was the "Tanganyikan Laughter Epidemic." Three girls attending a small, missionary-run boarding school in what is now Tanzania started laughing. Strangely, the laughter quickly spread to the other students and was accompanied by fainting, a rash, unexplained pain, and occasional screaming. The teachers never "caught" the laughing disease, but when it eventually affected 95 of the 159 students, the school had to be closed.

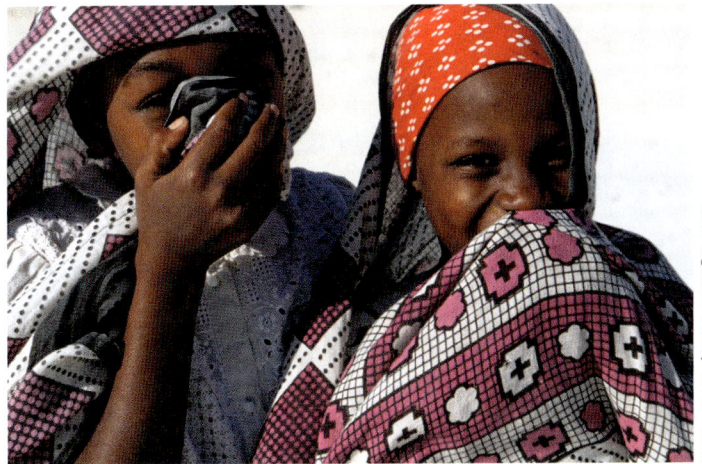

Laughing in Tanganyika (now Tanzania).

Things got worse, but only if you consider more laughter a bad thing. When the students went home, other people in their towns also started laughing. The laughter spread, as it often does. But it also persisted, affecting thousands of people in the region. After 18 months, it all stopped, but only after a total of 14 schools had to be temporarily shut down. About 1,000 people experienced the "symptoms" (Provine, 1996) that defied any medical explanation.

The laughing epidemic suggests that a wide variety of social behaviors—even laughter—can be distributed through social contagion. And don't stereotype young teenage girls as helpless gigglers. Television laugh tracks also rely on contagious laughter (Provine, 1992) as they subtly convey social norms (Rhodes & Ellithorpe, 2016).

Contagious Yawning: Humans, Chimps, and Dogs

Is yawning "catching"?

A new line of research is trying to scientifically answer this old question regarding contagious yawning, a form of facial mimicry. We're discovering that contagious yawning

- happens to many animals, including humans, chimpanzees, and dogs (see Anderson et al., 2004; Bowers, 2018);

- is probably related to empathy (Campbell & de Waal, 2011);

- may help coordinate group responses (see Franzen et al., 2018; Gallup et al., 2019); and

- can even be triggered in virtual reality (Gallup et al., 2019).

This quirky and intriguing example of social influence and, perhaps, an automatic instinct toward conformity may have surprising insights into empathy within and between species.

THE MAIN IDEAS

- Social influence can be either implicit (including conformity and behaving according to a social role) or explicit (including compliance and obedience).

- Informal social norms (also called group norms) are communicated through a process called social contagion and can lead to a herd mentality.

- One extreme form of social contagion or conformity is mass psychogenic illness.

CRITICAL THINKING CHALLENGE

- Explain a specific time in your life when you were influenced by (1) conformity, (2) expected behaviors within a social role, (3) compliance, and (4) obedience.

- Think of two examples when conformity to group norms helps the group but harms the individual. Now, think of two examples of the opposite—when conformity helps the individual but leads to problems for the group. Explain each.

- Identify and explain another time in history when you think a group of people experienced a mass psychogenic illness, beyond the examples provided in this book.

WHAT SOCIAL FORCES COMPEL CONFORMITY?

>> **LO 7.2:** Describe how informational and normative pressures to conform have persisted over generations and across cultures.

Imagine going to an unfamiliar religious ceremony with a friend.

You feel a bit nervous, so you glance at what others are doing. If they kneel or sit or stand, then it's likely that you will do the same. If they take off their shoes, again, it's likely that you will follow along. Most of us perform these actions because we (a) are uncertain about what the correct behavior is, and (b) have anxiety about fitting in. That is why the **theory of informational and normative influence** describes how information uncertainty and social norms compel conformity (Deutsch & Gerard, 1995).

We answer the core question "What social forces compel conformity?" by

(1) describing why informational uncertainty leads to conformity,

(2) demonstrating how social norms demand conformity, and

(3) exploring how culture shapes conformity.

Uncertain Information Promotes Conformity

In the face of uncertainty, we tend to look around, observe what others are doing, and then do whatever they are doing, just as the example above describes.

Informational social influence focuses on how information *un*certainty influences social conformity. We follow along with what appears to be the social norm because we want to be "correct." If you're unsure what this religion expects, you follow along. If you're at a fancy restaurant and you don't know what fork to use, you look around and copy others. If you're trying to buy a train ticket in a new city, you quietly watch other people in line to see what to do.

A classic research study on informational social influence came from Muzafer Sherif (1936). He took advantage of a strange optical illusion called the **autokinetic effect**, which occurs when we perceive a stationary dot of light as moving due to natural, intermittent movements of our eyes (called saccades). When people were tested alone in a room and asked how much the light moved, their average guess was about 4 inches. But when they were in a room with a *confederate* who gave an answer first, their uncertainty led them to be influenced by the confederate's answer—they conformed. To learn more, see the Spotlight on Research Methods feature.

"Because we've always done it that way."

About 25 years after Sherif's clever experiments, two researchers followed the thread of that research to an additional discovery. Jacobs and Campbell (1961) demonstrated how a cultural belief or norm can become a **generational influence** on social conformity. Their simple insight was to conceive of a "generation" as the replacement

---

Theory of informational and normative influence: The idea that there are two ways that social norms cause conformity (see *informational social influence* and *normative social influence*).

Informational social influence: When we conform to group standards because we want to be "correct."

Autokinetic effect: An optical illusion that occurs when we think a stationary light is moving.

Generational influence: A cultural belief or norm that continues as the people who started it leave and newer members of a group remain.

Sherif and the Autokinetic Effect

To study the autokinetic effect, Sherif created uncertainty in a *controlled experiment* by first placing participants in a darkened room. They all looked at a dot of light (Sherif, 1935, 1936). In a dark room, a dot of light will appear to dance about. The effect is due to your own eye movements, but participants in the control group who were tested alone estimated that the light had moved an average of 4 inches. Of course, the reality was that the dot of light had not moved at all. In the control group, people simply gave their best guess.

Next, Sherif arranged for a *confederate* in one *experimental group* to provide the group with a fake estimate of how far the light had moved: 15 inches. The confederate did this out loud, so that others in the room could hear the estimate. Soon, everyone else was conforming around the confederate's estimate

of 15 inches. But when the confederate in another experimental group estimated only 2 inches, the other participants conformed around this much smaller number.

Remember that the idea behind control groups and experimental groups is to provide meaningful comparisons. That requires keeping everything the same except for the variable of interest (the *independent variable*). In this experiment, the *only* thing that changed was the confederate's declaration of how far the dot of light had moved—and the experiment tested how that initial number caused participants to change their own estimates (the *dependent variable*). Why did the experimental group participants conform around 15 inches and 2 inches? Sherif said it was informational conformity.

of people rather than as generations based on birth, life, and death. With that small change, Jacobs and Campbell could now study generational transfer without having to wait 40 or 50 years.

They began by first *replicating* Sherif's autokinetic experiment. They found the same effect. If the first estimate was that a dot of light in a darkened room had moved 17, 11, or 6 inches, then the group conformed around that number. That first estimate was arbitrary, but it became the group's social norm. Everyone went along with it.

Then they added their generational twist: The first "elder" member of the group departed and was replaced by a new member. It was only a slight generational change, like the simultaneous birth of a grandchild and death of a grandparent within a large family. But would the tradition continue as the group was slowly replaced with new members?

As each new participant came into the room, the "older" members were always the first to offer an opinion; the newbies were always last. Importantly, the original confederate who had started the tradition was completely gone—yet conformity persisted. It required, on average, five to eight "generations" before it merged with the baseline perception. Remember: *Nothing happened.* The dot of light had never moved even one inch—but a single person had created a tradition that lasted for generations, with each new member of the group being convinced their perception was "right."

Three conclusions emerged from these autokinetic experiments:

1. participants can sincerely believe perceptions that are simply not true,

2. uncertainty (about how far the dot of light had moved) promotes social conformity, and

Traditions vary all over the world for socially normed events such as weddings. How did these traditions start? Why are they passed down from one generation to the next?

3. social conformity endured—across five to eight generations—even when the origin of the "tradition" was based on an inaccurate and arbitrary estimate and the person who started the tradition was long gone.

Social Norms Demand Conformity

In 2015, the beach in Mumbai, India, was disgusting.

Afroz Shah, 33, and his 84-year-old friend and neighbor Harbanash Mathur were walking along the beach. The beautiful beach Afroz remembered from his childhood was now filled with layers of garbage and topped with plastic refuse. They started picking up, one piece at a time. It was often heavy, hard, disgusting work, and for the first 2 to 3 weeks, it was lonely work, too.

But then, people started noticing what Shah was doing. A few more joined in, and then more. Soon, Shah had started what Sunstein (2019) refers to as a **social cascade**, a large social change in response to the beliefs or actions of a few early visionaries. The social norm went from mindless littering to spending part of your weekend cleaning the beach. It was still unpleasant work, but now a **normative social influence** had caused public conformity to achieve a public good. Normative social influence occurs not because we want to be "right" but because we want to fit in and be accepted by those around us.

Descriptive Norms and Injunctive Norms

There are two types of social norms; both are influential but in different ways.

Descriptive norms refer to what is commonly done—what most people do. The descriptive norm before Shah championed the beach cleanup was to ignore it, to emotionally throw up your hands and think, "Somebody ought to do something"—but not lift a hand personally. Research has established that sometimes littering persists simply because everyone else is believed to be littering (see Cialdini et al., 1991). We know we *shouldn't* do it, but we do anyway because everyone else is doing it.

Injunctive norms refer to what is socially sanctioned—what society says people are *supposed* to do, or what we *should* do. A simple way to influence injunctive norms against littering is to place trash or recycling bins in obvious areas. When one person goes against descriptive norms, like Shah on the beach, injunctive norms can kick in and be persuasive influences on our behavior.

The Pressure of Fitting In: Asch's Line Judgment Experiments

Sometimes, going against the group can be really uncomfortable.

After World War II, social psychologist Solomon Asch was desperate to understand what had just happened to humanity. His 1952 textbook discussed how education could either promote (a) "independent thinking and self-reliance" or (b) the kind of conformity created by the Nazis to "indoctrinate blind obedience to state and church" (Asch, 1952, p. 620). Asch believed that nonconformity and critical thinking were signals of a healthy society.

Sherif was studying the effects of informational *un*certainty. Asch, however, recognized that there was no uncertainty during the Holocaust. Most soldiers, citizens, bureaucrats, and death camp and concentration camp workers *knew* what they were doing. If nothing else, the undeniable smell of the camps floated into nearby towns (see Sergent et al., 2019). Uncertainty was not the problem.

Asch wanted to study what people would do when the "right" answer was clear, but social pressure was to do the *wrong* thing. In his study, "wrong" didn't have to be morally wrong, just obviously wrong—like giving the wrong answer to the question in Figure 7.2: "Which line on the right matches the length of the line on the left?" Asch believed that only a few people would ever answer anything other than Line B, the clearly correct answer (see Bond & Smith, 1996; Cialdini & Trost, 1998; Friend et al., 1990). He optimistically believed that people wouldn't conform in such circumstances. Asch (1952, 1956) was about to be surprised by the results of his own experiments.

Social cascade: A large social change in response to the beliefs or actions of a few early visionaries.

Normative social influence: When we conform to group standards to gain social acceptance and fit in.

Descriptive norm: Our perception of what most people do in a given situation.

Injunctive norm: Our perception of what we *should* do in a given situation.

FIGURE 7.2

Which line on the right matches the length of the line on the left?

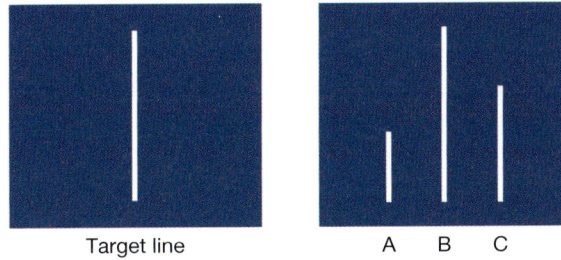

Target line   A   B   C

Source: Adapted from Asch (1952).

WHAT'S MY SCORE?

Measuring Conformity

Instructions: Please use the following scale to indicate the degree of your agreement or disagreement with each of the statements below. Record your numerical answer to each statement in the space provided preceding the statement. Try to describe yourself accurately and generally (that is, the way you are actually in most situations—not the way you would hope to be).

−4	−3	−2	−1	0	+1	+2	+3	+4
Very strong disagreement				Neither agree nor disagree				Very strong agreement

____ 1. I often rely on, and act upon, the advice of others.

____ 2. I would be the last one to change my opinion in a heated argument on a controversial topic.

____ 3. Generally, I'd rather give in and go along for the sake of peace than struggle to have my way.

____ 4. I tend to follow family tradition in making political decisions.

____ 5. Basically, my friends are the ones who decide what we do together.

____ 6. A charismatic and eloquent speaker can easily influence and change my ideas.

____ 7. I am more independent than conforming in my ways.

____ 8. If someone is very persuasive, I tend to change my opinion and go along with them.

____ 9. I don't give in to others easily.

____ 10. I tend to rely on others when I have to make an important decision quickly.

____ 11. I prefer to make my own way in life rather than find a group I can follow.

Scoring: First, reverse-score Items 2, 7, 9, and 11. For this scale, all you have to do is cross off the plus or minus in front of what you wrote and change it to the other sign (so, for example, a −3 becomes a +3). Zeros stay the same. Then, add up all the numbers to get your composite score, which should be between −44 and +44. Higher numbers mean more of a tendency to conform to others.

Source: Mehrabian and Stefl (1995), "Basic temperament components of loneliness, shyness, and conformity." *Social Behavior and Personality. 23*(3). 253–263. https://doi .org/10.2224/sbp.1995.23.3.253

Asch's Procedure

Imagine that you are one of seven participants seated around a table. One by one, you are each asked to report your perception about the length of a line. You are second to last.

Trial 1: The answer is obvious and everyone is in perfect agreement.

Asch's line judgment experiments.

Trial 2: Same thing. It appears to be an exceptionally boring experiment.

Trial 3: Once again, everyone who answers before you voices a unanimous opinion—but it is about the wrong line!

You look around the table at the others; they are all serious! What you don't know is that everyone else in this experiment is a *confederate*. Everyone is in on the *deception* except you. Asch's simple line judgment task thrust participants into a crisis. They had to choose between what they thought was clearly correct versus giving in to what seemed to be weird and surprising group pressure.

In control studies with no confederates, participants had provided the correct answer 98% of the time. The problem was not *un*certainty; the answer was obvious. The problem was certainty versus the pressure of the group. Roger Brown (1965, p. 671) called the experience of Asch's participants "an epistemological nightmare." Without warning, for them, "deeply rooted assumptions—of mutually shared perceptions and expectations—are decisively shattered" (see also Friend et al., 1990, p. 42). What would they do?

Asch's Results

When participants were run in groups where everyone else was a confederate, Asch had arranged for the confederates to give the wrong answer more than 50% of the time. The social pressure to conform was so powerful that over one third of the time (36.8%), the participants said what they knew was the wrong answer. In addition, 75% of them conformed to the wrong answer at least once (Asch, 1951).

To really understand the participants' mind-set, Asch (1955) combined both *quantitative data* (the percentage conforming) and *qualitative data* (comments they offered during debriefing). Table 7.1 shows how some of them explained their own behavior.

TABLE 7.1

Thoughts From Participants in the Asch (1955) Study

Nonconformists who expressed an obligation to tell the truth as they saw it:
They were wrong. Or, if I was wrong, I'd rather try to find out why I was wrong.
. . . they have a habit of laughing at you if you're wrong in class, but in this case I didn't care. It would be different if it were a question of ethics, but I wouldn't agree!
I've never had any feeling that there was any virtue in being like others. I'm used to being different. I often came out well by being different.
Nonconformists who expressed informational uncertainty:
Frankly I thought the mob were following the first man. Of course, it could be my eyes since I was the only one who disagreed.
I began to question whether my own perception was as acute as it seemed to be.
Yeah, I figured the lines contained some sort of illusion which I was not subject to and they were.
Conformists who went along with the group because of social desirability in research:
I wanted to conform. Was picturing in my mind the graph of results with a big dip in it—I wanted to make your results better.
I realized you'd know I'd been fibbing so thought I had better tell you and not spoil the statistics.
Hm-m-m. I wondered if it was a put-up job, because those guys were all up here when I arrived.
Conformists who went along with the group to fit in:
. . . we all want to be with the bandwagon.
I just sort of slipped along.
I was standing out . . . a sore thumb. I didn't particularly want to make a fool of myself . . . I felt I was definitely right [but] they might think I was peculiar.

Those who conformed noted two primary reasons: (1) the desire to help the researcher and be a "good subject" and (2) to fit in or not appear strange.

Years later, Bond and Smith (1996) reviewed 133 replications using the Asch conformity paradigm. The studies had been conducted over four decades and from 17 different countries. They noted that conformity in the United States had declined since the early 1950s, but conformity increased when

(a) the size of the majority increased,

(b) differences between the lines were more ambiguous,

(c) the majority group only included members of one's social ingroup, and

(d) the proportion of women participants increased.

Why might the presence of others in your social ingroup increase conformity? One explanation is that the risk of rejection is much greater. And for women, they may have been more socialized to conform, to "be nice" and "not make trouble." Cultural expectations and influence matter, so let's explore culture more in the next section. You can also read about gender and conformity in the Social Psychology in Popular Culture feature.

▶ Conformity in *The Marvelous Mrs. Maisel*

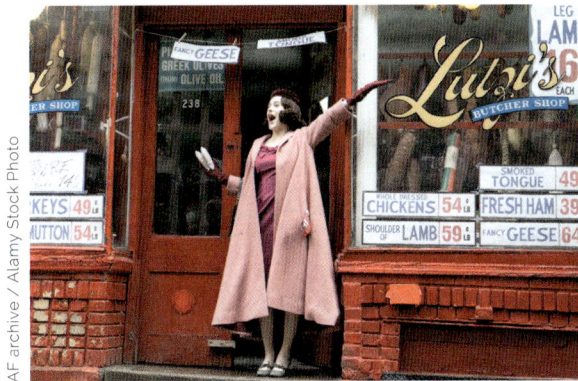

AF archive / Alamy Stock Photo

Midge Maisel did everything right: She graduated from a good college, maintained a perfect figure, married a nice Jewish boy, and had beautiful kids. She conformed to all the 1950s gender-based expectations thrown at her—until it all blew up in her face when her husband cheated on her.

In the breakout hit *The Marvelous Mrs. Maisel* (Sherman-Palladino, 2017–), Midge realizes that following "the rules" of how to act wasn't allowing her to embrace her true self: a sarcastic, rebellious, hilarious young woman who questions the value of tradition and stereotypes. She becomes an overnight sensation when she uses her observations about culture and conformity to launch her new career as a standup comedian. Part of her success is due to her manager and friend, Susie, who also breaks expectations with her masculine dress and demeanor.

The problem is that Midge is caught between loving her new, independent, nonconforming self and still feeling the pull of what everyone wants and expects of her. Her family disapproves, she's still attracted to her ex-husband, and it's clear that she misses the easy routine and social acceptance of her old life. It's hard to be a nonconformist, and she sometimes makes mistakes as she tries to navigate social influence and wonders whether she can really find happiness without authenticity.

Culture Shapes Conformity

Some people in Asch's study didn't conform.

Asch (1956) noted differences across his participants. Some of those differences appeared to be caused by personality (see also Kosloff et al., 2017). Other individual differences, in the original study and in replications, appear to be the result of cultural values (Triandis, 1989; see also Varnum & Grossmann, 2017). Remember, for comparison, that U.S. participants conformed about 33% of the time.

When Asch's study was replicated in Kuwait, conformity rates were almost identical: 33% (Amir, 1984). But Chandra (1973) found much higher rates of conformity (about 58%) in Fiji, a collectivistic culture that highly values conformity to the group. Whether a culture values conformity has interesting effects on individual people's behaviors. What makes a culture value conformity to social norms?

One intriguing idea is the **food accumulation hypothesis**, the idea that cultural views of conformity originate from that group's relationship with food. Consider Berry (1967), who compared two extremely different cultures: the Temne people from Sierra Leone (on the west coast of Africa) with Inuits (formerly sometimes called Eskimos) from Baffin Island (in the northernmost section of Canada). The Temne people demonstrated a strong tendency to conform, whereas the Inuits almost entirely disregarded group pressure.

Berry pointed out that the Temne are mostly rice farmers who can harvest only one crop per year. Their survival depends on accumulating a great deal of food during the brief harvest time. That's a lot of pressure, so everyone must participate. Children are trained to be obedient, dependable, and cooperative. Their conformity directly contributes to everyone's survival. A Temne participant in a replication of Asch's line judgment experiment said, "When Temne people choose a thing, we must all agree with the decision—that is what we call cooperation." To collectivist cultures, conforming isn't caving in; it is a virtuous social courtesy that puts the group's needs before your own (Markus & Kitayama, 1994).

The Inuits of Baffin Island have no vegetation, so their survival requires individualists. As soon as possible, a child should learn how to fish and hunt independently and to take care of themselves in the wild. Inuits are lenient with their children, encourage independence, and value self-reliance. When the Inuits from Baffin Island participated in the line judgment experiment, they would usually say nothing at all but "would often display a quiet, knowing smile" as they pointed toward the correct line (Berry, 1967, p. 17).

In the United States, cultural attitudes toward conformity have changed with time. In the 1950s, conformity was generally seen as a good thing; everyone worked together to recover from World War II. Attitudes changed when college students began to question authority during the Vietnam War era. Social conflict promoted independent thinking, and conformity was viewed as "selling out" (see Larsen, 1974, 1982, 1990; Perrin & Spencer, 1981). But ironically, even the "hippie" subculture that formed an identity

Food accumulation hypothesis: The idea that cultural views of conformity originate from that group's relationship with food.

The "hippie" era in the United States during the late 1960s and early 1970s was a time when young people attempted to question the status quo and be non-conformists. Is it ironic that so many of them generally dressed and acted the same as each other?

around nonconformity showed the pressure of group norms: "Make love, not war" and a uniform of bell-bottom jeans and long hair made all the nonconformists look alike. Rebellion was encouraged . . . as long as everyone else in the subculture approved.

Just how common is cultural conformity in the world? It may go all the way down to—drumroll—fruit flies! We know that wolf culture encourages loyal conformity to the pack. Elephants display grieving rituals. And chimpanzees act uncannily like their next-door genetic neighbors: us. But fruit flies!?

Perhaps surprisingly, Bridges and Chittka (2019) documented a cultural bias in mate selection among fruit flies. First, they painted some fruit flies different colors. Virgin females watched through a glass as a pink-painted or green-painted male fruit flies mounted another female. Those females observing behind the glass then preferred to mate with males of whatever color they had observed. Even though the paint colors weren't natural for fruit flies, seeing another female mate with them apparently influenced later females to prefer those males. They must be studs! Social norms, cultural expectations, and popularity matter, even to the smallest of us.

THE MAIN IDEAS

- Informational social influence occurs when we conform in order to be correct, while normative social influence occurs when we conform in order to gain acceptance and avoid rejection.

- A famous study testing informational social influence is Sherif's study on the autokinetic effect. A famous study that tested normative social influence was the Asch line judgment task, in which people conformed about 33% of the time, even when they knew they were stating an incorrect answer.

- Cultures vary in the degree to which they value conformity. Culture and conformity can be seen in humans, chimpanzees, canines, and even fruit flies.

CRITICAL THINKING CHALLENGE

- How do you think you would have behaved in the Asch line judgment experiment? Explain your answer. Then, name an example of when you've gone along with conformity to fit in (normative social influence) and a time when you went against the group. Did the latter situation make you feel uncomfortable or result in any social judgment from others?

- How has your cultural upbringing influenced whether you think of conformity as a good thing or a bad thing? Is nonconformity a way to break up the status quo and to live authentically—or is it simply being selfish and valuing your own needs more than the group's needs?

- Describe a behavior, tradition, value, or even a perception of the world that you think you've "inherited" through generational influence from your family or hometown. First describe what you do or think, then explain how your behavior or perception has been influenced by the "generations" of people who came before you and started this tradition.

HOW ARE WE INFLUENCED BY SOCIAL ROLES AND OBEDIENCE TO AUTHORITY?

>> LO 7.3: Analyze key experiments that demonstrate influence through social roles, obedience, and the power of the situation.

The rest of this chapter focuses on two of the most famous studies in all of social psychology: Phil Zimbardo's Stanford Prison Study and Stanley Milgram's obedience study. Both studies explored social influence (De Vos, 2010). Both were dramatic, well documented, and even filmed. And both studies—and their creators—have generated continuing controversy over the ethics of the studies and how the results should be interpreted.

This section explores the core question "How are we influenced by social roles and obedience to authority?" by

(1) connecting two of psychology's most well-known studies,

(2) discussing the influence of social roles on behavior,

(3) exploring how obedience might make us cruel, and

(4) analyzing alternative explanations for each famous study.

The Milgram-Zimbardo Connection: The Power of the Situation

Phil Zimbardo connected his own study with Milgram's during an interview with Professor George Slavich (2009, p. 282). According to him, the two studies

> are really bookends that elucidate the power of the situation. . . . Milgram's research was all about the power of individual authority over an individual person, the Stanford Prison Experiment was all about the ability for a system to repeatedly create situations that strongly influence behavior.

Milgram and Zimbardo were in the same high school graduating class at the James Monroe High School in the Bronx section of New York City. Both had an artistic flair and were acquainted with professional theatrical performances (Blass, 2004). They both brought a sense of dramatic theater to the science of social psychology.

Zimbardo had left the Bronx his junior year to live in California, where he was lonely and unpopular. When he returned to the Bronx for his senior year, he was voted the most popular boy in the class. He later noted (Slavich, 2009, p. 279),

> I talked with Milgram about my spike in popularity when I got back to Monroe, and together we wondered—in primitive terms—whether it was me or the situation that had changed. We agreed it was probably the situation.

Both Zimbardo and Milgram came from struggling, poor, immigrant families who knew what it meant to be the target of prejudice. As future social psychologists, both were deeply concerned about whether the Holocaust could ever be repeated. Both suspected that it could, if social pressure were powerful enough. So they each designed a study that tested their own ideas regarding what could bring out the worst in humanity, because of social influence.

The Power of Social Roles

Losing your self sounds like it might be a bad thing—and sometimes it is.

However, losing ourselves into a new social role happens repeatedly across our lives. We begin as an infant and eventually, if we are lucky, retire with some measure of life satisfaction. But there are many, mostly unavoidable social roles in between. They all will require, to some degree, that we commit our thoughts, emotions, and behavior to some role that is bigger than ourselves.

Theory in the Stanford Prison Study

In some situations, a few environmental hints are all we need to switch social roles.

Social role theory (see Chapter 9) proposes that we have widely shared stereotypes about how people act when they are assigned a certain position in society, like a label for expectations (Eagly, 1987; Eagly et al., 2000). We have expectations based on gender, for example: Men will be competitive and provide financially for their families, while women will be nurturing, provide guidance for children, and take care of the home. They are just stereotypes, but these labels and expectations shape our society and how we act.

Zimbardo wanted to test the power of social roles in a setting where some people would have complete power over others, a parallel to what had happened in World War II concentration camps. His chosen setting: a prison. The social roles in the Stanford Prison Study began to feel real when police cars arrived at the homes of the young men who had volunteered for this unusual experiment (see Zimbardo, 1973). The neighbors watched as the officers handcuffed them and took them away to the psychology building at Stanford University.

When they entered the basement, the volunteers found a 35-foot hallway and a few small rooms. The rooms were just big enough to hold a couple of cots, but not much more. The "prison hole" for misbehaving "prisoners" was a 2 × 2 × 7–foot closet. External signals of social roles were clear. Prisoners had to wear nets on their hair, a loose smock that didn't offer much protection or coverage, and symbolic ankle chains. Numbers replaced names.

In contrast, the guards—who were also college students—wore official-looking uniforms. They carried symbols of their authority, including mirrored sunglasses and nightsticks. They teamed up to control their pretend prisoners. Importantly, Zimbardo had selected every participant (prisoners and guards) because pretesting showed them to be healthy, well-adjusted young men. Then, he *randomly assigned* them to either the social role of prisoner or guard.

Random assignment meant that the simulated prison experiment could test whether social roles could overwhelm someone's personality (Haney et al., 1973). According to Zimbardo, both groups started out on an equal playing field, so anything that happened later was probably *not* the result of naturally aggressive people becoming guards or dependent personalities becoming prisoners. If personality differences were controlled, or limited, by random assignment, then what did influence the prisoners and the guards?

Phil Zimbardo, the social psychologist behind the Stanford Prison Study—perhaps the most controversial study ever done on the influence of social roles on behavior.

Gary Gershoff/Wireimage/Getty Images

Results of the Stanford Prison Study

One of the first outcomes in the Stanford Prison Study occurred with alarming speed.

Deindividuation occurs when self-awareness disappears into some alternative social role, especially when the role includes anonymity through things like a uniform. The guards' uniforms communicated implicit permission to play their role behind the protection of sunglasses, nightsticks, and stereotyped behaviors. The guards embraced their social role and translated it into deindividuation, psychological control, and cruelty.

The guards took away the prisoners' beds and school books (many had been planning to study for finals during the study). The guards woke the prisoners up throughout the night, forcing sleep deprivation. They placed some in the isolation hole and forced the others to pound on the door while yelling criticisms. The guards forced the prisoners to do several humiliating behaviors, including simulated sexual acts.

The prisoners also embraced their social roles. They identified themselves by their prison numbers rather than their names. They did not object when ordered to criticize their fellow prisoner. Another complied when ordered to sing the hymn "Amazing Grace" or to tell another prisoner "I love you." They quickly became enraged, rebellious, or zombie-like drones. A study designed to last 2 weeks had to be stopped after just 6 days.

Zimbardo concluded that social roles had overwhelmed both the prisoners and guards. Their individual identities, personalities, and backgrounds became irrelevant as they became absorbed into their randomly assigned social roles. "Role playing has become role internalization; the actors have assumed the characteristics and identities of their fictional roles" (Zimbardo, 2007, p. 142). He related this back to his original question about how the Holocaust could have happened when he wrote, "Evil acts are not necessarily the deeds of evil men, but may be attributable to the operation of powerful social forces" (Haney et al., 1973, p. 35).

Deindividuation: When self-awareness is replaced by a social role or group identity, resulting in the loss of individuality.

Ethical Issues and Other Criticisms

There's irony here.

Phil Zimbardo (2017) recognized—too slowly, he acknowledged, during the shortened experiment—that ethical standards had been violated. He later admitted,

> Volunteer prisoners suffered physical and psychological abuse hour after hour for days, while volunteer guards were exposed to the new self-knowledge that they enjoyed being powerful and had abused this power to make other human beings suffer. (p. 243)

What happened from the prisoners to the guards was absolutely unethical. But there are even more concerns.

When he reflects on the study now, Zimbardo claims that the social role of a passive prisoner took over such that even though the prisoners had been told they could request quitting the study whenever they wanted, none of them did. He claims they had been so psychologically enmeshed in the situation that they lost perspective and forgot they had rights. He says that in orientation, they had been told that they could simply ask to quit, and they would be released.

But now, that claim seems to be in doubt. There are no existing records of consent forms in which this part of the "rules" was explained to the prisoners. Zimbardo (2017) writes that the prisoners were desperate to escape and even went through grueling and humiliating "parole boards." One of them may have even faked a mental breakdown to be released. Why would they go through all of that if they thought they could leave by simply asking to?

Finally, it's unclear what theoretical conclusions we can safely draw from the study. Zimbardo's written papers and TED talks consistently claim that the only difference between the prisoners and the guards was due to random assignment and that it was simply the social roles and power of the situation that caused the guards to become power hungry and cruel.

Bartels (2019) disagrees. It turns out that the day before the experiment began, the guards received an orientation full of "expectations for hostile guard behavior, a flippant prisoner mindset, and the possibility of ending the study prematurely" (Bartels, 2019, p. 1). The guards were explicitly instructed to be tough and controlling. This was reinforced each day in the study, by Zimbardo himself and by consultants he brought in. In short, the guards may not have been cruel because they enjoyed it or because the situation allowed their natural cruelty to come out; they may have acted this way because they *were trying to help out the study*.

The infamous Zimbardo prison study is complicated and fascinating. Exactly how to think about it is ripe for debate and critical thinking (Bartels et al., 2016). If nothing else, it might be a case study in how *not* to run a study. There are several films based on it, as well as the original footage (Dunn, 2016). Its use may not be what Zimbardo originally intended, but it certainly allows us to ask questions about how we can "study harm-doing without doing harm" (see Haslam et al., 2015).

Applications and Extensions

While the procedure and results of Zimbardo's study make it hard to draw clear conclusions about the nature of social roles, it inspired hundreds of other studies on how situational forces can influence whether we act in socially sanctioned ways.

Environmental Cues Encourage Disinhibition. Feeling anonymous can lead us to questionable behavior.

Consider something as simple as trick-or-treaters who approach a bowl of candy that says, "Just take one" (Diener et al., 1976). Children are more likely to steal when they're in a group (and thus might not feel individually responsible—everyone else did it too!) and when they feel relatively anonymous by not providing their names and/or feeling like their costume protects their identity.

Deindividuation encourages disinhibition that loosens customary social restraints (see Diener, 1979; Prentice-Dunn & Rogers, 1982). As Figure 7.3 shows, anonymity helps us lower our self-awareness and hide behind deindividuation, making us feel like we can "get away with" bad behavior. When we're reminded of our identity, disinhibition disappears. For example, college students are less likely to cheat in a room with a mirror facing them, as a reminder of their identity (Vallacher & Solodky, 1979).

FIGURE 7.3

A possible path to social disinhibition.

Anonymity ⟩ Lower Self-Awareness ⟩ Deindividuation ⟩ Social Disinhibition

One of the most prominent modern examples of disinhibition is cyber-disinhibition, where the anonymity of the Internet encourages trolling, harassment, and cruelty without consequences (Bargh & McKenna, 2004; Steinfeldt et al., 2010). It's easier to say offensive or dishonest things when no one can trace the comments back to their author (see Toma et al., 2019). People with social anxiety are especially prone to the negative effects of cyber-disinhibition (Antoniadou et al., 2019), and people are more willing to lie in electronic communications than with an actual pen and paper (Naquin et al., 2010). It seems that simply using a computer helps people feel less personally tied to their actions—something to think about in an age when job applicants, tax returns, and bureaucratic reports are submitted electronically.

The rapid increase in online dating apps is also a field for deception. It can range from small lies (say, about your height or weight) to entirely false profiles known as "catfishing." It's easy to see why people might be tempted to embellish themselves, as Sharabi and Coughlin (2019) found that deception on a first date led to a second one. Internet anonymity has other benefits. Anonymity allows users to practice social skills, explore possible social roles, and experiment with "new behaviors and beliefs without fear of being judged" (Barnett & Coulson, 2010, p. 171). If your social role, sexual orientation, or political beliefs are quietly shifting, then anonymity allows you to try out your private transformations.

On the other hand, the documented, sweeping, systematic Russian interference in the American elections raises the stakes from personal abuse to state-sponsored warfare. Approximately 126 million citizens were contacted by Russian creators of fake news with a biased agenda (see Jensen et al., 2019). The anonymity of online interaction leads to some very bad outcomes.

Anonymity Can Encourage Aggression. Laws about whether people should wear masks during pandemics like COVID-19 represent a legal balancing act in the United States (and elsewhere) between constitutionally guaranteed freedom of speech and public safety.

Sometimes the legal origin of these laws were crimes committed by Ku Klux Klan members wearing hoods. More recently, laws have been passed banning people from wearing "Guy Fawkes" masks in public (named after a famous British political protestor). The online hacking group known as "Anonymous" has chosen this image as their icon.

Zimbardo's prison study only included men—what about women? In a different study, Zimbardo (1970) allowed one group of women to become deindividuated by wearing hoods and loose-fitting clothing. The comparison group wore their own clothes and large nametags. When given the opportunity to deliver an electric shock, the *de*individuated group of women hiding in hoods and lose clothing held

Disinhibition: Loosening of social restraints when someone feels anonymous or not identifiable.

Cyber-disinhibition: Lack of social restraints due to the anonymity of the Internet, leading to behaviors like trolling or online harassment.

AFP/Getty Images

Criminals sometimes wear masks. Certainly, this helps protect your identity, but it also may empower their planned antisocial behaviors. Here you can see people wearing a "Guy Fawkes" mask, made famous in the movie *V for Vendetta* (2005) and now associated with the online hacking group called "Anonymous."

the lever down twice as long, even "as their victims twisted and moaned right before them" (p. 300).

In another experiment by Lightdale and Prentice (1994), deindividuated women were just as willing as men to "let go" of their inhibitions and harm others. When hidden inside a car, men and women exhibit similar levels of mild aggression (Hennessy & Wiesenthal, 2001). The same is found in multiplayer online games: Women using fake names are equally as aggressive as men (Hughes & Louw, 2013). Anonymity in each case allowed these women to become just as nasty and aggressive as men. Perhaps most of the time, women and men seem more different than they really are, simply because they are both conforming to stereotypical social roles.

Social Roles Can Also Encourage Kindness

So far, this has been a pretty negative discussion.

Johnson and Downing (1979) wondered whether social roles could prime both antisocial behavior *and* prosocial behavior. They compared groups who saw a photograph of someone dressed either in a nurse's uniform (priming the stereotype of a prosocial, caring person) or a Klan-like uniform (priming antisocial, aggressive stereotypes). The people in both groups were further subdivided into another two groups: individuated (with a large nametag) or relatively deindividuated (no nametag, a *control group*).

The *experimental design* for this study is represented in Table 7.2. It is called a *2 × 2 factorial design* because there are two *independent variables* (type of uniform and the presence or absence of a nametag) and two levels of each independent variable. If the study had included people wearing some third type of uniform, say that of a soldier, then it would have been known as a *2 × 3 factorial design*.

TABLE 7.2

The Experimental Design for Johnson and Downing (1979)

	KKK UNIFORM (NEGATIVE STEREOTYPE)	NURSE UNIFORM (POSITIVE STEREOTYPE)
Large nametag (individuated)	Condition 1	Condition 2
No nametag (deindividuated)	Condition 3	Condition 4

The *dependent variable:* Participants were asked to decide whether to increase or decrease the amount of electric shock experienced by another person. The outcomes are in Figure 7.4. The anonymous, deindividuated participants (without a nametag) were more extreme in *both* directions. The clothes mattered. Nurse uniforms led to *kinder* behaviors; KKK uniforms led to more aggressive behaviors. Importantly, social roles lead to both positive and negative behavior that matches expectations.

Anonymity Can Encourage Intimacy. They didn't become aggressive or helpful.

When Gergen et al. (1973) enforced anonymity by putting unacquainted strangers, aged 18 to 25, in a darkened room, the participants showed a third possible outcome: They became affectionate. The participants in the experimental group never saw one another and never learned each other's names, before or after the experiment. In groups of seven to eight people, participants were asked to remove their shoes, empty

FIGURE 7.4

Type of clothing and deindividuation.

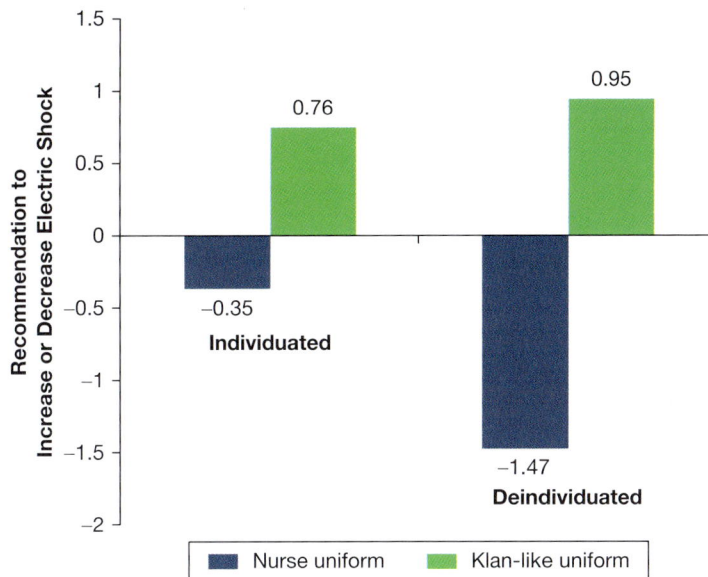

their pockets, and bring nothing else into the room with them. The room was about 10 × 12 feet with padded walls and completely dark except for a small red light over the door.

The control group received the same instructions—but the lights were on. So the *independent variable* was the lighting conditions: lights off (anonymous) or lights on (not anonymous). They assessed the effects of anonymity (the *dependent variables*) in three ways. They (1) tape-recorded the conversations, (2) used infrared cameras to track their movements in the room, and (3) asked them to write down their impressions at the end of the experiment.

The anonymity of darkness encouraged intimacy. About 90% "touched each other on purpose, while almost none of the lighted-room subjects did." Almost 50% in the darkened room hugged another person. About 80% reported feeling sexual excitement. One female participant wrote that after initial tension and nervousness,

> the darkness no longer bothered me. . . . [By the end of the hour] the group sat closely together, touching, feeling a sense of friendship and loss as a group member left. I left with a feeling that it had been fun and nice. I felt I had made some friends. In fact, I missed them.

One male wrote that he

> felt joy over the possibility of not having to look at people in clichéd ways. Enjoyed feeling of a self-awareness surrounded by a rich environment.

An important experimental variation occurred when participants in the darkened room were told that they would meet one another at the end of the experiment. The researchers reported that now the participants

> were less likely to explore, . . . more likely to feel bored, less likely to introduce themselves, less likely to hug . . . and more likely to feel panicky.

In this study, removing the promise of anonymity restrained their affectionate impulses. Their welcome disinhibitions began to disappear. Is this the reason most people turn off the lights when they're intimate with each other?

Obedience Can Encourage Cruelty

We promised a second famous study.

Nervous laughter is the norm when students first see original footage of Stanley Milgram's study. Ordinary people appear to deliver painful and probably lethal levels of electric shock to an innocent stranger. Why would anyone do that?

Milgram explicitly connected his experiments to the war crimes committed during the Holocaust. He recognized that it required social coordination, even creativity, from many thousands of people to murder so many millions of people so quickly (Cropley et al., 2010; Heinzen, 1995). The theory and structure of Milgram's experiments suggest that the nervous laughter comes from a recognition that we all are capable of such cruelty, given the right circumstances.

Milgram's Methods: Quantifying Obedience to Authority

Milgram started his experiment with an ad in the New Haven newspaper.

"Persons Needed for a Study of Memory." It was a *cover story,* a choice to use strategic *deception* that camouflaged the true nature of the experiment. Participants would be paid $4.50 (it had more buying power in the 1950s). When they arrived at prestigious Yale University, they were told that the study was about punishment and learning.

The participants met a *confederate,* someone who was part of the experiment but pretended to be just another person off the street. The deception continued: A third man, the experimenter, pretended to randomly assign one of them to the role of "Teacher" and the other to the role of "Learner." It was actually a rigged drawing; the real participant was always assigned the role of Teacher.

The job of the Teacher was to present the Learner with word pairs to be memorized (such as "clear/air" or "dictionary/red"). The Teacher's job was to punish the Learner for each memory failure. The punishment was an electric shock that became 15 volts more painful with every (prearranged) memory error. To make the deception seem real, the Teacher was allowed to experience a low-level voltage shock before the experiment began. There was no uncertainty about the pain that the Teacher would be delivering.

The electric shocks were another *deception*, though. As soon as the participant saw the Learner get hooked up to the machine, the experimenter took the participant to a different room. The participant didn't see that the Learner promptly got up and walked away, never receiving any shocks. But Milgram wanted to know: How far up the electric shock scale shown in Figure 7.5 would a Teacher go before refusing to go on?

Milgram thought that people who participated in the Holocaust may have done terrible things simply because they were ordered to do so. In his own study, then, he made sure the participants were ordered to keep going on the shock machine. If, at any point, they protested what they were supposed to be doing, the experimenter would respond with four verbal prods:

FIGURE 7.5

Levels of electric shock in Milgram's famous obedience studies.

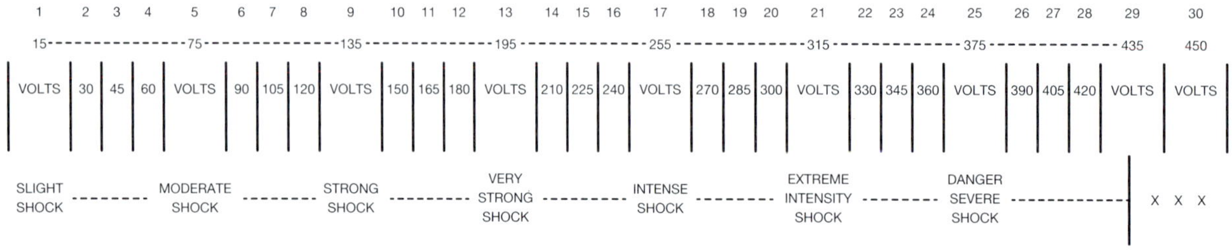

Source: © 1974 by Stanley Milgram; by permission of Alexandra Milgram.

Prod 1: "Please continue" or "Please go on."

Prod 2: "The experiment requires that you continue."

Prod 3: "It is absolutely essential that you continue."

Prod 4: "You have no other choice, you *must* go on."

Results of the Obedience to Authority Experiments

Milgram was surprised at the results.

When he conducted a preliminary test of the procedures with Yale college students, most of them raced past labeled warnings (on the phony shock machine) such as "DANGER SEVERE SHOCK," until they reached the maximum shock level of 450 volts. A few asked questions, but 26 out of 40 Yale students (65%) shocked to the maximum 450 volts.

Milgram thought maybe they didn't quite understand the effects these shocks were supposed to be having on the other person—maybe that's why they kept going. So he tried again, this time with middle-aged male volunteers from the community. They also heard the scripted responses whose highpoints you can see in Table 7.3. Milgram thought that the Learner's screams and heart problems would limit the Teacher's obedience (Milgram, 1974, pp. 56–57). But once again, 65% of the participants went all the way to 450 volts.

Variations That Reduced Obedience

Milgram replicated his own study 18 times, each time with a slight variation.

Those first studies with 65% obedience established a baseline. Now Milgram could test what situational factors, if any, might raise or lower that number (see Table 7.4). For example, would women act differently? Nope—they got exactly the same result (65% went all the way). But when the study was moved off the beautiful, prestigious Yale campus, obedience did go down, to only 48%. When the Teacher had to sit in the same room as the Learner, it went down again to 40%, and when the Teacher had to physically hold the Learner's hand to an electrified metal plate to get the shocks, only 30% of the participants went all the way to 450 volts. Note, though, that 30% of people still did it!

TABLE 7.3

The Learner's Scripted Responses in Milgram's Obedience Studies

SHOCK LEVEL	LEARNER'S SCRIPTED RESPONSE
75 volts	Ugh!
150 volts	Ugh!!! Experimenter! That's all. Get me out of here. I told you I had heart trouble. My heart's starting to bother me now. Get me out of here, please. My heart's starting to bother me. I refuse to go on. Let me out.
270 volts	[Agonized scream.] Let me out of here. Let me out of here. Let me out of here. Let me out. Do you hear? Let me out of here.
330 volts	[Intense and prolonged agonized scream.] Let me out of here. Let me out of here. My heart's bothering me. Let me out, I tell you. [Hysterically.] Let me out of here. Let me out of here. You have no right to hold me here. Let me out! Let me out! Let me out of here! Let me out! Let me out!
345–450 volts	[Silence]

Source: Milgram (1963).

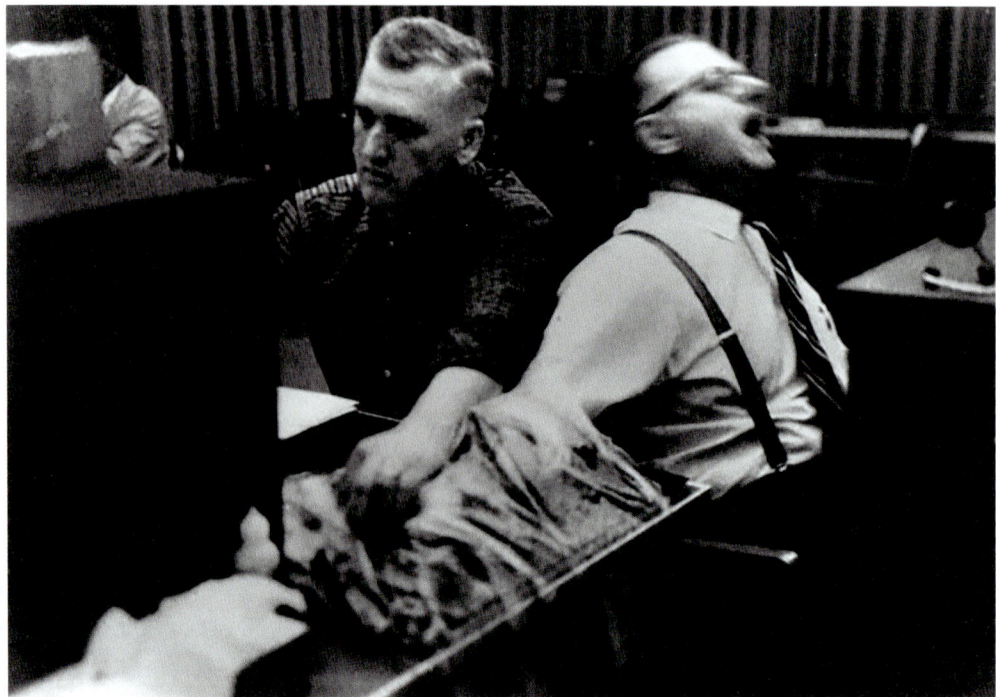

Obedience to authority declined to (a still disturbing) 30% when the participant had to physically hold the victim or "Learner" down to receive painful shocks.

TABLE 7.4

Replications and Variations of Milgram's Original Study

CHANGE IN SITUATION	PARTICIPANTS ALL WOMEN	STUDY MOVED OFF YALE CAMPUS	TEACHER AND LEARNER IN THE SAME ROOM	TEACHER HAS TO HOLD LEARNER'S HAND TO METAL PLATE	EXPERIMENTER LEAVES THE ROOM
% Obedient to 450 volts	65%	48%	40%	30%	21%

Ethical Issues in Milgram's Studies

Thanks to the popularity of Milgram's grainy black-and-white original film, the obedience-to-authority experiments have become "part of our society's shared intellectual legacy" (Ross & Nisbett, 1991, p. 55).

However, the ethics of those experiments have stirred considerable controversy (Baumrind, 1964; Mixon, 1972). In his own defense (also controversial), Milgram asserted that his procedures did not violate any of the research norms of that time period, and his procedures had been preapproved by the National Science Foundation (NSF).

Milgram's NSF grant application also had included a special section about ethical responsibility to the participants (see Blass, 2004). Milgram reported that he debriefed participants after the experiment and kept in touch with them long after the experiment had ended. That assertion is also controversial in light of recent evidence.

Australian journalist Gina Perry deserves significant credit for the 4 years she spent reexamining the Milgram archives (Brannigan, 2013). She listened to 140 audio recordings of the original experiments, to many hours of debriefings with participants, and to experts and family members of the actors playing confederates. Her conclusions challenge how scholars have interpreted (and textbook authors have presented) Stanley Milgram's experiments. Brannigan's (2013) summary of the criticisms included

1. minimizing or hiding the degree of trauma experienced by many participants,

2. providing deliberately misleading reports about those traumas,

3. not reporting participants' skepticism about the various deceptions,

4. misrepresenting how the prods were used,

5. failing to debrief most participants,

6. cherry-picking data, and

7. creating a pseudo-documentary film that whitewashed all these shortcomings.

These are serious charges. Stanley Milgram's death means that he cannot explain, modify, or rebut those assertions. However, the archives indicate that, in contrast to what he reported, Milgram did not debrief all participants and minimized negative consequences when he knew about them (see I. A. M. Nicholson, 2011, 2015; I. R. Nicholson, 2011; Perry, 2013).

For example, one participant indicated that he had lost his job "due to an emotional outburst during a discussion about the experiment. . . . Another reported that he had suffered a mild heart attack . . . implying that the extreme stress of the study was at least partially responsible" (Brannigan et al., 2015, p. 554).

The American Psychological Association's ethical guidelines are part of the legacy of both Milgram's and Zimbardo's experiments. They offer two practical lessons:

- First, use your *institutional review board* (IRB) to protect your study participants, yourself, and your institution. They will review the ethics of your procedures *before* you start conducting an experiment.

- Second, use Morling's (2015) ethical decision-making matrix (see Table 7.5) to help you evaluate risk as you make ethical decisions.

Three Theoretical Explanations

There are three ways to interpret the Zimbardo and Milgram studies.

Option 1: People are basically evil. We're all born with instincts for cruelty and destruction. The only reason we don't exhibit these tendencies more is because social norms prevent us from unleashing the animals within all of us. These two studies showed the true nature of people, because the circumstances gave the participants permission to behave badly.

Option 2: People are neutral. These participants were just average humans, like the rest of us, and the "power of the situation" molded their behavior. The social roles and authority figures told them to act badly, so they did. We're all capable of good or bad deeds if the situation is compelling.

But there's a third option: We're basically good and helpful. How could two studies that are famous for showing the worst in human behavior—cruelty and abuse—be evidence of this option?

Remember that one way to interpret the guards' behavior in Zimbardo's study is that they were explicitly encouraged to act the way they did. Zimbardo himself told the guards that he wanted to study how the prisoners would respond to cruelty—so the prisoners acted cruelly to *help the study*.

The same argument can be made for Milgram's participants. They followed orders from a prestigious-looking authority figure, a scientist wearing a lab coat who said

TABLE 7.5

Morling's (2015) Ethical Decision-Making Matrix

	LOW RISK	HIGH RISK
Low reward		
High reward		The Milgram Obedience Experiments

Milgram's obedience experiments involved high risk and high reward. When does a high reward justify taking a high risk?

Source: Adapted from Morling.

Daily workers at the Auschwitz World War II concentration camp take a break. Their capacity for happiness suggests that they were engaged and willing participants in the mass murder of at least 1.1 million people at Auschwitz. Perhaps they thought they were helping a "higher cause."

he was from Yale University. Maybe they helped because they wanted to be cooperative. Any maybe people in both studies did what they thought was the behavior the researchers wanted to see, because they wanted to be part of a noble cause.

The Higher Cause Explanation

The most radical new interpretation of the Milgram shock experiments comes from Haslam et al. (2015)—and from Milgram's own notes. They propose that participants were more than just obedient—they were engaged followers. They were proud to commit their time to the noble cause of science.

One participant tried to explain his nervous laughter and conflicted emotions as he continued delivering electric shocks. "In the interest of science," he explained, "one goes through with it" (Milgram, 1974, p. 54). Milgram's own notes express initial ambivalence about whether he is observing obedience or cooperation. Table 7.6 (from the Yale archives of the study) organizes sample quotations of what participants said about their level of engagement (see Haslam et al., 2015, p. 72).

Milgram was trying to understand people like Nazi officer Adolf Eichmann. Eichmann was a capable organizer, a man of influence and initiative. Even when the war was ending, Eichmann persisted. He organized an extraordinary 144 transports to Auschwitz for approximately 440,000 Hungarians in just 2 months. He felt such a strong sense of higher purpose that he even defied orders from his Nazi superiors to cut back.

How do you get ordinary people to behave with extraordinary evil? Grobman and colleagues (1983) report a speech by Himmler, generally regarded as the architect of the mass exterminations. His speech was to SS officers who every day were murdering Jews at Poznan, in Poland. Notice Himmler's appeal to "a spirit of love" for a higher cause:

> Most of you know what it is like to see 100 corpses lie side by side, or 500 or 1,000. To have stood fast through all this and . . . at the same time to have remained a decent person. . . . This is an unwritten and never-to-be-written page of glory in our history. . . . We have carried out this most difficult of tasks in a spirit of love for our people. (pp. 454–455)

TABLE 7.6

Participants' Experience in Milgram's Study

LEVELS (1–7)	DESCRIPTION	SAMPLE COMMENTS BY LEVEL OF ENGAGEMENT	NO. OF PEOPLE WITH SIMILAR COMMENT	% PEOPLE WITH SIMILAR COMMENT
7	Very highly engaged	*I feel I have contributed in some small way toward the development of man and his attitudes towards others. I would be glad to participate in other studies. I thoroughly enjoyed participating in the program and hope I will be called on again.*	33	23.6
6	Highly engaged	*The experiment was very interesting and worthwhile. I think that studies of this kind are very helpful and should continue.*	27	19.3
5	Moderately engaged	*Any study with an aim, if properly conducted, can do no harm and might be of some value.*	34	24.3
4	Neither	*It is good to know that you would not permit me to give the learner the actual shocks under the condition of this experiment.*	33	23.6
3	Moderately disengaged	*It was only after speaking to you on the phone that I concluded the experiment had been prearranged and in all truthfulness somewhat silly. I would suggest that more experiments are conducted but that they be conducted on the more serious side.*	8	5.7
2	Highly disengaged	*You might be interested to know that my opinion of Yale is quite low because of this experiment. Kindly furnish me with the name & address so that I can satisfy my own thought about this experiment.*	5	3.5
1	Very highly disengaged	[no comments]	0	0
	Total		140	100%

Source: Adapted from the Yale University Library.

This represents a new way to understand Milgram's experiments. If it holds up, then it has far-reaching implications—and not just for our understanding of the past. On one hand, it's scary. Viciousness is camouflaged as virtue. It can help us understand how modern terrorists privately make sense of and rationalize mass murder: It's for a higher cause. On the other hand, maybe there's a more optimistic view. People are willing to sacrifice their own comfort if they think they're helping a noble cause. It seems that situations are, indeed, powerful, but they can shape our perceptions and behaviors in very complicated ways.

Courage and Nonconformity

We need nonconformists.

Conformity can sometimes be good, when people do what's honestly best for the group. That's why conformity is valued by many countries and cultures. But other times, conformity means a lack of social progress and maintaining a status quo that is rooted in a past of prejudice. Think about the brave people who helped Jews and others hide or escape during the Holocaust: Their ability to stand up to both implicit and explicit social influence saved lives. There are many examples of this kind of courage in history.

Bettmann / Bettmann/Getty Images

Rosa Parks' arrest ignited a city-wide boycott of buses.

Rosa Parks was one of the early movers in a cascade of nonconformity that led to large-scale social changes (Sunstein, 2019). Parks helped ignite the larger civil rights movement when she refused to give up her seat on a bus in Montgomery, Alabama, in 1955 (see Theoharis, 2015, p. 62). The community of civil rights activists in Montgomery was not unified until her arrest brought them together. Ms. Parks explained the triggering event that became a large, enduring social movement:

> People always say that I didn't give up my seat because I was tired, but that isn't true. I was not tired physically, or no more tired than I usually was at the end of a working day. I was not old, although some people have an image of me being old then. I was only forty-two. No, the only tired I was, was the tired of giving in.

Notice the pattern of nonconformity that runs through this chapter:

- August Landmesser courageously folded his arms at a public Nazi rally rather than conform to the "Heil Hitler" that condemned his lover.
- About 25% of participants in Solomon Asch's line judgment experiments refused to conform to the pressure of the group.
- The Stanford Prison Study only ended when an observer criticized Zimbardo for allowing the cruelty to continue as long as it had.
- In the most well known of Milgram's studies, about 35% of participants refused to continue delivering electric shocks to innocent others.
- There are thousands of examples throughout history of people who had the courage to stand up to oppressive conformity. Often, their leadership inspired others to create massive social change.

Solomon Asch, Stanley Milgram, and Philip Zimbardo were all interested in why some people are able to rise above social influence to be nonconformists, disobedient to brutal authorities, and able to rise above a negative social role. To end this chapter, consider qualitative data from Milgram's study when he interviewed people who successfully stood up to the experimenter by refusing to continue. Here are three examples.

Interview 1: "I do have a choice." An industrial engineer stopped at 255 volts. When the experimenter said, "It is absolutely essential that you continue. . . . You have no other choice," this man said,

> I *do* have a choice. Why don't I have choice? I came here on my own free will. I thought I could help in a research project. But if I have to hurt somebody to do that, or if I was in his place, too, I wouldn't stay there. I can't continue. I'm very sorry. I think I've gone too far already, probably. (Milgram, 1974, p. 51)

Interview 2: "But not in America." One man, a professor of religion, stopped at 150 volts. When the experimenter told him, "You must go on," he responded, "If this were Russia maybe, but not in America" (Milgram, 1974, p. 48).

Interview 3: "Perhaps we have seen too much pain." A female immigrant from Germany had been raised in a culture of Nazi propaganda and participated in the Hitler youth program. She had witnessed the social disintegration and terror produced by blind obedience to an authoritarian leader. When asked why she had stopped at 210 volts, her calm answer was, "Perhaps we have seen too much pain" (Milgram, 1974, p. 85).

THE MAIN IDEAS

- The famous Stanford Prison Study explored social roles and deindividuation by randomly assigning students to pretend to be either a prisoner or a guard.

- Milgram's obedience to authority experiments demonstrate how many people will follow orders from an authority, even when it means engaging in behaviors they might consider immoral.

- Both Zimbardo's study and Milgram's study are considered unethical by today's standards. In addition, there are many possible interpretations of the results.

CRITICAL THINKING CHALLENGE

- Imagine you were given an opportunity to be a participant in a replication of the original Zimbardo or Milgram study. Would you do it? Why or why not?

- If you felt like ethical concerns could be addressed, think of three additional ways that the Milgram study could be replicated with different circumstances. For example, Milgram compared adult men and adult women who were both assigned the "Teacher" role. He also moved the study from a prestigious campus to a run-down building in the city. What other changes could be made in interesting ways, and what do you hypothesize would be the results in each of your three changes?

- The book offered three different conclusions from the Zimbardo and Milgram studies: (1) People are basically evil, (2) people are neutral and are guided by circumstances, or (3) people want to be helpful and cooperative, especially if they feel like they're part of a "noble cause." Which explanation is most convincing to you, and why?

CHAPTER SUMMARY

What Types of Social Influence Exist?

Social influence occurs when our thoughts, feelings, and/or behaviors change because of pressure from our social world. Implicit social influence occurs when we follow subtle, unwritten rules; conformity and social roles are examples. Explicit social influence happens when we follow clearly stated requests (compliance) or orders (obedience).

Social norms can lead to a herd mentality, or the tendency to follow the direction of a group without question. In general, conformity seems to be contagious; we feel more pressure to conform when the group is larger. This can sometimes even lead to a phenomenon called mass psychogenic illness, which is when psychological conformity leads to people experiencing physical symptoms of illness when there is no physical cause.

What Social Forces Compel Social Conformity?

Informational conformity or social influence occurs when people change their behavior because they want to be correct. Classic research was started by Sherif when he found that people's guesses for how much something appeared to move were influenced by confederates. This effect has been shown to occur over "generations" of participants.

On the other hand, normative social influence occurs when we go along with group behaviors in order to fit in or be accepted. The most famous example is a series of studies by Asch in which participants provided what was clearly the wrong answer to a perception task after confederates had provided a wrong answer. Participants indicated that they went along with the wrong answer because they didn't want to seem strange or not fit in. There are individual differences in how likely people are to conform, based on variables such as cultural values.

How Are We Influenced by Social Roles and Obedience to Authority?

Social roles guide us in how to think, feel, and act in a variety of situations, like characters in a play. The most famous social psychology study of social roles is the Stanford Prison Study created by Zimbardo. He turned the basement of the Stanford psychology building into a fake prison, then randomly assigned students to play either the role of prisoner or guard. The students quickly seemed to lose their individual identities and simply played the part, or they went along with their assigned social role.

Milgram conducted a series of studies regarding whether people are willing to deliver potentially painful and dangerous electric shocks to someone else, simply because they were ordered to do so. Approximately two thirds of the participants in Milgram's initial conditions went to the maximum shock level available.

Both studies are considered unethical by today's standards, and both have recently come under question regarding how the results should be interpreted. Either way, social change often occurs because a courageous individual is willing to stand up as a nonconformist.

CRITICAL THINKING, ANALYSIS, AND APPLICATION

- Identify two times in world history when someone stood up against a group (they exhibited nonconformity) and helped change the world for the better. Then, identify two times in world history where conforming to the values or needs of the larger group helped a community make a good or progressive decision, even if some people in the group disagreed or had to make a sacrifice.

- As times change, social roles change as well. For example, the social roles expected of "stereotypical" men and women have changed over the past 100 years. What are positive aspects of this change—and are there any negative aspects of this change?

- This chapter discussed several famous studies that some people consider unethical. Do you think an unethical study is more likely to become famous compared to an ethical one? Why or why not? Provide examples as evidence of your answer.

- The theories and phenomena in this chapter (conformity, social roles, compliance, and obedience) were presented as possible social psychological explanations for the Holocaust (or, at least, contributing factors). What other theories that you've learned about in this book so far might also be included as possible explanations for what happened?

8

Group Processes

Core Questions

8.1	Why are groups so important to us?
8.2	How do groups influence individuals?
8.3	How can individuals influence groups?

Learning Objectives

8.1	Explain the benefits of living in groups, including support, safety, and cohesion.
8.2	Describe both positive and negative effects that groups can have on individuals.
8.3	Analyze how social loafing, leadership, decision-making processes, and creativity occur in group settings.

Thirteen people painted the Sistine Chapel, but we credit the achievement to just one person (Michelangelo). The first computer software was written when six women were given a stack of wiring diagrams and instructed to "figure out how the machine works and then figure out how to program it" (Isaacson, 2014, pp. 97–98). Fantastic achievements have been reached by sports teams with incredible synergy, like the New York Yankees, L.A. Lakers, U.S. Women's National Soccer team, and more.

But groups can also go bad, and sometimes there is only a faint line between creating and destroying. History contains a long line of charismatic or powerful leaders who have turned one group against another through fear, prejudice, or nationalistic pride. On a smaller, but more personal level, many students dread group projects because of the imbalance of work, commitment, and motivation within team members. Groups can result in creative triumphs or to miserable defeats.

This chapter explores both the creative and the destructive potential of groups by asking and answering three core questions:

WHY ARE GROUPS SO IMPORTANT TO US?

>> **LO 8.1:** **Explain the benefits of living in groups, including support, safety, and cohesion.**

Groups develop whenever two or more individuals interact with one another or are joined together by a common fate.

Most of us were welcomed into the world by a family: our first group. Our family group is supported by even larger social groups of friends and neighbors. And they were organized into larger groups based on geography, beliefs, convenience, and cultural traditions.

The importance of groups is revealed by how humans punish one another. We isolate social offenders in prisons (in part to protect the community group) and send the most severe cases to solitary confinement. Another way groups punish individuals is to banish them. On an individual level, we might give someone the "silent treatment" or ghost them. We all crave social connection and validation.

This section answers the core question "Why are groups so important to us?" by

(1) describing how groups provide critical social supports, safety, and social cohesion and

(2) summarizing why we value groups more if they're hard to get into.

Groups Provide Support, Safety, and Cohesion

Groups provide their individual members with many kinds of social supports.

Table 8.1 summarizes how Glanz et al. (2008) think of different types of social support. We may have to belong to several different kinds of groups to give and receive all possible forms of social support. It would be difficult to live effectively or meaningfully without any social supports; we'd feel isolated and vulnerable. Being part of a group means our chances go up of having someone who can provide the type of support we need.

Groups Help Us Feel Safe

Think of it as the "Misery Loves Company" hypothesis.

What do you do when you feel threatened? Safety is a basic need, of course, but Stanley Schachter (1959) wanted to know whether we tend to affiliate with one another when we feel threatened. His experimental design was simple but a bit grim: He threatened study participants with the possibility of electric shock. Sure enough, the threatened people clustered together. When we're afraid, we like the comfort of a group.

Group: When two or more individuals interact or are joined together by a common fate.

TABLE 8.1

Types of Social Support

CONSTRUCT	DEFINITION	EXAMPLE
Emotional	Expressions of empathy, love, trust, and caring	Close friends and family members provide hope and a listening ear in times of trouble.
Instrumental	Tangible aid and service	A woman whose friend's apartment burned down lets him sleep on her couch until he finds another place to live.
Informational	Advice, suggestions, and information	A professor helps her niece decide what college to attend by providing information about how to compare dorm rooms, financial aid packages, and academic merit.
Appraisal	Information that is useful for self-evaluation	A close friend of a man with social skills challenges helps explain behaviors he's doing that frustrate people at his job and how he can be more understanding of others.

Source: Glanz et al. (2008).

But Schacter's observation wasn't the end of the research story. Two years later, Sarnoff and Zimbardo (1961) conducted an experiment that first *replicated* the Schachter study. But the researchers then used an experimental manipulation that made people feel anxious instead of afraid—and they found that anxious people did *not* tend to cluster with other anxious people.

Do anxious people want to be left alone? Actually, they don't. Firestone et al. (1973) found that anxiety still leads to a desire to be with others. But unlike fear, anxiety makes us want to be surrounded by people who are *not* anxious (so clustering around the other anxious participants in the study wouldn't help).

It seems that both fear and anxiety motivate us to affiliate with others. But when we're afraid, we like to be with people who feel the same way; this could help us bond together against a common enemy. In contrast, when we're anxious, we like to be with people who are *not* anxious because they can calm us down. Both responses appear to be driven by the need to feel safe and secure. Feeling safe is a major benefit of belonging to a group. So misery does love company, but the kind of company we crave depends on the kind of misery we are experiencing.

Social Cohesion in Groups

Some groups have an impact on every member.

Group cohesion is the degree to which every member feels connected with everyone else. It means people who work harmoniously together for some common cause enjoy a high quality of social cooperation, resist disruptive forces, and hold together when social forces try to separate them (see Dragolov et al., 2016; Durkheim, 1893; Festinger et al., 1950; Merton, 1994).

For example, you are likely to benefit by investing your time in groups offered by your college or university. There is probably a huge variety: groups based on academic interests, religious faith, athletics, ethnicity, community outreach, study abroad, and more. These groups are relatively cohesive simply because the members all immediately have something in common. At a practical level, those extra activities help develop long-term professional connections and build a distinctive resume. They also promote emotionally satisfying, lifelong friendships (see Coker et al., 2018; Dustin et al., 2019).

Groups can provide more than friendship or job connections, though; they can help you survive. In an interesting *case study* using *naturalistic observation* of the "bad" part of Chicago, graduate student Sudhir Venkatesh (2008) was allowed to follow a

Group cohesion: The degree to which members of a group feel connected to one another, work harmoniously, and resist threats.

gang leader's daily activities for an extended period of time. He reported his observations in the book *Gang Leader for a Day*.

Venkatesh's reports contradicted the television stereotype of macho male drug dealers wearing expensive jewelry and listening to music while being pampered by beautiful women. Kill the stereotype because Venkatesh found that most drug dealers lived with their mothers. They worked long hours for low pay, often in terrible weather, and at high personal risk. Many moved on to other jobs when they got older, but their gang was a cohesive group that satisfied deeper existential and evolutionary survival needs for friendship, money, and daily social support.

The fine-grained details that emerged from Venkatesh's (2008) observations demonstrated how cohesive groups of mothers squeezed the most benefits out of their meager resources. One apartment might have working plumbing, another a working stove, and a third a television, or heat, or air conditioning. Among them, they had approximately one working apartment, so they shared their resources and shifted their daily activities as required. Likewise, the young men—some of them drug dealers—also became emergency community ambulance drivers when residents became ill.

What looks careless and unkempt to an outsider is sometimes creative coping by the insider. For example, Venkatesh discovered that sometimes mothers would allow people to urinate in the stairwells immediately outside their apartments because the terrible odor kept the drug dealers, prostitutes, and gang members from hanging out near their doors—and their children.

So group cohesion increases our opportunities to survive by sharing food and shelter in times of scarcity. This even happens in the virtual world: Players of online games form strategic alliances, even when the other players are anonymous or strangers (Belz et al., 2013; DeScioli & Kimbrough, 2019). Groups allow individuals and subgroups to specialize, define social roles, develop an identity, share critical information, and provide a safer environment for everyone. On the flip side, group cohesion can lead to long-term harm when people join an abusive religious cult, a terrorist organization, or even a successful but cutthroat business headed by a strong personality (Snook et al., 2019; Wu, 2019). How groups influence individuals is the focus of the next section of this book.

We Value Groups More When They're Hard to Join

We admire the elite.

Many students in the psychology major or minor wait for the day they're invited to join Psi Chi, the national honors society (see www.psichi.org). To get that invitation, you have to meet several criteria, including a high cumulative GPA. It feels great if it happens, because you know your hard work has been acknowledged by your peers, your professors, and even people across the nation you've never met. Members are proud, as they should be; it's a great group. We feel more gratified when we're asked to join elite, selective, prestigious groups. Exclusivity makes us feel special.

But there are other groups that seem exclusive at first, only to let members down later. What happens if you've gone through the initiation, paid your dues, and then discovered that you don't like this group very much? It is a classic case of cognitive dissonance (see Chapter 6). We went through all the work to join, and we don't want to be disappointed.

One psychological reaction to this situation, based on cognitive dissonance, is the **initiation effect**: We value groups more when they were hard to join, even if membership doesn't provide much to us, objectively speaking. Sometimes this phenomenon is called **effort justification**. We simply tell ourselves that the group is fantastic, even if it's not. The Spotlight on Research Methods feature explains a classic study that explored this interesting reaction.

Recall that cognitive dissonance (see Chapter 6) predicts that when we have thoughts and behaviors that don't align, we'll feel uncomfortable and are motivated to change something—anything, really, that will reduce the dissonance. Once people have gone through embarrassing, effortful, or expensive efforts to gain membership

Initiation effect: We value groups more if they're hard to get into and/or if we had to go through a difficult initiation.

Effort justification: See *initiation effect*.

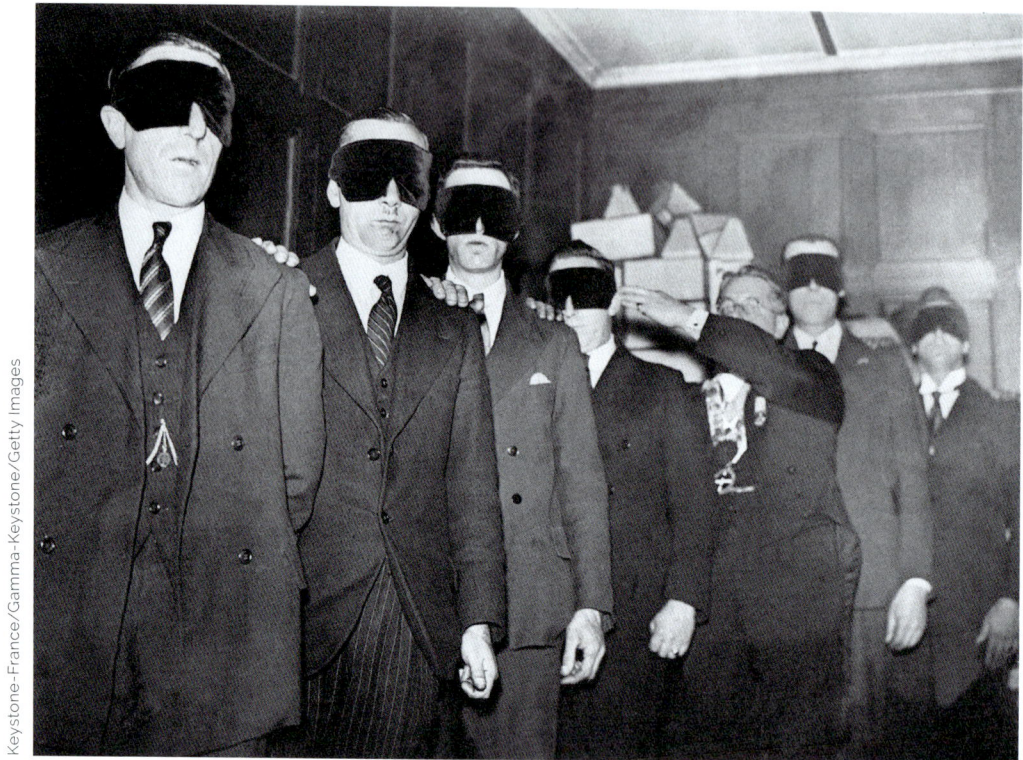

Some groups are more prestigious and elite—and harder to get into. The Freemasons, for example, have several famous political leaders and celebrities, including George Washington, Jesse Jackson, Buzz Aldrin, and the musicians Beethoven, Bach, and Mozart. Women are not allowed to join traditional lodges in the Freemasons.

in a group, it would create cognitive dissonance if they believed those efforts were a waste of time. So, instead, we simply convince ourselves that the group is wonderful! Just as cult members didn't want to admit they were wrong about an apocalypse that never came, we don't want to admit when an elite group has let us down. Groups are so important to us that we are motivated to maintain loyalty once they've become part of our identity.

The Initiation Effect

Aronson and Mills (1959) wanted to see if people would become more committed to groups if they were required to go through an initiation ritual, similar to many social groups in the "real" world (such as fraternities and sororities). They tested this hypothesis using an ingenious and now-famous research study with college women. The participants thought they were trying to join a small discussion group about sex—a topic that was socially taboo back in 1959 when the study was done, especially for a proper college lady. While talking about sex might seem titillating, Aronson and Mills purposely designed the actual conversation to be downright dull and boring. So how

did they get some of the participants to say the group was exciting and interesting?

Using *random assignment to groups,* the experiment started by placing participants into groups with different initiation experiences. Participants in the *control condition,* the lowest or easiest level, only had to state that they were willing to discuss sexually oriented material to join the group. In one *experimental group* (the mild embarrassment condition), participants read some mildly sexual passages out loud that included the words *prostitute, virgin,* and *petting*—again, fairly embarrassing for the deeply conservative 1950s.

However, in the severe embarrassment condition, participants read (out loud) vivid descriptions of explicit sexual activity—essentially, they had to read pornography aloud to the researchers.

After each woman completed her level of "initiation," she was allowed to "eavesdrop" on a conversation the discussion group was having. The *dependent variable* was each woman's attitude toward the group—was it interesting, and did they like the group? Figure 8.1 shows the results. The women who experienced the most severe initiation (reading pornography aloud) gave the most positive attitude ratings to the very dull discussion group (and to the people in the group). The women in the "porn" condition justified their embarrassing efforts to join by telling themselves that it was all worthwhile to join such an exciting group—even though the group was perceived as pretty boring by everyone else.

FIGURE 8.1

The effect of severity of initiation on attitude toward the group.

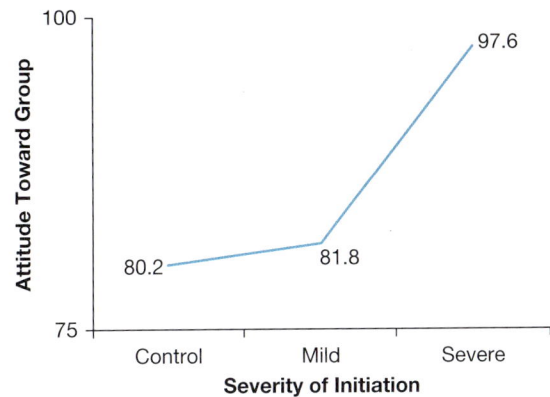

THE MAIN IDEAS

- We're instinctively motivated to form groups because they provide several survival advantages, including various forms of support, safety, and social cohesion.

- The initiation effect happens when we value groups more if they're hard to get into and/or if we had to go through a difficult initiation.

- After joining an exclusive group, we might continue to value it despite disappointing results because of cognitive dissonance.

CRITICAL THINKING CHALLENGE

- Provide examples of a time in your life when someone in your social world offered you each of the four types of social support listed in Table 8.1.

- Think of times in your recent life when you felt afraid or threatened, then think of times when you felt anxious. Did your social patterns match the research described in this section in terms of whether you wanted to be around other people versus alone?

- Describe a group you joined that was either elite and/or difficult to join because of an initiation ritual. Explain how you feel about the group now in terms of whether you believe this group is successful, well respected, and valuable. If you think positively about the group, do you think your view is partially due to the initiation effect? Why or why not?

HOW DO GROUPS INFLUENCE INDIVIDUALS?

>> **LO 8.2:** **Describe both positive and negative effects that groups can have on individuals.**

We know groups offer several advantages and that we value them so much we're willing to go through a lot to join them.

From the beginning of life, we need other people to survive. But groups can have both positive and negative effects on us. We've all felt the sting of social ostracization at some point in our lives, when a group turns against us. This section of the chapter summarizes two negative effects groups can have on individuals, but we'll end on how being in a group can also motivate us to do our best work.

This section answers the core question "How do groups influence individuals?" by

(1) describing how mistreatment effects such as hazing strengthen a group's authority over the individual,

(2) summarizing how the fear of being rejected transfers social power from the individual to the group, and

(3) describing how group settings facilitate individual effort.

Mistreatment Strengthens a Group's Authority

Many graduate students earning master's or doctorate degrees complain about the intimidating and harsh oral defenses they have to give of their research projects. But when those same people become professors, they may continue the tradition for the next generation of scholars. The same thing used to happen (and, in some cases, still does) in the military and when fraternities and sororities gain new members, although harassment laws have decreased this treatment over the years.

Hazing rituals occur across cultures and begin early in life (Martini, 1994). Two obvious questions: (1) Why is hazing so popular? and (2) Why do otherwise intelligent, caring people put up with it, both as victims and as perpetrators? We know from the previous section that harsh initiations make people value groups more, so that's a big part of why groups continue to use this technique. But hazing is complicated.

The Social Problem of Hazing

Hazing occurs whenever members of a group establish arbitrary rituals for new members that may cause physical or emotional harm.

Few university fraternities and sororities still perpetuate dangerous hazing activities, which is a good thing. However, one research team (Keating et al., 2005) happened to be collecting data about hazing when a student died during a ritual requiring him to drink large quantities of water through a funnel. Finkel (2000) described Greek organizations that required pledges to swallow nausea-inducing drinks, be branded with cigarettes, and submit to sexual assaults. According to ESPN, 40 young men on high school teams were subjected to sodomy sexual assault by different teammates across the country who claimed their actions were just "hazing" (Barr et al., 2012). A study of Canadian universities found that 58% of college athletes experienced hazing and perceived that it was "part of being a member of the team" (Johnson et al., 2018, p. 144).

Another case of hazing at a well-known university (see Gallo & DeRobertis, 2019) led to the death of a student. That case was complicated by a charge of obstruction of justice when a fraternity brother deleted images shortly after the authorization of a search warrant. He was one of nine students arrested. Administrators also were placed on leave when they did not respond to rumors of hazing rituals.

We shouldn't pick only on Greek fraternities, sororities, and sports teams. Hazing occurs throughout society. The *generalizability*, or social ubiquity, of hazing was documented when Winslow (1999) described how the Canadian Air Force employed rituals of binge drinking, demeaning tasks, and painful activities. Similar rituals occur in U.S. Marine paratroopers (Gleick, 1997), the Australian military (Wadham, 2016), college marching bands (Silveira & Hudson, 2015), and even in "nice" professions like nursing (Reynolds-Milon, 2019). Generally, people approve of hazing if it's part of a "tradition" and if they believe it makes people more loyal to the group (Thomas & Meglich, 2019).

Hazing: Whenever members of a group establish arbitrary rituals for new members that may cause physical or emotional harm, which can be a type of escalation trap for aspiring members (see *effort justification*).

Hazing and Mistreatment Effects

Initiation rituals and hazing strengthen a group's authority over the individual.

Keating et al. (2005), for example, pointed out that different kinds of groups require different kinds of initiation rituals. Fraternities and sororities tend to have hazing rituals that include high levels of social deviance and embarrassment; the point is usually humiliation. But athletic and military groups have hazing rituals that require more physical challenges and pain endurance. The end result is that each initiation ritual affirms the social hierarchy, values, and goals of that particular group. The message: If you don't like it, if you're not committed, then you're not welcome.

Why do otherwise intelligent, caring individuals put up with hazing? One explanation is **maltreatment effects**. Maltreatment is a fancier way of saying mistreatment, but they both refer to the ironic result of becoming more loyal to a group after it's treated us badly (Keating et al., 2005). By the end of the process, the abused person starts to connect with or even love the people who hurt him or her. It's the same cognitive dissonance we saw through the initiation effect. We think, "I must really like these people or this group to put up with so much." Psychologically, we go through the five-step process shown in Figure 8.2.

- Step 1: Maltreatment creates confusion, especially when delivered by friends or family members.

- Step 2: Confusion creates uncertainty about our value or place in a social world.

- Step 3: Uncertainty leads to emotional vulnerability.

- Step 4: Vulnerability creates a dependency on the people who hold such power over you; you need their acceptance.

- Step 5: Dependency creates gratitude when your needs are met. For example, a stale piece of bread and a cup of water can feel like a deep kindness when you are starving, even when it comes from the enemy that is starving you.

FIGURE 8.2

The maltreatment effect model.

Maltreatment > Uncertainty > Vulnerability > Dependency > Gratitude

Source: Adapted from Keating et al. (2005).

Stockholm Syndrome

A fascinating example of maltreatment effects is **Stockholm syndrome**, when a captive develops affection for their captors (West, 1993).

The name came from a 1973 bank robbery in Stockholm, Sweden. Four hostages resisted being rescued. After they were rescued, they defended the robbers and refused to testify against them in court. To most observers, that just seemed downright weird. But it turns out that Stockholm syndrome is more common than first appears.

According to the FBI, about 8% of hostages end up agreeing with their captors' demands or feeling friendship or romantic attraction to their captors (Sundaram, 2013). So, Stockholm syndrome may not be quite as weird or as uncommon as you imagine. A similar effect occurred in 1974 when newspaper heiress Patty Hearst was kidnapped by the Symbionese Liberation Army (SLA) and then joined their cause (Hearst & Moscow, 1988). Hearst used Stockholm syndrome as her defense in court and was later pardoned.

Maltreatment effects: When hazing elicits social dependency, which ironically promotes loyalty to the group.

Stockholm syndrome: When hostages develop affection for their captors.

Patty Hearst was famously kidnapped but then appeared to join the cause of her kidnappers. What would motivate her to become allies with a group that treated her badly?

British reporter Yvonne Ridley was kidnapped by the Taliban in 2001. After being held prisoner for 11 days, Ridley was released—and she proceeded to convert to Islam, praise the Taliban's practices, and denounce "Western" values. Unlike Hearst, Ridley refused the idea of Stockholm syndrome and claimed that her experience had simply awakened her understanding of a better lifestyle (Adorjan et al., 2012).

A particularly sad example of Stockholm syndrome appears to be at work in some cases of sex trafficking (Sanchez et al., 2019). Some of those victims will come to identify with their captors (see Hopper, 2017; Ueda, 2017). Sex trafficking is a robust, global business. It operates in all 50 states in the United States. About 70% of sex trafficking victims are under the age of 24 (30% under 18) and have run away from home or are homeless. Their situation obliges them to trade sex for basic needs of food and shelter (see Middleton et al., 2018). Sanchez et al. (2019) recognize that for these youthful victims of sex trafficking, their situation "interrupts identity formation in the adolescent, resulting in role confusion, which in turn diminishes self-esteem and destroys healthy boundaries." (p. 48)

Groups Can Ostracize Individuals: Rejection Sensitivity

Experiencing rejection can trigger deep-seated fears (see Sloman, 2000).

Much of what we've covered so far speaks to our need to be part of a group, to be socially accepted. Consequently, group norms become powerful influences because of **rejection sensitivity**, the fear of social rejection and ostracism (see Downey & Feldman, 1996). On some level, most of us have anxiety about whether our friends, associates at work, teammates, and even family members will accept us and validate us. When they don't, it can be heartbreaking.

Fear of Being Rejected

Fear of being rejected transfers social power from the individual to the group.

At a practical level, social rejection threatens our survival (Baumeister & Leary, 1995; Gruter & Masters, 1986; Van Beest & Williams, 2006; Williams, 2002). Like jabs from a four-pronged pitchfork, social rejection threatens our

1. need to belong by separating us from our group,

2. self-esteem because it implies that we are unlikeable,

3. need for control because we cannot influence the decision, and

4. sense of existence, both metaphorically and in reality.

Merely observing someone *else* being ridiculed produces increased social conformity in observers (Janes & Olson, 2000). Sometimes social conformity in public seems to be a way to privately beg not to be rejected. Most—and perhaps all—social animals appear to have developed some degree of rejection sensitivity. You can see how this is measured in psychological studies by checking out the What's My Score? feature.

Rejection sensitivity: The fear of social rejection and ostracism.

Measuring Rejection Sensitivity

How sensitive are you to social rejection or ostracism? Instructions: Consider each situation below and rate how concerned you would be that the other person involved would reject your request, using this scale:

1	2	3	4	5	6
Very unconcerned					Very concerned

___ 1. You ask someone in class if you can borrow their notes.

___ 2. You ask your romantic partner to move in with you.

___ 3. You ask someone you don't know well out on a date.

___ 4. You ask your parents for extra money to cover living expenses.

___ 5. You approach a close friend to talk after doing or saying something that seriously upset them.

___ 6. After graduation you can't find a job and you ask your parents if you can live at home for a while.

___ 7. You ask a friend to do you a big favor.

___ 8. You ask your romantic partner if they really love you.

Scoring: Add all of your responses; higher scores indicate a greater level of rejection sensitivity.

Source: Modified from Downey and Feldman (1996). The original scale includes 18 scenarios, and some terms were changed to be gender inclusive (e.g., "boyfriend/girlfriend" was changed to "romantic partner"). The original scale also includes more complicated scoring.

Rejection hurts. One study scanned participants' brains when they were suddenly excluded from a computer game of virtual ball-tossing. The social pain of being excluded occurred in the same part of the brain (the dorsal anterior cingulate cortex) that registers our physical pain (Eisenberger et al., 2003). In other words, the social pain of this mild form of virtual rejection was experienced as a real neurological event. Ouch.

We're so sensitive to rejection that participants in experiments experience painful rejection even when

- we're just seeing someone else be excluded (Giesen & Echterhoff, 2018);
- social exclusion comes from members of an outgroup (Eisenberger & Lieberman, 2005), even groups that the participants strongly *dislike*, such as the Ku Klux Klan (Gonsalkorale & Williams, 2007);
- rejection is caused by a "technical problem" (Eisenberger & Lieberman, 2005) that's not even perceived as the participant's fault or as personal;
- ostracism comes from a computer instead of from another person (Zadro et al., 2004); and
- being ostracized leads to a financial reward (Van Beest & Williams, 2006).

These irrational reactions signal that the self perceives rejection as an existential threat so important that it makes us question our entire value.

Optimal Distinctiveness Theory: Being the Same and Different

Clearly, we want to be a validated, supported member of a group. We fear social ostracism.

But we're also driven by the need to be unique. We want to be really *seen* as valuable individuals with our own, unique talents and perspective. On some level, these two needs (to be part of a group and to be individuals) are in opposite directions. How do we balance these two basic, instinctive psychological motivations?

In 2017, the Malaysian gymnastics team won the gold medal at the Southeast Asia Games. Each player is recognized for her individual skills, but the entire team was needed to win.

Brewer (1991) suggested a solution called **optimal distinctiveness theory**. Her original paper was called "The Social Self: On Being the Same and Different at the Same Time" (p. 475). Optimal distinctiveness is the idea that we can simultaneously achieve the advantages of being seen as a unique and important individual *and* of being in a group by being an identifiable member of a small and elite group. In this way, we're not "too" distinct (which might mean social isolation) or "too" anonymous (losing our individuality). We want a level of distinctiveness that's somewhere in the middle, the best of both worlds.

Small, elite groups provide all the advantages of groups in general (social support, a sense of identity, information, and safety). In addition, their elite status provides prestige and pride (and more commitment to the group, as we saw with hazing). At the same time, elite groups are small enough that we still maintain our individuality and sense of importance. Like each player on a world-class sports team, each individual is identifiable and needed—but the entire team is still needed to reach success.

Social Facilitation: Groups Can Help Performance

"Two heads are better than one."

That's the folk wisdom—but is it true? The idea is that more people equals better results. You've also heard the opposite idea, "Too many cooks spoil the broth." The second phrase implies that groups can cause disagreement and havoc, leading to a bad outcome. Can both be true? There is a two-sided story about how and why our behavior changes in group settings.

Here are three curious observations about athletic performance when an audience is watching.

1. When bowlers roll a strike, they probably won't smile about that achievement until they turn and face their friends (Kraut & Johnson, 1979).

2. People on exercise bikes do better in both sprints and endurance training when they get verbal encouragement from others during the task (Edwards et al., 2018).

3. Use of virtual reality (VR) can motivate athletes to work harder if the VR makes it seem like other people are watching, even when those people only exist digitally (Neumann et al., 2018).

Optimal distinctiveness theory: The idea that we can simultaneously achieve the goals of being unique and of being in a group through membership in a small and elite group.

Social facilitation is the increase in effort and performance in the presence of others. Often, we're more motivated to do our best when someone else is watching. Whether it be trying to impress a potential date, a simple competitive spirit, trying to show off, or any other motive, we often work harder if we know people can see us.

Social Facilitation: When It Works and When It Doesn't

Bicycle racing was becoming a big sport in the late 1800s.

The first Tour de France took place in 1903, and psychologist Norm Triplett was one of the early enthusiasts. From his own experience as a cyclist, he wondered why racing times were faster when racing against one another than when practicing alone, against the clock. His testable *hypothesis* was that "the bodily presence of another rider is a stimulus to the racer in arousing the competitive instinct" (Triplett, 1898, p. 516). He tested his hypothesis with a simple setup: He asked children to wind fishing reels either alone or in the presence of others also winding fishing reels. As expected, children in groups worked harder. Triplett is now credited as conducting one of the earliest experiments in both social and sports psychology (Vaughan & Guerin, 1997).

Another psychologist, Allport, also became intrigued with social facilitation but noted that it didn't have to happen in a sports environment (Allport, 1920). For example, social facilitation occurs when people give more money to charity in the presence of others (Hofmann et al., 2018; Izuma et al., 2010). Airport security staff speed up when doing simple tasks like pat downs if the lines are long and they know they're being watched (Yu & Wu, 2015). We also eat more when we're around other people (Ruddock et al., 2019), as shown in Figure 8.3.

But social facilitation doesn't always work. Research shows that it works best when we're doing simple or well-practiced tasks. If, instead, we don't feel confident or the task is complicated, the presence of others actually hurts. When firefighters are filmed by people watching, they report that it's distracting and decreases their success (Strojny et al., 2018). People learning a new Wii game with a balanceboard didn't do better when people watched (Lau et al., 2019), and the same thing happened with people learning new digital games in general (Emmerich & Masuch, 2018).

In one memorable and ethically questionable study (see Koocher, 1977; Middlemist et al., 1976, 1977), a research team hung signs in a men's restroom reading, "Don't use; washing urinal" to force male participants into one of three experimental situations in which they (1) stood alone, (2) were separated from another man by one urinal, or (3) stood right next to another man. (If you want a peek into the world of "Dude Rules" regarding male restroom etiquette, then search the Internet for "The Urinal Game.")

Have you ever attended an exercise class, such as a spin class for bicycling? If so, your efforts and exertion probably went up compared to when you exercise alone, due to social facilitation.

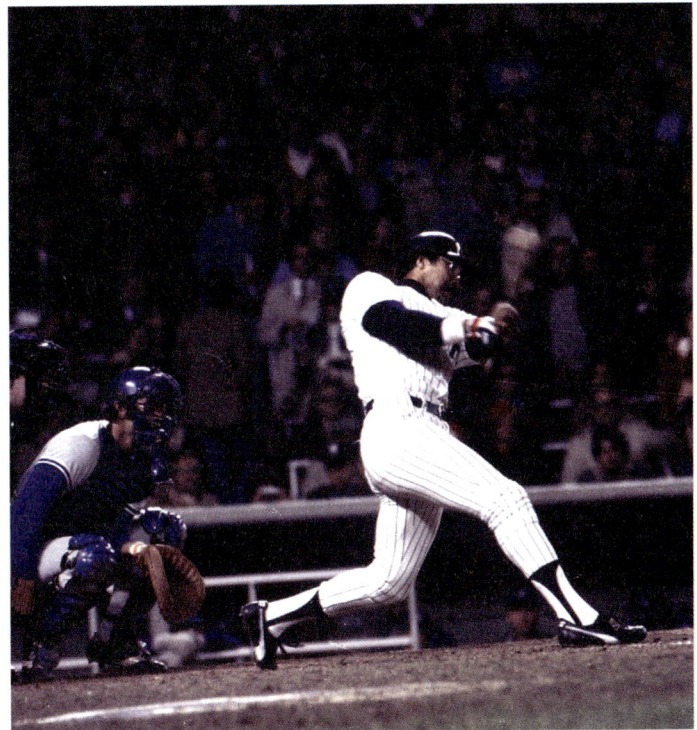

The pressure of World Series Game 6 appeared to improve Reggie Jackson's performance in 1977. After ending the previous game with a walk-off home run, Jackson walked on four pitches in his first at bat. But then he hit the first pitch of three consecutive at-bats with a home run off three different pitchers. Social psychologists might say that his hitting that day was helped by social facilitation.

Social facilitation: When we work harder in the presence of others than we would by ourselves.

FIGURE 8.3

How much do you eat in the presence of others?

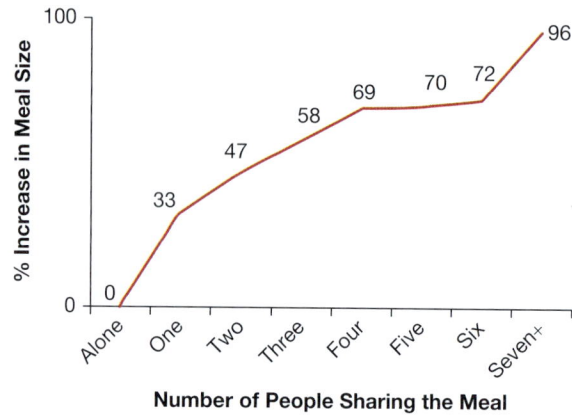

Source: Adapted from de Castro (2000).

FIGURE 8.4

Onset and persistence of urination.

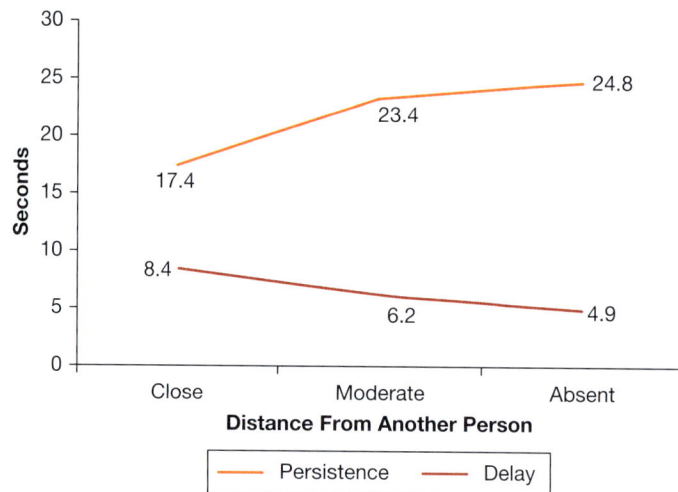

Source: Adapted from Middlemist, Knowles, and Matter (1976, 1977).

The data in Figure 8.4 show us that the presence of another person approaching the personal space of someone else did *not* facilitate the individual's "performance" at the urinal. In fact, the closer someone else was to a participant, the longer it took him to, well, get going. So even though this was an unusual *field experiment*, it suggested that the body does react physiologically to the presence of others. Other researchers made similar observations without resorting to such questionable ethical procedures (see Bond & Titus, 1983; Zajonc, 1965; Zajonc & Sales, 1966).

For example, four decades before the public restroom experiment, Pessin (1933) found that college students were worse at memorizing made-up words (nonsense syllables) in front of spectators. And while the airport security study cited above found that security agents sped up their simple tasks when other people were watching, they actually slowed down for complicated tasks when they knew they were being watched (Yu & Wu, 2015).

Researchers kept confronting the same confusing plot twist. Groups seemed to be helping in some situations but hurting in others. More research was needed to clarify how groups influence us to either choke or to achieve. Two different explanations have been offered for why groups sometimes help and sometimes hurt.

The Cockroach Experiments and Mere Presence

These famous cockroach studies are pretty weird, but memorable.

Comparative social psychology compares the social behavior of different species. To investigate his hypothesis for how social facilitation works, Zajonc (note: it's pronounced "Zy-ence," rhyming with "science") and colleagues (1969) constructed something unusual. It was like a transparent, enclosed cockroach sports stadium with luxury boxes that allowed cockroaches to watch each other. Experimenters could then watch the cockroaches in the stadium to see how they responded to noxious blasts of light (cockroaches don't like light).

"Mazes" were set up inside the stadium with starting points and "goals" where they could escape the light. In simple mazes like the one shown in Figure 8.5, cockroaches run faster when other cockroaches are present: social facilitation. However, in complex mazes (that require turns), cockroaches slow down when other cockroaches are present. Here, being watched by other cockroaches made their performance worse.

Zajonc (1965) concluded that the presence of others (humans or cockroaches) makes us physiologically aroused. This arousal improves performance for easy or well-practiced tasks (social facilitation), because we're physically confident. But for new or difficult tasks, arousal hurts. Basically, when you're being watched, easy things

Comparative social psychology: Species-level comparisons of social behavior usually used to determine the uniqueness of human behavior.

FIGURE 8.5

(A) A simple "cockroach maze." Light (which cockroaches don't like) is shined on the starting point, which makes cockroaches search for the darkness of the goal. (B) When other cockroaches are added in "audience boxes," a cockroach in the maze runs faster in a simple maze but runs more slowly in a complex maze (compared to when alone).

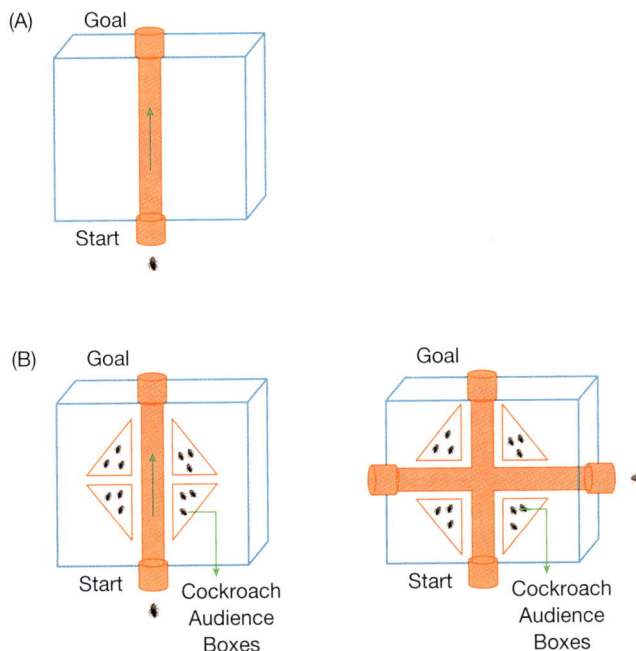

Source: Adapted from Zajonc, Heingartner, & Herman (1969).

FIGURE 8.6

Social facilitation.

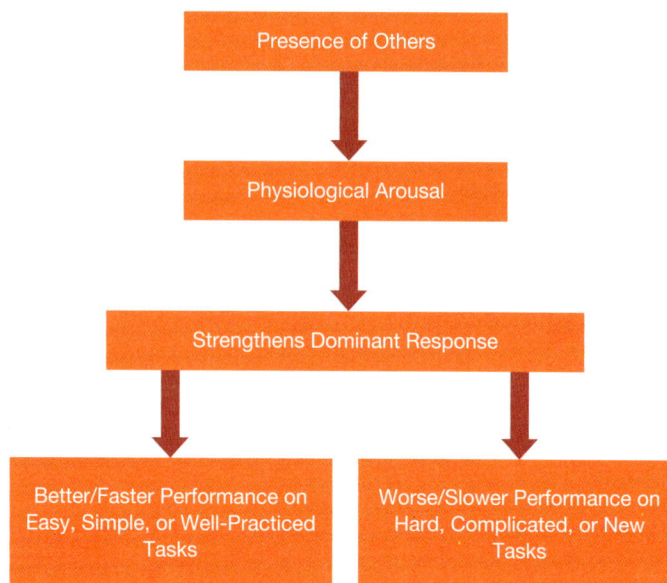

Presence of Others

↓

Physiological Arousal

↓

Strengthens Dominant Response

↓   ↓

Better/Faster Performance on Easy, Simple, or Well-Practiced Tasks   Worse/Slower Performance on Hard, Complicated, or New Tasks

get easier and harder things get harder. Figure 8.6 expresses the chain of events that leads either to superior or inferior performance. Over several experiments, this pattern happens with cockroaches and with humans.

Zajonc's explanation for why this happens is what he calls the **mere presence hypothesis**: that having other people (or cockroaches) in the room increases our physiological arousal, *even if the people aren't paying attention to us*. This arousal causes our body to "turn on" enough that it boosts our performance when we're comfortable with the task. It's like a little adrenaline shot that energizes us. But the same arousal can hurt us if we're nervous or trying to learn something new—we can't relax and our arousal becomes a hindrance.

Importantly, the famous cockroach study was recently done again (Halfmann et al., 2020). The procedure was as similar as possible except with even more cockroaches. The attempt at replication is generally considered a failure. The study did find that the roaches run faster in simple mazes than complicated ones, *and* they found that roaches run more slowly when other roaches are watching. But the important interaction wasn't found—they didn't run faster in easy mazes. So about half of the original findings were successfully replicated, but half weren't.

It was a different breed of cockroach, but it's unclear how much that matters. While cockroaches might not behave the way we want them to, other studies *have* found the general social facilitation effect in other species (Allee, 1938; Hoesey et al., 1985; Klopfer, 1985) and in humans, of course.

Another Explanation: Evaluation Apprehension

There's a second explanation.

Other researchers say that the reason our behavior gets better on simple/well-practiced tasks but gets worse on new/complicated tasks in the presence of others is because we're worried about impressing others (Geen, 1989). This explanation is called the **evaluation apprehension hypothesis** (Henchy & Glass, 1968). In plain language, this means that you're bothered when you think people might be judging you. More formally, anxiety about being judged causes physiological arousal and consequential changes in behavior. The key difference between evaluation apprehension and mere

Mere presence hypothesis: The idea that just having other people in the room will increase your physiological arousal and affect your task performance, even if they aren't actually watching you.

Evaluation apprehension hypothesis: The idea that having other people in the room will affect your task performance because of your anxiety that they are judging you.

presence is that for evaluation apprehension to affect you, you have to think that people are paying attention to you.

Cottrell and colleagues (1968) tested this idea by having other people in the room but blindfolded. The people were "present"—but they couldn't observe and judge your performance. Here, people being in the room didn't affect the participants' behavior because the participants knew they couldn't be seen (and therefore judged). So they argue that it's not "mere presence" of others but that other people affect us only when we feel like they can judge our performance. The explanations aren't settled; it's still a debate (see, e.g., Bond & Titus, 1983; Le Hénaff et al., 2015; Mesagno et al., 2012). If you have an opinion and a way to test it, you might be the next person mentioned in books like this one!

THE MAIN IDEAS

- When groups mistreat individual members, it can lead to ironic effects where they become more loyal to the group; this may occur because mistreatment strengthens the group's authority. Examples include hazing and the Stockholm syndrome.

- We are strongly affected by social rejection or ostracism from groups. Optimal distinctiveness theory predicts that we balance the need to be in groups against our need for individual validation by joining small, elite groups.

- Social facilitation occurs when the presence of others helps our performance. Research shows that others tend to increase performance on simple or well-practiced tasks, but they hurt performance on new or complicated tasks. This may be because of physiological arousal and/or because we're afraid of being judged.

CRITICAL THINKING CHALLENGE

- Consider a group in which you have a leadership position. Based on the ideas in this section of the chapter, what activities could you ask group members to do that would result in increasing their commitment to the group? Can you ask them to do these activities in an ethical way?

- This section showed you the self-report scale that measures rejection sensitivity. What predicts people who care about this a lot (high levels) versus those who don't seem to care as much (low levels)? Identify factors that you think predict scores on this measure (e.g., childhood experiences, self-esteem, and so on).

- There were two explanations offered for social facilitation effects: mere presence of others and evaluation apprehension. First, explain each in your own words; then, analyze which explanation seems more credible to you and why. Can you give an example from your own life of when you've experienced social facilitation?

HOW CAN INDIVIDUALS INFLUENCE GROUPS?

>> **LO 8.3:** Analyze how social loafing, leadership, decision-making processes, and creativity occur in group settings.

How can individuals affect the group?

In 1974, Bangladeshi economics professor Muhammad Yunus discovered that a group of local women, basket weavers, were borrowing money. The interest rate was so high that they never really made any profit (Yunus, 2007). They were hardworking, but they were perpetually impoverished, uneducated, and stuck in a male-centric culture that provided them almost no opportunity. So, Yunus took a small chance: He lent 42 women a total of approximately $30. He was creating what came to be called microloans with a social mission: to fund startup businesses that would empower hardworking people to become financially independent.

Muhammad Yunus, an individual who had an important impact on a group, starting with 42 women in Bangladesh.

Scott Olson/Getty Images

The women repaid the loans, supported one another as a group, began to make more profit, and then reinvested their money in themselves and their businesses. They soon began pulling themselves—and their families—up and out of poverty. In 1983, Yunus started Grameen Bank, founded on the practice of trust and group solidarity. The bank has enjoyed an extraordinary record of success with its small business loans: 94% of its borrowers are women, over 98% of loans are repaid, and the bank collected an average of $1.5 million in *weekly* installments that it keeps reinvesting in struggling people with ambition (Yunus, 2007).

In 2006, Yunus was awarded the Nobel Peace Prize, and in 2009, President Barack Obama awarded him the Presidential Medal of Freedom. Yes, groups affect individuals—but the success of Grameen Bank demonstrates that individuals can also have a profound influence on groups.

This section answers the core question "How can individuals influence groups?" by

(1) documenting how social loafers can hinder groups,

(2) recognizing that the most effective group leader depends on the situation,

(3) explaining why extremism tries to silence nonconformists and minorities, and

(4) describing how individuals can inspire group creativity.

An Individual Social Loafer Can Harm the Group

Our language suggests that American culture does not approve of social loafers.

Consider the words we have for them: avoider, bum, clock-watcher, couch potato, deadbeat, freeloader, free-rider, goldbricker, good-for-nothing, goof-off, idler, laggard, layabout, lazy bones, loafer, lounger, malingerer, ne'er-do-well, no-good, profligate, quitter, scrimshanker, skiver, slacker, slouch, slug, slugabed, sluggard, vagabond, waster, wastrel . . . and more recently, cyber-loafer and cyber-slacker.

Social loafing occurs when people working in a group reduce their individual level of effort (see Jackson & Williams, 1985; Sanna, 1992). They're coasting on the efforts of others. And if you're not the loafer, you have to work even harder to accomplish the work expected of two (or more!) people, which feels unfair as well as frustrating.

Individuals can influence groups in both negative and positive ways. Social loafers are why many students resent group projects. They are afraid they'll have to work harder to make up for someone else's social loafing. They will. And you better get used to finding ways to deal with it because that's what happens in just about every job that requires people to work together.

Ringelmann's Oxen Experiments and Other Applications

This time, it wasn't cockroaches; it was oxen.

French agricultural engineer Max Ringelmann (1913) studied social loafing with farm oxen. His studies relate to the phrase, "You're not pulling your weight." Ringelmann's experiments demonstrated that oxen (and then people) would pull less hard on a rope when working together than when working alone. Ringelmann also found that the larger the group size, the lower the individual effort (see Kravitz & Martin, 1986).

His early social loafing studies have been *replicated* in classic experiments involving rope pulling (Ingham et al., 1974), evaluation of poems and editorials (Petty et al., 1977), pumping air (Kerr & Bruun, 1981), and how loud cheerleaders yell (Hardy & Latane, 1988). More recently, psychologists have seen social loafing in youth soccer teams (Vaartstra et al., 2018), restaurant workers (Akgunduz & Eryilmaz, 2018), college students majoring in business (Mihelič & Culiberg, 2018), hotel staff (Hou et al., 2019), and more. Even more worrisome is when people decide not to get vaccines, thinking, "If everyone else gets a vaccine, then I don't need one" (Betsch et al., 2013).

Social loafing: When people working in a group reduce their individual level of effort.

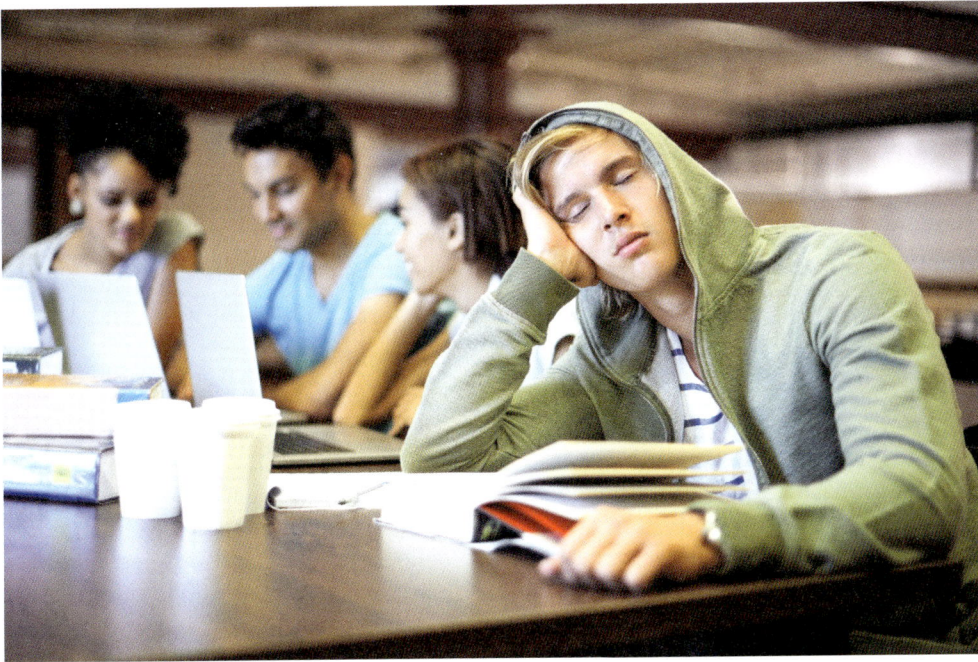

If you've ever been in a group project and one of the group members doesn't contribute—but still wants to share in a good evaluation or grade—then you know what it feels like to have a social loafer around.

Situational Influences on Social Loafing

Not everyone is a loafer.

People might not even do it on purpose. One study (Hardy & Latane, 1988) found that cheerleaders yelled louder when they thought they were alone, compared to when they knew they were in a group. But the leaks in their energy and cheerleading efforts weren't deliberate. So how did their reduced effort happen accidentally?

Steiner (1972) identified two general explanations for the loss of productivity when working in groups. Process loss is a reduction of effort in group settings that comes from a lack of motivation. Social loafing is a big contributor to process loss, but only when people slack on purpose. The second type of loss is coordination loss, which occurs when lack of cooperation and communication weakens the group's effectiveness. Everyone is willing to work, but the communication isn't there.

Coordinating a group may be as simple as getting people to say, "1-2-3 Lift!" so that everyone understands exactly when to put forth their maximum effort. Ancient sailors would sing rhythmic songs to coordinate their rowing, and marching bands began as a way to help armies stay coordinated. To fix the cheerleading problem, captains often yell, "Ready? OK!"

Karau and Williams's (1993) meta-analysis of 78 social loafing studies indicated that there are other situational variables regarding when you are *not* likely to be a social loafer. Social loafing is less likely when

1. The group is doing something difficult.
2. Your contributions can be identified as coming from you.
3. You believe that what you are doing is valuable.
4. You are working with people you know.

Social loafing also *increases* when there is diffusion of responsibility. This occurs when each individual in a group thinks, "I don't need to take care of it . . . someone else will." For example, diffusion of responsibility appears to kick in when listeners of public radio (such as NPR) fail to make a financial contribution to support the station. They can easily think, "Thousands of other people will send in money . . . so they don't need my $10." We'll come back to the idea of diffusion of responsibility in Chapter 10 when we analyze when people do (and don't) help others in an emergency.

Process loss: Reduction of effort in group settings that comes from a lack of motivation.

Coordination loss: When a lack of cooperation and communication weakens a group's effectiveness or increases social loafing.

Diffusion of responsibility: When we feel less responsible for an outcome due to the presence of others.

When we unite literatures based on college students (see Aggarwal & O'Brien, 2008) and full-time employees (see Liden et al., 2004), we find that diffusion of responsibility is *more* likely when

(a) students believe that the project is big,

(b) students believe that the project involves many students,

(c) students believe that the project does not require that students grade one another,

(d) employees do not believe that others will notice their lowered effort,

(e) employees notice other people's lowered efforts, and

(f) employees perceive unfairness within the organization.

Cultural and Personality Influences on Social Loafing

Social loafing may also vary by culture (Karau & Williams, 1993).

It occurs around the world but to a *lesser* degree among women (who have been socialized to be "nice") and among people from Eastern cultures (they studied people from China, Japan, and Taiwan). People from collectivistic cultures are less likely to allow social loafing because their cultures frequently emphasize the good of the group over the good of any given individual.

Kurt Lewin, of course, would not be surprised to discover that both personality and situations can systematically influence social loafing. Several personality variables have been linked to social loafing. For example, people high in **conscientiousness** are less likely to loaf (Schippers, 2014). Conscientiousness is a personality trait that includes a striving for achievement, attention to detail, and a sense of responsibility. People are also less likely to be social loafers if they are high in **agreeableness**, meaning they are willing to be flexible, to cooperate, and to try to please other people (Schippers, 2014).

Social loafing is also less likely among individuals who have a high **Protestant work ethic** (Smrt & Karau, 2011). They value discipline, honoring commitments, and doing a good job in any setting. Beyond guessing whether someone will be a social loafer indirectly through these traits, a simple and short scale has been developed to directly measure individual differences in tendencies to be a social loafer, which you can take in the What's My Score? feature.

Cyberloafing

Have you ever checked social media during class?

Access to technology has led to a new productivity problem: **Cyberloafing** or **cyberslacking** occurs in the workplace when employees (or students) excessively surf

---

Conscientiousness: A personality trait regarding attention to detail, responsibility, and striving for achievement.

Agreeableness: A personality trait regarding willingness to be flexible, to cooperate, and to try to please others.

Protestant work ethic: A personality trait valuing discipline, commitment, and hard work.

Cyberloafing: When people working in a group reduce their individual level of effort.

Cyberslacking: See *cyberloafing.*

Measuring Likelihood to Be a Social Loafer

Instructions: How much do you agree with each statement below? Respond to each using this scale:

1	2	3	4	5
Strongly disagree				Strongly agree

___1. In a team, I am indispensable.

___2. In a team, I will try as hard as I can.

___3. In a team, I will contribute less than I should.

___4. In a team, I will actively participate in the discussion and contribute ideas.

___5. In a team, it is okay even if I do not do my share.

___6. In a team, it does not matter whether or not I try my best.

___7. In a team, given my abilities, I will do the best I can.

Scoring: First, reverse-score what you wrote for Items 1, 2, 4, and 7. This means that if you wrote a 1, it becomes a 5, a 2 becomes a 4, a 3 stays the same, a 4 becomes a 2, and a 5 becomes a 1. Then, add up your answers; higher scores mean you are more likely to be a social loafer.

Source: Ying, X., Li, H., Jiang, S., Peng, F., & Lin, Z. (2014). "Group laziness: The effect of social loafing on group performance." *Social Behavior and Personality: An international journal, 42*(3). 465–472. http://dx.doi.org/10.2224/sbp.2014.42.3.465

the Internet during work hours for non-work-related activities. Online social loafing includes shopping, gambling, playing games, checking social media, reading the news online, or anything else that's not what you're being paid to do.

The productivity losses can be alarming (see Alharthi et al., 2019). The employee-experience causes of cyberloafing are predictable: "lack of organizational justice, lack of job involvement, attitude towards the job, and job monotony" (Basu & Pooja, 2017, p. 19). Some companies even create automated monitoring systems to check up on employees (see Khansa et al., 2017). Other companies just give up, unsure what they can really do about it (Lim & Chen, 2012).

Psychological solutions tend to aim at reducing cyberslacking by boosting motivation. For example, in college students, smaller groups tend to help people stay on task (Akcaoglu & Lee, 2016). In other work settings, one of the emerging critical variables is the degree to which employees perceive fairness within the organization (George & Wallio, 2017; Kim et al., 2016). From a wellness perspective, other research has found that employees are less likely to cyberloaf if they are well rested and feel less lonely (Lim et al., 2018). A company that truly cares about encouraging its members to be engaged, happy, and healthy seems to provide a lot of motivation for people, which probably isn't a big surprise but is good for CEOs to remember.

dbtravel / Alamy Stock Photo

Do you ever listen to National Public Radio or watch public television? If you do but fail to contribute to their fundraisers, you might be engaging in social loafing and diffusion of responsibility.

▶ Group Dynamics in *The Avengers*

BFA / Marvel Studios / Alamy Stock Photo

In an extremely popular blockbuster chain of movies, millions of people around the world have become acquainted with the Marvel comic book superhero group *The Avengers*.

This band of superheroes is always, inevitably, successful. What makes them so? To start, they first worked together to stop a trickster alien (Loki) from taking over the planet. It was a *difficult initiation*, and afterward, they were extremely proud to be in the group—just as Aronson and Mill's famous study would have predicted. The challenge they had to overcome to become an Avenger made them even more committed to working together.

Second, no member can ever be a *social loafer*. They know that if they try to slack off, the rest of the group will immediately chastise them. They also feel the pressure of working hard because they know their goal is so important (usually, it's saving the universe or at least the entire planet). The lack of social loafing also occurs because each person's contributions are identifiable, forcing individual action when needed (if you need something smashed, call the Hulk; if you need some high-tech gear, call Black Panther).

Finally, the group is certainly small, elite, and prestigious, and each member is famous and admired for their own special role. This means that being a member of the Avengers is a perfect opportunity for *optimal distinctiveness*. Each superhero can remain individually valued but also gain the benefits of being in a respected and supportive community. Remember: If you end up with superpowers, use them for good, not evil.

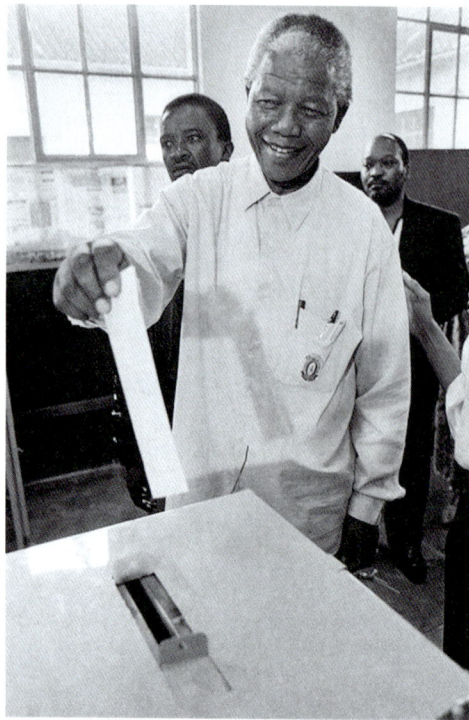

When is a transformational leader likely to be most effective?

Group dynamics: The social roles, hierarchies, communication styles, and culture that naturally form when groups interact.

Contingency theory of leadership: The idea that the "best" leadership style depends on the given group dynamics.

Task leader: A type of leader who focuses on completing assignments, achieving goals, and meeting deadlines.

Social leader: A type of leader who focuses on the people involved, building teamwork, and providing emotional support.

Transactional leader: A type of leader who uses rewards and punishments to motivate group members; these leaders help to maintain the status quo.

Transformational leader: A type of leader who uses inspiration and group cohesion to motivate members; these leaders are useful for challenging established rules or procedures.

The Most Effective Leader Depends on the Situation

Leaders certainly have a major influence on their group. **Group dynamics** refer to the culture that forms when members of a group interact. The culture will be shaped by social roles, hierarchies, communication styles, and much more. Some people will emerge as leaders; others prefer to stand back. The leaders may choose very different styles—and these choices will have an influence over how the group members perform and feel.

Again echoing Lewin's early equation about behavior, different situations call for different kinds of leaders. A business that is about to go bankrupt may require a leader with a forceful personality; a business that is growing smoothly may require a leader with a lighter touch. Young parents leading a family with four children under the age of 11 probably will need a different leadership style than the 35-year-old parents of just one child. The situation matters and so do the personalities—just as Lewin predicted.

Lewin was sensitive to the group dynamics in Nazi Germany when a fascist leader took advantage of a desperate economic situation. Lewin's (1948) experiment compared three leadership styles: autocratic, democratic, and laissez-faire. His methods were imperfect and may have been interpreted in a slightly biased manner. (Lewin favored democracy over authoritarianism and laissez-faire—and that's what his experiment discovered.) But his studies have largely stood the test of time (Taylor, 1998). Leaders have a profound influence on the groups that they lead—for better and for worse.

Following in Lewin's footsteps, Fiedler (1967, 1996) spent more than 45 years studying leadership in the military: ROTC, infantry squad leaders, Coast Guard officers, and Army and Navy personnel. He observed people making real decisions that had real consequences. Fiedler's ultimate conclusion: A leader's effectiveness depended "on how well the leader's personality, abilities, and behaviors match the situation in which the leader operates" (p. 242). The **contingency theory of leadership** acknowledges that the "best" leadership style depends on the given group dynamics.

Fiedler identified leaders who tended to be more effective in different types of situations. For example, a **task leader** focuses on completing assignments. By contrast, a **social leader** is focused on the people involved and invests time in building teamwork, facilitating interactions, and providing support. In an emergency, you probably want a task leader—you don't want the person in charge to stop and ask how you're feeling about everything. But when cooperative teamwork is required, you probably want a social leader who knows about and cares for each member of the group. The best type of leader is contingent on the situation.

A variation on the contingency view of leadership defines **transactional leaders** as those who use rewards and punishments to motivate group members. Transactional leaders can be useful when an organization or government wants to maintain the status quo. On the other hand, **transformational leaders** use inspiration and group cohesion to motivate group members (see Nye, 2008) and are useful for challenging established rules or procedures.

The balance of research (e.g., Bass, 1998) seems to support the idea that transformational leadership can influence society toward positive change. For example, Pittinsky (2010) identified Martin Luther King Jr. and Nelson Mandela as two classic historical examples of transformative leaders. Muhammed Yunus (who gave poor women small loans for their businesses) represents another transformational leader who influenced and inspired.

Individuals Can Influence Group Decision Making

Have you been asked to serve on a jury yet?

In the classic film *12 Angry Men* (1957; remade in 1997), a lone juror tries to convince the rest of the group to change their verdict. Can one person really have that much influence over a group?

World History Archive / Alamy Stock Photo

You probably will be. Even though it will definitely interrupt your life, it is one of the many citizen responsibilities in a democracy. Plus, as a student of psychology, you will find it fascinating to observe the court system, participate in the selection process, and engage in group decision making.

Does one person try to bully everyone else into an agreement? If the jury is allowed to decide on things like monetary damages, how do they reach a final number? Can one person really influence the final outcome if everyone else disagrees? Three lines of research have explored how an individual can influence group decision making: group polarization, groupthink, and minority influence through phenomena called the spiral of silence and pluralistic ignorance.

"Risky Shift" Research Becomes "Group Polarization"

Consider this scenario:

Mr. A, an electrical engineer, who is married and has one child, has been working for a large electronics corporation since graduating from college 5 years ago. His job is stable with a modest income but little chance of increasing. He's offered a job at a different, new company with a highly uncertain future. The new job would pay more to start and offers the possibility of shares in the company. What is the lowest probability you consider worthwhile for Mr. A to take the new job?

When participants (Stoner, 1961) saw it in research, they first provided their own, personal answer. Then they joined a group discussion to come up with a final, joint answer. After the discussion, answers shifted toward being more willing to accept risk. Risky shift was the term used for this change (Stoner, 1968; Wallach & Kogan, 1965), the tendency of groups to make riskier or more daring decisions than the average of individuals (Stoner, 1968; Wallach & Kogan, 1965).

Do group decisions always reflect more risk than individual ones? As you've probably come to expect at this point, it's complicated. Follow-up research showed that groups do shift individual decisions, but that movement can be *either* riskier or more conservative. The direction of the shift depends on which direction most individuals were headed in *before* they got together as a group (Moscovici & Zavalloni, 1969). So "risky shift" was updated with a new term: *group polarization*.

Risky shift: The tendency of groups to make riskier or more daring decisions after a discussion (see *group polarization*).

CNN is known for being a liberal news network, while Fox is known for being conservative. If you tend to watch only one of these networks, or your social media friends tend to post only one kind of political message, then your opinions will gradually become more extreme: group polarization.

Group polarization occurs when a group makes more extreme decisions than the average of individual decisions—in either direction. It seems that we can question our own, individual decision. Exposure to a group that starts with general agreement can "fuel the fires" and make people feel more assured and confident, thus moving their opinion toward a more extreme one.

For example, in one early study, moderately profeminist women became more feminist following a group discussion (Myers, 1975). Several more recent studies have shown that if you lean toward one political candidate or party, exposure to others who also favor that person or party will eventually lead your opinion to become much stronger and more extreme (e.g., Iyengar & Westwood, 2015; Keating et al., 2016; Stroud, 2010).

Why do we shift? Why can't we just stick with our own private opinion? Isenberg (1986) identified two explanations for *why* group decision making becomes more extreme: social comparisons (a normative influence) and persuasive arguments (an informational influence). First, social comparisons encourage us to push one another in the socially approved direction until we find ourselves advocating for an extreme perspective that is far from where we started. We feel comfortable arguing for an opinion that we now know is shared by others.

The second explanation for group extremism focuses on persuasive arguments. Any group we join is probably inclined toward a viewpoint we agree with—that's why we joined it in the first place. So, conservatives tune in to radio shows or podcasts that reinforce their conservative viewpoint while liberals associate with programs that present the other side. Both sides hear more and better arguments in the same direction (and are not exposed to counterarguments) and thus become increasingly persuaded toward that perspective.

Groupthink

George Orwell gave us new words.

His frightening dystopian novel *1984* (written in 1948) introduced phrases such as "Big Brother," "doublethink," and "thoughtcrime." They were all about how the suppression of ideas can lead to brainwashed, ignorant masses. In 1972, psychologist Irving Janis introduced another memorable term, **groupthink**, which describes the tendency for people in groups to minimize conflict by thinking alike and publicly agreeing with each other.

In general, people don't like to be disagreeable troublemakers or the only ones holding a contrary opinion—so they tend to stay silent. But if *all* the contrary opinions remain silent, then no one realizes the size of the doubt members have. We think, "If I'm the only one questioning this decision, maybe I'm wrong." This self-silencing can lead to groupthink, a false sense of group consensus that leads to a culture where no one questions group decisions.

Table 8.2 describes some of the historical events—and tragedies—in the United States that are identified as influenced by groupthink. This list suggests that one thing we learn from history is that we don't learn very well from history. A classic example is the explosion of the *Challenger* space shuttle in 1986. NASA wanted to reenergize the public's excitement about space exploration, so they created unnecessary rushes. They ignored any possibility that the launch wasn't safe or that the shuttle wasn't ready because of group momentum and pride. Their failure to stop, listen to warnings, or question their decision to keep going despite problems led to disaster.

When is groupthink most likely to occur? Janis identified three conditions:

- *High group cohesion.* Group members who feel connected to one another are less likely to criticize each other. They think of each other as friends and want to be supportive, despite doubts.

- *Strong, directive leadership.* A group structure with a strong, directive leader will tend to isolate the group from alternative opinions and discourage disagreement.

- *Stressful situations.* A crisis requires groups to make fast decisions based on incomplete information; this can promote the illusion that there is a clear consensus of opinion. People are less likely to question decisions if there's a rush.

Group polarization: When a group makes more extreme decisions after a discussion, toward either a more or less risky position.

Groupthink: The tendency for people in cohesive groups to minimize conflict by publicly agreeing with each other, despite any doubts they have.

TABLE 8.2

Tragic U.S. Events Attributed to Groupthink

EVENT	HISTORICAL CONTEXT
Attack on Pearl Harbor	1941: During the F. D. Roosevelt administration, groups analyzing intelligence data dismissed evidence about a possible attack on U.S. ships at Pearl Harbor.
The failed invasion of Cuba: Bay of Pigs	1961: Three months into the Kennedy administration, White House planners miscalculated Cuban resistance and underfunded the military effort.
Escalation of the war in Vietnam	1965–1968: During the Johnson administration, the president and his cabinet escalated U.S. troop commitments to Vietnam from 16,000 to 537,000 with an average of about 1,200 U.S. fatalities each month.
The Watergate coverup	1972–1974: During the Nixon administration, the president and his staff covered up their involvement in illegal "dirty tricks" during the 1972 reelection campaign.
Destruction of the space shuttle *Challenger*	1986: A group of NASA officials ignored specific warnings not to launch the space shuttle because O-rings separating rocket boosters were less resilient in cold temperatures.
9/11 terror attacks	2001: Groups analyzing intelligence data dismissed evidence suggesting that an attack was imminent.
Destruction of the space shuttle *Columbia*	2003: A group of NASA officials decided to ignore suggestions to look more closely at damage during launch to the heat-shielding tiles.
The U.S. invasion of Iraq	2003: The George W. Bush administration decided to invade Iraq to remove the threat of weapons of mass destruction that never existed.
Penn State sex scandal	2014: Coaches and professionals from the Penn State football team ignored concerns that Jerry Sandusky was sexually abusing children on campus.

The symptoms of groupthink seem obvious in retrospect, but they are subtle when groupthink is seducing you into a terrible decision. How can groups avoid making this mistake? They can look for the symptoms of groupthink and purposely try to avoid them. See Table 8.3 for a list of symptoms and matching example statements. Better decisions are made when the group's culture allows for questions, analysis, and doubt. In short, a group full of "yes men" (or yes people) often leads to problems.

Minority Influence: The Spiral of Silence and Pluralistic Ignorance

Have you ever felt afraid to voice an opinion in a group?

Groupthink is thought to produce what has been described as a **spiral of silence**. The metaphorical spiral is like a tornado, building on itself, fueled by fear of rejection that leads people to (1) keep silent about their private opinion, (2) misperceive the loudest opinion as a majority opinion, and (3) therefore become even less likely to express their private opinion (Noelle-Neumann, 1993; see Figure 8.7). People tend to feel more anxious when they think their opinion is the minority view (Morrison & Miller, 2008). This anxiety and the desire to be accepted results in the gradually increasing reluctance to express any thoughts other than those "allowed" by the group (Bassili, 2003): a spiral of silence.

Part of what keeps people with a minority opinion silent is **pluralistic ignorance**, the false impression that others do not share your private perspective. In one of many empirical studies testing pluralistic ignorance, students on a large Midwestern university campus falsely believed that their personal reservations about using alcohol were not shared by others (Suls & Green, 2003). Students believed that not drinking made them social deviants. Essentially, people changed their behavior because they thought—incorrectly—that their opinion was unique and that most others felt differently.

Spiral of silence: When fear of rejection leads people to keep silent about a private opinion.

Pluralistic ignorance: When a majority of individuals in a group get the false impression that others do not share their private perspective because no one is speaking up.

TABLE 8.3

Groupthink Symptoms and Example Statements

SYMPTOM	STATEMENT
Overestimating the expertise of the group and its leader	"We really are the best people for this job; our leader is wiser than other leaders."
Becoming close-minded toward alternative opinions	"Other people's ideas may have some merit, but our insights are special."
Using someone as a "mindguard" to pressure dissenters to conform	"How can I shut that person up? Don't they know their comments are bringing everyone else down?"
Self-censoring by not voicing disagreements or concerns	"My contrary idea probably isn't right anyway."
Perceiving a unity of opinion that does not really exist	"We must be right; no one has spoken up about a disagreement."
Limiting the range of alternative decisions	"We don't have to consider some of these weird ideas."
Being reluctant to question your objectives or reconsider dismissed alternatives	"We already made up our minds about that. Let's not go over it again."
Focusing on positive outcomes while minimizing risk assessment	"This is going to work great! I just know it is!"
Limiting the amount of incoming, potentially contradictory information	"We've heard enough. It's time to make a decision."
Failing to consider contingency plans in case things don't succeed	"What will happen if it doesn't work? It doesn't matter. It *has* to work."

Source: Adapted from Dugosh et al. (2000).

FIGURE 8.7

Spiral of silence.

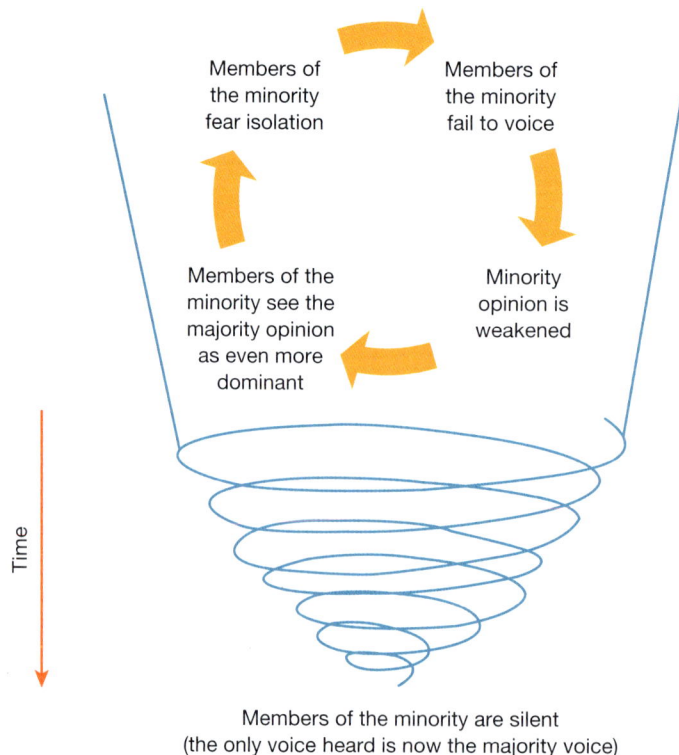

Members of the minority fear isolation → Members of the minority fail to voice → Minority opinion is weakened → Members of the minority see the majority opinion as even more dominant

Members of the minority are silent (the only voice heard is now the majority voice)

Source: Noelle-Neumann (1974).

Pluralistic ignorance sucks us deeper down into the spiral of silence. It seems that for many of the problematic group phenomena covered here, the truly brave person is the nonconformist who is willing to speak their mind. As we discussed in Chapter 7, a healthy society *needs* nonconformists. In sum, an individual can influence a group if they are strong enough to voice an opinion they believe is unpopular, thus avoiding the spiral of silence and pluralistic ignorance.

Individuals Can Inspire Group Creativity

There are many examples of how individuals can inspire group creativity. Consider:

- The eight women who created the first computer software (see Isaacson, 2014)

- The anonymous women code breakers of World War II (see Mundy, 2017)

- Walt Disney, who inspired hundreds of artists to work together to create the first animated film, *Snow White and the Seven Dwarfs* (Isaacson, 2014)

- Steve Jobs, who "revolutionized six industries: personal computing, animated movies, music, phones, tablet computing, and digital publishing" (Isaacson, 2011, p. xxi)

- Albert Einstein, who in just 4 months at the age of 26 authored four papers that transformed scientific understanding of time, space, mass, and energy (Schilling, 2018)

- Afroz Shah and his neighbor, who initiated a social cascade that transformed the beach in Mumbai, India, "from filthy to fabulous" (Pathak & Nichter, 2019)

- Muhammad Yunus (2017), who helped create micro-loans that allowed women to escape a cycle of poverty by building a banking system that relied on small loans and big trust

- Elon Musk, who sold his first video game at age 11, became a millionaire in his 20s, helped develop PayPal, and created the electric car company Tesla Motors (Schilling, 2018)

- Anne Wojcicki and Linda Avey, who founded the human genome research company 23andMe that helps individuals understand the impact of their own DNA (see Wojcicki et al., 2013)

- Jimmy Wales and Larry Sanger conceived the original idea for what is now Wikipedia (Lageard & Paternotte, 2018)

The Big Promise: Brainstorming

Where do creative ideas come from?

Using a term that's now famous, advertising executive Alex Osborn (1957) created procedures for **brainstorming**, a group approach to problem solving that emphasizes nonevaluative creative thinking. Osborn's methods were simple: Generate lots of ideas, encourage wild ideas, don't judge any idea, and modify or expand other people's ideas. In other words, no sneering or snickering was allowed when people said weird things—it was time to suspend judgment and let your creativity flow! The #1 rule: There are no bad ideas.

Osborn believed that brainstorming would produce ideas that would collide in ways that sparked imaginations and fueled creativity. It certainly went against problems like the spiral of silence. Early research results mostly supported Osborn's idea. Brainstorming increased both the quantity and quality of ideas and even more so if individuals were first trained in brainstorming techniques (see Parnes & Meadow, 1959).

But there are limitations. For example, Dunnette et al. (1963) tested it among research scientists and advertising personnel employed by the Minnesota Mining and Manufacturing Company. The sum of creative ideas produced by *individuals* brainstorming was greater than that of people brainstorming in groups. It was the opposite of what was supposed to happen. Why wasn't brainstorming working as well as advertising executive Alex Osborn had, well, advertised?

Brainstorming: A group approach to problem solving that emphasizes nonevaluative creative thinking where members don't judge any idea.

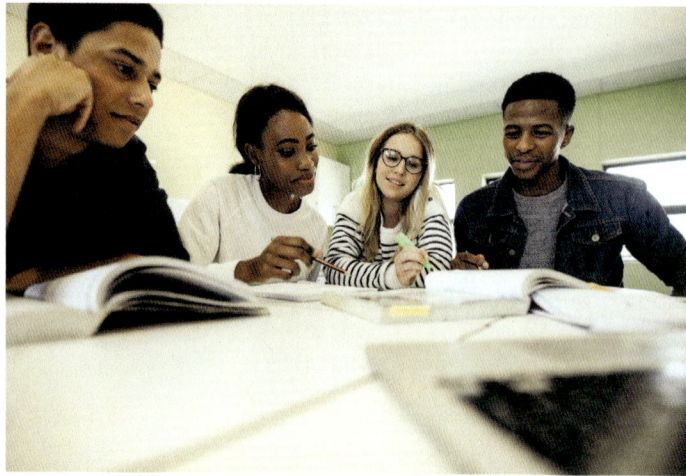

iStockPhoto/jacoblund

One of the keys to successful brainstorming is that everyone maintains a supportive and positive attitude.

Obstacles to Effective Brainstorming

Two explanations for the weak performance of brainstorming will sound familiar.

The first is diffusion of responsibility (Mullen et al., 1991; Paulus et al., 2006). In theory, people in brainstorming groups are free of individual responsibility and are not supposed to judge any ideas or the people who produce them. But the rules of brainstorming are often unrealistic. People can be tired, distracted, or think that the entire exercise is trying to solve a futile problem, so it's easier to just sit back and generate one or two mundane ideas than to really push yourself toward creativity.

The second is evaluation apprehension. Even though the rule is no judgment, participants can still be afraid that their contributions will be seen as silly, so they just don't say them out loud. The fear of evaluation is especially salient to people with social anxiety. In a *quasi-experiment*, Comacho and Paulus (1995) found that groups of four people who had tested high in social anxiety were less productive than groups of four people who were all low in social anxiety. While online brainstorming groups seem to generate more ideas than face-to-face groups (Connolly et al., 1993), self-censoring due to social anxiety remains a problem even in these settings.

Guidelines for Successful Brainstorming

Shall we give up on brainstorming?

Some research indicates that brainstorming doesn't work. But we don't want to brush it off, because—as we've already said many times—it depends on the situation. Especially with advances in technology (Sharp & Whaley, 2018), many problems can be curtailed. For example, evaluation apprehension is decreased when people generate ideas anonymously.

We also don't want to give up on brainstorming because there are so many quiet success stories. Sometimes, it does work (Al-khatib, 2012). Patients with cancer who brainstormed with counselors about ways to talk with their families appreciated the sessions (de Geus et al., 2016). Middle school children who brainstormed were judged to be more creative than a control group (George & Basavarajappa, 2016).

Success depends on how the session is set up. For example, alternating between individual and group idea generation produces more creative solutions to problems (Korde & Paulus, 2017). Results are also increased when people think of themselves as creative (Buisine & Guegan, 2019). Dugosh and colleagues (2000) suggested four practical guidelines, shown in Table 8.4. In the right situation, brainstorming can be an effective way for individuals to propose and implement creative solutions to stubborn problems. This is the ideal group setting.

TABLE 8.4

Practical Guidelines for Successful Brainstorming

Use a facilitator to remind everyone of the rules of brainstorming and keep their attention focused on the task.
Encourage people to take an "incubation break," a rest period following intense effort to solve a problem.
Begin brainstorming with "brainwriting," an approach that generates ideas by having group members independently write down their ideas on paper and then sharing them with the group.
Embed independent diversity of viewpoints when selecting members of the group.

Source: Dugosh et al. (2000).

THE MAIN IDEAS

- Social loafing occurs when people working in a group reduce their individual level of effort. This may occur because of diffusion of responsibility, when people work less because they think others will make up for it.

- Contingency leadership is the idea that different kinds of leaders are useful for different kinds of situations. Four leadership styles are task, social, transactional, and transformational.

- Group decisions tend to be more extreme than individual decisions, a general tendency called group polarization. Groupthink occurs when people in a cohesive group fail to publicly disagree with each other, which can lead to bad decisions.

- Finally, brainstorming can generate creative solutions when the circumstances allow for true lack of judgment and other rules, such as alternating between individual and group idea generation.

CRITICAL THINKING CHALLENGE

- Think of specific times when you've had to work in a group at school, at work, or even socially. Identify people in the group who seemed to work harder versus people who seemed to work less. What differences can you identify in the two different responses, and do the ideas in this section align with your experiences? If not, what other variables should be studied by social psychologists to fully understand social facilitation versus social loafing?

- Identify your own leadership tendencies and analyze whether your leadership style changes depending on the situation (reinforcing the idea of contingency leadership). Then, describe whether you are a task, social, transactional, or transformational leader. Give a specific example as evidence of your leadership style.

- Four ways to increase successful brainstorming were offered in Table 8.4. What's missing from this table, based on your experience or your understanding of social psychological principles? What other concepts from the book so far could be applied to research studies on brainstorming that you hypothesize would help or hurt the process or outcome?

CHAPTER SUMMARY

Why Are Groups So Important to Us?

Groups occur when two or more people interact with each other or share a common experience or fate. We have a natural instinct to form groups because they offer several advantages, including social support, safety, and a sense of cohesion with others. We're especially loyal to groups that were hard to get into, something called the initiation effect. In short, cognitive dissonance occurs if we work hard to get into a group we don't like, so we convince ourselves the group is great (even if it isn't).

How Do Groups Influence Individuals?

Ironically, we're sometimes more committed to groups that have treated us badly; examples are hazing and the Stockholm syndrome (when captives end up agreeing with their captor's motives or even become attracted to them). We are also particularly sensitive to social rejection and ostracism. Optimal distinctiveness theory suggests that we will particularly value small, elite groups because they balance our needs to (a) affiliate with a group but also (b) feel unique and special.

Social facilitation occurs when our performance on simple, easy, or well-practiced tasks goes up in the presence of other people (compared to when we're alone). However, the presence of others also makes our performance on new or difficult tasks go down. There are two major explanations for this effect. One, the mere presence hypothesis, is that other people simply being around increases our physiological arousal; this arousal affects our performance. The other, evaluation apprehension, says our performance changes because we're afraid of being judged.

How Can Individuals Influence Groups?

Social loafing occurs when people working in groups put in less effort, believing other people will make up for their slack. The likelihood of someone being a social loafer depends on the situation as well as on culture and personality.

The contingency theory of leadership is the idea that different leadership styles will be needed depending on the given situation. Four types of leadership are described, including task, social, transactional, and transformational. Each has advantages and disadvantages.

Sometimes, discussions in groups make people's initial opinions change. If someone were leaning toward one decision, talking with people who also leaned toward that decision would likely make everyone in the group more confident regarding their decision. This tendency is called group polarization: when a group makes more extreme decisions than the average of the individual decisions.

Finally, brainstorming is the idea that groups can generate creative solutions if people are willing to offer new ideas and not judge each other. Brainstorming has mixed results, with research indicating "rules" or circumstances in which it's more likely to be effective.

CRITICAL THINKING, ANALYSIS, AND APPLICATION

- Groups offer many benefits, as described in the first section of this book. However, a previous chapter described how groups can also offer the opportunity for anonymity and deindividuation, which can sometimes lead to negative behavior (e.g., online trolling or crime). Do the advantages that groups offer society outweigh the disadvantages? Provide specific examples to support your answer.

- Social facilitation was first explored with cockroaches; social loafing was studied with oxen. Analyze whether you think comparative social psychology (studies with nonhuman animals) is or is not useful and relevant to a better understanding of human social psychology. Defend your answer with at least one specific example beyond those from this chapter.

- This chapter introduced four specific leadership styles (task, social, transactional, and transformational). Identify one famous person who is an example of *each* of those four styles, then provide examples of why you think this person matches that style.

- First, identify a group from your own life. Then, specifically relate at least three of the theories or ideas from this chapter to that group. Explain how you saw these ideas come to life in your own experience through that group.

Don Bartletti/Los Angeles Times/Getty Images

9

Stereotyping, Prejudice, and Discrimination

Core Questions

9.1 Why do we keep using stereotypes?

9.2 How do stereotypes turn into prejudices?

9.3 How can we reduce prejudice and discrimination?

Learning Objectives

9.1 Identify why we seem to have stereotyping instincts and the dangers they can lead to.

9.2 Understand types of prejudice and how four theories explain the motivation behind it.

9.3 Analyze various research-based interventions to reduce prejudice and discrimination.

If stereotypes are so bad, then why do we keep using them?

Hold that first core question for this chapter in mind as we remind you of the dangers associated with stereotypes.

Mesa, Arizona: FR was working at a Boeing aircraft plant when he learned about the terror attacks of September 11, 2001. He told coworkers and a waitress at Applebee's that he wanted to shoot some "towel heads." FR's stereotype was that a member of the Sikh faith, Mr. Balbir Singh Sodhi, was a threat. So, he shot and killed Mr. Sodhi as he was planting flowers outside his gas station. Like many of the male members of the fifth largest religion in the world, Mr. Sodhi's head was covered with the traditional Sikh—not Muslim—turban.

Pittsburgh, Pennsylvania: RB posted an online statement before murdering 11 people (ages 54 to 97) inside their synagogue. "I can't sit by and watch my people get slaughtered, screw your optics, I'm going in." RB's stereotype blamed all Jewish people for helping unarmed Central Americans as they walked toward the U.S.-Mexico border. The congregation contributed to the Hebrew Immigrant Aid Society (HIAS), which has helped resettle refugees from all over the world.

El Paso, Texas: PC drove to a Walmart intending to counter what he called the "Hispanic invasion" by murdering innocent shoppers. He had to travel more than 600 miles to reach El Paso from his home near Dallas, Texas. The ages of his shooting victims ranged from 2 to 90. PC's stereotype promoting the superiority of White people allowed him to justify murdering 22 unarmed strangers, many of them probably shopping for back-to-school supplies.

WHY DO WE KEEP USING STEREOTYPES?

>> **LO 9.1:** **Identify why we seem to have stereotyping instincts and the dangers they can lead to.**

FR, RB, and PC (the people just described) were living a familiar, but sad, social psychological story. To start, let's define some important terms. Stereotypes are oversimplified *beliefs* that all members of a group have the same characteristics. They describe the expected traits and behaviors of group members. **Prejudices** are emotion-centered evaluations and *judgments*, based on someone's perceived membership in a group. The word means you've "prejudged" someone without knowing much, if anything, about them. Stereotypes and prejudice lead to **discrimination** when they become an action or *behavior* targeted at someone because of their perceived group status.

Psychology differentiates between what we call "positive" and "negative" stereotypes. We're more familiar with negative stereotypes, which are beliefs that a group has some kind of bad trait. In contrast, "positive" stereotypes are beliefs that are in a positive, complimentary direction (Siy & Cheryan, 2016). Examples are that doctors are smart, Black people are athletic, Asians are good at math, gay men are stylish, or women are naturally good caretakers of children.

But it's essential to note that even with "positive" stereotypes, the *outcome* is negative. Any stereotype makes assumptions about people, assigns them roles we feel comfortable with, and judges people if they don't live up to our expectations or try to break out of the box we've assigned them to live in. Stereotypes encourage prejudice, which leads to discrimination.

Each of these terms (stereotyping, prejudice, and discrimination) is sometimes used to describe the combined effects of all three. But when we use the words more precisely, stereotyping usually refers to how we think (the cognitive component). Prejudice refers to our feelings (the affective or emotional component). Discrimination refers to our actions (the behavioral component); see Table 9.1. Combined, we have the "ABCs" of intergroup relations (affect, behaviors, and cognitions).

How might we end—or at least limit—harmful discrimination? One answer seems to be to cut it off at the beginning of the process: stereotyping. The main problem with that sensible strategy is that we humans can't seem to stop stereotyping; it appears to

Prejudice: Emotion-centered judgments or evaluations about people based on their perceived membership in a group.

Discrimination: Behaviors toward a people because of their perceived membership in a group.

TABLE 9.1

Making Distinctions Among Stereotypes, Prejudice, and Discrimination

TERM	COMPONENT	EXAMPLE	EXAMPLE	EXAMPLE
Stereotype	Beliefs (cognitive)	Belief that men wearing any kind of headscarf are Muslim	Belief that women are emotional	Belief that gay people are stylish
Prejudice	Feelings (affective)	Negative emotions toward Muslims; judgment that they are all "terrorists"	Negative judgment that women make for bad leaders	Positive judgment of gay people and their fashion sense
Discrimination	Actions (behavioral)	Refusing to board an airplane with anyone perceived to be Muslim	Not voting for female political candidates	Choosing a gay man as your hairdresser

be a basic human instinct. This section answers the first core question, "Why do we keep using stereotypes?" by

(1) reviewing why stereotypes might be an automatic instinct,

(2) understanding how stereotypes support personal and group identity,

(3) recognizing how stereotypes can become self-fulfilling prophecies, and

(4) analyzing how cultural forces and institutional discrimination keep stereotypes going.

Stereotyping Makes Our Mental Lives Easier

Maybe stereotypes are an automatic instinct.

You probably haven't been paying attention to the small sounds all around you. It could be an old ticking clock, passing traffic, or someone climbing stairs. Your vision, smell, sense of touch, and even your thoughts are constantly sending you information, but we don't pay attention to every single little thing—and that's good. We couldn't cope if we had to pay attention to every sensation and perception. It would be overwhelming.

Instead, our automatic mental spam filter takes the easy way out. It throws out most sensations and perceptions and organizes them into folders of what should be given priority. It's what Allport (1979, p. 173) called "the principle of least effort." It's just what you would expect from cognitive misers who adopt mental shortcuts whenever possible (see Chapter 4). In short, stereotypes allow us to be mentally lazy by quickly making decisions about how to think about the people around us, freeing up our attention for other things.

Adaptive Categorization

Filtering what is and isn't important for our attention is an automatic instinct.

We do this, at least in part, because it helps our survival to label things as quickly as possible in terms of whether they present a threat to our survival. In other words, it's adaptive to make the snap decisions because if something *is* a threat, we need to respond quickly to it (e.g., fight or flight). Thus, use of quick labels like stereotypes is predicted by an idea called **adaptive categorization**: We automatically label things because it helps our survival to do this as quickly as possible.

Adaptive categorization: The idea that the instinct to group and label other people and things arose because it was a benefit to survival.

When you first meet someone, the *very first* information you get about them will be their outer appearance. Thus, according to adaptive categorization, the fastest way to label them is to use stereotypes based on things like their apparent age, sex, skin color, or even clothing (which might indicate things like socioeconomic status). Once we spot these initial features about someone, we start to immediately and automatically predict what kind of person they'll be. These external features allow us to make efficient, split-second, cognitively lazy decisions—that sometimes are wrong.

For example, think about the strange mashup in RB's mind that put two profoundly dissimilar groups into the same category. RB grouped elderly Jewish worshippers in Pittsburgh with foot-weary Central Americans in Mexico. If there had somehow been a stereotype-declaring sticker pasted on RB's forehead, then the category probably would have been labeled something like "My Enemies." This "us versus them" thinking is a theme throughout this entire chapter.

Stereotypes Are Supported by Automatic Neural Signatures

Stereotypes may be so common because they seem to be built into our brains.

Neural signatures are established pathways through regions of the brain. These pathways process particular types of information and can be processed without our conscious awareness (Cassidy & Krendl, 2016; Stolier & Freeman, 2016). Stereotypes can be automatically processed and can then influence our behavior automatically without us even realizing what's happening (Pesciarelli et al., 2019). Importantly, though, an established neural pathway does not mean that our thoughts will be permanently imprisoned by stereotypes. One study suggests that we can be liberated from stereotypes by simply slowing down and using logic.

Researchers (Cunningham et al., 2004) showed White participants images of either Black faces and White faces (the first *independent variable*). They also showed some participants the faces for 525 milliseconds (just over half a second) or 30 milliseconds (3/100 of a second!); timing was therefore the second *independent variable*. So this study was a *2 × 2 factorial design*.

Thirty milliseconds is a very brief exposure. But brain imaging showed that even during that tiny flash of time, participants in the 30-millisecond conditions had a reaction. Their fear responses (the *dependent variable*) in the amygdala were significantly greater for Black faces than for White faces.

That's depressing—but there's a silver lining. Participants who saw the same faces for 525 milliseconds showed brain activation in the complex neural pathways in the prefrontal cortex and the anterior cingulate—the thinking, logical parts of the brain. With just a half second delay, logic had an opportunity to influence and reduce the automatic fear response. While we may not be able to escape our automatic response to categorize and label other people, it takes only half a second of logical and effortful thought to start restraining those automatic impulses (see Harris & Fiske, 2018; Kubota et al., 2012).

Stereotypes Strengthen Our Identity

Maybe we stereotype others because it helps us understand our own identity.

Remember from Chapter 8 that groups provide a variety of benefits to their members. Groups provide personal access to resources, emotional comfort, physical safety, recreation, potential mating partners, and . . . well, lots of stuff that make our lives easier. We love our groups . . . even when they are logically meaningless.

Ingroups and Outgroups: Social Identity Theory

You're already a member of dozens of groups.

Some of these groups you chose, like your political party, college major, religion, extracurriculars, and so on. Others, you didn't (like your ethnicity and sexual orientation). **Ingroups** are all of the groups in which you are a member ("us"), while your **outgroups** are any groups in which you are not a member ("them").

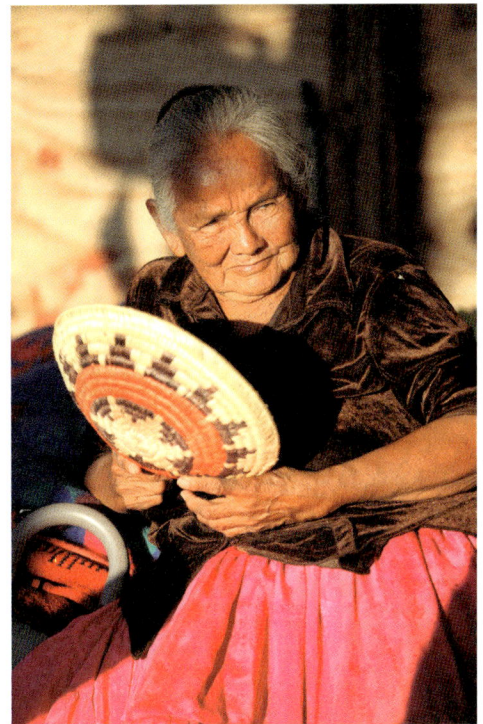

Feije Riemersma/Alamy Stock Photo

Just by looking at this person, what stereotypes might pop into your head? You already know she is old, female, and Native American, so assumptions about her personality, behaviors, and so on can begin to form immediately.

Neural signatures: Established pathways through regions of the brain.

Ingroup: Any group in which you're a member.

Outgroup: Any group in which you're not a member.

We appear to have the tendency to gather in groups of people we think are similar to each other.

You may have heard the phrase, "Birds of a feather flock together." We like spending time with people who are similar to ourselves, and that tendency reinforces stereotypes. When other people share experiences, agree with our opinions, and tell us that we're right, we feel comforted and validated. Our grouping tendencies became the theme of a controversial book written by social psychologist Beverly Tatum (2017) called *Why Are All the Black Kids Sitting Together in the Cafeteria?*

Our identities blend a personal identity (including our individual traits and what makes us unique) with a social identity (the parts of our "self" that include our group memberships). Remember from Chapter 3 that social identity theory (Tajfel & Turner, 1979) explains our automatic tendency to form "us versus them" groups that validate our perceptions of ourselves in ways that are both flattering and useful. We learn about ourselves and where we fit into our larger society by aligning ourselves with groups that we decide are meaningful to who we are and what we believe in.

But for social identity to bring us self-esteem, we have to think that our ingroups are valuable, useful, and/or skilled. One easy way for us to form this opinion is to think that our ingroups are *better* than our outgroups—and this requires stereotyping the outgroup as somehow lesser. Maybe they're not as hardworking, not as intelligent, more likely to be aggressive criminals, or whatever other belief we conjure up to reinforce that our group comes out on top.

The Minimal Group Paradigm

Minimal group paradigm: An experimental method creating groups based on meaningless categories to study intergroup dynamics.

Our motivation to protect our ingroups is strong—even stronger than logic.

Tajfel (1970) wanted to scientifically show that our bias toward ingroups is so strong that we'll protect people in our group even when the group is meaningless. He invented the **minimal group paradigm**, an experimental method to create groups that are so loosely tied together they are based on meaningless categories. To start, he showed

Do you prefer the painting on the left, by Klee, or the one on the right, by Kandinsky? Do you think you deserve more money, land, or food than people who disagree with you?

some English schoolboys (14 to 15 years old) very brief images of dots and asked the boys to estimate how many dots they had seen.

The catch was that the boys were given *bogus feedback* about their answers. In this case, the boys were told that they were either "overestimators" or "underestimators" of how many dots they had seen. It was a ridiculous, fictional, randomly assigned label. But the group label meant something to these boys. The members of each group used points (that represented real money) to discriminate unfairly to their outgroup. Just being told that "those kids" were different from you led to stereotypes, prejudice, and discrimination.

Tajfel *replicated* the experiment by leading another group of schoolboys to believe that they preferred the abstract paintings of either artist Paul Klee or Wassily Kandinsky. It happened again: ingroup favoritism and outgroup bias. How low was the bar needed to create this kind of discrimination? In a third experiment, bias emerged again even when participants *could observe* that assignment to a group was based on random chance—pulling a lottery ticket out of a can. Participants *still* rewarded other members of their new ingroup at the expense of the perceived outgroup (Billig & Tajfel, 1973; Tajfel et al., 1971).

The minimal groups experiments suggest that an "us versus them" mentality is unavoidable. We protect people we perceive to be "us." And behave as if "we" somehow deserve more than "they" do.

Stereotypes Can Become Self-Fulfilling Prophecies

Maybe we keep using stereotypes because their existence makes them come true (at least, in part).

In Chapter 5, we talked about self-fulfilling prophecies. Expectations about how we'll act influence us, sometimes making those expectations happen. If our teacher believes in us, we'll do better. If we think beautiful people are socially gifted, we're nice to them and we make them feel comfortable—thus making them socially gifted. And remember from Chapter 5 a study (Glover et al., 2017) that found managers who expected poor performance from immigrants found just that—while managers without this bias had immigrant workers who were great.

In order for self-fulfilling prophecies to occur based on stereotypes, we have to start with a stereotype. Some social psychologists argue that the stereotype originally came from some tiny truth. **Kernel of truth theory** notes that stereotypes might have been true for a small group of people (maybe even one person!) at some point in history, creating a starting point for the belief. It becomes a stereotype when we assume it's true for everyone in a group, or we believe it's still true thousands of years later. That kind of perpetual generalization is the problem.

Think about some possible examples of kernel of truth theory. "People who wear glasses are smart." That's a stereotype. Reading a lot can strain the eyes and educate you, simultaneously. So people who read a lot might need to get glasses, but they're also smart because of all that reading. Of course, there are smart people without glasses and dumb people with glasses—so the stereotype isn't really true, but it started from somewhere. Once we get an idea in our heads, we tend to keep that idea going. Two ways these ideas can become so ingrained in our culture that they become self-fulfilling prophecies are explained in social role theory and in stereotype threat (the next two parts of this section).

Social Role Theory

Men are good at business, and women are good at taking care of kids. Right?

Let's start with this kernel of truth: Women are the ones who give birth. Of course, not all women give birth. Some women choose not to have children, and some women don't have functioning reproductive systems (e.g., women who've had a hysterectomy, transwomen). But because some women biologically bear children, many people assume that women are also psychologically more capable of taking care of

Kernel of truth theory: The idea that stereotypes originated with truth for a small group of people at some point in time but are now exaggerated and potentially out of date.

those children later. Sexism predicts that women will be nurturing, kind, empathetic, and so on, all traits helpful in raising kids.

Based on this stereotype, we raise little girls to be future mothers and wives. We give them dolls, toy kitchens, Easy Bake ovens, and so on. And consider how we train little boys: We give them army sets, LEGOs to build, toy cars and trucks, and guns. Because we believe girls are kind and nurturing, and boys are aggressive and competitive, we *train them accordingly*.

Social role theory proposes that we (1) observe the roles people already have in our society, (2) assume people are inherently suited to those roles, and (3) reinforce traits that help people prepare for those roles (Eagly, 1987; Eagly et al., 2000). Gender roles are a clear example of how we see that women give birth and men (on average) are physically bigger and stronger. That biological divide leads to self-fulfilling prophecies when we assume that men and women are fundamentally different in lots of other ways, and we then reinforce those differences. This happens both at work (we assume men and women are differentially suited for various jobs) and at home (men and women take on different household responsibilities; Moulton-Tetlock et al., 2019). We make our stereotypes come true.

Social role theory: The idea that stereotypes form when we observe what people are doing, assume they are good at that, and then reinforce them to keep doing it.

Toys are frequently marketed toward boys versus girls—and they often send messages about what each sex should be learning and practicing for adulthood.

We start the self-fulfilling prophecy early, partially through toys. When the Mattel toy company released its "Teen-Talk Barbie," the doll was programmed to say stereotypically feminine phrases such as, "Do you have a crush on anyone?" "I will always be there to help you," and most famously, "Math class is tough!" The challenge to raise awareness of gender stereotypes and the messages we send little girls inspired some social activists to form the Barbie Liberation Organization (BLO).

BLO members purchased talking Barbies and GI Joes and performed "corrective surgery" on their voice chips before sneaking the dolls—in their original packaging—back onto the store shelves. Now the surgically modified Barbie declared in a gravelly voice, "Gung Ho!" "Cobra! Attack!" and "Dead men tell no tales." And GI Joe was eagerly asking, "Do you want to go shopping?"—and bemoaning the fact that math class was so hard.

If you think that dolls don't have any kind of influence about how children perceive the world around them, check out the Spotlight on Research Methods feature, which summarizes a study done with dolls that made it all the way to the U.S. Supreme Court.

💡 Dolls, Prejudice, Schools, and the Supreme Court

In 1954, the Supreme Court made what was possibly the most consequential constitutional decision of the 20th century: *Brown v. Board of Education,* which led to racial desegregation of schools. One of the ways the justices came to their conclusion was by considering research from psychology (Benjamin & Crouse, 2002). The Court concluded that "to separate [African American children] from others of similar age and qualifications . . . may affect their hearts and minds in a way unlikely ever to be undone."

The pivotal research cited by the Court, now known as the "doll studies," was first conceived by Mamie Phipps Clark as part of her master's degree. She and her husband, Kenneth Clark, were the first two African Americans to earn doctorates from Columbia University (see Johnson & Pettigrew, 2005). In their experiments, the Clarks presented African American children with dolls that were identical except that one doll was white-skinned and the other was brown-skinned (Whitman, 1993). It was a *within-subjects design* because the same children saw both a white-skinned doll and a brown-skinned doll. Then they asked the children a series of questions (the *dependent variables*) about which doll they preferred: "Give me the doll that you like to play with," ". . . you like best," ". . . is a nice doll," ". . . looks bad," ". . . is a nice color"—and, finally, ". . . is most like you?"

Some 90% of these 3- to 7-year-olds accurately indicated they were like the brown-skinned doll— but about two thirds preferred the white doll. In examining their results, the researchers compared the responses of children attending segregated schools in Washington, DC, and those of children attending racially integrated schools in New York. Comparing these two preexisting groups made their research a *quasi-experimental design*. The preference for the white doll—indicating a negative prejudice toward their own race—was much more pronounced in the children from segregated schools. Culture had taught them self-hatred, and they transferred those feelings to the dolls.

Some of the children's reactions were disturbing. One girl who had described the brown doll as "ugly" and "dirty" burst into tears; others refused to continue the experiment; some giggled self-consciously; one little boy tried to escape his dilemma by insisting that he had a suntan. The fact that this internalized racism was greater for children from segregated schools was a pivotal piece of information in the Court's decision that segregation led to negative outcomes.

The American Psychological Association (APA) was disturbingly quiet in the aftermath of *Brown v. Board of Education* (see Benjamin & Crouse, 2002). In 1970, Kenneth Clark was elected president of the APA and in 1994 was honored for his lifetime contributions. In his acceptance speech, he admitted that "thirty years after *Brown*, I must accept the fact that my wife left this earth despondent at seeing that damage to children is being knowingly and silently accepted by a nation that claims to be democratic" (from Benjamin & Crouse, 2002, p. 48).

Becoming Our Own Worst Enemy: Stereotype Threat

We're usually aware of negative stereotypes about our ingroups.

Consider a problem that Steele (1997) pointed out: A girl in a math class dominated by boys and a Black student in an all-White classroom face similar problems. Materially, everything could be the same—same textbook, same teacher, and even how the teacher treats everyone. But there is "a threat in the air"—stereotypes—that creates a more distracting classroom experience to some students. The girl might feel pressure because she knows she is not expected to do as well as the boys in math. The Black student might feel the same with respect to the White students.

Stereotype threat occurs when people worry about confirming a negative stereotype about their group (see Lee & Ottati, 1995; Steele & Aronson, 1995; Wheeler & Petty, 2001). In classrooms, this anxiety creates an extra layer of worry that's distracting. The irony here is that the anxiety resulting from fear of doing badly can lead to poor performance. Stereotyping has led to a self-fulfilling prophecy.

Almost 300,000 articles have been published regarding stereotype threat and its consequences. Some recent examples find it to be a problem for gender and racial minorities in STEM careers (Block et al., 2019; Starr et al., 2019), people of color in health care (Williams et al., 2019), older employees at work (von Hippel et al., 2019), and people who are trying to stop smoking (Cortland et al., 2019).

Stereotype threat: Anxiety about confirming a negative stereotype about our group, which is distracting and ironically leads to poor performance (confirming the negative stereotype).

Golfers and the Yips. Surprise! Golfers may be able to help students deal with stereotype threat.

That's because golfers sometimes experience the "yips"—becoming self-conscious about choking under pressure. The yips show up when basic, familiar motor skills suddenly became difficult to perform (see Roberts et al., 2019; Roberts et al., 2013). The distraction of worrying about choking will make them more likely to choke again (see Hill et al., 2009). In other words, the yips might become a self-fulfilling prophecy.

However, golfers and other athletes are not condemned to live down to their expectations. One study relied on *qualitative interviews* that allowed athletes to describe both short-term and long-term subjective experiences of choking. These particular athletes were intermediate-level golfers (those with low handicap scores) who previously had choked under pressure. Their fellow competitors knew they had choked under pressure. So they were now worried about fulfilling the low expectations of others (stereotype threat).

The golfers reported negative short-term consequences (losing, embarrassment), but only a few reported long-term negative consequences. One long-term case led to withdrawal from the sport and a lowered sense of self-worth. However, most golfers described long-term benefits related to "adversity-related growth" as a critical long-term benefit (Cheesebrough et al., 2019). People who said that they fought the stereotype, rose above the negative expectation, and proved themselves felt even better about their accomplishments.

Reframing Stereotype Threats. Reframing is an established feature of many effective therapies. It's thinking about the problem in a different way.

For example, you can reframe stereotype threat as a cultural challenge—which it certainly is. Seeing stereotype threat as an opportunity to overcome prejudice rather than a life sentence works well (see Alter et al., 2010). For example, one study found that a 9-week intervention to decrease math-gender stereotypes helped improve girls' confidence and their math scores (see Zhao et al., 2018).

Spencer et al. (1999) found another way to reframe and remove stereotype threat. The result was to equalize the math performance of different at-risk groups. How did they do it? They simply told participants at the beginning of the study that the test they were about to take had never shown different results from different groups. Here, people who reframed their beliefs were no longer distracted. The test was really about individual ability, so they no longer needed to worry about being a token representative of their group. They were free to focus on achievement—and achievement improved.

Finally, some studies have shown that even when stereotype threat is acknowledged by individuals, they can overcome their anxiety by thinking about the situation with a sense of humor. Humor, in at least one study, helped increase women's math performance and men's verbal performance (Ford et al., 2004). A sense of humor reframes difficult or awkward situations, such as stereotype threat, with the kind of thinking represented by one of the scale items: "I can usually find something to laugh or joke about even in trying situations."

Stereotypes Are Reinforced by Culture and Institutional Discrimination

Maybe stereotypes endure because they're reinforced by our culture and through institutional discrimination.

Culture is a collection of shared beliefs, customs, and social norms passed down from one generation to the next. One of those sets of beliefs can be stereotypes. Culture is "like a fish's understanding of the notion of water" (see Whitley & Kite, 2010, p. 6), something we usually don't bother to question until someone takes us out of our metaphorical water. It simply surrounds us, often without us noticing it's there or questioning its nature.

For example, Sue (2003) used a *qualitative methodology* to ask White people in the United States—part of the dominant culture—"What does it mean to be White?" Common

Culture: A collection of shared beliefs, customs, and social norms passed down from one generation to the next (including stereotypes).

responses were, "Is this a trick question?" "I've never thought about it," and "I don't know what you are talking about." Stereotypes can be intrinsic parts of culture that are reinforced by group privilege, social rewards and punishments (social learning theory), and institutional discrimination. Let's quickly examine each.

Group Privilege

Life is easier for the dominant group—and they don't even have to realize it.

People born into rich families have all kinds of advantages. They have access to good schools, plenty of money for clothes, high-quality food, expensive hobbies, safe neighborhoods, and more. They didn't earn their status, but they do benefit from it. In the same way, culture allows other groups to have more privilege than others. In most countries around the world, men have power access to high-paying, high-status jobs and a voice in politics, compared to women. And in most countries, one race has more privilege than the others.

The dominant group in society has privileges like resources and status—but it also has the privilege of not necessarily being aware of its privilege. One example that's often cited in research is **White privilege**, the social benefits of being White in a White-centric culture (Dyer, 2016; Lipsitz, 2016; Mills, 2016). White people might not even realize the kind of privileges they have until someone points it out. For example, White people usually aren't afraid that they've been "targeted" or "profiled" when they're pulled over by the police. That's not true of many other groups.

Peggy McIntosh (2011) recognized that one way to help Whites realize their privilege is to provide a list of examples of ways culture is set up to quietly benefit you, relative to other races or ethnicities. Here are some privileges from a much longer list of difficult-to-see-if-you-are-White advantages:

- Going shopping without being followed or harassed by store detectives

- Being sure that your children will get school materials that testify to the existence and achievements of people from their race

- Knowing you won't be asked to speak on behalf of your entire race

- Criticizing the government without seeming resentful on behalf of an entire group

- Not receiving backhanded compliments such as, "You speak so well!"

- Buying things in "flesh" color or "nude" and having them match my skin (e.g., clothes, bandages)

Simply being in a group with privilege isn't your fault, and it doesn't make you a bad person. And of course, there are White people who come from poor backgrounds who find it difficult to see how exactly they are "privileged." White privilege means that even if you are poor or come from a bad neighborhood, White people in that situation will still have more opportunity than people of color from that same situation. Much of privilege is not even thinking about how your group status might help or harm you, because it just hasn't occurred to you. If you had been in a marginalized group, you'd have seen how prejudice affects your life.

Privilege comes in other forms (beyond race) as well, based on which group has social power. Women might worry about not being paid the same amount as men in the same job—but men don't have to think about the wage disparity. Gay spouses might worry about putting pictures of each other on their desk at work—but heterosexual

One bee sting can hurt. Even though each sting is small, many small stings over and over can feel overwhelming.

iStockPhoto/bo1982

White privilege: The cultural benefits of being White in White-centric societies.

spouses don't even think about it. Jewish people will probably have to work on Yom Kippur, while Christians usually assume they'll get Christmas off.

These subtle, persistent parts of privilege accumulate into an experience for the oppressed that can be depressing. Each single instance can be like an annoying bee sting—but hundreds of bee stings over years can be pretty overwhelming. It's hard to grow up in a culture where you're often reminded that your group is not on top.

Intergenerational Transfer: Social Learning Theory

Stereotypes also get passed along to the next generation.

Social learning theory is the idea that we observe what others do and copy them, especially when those behaviors lead to success or rewards (Bandura, 1986). Cultures subtly reward specific stereotypes in subtle ways that are transmitted from one generation to the next. **Social agents** are the ones sending the messages about cultural beliefs and expectations. They can be parents, the media, or any source that transmits information to others.

For example, across more than 900 Hollywood movies, Arabs have been stereotyped as uncivilized, savage, religious fanatics (Shaheen, 2003). In television and news coverage of athletes, the focus on female athletes is often how physically attractive they are, whereas the focus on male athletes is their skill (Messner, 1988). Television shows frequently endorse stereotypical gender roles, as well as stereotypes of the wealthy and the poor (Newman, 2007). Video games focus on male characters, often in hypermasculine or "macho" roles and body types (Huntley & Goodfriend, 2019; Melzer, 2019).

Social learning recognizes that merely observing these behaviors helps transfer them from one generation to the next. When we see the beliefs our culture endorses, we know that we'll be largely rewarded for espousing these same beliefs. But these stereotypes can lead to important problems.

For example, many modern cultures portray men as "fighter, hunter, provider and protector" (Seager, 2019, p. 227). When individual men feel that they can't admit any weakness, can't ask for help, and can't show any vulnerability because they fear social rejection or punishment due to this stereotype, it can lead to mental health problems and even suicide (Seager, 2019). This example shows another sad example of how stereotypes are reinforced by culture and how that culture can hurt everyone inside it.

Institutional Discrimination

Finally, stereotypes are endorsed and supported by some institutions throughout our culture.

Institutional discrimination is unfair treatment of individuals or certain groups by society or organizations through unequal selection, opportunity, or oppression. In the United States, some people believe that institutional discrimination occurs throughout many layers of the culture, including the legal system, health care, social services, political representation, media representation, and more. It's bias that built into the system itself.

In 2016, a study found that in "routine" traffic stops by the police, Black and Hispanic drivers were more likely to be stopped and to have their vehicles searched, compared to White drivers (even though those searches didn't lead to any more illegal drugs or weapons; Andrews, 2016). People of color are sometimes denied health care or certain prescriptions by medical doctors (Tello, 2017). In 2019, women (on average) still made only $0.79 for every dollar a man earned (Payscale.com, 2019). And note that this differential changes with race: Asian women make $0.93, White women make $0.80, and Hispanic or Black women make $0.74. Structural barriers that keep women from advancing in the workplace, such as low expectations and stereotype threat, are one reason for this continued discrepancy.

One by-product of institutional discrimination is that it keeps stereotypes going by keeping groups largely separated from each other. When we spend time only with people who look and think like us (our ingroups), we experience **ingroup heterogeneity**, the perception of diversity among our own group. We see how all the students at

Social agents: People who send messages about cultural beliefs and expectations that help transmit ideas from one generation to the next.

Institutional discrimination: Unfair treatment of individuals or certain groups by society or organizations through unequal selection, opportunity, or oppression.

Ingroup heterogeneity: The tendency for individuals to see wide diversity within their ingroups.

our own school, for example, differ in various interesting ways. But if we never spend time with people from other groups, we experience **outgroup homogeneity**, the perception that everyone in an outgroup is the same as everyone else in that group. All we have to go on are stereotypes, so the stereotype continues.

If you play on the women's basketball team, then ingroup heterogeneity will help you see the different personalities of each player on your team—their strengths and weaknesses on the court and their complicated lives away from the team. But if you know or care little about basketball, then outgroup homogeneity will make you perceive that everyone on the basketball team is pretty much the same. If someone asks, "Who is she?" then your outsider's view can only say, "I don't know. She plays hoops."

For more examples of institutional discrimination, see the Social Psychology in Popular Culture feature.

Outgroup homogeneity: The perception that all members of a particular outgroup are identical to each other.

SOCIAL PSYCHOLOGY IN POPULAR CULTURE

▶ Institutional Discrimination in *Mulan* and *The Handmaid's Tale*

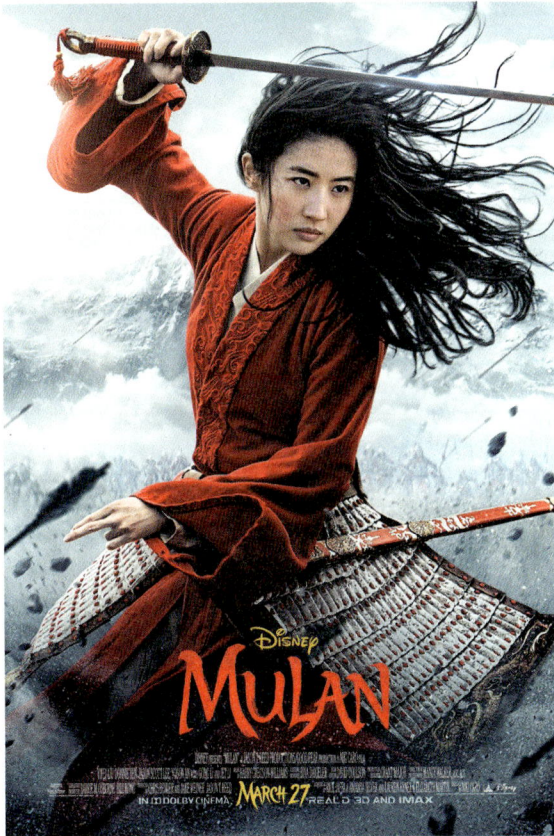

BFA / Alamy Stock Photo

JIM WATSON /AFP/Getty Images

Two stories. One from the past, one from the future. One for children, one for adults. Both based on a world run by powerful men.

Institutional discrimination can be seen in two settings from recent popular culture. In Disney's *Mulan* (both

the animated version and the new, live-action version), ancient China is besieged by invaders. Every family is required to send one male member to serve in the military. The film follows the legend of Hua Mulan, a young woman who disguises herself as a man so that her elderly father won't have to go. Overcoming every challenge presented to her, Mulan proves that women can be just as dedicated, loyal, and intelligent as any man. It's a heartwarming and empowering story, especially for young women who might be used to seeing pretty but helpless princesses in Disney films.

We also see institutional discrimination in an extreme dystopian form in the best-selling book *The Handmaid's Tale* (Atwood, 1986) and award-winning Hulu series. Here, the fictional future is a world in which extreme pollution has made 99% of women infertile. For women who are still able to bear children, instead of being given extra privileges and honor in society, they

(Continued)

(Continued)

are considered property of the state. These women are essentially subjugated to the role of sex slave and are given as rewards to rich, powerful men who keep the government going.

The entire culture is based on institutional discrimination. Women are forced into roles such as Handmaid (fertile women who have no choice about the men who are sanctioned to rape them once a month), Marthas (house servants and cooks), and Wives (who are married to the rich, powerful men but have no rights or power themselves). Each role has a color they must wear, identifying themselves immediately to strangers. It is forbidden for any women to read.

The culture is one of oppression and discrimination, veiled behind "tradition" and extreme religiosity. Really,

it's just misogyny. One of the most effective ways the Handmaids are kept in line is by training them to turn against each other using victim blaming and ostracism. In the novel, only White people have value (it's both sexist and racist), although in the show, the White supremacy is largely removed. The show's storyline follows both women and men who try to fight against the status quo—a crime that could lead to surgery, banishment to highly polluted rural work farms, or humiliating public deaths.

As Dr. Kara Ellerby, professor of political science and gender studies, notes, "Domination is complex and it takes a complex and inclusive social movement that recognizes the magnitude of oppression in order to truly emancipate anyone" (Ellerby, 2017). Or, as the author Atwood puts it in the novel itself: "Don't let the bastards grind you down."

THE MAIN IDEAS

- Stereotypes are beliefs about members of a group, prejudice is evaluations of the group, and discrimination is unfair behaviors toward someone based on their group membership.
- Adaptive categorization is the idea that the instinct to group and label other people and things in the environment arose because it was a benefit to survival.
- Our instinctive tendency to prefer ingroups over outgroups can be seen even in groups that are arbitrary and meaningless, a point supported by research called the "minimal group paradigm."
- Stereotypes can also become self-fulfilling prophecies. Social role theory notes that we train people to be good at the roles we expect them to fulfill as adults. Stereotype threat is the idea that we can be anxious about fulfilling negative expectations about our own group, but this anxiety can be distracting and can lead to ironically poor performance (thus, a self-fulfilling prophecy).
- Finally, our culture and institutional discrimination endorse stereotypes by setting up structures that continue these beliefs over time and across individuals. Specific examples come from social learning theory (that we copy what we observe in others) and from group privilege.

CRITICAL THINKING CHALLENGE

- Examples of stereotypes, prejudice, and discrimination often focus on either race or sex. What *other* important categories or group labels and assumptions about groups affect your own life? You might think of religion, people in your major, people in your chosen extracurriculars, or any of your other interesting ingroups.
- Have you ever experienced stereotype threat when you were afraid of confirming a negative stereotype about one of your ingroups? Was it distracting? How did you respond? Describe how this effect can be seen in your own life.
- Identify three specific ways that growing up in a certain culture led you to learn stereotypes about different groups (e.g., media messages, how you were treated in various settings). Looking back on these messages now, can you identify any negative influences they had on your perceptions or behaviors regarding yourself or people from your outgroups?

HOW DO STEREOTYPES TURN INTO PREJUDICES?

>> **LO 9.2:** **Understand types of prejudice and how four theories explain the motivation behind it.**

Let's review:

- We categorize in ways that produce stereotypes. It seems to be an automatic behavior pattern.

- We prefer to live in groups. It's safer, is more comfortable, and provides many benefits, including an integrated identity.

- Cultures teach the next generation how to think about one group versus another.

But those three characteristics don't make us prejudiced—or do they? This section answers the core question "How do stereotypes turn into prejudices?" by

(1) discussing different forms of prejudice and

(2) analyzing four theories regarding how stereotypes, emotions, and situations turn into prejudice.

Three Types of Prejudice

Some people believe that the current world no longer suffers from prejudices like racism or sexism.

They believe that we've reached a society where everyone really has equal rights and opportunities. Others argue that prejudice still exists, but it has (at least in part) changed over time to be more hidden. To analyze your own view on this debate, consider three types of prejudice.

Old-Fashioned Prejudice

First: Open, obvious prejudice is easy to spot.

Signs in a window saying "Irish Not Welcome" or having different water fountains for different races are a thing of the past. This blatant prejudice is called **old-fashioned prejudice** in psychology, because it's largely not socially acceptable in today's "politically correct" world. It's probably true that old-fashioned prejudice has decreased a lot over the past several decades in the United States, partially because of the civil rights movement. But just because this form of prejudice has decreased doesn't mean prejudice is gone completely. Maybe it's just become more subtle—and certain types of prejudice are still more acceptable than others.

For example, many media representations of overweight people are negative or contemptuous. Some states have passed laws that business owners can refuse to provide services to potential customers whose practices do not align with the owners' religious beliefs. A baker, for example, might refuse to make a wedding cake for a gay couple in such a state. These examples lead us to two other forms of prejudice.

Modern-Symbolic Prejudice

Denying that prejudice still exists in the world is considered a form of prejudice itself.

Modern-symbolic prejudice (McConahay, 1983, 1986) comes from people who think of themselves as valuing equality for all people but who simultaneously oppose

Explicit prejudice like that displayed on this sign is much less likely to be seen today. Does that mean prejudice has decreased—or simply that it has changed to more subtle forms?

Old-fashioned prejudice: Obvious, overt prejudice that is considered inappropriate by modern social standards.

Modern-symbolic prejudice: Prejudice from people who think they value equality but oppose any social change that would go away from "tradition" to make equality possible.

social change that would allow this equality to occur. They believe that modern culture has eliminated prejudice and oppression, so they resent minority groups who ask for attention and additional resources. They also believe in maintaining "traditions" that unfortunately keep some groups from having the same opportunities as others.

Sears and Henry (2005) summarized the beliefs within modern-symbolic prejudice as follows:

- Most forms of prejudice and discrimination no longer exist or are rare.

- Any remaining group differences in socioeconomic outcomes or class are the result of some groups' lack of motivation to work hard.

- Because those groups are unwilling to work toward goals, their continuing anger or claims of discrimination are not justified.

- Rather than committing to more effort, those groups seek special favors (e.g., "reverse racism").

- Due to their complaints, minorities now get more than they deserve due to these special favors.

This form of prejudice blames groups without power for being powerless. They are in that situation due to their own lack of effort. Because people high in modern-symbolic beliefs perceive that prejudice is no longer a problem, they resent anything that appears to "favor" minorities, such as affirmative action policies and scholarships for people of color. In their view, such policies are no longer necessary and represent "reverse" discrimination. People high in modern-symbolic prejudice reject the idea that they, personally, have any prejudice but hold tightly to "traditions" and often believe that things are already good, so why make any changes (Fish & Syed, 2019)?

Benevolent + Hostile = Ambivalent Prejudice

Finally, a third form of prejudice combines two subforms.

Benevolent prejudice is the perception that members of certain groups have positive qualities that should be praised and valued. But remember the problem with positive stereotypes: When group members fail to live up to these unfair standards, they will be judged particularly harshly. Another problem is that the stereotype of what people in that group "should" be still restricts opportunities for the group. Finally, some of the values inherent in benevolent prejudice may be condescending and paternalistic toward the relevant outgroup.

A common example is that women are "pure," "nice," and "kind" (Glick & Fiske, 1996, 2001). People with high levels of benevolent sexism believe that most women possess these qualities—and that women *should* possess these qualities. Women who fit this model are then especially liked and praised.

The backlash comes when some women do not fit this stereotype. They are then judged particularly harshly, an attitude called **hostile prejudice**. If women present themselves as competitive, aggressive, feminist, and/or "masculine," they can be judged especially harshly (e.g., Masser & Abrams, 2004; Oh et al., 2019; Rudman, 1998; Yildirim et al., 2019). Men who are high in hostile sexism are more accepting of both sexual harassment (Begany & Milburn, 2002; Russell & Trigg, 2004) and domestic violence toward women (Glick et al., 2002). They also are more likely to blame rape victims for what happened (Viki & Abrams, 2002).

The combination of benevolent and hostile prejudice is **ambivalent prejudice**. It's maintaining stereotypes and judgments about people from a certain group as either very positive (when they fit into how we think they "should" act) or very negative (when they dare to fight against the boxes we want to put them in). Again with the example of sexism, the idea that women are either virtuous angels or sinful devils has been called the "virgin/whore false dichotomy" or the "Madonna/whore complex" (in which "Madonna" refers to the Christian Virgin Mary). In the 2016 U.S. presidential election,

Benevolent prejudice: Positive judgments of group members who have traits we value and align with our expectations.

Hostile prejudice: Negative judgments of people who do not fit prescribed group stereotypes or push boundaries of what people in their group "should" do.

Ambivalent prejudice: A combination of hostile and benevolent prejudice that means some group members are judged very positively while others are judged very negatively, depending on whether they fit our expectations.

scores on a measure of ambivalent sexism were found to be significantly strong predictors of whether people intended to vote for Hillary Clinton (Blair, 2016; Cassese & Holman, 2019).

Other forms of ambivalent prejudice exist. We like gay men when they're helping us be fashionable or have trendy cocktails (benevolent prejudice), but we don't like it when they make legitimate demands for equal rights and respect (hostile prejudice; Brooks et al., 2019). We like people with "disabilities" when we think of them as inspirational or when we can "help" them and feel good about ourselves, but we don't like it when they ask to be equally represented in the media or when they complain of being pitied (Nario-Redmond et al., 2019). In short, we maintain positive views of people from social minorities (they're wonderful!)—but we only like a *certain kind* of people: those who know their "place" and don't get too "pushy."

Now that we've covered a few types of prejudice, let's consider the big picture question of the motivation behind this type of social judgment of others: Why do we feel particularly positive or negative toward outgroup members?

I Deserve It More Than You: Realistic Conflict Theory

What's happening psychologically when multiple people want that last slice of pizza?

The answer to that question sums up **realistic conflict theory**, the idea that prejudice results from competition over scarce resources (Sherif, 1966a; Sherif & Sherif, 1969). Others around the table may start to judge the person grabbing that last slice: "no self-control," "rude," "selfish," or even "greedy." Alternatively, we also think about how we somehow deserve it more than everyone else. While pizza is clearly a trivial example, realistic conflict theory can become dangerous when played out on a larger community or national scale.

Prejudice has helped colonizers of almost every nation and time period justify taking land and resources from native peoples. They justify their own behavior by calling people "savages," believing that they practiced the wrong religion or that they needed to be "civilized." People rely on prejudice to convince themselves that they "deserve" scarce resources more than someone else.

In a more modern example, realistic conflict theory can explain the behavior of some Canadian landlords. Researchers (Hilton et al., 1989) asked landlords in Greater Montreal two simple questions: (1) How willing are you to rent to people of a particular ethnic background (see Figure 9.1)? (2) How might renting to that group affect the value of your rental properties?

The context of this study matters: At the time, apartments in Montreal were scarce, and landlords wanted to maximize the value of what they owned. All of the landlords were French-Quebecers (the ingroup), and only 15% had previously rented to non-French-Quebecers (the outgroups). The landlords wanted to protect their scarce resources and keep the values of their apartments high. So they justified prejudice against outgroups by convincing themselves that renting to minorities would decrease the value of their property. They told themselves that it wasn't personal; it was just business.

Consider whether realistic conflict over limited resources might explain other historical examples of prejudice. When European explorers came to North America, they took the land they wanted and were told to "subdue the Saracens, pagans, and other enemies of Christ" (Davenport, 1917, p. 20). During the Crusades, both Christians and Muslims fought over resources and considered each other barbarians (Halperin, 1984). In 1994, a genocide in Rwanda occurred between two ethnic groups who resented each other because of perceived unfairness in power, land ownership, and government

While the "Madonna/whore complex" refers to the New Testament Madonna (the Virgin Mary), enduring pop star Madonna has played on this concept to help her achieve fame.

Kevin Mazur/WireImage/Getty Images

Realistic conflict theory: The idea that prejudice results from the justifications we create to determine that our ingroup "deserves" limited resources.

FIGURE 9.1

Economic prejudice by landlords in Montreal.

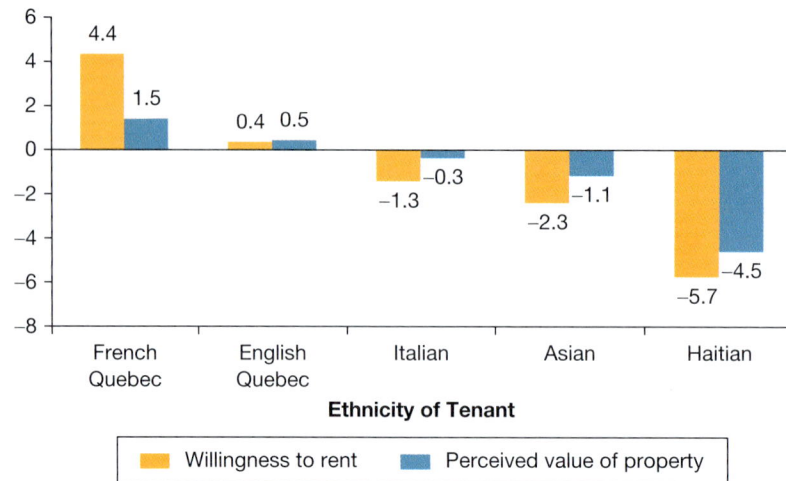

Source: Data from Hilton et al. (1989).

representation (Buckley-Zistel, 2009). And in modern Israel, people from Jewish, Christian, and Muslim religious traditions all feel a rightful claim to certain landmarks and regions (Hajir, 2019).

It's Your Fault: Scapegoating

A second theory about prejudice focuses on how it feels good to blame someone else for our problems.

Frustration-aggression theory proposes that mounting frustrations will lead to aggression (Dollard et al., 1939; Hogg, 2016). Any obstacle can generate frustration: poor economic conditions, personal failures, humiliating losses, romantic disappointments . . . it doesn't matter. Frustration builds a physical and psychological tension that we feel must be let out, and frequently the outlet is aggression.

Prejudice comes into the picture when we *justify* our aggression by choosing a target we believe causes our problems and deserves to be punished. **Scapegoat theory** is the idea that prejudice is the result of one group blaming another for its problems and frustrations (Allport, 1954; Joly, 2016). We choose targets who (1) are weaker than us (so they can't put up much of a fight) and (2) can somehow be tied to our problem (so we can justify the prejudice and aggression).

The early example in the history of social psychology was the Nazi party. They blamed Jews, gypsies, Communists, homosexuals, and many other groups for their nation's poor economy after World War I. Hitler characterized these groups as greedy, dirty, and diseased. He also managed to convince millions of people that all their problems would go away if these groups were eliminated. Recent events continue to use Jews, Blacks, Mexicans, and immigrant groups as scapegoats.

In the history of the United States, economic frustrations were transformed into prejudice and then aggression after the American Civil War. Many Whites were financially devastated when slaves were freed. Between 1882 and 1930, patterns of violence against African Americans showed that anti-Black prejudice increased when the economy was troubled. During that time period, the price of cotton and the number of lynchings of Black men by White men were *negatively correlated* between –0.6 and –0.7 (quite a high correlation!). As the price of cotton went down, the number of lynchings went up (Hovland & Sears, 1940). As the price of cotton declined and Whites became

Frustration-aggression theory: The idea that our frustrations build until they are released through aggression toward weaker targets we can blame.

Scapegoat theory: The idea that prejudice results from blaming an outgroup for our frustrations (see *frustration-aggression theory*).

frustrated over their financial situation, they blamed the former slaves and aggressed against them with shameful murders.

More recently, prejudice toward immigrants in the United States increases when people believe that the economy is bad and that jobs may be limited (Filindra & Pearson-Merkowitz, 2013). In another study, prejudice against Asian Americans increased when participants were led to think about economic threats (Butz & Yogeeswaran, 2011). Merely thinking about economic threat increased their prejudice only toward Asian Americans—a group perceived as potentially taking higher-paying and higher-status jobs. The belief that immigrants from Latinx countries threaten job security and will lower U.S. wages is tied to prejudice toward immigrants and support for stricter border control between the United States and Mexico as well (Finley & Esposito, 2019). The prejudice appears to be linked to fear, frustration, and resulting aggression.

One reason prejudice exists is because we like to blame other people for our problems, a tendency called scapegoating.

You're Nice, but Incompetent: The Stereotype Content Model

Stereotypes are based on beliefs. Prejudices are based on emotions.

Some stereotypes are so cruel that they make it easy to experience automatic, negative emotions. For example, the Jewish stereotype is one of shrewd wealth—and the emotions that trigger anti-Jewish prejudice are envy and a fear of losing resources. The stereotype of African Americans is one of criminals and sexual predators—and the emotions that trigger anti-Black prejudice are often fears of being physically harmed. Different stereotypes trigger different emotional profiles (Cottrell & Neuberg, 2005).

Fiske et al. (2002) wondered whether all prejudices could be tracked based on their emotional foundations and categories of judgment. Their stereotype content model proposes two categories of judgment: warmth and competence. Groups that do not compete with us pose no threat, so it's easy to like them—to perceive them as warm (and remember, warmth leads to a halo effect of positivity). At the same time, groups that aren't threatening are perceived as relatively ineffectual or incompetent. We can look down on them with condescension and/or pity.

In contrast, groups that are high in status have resources, so it's easy to admire them and to perceive them as competent. As the same time, we might resent them. Table 9.2 names and describes the four possible combinations that these two categories (warmth and competence) can create. The table also identifies the corresponding emotional responses and types of prejudices, as well as suggests representative groups in current U.S. culture. Note that Table 9.2 is from the perspective of the group currently in power—and that any of the four combinations results in some form of emotional judgment or prejudice toward people in our outgroups.

I Don't Like People Who Are Different: A Prejudiced Personality

Maintaining positive self-esteem is important to most of us.

Social psychology's interactionist perspective focuses on how particular personalities make sense of each situation. Many researchers have suggested personality traits that either directly or indirectly relate to an individual's personal tendency to be more or less prejudiced toward outgroups. Theoretically, someone with a prejudiced personality will have a general tendency to dislike any outgroups and members of those outgroups, across the board.

Stereotype content model: The idea that two categories of judgment, warmth and competence, interact to form four different types of prejudice and emotional reaction to outgroups.

Interactionist perspective: The idea that personality and situations jointly affect an individual's social behavior.

Prejudiced personality: The idea that certain traits are linked to a general tendency to dislike all outgroups.

TABLE 9.2

The Stereotype Content Model

	LOW IN COMPETENCE	HIGH IN COMPETENCE
High in warmth	***Paternalistic prejudice*** toward people who are low in status and do not compete with the ingroup. Our emotional responses include pity and sympathy. Examples: elderly people, people with disabilities, and housewives.	***Admiration prejudice*** for people who have high status and do not compete with the ingroup. Our emotional responses include pride and admiration. Examples: our ingroups or allies.
Low in warmth	***Contemptuous prejudice*** toward people with low status who compete with the ingroup. Our emotional responses include contempt, disgust, anger, and resentment. Examples: Welfare recipients and very poor people	***Envious prejudice*** toward people with high status who compete with the ingroup. Our emotional responses include envy and jealousy. Examples: Asians, Jews, rich people, and feminists

Source: Fiske et al. (2002).

Some people may have "prejudiced personalities." Cartman from *South Park* explicitly believes anyone not like himself is not as good.

Personality alone does not explain particular prejudices against different classes of people. We turn once again to Kurt Lewin's interactionist perspective: Behavior is best predicted by understanding how an individual personality causes us to respond to given situations. Three personality traits that may be tied to prejudice toward outgroups are authoritarianism, social dominance orientation, and religiosity.

The Authoritarian Personality

Someone who "kisses up" and "kicks down" is the shorthand description of the authoritarian personality.

Exploring the authoritarian personality was the first and most influential attempt after World War II to define and measure a prejudiced personality. Psychologists wanted to know what type of person would eagerly join the Nazi party, believe its outlandish propaganda, and then act on those beliefs in such destructive ways. Researchers (Adorno et al., 1950) suggested that the **authoritarian personality** generalizes prejudices across many different groups using a structure of authority and order. The authoritarian personality includes three major behavioral tendencies:

(1) submitting to authority (when that authority is perceived as legitimate),

(2) disciplining those who defy authority, and

(3) conforming to conventional beliefs.

Authoritarian personality: A personality characterized by submission to authority, discipline toward those who defy authority, and conforming to conventional beliefs.

Pettigrew (2016) observed that authoritarianism has continued to be a consistent predictor of personal prejudice for well over half a decade, including current political and social anxieties (see also Smith, 2019). Dunwoody and Plane (2019), for example, found that individuals with more authoritarian beliefs were more likely to perceive members of outgroups (Mexicans and Muslims) as threatening and more willing to abandon the rule of law to cope with perceived threats from immigrants.

PjrStudio/Alamy Stock Photo

It is easy to think that Germany's descent into authoritarianism is the poster child for this disturbing personality trait. But Parker and Towler (2019) point out that American slavery, Jim Crow laws, and campaigns of voter suppression also required commitment to authoritarian beliefs. Authoritarianism is embedded in passionate cultural traditions and appears prominently in political debates.

Consequently, finding a way to measure this important social tendency is sometimes charged with political bias. The most popular scale now to measure authoritarian personality was first developed by Altemeyer in 1981 and updated in 1994; you can see several of the items in the What's My Score? feature. But it has two major criticisms.

First, some of the items include more than one idea. For example, one item is "Homosexuals and feminists should be praised for being brave enough to defy traditional family values" (this item is *reverse-scored*). When a scale item includes more than one basic idea, people have difficulty knowing how to respond if they agree with one of the ideas but not the other. Such an item is called a **double-barreled item**. Second, the scale is criticized for assuming that prejudice only comes from right-wing politics instead of acknowledging that either side can be close-minded and judgmental of the other (Altemeyer, 1990; Ray, 1990). Social psychologists are still trying to develop a good way to measure authoritarianism (Bizumic & Duckitt, 2018).

Criticisms aside, authoritarianism does appear to predict a variety of social prejudices.

High scores are *correlated* with prejudice against environmental and community activists (Middeldorp & Le Billon, 2019), African Americans (Rowatt & Franklin, 2004), feminists (Duncan et al., 1997), gay people (Cramer et al., 2013; Crawford et al., 2016), overweight people (Crandall, 1994), Muslims (Wilson, 2019), and immigrants (Duckitt & Sibley, 2010).

Social Dominance Orientation

Authoritarianism is all about knowing who is in charge.

Similarly, **social dominance orientation** (or SDO; Pratto et al., 1994) is a preference for social hierarchies and a clear understanding of which groups do and do not possess social power. It also includes "the extent to which one desires that one's in-group dominate and be superior to out-groups" (p. 742). People high in SDO believe that their own group should be at the top of the social ladder and that others should "stay in their place."

Again, you can see items from the SDO scale in the What's My Score? feature. A disturbing pattern here is that people high in SDO are more likely to make a variety of unethical decisions such as polluting the environment, exploiting workers in a less developed country, or marketing a profitable but harmful drug (Son Hing et al., 2007). People high in SDO believe governments should *not* issue official "apologies" to groups that have been oppressed (Mifune et al., 2019). And students high in SDO believed that harsh tactics from their professors were more reasonable, compared to students low in SDO (Tesi et al., 2019).

Keep in mind that correlations only hint at what might be causal relationships. Like authoritarianism, high SDO scores are *positively correlated* with a variety of social prejudices (a *true experiment* is needed to verify any causal relationship; Kteily et al., 2011). Interestingly, one study found that people high in SDO resent it when African Americans claim to be victims of discrimination, but those same people support Whites who claim discrimination (Unzeuta et al., 2014). This particular pattern shows a clear preference for helping groups that are already privileged.

Religiosity

Religion isn't a personality trait, like authoritarianism or SDO—but religiosity might be. **Religiosity** is an individual difference that explores the degree to which a person is religious and why. The question isn't whether any particular religion is tied to prejudice. Instead, social psychologists ask if motivation behind believing in any given faith is tied to negative judgments about outgroups. At first, this may seem ironic or

Double-barreled item: A scale item that includes more than one basic idea, making it difficult for individuals to know how to respond if they agree with one of the ideas but not the other.

Social dominance orientation: A preference for social hierarchy and having power over outgroups.

Religiosity: The degree to which one is religious and why.

even offensive; after all, most religions teach tolerance and forgiveness. So the research results are complicated.

Start with the interesting finding (Allport & Ross, 1967) that while most regular churchgoers are *more* prejudiced toward outgroups than nonattenders, a significant minority of church attenders are *less* prejudiced. Other research also linked extreme religiosity to prejudice. One study (Pettigrew, 2016) showed that high religiosity is positively correlated with dogmatism, zealotry, self-righteousness, and believing that the world is a dangerous place (Altemeyer & Hunsberger, 2004). A review of 38 studies (Batson et al., 1993) concluded that "religion is not associated with increased love and acceptance but with increased intolerance, prejudice, and bigotry" (p. 302). But there was another complicating detail to the research story about religion and prejudice.

It turns out that the link between religiosity and prejudice depends on people's motivation to be religious. Social psychologists have now identified four distinct types or forms of religiosity:

- **Intrinsic religiosity**: People who have a sincere belief in their faith and try to incorporate its teaching into their daily life (Allport & Ross, 1967; Batson et al., 1993). Correlations between intrinsic religiosity and prejudice tend to be small or nonexistent in either positive or negative directions.

- **Extrinsic religiosity**: This refers to people who engage with a faith because of social or practical rewards (e.g., impressing their boss, making business connections, access to food or clothing banks). Being higher in extrinsic religiosity is *positively correlated* with various forms of prejudice, such as racism (Herek, 1987) and homophobia (Lough, 2006). In some ways, extrinsic religiosity is hypocrisy (Donahue, 1985).

- **Fundamentalism**: This is the belief that only one religion is correct, all teachings should be taken literally, and that forces of evil are active and all around us (see Altemeyer & Hunsberger, 1992, 2004; Brandt & Reyna, 2014). Fundamentalism can be found in most, if not all, major religions (Armstrong, 2000). Fundamentalism is *positively correlated* with several types of prejudice (Spilka et al., 2003), especially when outgroups are seen as "sinful."

- **Religion as quest**: Finally, this form of religiosity is that faith is really about philosophy and spirituality. Here, asking questions is more important than finding answers. Skepticism and doubt are welcomed. Quest orientation is often *negatively correlated* with prejudice (Batson et al., 1978; Hunsberger, 1995; McFarland, 1989), perhaps because they acknowledge that their own beliefs may not be the only "truth" in the world.

Intrinsic religiosity: Sincere belief in a faith and attempts to apply those principles to everyday behaviors.

Extrinsic religiosity: Practicing a faith only because of social or practical rewards.

Fundamentalism: Belief that one's faith is the only true religion, that teachings should be taken literally, and that evil is all around us.

Religion as quest: A spiritual or philosophical approach to religion that values skepticism and exploration.

The Westboro Baptist Church is well known for its racist and homophobic demonstrations. Many other Christians do not want to be associated with members of this group due to their prejudices.

Mark Reinstein/Corbis News/Getty Images

Measuring "Prejudiced" Personality Traits

Below you'll see several statements that are example items from scales that some people believe measure aspects of a "prejudiced personality." After you take the scale, see the scoring instructions to know which items measure which traits. Rate how much you agree or disagree with each statement using this scale:

1	2	3	4	5	6	7
Disagree strongly			Neutral			Agree strongly

___ 1. Our country desperately needs a mighty leader who will do what has to be done to destroy the radical new ways and sinfulness that are ruining us.

___ 2. The only way our country can get through the crisis ahead is to get back to our traditional values, put some tough leaders in power, and silence the troublemakers spreading bad ideas.

___ 3. Our country will be destroyed someday if we do not end the perversions eating away at our moral fiber and moral beliefs.

___ 4. What our country needs is more discipline, with everyone following our leaders in unity.

___ 5. God's laws about abortion, pornography, and marriage must be strictly followed before it is too late, and those who break them must be strongly punished.

___ 6. Some groups of people are simply inferior to other groups.

___ 7. In getting what you want, it is sometimes necessary to use force against other groups.

___ 8. It's OK if some groups have more of a chance in life than others.

___ 9. It's probably a good thing that certain groups are at the top and other groups are at the bottom.

___ 10. Inferior groups should stay in their place.

___ 11. It is important to me to spend periods of time in private religious thoughts and meditation.

___ 12. I try hard to carry my religion over into all my other dealings in life.

___ 13. Religion is especially important to me because it answers questions about the meaning of life.

___ 14. The church is most important as a place to formulate good social relationships.

___ 15. I pray chiefly because I have been taught to pray.

___ 16. Occasionally, I find it necessary to compromise my religious beliefs in order to protect my social and economic well-being.

___ 17. God has given mankind a complete, unfailing guide to happiness and salvation, which must be totally followed.

___ 18. The long-established traditions in religion show the best way to honor and serve God and should never be compromised.

___ 19. Whenever science and sacred scripture conflict, science must be wrong.

___ 20. As I grow and change, I expect my religion to grow and change.

___ 21. It might be said that I value my religious doubts and uncertainties.

___ 22. Questions are far more central to my religious experience than are answers.

Instructions: These items are just examples from the original, longer scales. Note that the original scales had different answering scales; these have been modified for simplicity to all use the same scale. For each set of items below, add up your responses (higher scores indicate stronger beliefs in favor of that concept).

Authoritarianism: Add Items 1 to 5

Social dominance orientation: Add Items 6 to 10

Intrinsic religiosity: Add Items 11, 12, and 13

Extrinsic religiosity: Add Items 14, 15, and 16

Fundamentalism: Add Items 17, 18, and 19

Religion as quest: Add Items 20, 21, and 22

THE MAIN IDEAS

- While "old-fashioned" or blatant prejudice has gone down over time, other forms of prejudice may still exist. Modern-symbolic prejudice comes from people who say they value equality but oppose social changes that would make that equality possible. In addition, ambivalent prejudice judges some members of an outgroup positively (when they align with how we think they "should" behave) but judges other members of the same outgroup negatively.

- Realistic conflict theory proposes that prejudice results from the justification we create to determine that our ingroup deserves limited resources.

- Scapegoat theory says we blame outgroups for our problems, especially when frustrated, and that prejudice justifies aggression toward those outgroups.

- The stereotype content model is the notion that different forms of prejudice develop when we perceive groups to be high or low in warmth and competence, and we have emotional reactions based on those perceptions.

- Finally, some researchers have explored the idea of a prejudiced personality, one that is generally negative toward all outgroups. Three specific traits that have been explored are authoritarianism, social dominance orientation, and religiosity.

CRITICAL THINKING CHALLENGE

- Identify two historical events that may have been caused, at least in part, by realistic conflict over limited resources (such as land, jobs, oil, gold, etc.) and how this conflict led to prejudice between the parties involved.

- List four groups that were not included in Table 9.2 describing the stereotype content model. Then, try to identify which of the four categories each group would fall into, and explain why.

- Are there people in your life who seem to have high or low amounts of prejudice toward outgroups in general, supporting the idea of a "prejudiced personality"? If not, can you think of other television/film characters or even celebrities who appear to have high or low levels of a prejudiced personality?

HOW CAN WE REDUCE PREJUDICE AND DISCRIMINATION?

>> **LO 9.3:** **Analyze various research-based interventions to reduce prejudice and discrimination.**

JF is now in prison and probably will be for the remainder of his life.

He was a neo-Nazi with White supremacist beliefs. He pled guilty to 29 out of 30 federal hate crimes in a 2019 courtroom. He was also convicted of murdering Heather Heyer when he purposely drove his car into a crowd of people who were counterprotesting a White power rally in Charlottesville, Virginia. In May 2019, Heather's mother Susan Bro offered poignant testimony to the House Committee on Oversight and Reform, including the following words:

Anna Moneymaker/Getty Images News/Getty Images

Many people think that being non-racist is okay. . . . Non-racist is saying "I don't recognize anybody's color, I think that we're all equal, and we should all be treated fairly." And that's kind—to a point. I understand what they're trying to say, and it comes from a place of good intention.

However, we need to recognize our differences, we need to rejoice in our differences, America is stronger for all of our differences brought together and we need to accept that and go out of our way to stand up against racism when we see it. To be anti-racist means to say I am not going to tolerate that in my presence.

What can social psychology offer as solutions to the terrible outcomes of prejudice? This section answers the core question "How can we reduce prejudice and discrimination?" by

(1) identifying and evaluating an early solution suggested by social psychologists to reduce discrimination and

(2) analyzing later possible solutions, including classic research and modern applications.

An Early Hope: The Contact Hypothesis and the Robbers Cave Experiment

When Allport (1954) formalized the study of prejudice in his classic book *The Nature of Prejudice*, he summarized the problem with the following conversation:

"See that man over there?"

"Yes."

"Well, I hate him."

"But you don't know him."

"That's why I hate him."

To Allport, that brief exchange also pointed toward a potential solution. His logic was that prejudice was based on misunderstanding other people because you don't know them, personally. If you hate people because you don't know them, then the solution is to get to know them. Allport's (1954, p. 281) contact hypothesis proposes that prejudice may be reduced by increasing contact—or exposure—to outgroups. Recall from earlier in this chapter that one of the reasons why stereotypes form is because we're more comfortable interacting with similar others.

Amir (1976) summarized the spirit of the contact hypothesis:

> Interaction between people changes their beliefs and feelings toward each other. . . . Thus, if only one had the opportunity to communicate with others and appreciate their way of life, understanding and reduction of prejudice would follow. (p. 245)

Boys at Sherif's famous Robbers Cave study, playing baseball.

Is it just a matter of leaving our comfort zones by spending time with others who are different from us? One of the early and most famous tests of the contact hypothesis has an intriguing name: the Robbers Cave Experiment. Muzafer Sherif and his team (Sherif, 1956) wanted to study how prejudice forms between two newly created groups and whether the contact hypothesis can help to erase this prejudice. To do this, they carefully selected several 11-year-old boys and invited them to a 3-week summer camp held in Robbers Cave State Park in Oklahoma.

Sherif wanted to experimentally manipulate prejudices. So he made sure the boys were all as identical to each other as possible. His goal was to eliminate *confounding variables* such as preexisting ingroup prejudices based on factors such as religion, social class, or race. The boys had no idea they were about to become participants in a study; they thought they were simply going to a regular summer camp for boys. They

Contact hypothesis: The idea that prejudice will decrease with exposure to members of a disliked outgroup.

did not know each other, and they were split into two equivalent groups not by *random assignment* but by *matched pairs,* ensuring that each group had parallel characteristics.

The camp counselors were *participant observers* trained not to influence the boys' behavior (unless they were in danger). Safely tucked away in separate campsites, each group of boys initially believed that they were the only group camping at Robbers Cave. No one told the boys that they should name their groups, but one group became the Rattlers and the other became the Eagles. By the end of the first week, the boys were proud of who *they* had become, but their cabins were far enough apart that the groups still did not know that the other group even existed. That was all about to change.

In Week 2, the counselors arranged for the two groups to discover one another at the baseball field. The members of each group clustered close together and eyed the other group with apparent suspicion. The two groups soon started competing over everything: baseball, tug-of-war, tent pitching, and other typical camp activities—all with minimal adult supervision.

The competitions escalated to accusations of cheating. During a tug-of-war, one group sat down and dug in their heels so that they could neither lose nor win. Prejudiced feelings oozed out of such situations: The two groups started calling each other bad names. One made a flag that put down the other group. A stolen pair of pants was dragged through the dirt, cabins were raided, and accusations of bad character ("stinkers" and "sneaks") filled the air.

By the end of their second week, these two groups of boys—who had every demographic reason to become friends—were at war with one another. They marked their territories, sent spies to gather information about enemy movements, and conducted more cabin raids. The camp counselors only intervened when the boys prepared for a major battle by building stockpiles of rocks and escalating their weaponry: swinging socks filled with rocks. They were one incident away from serious, life-threatening violence.

Could the contact hypothesis now make this prejudice go away? Sherif first attempted to bring the boys together during meals. It didn't work; the two groups battled with each other to be first in line, and the losing team tried to save face by yelling "Ladies first!" at the winners. When an Eagle bumped into a Rattler, the Rattler would make a display of brushing "the dirt" off his clothes (p. 418). Similar conflicts continued in other settings, such as trying to watch a movie together.

Sherif was not surprised; he hadn't really expected this kind of contact to help. In fact, it seemed to have only made the prejudice stronger. At this simple, unsupervised level, contact seemed to backfire: It only made their prejudice and discrimination worse. What could he try next?

Sherif's Solution: Superordinate Goals

Not even Allport would have been surprised by Sherif's findings at that point in the Robbers Cave Experiment.

Allport recognized that not all forms of contact would be positive. He specified that interaction between two hostile groups would, in fact, only lead to decreased prejudice if four criteria were met:

- The groups had to have equal status (one group couldn't have more power than the other).

- Group members had to be able to get to know each other on an individual level (not just as anonymous members of the "other" group).

- Any authority figures in the situation had to support the groups' positive change.

- The groups had to work together, cooperatively, on a common goal. They had to *need* each other to succeed.

Sherif's next step in the Robbers Cave Experiment was to make sure all of these criteria were met, and he focused in particular on the final criterion. Prejudice had spontaneously occurred in a context of *competition* between the two groups. Could cooperation be the answer to that same prejudice going away?

Sherif and the camp counselors brought the boys back from the brink of violence by creating situations that promoted individual contact *and* cooperative tasks that made it difficult for stereotypes and prejudice to survive. Sherif called these tasks superordinate goals—objectives that neither group could achieve without the other's cooperation. To move forward, "us versus them" had to become "we."

For example, the camp counselors went to the large holding tank that supplied water to the camp and turned it off. Then they sent teams of boys to survey different parts of the line for a leak. Only a few of the Eagles voluntarily worked with a Rattler. But when they discovered that the valve had been turned off at the source, they turned it back on and cheered their victory—as a group. When a vehicle supposedly got stuck in the mud, first one group and then the other tried to push it out. But the driver discreetly kept his foot on the brake until both groups of boys got out and pushed together. Only their combined efforts got the truck out of the mud. Finally, when the boys wanted to rent a movie, they could only afford it by pooling their money together.

By the end of the third week, they were all friends and appeared to have enjoyed a wonderful 3 weeks of summer camp (see Figure 9.2). Cooperation and superordinate goals had saved the day and made the boys appreciate each other.

FIGURE 9.2

During conflict between the two groups in the Robbers Cave Experiment, there were few friendships between cabins (left). After cooperation toward common goals had restored good feelings, the percentage of boys reporting friendships across cabins rose significantly (right).

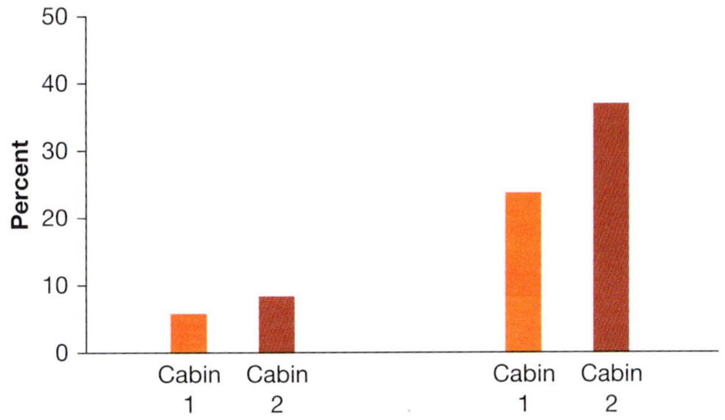

Source: Sherif (1956).

Superordinate Goals in Modern Applications

Allport's criteria for successful intergroup contact and Sherif's demonstration of their power have been inspirational in a variety of contexts.

Acknowledging that "us versus them" is a harmful mindset is a good start. Combining efforts and identities with people who might have been considered outgroups in the past is helpful in terms of working against common enemies, pooling resources, or simply moving past historical prejudices. Examples on a national scale include overcoming problems in different religious groups in Israel (Somech & Sagy, 2019) and helping native tribes in Canada maintain both a specific community culture (for their specific tribe or family group) as well as an overarching native culture

Superordinate goals: Objectives that cannot be achieved without the cooperation of an outgroup; they often reduce prejudice when the goal is achieved.

(Neufeld & Schmitt, 2019). On a smaller scale, thinking from a cooperative mindset can help business managers to be empathetic instead of impulsive and aggressive (Mukherjee & Upadhyay, 2019) and help employees work together more harmoniously (Ho & Yeung, 2019).

Jigsaw Classrooms

Reducing prejudice as early as possible is a good goal.

For example, if we could reduce prejudice in children, perhaps the next generation could avoid some of our enduring intergroup problems. This is exactly what was attempted when Aronson and his colleagues (1978) invented an elementary school technique based on superordinate goals called the **jigsaw classroom** (see Figure 9.3).

In a jigsaw classroom, the students are first divided into small "expert groups." These groups all learn about some aspect of the day's lesson. If the lesson is about Eleanor Roosevelt, for example, one expert group learns about her early life, one group learns about her activism in the civil rights movement, and so on. Then, the expert groups are broken up and new groups are formed—the "jigsaw" groups. Each of these groups has one representative from each of the expert groups.

The key here is that the students have to teach each other what they learned earlier in their expert groups—the "expert" in each jigsaw group is the only one who knows that particular set of facts. To succeed in the class, they must rely on each other, respect each other's knowledge, be patient with each other, and so forth. It no longer matters what race or religion another student is—prejudices go away as the jigsaw groups work cooperatively toward a superordinate goal (Blaney et al., 1977).

Jigsaw classroom: A teaching technique in which students are divided into groups that must teach each other class material. Students must rely on each other and work cooperatively to pass tests.

FIGURE 9.3

In a jigsaw classroom, first teams are "expert groups" that all learn a certain set of information. Then, groups are mixed up such that the second set of teams, the "jigsaw groups," each includes one member from the expert groups. Each jigsaw group must then rely on the other members of the team to teach them the needed material.

(a) Expert Groups

Team 1   Team 2   Team 3   Team 4

(b) Jigsaw Groups

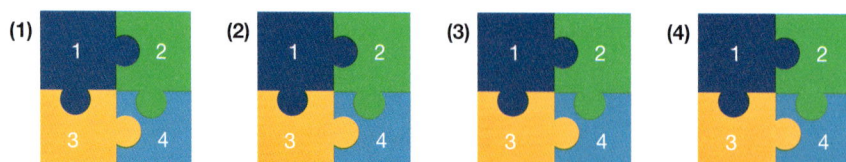

A perfect jigsaw setup is complicated. For example, if students don't do well, they might blame each other, which would only increase prejudice. Some studies have found that it simply doesn't work (e.g., Bratt, 2008; Moskowitz et al., 1983, 1985). In addition, the environment will make some students more competitive instead of cooperative (Roseth et al., 2019). But it works sometimes, and it might be worth a try, especially if teachers do research on how to structure it to reach maximum effectiveness (see Roseth et al., 2019, for some tips).

Try This Away From Home: Forming Friendships

Could it be as simple as making friends?

A sneering tone of voice typically makes fun of the idea of "holding hands and singing Kumbaya." But perhaps friendship provides a way to reduce stereotyping, prejudices, and discrimination. In 1978, President Jimmy Carter's stubborn determination to keep Egypt and Israel talking to one another produced the only significant peace agreement in the region. A handshake between enemies helped end the deadly violence in Ireland after 30 years of bloody conflict. Telling one another's stories helped South Africa make a difficult transition away from apartheid. And writing a biography of someone from an ingroup helps college students empathize with them, significantly reducing prejudice (Nordstrom, 2015).

Friendship is powerful—and risky. Binder et al. (2009) reported how **friendship contacts**—individual, positive, personal interactions—reduced prejudice among students. This impressive study involved people from 33 different schools and three different countries (Belgium, England, and Germany). Minority groups were Turkish, Bangladeshi, Afro-Caribbean, and more—and despite this diversity, simple friendships led to less prejudice almost across the board.

Friendship contacts reduced prejudice, but the fine print in this study was even more revealing in two ways. First, the *quality* of those ingroup and outgroup contacts was more important than the *quantity* of contact. A friendship can become intensely influential if it is deeply meaningful, even if you only see your friend once every year or even less. Second, friendship contact reduced the prejudice of the majority group member more than it did for the minority group member.

Perhaps the friend with a life of privilege has a bit more to learn, a bit more to realize, a bit more empathy to gain. The bottom line was that quality friendships reduced prejudice (over a relatively long-term, *longitudinal* 6-month study) among people from extremely different backgrounds. All people, at any time, can choose to apply this lesson to their own life circumstances.

THE MAIN IDEAS

- The contact hypothesis is the idea that prejudice will be reduced with more exposure to members of outgroups. Allport noted that for this to be successful, certain criteria must be met regarding the type of contact.

- Sherif's famous Robbers Cave Experiment involved boys in a summer camp setting. The experimenters created prejudice between groups through competitive contexts, then reduced prejudice through cooperative contexts and superordinate goals.

- Two modern applications of prejudice reduction through cooperative contact are jigsaw classrooms in schools and intergroup friendships.

CRITICAL THINKING CHALLENGE

- Many students in our social psychology courses over the years have complained that Sherif only used White, male preteens in his study. What would your hypotheses be if we replicated this study using a different type of participant, such as all girls, all poor children, or all adults? What might happen if the participants were not selected to be similar to each other but were allowed to come from different outgroups?

Friendship contacts: Individual, positive, personal interactions that reduce prejudice.

- Try to be honest in identifying prejudiced attitudes you hold right now. What groups make you uncomfortable or seem to live in a way you don't approve of? Would you be comfortable in purposely seeking out members of those groups to learn more about them, or even befriend them, as an attempt to reduce this prejudice? If not, why not?

- Think of a popular culture example (from a book, TV show, movie, etc.) that shows two people who originally disliked each other because they were from different backgrounds or ingroups but that eventually reduced that prejudice because of a meaningful friendship. Describe how their perceptions of each other changed over time.

CHAPTER SUMMARY

Why Do We Keep Using Stereotypes?

Stereotypes are beliefs about members of a group; prejudices are judgments or evaluations of members of a group, and discrimination is behavior toward people because of their group membership. Stereotypes are pervasive for many reasons. One is because they make our mental lives easier, because labels are cognitively efficient (adaptive generalization). Another is that stereotypes strengthen our own group identity by helping us categorize "us" versus "them" (social identity theory). Third, stereotypes may persist because of self-fulfilling prophecies, where our expectations shape our own and others' behaviors. We might train children to fulfill roles we expect of them later (social role theory). We might also feel anxious about fulfilling negative stereotypes about our own group, such that the anxiety distracts us and leads to poor performance (stereotype threat). Finally, stereotypes endure because they are reinforced by culture (privilege, social learning theory) and by institutional discrimination.

How Do Stereotypes Turn Into Prejudices?

First, while blatant or "old-fashioned" prejudice may be less common today, other more subtle forms of prejudice still exist (e.g., modern-symbolic and ambivalent prejudice). Four major theories explain the subtle shift from belief-based stereotypes into emotional prejudices: conflict over limited resources, scapegoating, the stereotype content model, and the idea of a "prejudiced personality." Realistic conflict theory states that we form prejudices to justify taking control of limited resources, such as land. Scapegoating is the idea that when we are frustrated, we become aggressive, and we take our frustration out on a group we can blame for our problems. The stereotype content model argues that our emotional reactions and prejudice toward outgroups is based on judgments of whether they are warm and whether they are competent. Finally, some researchers argue that certain individuals will be prejudiced toward anyone different from themselves, thus displaying a generally prejudiced personality. Particular traits examined in this chapter are authoritarianism, social dominance orientation, and religiosity.

How Can We Reduce Prejudice and Discrimination?

An early idea in social psychology regarding how to reduce prejudice was the contact hypothesis, the idea that more interaction with outgroup members would reduce prejudice. A famous study done by Sherif called the Robbers Cave Experiment tested this hypothesis. He found that prejudice could be created through competitive interactions between groups. When he tried to bring them together peacefully (the contact hypothesis), simply having them spend time together did not work. Sherif eventually did reduce prejudice between the groups by forcing them to work together on what he called superordinate goals.

One application of the superordinate goal research is a classroom technique called the jigsaw classroom. Here, students must depend upon each other to fully learn any given lesson and achieve a good grade. Other research indicates that simply forming a close friendship with someone from an outgroup can also increase respect and liking for people in outgroups.

CRITICAL THINKING, ANALYSIS, AND APPLICATION

- We typically think of stereotypes, prejudice, and discrimination as negative thoughts, judgments, and behaviors (respectively) toward people due to group membership. What are examples of "positive" stereotypes, prejudice, or discrimination? Can you identify short-term or long-term negative effects of these "positive" thoughts, emotions, or actions?

- Consider again Table 9.2, which shows the stereotype content model. Can you identify any stereotypes or prejudices toward groups that have changed categories over time? Why did this change occur—and do you think it led to positive or negative outcomes for the group in question?

- Identify three fictional characters you believe exemplify concepts from this chapter. Write a paragraph about each that explains who the character is and examples of how their thoughts or actions display one of the ideas in the chapter.

- Sherif's famous study showed that working together on superordinate goals helped reduce prejudice between two groups of boys. Other examples throughout history have shown that warring groups can put aside animosity if they suddenly have to bond together against a common or shared enemy. Does this mean that the best hope of eliminating human prejudice is an outside threat, such as an alien attack or zombie uprising?

Christopher Furlong/Getty Images News/Getty Images

10 Helping and Prosocial Behavior

Core Questions

10.1 What motivates people to help others, in general?

10.2 Why are some people more helpful than others?

10.3 What circumstances make helping more or less likely?

Learning Objectives

10.1 Explain several general motives for why helping behavior occurs.

10.2 Identify individual differences that explain why some people are more likely to help.

10.3 Analyze what situational variables lead to more or less helping in different settings.

WHAT MOTIVATES A HERO?

Malala Yousafzai

Malala Yousafzai was 11 years old when she started blogging about girls' education.

The extremist religious Taliban had taken over her region of Pakistan. They opposed education for women and had destroyed more than 400 schools. A man boarded her school bus and asked, "Who is Malala?" The assassin shot her in the face and left her to die. But she didn't die. After a long recovery, Malala continued writing, speaking, and defying the antieducation extremists. In 2014, she became the youngest person to become a Nobel laureate. The threats on her life continue. Malala Yousafzai continues to advocate for other girls around the world.

Kendrick Ray Castillo

Kendrick Ray Castillo and Brendan Bialy were sitting near the door during ninth-period English class.

Two late-entering students closed the door, pulled out guns, and told everyone not to move. "That's when Kendrick lunged at him," senior Nui Giasolli said, "giving all of us enough time." But Kendrick took a bullet at point-blank range. "I wish he had gone and hid," his father said, "but that's not his character." A 4-year member of the robotics team, Castillo spoke both Spanish and English and was planning a career in engineering. Bialy reported that "it was immediate, non-hesitation, immediate jump into action."

Guardian Angels

Five people were wounded during a stabbing attack during a Hanukkah party in New York City (Romero, 2019).

Between December 13 and 28 in 2019, a total of eight attacks against Jewish people occurred in the city. In response, a private crime prevention group called the Guardian Angels started patrolling. They are unarmed and simply walk the streets, trying to prevent hate crimes through their presence. They wear red berets and red jackets to make their presence known. Their entire goal is to keep the city safe.

Stephen Chernin /Getty Images News/Getty Images

The Kelly Twins

"You just reach out and grab the blobs of blood."

The minor blood spill in zero gravity came while astronaut Scott Kelly was drawing blood during his 340 days on the International Space Station. To make comparisons, another astronaut on Earth mimicked every mental and physical test: Mark Kelly, Scott's identical twin. When he returned to Earth, Scott experienced greater cognitive declines, slower reaction times, DNA mutations, and changes in his immune system. Many, but not all, symptoms resolved not long after he returned to Earth (see Garrett-Bakelman et al., 2019; Zimmer, 2019). Scott knew that living in space for a year would expose him to unknown risks.

NBC NewsWire / NBCUniversal/Getty Images

WHAT MOTIVATES PEOPLE TO HELP OTHERS, IN GENERAL?

>> **LO 10.1:** Explain several general motives for why helping behaviors occur.

Have you ever given blood? Donated to a charity? Spent a weekend doing community service?

Prosocial behavior is how social psychologists refer to what others call "helping" or "altruism"—and the opposite of antisocial (see Aghababaei et al., 2014). It's any action performed to help others, either on an individual or group level. Why people make sacrifices to help others is an intriguing question (see Batson, 1987), so let's start with some observations.

Observation 1. Humans are a paradox. Humans are capable of great goodness, sacrifice, and heroism. But we also have a dismal history of cruelty and destruction. When historian Yuval Noah Harari (2014, p. 67) surveyed the long history of how humans affected other species, he had to describe humans as "ecological serial killers."

Observation 2. Humans are sometimes surprised by their own goodness. People who help often don't consider themselves heroes, but other people do. Sometimes, people who help say it wasn't a choice—it was intuitive and automatic (see Kahneman & Tversky, 1979). If that's true, why doesn't everyone help?

Observation 3. Helping is satisfying. Everyday helping keeps societies running smoothly and promotes life satisfaction (see Dulin et al., 2001; Kee et al., 2018). Many teachers, for example, describe their own success at helping students as satisfying despite high levels of stress (Olčar et al., 2019; Patulny et al., 2019).

Observation 4. Prosocial behavior is not limited to humans. Charles Darwin, for example, observed that sterile worker honeybees altruistically sacrifice their lives to preserve the hive (Darwin, 1859, p. 236; see also Dugatkin, 2007, p. 1375). Rats have been known to display what appears to be empathy and helping behavior toward other rats (Cox & Reichel, 2019). As you'll soon read, helping is highly evolved in vampire bats as well.

Observation 5. Helping others was a life-or-death choice for many during the COVID-19 pandemic. Millions of relatively healthy people wore masks and stayed at least 6 feet away from others. Many of the people doing this weren't particularly vulnerable to the disease themselves; they wore masks to protect *other people* and to keep the good of the larger community prioritized over their own convenience or comfort (Tufekci et al., 2020).

This section answers the core question "What motivates people to help others, in general?" by

(1) distinguishing between pure and egoistic altruism and

(2) comparing four overlapping explanations based on (a) evolution, (b) social norms, (c) negative state relief, and (d) empathy.

Pure Versus Egoistic Altruism

The central question is simple: Why do people help others?

The question is simple, but getting to the answers is difficult. Why? Because people's thoughts are complicated, our emotions are changeable, and our behavior is slippery. We sometimes do surprising, heroic things. But sometimes, we intend to help someone with a simple task but get distracted by the smell of pizza or urgent need for a nap. What pushes us away from selfishness toward selflessness?

The answers tend to fall into two categories (see Batson, 1990, 1998). **Pure altruism** describes actions motivated *only* by the desire to help, with zero expectation for any kind of reward at all. That may be what we would like to believe about ourselves, but that doesn't make it true.

Prosocial behavior: Any action performed to help others, either on an individual level or a group level.

Pure altruism: Helping others purely out of selfless concern for their well-being, with no expectation of a reward.

Slightly more cynical (realistic?) people argue that pure altruism is a myth. Philosopher Francis Bacon (1561–1626) observed (in the sexist language of his day) that "man prefers to believe what man prefers to be true." So prosocial behaviors could come from **egoistic altruism**, helping behaviors done with an expectation of some kind of personal (or group) benefit.

You might protest at this point, thinking, "But I do help others, expecting nothing in return!" Does thinking that and doing those wonderful things make you feel like a better person? If so—isn't that a reward? If you don't help, will you feel guilty or sad? If so, is avoiding those negative emotions just a different kind of reward? These indirect or emotional rewards for helping are part of egoistic altruism.

Four Explanations for Prosocial Behavior

Social psychologists have developed four explanations for prosocial behavior (see Table 10.1).

Three of those explanations represent types of egoistic altruism. These are not competing theories; they can work together. The upcoming evidence about altruistic vampire bats, for example, suggests that both evolutionary and social norm explanations are mutually supportive in understanding their prosocial behavior.

The Evolutionary Perspective: Prosocial Behaviors Strengthen Group Survival

Life is a little easier if you have good neighbors.

During a recent blizzard in Iowa (where Wind lives), my snowblower broke. Almost immediately, my next-door neighbor came by to clear out my sideway and driveway so that I could get to work. Later, I made him cookies as a thank you.

It doesn't matter whether you live on the neighboring farm three miles down the road or in the opposite apartment three steps across the hall. For social animals, there are evolutionary advantages to having and being a good neighbor. Among our ancient ancestors, these daily prosocial exchanges probably began over food.

What if you had killed more meat than you could consume before it got rotten? You probably would try to trade it for someone else's excess fruit, grain, or other resources. At some point, you might have given someone extra resources without immediately expecting something in return. Food sharing could easily evolve into other types of sharing that made life easier: communal childcare, cooperative hunting, mutual defense, and so on. It looks like a society full of at least part-time altruists.

Evolution Requires Social Exchange. **Social exchange theory** adds details to why and how evolution promotes prosocial behaviors that strengthen the group. It suggests that people form dyads or larger groups because of mutually shared benefits.

Egoistic altruism: Helping others in exchange for some personal benefit.

Social exchange theory: The idea that people form dyads or larger groups because of mutually shared benefits. See *interdependence theory*.

TABLE 10.1

Four Explanations for Prosocial or Helping Behaviors

THEORY	MOTIVATION FOR HELPING	TYPE OF ALTRUISM
Evolutionary perspective	To help our group survive and to have more opportunities to mate	Egoistic
Social norms	To fit into our group's expectations of social behavior	Egoistic
Negative state relief	To avoid feeling sadness or guilt	Egoistic
Empathy-altruism	To help someone in need	Pure

Over time, social exchanges between humans became "universal and highly elaborated across all human cultures" (Cosmides & Tooby, 1992, p. 164). You can recognize, for example, that we exchange favors with neighbors, exchange money for electronic devices, exchange personal promises at marriage, and exchange complex group commitments when negotiating treaties between nations. Social exchanges are everywhere.

Evolution Made Altruism Sexy. In groups, the selfish loners are more likely to starve to death or be eaten by prey.

They also become less available and less attractive as sexual and relationship partners. From an evolutionary perspective, their tendency for selfish behavior would slowly be washed out of the gene pool. Being a selfish jerk just isn't very sexy.

By contrast, helpful, cooperative, generous altruists would survive by becoming skilled at group living. They would attract strong sexual and relationship partners. Their genes would slowly come to dominate the gene pool (see Nesse, 2001; Van Vugt & Van Lange, 2006).

Altruism is sexually attractive for all genders, especially for long-term relationships (see Farrelly & King, 2019), although women seem to value it the most (Bhogal et al., 2019). Physically attractive people of any gender are also more likely to receive help from others (Bhogal et al., 2019). In this view, then, prosocial behaviors offer two strategic survival advantages. Prosocial behavior

(1) helps individuals survive by promoting opportunities to reproduce and thus pass on one's genes and

(2) helps groups survive by sharing food, social supports, and defenses against enemies.

Evolution Takes Advantage of Kinship Selection. Good neighbors are nice, but we do help some people more than others.

Kinship selection refers to the evolutionary urge to favor those with closer genetic relatedness. Kinship selection is how Darwin explained honeybees. The self-sacrificing worker bees were doing what was best for their closest genetic kin: the hive.

In *On the Origin of Species*, Darwin (1859, p. 238) pointed out that cattle breeders wanted cattle with "flesh and fat well marbled" together. But when they found such an animal, farmers couldn't breed it—because they had already slaughtered it. What does the smart farmer do? They breed the dead animal's closest living relatives.

Darwin realized that these English cattle (and dog) breeders understood kinship selection. They made breeding decisions based on the evolutionary principle of **inclusive fitness**. Our genetic heritage will be preserved, at least in part, in the offspring of our relatives.

Evolutionary Prosocial Behavior Can Be Described Mathematically. A biologist named Hamilton provided an interesting follow-up to Darwin.

He created a mathematical formula to predict helping. He proposed that prosocial behavior could be predicted by the following formula:

$$(r \times b) > c$$

The formula, known as **Hamilton's inequality**, predicts that prosocial behavior will emerge whenever r (the genetic relatedness of the person needing help) multiplied by b (the benefits of helping) are greater than c (the costs of helping). Living things from honeybees to cattle to humans will be altruistic when the benefits to ourselves and our nearest kin outweigh the costs.

The idea is simple: Benefits outweigh costs. It appears to have *ecological validity* because it explains real-world observations. For example, Essock-Vitale and McGuire (1985) interviewed 300 randomly selected White, middle-class Los Angeles women about patterns of helping between kin (family members) and nonkin. They discovered

Kinship selection: The evolutionary urge to favor those with closer genetic relatedness.

Inclusive fitness: The probability that our genetic heritage will be preserved in the offspring of relatives.

Hamilton's inequality: A formula that predicts helping will occur when the benefits to ourselves or our genetic relatives outweigh the costs.

Reciprocal altruism: Altruistic behavior that occurs because we expect to be "paid back" in the future.

that the women were more likely to help (a) those who were more closely related and (b) those with high reproductive potential.

More ecological validity comes from people asked for recommendations when presented with life-or-death moral dilemmas (Burnstein et al., 1994). They consistently recommended more help for close kin and for younger people. They even recommended more help for premenopausal rather than postmenopausal women.

Human decision making seems to include an intuitive sense of inclusive fitness. But the mathematical idea can be expressed with plain words: when benefits outweigh costs, especially when it comes to family. We conform to Hamilton's formula by passing on our genes to the next generation—even if we have to do it indirectly through our nearest blood relatives.

Prosocial Social Norms Increase Helping

Taking risks for others is a social norm for some groups of people.

Recall from Chapter 7 that social norms are the unwritten rules about how members of a group are expected to behave. The Kelly twins were astronauts, expected to take risks. So are soldiers, firefighters, police officers, and many others. Some of these norms are specifically about helping, such as the norm of reciprocity, belief in a just world, and the social responsibility norm.

Reciprocal Altruism: Social Norms Among Prosocial Vampire Bats. You may have to give up some of your stereotypes about vampire bats.

Reciprocal altruism is the expectation that our helpfulness right now will be "paid back" in the future. Humans are not the only creatures to practice reciprocal altruism (Van Vugt & Van Lange, 2006). Vampire bats, for example, also practice reciprocal altruism. They sustain reciprocal altruism with what appear to be strict social norms for appropriate behavior.

Yes, vampire bats famously feast on blood. They usually collect their blood meals from large mammals such as wild pigs, cows, and horses (but rarely from humans). They need a lot of blood. Vampire bats will drink about half their body weight during an uninterrupted feeding—so much that they may have difficulty taking flight.

Vampire bats are so bloodthirsty because they will die if they go more than 48 to 72 hours without a blood meal (DeNault & McFarlane, 1995). But, in an apparent act of reciprocal altruism, both male and female vampire bats will regurgitate and share some of their blood meal with starving neighbors where they roost. And there's more to the story.

Vampire bats are selective about sharing their blood. When Wilkinson (1984) studied them in Costa Rica, he discovered they were more likely to donate blood to those bats with the greatest need for a meal. Furthermore, their altruistic food sharing was not limited to their immediate kin. Frequent roost-mates were more likely to be the beneficiaries. And there is still more to the story of vampire bat altruism—and it makes them sound, well, almost human.

Vampire bats are able to identify, remember, and *not* help those vampire bats that had *not* donated blood to other starving bats. Essentially, "cheaters can be detected and excluded from the system" (Wilkinson, 1990, p. 82). Reciprocal altruism among vampire bats can directly lead to increasing the probability of their own survival in tough times.

In sum, vampire bats appear to have and strictly reinforce social norms for altruistic behavior.

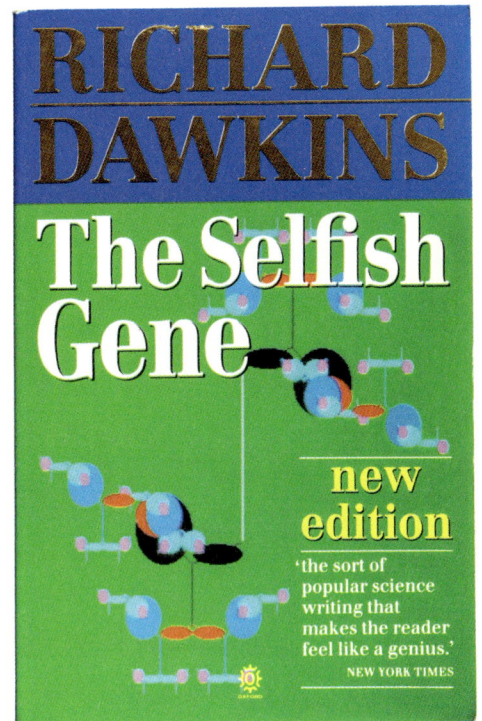

Dawkins's (1976) book *The Selfish Gene* discusses the genetic benefits of helping others—but only if the people you help are related to you and thus share your genes.

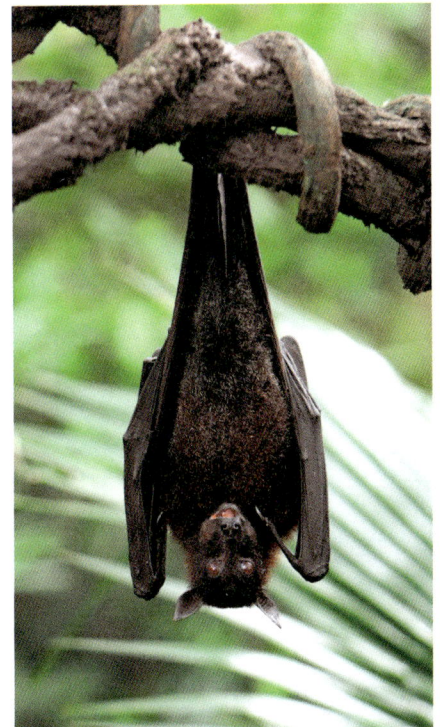

It may surprise you that vampire bats have a highly evolved system of helping each other, through a system called reciprocal altruism.

Civil rights icon Rosa Parks participated in a movement to end racial discrimination, probably in part because she believed that the world should be just and fair.

Social responsibility norm: The idea that we each have a duty to improve the world by helping those in need.

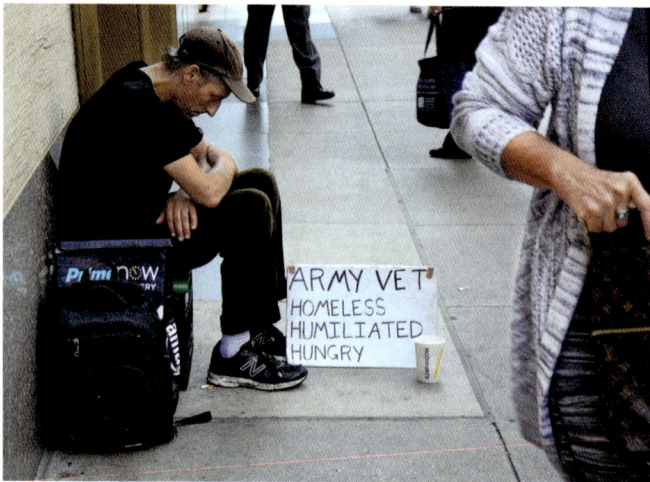

Are you more likely to give money to a homeless person who doesn't appear to "deserve" being homeless? If so, the dual norms of a just world and social responsibility may be at work.

Prosocial Behavior and Belief in a Just World. Whose job is it to make the world a just and fair place?

In 1943, a Montgomery, Alabama, bus driver named James Blake gave an order to a Black passenger: Rosa Parks. She was to get off and then reenter through the rear door. She obeyed and was headed toward the rear door when James Blake drove away.

Fast forward to December 1, 1955. James Blake was once again the driver when Bus No. 2857 picked up a White man. Blake ordered a Black woman to give up her seat: Rosa Parks. This time, Rosa Parks refused to obey. She was arrested. Her defiance eventually helped make her a heroine of the civil rights movement.

The success of the foot-weary bus boycott that followed depended on hundreds of altruistic sacrifices. People had to get up earlier, endure long walks to work, shop, go to church, and so forth. In the short term, it was painful for each individual. In the long term, it benefited the larger community, especially when their efforts spread around the country.

The behavior of the people in the bus boycott was not because they expected some kind of reciprocity. Instead, they believed that it was their job to make a more just world. Belief in a just world (see Chapter 5) is the idea that good things eventually happen to good people—and bad things happen to bad people (Lerner, 1980). The just world hypothesis suggests a cosmic yet practical sort of a social exchange (see Jiang et al., 2017; Roch et al., 2019). Belief in a just world provides individuals with a sense of purpose and long-term investment in making sacrifices for the good of a larger community (Hafer & Rubel, 2015). If you treat the universe well, the universe will be kind back to you.

Altruism and the Social Responsibility Norm. The civil rights movement relied on a powerful force for prosocial behavior.

Even if you don't believe the world is fair, the social responsibility norm asserts that we each have a duty to improve the world by helping those in need. If you are on an elevator with someone who is unable to push a button, it's a social expectation that you should ask them what floor they want and push the button for them. However, the social responsibility norm can be tricky.

Have you ever held the door open for someone, only to find yourself standing there holding the door for many more? How long are you expected to stay there, making yourself late or separating you from your friends? You might have experienced a similar problem in a city with homeless people asking for spare change . . . You can't give away all of your money or help every homeless person you see!

The social responsibility norm must be strong enough to "compel people to provide aid" but sensitive enough to help only "those who deserve help" (Simmons & Lerner, 1968, p. 224). This may be where the social responsibility norm overlaps with the just world norm. For example, some homeless people make signs reading "homeless vet" or "God bless you," hoping that you will be more likely to help them if you believe that they don't "deserve" to be homeless.

Feeling Bad? Try the Negative State Relief Model

Abraham Lincoln understood egoistic altruism.

After a companion praised him for rescuing some baby pigs from drowning, Lincoln said that his behavior was "the very essence of selfishness." When his companion asked him why, he replied, "I should have had no peace of mind all day had I gone on and left that suffering old sow worrying over those pigs. I did it to get peace of mind" (Sharp, 1928, cited in Batson et al., 1986). Whether folklore or fact, the Lincoln story suggests that sometimes the purpose of helping is to avoid negative feelings we'd have if we didn't help, such as sadness or guilt.

The egoistic **negative state relief model** proposes that our prosocial behavior decreases a variety of negative emotions (Dovidio & Penner, 2001; Schaller & Cialdini, 1990). We can all relate to helping someone to avoid feeling guilty later, but the model also predicts that we might help more even if we were already feeling bad for completely different reasons. Specifically, simply being in a negative mood doesn't seem to reliably increase helping behaviors (Forgas, 1998; Habashi et al., 2016), but sadness and guilt do seem to increase compliance when someone directly *requests* help.

Negative state relief model: The idea that seeing another person in need causes us emotional distress, and helping decreases those negative emotions.

SOCIAL PSYCHOLOGY IN POPULAR CULTURE

▶ Captain America: A Paragon of Prosocial Action

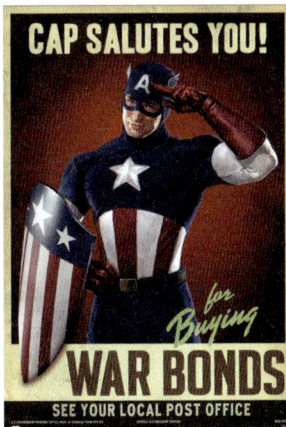

AF archive/Alamy Stock Photo

In the world of comic book superheroes, Captain America is one of the most pure of heart. Consistently ethical, loyal, and the epitome of patriotism, he also encapsulates the idea of pure altruism, or willingness to sacrifice himself to help others with no expectation of reward.

This altruism is highlighted in an early scene from *Captain America: The First Avenger* (Feige & Johnston, 2011), in which the military is attempting to decide which new recruit they will choose for their experimental program to create a super-soldier. The military officers argue with the scientists regarding which traits are most important, and they seem to settle on "guts" and heroism. To test the candidates, one of the officers throws a dummy grenade at the group of soldiers. While most of the men immediately run for cover, Steve Rogers jumps onto the grenade in an attempt to save everyone else. This ultimate altruism and self-sacrifice is what distinguishes him from the crowd and ultimately leads to him becoming Captain America.

Researchers tested the negative state relief model by creating an experiment that used a little deception and a confederate. They wanted to trick students into feeling guilty to see if they would make more prosocial decisions. They arranged for a confederate to give students answers ahead of time to an extra credit test (McMillen & Austin, 1971). When asked if they had any knowledge ahead of time, some participants said "no"—a harmless little lie, right?

Then all the student participants were asked to help score some of the tests. Participants who had *not* lied helped for an average of about 2 minutes. But the people who had lied helped for an average of 63 (altruistic?) minutes!

The negative state relief model makes three related predictions (Dietrich & Berkowitz, 1997; Fultz et al., 1988). We will display more prosocial behavior in order to

(1) reduce negative emotions and perceptions about ourselves if we don't help,

(2) relieve our own discomfort when seeing others suffer, and

(3) escape a bad mood (which might have already existed for completely different reasons).

We Help Because We Care: The Empathy-Altruism Hypothesis

So far, you might think that social psychology is a pretty cynical science.

The first three theories concluded that people only help (a) for self-serving, egoistic reasons; (b) because we want to comply with social norms; or (c) because we want to avoid feeling guilt or sadness. However, this fourth theory suggests that sometimes, people help others simply out of "the goodness of their hearts." The **empathy-altruism hypothesis** proposes that feelings of compassion create a purely selfless motivation to help (see Batson, 1991, 1998; Toi & Batson, 1982).

Empathy and Behavior. Two women on a commuter train in Portland were being harassed (see Dobuzinskis, 2017).

They appeared to be Muslim, and their harasser was yelling racial and religious slurs. Three men who saw the harassment intervened. All three were stabbed; two died. Each risked his life for complete strangers. The accompanying feature, Social Psychology in Popular Culture, discusses the fictional altruism of the comic book superhero Captain America. But knowing that there are real-life heroes like these men can be even more inspiring.

Batson (1991, 1998) has been the major proponent of the empathy-altruism hypothesis. Batson's foundational idea is that when we see people who need help, we empathize with them; we put ourselves in their shoes and feel compassion. Batson recognizes that all the egoistic reasons for helping exist; he doesn't deny these ideas. He simply says they can coexist with pure altruism.

Empathy Isn't Enough. Let's get practical. In many cases, empathy is not enough.

More is needed before people who feel compassion can provide authentic help. Providing tangible help requires that you

- are capable of helping (e.g., we may not offer to help a friend with calculus homework if we don't understand the subject),

- perceive that our help will actually benefit the person (e.g., we might not give $1 to someone who needs to quickly earn $10,000), and

- perceive that our help will be more beneficial than someone else's help (e.g., we might not volunteer to lead a group if someone else is available who has more experience or expertise).

Thus, the empathy-altruism hypothesis suggests that pure altruism is *possible*, under the right circumstances. A classic experiment asked women to listen while another young woman received painful electric shocks (Batson et al., 1981). As you probably suspected, no one actually got shocked in the study. The shocks were just the *cover story*, a *deception* cleared ahead of time by the institutional review board (IRB). Participants also heard the woman explain that due to a childhood accident, she was particularly sensitive to shocks.

When the experimenter asked each participant if she was willing to take the other woman's place, most of them agreed. This happened even though the participants

Empathy-altruism hypothesis: The idea that feelings of compassion create a purely selfless motivation to help.

thought their own part of the study was done and they could go home. There was a rational, easy way for them to escape.

Indeed, the women were especially likely to volunteer to take the shocks *if* they believed that the other woman was very similar to themselves. Sharing attitudes and interests presumably helped the participants empathize. Notice these important experimental conditions in this search for pure altruism:

- Participants volunteered to experience painful shocks for someone else (quite a sacrifice).

- The woman was a stranger.

- There was no compensation.

So, did this experiment capture pure altruism? Perhaps these women were fulfilling some gender-stereotyped social norm of helpfulness. Maybe they were avoiding feelings of guilt that they knew would come later (Schaller & Cialdini, 1988). Or, perhaps pure empathy is poured into an ever-shifting mixture of emotions that also influenced the behavior of Kendrick Castillo, the Guardian Angels, the Kelly twins, Malala Yousafzai, and the three men on the train.

Mirror Neurons and Empathy. The secret of discovery was peanuts.

Wherever it comes from, we know that empathy is not literally bubbling away somewhere in our heart. Instead, it's in specific neurons referred to as **mirror neurons** (Kaplan & Iacoboni, 2006; Rizzolatti & Craighero, 2005; Rizzolatti et al., 1996). These neurons respond in kind when observing what others are experiencing. That's why you flinch when you observe a car crash, feel hungry watching others eat, and yawn when others yawn.

Peanuts were the catalyst behind the almost accidental discovery of mirror neurons. A team of Italian researchers were already studying neural responses in macaque monkeys. They noticed neural stimulation in a monkey, typical of what happens when they eat. But this neural stimulation occurred when the monkey only observed them, the researchers, picking up peanuts.

As they investigated, the research team discovered that experimenter movements activated neural stimulation in the monkeys under many circumstances, such as "placing or retrieving a piece of food from the table [and] grasping food from another experimenter's hand" (Di Pellegrino et al., 1992, p. 176). They reasoned that the neural action resulted from interpretation of the observed actions.

The macaque monkeys were experiencing something of the researchers' world as their own: empathy. The implications of the discovery of mirror neurons reach far beyond a better understanding of empathy between humans.

Mirror Neurons Call for Empathy Between Species. Harari (2014) is not alone in recognizing that humans can be accidental ecoterrorists.

Scientists across disciplines are arguing for more empathy between humans and other animals. Ironically, these appeals against extinction are coming as studies of mirror neurons tell us that many birds, for example, compete and surpass humans' cognitive and affective abilities (Kaplan, 2019). The same call for across-species empathy is being voiced toward marine life (Wharton et al., 2019).

Perhaps it's a blow to the human ego to recognize that birds can empathize, that elephants can grieve, and that fish in water are more intelligent than humans in water. An alternative view is that the entire world is made up of empathetic, intelligent species and that we (humans) don't have the right to destroy others. Perhaps our helping behaviors should expand just a little bit further.

Mirror neurons: Neurons that respond in parallel when we observe others experience something (e.g., we feel hungry when watching someone eat).

THE MAIN IDEAS

- Prosocial behavior is designed to help others. Two theoretical reasons for helping are (1) pure altruism, helping simply to benefit another person with no expected reward, or (2) egoistic altruism, helping because it somehow benefits us.

- Three egoistic explanations for prosocial behavior are the evolutionary perspective (that helping others increases our survival, mating opportunities, or chance to pass genes on), social norms (that we help to fit in or because of our worldviews), and the negative state relief model (that we help because it makes us feel better).

- Pure altruism is supported by the empathy-altruism hypothesis, that feelings of compassion compel us to help others. Recent research shows that several species (not just humans) have mirror neurons, indicating the ability to empathize with others, even across species.

CRITICAL THINKING CHALLENGE

- Consider the debate regarding true versus egoistic altruism. First, define each idea in your own words. Then, analyze whether true altruism is really possible. Give examples to back up your opinion either way.

- One implicit idea behind social norms for prosocial behavior is that if you do not engage in these norms, people in your social groups may judge you negatively or punish you in some social way (e.g., ostracize you from the group). Have you ever experienced this? Have you ever failed to help someone and then perceived that other people were perceiving you negatively—or have you made this judgment about someone else?

- Consider the examples of helping behavior from the opening of this chapter. For each example, which theories or ideas from the first section of the chapter best explain that individual or group's choice to help? Try to match each example with one specific idea from the first section of the chapter.

WHY ARE SOME PEOPLE MORE HELPFUL THAN OTHERS?

>> **LO 10.2:** Identify individual differences that explain why some people are more likely to help.

The theories you just learned explain general helping behaviors.

But you know from life experience that some people are more likely to help than others. Malala Yousafzai declared that "we need to encourage girls that their voice matters. I think there are hundreds and thousands of Malalas out there" (see Collard, 2017). What motivates some people to help, while others simply walk on by?

This section answers the core question "Why are some people more helpful than others?" by

(1) describing the constellation of traits associated with helping and not helping and

(2) documenting how different social norms influence helping, including a focus on religion, gender, and culture.

The Complicated Prosocial Personality

Is there a "helping" personality trait?

You would expect that people with a prosocial personality would be more likely to help different people across a variety of situations. However, personality traits aren't as simple as one dominant, isolated feature of our personality. And of course, as Lewin reminded us, personality will always combine with the situational circumstances to predict behavior (circumstances are the topic of the final section of this chapter). That said, what traits have been linked to more consistent helping behaviors in individuals?

The Big Five and the Prosocial Personality

OCEAN is an easy way to summarize the five components of anyone's personality.

OCEAN is a small gift to your memory because the letters conveniently describe the **Big 5 Model** of personality. **O**penness to experience, **c**onscientiousness, **e**xtraversion, **a**greeableness, and **n**euroticism are five fundamental personality traits that have been shown to predict behavior across cultures and over time (see McCrae & Costa, 1987; Mooradian et al., 2011).

The study described in the Spotlight on Research Methods provided evidence that out of these five traits, agreeableness was the single best predictor of who would be helpful. Agreeableness is a trait associated with people who are highly cooperative, have high empathy and compassion for others, and are generally "people pleasers." It makes sense that folks high in agreeableness might be most likely to help others, in general, regardless of the circumstances. Agreeable people might be more likely to help because they have a high need for approval or acceptance from others (Deutsch & Lamberti, 1986). It's also possible their increased empathy is the root of their helping (Krueger et al., 2001).

But let's also explore the personalities of people who are *not* helpful.

Big 5 Model: A theory that five fundamental personality traits make us distinct and predict behavior: openness to experience, conscientiousness, extraversion, agreeableness, and neuroticism.

Personality and Prosocial Behavior

"The search for the prosocial personality has been long and controversial" (Habashi et al., 2016, p. 1177). This is the first sentence in an article devoted to studying whether different personality traits really can be linked to helping others. Habashi and her colleagues started with the most popular general theory on personality, which most researchers call the Big 5 Model of Personality (McCrae & Costa, 1987; Mooradian et al., 2011). According to this model, five culturally universal personality traits predict behavior fairly reliably:

- **Openness to experience:** enjoyment of adventure, new experiences, independence, curiosity

- **Conscientiousness:** attention to detail, responsibility, self-discipline, high achievers

- **Extraversion:** highly social, energetic, assertive, spontaneous

- **Agreeableness:** cooperative, peacemakers, compassionate toward others

- **Neuroticism:** anxious, prone to stress, more likely to be depressed and socially insecure

When you consider these five traits, which would you hypothesize is most likely to be associated with more prosocial behaviors?

The research team asked college students at Purdue University to come to a session under the *cover story* that they would be reviewing a new program for the university's radio station. The broadcast was an interview with a senior student, "Katie." She had lost both parents and a younger sibling in a car accident. Now she was left with no financial resources and no family support. Not surprisingly, Katie was struggling to graduate while caring for her remaining younger siblings. The participants didn't know that "Katie" was not a real person.

All of the participants completed self-report scales of the Big 5 personality traits. The major outcome of the study was measured when the participants were given the opportunity to help Katie. The participants wrote down how many hours they would volunteer to help her personally, how many hours they would work on trying to get others to help, and how much money they would donate.

(Continued)

(Continued)

TABLE 10.2

Statistically Significant Correlations

	OPENNESS TO EXPERIENCE	CONSCIENTIOUSNESS	EXTRAVERSION	AGREEABLENESS	NEUROTICISM
# Hours willing to volunteer	+.03	+.09	+.11	**+.17**	+.03
# Hours willing to get others to help	+.13	+.12	+.06	**+.20**	+.13
Amount of money willing to donate	+.07	+.12	+.13	**+.15**	+.07
Personal distress	+.03	−.03	−.05	**+.18**	**+.19**

Source: Data from McCrae and Costa (1987); Mooradian et al. (2011).

The participants also rated how much personal distress they felt when thinking about Katie's story. Each of these variables was *correlated* with each of the Big 5 personality traits; the results are shown in Table 10.2. Remember that correlations can range from −1.0 to +1.0, and numbers closer to 1 in either direction mean that the two variables are more closely associated with each other.

As you can see, only agreeableness was significantly correlated (shown in bold in the table),

with people being more likely to donate their time and money to a person in need. Being higher in openness to experience, conscientiousness, or extraversion had no relationship with prosocial behaviors in this study. Interestingly, people who were high in either agreeableness or neuroticism were likely to say that Katie's story caused them personal distress—but only those high in agreeableness followed that up by expressing a willingness to help.

Not Helpful: The Dark Triad

The combination of three other traits is called the **dark triad**.

It's a scary-sounding group of personality traits labeled Machiavellianism, narcissism, and psychopathy (see Paulhus & Williams, 2002). The first, Machiavellianism, is named for the Italian diplomat Niccolò Machiavelli (1469–1537), who wrote a book *The Prince*. It's basically a handbook for unethical politicians on the ruthless use of political power (see Dietz, 1986; Jackson & Grace, 2018). The term is now used as a personality trait relevant to people who believe that any behavior is justified by the ambition to gain and maintain social power. In other words, lying and manipulation of others is the key to power. It won't surprise you that prosocial behaviors are *negatively correlated* with Machiavellianism.

The Machiavellian personality exercises power through flattery, cheating, manipulation, and plotting. It combines distrust of others with callous uncaring toward friends and foes alike (Collison et al., 2018). College students with Machiavellian impulses are more likely to cheat on tests, but only if they don't think they'll be caught (Barbaranelli et al., 2018).

Dark triad: A group of three personality traits associated with lack of ethics and need for power: Machiavellianism, narcissism, and psychopathology.

The next two traits, narcissism and psychopathy, can each reach extreme levels when tied to clinical mental disorders. Common measures of the dark triad expect that most people will only reach "subclinical" levels. Narcissism is feelings of entitlement, superiority to everyone around you, and the desire for dominance. Psychopathology, in this context, refers to high impulsivity and thrill-seeking as well as low levels of empathy and anxiety. In other words, people high in psychopathology like to take risks and don't worry about the consequences, especially in terms of how those risks might hurt others.

People who score high on the dark triad, especially psychopathy, are less likely to be good citizens (Pruysers et al., 2019). In general, people who fit the dark triad are relatively unconcerned about prosocial behavior (Djeriouat & Trémolière, 2014); they really don't care about "being a good person." In addition, people who score high on the dark triad tend to be bullies (Dåderman & Ragnestål-Impola, 2019).

Warning: Try not to be tricked by someone with a dark triad personality. They seem to have an intuition (Gordon & Platek, 2009) that helps them find gullible people they can victimize. They can sense vulnerability when they troll profiles on Facebook (Lopes & Yu, 2017) and when ethics are required in business (see Harrison et al., 2018). To see where you might fall on these traits, check out the What's My Score? feature.

Measuring Personality Traits Relevant to Helping

In the Spotlight on Research Methods feature, you read about a study (Habashi et al., 2016) showing that two personality traits are positively correlated with feelings of personal distress on hearing about someone in need of help: agreeableness and neuroticism. However, only people high in agreeableness actually offered to help. You also learned about the dark triad, personality traits negatively correlated with helping others. Where do you fall on each trait?

Instructions: Next to each item, write a number indicating whether the word or phrase describes how you see yourself, using this scale:

1	2	3	4	5
Strongly disagree		Neutral		Strongly agree

I see myself as someone who . . .

____ 1. Is helpful and unselfish with others.
____ 2. Has a forgiving nature.
____ 3. Is considerate and kind to almost everyone.
____ 4. Likes to cooperate with others.
____ 5. Uses deceit or lies to get my way.
____ 6. Tends to manipulate others to get my way.
____ 7. Uses flattery to get my way.
____ 8. Tends to exploit others toward my own end.

____ 9. Tends to want others to admire me.
____ 10. Tends to want others to pay attention to me.
____ 11. Tends to expect special favors from others.
____ 12. Tends to seek prestige or status.
____ 13. Tends to lack remorse.
____ 14. Tends to be callous or insensitive.
____ 15. Tends to not be too concerned with morality or the morality of my actions.
____ 16. Tends to be cynical.

Instructions: Add up your answers for the following subscales; your score should range from 4 to 20 for each personality trait, with higher numbers indicting higher levels of that trait.

- Agreeableness: Items 1 to 4
- Machiavellianism: Items 5 to 8
- Narcissism: Items 9 to 12
- Psychopathology: Items 13 to 16

These scales have been modified from the original measures. Higher scores in agreeableness are tied to more helping, while higher scores in the other three traits are tied to less helping.

Source: Modified from Jonason and Webster (2010); John and Srivastava (1999).

Social Norms

Social norms guide a surprising amount of prosocial behavior.

Religious norms provide existential reasons to be "good" people. Gender norms dictate what it means to fit inside "masculine" or "feminine" expectations. Cultural norms tell us how to be a good citizen across a variety of situations. All three influence our decisions and behaviors.

Religious Norms

Most major world religions profess social norms that support prosocial behavior.

Giving a percentage of your wealth to the poor is one of the five pillars of Islam. A similar obligation within Judaism, Tzedakah, emphasizes that giving is a matter of justice rather than generosity. Hinduism promotes Yajna, a term that suggests that sacrificing for others is a way of behaving in harmony with universal laws. The Christian requirement advises extreme altruism: "Love your enemies, and do good to those who hate you," "Turn the other cheek," and "Sell your possessions and give to the poor." All these religious ideals influence prosocial behavior, but exactly how is a little complicated.

Intrinsic Versus Quest Religiosity. Batson and Gray (1981) discovered that *why* you are religious influences *how* you are religious. Recall from Chapter 9 that people high in intrinsic religiosity attempt to internalize their faith's teachings—and live accordingly. In contrast, quest religiosity uses religion as a way to question, doubt, and reexamine values and beliefs. In other words, it might not matter what religion you belong to—what matters is what motivates your religious belief.

In their study (Batson & Gray, 1981), 60 religiously oriented women were presented with someone in emotional distress. Those who were oriented toward intrinsic religiosity offered their help whether or not it was welcome; they were responding to their own internal need to be helpful (a more egoistic response).

However, those women oriented toward religion as a quest offered help only if the person wanted help; they were responding to the expressed needs of the victim (a more purely altruistic response). This pattern has been replicated by others (e.g., Hansen et al., 1995). In other words, why you are religious influences how you provide prosocial behavior.

When Religious Norms Aren't Enough: The Good Samaritan Experiment. Being religious does not automatically lead to moral behavior.

Consider the famous "Good Samaritan" *field experiment* (Darley & Batson, 1973). It tried to test (1) whether being reminded of religious norms influences helping and (2) whether situational circumstances influence helping. Here's the setup. The Christian Bible has a parable about altruism called "The Good Samaritan." A traveler is stripped, beaten, and left to die next to a road. Two different religious men, a priest and a Levite, both pass by and fail to help the man. Finally, a man from Samaria (considered unworthy by the priest and the Levite) stops and helps the traveler.

The participants were 40 students at the Princeton Theological Seminary. That means they were already people who presumably wanted to be helpful, stand-up, religious leaders of their communities. These 40 ministers-in-training didn't know it, but each had been assigned to different experimental conditions. Importantly, each man was tested by himself.

The first *independent variable* divided the participants into two groups. Half were asked to prepare a brief talk about careers for ministers (the control group). The comparison or experimental group also prepared a brief talk, but this time they were asked to focus on the Good Samaritan story. In other words, the experimental condition primed them to think about prosocial, religion-based behaviors.

The second *independent variable* came in Part 2 of this study. They were all told that the rest of the study was in a different building on campus and they needed to walk there now. The participants were further randomly divided by the instructions they got at this point:

- Group 1. "They were expecting you a few minutes ago. . . . The assistant should be waiting for you, so you'd better hurry."

- Group 2. "The assistant is ready for you, so please go right over."

- Group 3. "It'll be a few minutes before they're ready, but you might as well head on over."

In other words, independent variable 2 manipulated the situation by making them feel high, medium, or low levels of urgency.

Finally, the *dependent variable* came as the men walked across campus. They each passed a man (a *confederate* actor) slumped in a doorway who coughed and groaned as the students passed by. Would they stop to help? The results (see Figure 10.1) were reported as both quantitative and qualitative observations. Quantitatively, only about 40% of the seminary students stopped to help the groaning man. People who had just been reminded of the Good Samaritan story were always a little more likely to help (the blue bars are always a little higher than the red bars; Greenwald, 1975).

However, you can see that the essay they wrote had the biggest effect when the future ministers didn't feel any urgency. Being in a hurry mattered: Even when slightly rushed, people were less likely to stop and help, even if they had just been reminded of prosocial religious norms.

In addition to these *quantitative observations*, Darley and Batson (1973) also made *qualitative observations*. They wrote that "on several occasions, a seminary student going to give his talk on the parable of the Good Samaritan literally stepped over the victim as he hurried on his way" (p. 107). In this experiment, religious social norms or religiosity might make some people a little more likely to help, but only if they don't have other urgent things to do.

FIGURE 10.1

Do religious motivations increase helping behavior? The results from Darley and Batson's (1973) "Good Samaritan" study.

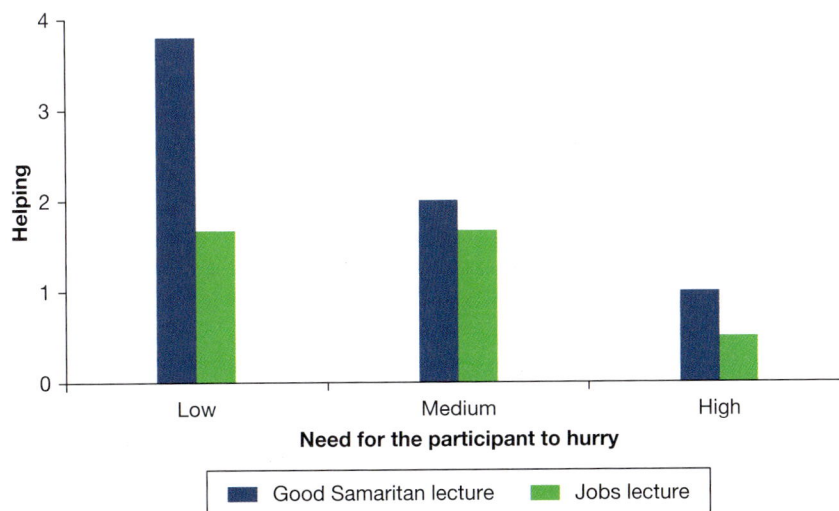

Source: Adapted from Darley and Batson (1973).

Moral Hypocrisy and Integrity. From the study just described, we learned that people with a religious commitment can live up to their ideals, but it doesn't always happen.

Sometimes people will display moral hypocrisy, which is appearing to have high moral and ethical standards while their behaviors don't actually match these standards. Situational circumstances might explain this mismatch, but it's also possible that some people claim to follow their religious standards when they simply don't. On the other hand, some of the participants really did stop to help, even when in a hurry. Those people displayed moral integrity, the motivation to actually live up to one's own standards of morality and ethics.

Gender Norms

Who helps more—men or women? And why?

It's only recently that both researchers and general society have acknowledged that sex and gender are more complicated than just "men versus women." This false gender binary oversimplifies a complex and nuanced reality that includes transgender people, queer people, and more. So it's going to take some time for research studies to catch up; most only examine cismen and ciswomen.

That said, gender is a powerful influence across different cultures. For example, women around the world tend to behave with greater social and ethical sensitivity, a higher degree of nurturance, and less combativeness than men (Kamat & Kanekar, 1990; Miranda & Kanekar, 1993). While many cultures include social norms around caring for aging parents, this obligation often falls to women more than men in terms of everyday tangible support (Lee et al., 2003; Silverstein et al., 2006). What makes men and women act differently when situations demand prosocial behavior?

Gender Socialization: Agency and Communion. Much of your life is on automatic pilot.

Just as different countries have different cultures with different social norms, men and women also have different social expectations. Gender socialization establishes the expected patterns of behavior deemed appropriate for men and women (see Bakan, 1966; Eagly, 2009) by rewarding each sex for doing what is considered "appropriate." This includes how—and when—to be helpful.

One key dimension of gender socialization is agency, the stereotypically male-oriented pattern of behavior that emphasizes being masterful, assertive, competitive, and dominant (see Spence & Buckner, 2000). In contrast, communion is a stereotypically female-oriented pattern of behavior that emphasizes being friendly, unselfish, other-oriented, and emotionally expressive.

Agency and communion describe a pattern of gender differences that is common across cultures (Kite et al., 2007). Agency promotes the self; communion emphasizes the good of the group. Several researchers have suggested that girls are raised to have higher moral reasoning and empathy than boys, which leads to more helping and prosocial behaviors (see Eisenberg et al., 1989; Kumru et al., 2012).

Gender norms direct boys and girls to different prosocial paths. A study in Polynesia found that girls engage in more prosocial behavior than boys. Girls are required to engage in cooperative housework for the good of the family; boys are allowed to be more independent (Graves & Graves, 1985). We train both boys and girls to be helpful. But the definition of helpful depends on whether we're training boys or girls.

Male and female career choices in "helping" professions suggest how agency and communion influence behavior. Eagly (2009) drew on the U.S. Bureau of Labor Statistics reported in Table 10.3 to identify how many women were in various prosocial occupations. Women are a minority within prosocial professions that stereotypically require initiative and physical strength. By contrast, women are a significant majority within professions that stereotypically require cooperation and nurturing such as preschool and kindergarten teachers.

Eagly's (2009) review concluded that "men tend to extend heroic help in dangerous emergencies" (p. 649), intervene in accidents to help strangers, are chivalrous to

Moral hypocrisy: When someone's behavior doesn't match their stated moral and ethical standards.

Moral integrity: When people are motivated to live up to their own stated morals and ethics.

Gender socialization: The expected patterns of behavior deemed appropriate for men and women.

Agency: A stereotypically male-oriented pattern of behavior that emphasizes being masterful, assertive, competitive, and dominant.

Communion: A stereotypically female-orientated pattern of behavior that emphasizes being friendly, unselfish, other-oriented, and emotionally expressive.

TABLE 10.3

Percentage of Women in Various Careers

MALE STEREOTYPE: REQUIRES STRENGTH AND INITIATIVE	FEMALE STEREOTYPE: REQUIRES COOPERATION AND NURTURING
Firefighters (5%)	Preschool/kindergarten teachers (98%)
Police officers (15%)	Social workers (79%)
Soldiers (14%)	Registered nurses (92%)

Source: Eagly (2009), when she referred to the Bureau of Labor Statistics (2009).

help women, and are more likely to serve their nation in war. Women may be less inclined to stop to offer help to someone on the side of the road, for example, due to fears of assault. But in a 2010 survey of over 200,000 students first entering college, 62% of men and 75% of women said that helping others is either "essential" or "very important" (Pryor et al., 2010).

Changing Patterns of Gender Socialization. Over the past 50+ years, gender expectations around the world have changed dramatically.

Warfare, for example, relies more on technology than brute strength. That has opened opportunities for and acceptance of women in the military. These changes may affect other gendered helping behaviors.

Changing gender roles were examined in depth by Diekman across a series of studies. Diekman and Eagly (2000) found that both men and women perceive the same pattern over time: Women remain fairly stable in their high levels of communion, but they are simultaneously increasing their levels of agency. In other words, women are perceived to be high in both traditional "masculine" and "feminine" personality traits and cognitive abilities.

In a series of follow-up studies, Diekman and Goodfriend (2006) found that both men and women are relatively accepting of these changes, although some women report disappointment about the pattern in men. These women note that as they, themselves, appear to be capable of any task, they don't see as many men doing things like changing diapers and being secretaries at work. They want men to make more efforts to be nurturing and relationship focused.

As time progresses, traditional ideas of how and when women versus men help others may change.

Cultural Norms

Prosocial behaviors can vary widely across cultures (Chen et al., 2012).

You're probably not surprised to learn that collectivistic cultures lead to more prosocial behaviors than individualistic cultures (Barrett et al., 2004; Bontempo et al., 1990). However, individuals in collectivistic cultures are especially likely to help people in their own group (Kemmelmeier et al., 2006). One review covering 21 different nations showed a similar pattern. Cultures that focused on the good of their own group were less likely to help strangers but more likely to help family members. The examples below demonstrate some interesting additional examples of cultural differences.

Comforting Others. Playing with toddlers became a scientific study.

This *quasi-experiment* compared the prosocial behavior of 19-month-old toddlers being raised in individualistic German and collectivistic Indian cultures (see Kärtner et al., 2010). Researchers played with the toddlers and pretended that a teddy bear's arm had broken off. Prosocial behavior from the toddlers was measured by whether they tried to comfort the researcher (by hugging, kissing, etc.) or by offering a new toy to replace the bear. In both samples, about 30% of the toddlers showed prosocial behavior—the two different cultures did not show *statistically significant* results.

However, the researchers suggested that there were different motives driving helping behaviors, based on culture. When the toddlers' mothers were compared, mothers from India emphasized relational social norms (such as obedience and helping) more than German mothers. This difference seemed to motivate the Indian children to help due to situational cues, while the German children seemed motivated by empathy. Objectively, the helping behaviors of these toddlers looked the same from the outside, but motives for helping may change based on culture (Kärtner et al., 2010). The researchers proposed that "there may be culture-specific developmental paths to prosocial behavior" (p. 913).

The Influence of School Lessons. The final two studies in this section both emphasize the impact of school on prosocial behavior.

First, one study focused on **prosocial moral reasoning** of 5th- through 10th-grade students. They explored children's ability to analyze moral dilemmas in which two or more people's needs conflict with each other and where formal rules of what to do are absent (Carlo et al., 1996). Their *quasi-experiment* gave U.S. and Brazilian participants seven dilemmas such as this one:

> One day Mary was going to a friend's party. On the way, she saw a girl who had fallen down and hurt her leg. The girl asked Mary to go to the girl's house and get her parents so the parents could come and take her to a doctor. But if Mary did run and get the girl's parents, Mary would be late to the party and miss the fun and social activities with her friends. (p. 233)

After each dilemma, the children indicated what the main character should do and why. Regardless of culture, individual participants with self-focused concerns about maximizing pleasure were *negatively correlated* with helpfulness, whereas other-oriented, communal concerns were *positively correlated* with helpfulness. That said, in general, the U.S. children got higher internalized moral reasoning scores, on average, than Brazilian children—a finding that was a *replication* of other studies (e.g., Hutz et al., 1994). The researchers suggested this difference may be due to the emphasis on critical thinking in U.S. school systems.

A second study compared adolescents from Spain and Turkey (Kumru et al., 2012). Spain and Turkey were chosen specifically because both are quickly moving from agricultural, patriarchal, and traditional cultures to more egalitarian cultures. However, Spain has moved along this continuum more quickly. As the researchers expected, the Spanish adolescents displayed higher levels of prosocial moral reasoning and prosocial behavior.

Their main explanation for these differences was the different emphasis in the school systems. Spanish schools emphasize abstract and deductive reasoning. They also noted, however, that motives for helping might change based on culture. Their data indicated that in Spanish culture, helping seemed to be motivated by gaining the approval of others. If this is true, the helping is egoistic and not truly altruistic. Either way, cultural differences in helping motives and behaviors is an area ripe for further research.

Prosocial moral reasoning: Our ability to analyze moral dilemmas in which two or more people's needs conflict with each other and where formal rules are absent.

THE MAIN IDEAS

- Prosocial behavior is associated with certain personality traits. Specifically, helping is positively correlated with agreeableness but negatively correlated with Machiavellianism, narcissism, and psychopathology.

- While some research shows that certain types of religiosity are associated with prosocial behaviors, other studies find that situational demands (such as whether people are in a hurry) are more predictive of who is most likely to help.

- Culture encourages men to be more agentic (independent and competitive) and women to be more communal (concerned with caring for others), but both traits are associated with helping in different settings. Research has also investigated whether national culture affects the likelihood of helping and motives behind helping.

CRITICAL THINKING CHALLENGE

- Research in this section noted that some personality traits are associated with more prosocial behavior (like agreeableness) while others are linked to less prosocial behavior (like Machiavellianism). If you wanted to design school activities for children that would promote agreeableness and decrease Machiavellianism, what kinds of activities would you create? What would you suggest parents could do to encourage agreeableness and discourage Machiavellianism in their children at home?

- What hypotheses do you have about whether religious people are more likely to have moral integrity versus moral hypocrisy? Can you think of people in your life who display one tendency or the other—and can you see patterns in the two types of people? Do you think one path over the other is based on life experiences, related personality traits, forms of religion, or other variables?

- Do you agree with Diekman's research participants that women are changing over time to be high in both communion and agency? And do you agree that men seem to be staying high in agency while staying relatively low in communion? Explain your view and provide at least two examples.

- What aspects of your national culture or particular subcultures either encourage or discourage helping of others? Does your culture encourage helping some kinds of people, or helping in some situations, more than others?

WHAT CIRCUMSTANCES MAKE HELPING MORE OR LESS LIKELY?

>> **LO 10.3:** Analyze what situational variables lead to more or less helping in different settings.

The scientific study of what situations make people more or less likely to help started with a grisly murder in 1964.

In Queens, New York, a young bartender named Kitty Genovese arrived home to her apartment complex around 3:00 a.m. A man chased her across the parking lot with a hunting knife and stabbed her twice. When she screamed for help, the man ran away . . . but he came back a few minutes later, stabbed her several more times, sexually assaulted her, and stole $49. He then left her in the hallway, bleeding. Overall, the attacks took place over half an hour. Kitty Genovese died about an hour later.

Two weeks after her death, the *New York Times* ran a story with a disturbing headline: "37 Who Saw Murder Didn't Call the Police" (Gansberg, 1964). According to the story, 37 people in Genovese's apartment complex either heard her screams for help or saw the attack happening. Not a single one called the police.

New York Daily News Archive/New York Daily News/Getty Images

Kitty Genovese, who was murdered in 1964.

The story had convincing details. It reported, for example, that one neighbor turned up his radio to avoid the annoying noise of the attack. Several people used the story as an example of society's increasing apathy and callousness toward victims. It was portrayed as part of an epidemic of dangerous, antisocial behaviors in big cities like New York.

The story about Genovese's uncaring neighbors was sensational—and wrong (Manning et al., 2007). Several people did call the police. One neighbor yelled at the attacker to leave her alone, the reason he initially ran away. Interviews with the rest of the neighbors revealed that while they admitted they had heard something, they had no idea it was a murder. They simply thought it was a couple arguing or a group of drunk friends. Years later, newspaper executives admitted to exaggerating the story to sell papers. You can read more about the Kitty Genovese story in the accompanying Social Psychology in Popular Culture feature.

Even if the details weren't accurate, several social psychologists heard about the case and were inspired to scientifically study helping—and not helping. This section answers the core question "What circumstances make helping more or less likely?" by

(1) describing how (a) the urban overload hypothesis, (b) diffusion of responsibility, and (c) pluralistic ignorance all can influence our behavior;

(2) explaining that we're more likely to help certain kinds of people; and

(3) describing a five-step model of helping.

SOCIAL PSYCHOLOGY IN POPULAR CULTURE

▶ Kitty Genovese's Story on Film

The murder of Kitty Genovese—and the headlines about how many people witnessed it without helping or even calling the police—are infamous. Even though later investigations questioned whether it was really true that 37 people failed to help, the Genovese story has inspired not only social psychology research but also two films. Both were released in 2016; the first is called *37* (Grasten et al., 2016) and the second is called *The Witness* (Solomon et al., 2016).

37 is a fictional version of the famous murder in which the characters represent the types of people who might have lived in Genovese's apartment building. It suggests a wide variety of reasons why people might not have helped. Characters experience all the following situations (and more) that lead them to not help:

- Interpreting her cries for help as a radio program

- Not hearing the noise due to family arguments

- Mental illness leading to incorrect attributions that the cries were hallucinations

- The belief that the noises were simply children playing a prank

- Concern that the police might ask uncomfortable questions about the neighbors' personal lives

In a review of the film for the *New York Times* (2016), critic Andy Webster comments about the final scenes, "Pressure builds in a protracted sequence of sputtering lobby lights, leaky fixtures, dying dowagers, the assault

New York Daily News Archive/New York Daily News/Getty Images

itself and the hysteria of [a] young girl. Implicit is the idea that the murder embodied a neighborhood's moral decay."

The second film, *The Witness*, was the result of Genovese's brother Bill, who was only 12 years old at the time of her murder. He was able to speak with some of the former friends of his sister and with people still living in the neighborhood, as well as with his extended family. The film raises some of the same doubts as the film *37* about the accuracy of the original report. It also explores the effect of so much public and research attention on the remaining family members.

What really happened that night is still controversial. But it is gratifying to see that the searching questions raised by this case study and the subsequent films continue to provoke deep conversations about social responsibility.

More People = Less Helping

When is helping most likely?

An obvious answer might be the more people, the better! If 100 people see someone faint suddenly, aren't the chances of the person getting help 100 times better than if only one person is there to witness the problem? It turns out that the answer is no. Why not?

Too Much! The Urban Overload Hypothesis

Big cities like New York are full of people, many of whom need help.

But if you tried to help every homeless person you saw in a big city, you would quickly be out of money—and thousands would still need your help. And if you keep giving away your money, then *you* might become one of those needy individuals. Often, people from a rural area who visit a big city for the first time feel that the city-dwellers seem harsh, callous, and unfriendly . . . but there are psychological reasons for their behavior.

One explanation is the **urban overload hypothesis**. People in cities avoid social interactions with strangers simply because they are overwhelmed (Milgram, 1970). Someone in a city may pass thousands of others on the street, in the subway, or in public parks. They don't have time to smile and say hi to everyone, much less help every tourist with a map and a confused look or every homeless person they pass.

The urban overload explanation recognizes urban-rural cultural differences. When researchers pretended to be bleeding and yelping in pain, about half of people in small

Urban overload hypothesis: The idea that people in cities avoid social interactions like helping strangers because they are overwhelmed by the number of people they encounter each day.

REUTERS/Juan Medina

The bystander effect is the ironic tendency for people to receive less help when more people are there to witness the problem.

towns stopped to help—but only 15% of people in large cities (Amato, 1983). A review of 35 studies suggests that learning "small town values" as a child doesn't seem to increase helping. Prosocial behavior occurred more in rural areas than in urban areas, regardless of where the witnesses grew up as children (Steblay, 1987). Instead of a values explanation, it seems that people who live in cities may simply feel that the need for their help is overwhelming.

Diffusion of Responsibility: The Bystander Effect

Urban overload explains why thousands of people in need might not get help. But what if there's only one person who needs help?

The **bystander effect** occurs when the likelihood of being helped in an emergency is *negatively correlated* with the number of people who witness that emergency (Darley & Latané, 1968; Latané & Darley, 1970). The more people around, the less likely you are to get help. Why?

A popular psychological explanation is diffusion of responsibility (Darley & Latané, 1968; Latané & Darley, 1970). Remember from Chapter 8 that diffusion of responsibility occurs when each person in a group feels less accountable to take action because there are other people who can do something (it was at play during what we called social loafing). Ironically—and sometimes tragically—you sometimes are more likely to be helped with fewer people around.

Diffusion of responsibility suggests why Kitty Genovese's neighbors might have heard the emergency but did not do anything about it. They could easily have thought, "Someone else must have already called the police." It's not that people didn't care. They just assumed others would help.

The bystander effect has influenced business practices and organizations. One study showed that managers who know of fraud occurring in their organizations are more likely to report it when they alone have the relevant information (Brink et al., 2015). Another study found the bystander effect in witnesses to theft (van Bommel et al., 2014). Employers also are reevaluating how to respond to bystander apathy in the face of increasing numbers of complaints (Zugelder et al., 2018).

Bystander effects also influence whether children will report problems (Plötner et al., 2015). For example, the number of witnesses to cyberbullying has been shown to have a negative correlation with each witness's sense of responsibility and intention to intervene (Obermaier et al., 2016). Other research has found that less helping behavior occurs when people play multiplayer video games than when they play single-player games, both during game play and afterward (Stenico & Greitemeyer, 2015). Middle school children are being trained to understand the bystander effect relative to helping prevent sexual violence (Cardona & Napierski-Prancl, 2019).

Bystander effect: The finding that the likelihood of being helped in an emergency is negatively correlated with the number of people who witness it, probably due to diffusion of responsibility.

The #MeToo Movement Promotes Helping. The #MeToo movement undermines these negative bystander effects.

The movement has empowered reports of sexual assault, mostly against men in positions of power: religious leaders, coaches, media personalities, business leaders, and movie producers. For example, Abrams and Bartlett (2019) describe the implications of the #MeToo movement within the world of sport. When Emily Kroshus (2018) surveyed college athletes, she found that both male and female athletes perceived that their campus didn't particularly support sexual assault prevention—but that these perceptions were wrong. By emphasizing a true team spirit mentality and that everyone should care about prevention and intervention when they see something going wrong, perhaps fewer crimes will be prevented.

When individuals avoid feeling personal responsibility, vulnerable women continue to suffer (e.g., in Bangladesh, where the #MeToo movement hasn't reached general popularity; Hassan et al., 2019). That helps explain why some researchers (e.g., O'Neil et al., 2018) see the #MeToo movement as an opportunity to promote public health. Acknowledging individual survivors and emphasizing that sexual assault should matter to everyone is key to making people feel personally responsible when they have the opportunity to prevent it.

Exceptions to the Rule.   Importantly, there are exceptions to the rule of the bystander effect, where more people usually lead to less helping.

For example, in an experiment that staged bike theft, bystanders were *only* more likely to stop a dangerous-looking thief when other witnesses were present. The participants in this setting may have felt that the presence of other people made it safer to confront a dangerous-looking criminal (Fischer & Greitemeyer, 2013). Another study showed that people will help, regardless of whether other people are around, if they know they're being filmed (van Bommel et al., 2014). Diffusion of responsibility also seems to decrease when the specific situation requires help from multiple people, such as lifting something heavy (Greitemeyer & Mügge, 2013, 2015).

Finally, in a *field study* conducted in bars throughout Amsterdam, researchers purposely dropped items to see who would help pick them up. Results showed that the size of the bar's crowd had no influence on helping (a lack of the traditional bystander effect). However, the amount of alcohol consumed before the help was needed *did* influence how quickly help was offered: Drunker people helped faster (van Bommel et al., 2016).

The Smoke-Filled Room: Pluralistic Ignorance

In Chapter 8, we reviewed how pluralistic ignorance occurs when we think we're the only person thinking in a certain way.

What do most of us do in uncertain situations that might be interpreted as an emergency? We often look around to see if other people are also interpreting the situation in the same way. If they don't appear to be worried, we tell ourselves that everything must be okay. A clever experiment by Latané and Darley (1970) put participants in a room to complete a survey without supervision of an experimenter. The room began filling with (nonharmful) smoke.

Table 10.4 tells you the quantitative data story that supports the idea of pluralistic ignorance.

In over half of the groups, all three participants sat quietly, even when the smoke was so thick they couldn't see what they were writing on their surveys. Apparently, these participants felt that if the other two people didn't think there was a problem, then they didn't want to look like a fool or a troublemaker.

TABLE 10.4

Quantitative Data Story

# OF PEOPLE IN A ROOM FILLING WITH SMOKE	BEHAVIORAL RESPONSE
1 person	75% quickly got up and reported the problem
3 people	38% had one person report the problem within 6 minutes

Strangely, people can be less likely to act in an emergency if more people are there to see it.

We Help People We Like
(and Who Appear Similar to Us)

You're probably not shocked by this news: We're more likely to help people we like.

Obviously, you'll be more inclined to make sacrifices for people who are friends or family. The more interesting news might be that we're also more likely to help people we *assume* we would like, even when they are complete strangers. How do we decide how likeable we think they might be? One answer is that we assume we'd like people who are similar to ourselves.

Figure 10.2 demonstrates a strange path to prosocial behavior: clothes. We use clothes to estimate similarity and liking. It doesn't have to be clothing, of course. Any perceived similarity will promote liking and then prosocial behavior. Here's why similarity promotes prosocial behavior.

- We rely on available information (e.g., clothing) to decide who is similar to us (belongs to our ingroup).

- We spend more time with people belonging to our ingroups.

- Spending time selectively promotes positive evaluations of ingroups and negative evaluations of outgroups (see Chapter 9).

- We are more likely to help people we think are like us: members of our ingroups (Dovidio & Morris, 1975).

FIGURE 10.2

One possible path to helping.

Clothing Similarity → Liking → Helping

An early study done in 1970 on a Midwestern university campus showed this tendency with a very simple procedure. *Confederates* of the study dressed in either conservative or "hip/counterculture" clothes. (Note: this was the time of hippies and colorful clothing.) They walked around campus asking other students for some spare change to make a phone call. When the confederate asked for help from someone wearing the same type of clothes, about two thirds of them helped. Less than half provided help when approached by someone dressed differently (Emswiller et al., 1971).

Anyone familiar with international soccer ("football" to everyone except people living in the United States) knows that team loyalty and rivalries are extremely important. But how important, when it comes to helping? Do team loyalties mean that we are *less* likely to offer help to someone who favors a different team?

In 2005, a research group (Levine et al., 2005) tested this question with participants who preidentified as fans of the Manchester United team in England. Each participant seemingly happened upon a person (a *confederate,* again) who was jogging—but then slipped and appeared to be hurt—and in need of some help. The jogger was wearing a jersey that was either (1) a blank, generic sports jersey; (2) one supporting Manchester United; or (3) one supporting Liverpool, which is Manchester United's rival team.

The results can be seen in Table 10.5 in the Study 1 rows. The confederate was much more likely to be helped if he was wearing a shirt indicating at least one similarity to the participant. In fact, only one participant failed to help a fellow fan of the team. In contrast, people wearing a plain jersey or a rival team's jersey were helped by only about one third of the participants.

Take another look at Table 10.5 and focus on Study 2. In this second study, helping behaviors for the confederate wearing a Liverpool jersey showed the opposite effect!

TABLE 10.5

Team Loyalty of Manchester United Fans

	TYPE OF JERSEY		
	MANCHESTER UNITED	**PLAIN**	**LIVERPOOL**
Study 1			
Not helped	1	8	7
Helped	12	4	3
Study 2			
Not helped	2	7	3
Helped	8	2	7

Source: Levine et al. (2005). Copyright by SAGE Publishing.

What made them flip? Before these participants came across the hurt jogger, they filled out a survey that was really an experimental intervention. The survey focused attention on the good qualities shared by all soccer fans, regardless of team alliance.

Study 1 participants probably thought of Liverpool fans as rivals. But Study 2 participants were primed to think about Liverpool fans as fellow fans of English football. They had something important in common with *all* soccer fans. This altered perception was the result of a simple manipulation: filling out a survey. But that's all it took to make this perception of similarity effective. Participants changed behavior to helping rather than ignoring an injured jogger. Perhaps this is the lesson, then: If you need help from someone, try to highlight what you might have in common with them.

Latané and Darley's Five-Step Model of Helping

What can we conclude about when people are most likely to help?

Let's be practical by returning to the work of Latané and Darley, the two researchers who helped kick off research about prosocial behavior. They stayed with this topic by trying to discover when people will (or won't) help in emergencies. As a result, they were able to create a five-step model predicting the specific circumstances that lead to prosocial engagement. A summary of their model (Latané & Darley, 1970) is shown in Figure 10.3.

FIGURE 10.3

Latané and Darley's five-step model of helping.

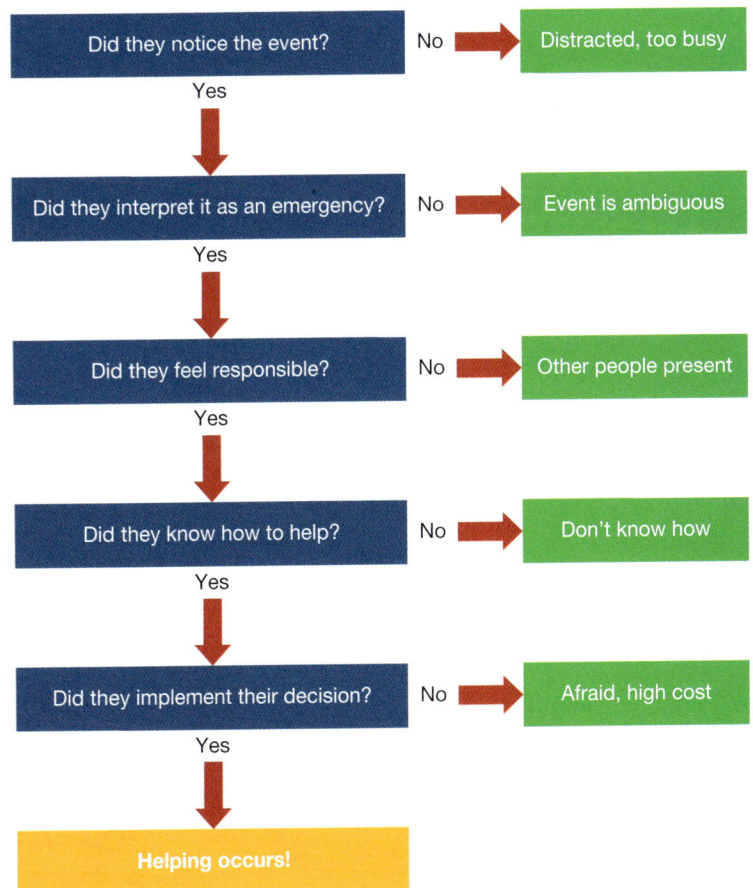

Source: Adapted from Latané and Darley (1970).

People are more likely to help if the answer is "yes" to each of the following five questions:

Step 1: Did You Notice the Event? To help, we must first realize that help is needed. People might fail to help simply because they're distracted or not paying attention. They may be distracted, for example, because they're in a hurry (one explanation for the findings of the "Good Samaritan" study).

Step 2: Did You Interpret the Event as an Emergency? To help, we must correctly interpret that help is needed. Many of Kitty Genovese's neighbors heard noises at 3:00 a.m. But some reported that they thought it was a romantic couple having a fight or drunk friends staggering home. To help, we must correctly interpret the situation as one in which help is needed.

Step 3: Did You Take Responsibility? Prosocial behaviors increase when people feel responsible. This is more likely to be the case when they are alone and no diffusion of responsibility can take place. It also seems to be the case when they feel compelled to help others who are, at least on the surface, similar and therefore potentially a member of their ingroup. Emergency training (such as CPR classes) often emphasizes increasing responsibility by instructing us to point to a single person in the room and say, "You! Call 911!" Yelling, "Someone call 911!" might lead to diffusion of responsibility.

Step 4: Did You Know How to Help? Even if we know an emergency is happening and we want to help, we might not be able to. I [Wind] was once on an airplane in which another passenger passed out and the flight attendant asked if there was a doctor on the plane. I stayed silent, knowing they didn't mean my kind of doctor. Even the most empathetic, agreeable person won't be able to help in every situation.

Step 5: Did You Decide to Help? Time to decide. Make a rapid calculation of the costs and potential benefits of helping. For example, earlier we noted that women may hesitate to help a stranded motorist on a rural road. Why? Fear of being assaulted. To help or not to help—that will be the question you must answer.

When I [Wind] was in high school, a rumor circulated that if you saw another car at night without its headlights on, you shouldn't flash your own lights to help the other driver. Why not? I was told that certain "dangerous gangs" had decided to purposely drive without their lights on—and then murder the first person who flashed at them. (This was unlikely in the middle of Iowa in the 1980s, but it was troubling enough to keep me from helping by flashing my lights.)

Sometimes, these fears may be justified. Ted Bundy, the famous serial killer, used to pretend to be injured until a young woman offered to help—and then he would choose her to be his next victim (Byrne & Pease, 2003). Intervening is risky. First responders live with those risks every day to help others. One lesson from this chapter is that there are lots and lots of reasons why any given person might decide not to help when help is needed—which should only make our admiration for those who *do* help grow.

THE MAIN IDEAS

- Social psychologists were motivated to study prosocial behavior after a woman named Kitty Genovese was murdered and reports (falsely) claimed that 37 people witnessed it without helping.

- Ironically, helping is less likely when more people are present. This effect may be due to urban overload (the idea that in cities, the number of people who need help is overwhelming), the bystander effect (which says people don't help because of diffusion of responsibility), and/or pluralistic ignorance (if others don't seem to think it's an emergency, we don't either).

- We are more likely to help people we like and people who are (or appear to be) similar to ourselves.

- Latané and Darley proposed that helping will only occur when five steps are all in place. To help, a person must notice the situation, interpret it as an emergency, feel responsible, know how to help, and implement the decision.

CRITICAL THINKING CHALLENGE

- Imagine that you find yourself in a big city, in need of help. Explain four specific ways that you could increase the chances of getting the help you need, based on concepts from this chapter.

- Do you think that the "five steps" toward helping outlined in this section are comprehensive? In other words, what steps might be missing from this model? When you are considering whether to help someone else, are there other circumstances or decisions that you make beyond the five identified here?

- This chapter discussed (1) general helping motives, (2) how different kinds of people are more likely to help than others, and (3) situational circumstances that lead to more or less helping. Consider all three factors and determine how important you think each one is, relative to the others, in terms of how much it influences helping. If you had 100 "points" that you could assign to these three factors, with more points indicating a stronger influence, how would you distribute those points? Defend your answer.

CHAPTER SUMMARY

What Motivates People to Help Others, in General?

Prosocial behavior is the general term for helping others. Social psychology differentiates between pure altruism, which is helping purely out of selfless concerns, versus egoistic altruism, which is helping that leads to some kind of personal benefit. There are four major theoretical explanations for why people engage in prosocial behaviors. The first three are all considered egoistic explanations: the evolutionary perspective, social norms, and negative state relief. The fourth, called the empathy-altruism hypothesis, is based on pure altruism because it argues we help others when we feel compassion for them. Recent research from neuropsychology on "mirror neurons" supports the idea that helping is at least sometimes based on empathy or compassion.

Why Are Some People More Helpful Than Others?

This section of the book considered variables that might have an influence on whether individuals are more or less likely to display prosocial, helping behaviors. The first variable was personality. While agreeableness is positively correlated to helping, the "dark triad" of traits called Machiavellianism, narcissism, and psychopathology is negative correlated to helping. A second variable is religious norms. People motivated by intrinsic religiosity seem to help due to personal needs, while people motivated by religion as quest seem to help out of empathy to the victim. A classic study called the "Good Samaritan experiment" showed that religious norms increase helping, but only when the participants weren't distracted by being in a hurry. Gender and cultural norms have also been examined in terms of prosocial behaviors. People high in "communal" traits are more likely to help in general, but people with "agentic" traits may help more when physical strength is needed or the situation is dangerous. People in collectivistic cultures are more likely to help family members, but they are less likely to help strangers.

What Circumstances Make Helping More or Less Likely?

A famous case study of people supposedly not helping is the Kitty Genovese story, in which 37 people supposedly witnessed a young woman being stabbed without helping. While at least somewhat exaggerated, these reports inspired research on situational circumstances that increase or decrease helping. One well-replicated finding is that ironically, we are less likely to be helped when there are multiple people present. Three explanations for this effect are urban overload, the bystander effect (or diffusion of responsibility), and pluralistic ignorance. Other research shows that we are more likely to help when we like the person who needs it or when we simply perceive that they are similar to us (and therefore we might be more likely to like them). Finally, Latané and Darley created a five-step model to explain the process that needs to occur in order for people to help. They suggest that for anyone to help in a given situation, that person must (1) notice the event, (2) interpret the event as an emergency, (3) take responsibility, (4) know how to help, and (5) implement the decision to help.

CRITICAL THINKING, ANALYSIS, AND APPLICATION

- Identify three specific examples of people making significant sacrifices to help others (at least one of your examples should be nonfiction). For each example, analyze the person's motives for helping based on the four theoretical explanations from the first section of this chapter (promoting our own genes, social norms, avoiding negative emotions, and pure altruism).

- Think about the different circumstances in which people are more likely to help—and tie each into one of the helping motives. Are these circumstances going to lead to egoistic or altruistic helping behaviors?

- Levine et al. (2005) showed that priming people to think about how all soccer fans are good people led participants to help fans of a rival team. How could this simple procedure be used in the real world to motivate individuals to help those in need such as refugees from other countries or people living in poverty?

- As technology advances and travel to other parts of the world becomes easier, do you think that views of other countries and cultures will change as well? How will these advances in technology influence the likelihood of helping people from other cultures? For example, will citizens of other countries still be considered part of an outgroup, or will the emphasis on being a "global citizen" change how we view others and whether we're likely to help them?

Christopher Furlong/Getty Images News/Getty Images

Time & Life Pictures/The LIFE Picture Collection/Getty Images

11 Aggression

Core Questions

11.1	What is aggression?
11.2	Why are humans aggressive?
11.3	How can we manage or reduce aggression?

Learning Objectives

11.1	Use typologies and the General Aggression Model (GAM) to define and describe how humans harm one another.
11.2	Distinguish among biological, cultural, and situational explanations of human aggression.
11.3	Analyze ideas for managing aggression.

The stakes could not be any higher.

We need to be real as we turn the spotlight of social psychology to aggression. Aggression is more than an interpersonal problem. The mixture of proliferating nuclear weapons and our poor track record at managing our own aggression represents a catastrophic threat to human existence. Not only do we have to think about aggression on this global level, but we also know that it affects our everyday lives.

Victims of interpersonal aggression can be scarred both physically and mentally. It's a sobering topic, but one that social psychology is obligated to understand and—hopefully—do something about. We focus on just three core questions as we share social psychology's insights into human aggression.

WHAT IS AGGRESSION?

>> **LO 11.1:** **Use typologies and the General Aggression Model (GAM) to define and describe how humans harm one another.**

Would you categorize the examples below as "aggressive"?

- A group who feel oppressed by the government holds a protest.

- Someone who doesn't like rabbits in their yard shoots them.

- A relationship partner leaves dirty dishes all over as a "signal."

- One roommate steals from another.

- A sports fan paints their face and yells at the opposing team's players.

- An unhappy employee hides dead fish in their boss's office.

In social psychology, **aggression** is behavior intended to harm others who do not wish to be harmed. The phrase "intended to harm" excludes situations such as a child receiving painful but helpful vaccinations or athletic competitions like boxing or wrestling. In both cases, no harm is intended. But this definition *does* include crimes like sexual assault and non-physical forms of aggression such as backstabbing office politics (Neuman & Baron, 2011) and **cyberbullying**, aggression through electronic sources like social media (Silva et al., 2018; Zois et al., 2018).

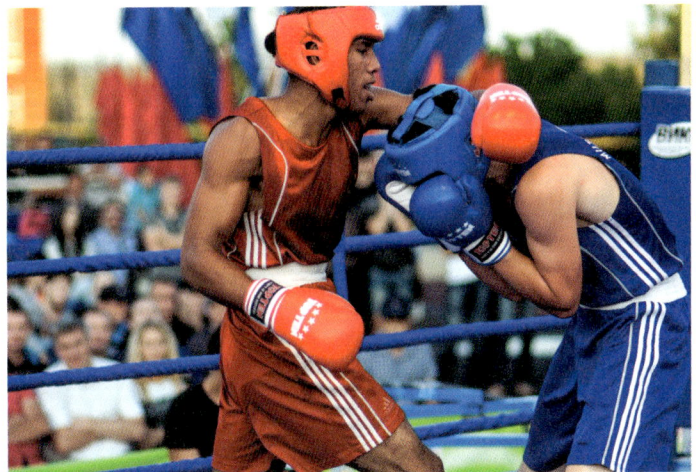

© istockphoto.com/vladimirvasil

Aggression can be hard to define. While some might consider boxing aggressive, the boxers certainly don't want to inflict actual harm on each other.

Aggression: Behavior intended to harm others who do not wish to be harmed.

Cyberbullying: Aggression through electronic outlets, like social media.

Typologies: Categorical systems that help us organize complex but related events.

This section answers the core question "What is aggression?" by

(1) describing typologies and a general framework that help us define aggression,

(2) documenting the historical persistence of aggression,

(3) recognizing that situational aggression tends to escalate, and

(4) reporting the (perhaps surprising) worldwide decline of aggression.

Typologies Help Define Aggression

We humans are constantly inventing new ways to harm one another.

We use **typologies** to organize the long list into categories. Typologies are categorical systems that help us think more clearly about complex but related events. The first typology organizes aggression into three content areas. The second describes how humans are aggressive. The third recognizes motivations for aggression. The fourth divides controversial microaggressions into subtypes. Finally, the General Aggression Model (GAM) unites these typologies under a larger theory.

Typology 1: Aggression Content

Science prefers definitions that are as simple as possible—and no simpler.

The first descriptive typology recognizes three types of behavioral aggression: physical, verbal, and relational (see Allen & Anderson, 2017). **Physical aggression** is intentionally causing harm to someone's body or property. Hitting, kicking, and beating are obvious examples. So is using weapons to cause bodily harm, including breaking car windows or damaging something that has value to the other person.

Verbal aggression relies on communications to cause harm. Name-calling is one form of verbal aggression. So is yelling and malicious gossip.

Relational aggression harms others by damaging their social networks or relationships with others. People can become creative in their meanness by excluding others, spreading gossip, undermining someone at work, or posting an unattractive photograph of someone on Facebook. You can see that these three forms may overlap.

Typology 2: Forms of Aggression

Table 11.1 presents a more detailed descriptive typology of how we are aggressive (adapted from Buss, 1961, p. 8).

TABLE 11.1

Buss's Typology of Eight Different Forms of Aggression

	DIRECT		INDIRECT	
	ACTIVE	**PASSIVE**	**ACTIVE**	**PASSIVE**
Physical aggression	Hitting, stabbing, beating, etc.	Positioning your car to prevent someone else from changing lanes	Cheating in a competition or hiring a "hitman"	Refusing to stop the bleeding of an enemy soldier
Verbal aggression	Putdowns and insults	Giving someone the silent treatment to punish that person	Spreading mean rumors or negative gossip	Failing to defend someone who you know is being accused unfairly

Source: Adapted from Buss (1961).

This typology subdivides aggression according to three categories: (1) physical or verbal, (2) direct or indirect, and (3) active or passive. It will help your understanding to create your own examples for each category.

Again, real-life aggression often blurs the lines between the categories. In a nursery school, one child called another "a big poopie-head!" and then giggled with his friends: direct, active, verbal aggression. And excluding that child from a group of friends was also indirect, passive aggression.

Typology 3: Aggressive Motivations

A third typology identifies motivations for aggression.

Hostile-reactive aggression is an impulsive, emotion-based reaction to perceived threats. It's driven by feelings like jealousy, humiliation, or anger. In contrast, **instrumental-proactive aggression** is a thoughtful or reason-based decision to harm others

---

Physical aggression: Intentionally causing harm to someone's body or property.

Verbal aggression: Using communication to cause harm.

Relational aggression: Harming others by damaging their social networks.

Hostile-reactive aggression: An impulsive, emotion-based reaction to perceived threats.

Instrumental-proactive aggression: A thoughtful, reason-based decision to harm others to gain resources such as territory, money, self-esteem, or social status.

FIGURE 11.1

A motivational typology of aggression.

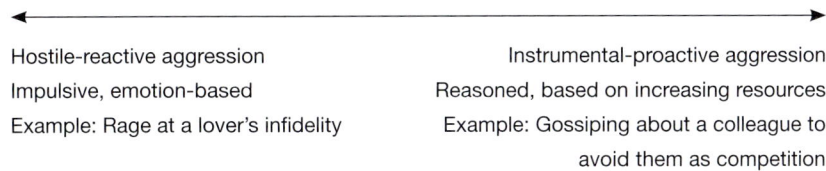

Hostile-reactive aggression	Instrumental-proactive aggression
Impulsive, emotion-based	Reasoned, based on increasing resources
Example: Rage at a lover's infidelity	Example: Gossiping about a colleague to avoid them as competition

to gain resources such as territory, money, self-esteem, or social status (see Berkowitz, 1989; Dodge et al., 1997; Feshbach, 1964).

As shown in Figure 11.1, Bushman and Anderson (2001a) think of hostile and instrumental aggression as a continuum anchored at one end by our brain's automatic impulses (hostile aggression) and at the other by reasoned, purposeful responses (instrumental aggression).

Typology 4: Microaggressions

The final typology is controversial.

Microaggressions have been defined as brief and "everyday" types of "verbal, behavioral, and environmental indignities . . . that communicate hostile, derogatory, or negative slights and insults" (Sue, 2010, p. 5). Microaggressions are said to be the result of subtle or covert prejudice and discrimination (Wang et al., 2011).

Examples might be asking an Asian American if they were born in the United States or refusing to call a transgender person by their preferred name or pronouns. You might hold more tightly to a purse when a person of color gets in an elevator. A professor could tell female students that they might not be suited for majors in the sciences, math, or technology. Microaggressions are each small, but a lifetime of them can really hurt (see Chapter 9).

A typology of three forms of microaggressions was developed by Sue and colleagues (Sue, 2010; Sue et al., 2007):

- Microinsults: Rude statements that demean someone's heritage (e.g., asking Latinx students if they are legal citizens; refusing to sit next to someone wearing a headscarf on an airplane)

- Microassaults: Behaviors meant to psychologically harm and/or insult someone (e.g., calling someone by a racial slur; spray-painting hate symbols such as a swastika on their property)

- Microinvalidations: Statements or behaviors that invalidate the target's feelings on an individual or group level (e.g., telling a person of color that you don't "see color"; telling an LGBTQ person that they need therapy)

Derald Wing Sue (2017, p. 170) asserts that we must pay attention to subjective microaggressions. "Microaggressions are about experiential reality and about listening to the voices of those most oppressed." His argument is persuasive because it is raw and urgent: Real people are suffering from microaggressions while academics debate relatively trivial issues about terminology, the motivation behind microaggressions, and what to do about them.

Why are microaggressions controversial? Social scientists still haven't decided exactly what they are, why they occur, or how they affect their targets. Science also hasn't found a particularly valid or reliable intervention to stop or prevent them from happening (see Lilienfeld, 2007, 2017). This is one area of our field where we need you, the rising generation of psychologically literate citizens (see Dunn, 2013).

Microaggressions: Subtle behaviors or insults that marginalize or negatively stereotype group members. They include microinsults, microassaults, and microinvalidations.

Putting Them Together: The General Aggression Model (GAM)

The content of these typologies overlaps.

Microaggressions, for example, often overlap with indirect, nonverbal forms of aggression. Fortunately, these (and other) typologies are integrated into a coherent understanding of aggression called the **General Aggression Model (GAM)**. The GAM unites biological, social, and cognitive theories to explain aggression by recognizing that aggression is a developmental process.

Each factor is more or less influential at different stages of aggression (Anderson & Bushman, 2002; Anderson & Carnagey, 2004; DeWall et al., 2011). Anderson and Bushman (2018) identified major theories integrated into the General Aggression Model, some of which are covered in other parts of this book (including social learning, scripts, excitation transfer, and more).

The GAM describes how any given episode of aggression develops over three phases: (1) inputs, (2) routes, and (3) outcomes (see Figure 11.2). "Inputs" are factors going on in the immediate environment, including biological, environmental, psychological, and social factors. Just like Lewin suggested in his famous equation, those inputs can be from the situation or from the person/people there. It includes the people's values, personalities, goals, and so on, as well as situational cues such as whether weapons are in the room, whether the people have just been frustrated, and so on.

FIGURE 11.2

The three phases of the General Aggression Model.

Source: Adapted from Anderson and Bushman (2002).

"Routes" are how the inputs are cognitively processed and the psychological state created in each person's mind. What mood is created? Do people feel provoked? Do they interpret the situation as hostile? Finally, "outcomes" are the behavioral actions taken by the people involved. They can be either impulsive or thoughtful, using heuristics, logic, or a combination of both.

In sum, the GAM notes that aggressive outcomes are the result of person and situational factors (inputs) combining to influence cognitive interpretations (routes) of a given situation. We'll come back to this model in a few minutes; for now, know that it's increasing in popularity as a nicely structured way to think about aggression from a "big picture" perspective.

The Persistence of Aggression

Aggression always has been part of the human story—and that's not likely to change.

For example, we see disturbing cruelty in ancient religious texts, evidence of violence in archeological digs, and industrialized killing in recent history. Let's consider each briefly.

Ancient Aggression

Episodes of brutal social aggression are reported in books that many people revere as holy.

Many view religion as an opportunity to promote human goodness. Hinduism and Buddhism, in particular, have relatively strong traditions and texts that encourage

General Aggression Model (GAM): The theory that aggression is a developmental process including biological responses to the environment, cognitive processing, and decisions about how to behave.

nonviolence. However, sociologist Charles Selengut's (2017) *Sacred Fury* exposes how religious texts can sometimes justify violence:

> Religion has another side: a sense that its truth is so correct and so divinely ordered and universal that all peoples must follow it. . . . The history and scriptures of the world's religions tell stories of violence and war as they talk of peace and love. (p. vii)

Both the Old and New Testaments of the Christian Bible, for example, frequently express commandments to sacrifice, knife, stone, and burn people. Examples are offering daughters to be raped by a mob, commandments about plucking out eyes, and cutting off various body parts (see Genesis 19, 22; Deuteronomy 22; and Matthew 5). The Koran also justifies violence with a commandment about how to deal with the enemies of Islam. "Fight them. Allah will punish them by your hands and bring them to disgrace and assist you against them and heal the hearts of a believing people." Selengut (2017, p. 35) recognizes that human insults, economic envy, and widespread injustice often inspire religious justifications for violence. Unfortunately, many people try to use ancient rules to justify modern aggression.

Archeological discoveries of weapons also reveal the long history of human aggression. In 1991, two hikers in the Italian Alps stumbled over "one of the most sensational archeological discoveries ever" (Baroni & Orombelli, 1996). The almost perfectly preserved 5,300-year-old skeleton of a man came to be known as the "Iceman." The Iceman died with a dagger in his right hand, the preserved blood of two other people on his body, a bow and quiver with 14 arrows by his side—and a 1-inch arrowhead that had entered through his back (see Buss, 2005).

Buss and Duntley (2006) also described the discovery of 59 skeletons in an Egyptian cemetery, estimated to be 12,000 to 14,000 years old. Almost half the skeletons had embedded stone projectiles indicating violent deaths, particularly of the male victims. Large collections of stone axe heads have been discovered at sites occupied by our ancestors. These primitive peoples probably stockpiled these axe heads to use as weapons (Clarkson, 2010). Human-to-human aggression stretches as far back in time as our historical indicators allow us to see.

FIGURE 11.3

Number of deaths in three historic events. As time progresses, the efficiency of killing during war has increased.

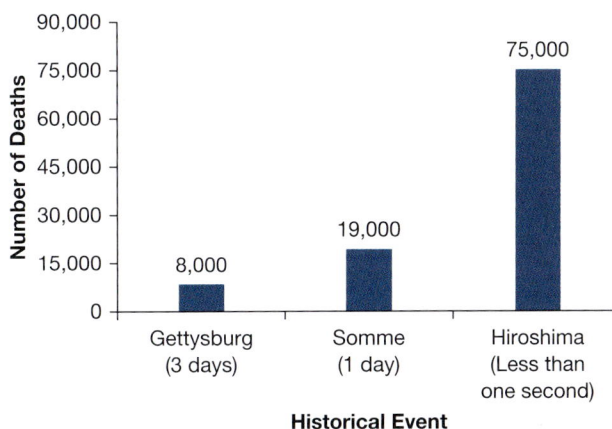

The Efficiency of Modern Weapons

Humans have become efficient killers.

At the Battle of Gettysburg in 1863, it required 3 days to kill approximately 8,000 Union and Confederate soldiers. Most deaths occurred in hand-to-hand combat or from gun blasts at close range. Many others died later from infected wounds.

On the first day of the Battle of the Somme in 1916, it required only 1 day to kill approximately 19,000 British soldiers. Most died from machine guns positioned about 200 hundred yards (185 m) away. It was killing with industrial efficiency.

Near the end of World War II in 1945, it required less than 1 second to vaporize approximately 75,000 Japanese soldiers and civilians. The *Enola Gay* was flying approximately 5 miles above the Earth when it dropped the atomic bomb named *Little Boy* on the city of Hiroshima (see Figure 11.3). Two of these super-destructive bombs ended World War II.

We are far more efficient killers than our ancestors, but our aggressive impulses do not appear to have changed. Modern stockpiles include nuclear devices rather than axe heads (see Figure 11.4).

FIGURE 11.4

Estimated global nuclear warhead arsenals in 2016. Do Russia and the United States need approximately 7,000 nuclear warheads each?

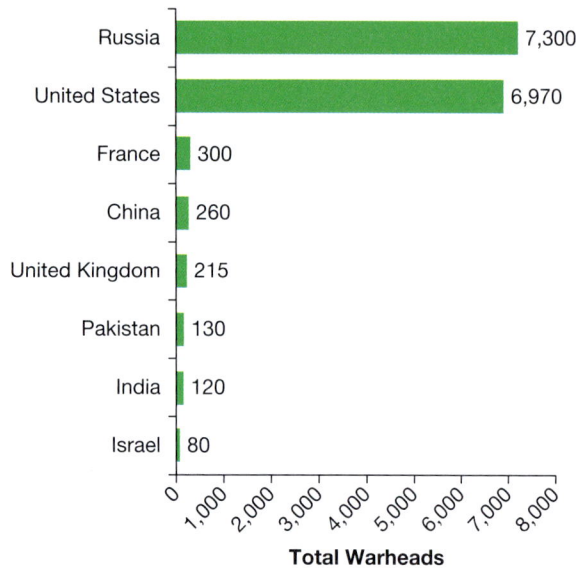

Source: Created using data from Chuck (2016).

Aggression Tends to Escalate: Stages of Provocation

What can we do to check our own destructive impulses?

One promising approach is to first recognize how aggression develops. The **escalation of aggression effect** describes an upward spiral of increasingly aggressive exchanges from which the antagonists are seemingly unable to free themselves (Goldstein et al., 1975). You can see the routine escalation of aggression all around you.

For example, based on film footage, Russell (2008) observed that fights between sports fans often have "exceedingly trivial beginnings, . . . a stare, or perhaps a gesture" (p. 19). Zillmann's (1994) three **stages of provocation model** (see Table 11.2) describes how thoughts (cognition), feelings, and behaviors collectively contribute to the escalation of aggression.

In Stage 1, provocation doesn't lead to particularly aggressive responses. Our cognitive response is annoyance. It's no big deal.

Escalation of aggression effect: The tendency for aggression to spiral and increase in a situation.

Stages of provocation model: Proposes that thoughts, feelings, and behaviors collectively contribute to the escalation of aggression in three stages.

TABLE 11.2

Zillmann's Stages of Provocation

	STAGE 1	STAGE 2	STAGE 3
Cognition	Irritated, but capable of good judgment	Angry thoughts and less empathic	Biased conclusions, no empathy, with illusions of power
Emotional arousal	Low to moderate	Moderate to high	Extremely high
Behavior	Cautiously assertive with self-control	Strongly assertive, unyielding, hostile	Impulsive, explosive, and irresponsible

Source: Adapted from Zillmann (1994).

In Stage 2, we experience angrier thoughts. We become mildly aroused physiologically and emotionally. Our heart beats a bit faster with mild anger. We may become more assertive in our verbal interaction.

By Stage 3, our thoughts are clouded by biased perceptions and overreactions. Our physiological and emotional response is to feel a surge of adrenaline and rage. Our behavioral response is explosive physical or verbal attack. We intend to harm the person who "started it" or "deserves to be taught a lesson."

Notice the escalation of aggression in the Robbers Cave Experiment (Sherif et al., 1961) described in Chapter 9. In just 2 weeks, two groups of 11-year-old boys escalated from competition in baseball and tug-of-war to marked territories, mud-smeared faces, stockpiles of stones, and potentially lethal weapons (rocks in socks).

But things turned during the third week of summer camp. A few strategic interventions based on superordinate goals deescalated the aggression. The boys all returned home with, apparently, mostly happy memories of their summer camp experience. Let's end this section of the chapter with more discussion about the decline of aggression.

The Statistical Surprise: The Decline of Worldwide Aggression

Here's a surprise.

There has been a persistent, long-term decline in worldwide violence. Do you find that hard to believe? Our impressions of the present are biased by the vividness of instant communications, high-resolution digital photos, and the ability to see modern conflicts on live television. This chapter even primed the idea of increasing violence and efficiency in killing (such as the escalation shown in Figure 11.1).

FIGURE 11.5

Homicide rates throughout Europe from 1300–2010. Homicides per capita have dramatically decreased around the world over the past several centuries. Are humans becoming less aggressive as technology and education increase?

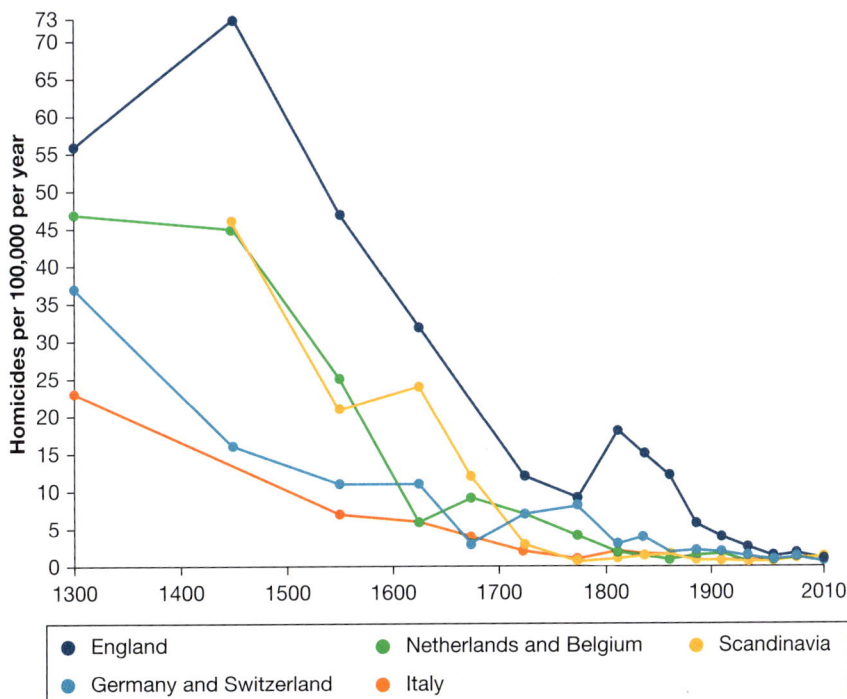

Source: Roser (2017).

However, the book *The Better Angels of Our Nature: Why Violence Has Declined* offers a social psychological version of hope (Pinker, 2011). This research into worldwide violence suggests that, over time, humans have become more intelligent—and with increased intelligence comes a decreased need for violent aggression (see Figure 11.5). So, although we have become far more *efficient* at killing one another, our *actual* killing of one another through homicides, genocide, wars, terrorism, and the like has been decreasing.

Think about aggression at a personal level: Do you tend to have aggressive responses to others? The next part of this chapter discusses different explanations for why we are aggressive—but the final section discusses how we might continue to manage and decrease violent behaviors.

THE MAIN IDEAS

- Aggression, intentional harm to others, can be defined and categorized using typologies. Examples break aggression down by content, form, and motivation. Another discusses forms of microaggression. Finally, the General Aggression Model (GAM) suggests aggression arises from personal and situational factors plus cognitive processing.

- Ancient religious texts and archeological discoveries show that humans have been aggressive for thousands of years. The escalation of aggression effect is an upward spiral of increasingly aggressive thoughts and/or actions; it can be broken into three stages that progress toward more extreme reactions.

- While humans have become more efficient in killing over time, data indicate that interpersonal human aggression has decreased overall in the past several centuries; this may be due to increased intelligence.

CRITICAL THINKING

- Educators are increasingly concerned about cyberbullying in children. Cyberbullying occurs when aggression takes place through social media (such as mean messages posted to Facebook), email, Snapchat, or other online venues. When you consider this type of aggression, which category in Buss's typology would you say applies and why?

- Of the four typologies discussed in this section, plus the GAM, which typology do you find the most useful, interesting, or applicable to real-world examples? Explain why you prefer that typology over the others.

- In Pinker's (2011) book, he argues that in humans, aggression is negatively correlated with intelligence, education, and reasoned thought. Based on your own knowledge of history, do you agree or disagree and why? Provide at least one concrete example to support your opinion. Also consider this question on an individual level—do you see this trend in certain individual people?

WHY ARE HUMANS AGGRESSIVE?

>> **LO 11.2:** Distinguish among biological, cultural, and situational explanations of human aggression.

Check out YouTube's video, "Top 10 Most Violent Celebrity Outbursts."

It highlights physical outbursts from Russell Brand, Chris Martin, Zsa Zsa Gabor, Russell Crowe, Eminem, Alec Baldwin, Gary Coleman, Conor McGregor, Solange Knowles, and Björk. Why did these celebrities lose their cool? Why does anyone?

This section answers the core question "Why are humans aggressive?" by

(1) explaining biological influences on aggression,

(2) reviewing evidence for cultural explanations, and

(3) describing experiments that indicate the power of situations.

Biological Influences on Aggression

The evolutionary goal of aggression is simple: Survive so you can reproduce.

Genetic determinism proposes that a gene's influence alone determines behavioral outcomes—a biological fate. Genetic determinism is a compelling force. Monarch butterflies, for example, fly to the same place in Mexico every year. The butterfly who starts the journey never arrives. It takes four generations of Monarch butterflies to complete just one annual journey (see Reppert & de Roode, 2018). But humans are more complicated than butterflies.

Four Responses to Threat: Fight, Flight, Freeze, Befriend

We inherited four possible aggression-related biological responses whenever we experienced threats to our survival (see Table 11.3).

The first two responses, "fight" and "flight" (Taylor & Gonzaga, 2006), are the result of a rush of adrenaline. Both involve high-energy action. A third, nonaggressive survival strategy also evolved: freezing until enemies or predators pass them by. Many species practice camouflaging and staying absolutely still to avoid danger. Shelley Taylor's (2002) book *The Tending Instinct* frames the scientific argument for a fourth survival strategy: "tend and befriend" for security purposes.

A "tend and befriend" response is common among social animals such as honeybees, prairie voles, and squirrel monkeys (see Taylor, 2002, pp. 91–92). In human societies, it is an impulse sometimes favored by people who are more likely, for example, to form clubs or create events around food, conversation, and mutual support. Several examples support the notion that tend and befriend might be more common in women than in other genders.

The Mundurucu women of Brazil, for example, travel in friendship groups for mutual protection (Murphy & Murphy, 1974). When women in the Wape area in Papua, New Guinea, hear the sounds of an escalating domestic argument, they have been known to "descend upon the house and stand around it until the woman joins them outside" (Mitchell, 1990, p. 148). Women who form bonds with other women are more likely to survive a wide variety of potentially aggressive threats.

Genghis Khan (1167–1227) stated, "The greatest pleasure is to vanquish your enemies, to chase them before you, to rob them of their wealth, to see their near and dear bathed in tears, to ride their horses and sleep on the white bellies of their wives and daughters."

World History Archive/Alamy Stock Photo

TABLE 11.3
Four Instinctual Responses to Threat
Fight
Flight
Freeze
Tend & Befriend

Animals—including humans—appear to have four biological responses to threat: fight, flight, freeze, and tend and befriend.

iStockPhoto/AndreAnita

Genetic determinism: The idea that genetic influence alone determines behavioral outcomes.

Low Heart Rates

This biological predictor of aggression is surprising.

We can predict extreme adolescent antisocial and aggressive behavior by measuring a child's resting heart rate (Patrick & Verona, 2007). Wadsworth (1976) studied 1,800 British schoolboys and found that a low resting heart rate at age 11 was a fairly strong predictor of delinquency at age 21. Subsequent *meta-analyses* have confirmed this counterintuitive negative correlation (Ortiz & Raine, 2004).

You might think that a low heart rate would mean that someone is not very excitable and therefore prone to be peaceful. That makes sense, but it doesn't fit the data story. And the data always win out in the end. Here are two possible explanations.

First, perhaps children with a low resting heart rate are "less sensitive to the negative consequences of their behavior." That could make them less likely to develop a moral conscience. They might be less responsive to their environment—and less empathetic toward others. Second, these children also might be more sensation seeking. They're bored, so they use aggression to create their own excitement (Hammerton et al., 2018; Patrick & Verona, 2007, p. 114).

Second, a lower moral conscience and lack of impulse control are symptoms of antisocial personality disorder. In extreme forms, the antisocial personality is associated with serial killers and people who torture animals. Notice the scary details and the tie to low heart rates in a study with perpetrators of domestic violence in the Spotlight on Research Methods feature.

SPOTLIGHT ON RESEARCH METHODS

Heart Rate and Domestic Violence

This insight into aggression was discovered by accident.

The insight is the mysterious connection between people's resting heart rates and violent tendencies. Jacobson and Gottman (1998) were studying perpetrators of domestic violence. They recruited participants in the Seattle, Washington, area by posting fliers asking for people to participate in a study on relationship conflict—and both couple members had to attend the sessions.

They first selected couples who admitted to domestic violence—including some cases of severe abuse. All the couples were heterosexual, and the man was the primary abuser. (This is not always the case; see Johnson, 1995; Leone et al., 2007.) Then they asked the couple to get into an argument! Imagine being part of this strange study.

During the conflict, the researchers observed the men's physiological arousal through heart rate monitors and galvanic skin response (sweaty palms). Their *hypothesis* was that as the argument got more heated, the men's physiological arousal would also go up. They predicted a *positive correlation*.

Results confirmed the hypothesis for about 80% of the participants. Jacobson and Gottman called these men the "pit bulls," because their increasing anger and aggression were obvious (note, the actual dog breed may not be any more aggressive than several other breeds). The men would yell, their faces would become red, and their posture leaned forward and clearly expressed anger. The surprise, however, was that about 20% of men showed the opposite pattern: a *negative correlation*. For these abusers, as conflicts with their wives or girlfriends progressed, their physiological responses got calmer and more peaceful.

Here's the scary part: The calmer, lower-heart-rate men were the most abusive. Jacobson and Gottman labeled these men "cobras," because they sat back calmly, waiting to strike. Their calm demeanor masked more extreme violent tendencies, a pattern also found in psychopaths and people with antisocial personality disorder.

This next observation may be even scarier: The wives of cobras were less successful in leaving their abusive partners, compared to pit bulls. Rationally, that's not easy to understand. But emotionally, perhaps these women understood just how scary their partners could become. For more information, see the mini-chapter on Social Psychology and Relationship Violence.

The pit bull may appear more aggressive, but the cobra is calmly waiting to strike with a deadly attack.

Alcohol

Alcohol consumption: Unlike a low resting heartrate, this biological predictor of aggression is not surprising.

Basketball player Charles Barkley was in a bar when a local man, Jorge Lugo, tossed some ice cubes at him. Barley responded by throwing Lugo out the window (see Griskevicius et al., 2009). More than any other illicit drug, alcohol is implicated in aggressive behavior (Kretschmar & Flannery, 2007). After throwing him through the window, the *Washington Post* ("Barkley Is Arrested," 1997) reported what Barkley said next: "You got what you deserve. You don't respect me. I hope you're hurt."

Alcohol affects GABA, the brain's main inhibitory neurotransmitter. After a few drinks, things that normally seem to be a bad idea suddenly might not seem so bad—such as a bar fight. The **alcohol disinhibition hypothesis** proposes that alcohol interferes with the brain's ability to suppress violent behavior by lowering anxiety and harming our ability to accurately assess a situation. However, disinhibition is not the only way that alcohol influences aggression.

In one study, intoxicated people had more trouble seeing their romantic partner's point of view in a conflict (MacDonald et al., 2000). Apparently, a soggy brain has difficulty resolving even minor disagreements. And that's only the start of the alcohol-violence connection. Among 1,401 women surveyed in a family practice clinic, 20% reported currently experiencing some type of intimate partner violence.

Most of the time, these were cases of physical or sexual violence. Not surprisingly, substance abuse was the strongest predictor of that violence (Coker et al., 2000). More optimistically, aggression is less likely among recovering alcoholics (Murphy & O'Farrell, 1996). But it also confirms the danger of alcohol as a predictor of aggression.

Testosterone

The (mostly) male hormone testosterone influences aggression.

However, the connection between testosterone and physical aggression is stronger among nonhuman animals than among humans. In an early (1939) testosterone

The stereotype of a bar fight may come from the tendency of people to be more aggressive after consuming alcohol.

Alcohol disinhibition hypothesis: The idea that alcohol interferes with the brain's ability to suppress violent behavior by lowering anxiety and harming the ability to accurately assess a situation.

study, low-ranking hens were administered testosterone and then began crowing—and acting—like roosters. In fact, the social order of the entire flock began to change (Allee et al., 1939).

Since then, two meta-analyses of the many studies about testosterone and aggression have found a strong *positive correlation* in nonhuman animals and a smaller (but still positive) correlation in humans (Archer et al., 1998; Book et al., 2001; Knickmeyer & Baron-Cohen, 2006). A third meta-analysis by Archer (2004) focused on gender differences in real-world settings and with a more cross-cultural sample. Archer found that early in their lives, boys tend to be more physically aggressive than girls, but aggression peaked in both men and women when they were in their 20s (when testosterone is at its highest point).

Björkqvist's (2018) review noted that the effects of hormones appear to change over one's lifetime. For example, there were higher-than-average levels of testosterone among a psychiatric group of older boys with disruptive behavior (ages 9–11; Chance et al., 2000). Testosterone levels among female inmates in a maximum-security state prison were also related to aggressive dominance. However, both aggression and testosterone declined as inmates got older.

For ethical reasons, we can't study aggression using a true *experiment with random assignment* to groups. Because of that, we can't say "testosterone causes aggression." However, there are other strategies for testing the connections between testosterone and sex differences in aggression. For example, the increasing number of transgender individuals receiving hormone treatments (both male-to-female and female-to-male) creates some interesting research opportunities.

A Dutch research team measured the aggression, sexual motivation, and other cognitive abilities of both groups (Van Goozen et al., 1995). Increases in testosterone were *positively correlated* with several variables: increased aggressive inclinations, likelihood of becoming sexually aroused, and some spatial abilities—a pattern that reversed among people who were suppressing testosterone.

That said, neurologist Sapolsky points out the subtleties and misunderstanding of the simple conclusion "testosterone = aggression." In his groundbreaking book *Behave: The Biology of Humans at Our Best and Worst* (2017), he provides evidence that testosterone only increases aggression when someone feels challenged. At other times, testosterone prompts "whatever behaviors are needed to maintain status" (p. 106). For example, more testosterone can actually make people more *generous* if their charity is publicly praised and helps their reputation.

So instead of saying that testosterone makes us aggressive, it might be more accurate to say that it makes us competitive—and that sometimes being the nicest person in the room wins us the social rewards we seek.

Interactions: Aggression Is the Result of Multiple Influences

"Nature versus nurture" is a false dichotomy.

It's almost never just one or the other; the issue is really how biological and environmental influences interact with each other. Aggression is the result of multiple interacting variables. For example, what is true for one group or culture about aggression may not be true for another group. Or the variables that influence aggression at one stage of life may not have any effect just a few years later.

One interesting example is how our "biological clocks" influence the form of aggression we choose. As teenagers mature, they start to prefer indirect and verbal aggression as potential mating strategies (Lee et al., 2018). Both men and women say that when they want their potential mate to commit, they're more likely to gossip about rivals, calling them promiscuous (Wyckoff et al., 2019). Adolescents whose parents have bad emotion regulation are more likely to be either a perpetrator or a victim of teen dating violence like sexual aggression (Ahonen & Loeber, 2016).

The link between biological factors and other factors, such as cultural or situational, is complicated—so let's consider those other factors a bit more now.

Cultural Influences on Aggression

Consider the following examples of how culture might encourage aggression:

- In countries where football (soccer in the United States) is popular—such as England—a culture of "football hooliganism" promotes aggressive, unruly, unpredictable, destructive behavior. Riot police resort to body armor, tear gas, dogs, water cannons, and armored vehicles. Intense rivalries have caused deaths of fans, police, and innocent bystanders (Podnar, 2007; Wainwright, 2015).

- The Yanomamö tribe of South America is a particularly violent group in a "state of chronic warfare" with other local tribes (Chagnon, 1983). They sing songs about killing and how they "hunger for flesh" (p. 183).

- American educator and documentarian Jackson Katz warns about a U.S. culture that creates a "crisis of masculinity." Young boys are expected to be aggressive, misogynistic, and homophobic; statistics and examples are highlighted in his popular film *Tough Guise* (Jhally et al., 1999).

Culture helps explain group differences in aggression. Culture can be on a national scale or smaller—like the culture of a given school. For example, some students may be plagued by a school culture that is relatively accepting of cyberbullying. Often cyberbullying occurs on social media sites (see Roland & Munthe, 1989/2017; Vandebosch & Van Cleemput, 2008; Wolke & Lereya, 2015). This form of aggression can be greatly reduced when school officials or student peers make it known that it's not acceptable behavior—in other words, they can create a culture of respect and safety for all students.

Previous chapters have pointed out a variety of cultural differences. This section relies on the insights from experiments and other social psychological tools to specifically examine three cultural influences: cultures of honor, gender roles, and sports-related violence.

In England, concerns about the aggression of "football hooligans" are frequently discussed in media outlets.

REUTERS/Pawel Kopczynski

Cultures of Honor

How offended would you be if somebody bumped into you and then called you an insulting name?

That was the unusual *field experiment* conducted at the University of Michigan. The participants did not know, of course, that their "bump" and insult were part of experimental procedures (Cohen et al., 1996). The men who had been deliberately bumped came from either the northern or southern regions of the United States. After being bumped and called a name, the men from the South were more likely to

(a) think their masculine reputation had been threatened,

(b) be emotionally upset (measured by their cortisol levels),

(c) become physiologically primed for aggression, and

(d) engage in more aggressive and dominant behaviors.

A **culture of honor** is one in which insults are perceived as threats to one's reputation. Often, this comes through specifically as men feeling that their masculinity is being questioned. These perceived threats sometimes result in aggression. One place where cultures of honor are seen in the United States is in Southern states (like Texas, Alabama, and Georgia). For example, two weeks after the 9/11 tragedies, students at the University of Oklahoma desired the deaths of the terrorists responsible more than students from Penn State, even though Penn State is geographically much closer to where the attacks occurred (including the crashed flight in Shanksville, Pennsylvania; Barnes et al., 2012).

The problem isn't geography; it's the personal and cultural values that can vary both within and between cultures. Some cultures teach that violence is manly, others that it is a sign of weakness and insecurity. Within a culture of honor, the socially appropriate responses are displays of dominance and aggression. Think of the celebrities from the YouTube video mentioned earlier who acted out due to perceived threats to their wives or girlfriends.

Saucier et al. (2016) explored the different values supported in a culture of honor; see Table 11.4. The values supported by cultures of honor are part of another societal problem called "toxic masculinity" (e.g., Kirby & Kirby, 2019; Parent et al., 2019), the idea that cultural expectations for boys and men are poisonous to their mental health and well-being.

TABLE 11.4

Values in a Culture of Honor

Masculine courage (e.g., men should be able to take pain)
Pride in manhood (e.g., men should be independent)
Socialization (e.g., men with honor stand up to bullies)
Virtue (e.g., fighting is admirable if done out of honor)
Protection (e.g., men should protect women)
Provocation/insult (e.g., men should not accept insults)
Family and community bonds (e.g., family is a man's first priority)

Source: Adapted from Saucier et al. (2016).

Men living in cultures of honor report a tendency to respond with physical aggression whenever their masculinity is threatened (Saucier et al., 2015). This trend happens around the world. For example, sociologist Venkatesh (1997) studied male gangs in Chicago housing projects. He found a similar culture of honor in densely populated (northern) Chicago housing projects—that police seldom patrolled. Within Latinx samples, participants who endorsed culture of honor values were more likely to accept relationship violence (Dietrich & Schuett, 2013). In one study of Brazilian inmates, most of the men convicted of murder said that their motivation had been "honor" (Souza et al., 2011).

You can see how culture of honor values are defined and measured—and you can score yourself on this scale—by referring to the What's My Score? feature. Cultures of honor are closely tied to gendered beliefs, and the next section discusses how gender roles influence aggression on a larger scale.

Culture of honor: A culture where individuals, especially men, tend to perceive insults as a threat to their masculinity and often engage in aggression.

Measuring Belief in a Culture of Honor

Instructions: Consider each statement and mark your level of agreement using this scale:

1	2	3	4	5	6	7
Disagree very strongly						Agree very strongly

___ 1. It is very important for a man to act bravely.

___ 2. A man should not be afraid to fight.

___ 3. It is important for a man to be able to take pain.

___ 4. It is important for a man to be more masculine than other men.

___ 5. A man should be embarrassed if someone calls him a wimp.

___ 6. A man should be expected to fight for himself.

___ 7. If a man does not defend his wife, he is not a very strong man.

___ 8. If your son got into a fight, you would be proud that he stood up for himself.

___ 9. As a child, you were taught that boys should defend girls.

___10. You would praise a man who reacted aggressively to an insult.

___ 11. Physical aggression is always admirable and acceptable.

___ 12. Physical violence is the most honorable way to defend yourself.

___ 13. A man should stand up for a female who is in his family or is a close friend.

___ 14. It is a male's responsibility to protect his family.

___ 15. If a man's wife is insulted, his manhood is insulted.

___ 16. If a man is insulted, his manhood is insulted.

___ 17. It is important for a man to be loyal to his family.

___ 18. A man's family should be his number one priority.

___ 19. It is important to interact with other members of your community.

___ 20. It is a man's responsibility to respect his family.

Scoring: Add up your answers to get your total score, which can range from 20 to 140 (higher numbers mean more endorsement of the values in a culture of honor).

Note that the original scale includes more items and has subscales for each aspect of the culture of honor (e.g., masculine courage, pride in manhood).

Source: Adapted from Saucier et al. (2016).

Gender Roles and Aggression

Archer (2006) studied the struggle for female empowerment.

At a global social level, female empowerment is tied to how frequently women are victimized by aggression. Using *archival data,* Archer (2006) found that as gender equality and individualism increased within a culture over time, female victimization decreased: a *negative correlation.* Less female victimization is good news, and Archer's findings produced even more nuanced insights into *how* culture influences aggression. Cultures that value individualism (more than collectivism) experience less female victimization, along with slightly more *male* victimization.

That last part might surprise you—why would more individualistic cultures have slightly more male victimization? Are some "liberated" women "getting even"? Archer also found that sexist attitudes and approval of wife beating increased women's victimization (no surprise there) but were *not* associated with *general* levels of violent crime. In some cultures, apparently beating your wife was okay—but being aggressive in general was not. Carefully defined gender roles within particular cultures influenced how aggression was expressed.

The link between gender and culture is complicated; Sweden is an interesting case study. The employment rate of women in Sweden is the highest in the European Union.

In addition, women in Sweden gain more education, have higher salaries, and are more likely to be board members of companies than the average woman in Europe ("The Current Situation," 2013).

At the same time, Sweden is the rape capital of Europe ("Case Closed," 2010); there are 46 reports of rape for every 100,000 Swedish citizens. This is twice the rate in the United Kingdom and four times the rate of Germany and France. Some people believe that women's relative equality in Swedish culture creates a "backlash" when some men are threatened and feel the need to aggress toward them as a way of regaining power.

Lifetime number of aggressive acts recalled. Men slightly favor direct aggression; women strongly prefer indirect aggression.

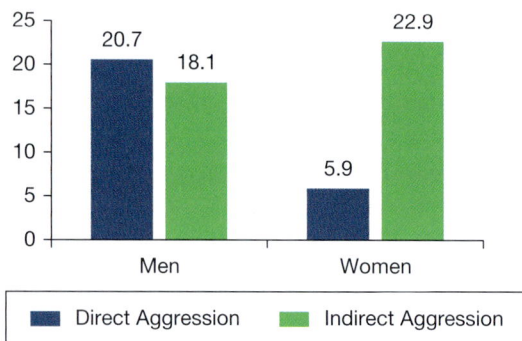

Source: Griskevicius et al. (2009).

Head impacts per 1,000 AEs per practice and game on a youth football team.

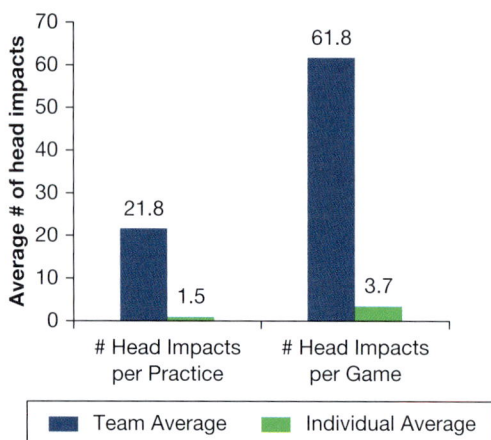

Source: Wong et al. (2014).

Both status and mating motives interact to influence how men and women are aggressive. For most men, status and mating motives lead to an increase in direct (face-to-face) aggression—but only when they know that other men are watching (Griskevicius et al., 2009). For women, status and mating motives lead to increases in *in*direct aggression (like social exclusion or giving someone the "cold shoulder"). The same pattern (see Figure 11.6) emerged when they asked male and female college students to recall their personal experiences of aggression. The frequency and types of aggression experienced by men tended toward direct aggression and women toward indirect aggression.

Björkqvist (2018) found that physical aggression was more common among males. However, different types of verbal aggression were practiced by men and women. Both men and women seemed to benefit because aggression raised their social status. It seems that men and women have figured out how to use certain types of aggression to their social advantage.

Sports Culture

Many sports require participants to risk serious injury.

Auto racing, boxing, American football, gymnastics, and soccer all require participants to risk serious injury. More and more attention is going toward the possibility of athletes receiving multiple extremely dangerous concussions; the most concussions occur in football, hockey, and women's soccer.

For example, Figure 11.7 displays the average number of head impacts per practice and per game experienced by one youth team (ages 7–14) practicing and playing American football. Head impacts, of course, can lead to concussions. Figure 11.8 reports the number of medically diagnosed concussions per 1,000 athletic exposures (AEs; 1 AE = one practice or game). In the absence of medical personnel capable of making a diagnosis at each practice and game, these data are probably severe underestimates of the actual incidence rate of concussions experienced.

There are now more rules about what to do and how to treat a player who may have suffered a concussion. But sports-related aggression extends far beyond the rules that regulate those competitions.

Perpetrators and Targets. There are a variety of positive benefits to participating in athletic activities (Findlay & Coplan, 2008).

There are even potential benefits to fans when they closely identify with a team (Wann, 2006). These benefits will continue to be pursued given centuries of enthusiastic, cross-cultural participation in athletic activities. But athletic competition can also create a dangerous subculture of aggression. Athletes, their support staff, their coaches, and their fans have all displayed purposeful aggression that undermines the higher ideals of athletic competition.

Prior to the 1994 Olympics, figure skater Tonya Harding apparently escalated her aggression from competition on the ice to aggression in a hallway. She arranged for her former husband to cripple the knee of her rival, Nancy Kerrigan, with a telescopic baton. Mike Tyson bit off 1 inch of Evander Holyfield's right ear during a boxing match. This kind of aggression occurs across cultures.

In France, Christophe Fauviau confessed to spiking the water bottles of 27 of his daughter's tennis opponents—one defeated rival died after falling asleep while driving. In Brisbane, Australia, a 19-year-old female referee officiating a 13-and-under rugby competition was chased into the dressing room by angry parents. Tennis star Monica Seles was stabbed in the back during a match by a fan of her rival Steffi Graf. Coaches, parents, players, and fans need to understand how easily sports passions can escalate into overt hostility.

FIGURE 11.8

Number of medically diagnosed concussions per 1,000 AEs.

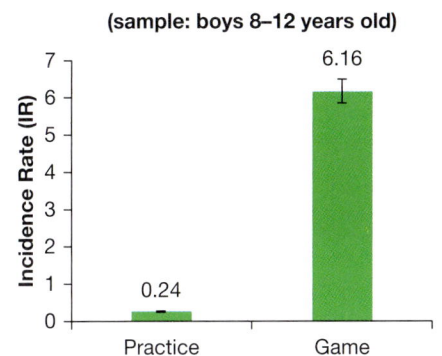

Source: Kontos et al. (2013).

The Color Black: A Cultural Cue for Aggressive Behavior.

The word "black" is loaded with mostly negative prejudices.

Frank and Gilovich (1988) pointed out that the Great Depression began on "Black Thursday." It is a bad thing to be "blackballed," "blacklisted," or "blackmailed." Baseball suffered through a "dark" chapter when a betting scandal "blackened" baseball's reputation in the infamous "Black Sox" affair. We even eat white angel food cake and black devil's food cake.

These observations led Frank and Gilovich (1988) to analyze 17 years of penalty records in the National Football League and the National Hockey League (another *archival study*). They focused their attention on teams in black uniforms. Both experimental and archival studies found consistently high rankings in penalties for teams switching to black uniforms or already wearing black uniforms. We either see or wear black uniforms and then expect violence. Why?

Some might argue that modern culture's connection between the color and perceptions of aggression is tied to racism against African Americans. But priests, Hassidic Jews, and stereotypical New York actors don't seem to behave more aggressively because of their black clothing. The meaning of black on a priest conveys a different social meaning than black on a member of the Hell's Angels motorcycle club.

It appears that black cues in the environment, such as black uniforms, take on particular cultural meanings. Unfortunately, this peculiar cultural bias about blackness can be harmful, especially when applied to Black children.

An article titled "The Essence of Innocence" (Goff et al., 2014) showed that Black children are **dehumanized** more than White children. That means a person is perceived as lacking positive human qualities and instead is seen more like an animal or an object. If a Black child is compared to an objectively equal White child, the Black child will be perceived as (1) less innocent, (2) older, (3) more responsible for their actions, and (4) more appropriate targets of police violence.

Bringing the discussion directly back to sports, another study (Wilson et al., 2017) found that photos of African American college quarterbacks are perceived as physically bigger and more "formidable" than White college quarterbacks, even when those photos are matched on actual size, weight, and muscularity.

Sports Can Be a Humanizing Influence.

So far, sports sound bad—but they can also be wonderfully good.

In World War I, trench soldiers were deliberately kept occupied with "football for the men and rugby and cricket for the officers" (Ellis, 1976, p. 142). The original intent of these sports was to emphasize aggression and obedience, but sports ended up having a surprising effect on men from both sides of the war.

Dehumanize: When a human is perceived as lacking positive human qualities and is seen more like an animal or object.

It was called the Christmas Truce of 1914, an expression of mutual goodwill. It was initiated, maintained, and expanded by individuals in the trenches—without permission from high command. One of its highlights was a game of soccer between the Lancashire Fusiliers and a Saxon unit (reportedly won by the Lancashire team 3–2).

The effect of playing soccer against the enemy was sobering. Ellis (1976) observed that "many soldiers were surprised to find that their enemy seemed quite human" (p. 172). An officer from the London Rifle Brigade described their enemy as "jolly good sorts. . . . I now have a very different opinion of the Germans."

In this case, sports competition had supplied a humanizing framework for peace between combatants. Soccer substituted for fighting and was a good-natured way to simply take a day off from the hard work of killing one another. Indeed, the true definition of "good sportsmanship" is an expectation of honoring and respecting your sports rival—the traditional, idealistic view of the international Olympics. Understanding how sports culture both increases and reduces aggression is as fascinating as it is complicated.

Situational Influences on Aggression

Do certain situations just "tick you off"?

For some people, it's careless drivers. For others, the triggering situation can be a perceived microaggression, threat to their manhood, or the success of a rival. Maybe you do something that ticks off others. Are you an aggressive person? Would you know it if you were?

So far, we've discussed two explanations for aggression. First, aggression is a biological instinct or drive that helps us survive. Second, cultural differences influence our behavior. This third explanation explores the power of situations to trigger aggression.

We explore four of the more obvious situational triggers for aggression: war hysteria, copying role models, media violence, and environmental cues. In certain situations, for example, the simple presence of weapons seems to cue thoughts and emotions associated with aggression (see Bushman, 2018).

Situation 1. War Hysteria and Moral Panic

Great crowds of cheering men and women were sending their sons off to war.

The great writer Rudyard Kipling pleaded poetically for the British nation to prepare for what decades later came to be called World War I. At the time, even the energetic movement to grant women the right to vote—so close to victory—was swept aside by war fever. Even many pacifists got caught up in the swell of patriotic aggression.

The peer pressure to join each army was like a swimmer in a riptide. Young women were prerolling bandages to heal any future wounds. Friends enlisted together. Great crowds gathered to send their young men off to war with cheers, tears, and confidence that they would be back very soon (see Remarque, 2013).

War hysteria is a kind of moral panic when a particular group is labeled the enemy, singled out as evil, and portrayed as needing to be punished (Bonn, 2010; Hawdon, 2001). You probably could be swept up in a moral panic. At its most intense, every day witnessed approximately 30,000 volunteers joining the British army (see Hart, 2010, p. 40). For these young men, killing and risking being killed became a courageous necessity in service of a nobler cause (see Hochschild, 2011). That was just one (very powerful) situation that cost approximately 16 million lives.

Propaganda posters from World War I emphasize the "patriotic duty" to become aggressive to fight the enemy during war.

Situation 2. Modeling Aggressive Role Models: The Bobo Doll Studies

A very different kind of fear was salient in the United States after World War II: Television was invading the family home.

Even relatively tame shows took advantage of television's ability to safely portray violence. These were not war documentaries: *Tom and Jerry, Gunsmoke, The Lone Ranger, Have Gun Will Travel,* and even *The Adventures of Superman.* So, understanding the possible effects of viewing violence on television became more urgent.

A Familiar Problem: Correlation Does Not Imply Causation. Psychology students know better than most people that *correlation does not imply causation.*

Assume, for the moment, that there really is a correlation between watching violence on television and behaving violently. We still can't say that watching violence on TV *caused* more violent behavior. Here are two alternative explanations:

- Maybe people who enjoy violent acts want to watch more violence on TV. Causation might be working in the opposite direction.

- Maybe being home alone (without parents) gives children more opportunities to do both (watch adult programming and get into trouble). A third variable involved might be causing the correlation.

A Familiar Solution: Controlled Experiments. As you read in Chapter 2, establishing causality requires *experiments* with things like *control groups, random assignment to condition,* and so on.

Luckily for science, someone rose to that challenge: Albert Bandura. Bandura and his research team (Bandura et al., 1961) devised a laboratory experiment that supplied a room full of toys. One of them was a large, bouncy, clown-faced doll that was weighted at the bottom. Anyone could punch, push, and pull it as many times as they liked, but it would always return to an upright position. If children watched someone on television being aggressive to this doll, called a Bobo doll (because the clown's name was Bobo), would they copy that behavior?

The famous Bobo doll, used by Bandura in his series of studies regarding what situations will lead to children displaying aggressive tendencies.

Replication. Over several studies, different children watched various potential role models on a television.

Adults were the first role models. They modeled aggression for the viewing children by punching and hitting Bobo with a mallet and throwing him in the air. They said things like, "Sock him," "Hit him down," and "Kick him." The experiments randomly assigned children to various conditions that tested how much they would copy the model's behavior (the *dependent variable*).

Study 1: Imitating Adults. In an initial study, one experimental group of little boys and girls watched an adult beat up the Bobo doll. Not surprisingly, when they were given the chance to play in the room of toys, children who had seen the adult displaying aggression toward the doll were more likely to do it themselves, compared to a control group.

Study 2: Imitating Adults on Television. Two years later, they found that aggressive models on television produced the same effects (Bandura et al., 1963a). The adult model was either a man or a woman (the first *independent variable*). The end of the film also showed different consequences to the aggression—a reward, punishment, or nothing at all (the second *independent variable*). Results showed that

- boys were, in general, more aggressive than girls, but that

- both boys and girls were more likely to copy the aggressive behavior they saw in adults when the adult role model was the same sex as themselves, and that

- both boys and girls were more likely to copy the aggression when they saw the adult being rewarded for the behavior.

Study 3: Imitating Children on Television. A third study (Bandura et al., 1963b) clarified *why* children imitated other children on television. These children watched a conflict between two boys: Rocky and Johnny.

Contrasting Experimental Conditions Lead to a Better Hypothesis. In that study (Bandura et al., 1963b), there were two filmed versions of a conflict between two boys.

They both started out the same: Rocky bullies Johnny. Rocky strikes Johnny with a rubber ball, kicks a plastic doll, and shoots darts at Johnny's cars and plastic farm animals. Then Rocky stumbles over Johnny's toys, sits on Johnny, tries to spank him, hits him with a baton, lassos him with a hula hoop, and pulls him to a far corner of the room!

In one experimental condition, the film ends with Johnny seated in a corner while Rocky triumphantly plays with all the toys. Then Rocky helps himself to snacks and happily rides a rocking horse singing, "Hi ho, hi ho, it's off to play I go." Rocky disappears off screen carrying a big bag of loot while an announcer declares Rocky the victor.

It's the same film in the comparison condition, but with a different ending. When Rocky tries to spank Johnny, Johnny turns the tables and thrashes Rocky. This time it is Rocky who flees to the corner while Johnny collects toys in his sack and walks triumphantly away. An announcer comments on Rocky's punishment.

Once again, the boys who saw Rocky being rewarded for his aggression displayed the highest levels of aggression. However, the girls who saw Rocky triumph did not imitate him. Their overall level of aggression was similar to those who had seen Johnny turn the tables and beat up Rocky. For the children in this particular study, gender identification was an important component of role modeling aggression.

Insights From Qualitative Interviews. The researchers asked the children an important question.

Who did they most want to be like: Rocky or Johnny? In the condition where Rocky the bully was rewarded for his aggression, he won big in the eyes of 4-year-olds (see Figure 11.9). They said:

"Rocky is harsh, I be harsh like he was."

"Rough and bossy."

"He whack people."

"He come and snatched Johnny's toys. Get a lot of toys."

"Rocky beat Johnny and chase him and get all the good toys."

"No one would ever get the toys from Rocky."

"He was a fighter. He got all good toys."

FIGURE 11.9

Who do you want to be like?

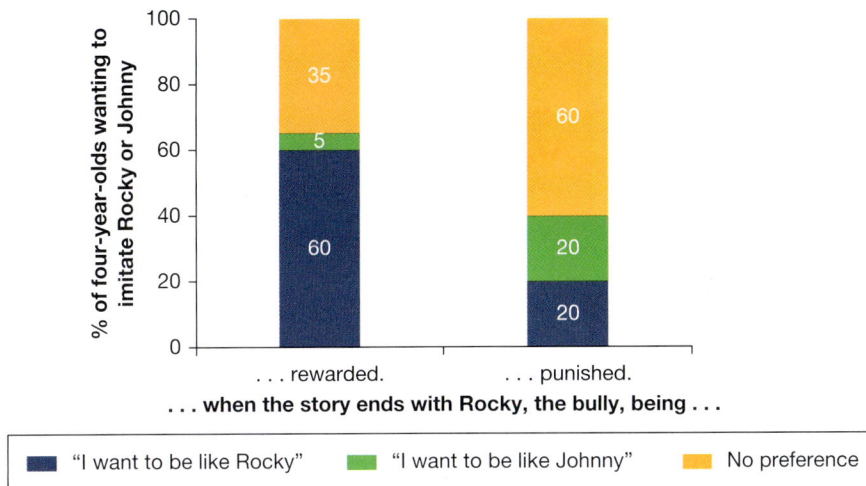

Source: Data from Bandura et al. (1963b).

They observed—and learned—that aggression was rewarded.

One little girl even asked for a sack like the one Rocky used to haul away his loot! The children rationalized their support for Rocky by blaming Johnny for being weak. For Johnny, they said:

"He was a cry baby. Didn't know how to make Rocky mind."

"If he'd shared right in the beginning, Rocky might have played nice. He didn't share."

Johnny, the victim, was described as "sulky," "selfish," "mean," and "sort of dumb."

For children who had watched other adults and children be aggressive—especially in conditions in which that aggression was rewarded—the take-home message was clear: Aggression works, and the victim is to blame.

Situation 3. Media Violence: Starting With *The Great Train Robbery*

Aggression has always been part of television history.

In 1903, many years before the Bandura studies, *The Great Train Robbery* (Porter, 1903; available on YouTube) was the very first moving picture to tell a story. Only 10 minutes long, the silent film begins when a stationmaster is beaten unconscious and then tied up by a gang who secretly board the train. They exchange five shots with a guard before killing him, exploding a safe, and taking the loot. (The actor playing the dead guard wiggles around until he gets his arm in a more comfortable position, but he is *supposed* to be dead.)

The film shows approximately one act of violence per minute. There is one gunshot for every 12 seconds during history's first storytelling film. The audience was thrilled during the final scene. The bad guy looked directly at the camera and fired his gun repeatedly until he ran out of bullets. The first audience ran from the theater—and then demanded another showing. For more on violence in movies, see the Social Psychology

The final shot of *The Great Train Robbery* (1903).

in Popular Culture feature that discusses a study that analyzed interpersonal violence in the 90 top-grossing teen films of the 1980s, 1990s, and 2000s.

Media Violence: Do You Really Want to Know? Do you really want to know?

Today, of course, violence is seen in movies and TV shows, and it is extremely popular in the form of video games. Discovering and communicating scientific answers to questions about playing violent video games bumps into political obstacles. For example, politicians were on television only a few hours after the 2019 shootings in Dayton, Ohio (9 dead; 27 injured), and the Walmart shooter in El Paso, Texas (22 dead; 26 injured). The likely cause, according to them? Violent video games.

Neither politicians nor reporters were in a position to know any answers. But that did not delay their opportunity to inject a political analysis even before many families knew whether they would be grieving. Was their hypothesis valid? As usual, the scientific summary is more complex than the three-word analysis "violent video games." Anderson and Bushman (2018) divided the effects of media violence (not just playing violent video games) into short-term and long-term effects.

Transient, Short-Term Effects of Media Violence. Exposure to violent media can lead to short-term increases in aggression through three psychological processes:

(1) Priming that activates existing memories and mental connections

(2) Mimicking or imitation of others' aggressive responses

(3) Changes in physiological arousal

Recall from Chapter 4 that priming describes what happens to the network of ideas already stored in our heads. Exposure to media violence activates and thereby strengthens our personal mental network of concepts.

Mimicking is the feature we see so easily when children imitate adults or other children in their lives. Mimicry is influenced by similarity; we tend to imitate those we perceive as similar to ourselves. Children are less able to distinguish between fantasy and reality, so they are more likely to mimic exposure to media violence even when it is a cartoon character (Bandura et al., 1963a).

Physiological arousal in response to action-packed media violence can raise both heart rate and blood pressure. Exposure to media violence can lead to aggression if the arousal experience (a) is unpleasant, (b) focuses attention on the aggressive cues, (c) triggers a dominant response, and (d) is perceived as provocative.

Enduring, Long-Term Effects of Media Violence. Exposure to violent media can lead to long-term increases in aggression through three psychological processes:

(1) Observational learning

(2) Desensitization

(3) Decreased empathy

Like mimicry, observational learning develops best when the media role model being observed is similar to the viewer. That may help the viewer pay closer attention and learn violence more quickly, especially if the rewards for violence are many and desirable (such as observing a socially rewarded hero).

Desensitization to media violence develops when the viewer is repeatedly exposed to violence. With repeated exposure, we become accustomed to viewing violence and its negative consequences. We gradually "get used to it."

Along with desensitization, repeated exposure to media violence diminishes our capacity for empathy. One form of passive, indirect aggression potentially linked to loss of empathy occurs when we fail to help people in need.

On the positive side, playing video games is contributing to education in many creative ways. For example, video games have contributed to our understanding of artificial intelligence (Lake et al., 2016) and more effective ways to teach (Epstein et al., 2016). This may be because the principles of good game design parallel established learning principles of psychological science (see Heinzen, Gordon, et al., 2015). Video games are powerful tools that can have both negative and positive consequences, depending on how and why they are used.

SOCIAL PSYCHOLOGY IN POPULAR CULTURE

▶ Aggression in the Movies

To complete her master's degree at Brigham Young University in 2011, Halie Foell Stout completed a content analysis of the 90 most profitable teen movies produced in Hollywood from 1980 to 2009. She focused on how each movie portrayed aggression between the characters that was specifically intended to affect social relationships and/or social status. This aggression included three forms:

- Direct—such as exclusion from a social group or bullying

- Indirect—such as gossiping, spreading rumors, or lying to the person's love interest

- Nonverbal—such as ignoring, rolling eyes, and dirty looks

Overall, she found that 85 of the 90 teen movies included some form of relational aggression, with girls being portrayed as the aggressor more often than boys—and that this gender trend became stronger over time. Results also showed that girls most often used indirect relational aggression. The four movies with the highest amount of aggression were the following:

> #1: *Mean Girls* (Michaels & Waters, 2004; 59 acts of aggression)
>
> #2: *The Mighty Ducks* (Avnet et al., 1992; 30 acts)
>
> #3: *My Bodyguard* (Simon et al., 1980; 21 acts)
>
> #4: *Just One of the Guys* (Fogelson & Gottlieb, 1985; 20 acts)

Note, while Stout identified five movies with no acts of relational aggression, even these films showed *some* form of aggression (e.g., *Transformers* [Murphy et al., 2007] and *Red Dawn* [1984 version; Beckerman et al., 1984] both have war-like battle scenes). Is it possible to make a Hollywood movie without *any* form of aggression? Maybe—but it might not make a profit.

Situation 4. Environmental Cues: Why the GAM Is a Good Theory

A good theory is like the border around a jigsaw puzzle. It provides a structure on which to build.

The General Aggression Model described earlier in this chapter is a good theory because it organizes many other observations into three understandable groups: inputs, routes, and outcomes. And that organizing clarity helps us ask and answer better questions.

The GAM: Environmental Cues Promote Aggression. Aggression has many, different triggering cues.

They include the shape of a game controller, black uniforms, hot temperatures, loud noises, unpleasant odors, ozone levels, crowding, pain—and many more. They all are associated with negative feelings that lead to increased aggression (see Anderson,

Many modern video games highlight extremely aggressive situations.

1989; Anderson et al., 2010; Berkowitz et al., 1981; Griffit & Veitch, 1971; Rotton et al., 1979).

So, here's our question: Why do such different environmental cues have similar effects? For the answer, we can return to the phases of the General Aggression Model (GAM). Aggression (a) begins with inputs that (b) take particular mental routes as we process them and (c) lead to aggressive decisions and behaviors. Consider three specific possible environmental inputs: the presence of weapons, alcohol, and heat.

The Weapons Effect. Berkowitz and Le Page (1967) conducted one of social psychology's classic experiments by comparing three groups. The short version of this classic study is that they placed on a table (a) badminton rackets, (b) a rifle and a revolver, or (c) nothing at all (the *control condition*). An experimental group of participants who had been angered ahead of time *and* primed for aggression by seeing weapons on the table delivered the most and longest electric shocks to other people. Weapons that happened to be lying on a table were an artificial, obvious cue for aggression.

A *field study* version of this experiment *operationalized* (or measured) aggression by counting whether drivers honked their horns at a pickup truck that did not move for 12 seconds after the light had turned green (Turner et al., 1975). There was more honking when the pickup truck had a rifle in the back and a bumper sticker reading "VENGEANCE," compared to no rifle and a bumper sticker reading "FRIEND." It was a slightly different triggering cue, but it produced a similar effect.

This weapons effect demonstrates a cognitive route from weapons to aggression. It has been replicated many times since 1967. A meta-analysis by Benjamin et al. (2018) included 78 studies and 7,668 participants. The results affirmed the prediction GAM would make, that environmental inputs can change our cognitive processing routes, thereby also changing our behavior. The presence of weapons stimulates thoughts and feelings that make aggression more likely, especially among previously angered individuals.

Alcohol. You're driving past a billboard.

You glance up and see an image of someone drinking alcohol. It doesn't matter if it's a fancy craft beer, the cheap stuff from the gas station, or a martini drinker reclining in an expensive armchair. You've probably seen thousands of such images. Alcohol is associated with aggression in your brain, if only because you've probably seen so many bar fights on television. That probably explains why Bartholow and Heinz (2006) found that images of alcohol could trigger aggression even when no alcohol had been drunk.

Another study showed participants subliminal images of alcohol and found that these individuals later showed more aggression toward the experimenter than people who saw neutral subliminal messages (Subra et al., 2010). Thus, you don't have to actually drink alcohol to be aggressive—just being around it (even on a subliminal level!) helps prime aggression.

Heat. I [Tom] was not teaching psychology when the riot broke out.

I was at home on a hot summer day when I received a call from the maximum-security prison where I was working at the time: Don't come to class. Although set in a wooded area, none of the shade reached the buildings made only of brick, concrete, and steel. The place held onto its heat like an oven, even into the night when my classes met. It was extreme discomfort, for both the prisoners and the guards. The riot happened on a particularly hot day.

Weapons effect: The tendency for the presence of weapons to prime aggressive thoughts, feelings, and behaviors.

Research evidence supports this story. Anderson's (1987) *archival data* suggest that heat is associated with increases in violent crimes. Rates for murder, rape, assault, robbery, burglary, larceny-theft, and stealing cars all went up with higher temperatures. Some of the evidence is curious. For example, when it's hot outside, more baseball pitchers hit the batter with the ball (Larrick et al., 2011).

The evidence is also distributed across many different activities. When it is hot, more children in daycares cry and hit each other (Ciucci et al., 2011). People feel more negatively toward immigrants (Cohen & Krueger, 2016). And more people commit violent crimes (Gamble & Hess, 2012). But most of this evidence is correlational, so we are uncertain about cause and effect.

For example, the heat may also simply mean that more people are outside in group areas (compared to in the middle of winter or during a thunderstorm). Thus, there may be more opportunities for riots, fights, conflicts, and so on. But, considering the research reviewed in this section, it's probably best to think twice before you bring your loaded guns into a crowded whisky bar during a gun convention in the middle of August.

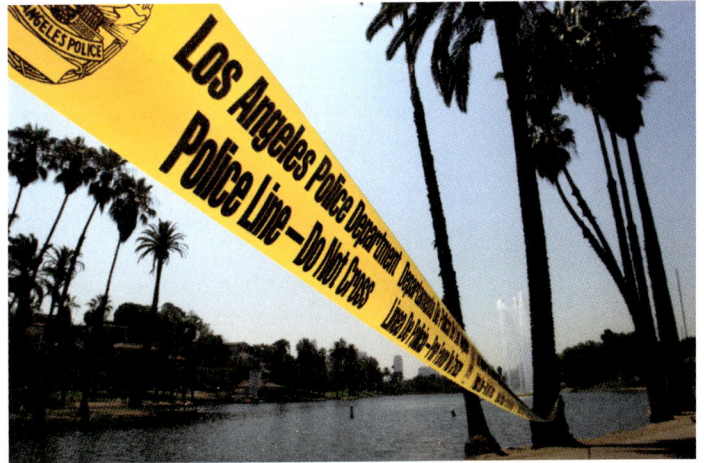

Heat and violence are positively correlated—what explains this trend?

THE MAIN IDEAS

- Several biological factors have been tied to aggression. Genetic determinism is the idea that genes alone predict our behaviors, but many other factors seem to matter. Some discussed in this section of the book are heart rate, alcohol, and testosterone.

- Culture also influences aggression. "Cultures of honor" see aggression when people (especially men) perceive that insults are threats to their reputation. Gender culture and sports culture also matter.

- Situational influences can make aggression go up or down as well. Examples discussed here are war settings, copying role models, media violence such as TV and video games, and environmental cues like the presence of weapons or alcohol or hot temperatures.

CRITICAL THINKING

- If ethics were not a concern, what experimental study would you design to test causal effects of biological influences on aggression? Choose one specific type of biological influence (such as testosterone). Identify the independent variable and dependent variable, and operationalize each by explaining your procedure.

- Consider the values included in a culture of honor. For each, do you agree or disagree (e.g., that family should be a man's first priority)? Can these values be endorsed *without* leading to aggression? Does defending one's "honor" always require physical aggression? Why or why not?

- Some very popular movies and books feature aggressive female protagonists (Black Widow from *The Avengers*, Katniss Everdeen from *The Hunger Games*, etc.). How do audiences seem to react when a woman expresses the same amount of violent behaviors as a man? Is it more culturally acceptable or less? Why?

- Reflect on how popular sports are in modern culture. Do you think sporting events encourage aggression and violence, or do they maintain respectful competition through endorsement of rules and regulations? How might sports culture focus more on peaceful, but still exciting, play and competition between athletes and teams?

HOW CAN WE MANAGE OR REDUCE AGGRESSION?

>> **LO 11.3:   Analyze ideas for managing aggression.**

A Popeye's chicken sandwich didn't cause the murder.

But in 2019, one Maryland man was stabbed to death after confronting another man cutting in line to get a chicken sandwich. The escalation required only about 15 seconds from the in-store confrontation to the stabbing in the parking lot. Aggression may be influenced by a lot of different factors (biology, culture, the environment) . . . but a chicken sandwich? By most people's standards, stabbing the guy is an extreme reaction.

Social psychologists have invested decades into the study of aggression—and how to reduce it. We'll begin with what *doesn't* work and then talk about what does. This section answers the core question "How can we manage or reduce aggression?" by

(1)   explaining why a popular way to reduce aggression often backfires and

(2)   describing modest but more promising social psychological insights.

Catharsis: A Tempting but Bad Idea

It is better to rip apart a pillow than a person.

Few would disagree with that sensible advice. One leads to replacement shopping; the other leads to prison. But does pillow-hitting really reduce aggression? A theory-driven hypothesis is lurking beneath that pillow-hitting advice. The original frustration-aggression theory (see Dollard et al., 1939) proposed that frustration leads to aggression (a concept we covered in Chapter 9). The resulting **catharsis hypothesis** proposed that releasing the pressure will reduce aggression (see Breuer & Freud, 1955).

Catharsis Is a Popular—and Dangerous—Belief

Catharsis is a popular belief—and it makes intuitive sense.

Earlier when we talked about violent video games, you may have thought, "But I prefer to get my aggression out by shooting on-screen people! It works for me." But as the research above implies, that might be a convenient myth you're telling yourself as an excuse to play them.

Athletic coaches, parents, and school administrators have long maintained that playing (and watching) football releases youthful aggressive impulses. Participation in sports offers many benefits, but aggressive sport catharsis (for both men and women) is probably not one of them—and often has the opposite effect (Bennett, 1991; Busnman, 2002; Chick et al., 1997; Nucci & Young-Shim, 2005; Shariff et al., 2017; Tandy & Laflin, 1973).

For example, one of the early classic studies testing catharsis (Hornberger, 1959) angered participants by having a confederate insult them. Half the participants were then *randomly assigned* to a "catharsis" *experimental group* where they would work out their anger by hitting nails with a hammer for 10 minutes; the *control group* had no catharsis opportunity. Contrary to the hypothesis, individuals allowed to "vent their anger" through hammering were significantly more hostile toward the confederate afterward.

Decades of similar experimental studies mostly tell the same basic story (but see Brans et al., 2014; Scheff, 2007). Bushman (2002) summarized an experiment that compared (a) catharsis, (b) specific "rumination" (thinking hard about the person who offended you), and (c) distraction:

> For reducing anger and aggression, the worst possible advice to give people is to tell them to imagine their provocateur's face on a pillow or punching bag as they wallop it. . . . Such advice will only make people angrier and more aggressive. (p. 730)

Catharsis hypothesis:
The idea that purposefully engaging in small aggression will reduce larger aggressive behaviors overall.

More evidence: Websites designed to let users write angry rants actually led to worse moods (Martin et al., 2013). "Venting" anger by complaining to a third party also produced more anger (Parlamis et al., 2010). Playing violent games tends to encourage aggression (Bushman & Whitaker, 2010). With few exceptions, research tells the same story: Catharsis doesn't reduce aggression; catharsis promotes aggression.

Revenge Is Sweet but Only Briefly

But sometimes aggression catharsis feels good, right?

Carlsmith et al. (2008) quoted from a blog by a parent whose child died when Virginia Tech student Seung Hui Cho massacred 32 people before killing himself. "I don't think there would be anything temporary about the satisfaction I would feel in being permitted to execute the person who killed my child." Cho's suicide denied this grieving parent cathartic satisfaction. However, predicting our own emotions while grieving is like forecasting rain next month because it is raining right now (see Carlsmith et al., 2008).

At best, we merely maintain our own misery. At worst, "getting even" becomes an escalation trap: murder over cutting in line for a chicken sandwich (Bushman et al., 2001; Bushman et al., 1999; Guerin, 2001; Verona & Sullivan, 2008). Expressing our aggression apparently only energizes more aggression. It's tricky because catharsis really does feel good in the immediate moment.

If catharsis and revenge don't decrease aggression, what does?

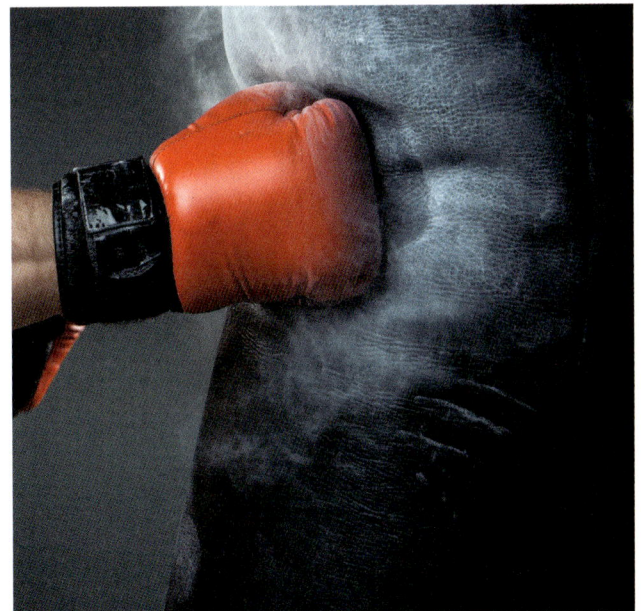

Releasing some steam from a pressure cooker helps it not to explode, but is this a good metaphor for reducing aggression by letting a little bit of it out?

Creating Cultures of Peace

Wishful thinking will not reduce aggression.

Bullies are real. Misunderstandings are pervasive. People with good intentions can be selfish. So, we're ending this chapter with research suggesting some social psychological explanations that take the long view of human history. They may help us understand ourselves and perhaps Steven Pinker's (2011) startling documentation that worldwide violence is declining.

Cultures of Peace Are Possible

Violence is no way to be happy.

Peaceful relations between once-warring and still competitive cultures are not just possible; they are the norm. For example, Darwen and Yao (2002) pointed out that

> the world's longest undefended border is between Canada and the United States. But over several days in August 1814, troops from Canada and Britain captured and sacked Washington DC, in retaliation for the American destruction of Canada's then-capital city of York in April 1813. Two bitter enemies can become close friends even after destroying each other's capital cities. It can be done. (p. 83)

Bonta (1997) identified 25 relatively peaceful societies, 7 of which are described in Table 11.5. They range across continents and varied geographies, from the Arctic to Tahiti. They also vary in how they obtain food, how much they interact with the outside world, and the degree of aggression in their communal stories about themselves. Their only

Will punching a bag or pillow really relieve stress and anger? Most research indicates it will only make it worse.

TABLE 11.5

Relatively Peaceful Societies

SOCIETY	LOCATION AND TYPE OF SOCIETY	CONFLICT MANAGEMENT TECHNIQUES
Balinese (Belo, 1935; Howe, 1989)	Agricultural and commercial on the Indonesian island of Bali	Use self-control to suppress conflicts, usually successfully
Birhor (Adhikary, 1984a, 1984b; Bhattacharyya, 1953)	Nomadic hunters, gatherers, and traders in the forests of central India	Rarely fight, do not commit crimes, and have harmonious relations with neighboring Hindu villagers
Chewong (Howell, 1984)	Agricultural communities in the mountains on the Malay Peninsula	Have no mythology of violence or words for quarreling, fighting, aggression, or warfare
Hutterites (Bennett, 1967; Deets, 1931; Van den Berghe & Peter, 1988)	Communal farmers on the central plains of the United States and Canada (unlike Amish, they use modern farming equipment)	Believe that their Anabaptist faith promotes resolving conflicts without open disagreement
Inuit (Briggs, 1994)	Fishing and hunting communities in northern Alaska, Canada, and Greenland	Fear interpersonal aggression, perhaps because murder had been frequent in some Inuit societies
Piaroa (Overing, 1986, 1989)	Native Americans of Venezuela formerly living in forest villages	Are appalled by aggression and treat disease as a sorcery attack from another village deserving a counterattack using sorcery
Tahitians (Levy, 1973, 1978)	Fishing and farming in the Society Islands of Tahiti	Behave with gentleness even during festivals; although alcohol occasionally contributes to hitting within a family

commonality is that each evolved its own distinctive ways to reduce conflict. Peace comes in a variety of forms, and they are all solutions to cultural aggression.

Constructive Journalism: Promoting Cultures of Peace

"If it bleeds, it leads," is the folk wisdom for headline writers.

It suggests a financially influenced reporting bias: Report audience-building sensationalism over complex analysis of causes. The end result is that how journalists cover conflicts focuses on aggression, injury, and death (see Horvit et al., 2018). By contrast, **peace journalism** (sometimes called constructive journalism) focuses news reporting on the structural causes of conflict and the opportunities for conflict resolution.

Peace journalism aims to fulfill traditional journalistic roles that include informing and educating the public. Peace journalists also report on solutions to complex social problems and promote restorative narratives, "stories that foster hope, healing, and resilience" (McIntyre & Sobel, 2018, p. 2126). Such stories appear to have contributed, for example, to Rwanda's postgenocide reconstruction. Maybe reading the news would be more inspirational and would influence our culture in positive directions if it emphasized how to end aggression instead of blood and anger.

MAD Wisdom and Game Theory: The Prisoner's Dilemma

MAD stands for mutually assured destruction. It's a scary prospect.

MAD may have prevented enemy nations with nuclear weapons from launching them at one another (Saijo et al., 2015; Wolf et al., 2008). Each side is uncertain about whether their enemy will launch a nuclear attack. If I try to destroy you, then you

Peace journalism: News reporting focused on ending conflict and its causes, instead of emphasizing aggression and injury.

will try to destroy me—and we both will probably be destroyed. So, we might as well cooperate enough to stay alive.

The logic of MAD is explored in experiments based on the two-person game called the Prisoner's Dilemma. Two captured prisoners are uncertain about whether their comrade in crime will snitch or keep their mouth shut. Police promote their uncertainty by putting suspects in different rooms. In the game, if both prisoners refuse to snitch on the other, then both sentences will be light. But if one snitches, that prisoner goes free while the other gets a much longer sentence. The temptation is, of course, to snitch—but if they both snitch, they're both in for a long time in prison. Once again, MAD dictates that it is better, on average, for both to cooperate with each other.

Bobo Doll Wisdom and Role Modeling

Perhaps we, also, have been paying too much attention to the experimental group.

Bandura's Bobo doll studies tell us about imitating aggression from role models. But they also tell us something about role modeling and nonaggression. When children saw nonaggression, they were *less* likely to be aggressive. Children were also less likely to copy aggressive behavior if they had seen that behavior was punished.

Another early study (Baron, 1972) was a variation on the famous Milgram shock experiments. But this time, when the participants saw the "teacher" give low-level shocks, they chose significantly lower levels of shock themselves (Baron, 1972). Once again, simple role modeling worked. And this time it decreased aggression. The pattern of peacemaking, helping, and forgiveness has been supported by many other studies (e.g., Crowder & Goodfriend, 2012; Donnerstein & Donnerstein, 1976; Vidyasagar & Mishra, 1993).

Media Violence: Fight False Fairness With Facts

The mass media is role modeling on steroids.

Social media, popular movies, serial shows, video games, and online banner ads that advertise products are pervasive. The television industry, for example, charges advertisers hundreds of thousands of dollars for a few minutes of commercials. So, the industry argument is weak when it claims that violent programing has no influence on children, for example, who may view many hours every day.

Bushman and Anderson compared 50 years of violence in the "reel" world of media to the "real" world of everyday life. They found that "even in reality-based TV programs, violence is grossly overemphasized" (Bushman & Anderson, 2001b, p. 479). Their chief disappointment, however, was that psychology's many data-driven insights were not being heard:

> An attempt to get both sides of the story may itself lead to a final story that puts too little emphasis on the findings and opinions of leading researchers and puts too much emphasis on the few dissidents who can be found on any scientific issue.... This fairness doctrine extends even to the public opinions of people who clearly have a monetary interest in befuddling the general public. (p. 487)

We, the authors of this book, hope that research wins out in the long run. Finding evidence-based ways to reduce individual and worldwide aggression are important goals.

THE MAIN IDEAS

- The catharsis hypothesis is the idea that engaging in small aggressive behaviors will reduce it overall; however, several studies have not supported this hypothesis. In addition, studies show that getting revenge leads to short-term satisfaction but only increases aggression in the long term.

- Cultures can influence aggression in a positive or negative way; just as some cultures promote violence, other cultures discourage it and find alternative ways to solve problems.
- Modeling peacemaking and forgiveness has also successfully decreased aggression in observers.

CRITICAL THINKING

- Think about catharsis or revenge on an international scale. Can you identify historical events that occurred due to one culture seeking "revenge" or "justice" for a past transgression? Did this response lead to positive or negative outcomes?

- Analyze the culture of your own school, family, or local community. Do these cultures encourage or discourage violence as a response to others? Identify three specific examples to support your view.

- Considering research showing that modeling forgiveness helps others choose to forgive, what could parents or teachers do to explicitly decrease aggressive tendencies in children? Discuss two specific scenarios that apply what you've learned from this section.

CHAPTER SUMMARY

What Is Aggression?

Aggression is behavior intended to harm others who do not wish to be harmed. There are many ways to categorize different forms of aggression. Descriptive typologies clarify different forms of aggression, such as physical versus verbal or direct versus indirect. A motivational typology can instead identify why people are aggressive; here, we can distinguish between hostile/reactive aggression and instrumental/proactive aggression. Finally, recent ideas on microaggressions (more subtle, "everyday" forms of aggression such as racist graffiti) can take on the forms of microinsult, microassault, and microinvalidation. The General Aggression Model (GAM) helps organize these different typologies by suggesting that aggression is a process going from (1) environmental inputs through (2) cognitive processing or routes to (3) aggressive outcomes or behaviors.

Evidence from several other academic disciplines, such as archeology or religion, indicates that humans have a long history of aggressive impulses and behaviors. Escalation of aggression can occur through stages of provocation. That said, some people argue that in general, human aggressive tendencies have gone down over time, potentially due to increases in intelligence and reasoned thought.

Why Are Humans Aggressive?

One explanation for aggression in humans (and other species) is biological influences. Genes, heart rates, alcohol, and testosterone have all been linked to more or less aggression. Another possible influence on our aggression is our culture. For example, a "culture of honor" in the U.S. South appears to encourage men to consider insults as a threat to their masculinity/reputation and as deserving of a violent reaction. Along the same lines, gendered culture seems to encourage men to be more aggressive in general, compared to women. Finally, sports culture seems to encourage violence in certain contexts (although sports can decrease aggression as well). Situations also matter. People can become more aggressive during times of war, even if they aren't directly fighting the "enemy." Children and adults are both likely to imitate aggressive role models, especially when those role models are perceived as similar to the self and are rewarded for their behavior. Violence in the media (such as movies or video games) also appears to increase aggression. Finally, small cues can trigger violence such as the presence of weapons, images of alcohol, and hot temperatures.

How Can We Manage or Reduce Aggression?

The catharsis hypothesis is the idea that engaging in aggressive behavior will reduce it, like venting or "letting off steam" to avoid an explosion. While catharsis may feel good and seem to work on an intuitive level, research shows that expressing aggression and anger only increases it. Catharsis can feel good in the short term, but it increases aggression in the long term. Instead of expressing anger, cultures can model forgiveness and peace in the same ways that cultures can encourage aggression. Research on various cultures around the world indicates that cultures with established conflict management techniques can decrease aggression. In addition, if modeling can increase aggression in television, movies, and video games, perhaps these media could be used to model forgiveness as well.

CRITICAL THINKING, ANALYSIS, AND APPLICATION

- Table 11.1 presented a descriptive typology (Buss, 1961) of eight forms of aggression. Think of an example of each type. Then, make a rank-ordered list of your examples in terms of how harmful they are to society in general. Be sure to note which end of the list is the most and least harmful.

- Pinker (2011) suggested that aggression is negatively correlated with intelligence, education, and reasoned thought. Archer (2004) found that aggression peaked in both men and women when they were in their 20s (when testosterone is at its highest point). How do these two findings go together—or not?

- This chapter covered ideas regarding how aggression is influenced by biological factors, cultural factors, and situational factors. Which potential causes of violence did you find the most convincing and why? Analyze your opinion on which of these three general categories is most influential in predicting aggression and violence. Give a few examples of your opinion as well.

- The final section of this chapter is "How Can We Manage or Reduce Aggression?" Does the answer depend on what caused aggression in the first place? For example, if aggression is more caused by biological factors than cultural or situational factors, will it be harder to decrease aggression in general? Discuss.

Kevin Mazur/Getty Images Entertainment/Getty Images

12

Intimate Relationships

Core Questions

12.1 What causes attraction?

12.2 How do we decide to commit to a particular relationship?

12.3 How do gender and culture influence relationships?

Learning Objectives

12.1 Explain situational and physical factors that predict attraction.

12.2 Compare and contrast three different models of relationship type and commitment.

12.3 Analyze ways that gender and culture influence relationships.

They're some of the most successful musical artists of all time: Beyoncé and Jay-Z.

But their relationship hasn't always been so successful. They dated in secret for 3 years and eventually married. Rumors of Jay-Z having an affair were confirmed with Beyoncé's powerful album *Lemonade,* in which she called him out for adultery but claimed to forgive him. He followed up with *4:44,* in which he begged for her understanding. In 2018, they co-released a third album, *Everything in Love.* Jay-Z said making it together was using "art almost like a therapy session" (see Legaspi, 2017).

Love, sex, and romantic relationships intrigue us because they are such an important part of our personal experience. What does science have to say about matters of the heart?

WHAT CAUSES ATTRACTION?

>> **LO 12.1:** **Explain situational and physical factors that predict attraction.**

We're all attracted to other people, sometimes without really understanding why. If "love at first sight" is most honestly "lust at first sight," what predicts these feelings we can neither deny nor always explain?

This part of the chapter answers the core question "What causes attraction?" by exploring

(1) situational predictors of attraction and

(2) factors related to physical attraction.

These situations and physical features appear to make us feel an attraction to others, regardless of our gender, sexual orientation, or culture. But don't worry; we'll talk about those kinds of differences in the last section of this chapter.

Situational Predictors of Attraction

You've seen it many times before: Lewin's famous equation, $B = f(P, E)$.

It seems that the equation could also be true if we substituted B (behavior) for A (attraction). Let's start by focusing on how similarity between people leads to attraction (something that probably won't surprise you) and then discuss two possibly more surprising ways that your environment can influence attraction.

Similarity

You may have heard the phrase "opposites attract."

It's a popular plot device in the movies to have the innocent rich girl fall for the street-smart bad boy (or vice versa). But social psychology tells us that the phrase "birds of a feather flock together" is a more accurate description of how real people connect with one another. This general idea, called the **similarity-attraction hypothesis**, predicts that people tend to form relationships with others who have the same attitudes, values, interests, and demographics as themselves (Morry, 2005, 2007). This is true for both friendships and romantic relationships—and within romantic relationships, the same idea is called assortative mating.

Demographic variables such as age, social class, political leanings, and race or ethnicity may be important. Many of us want to date someone who can share our interests and dreams as well as understand our perspective on the world. We want to be with someone who "gets" us. Planning simple date activities (what movie should we see?) and planning an entire life together are easier and more meaningful when two partners can agree. Similarities decrease arguments between couples. Morry (2005, 2007) also asserts that similarity matters because it validates our worldview. People with similar beliefs make us more comfortable with our opinions and affirm that we are logical, smart human beings.

Similarity-attraction hypothesis: The tendency to form relationships with others who have similar attitudes, values, interests, and demographics (see *assortative mating*).

Of course, people can be attracted to and have relationships with others who are different, and these relationships offer some benefits. For example, someone with a weakness in an area like verbal communication can improve this skill if their partner is strong in it (Gruber-Baldini et al., 1995). Baxter and West (2003) also tested couples to see how they perceived any differences between them. They found that most couples *can* see the differences between the two people involved—and couple members who perceive these differences as an opportunity to learn from each other viewed this lack of similarity as a positive instead of as a negative. So similarity makes things easier, but learning from each other might help us grow.

Mere Exposure and Proximity: The Westgate Housing Study

So, we tend to be attracted to people . . . like us!

That's not a major revelation, but the next two factors may be more of a surprise. Our situational environment might have more of an effect than we think on our friendships and relationships.

One interesting factor you might not have considered before is called **mere exposure**, or the tendency to like things and people more, the more we are around them. It seems that we like people who are familiar; again, it might be because we're comfortable with them. Sometimes this is called the **proximity effect** or the **propinquity effect** when it refers to increased exposure and liking due to people being in the same physical area as yourself (such as people who live in your dorm or neighborhood, or people you see frequently in classes or at work). In general, the more we know people and the more we're around them, the more we like them (Goodfriend, 2009).

Think about one of your favorite current singers or bands. The first time you hear a new song on the radio, you might think, "This song is OK, but not nearly as good as their previous tracks." Then you hear the song again a few times and start humming along, without even realizing you're doing it. A few more musical exposures later and you could be downloading your new ringtone. You love it!

The mere exposure effect predicts that as we become more familiar with an object or person, our liking for it/them increases (Festinger et al., 1950; Monahan et al., 2000; Van Horn et al., 1997). (Note that this is true only when our original impression was fairly neutral; if we originally hated something, we might just grow to hate it even more.) The mere exposure effect explains why we prefer photos of ourselves that have been reversed instead of actual, original photos—because we're used to looking at ourselves in a mirror. Photos are backward from how we usually see our faces, so they seem "off" without most people realizing why (Mita et al., 1977).

But does repeated exposure, by itself, really influence attraction between humans? A classic study called the **Westgate Housing Study** from early social psychology tested this hypothesis in a creative way. Festinger and two colleagues (Festinger et al., 1950) studied a small community named the Westgate Housing Project on the campus of the Massachusetts Institute of Technology (MIT). Each apartment building included 10 single-family units, with five apartments on each of two floors (see Figure 12.1). Although they were strangers at first, the residents of Westgate were similar in terms of background, interests, stage of life, and life goals. They were also living in very close proximity to each other.

Festinger et al. (1950) pointed out that there were two kinds of exposure in these apartments: (1) **physical distance** from one apartment to another—how many steps you'd have to take to get there—and (2) **functional distance**. Functional distance refers to the fact that, because of the buildings' design, some apartments were more likely to be passed by than others. The occupants of these apartments were more likely to be seen by other occupants because of the nature of how the apartments had to be used (in other words, you need stairs to get to the second floor).

Festinger asked people in Westgate to choose the three people in the entire complex whom they were most likely to see socially (in other words, their friends). They listed residents with closer physical and functional proximity to themselves. By looking at Figure 12.1, you can see why people in Apartments 1 and 5 were liked the most. These

Mere exposure: The tendency for us to prefer familiar objects and individuals, especially as exposure to them increases.

Proximity effect: The tendency for us to like people who are in close geographic proximity to ourselves, due to the mere exposure effect (see *mere exposure*).

Propinquity effect: See *proximity effect*.

Westgate Housing Study: A research project on how liking increases based on physical proximity and mere exposure to one's neighbors.

Physical distance: How far apart two people are from each other.

Functional distance: How often two people see each other, due to things like architectural design (e.g., who lives next to the stairs in a building).

Schematic diagram of a type of Westgate apartment (Festinger et al., 1950). When people in the buildings were asked to rate their neighbors, people in Apartments 1 and 5 were liked the most, while people in Apartments 6 and 10 were liked the least.

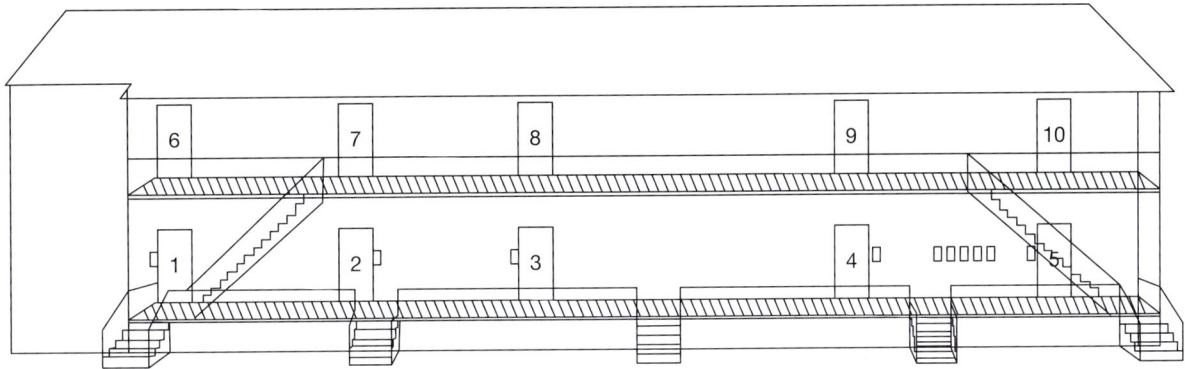

apartments were at the bottom of staircases leading to the second floor, so all the residents who lived on the second floor would have to pass those doors (Festinger et al., 1950).

People in Apartments 6 and 10 were usually liked the least, perhaps because the location of their apartments isolated them from their neighbors. Others felt that they didn't really know them. Importantly, this pattern was found across multiple buildings in the complex. That is important because the observations were *replicated*. Observing the same pattern across buildings suggested that the results weren't due to particularly nice people who happened to live in Apartments 1 and 5 (or jerks in Apartments 6 and 10). The researchers concluded that when all else was equal, mere exposure led to more liking (Festinger et al., 1950).

The mere exposure effect for interpersonal attraction has been replicated in many other ways, in both *controlled laboratory experiments* (e.g., Reis et al., 2011) and in *field studies*. For example, one field study found that friends who lived in the same room or same town were more likely to remain close than friends who lived apart (Batool & Malik, 2010). Two studies found that cross-ethnic friendships were more likely between adolescents if they lived in the same neighborhood (Echols & Graham, 2013; Kruse et al., 2016). So you might end up being friends with someone, or even dating them, just because luck happened to lead you to cross their path repeatedly.

💡 Misattribution of Arousal in the Shaky Bridge Study

How accurate are you at interpreting physical signals from your body? A famous research study explored this question and the fascinating phenomenon called misattribution of arousal, which happens when people make mistakes about the cause of physiological excitement they are experiencing.

Dutton and Aron (1974) asked a physically attractive female experimenter to spend time waiting in a park, then approach men who might be willing to complete a survey for a study. She told the men that the survey was investigating whether scenic settings affect creativity and that, after they completed it, she would

(Continued)

(Continued)

Would walking across these two bridges cause you different levels of anxiety and physiological arousal? Research indicates that some people might misinterpret that kind of arousal as attraction to other people who happen to be nearby.

be happy to answer additional questions. To emphasize her willingness to see more of each man, she wrote her phone number on a piece of paper and handed it to the men while smiling.

Remember that this experiment was meant to study *misattribution*. The key to how it worked was that the pretty young experimenter approached the men in two different park locations, making this a *quasi-experimental design*. The locations became the *independent variable*. But it's not a true experiment because the locations weren't *randomly assigned* to the different men. Still, Dutton and Aron predicted that one of the locations would lead to more physiological arousal—and thus more attraction to the woman—than the other. Attraction to her therefore became the *dependent variable*.

The locations were near two different bridges. The first bridge, considered the *control group* bridge, was sturdy and made of solid wood. It was wide, had high handrails, and the drop was only 10 feet. The second bridge, however, was a 450-foot suspension bridge made of individual wooden boards strapped together with cables. To cross it, participants had to walk over a 250-foot canyon full of sharp and scary rocks; the bridge also had the tendency to "shake" and sway in the wind. Imagine what it would be like to cross this shaky bridge. In most participants, it would produce anxiety

and fear—which in turn would produce physiological changes such as increased heart rate, faster breathing, sweat, and nausea. Sound familiar?

The pretty female experimenter would wait for a young man who was by himself to cross one of the bridges and then would approach him. Next, he would complete the survey and walk away with the woman's phone number. The research team measured how many of these men called the experimenter later and asked her on a date, their way of measuring or *operationalizing* his level of attraction. You can probably predict what happened. Of the men who had crossed the shaky, arousing bridge, 50% called the experimenter, while only 12.5% of the men from the stable bridge called, a difference that was *statistically significant*.

The scientific question to ask is: What accounted for this large difference? Misattribution of arousal suggests that the men who had just crossed the shaky bridge were physiologically aroused due to fear and anxiety caused by the bridge itself. However, when they interacted with a pretty woman immediately after crossing, they may have misinterpreted that physiological arousal as sexual interest. My heart is beating, I'm sweaty . . . I guess I find this woman sexy! Not as many men from the stable bridge called because they didn't feel as physiologically aroused.

Physiological Arousal and Misattribution of Arousal

Sexual attraction.

It's certainly part of overall attraction. Think back to the last time you were around someone you found extremely attractive. Your mind was probably racing with excitement—but so was your body. Did your heart beat faster? Did your breathing become short and fast? Maybe you were sweating or had a feeling of vague nausea. When we're sexually attracted to another person, we experience physiological arousal, the third predictor of attraction.

▶ Misattribution and Love in *The Hunger Games*

Moviestore collection Ltd/Alamy Stock Photo

In the popular movie series *The Hunger Games* (Collins, 2008, 2009, 2010), Katniss Everdeen is torn between love for two men. Why does she ultimately choose one over the other? If similarity were the focus of the film, she would probably choose Gale. Gale is very similar to Katniss; they both put protecting family first, they hunt together, and they stand up against the evil government together. But Gale doesn't capture her heart in the same way that Peeta, the other man, does.

Why does Katniss fall for Peeta instead? Peeta has many positive qualities (such as altruism and loyalty), but misattribution of arousal may also play a large part. Katniss and Peeta are constantly thrown together in a series of highly dangerous situations, both fighting for their lives. In a long-term and consistent state of physiological arousal, they are trying to survive multiple attempts the government designs to murder them. Being around Peeta in the midst of this chaos might lead Katniss to perceive more attraction to him than she would have felt in calmer conditions. Perhaps she interprets her beating heart as caused by love instead of the adrenaline of survival.

Usually we know exactly why we're experiencing this sort of physiological arousal. But is it possible for us to make an incorrect assumption about why we're sweaty and out of breath? In other words, we might make a **misattribution of arousal**. Physiological arousal from something in the environment might be misinterpreted as sexual arousal. Some researchers call this the **excitation transfer effect** because we tend to transfer our excitement over the situation to excitement about another person. To learn more about a famous study that tested this effect, see the Spotlight on Research Methods feature.

Physical Predictors of Attraction

Have you experienced an immediate spark of sexual attraction toward some stranger? There were no words, no information, just their appearance. What was it about the other person's physical features that hijacked your attention? You already know about the "what-is-beautiful-is-good" effect (see Chapter 5), in which physically attractive people are perceived as having several other positive qualities as well.

There are certainly individual differences regarding what we find attractive in others. You might be attracted to someone with dark coloring or very pale skin, short or long hair, muscular or delicate features. Despite these individual variations in what we consider our "type," certain physical characteristics seem to be universally appealing to everyone regardless of age, ethnicity, or culture. What explains these cross-cultural similarities in perceived beauty?

Buss is probably the most famous modern social psychologist studying how evolutionary theory applies to human dating and mating. He has published dozens of books and articles about this topic (e.g., Buss, 1985, 1989, 1994). His reasoning goes like this: If researchers can identify certain physical characteristics or traits that are universally considered attractive—regardless of one's upbringing or culture—then these traits probably come from ancient, inherited instincts. Moreover, we experience all these attraction impulses on an unconscious level; we don't even realize why we like someone or something.

Misattribution of arousal: Our tendency to assume physiological reactions to our environment is really due to sexual attraction to another person (see *excitation transfer effect*).

Excitation transfer effect: Our tendency to interpret excitement over a situation as excitement about another person (see *misattribution of arousal*).

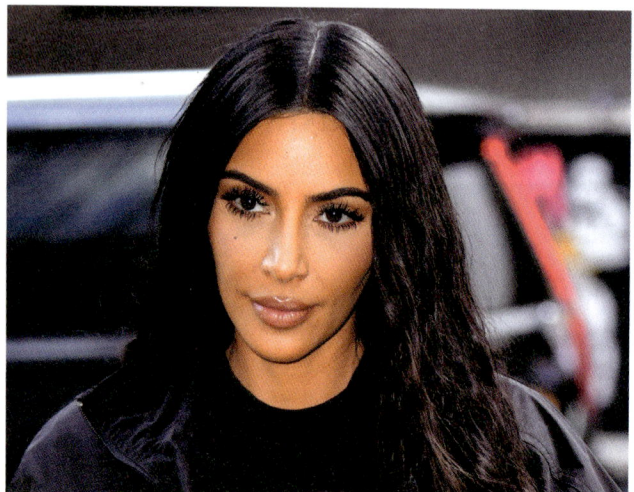

Scientifically speaking, George Clooney and Kim Kardashian have an almost "perfect" face, including an unusually high amount of symmetry (Cashin, n.d.).

Gareth Cattermole/Getty Images Entertainment/Getty Images

James Devaney/GC Images/Getty Images

Despite our lack of awareness, preferences for certain physical traits have endured over time and across dozens of different countries. What are the traits that seem to be almost universally appealing or beautiful? Psychologists have discovered three interesting patterns of appeal, regardless of culture.

Symmetry

Have you ever noticed a person whose facial features are not symmetrical?

Perhaps one eye is bigger than the other, there's a scar on one cheek, or one ear sticks out farther than the other. Do you think this factor affects how attractive you perceive the person to be? Several studies indicate we experience **bilateral symmetry** as attractive on an instinctive level. An object, face, or body is bilaterally symmetrical when the left half perfectly matches the right half. One study found the amount of symmetry in college students' faces was significantly (and positively) correlated with how attractive other people thought they were (Gangestad et al., 1994). The effect was stronger for men than for women.

They replicated the effect in a second study (Grammer & Thornhill, 1994). Perhaps most interestingly, a third study (Thornhill & Gangestad, 1994) measured men's and women's body and facial symmetry by comparing their left-side and right-side feet, ankles, hands, wrists, elbows, and ears. Results showed that for both sexes in the study, greater symmetry was associated with a higher number of sex partners. For men, symmetry was also correlated with having sex at an earlier age. The same trend was true for women but was not strong enough to be *statistically significant*.

Why is bilateral symmetry attractive? From an evolutionary perspective, symmetry may be an easy-to-see indicator of genetic quality—a heuristic cue that helps us make fast (but often unfair) judgments about others. If your potential mate is asymmetrical, perhaps they have a genetic disorder that could be passed on to any offspring. For example, in scorpion flies, lopsided individuals are more likely to have negative reactions to environmental pollution and to carry disease ("Biology of Beauty," 1996). Honeybees even prefer to pollinate symmetrical flowers (Wignall et al., 2006).

Bilateral symmetry: When left and right halves of a face or body match; symmetry is positively correlated with perceived attractiveness.

iStockPhoto/Tiorina

Symmetry is linked to within-species attraction for several animals—including humans.

We may not realize that we're attracted to symmetry. But symmetry may be an instinct at work when we find ourselves mysteriously attracted to someone. Note the quirky finding that in one study, sober people were good at detecting asymmetry in faces and found them less attractive. Drunk people, however, couldn't even tell when faces were asymmetrical (Halsey et al., 2010). Perhaps this explains one reason why drinking seems to make others suddenly more attractive.

"Averaged" Faces

Being "just average" doesn't sound that great in terms of your physical attractiveness, but in this case, being average might be a good thing.

Just as symmetrical faces and bodies might be heuristic cues to genetic health, so might **composite or averaged faces**, faces that do not include any unusual or strange features. Researchers test this hypothesis by having participants rate the attractiveness of many different faces. Included in the lineup is one computer-generated face that is the composite or morphed "average" of all the other faces (Perrett et al., 1994). When this is done, the computer-generated "averaged" face is typically rated as the most beautiful or attractive, compared to the individual faces of actual people (Langlois & Roggman, 1990; Langlois et al., 1994).

Check out the computer-generated faces in Figure 12.2; these were created by Langlois for her research lab (you can visit her website to learn more). As you can see, the face on the far left is a composite of 2 individual photos, while the photo on the far right is made up of 32 individual photos. People tend to rate the 32-face average as more attractive than the 2-face average (Langlois & Roggman, 1990; Langlois et al., 1994). In addition, the averaged faces are rated as more attractive than any of the individual faces used to make them, as long as the averaged face is a computer-generated composite of at least 16 faces.

But here's our usual question: Why? Why are "averaged" faces rated as more attractive? Here are three possibilities. First, it could be a **procedural artifact**, a finding that results from *how* we conducted the experiment. For example, it could be an *order effect* because seeing an "averaged" face *after* seeing so many similar faces engages the mere exposure effect you just read about. (This would only be true for *within-participants designs*.) Second, averaged faces may only be attractive because they are also more symmetric. Finally, we may experience "averaged" faces as comforting because they fit our cultural expectations. Most people are attracted to what their culture and media images tell them is attractive.

Waist-to-Hips and Waist-to-Shoulders Ratios

Which of the bodies shown in Figure 12.3 do you think is the most attractive?

These bodies differ in an important variable called **waist-to-hips ratio**, which is the ratio comparing the circumference of the waist to the circumference of

Composite face: See *averaged face.*

Averaged face: A computer-generated face created by combining several individual faces. Averaged faces are often perceived as more attractive than individual faces.

Procedural artifact: A finding that results from how a researcher conducted the experiment, rather than introduction of the independent variable.

Waist-to-hips ratio: The ratio comparing waist circumference to hips circumference, which often plays a role in determining female body attractiveness.

FIGURE 12.2

Averaged female faces. Computer-generated averaged faces are often perceived as more attractive than the individual faces used to create them.

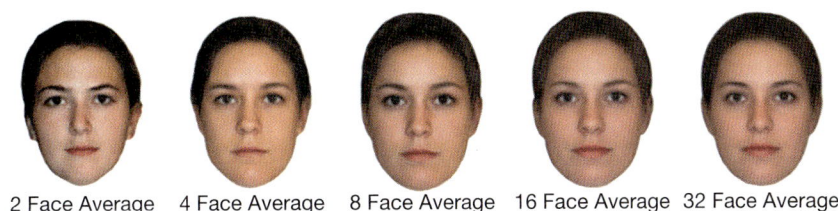

2 Face Average   4 Face Average   8 Face Average   16 Face Average   32 Face Average

Source: The University of Texas at Austin, Department of Psychology.

Which body type do you find the most sexually attractive? In research, "C" is the most popular answer.

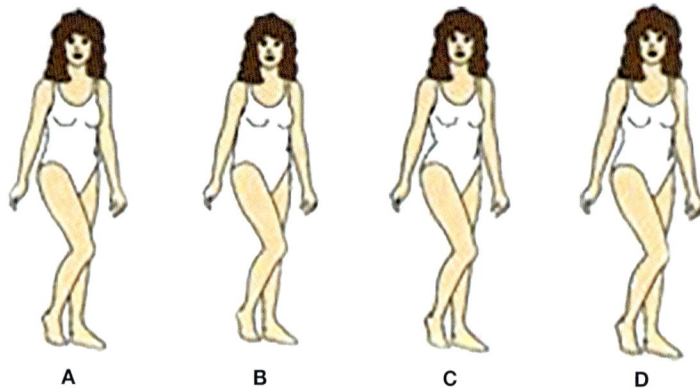

A   B   C   D

Source: Singh (1993).

the hips. If, for example, your waist measured 30 inches and your hips measured 40 inches, then your waist-to-hips ratio would be 3 to 4, or 0.75.

Several studies have shown that across cultures, the most desirable waist-to-hips ratio for women is about 0.7 (Bovet & Raymond, 2015; Singh, 1993a, 1993b; Singh & Randall, 2007). When men are asked to judge the attractiveness of line drawings of women, such as the one in Figure 12.3, the women with a ratio of 0.7 were rated healthier, more youthful, and to have a higher reproductive capacity (LaForge & Goodfriend, 2012). Interestingly, famous beauties Marilyn Monroe, Sophia Loren, and Jessica Alba all had, at least at one point in their popular careers as actresses and models, a 0.7 waist-to-hips ratio.

What about preferences for men's bodies? For them, too, a certain ratio matters. For men's bodies, it's the **waist-to-shoulders ratio**, or the ratio comparing the width of the waist to the width of the shoulders. The number for the ratio is about the same: between 0.70 and 0.75. That is, for men, the waist should be 70% of the width of the shoulders to be most universally appealing to women (Braun & Bryan, 2006; Dixson et al., 2003). Gay men also find this ratio the most attractive in other men (LaForge & Goodfriend, 2012).

Does an evolutionary explanation work for both ratios? According to this perspective, heterosexual men are attracted to women with large hips because they suggest a healthy gateway for babies; the small waist indicates aerobic health. So, the most attractive women will be those who are physically fit and more likely to survive childbirth and the following year of raising an infant. Heterosexual women are attracted to men with a small waist because it also indicates aerobic fitness while broad, strong shoulders indicate physical strength. This strength would certainly be an advantage for any physical tasks and might be important when a pregnant woman or a child needs protection.

It's important to remember that these preferences typically exist on an unconscious level. According to the evolutionary perspective—which is criticized by many in the field of psychology—they are the legacies of what benefited our ancestors in terms of genetic and reproductive fitness. Social psychology asserts that *both* nature (our biological impulses) and nurture (cultural preferences) are hard at work creating our attraction to others.

THE MAIN IDEAS

- Three variables that social psychology says contribute to attraction are similarity, mere exposure, and physiological arousal. Two famous studies testing these factors are the Westgate Housing Study (for mere exposure) and the "shaky bridge study" (for arousal).

- The evolutionary perspective predicts that some attraction preferences will be universal or cross-cultural due to their benefits to us as a species. Note that there are criticisms of this perspective, however.

- Three traits that are considered attractive, regardless of culture, are bilateral symmetry, composite or "averaged" faces, and specific waist-to-hips or waist-to-shoulders ratios.

Waist-to-shoulders ratio: The ratio comparing waist width to shoulder width, which often plays a role in determining male body attractiveness.

- The research reviewed above suggests that similarity, mere exposure, and physiological arousal all contribute to attraction. Of these three variables, which do you think is the most important in predicting whether you'll want to date someone? Do you think that the answer is the same for everyone?

- Consider the "shaky bridge study." First, point out at least one alternative explanation for the results. Could the men in the study have called the woman next to the "shaky" bridge more for any other reason, besides being attracted to her? Next, assuming this study's conclusions are correct, discuss how you might use them to get your next date to be more attracted to you.

- Now that you know about traits that are considered "universally" attractive, are there things you would consider changing about your own appearance or dress that might highlight your own features or disguise things about yourself that go against these desirable traits? Explain why or why not, using terms from this section of the book.

HOW DO WE DECIDE TO COMMIT TO A PARTICULAR RELATIONSHIP?

>> LO 12.2: **Compare and contrast three different models of relationship type and commitment.**

If you're lucky, lots of people will want to date you.

How do we decide which relationships are worth commitment and which aren't? Several models of relationship types exist in the world of social psychology; in this chapter, we'll cover three of the most popular. Each explains how two people in a relationship might achieve happiness and long-term commitment, but they all arrive at the answer from very different views. As we cover each, consider what you like (and don't like) about each model.

This section answers the core question "How do we decide to commit to a particular relationship?" by exploring

(1) Sternberg's "triangular" theory of love,

(2) a model that says our early childhood predicts our adult relationship patterns (attachment theory), and

(3) a theory that commitment comes from high satisfaction, low alternatives, and high investments (interdependence theory and the investment model).

Sternberg's Triangular Theory of Love

One of the most well-known relationship theories is **Sternberg's triangular theory of love** (Sternberg, 1986).

It's called the "triangular" theory because Sternberg suggested that love is made up of three components and that the degree to which each of these components is present in any given relationship will determine its nature. The three components are

- *Intimacy:* The emotional component. Intimacy is feelings of closeness, connection, bonding, and warmth toward a partner.

- *Passion:* The physical, motivational, or behavioral component. Passion is sexual drive or attraction toward a partner.

- *Commitment:* The cognitive component. Commitment is a thoughtful, reasoned decision to stay with a given partner and maintain the relationship, often exclusively.

Sternberg's triangular theory of love: Suggests all intimate relationships are made up of a combination of intimacy, passion, and commitment.

FIGURE 12.4

Eight types of love in Sternberg's triangular theory. In this theory (Sternberg, 1986), there are eight kinds of love that vary based on whether they have intimacy, passion, and commitment.

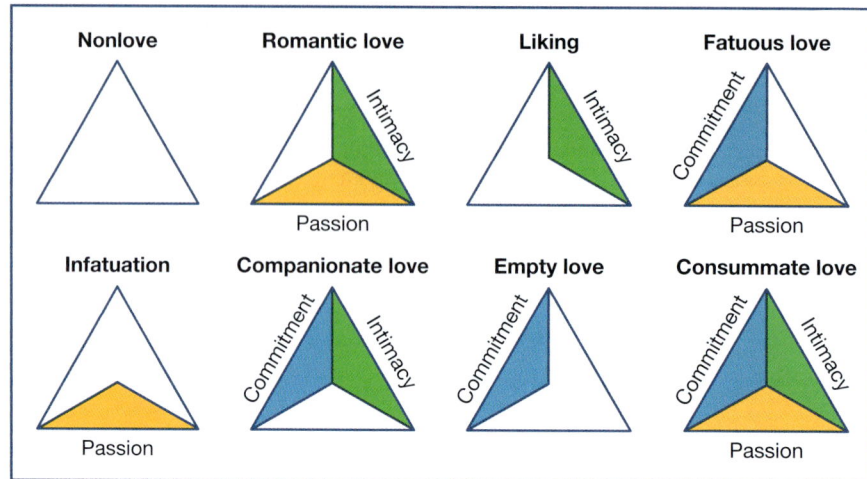

If you think about these components as being simply present or absent, there are eight different types of relationship that are theoretically possible; these are shown in Figure 12.4.

If a relationship has none of the components, Sternberg calls it "nonlove." These would be relationships with casual acquaintances, such as people in your class whom you don't know personally. Sternberg notes that "the large majority of our personal relationships" are nonlove (Sternberg, 1986, p. 123). The opposite would be "consummate love," or complete and perfect love.

In Sternberg's theory, ideal romantic relationships have commitment, intimacy, and passion. If you only have one or two of these three essential components, you get one of the other six types of relationship. For example, "companionate love" is more like a deep friendship; it's missing sexual or physical attraction, but it has all the other aspects of being with a partner. The other forms are romantic, liking, fatuous, infatuation, and empty love, which you can see result from different combinations.

Sternberg also notes that any given relationship will change over time and that each component will fluctuate. So while an ideal relationship has high levels of intimacy, passion, and commitment, that kind of relationship may be hard to maintain. Consummate love is a nice goal, but it requires effort between both people involved.

Attachment theory suggests that the relationship infants have with their primary caregiver (such as their mother) will serve as a template for all future relationships.

Attachment Theory

Perhaps the most popular theory explaining intimate relationships is attachment theory.

Inspiration came from London in World War II, when the city was being bombed by Germany. Parents had only one fear greater than their own death: the death of their children. To keep London's young ones safe, the British government evacuated the children to the countryside. After the war, the families who survived were reunited. Physically, the children were fine—but an unforeseen side effect had occurred. Some had been separated from their parents at a crucial time in their development, and as young adults, they displayed a variety of psychological problems. Many had trouble forming strong, loving ties with other people.

The theory evolved as psychological researchers tried to explain this pattern of behavior (Berscheid & Regan, 2005; Bowlby, 1958, 1988; Hazan & Shaver, 1987). Since then, thousands of research studies have explored how childhood experiences affect relationship behaviors, decisions, and interactions between couple members. **Attachment theory** says that our early family environment affects our ability to begin and maintain healthy, adult relationships—including romantic relationships.

The Strange Situation and Three Attachment Styles

British psychologist John Bowlby and his protégé Mary Ainsworth developed a unique way to test interactions between parents and infants (Ainsworth, 1979; Bowlby, 1958).

They believed if an infant-parent relationship was happy and healthy, then the child would learn to trust others and to grow up to have healthy relationships with others. To test this, they used a procedure called the **strange situation**. Infants and their primary caregiver (usually their mother) were observed as they sat in a room filled with new, interesting toys. Then, a series of exchanges would occur in which the mother left and returned after a few minutes. The babies were observed to see how they responded. Did they cry? Did they explore the room and play with the toys? How did they act when she came back?

The strange situation and follow-up research identified three different patterns, which are called **attachment styles**. These are summarized in Table 12.1 (Berscheid & Regan, 2005; Hazan & Shaver, 1987). The three styles are

- *Secure:* Produced by consistently supportive parents, these infants grow into adults with healthy self-esteem and the ability to have loving, trusting relationships with others. They don't get overly anxious or jealous.

- *Anxious/ambivalent:* The result of inconsistent parents, these infants later have low self-esteem. They tend to be highly jealous and anxious but crave love and support from others.

- *Avoidant/fearful:* When parents are consistently absent or abusive, children grow into adults who generally lack healthy attachments to others. They shut off trust and may avoid long-term commitments.

Just in the past 10 years, over 4,000 studies have been published on attachment styles. You can measure your own attachment tendencies with the What's My Score?

Attachment theory: The idea that our early family environment affects our ability to form and maintain healthy adult relationships.

Strange situation: Refers to either the experimental method in which a mother and child are observed in a room as the mother leaves and returns or to the room itself where this occurs.

Attachment style: Our pattern of trust and self-esteem within relationships; we can be secure (healthy), anxious-ambivalent (insecure), or avoidant-fearful (generally avoiding long-term commitment to others).

TABLE 12.1

Three Distinct Attachment Styles

ATTACHMENT STYLE	PARENTS WERE . . .	LEVEL OF ANXIETY WHEN PARENT LEAVES	EXPLORE THE STRANGE SITUATION ROOM?	LEVEL OF ADULT SELF-ESTEEM	TENDENCY TO BE JEALOUS OF ROMANTIC PARTNERS
Secure	Consistently good	Moderate	Yes	High	Low
Anxious/ ambivalent	Inconsistent	High	No	Low	High
Avoidant/fearful	Consistently bad	Low	Yes	Low	Low

feature. Here are some of the most interesting findings about how attachment style affects relationships in college students:

- Students with a secure style are more likely to send regular texts to a partner, whereas avoidant/fearful students are more likely to send "sext" messages (texts with sexual content or illicit photos; Drouin & Landgraff, 2012).

- Anxious/ambivalent people are more likely to jealously check on their partner's social media (e.g., Facebook or Snapchat) messages (Marshall et al., 2013).

- Secure people are less likely to accept violence or abuse in their relationships (McDermott & Lopez, 2013) and are more likely to display emotional sensitivity and social skills (Dereli & Karakuş, 2011).

- In gay couples, anxious/ambivalent men are less likely to require a partner to use a condom during sex (Starks et al., 2017).

WHAT'S MY SCORE?

Measuring Your Attachment Style

A good way to understand the different styles of attachment is to see how research psychologists measure them. One of the most popular is a scale called Experiences in Close Relationships (Brennan et al., 1998; updated by Wei et al., 2007). Some of the items have been modified slightly to make them easier for you to score.

Instructions: As you read each statement, write a number next to the item to indicate how much you agree with it, using this scale:

1	2	3	4	5	6	7
Strongly disagree			Neutral			Strongly agree

Anxiety Items

_____ 1. I worry that romantic partners won't care about me as much as I care about them.

_____ 2. My desire to be close sometimes scares people away.

_____ 3. I need a lot of reassurance that I am loved by my partner.

_____ 4. I find that my partner(s) don't want to get as close as I would like.

_____ 5. I get frustrated when romantic partners are not available when I need them.

_____ 6. I often worry about being abandoned.

Avoidance Items

_____ 7. I want to get close to my partner, but I keep pulling back.

_____ 8. I am nervous when partners get too close to me.

_____ 9. I try to avoid getting too close to my partner.

_____ 10. I don't usually discuss my problems and concerns with my partner.

_____ 11. I do not turn to my partner in times of need.

_____ 12. I do not rely on my partner for things like comfort and reassurance.

Scoring: The more you _disagree_ with these sentences, the more "Secure" you are. In other words, if you agree with Items 1 to 6, you would be classified as "Anxious/Ambivalent." If you agree with Items 7 to 12, you would be classified as "Avoidant/Fearful." If you don't really agree with any of the items, or your total score for each section is a low number, you are "Secure" and are more likely to have happy, healthy relationships.

FIGURE 12.5

An updated, four-category model of attachment.

		VIEW OF SELF	
		POSITIVE	**NEGATIVE**
VIEW OF OTHERS	**POSITIVE**	**Secure** (Comfortable with intimacy)	**Preoccupied** (anxious and jealous)
	NEGATIVE	**Dismissing** (narcissistic, avoids long-term intimacy)	**Fearful** (avoids social connections in general)

Source: Modified from Bartholomew and Horowitz (1991).

A New Model: Four Styles Instead of Three

Attachment theory is very popular.

However, some critics have noted that the original model didn't adequately explain *why* people end up with different attachment styles. So, an important update was offered by Bartholomew and Horowitz (1991). They believe that attachment style is generally produced by two key questions we all ask. First: Do I have a positive or negative view of myself? Second: Do I have a positive or negative view of others?

The answers to these questions produce four possible outcomes, shown in Figure 12.5. Each outcome is labeled as an attachment style. A positive view of self is like high self-esteem; it means you feel worthy of being loved and believe you would make a good relationship partner. A positive view of others means that you find other people trustworthy in general and seek out healthy relationships. Having both leads to a secure attachment style. They also found (Bartholomew & Horowitz, 1991):

- *Secure* people were most likely to have high levels of intimacy in both romantic relationships and friendships; they also showed self-confidence, warmth, and balance in their relationships.

- *Dismissing* people showed the highest levels of self-confidence but also showed very low levels of emotional expressiveness, empathy, and warmth toward others. They were less likely to rely on others in times of need and were less likely to share personal information with other people.

- *Preoccupied* people were the opposite of dismissing in almost every variable. They showed particularly low self-confidence but particularly high levels of personal self-disclosure, emotional expressiveness (such as frequent crying), and excessive caregiving behaviors.

- Finally, *fearful* people were very low on self-disclosures, intimacy, level of relationship involvement, reliance on others, and self-confidence. In general, they did not put much effort into relationships or expect others to do so.

Interdependence and the Investment Model

Both Sternberg's triangular theory of love and attachment theory predict different kinds of relationships and dynamics between two people.

But some researchers wanted more. Neither theory provides specific insight regarding *how* each of us decides whether a given person is "the one." How do we consciously decide whether to commit to a relationship? What factors do we consider? Can social psychology predict whether a relationship will last over time?

Thibaut and Kelley (1959) created **interdependence theory**, a model of romantic relationships that suggests relationship stability is predicted by commitment. Sometimes called social exchange theory, interdependence theory starts with the basic premise that once you enter into a relationship with another person, you are no longer an independent entity. Now your happiness or unhappiness is, at least to some degree, *interdependent* with that of the other person. If your partner gets fired or promoted, that affects you. If you come home in a good or bad mood, that affects your partner.

Two Predictors of Commitment: Satisfaction and Alternatives

Once a relationship is formed and people are interdependent, how do they decide whether to commit? This theory says that there are two factors we consider.

The first is **satisfaction**, which the theory defines as an individual's perception of whether their relationship is better or worse than average. If we perceive our relationship to be better than average, we're satisfied—and therefore more likely to commit to the relationship. The *positive correlation* between satisfaction and commitment has been supported in several research studies, including a *meta-analysis* that reviewed 52 individual tests of the connection (Le & Agnew, 2003).

The second factor is **alternatives**. If you weren't with this person, what are your other options? Whom else could you be dating—or would you rather just be single for a while? The more alternatives we have (or the better quality they are), the less committed we'll be to our current partner and relationship. So, alternatives and commitment are *negatively correlated:* As the number and quality of alternatives go up, commitment goes down (Le & Agnew, 2003).

Remember, correlation doesn't imply causation. So, the association between alternatives and commitment also goes the other way. One is that lots of alternatives might lead us to be less committed. But it's also true that if we're highly committed to a current partner, we tend to downgrade possible alternatives, telling ourselves that they aren't so great and thus avoiding temptation (Rusbult & Buunk, 1993). This cognitive bias is called **derogation of alternatives** (Johnson & Rusbult, 1989; Simpson et al., 1990).

A Third Predictor: Investments

It makes sense that commitment is predicted by satisfaction and alternatives.

But those two factors aren't always enough. Can you think of couples who stay together even though they don't seem very happy (low satisfaction) and could probably do better (high alternatives)? If so, you might like the addition to interdependence theory that came along in the 1980s: the investment model (Rusbult, 1980).

Investments are the time, energy, and resources put into a relationship that would be lost if the relationship were to end. It's things like a shared apartment, furniture you bought together, sacrifices you made to be in the relationship, or shared friendship networks. It's also the emotional investments and efforts you've made. Investments are *positively correlated* with commitment: The more investments we have, the more likely we are to stay in a relationship. The **investment model** adds this third component as an equally important predictor of commitment, along with satisfaction and alternatives (see Figure 12.6).

In another *meta-analysis* including data collected from 37,761 participants and 137 studies over 33 years, satisfaction, alternatives, and investments did successfully predict relationship breakup (Le et al., 2010). While it might not seem particularly romantic to think of love in these mathematical terms, the model shown in Figure 12.6 does appear to have predictive power concerning relationship commitment.

Interdependence theory: A model that predicts relationship commitment is based on (1) how satisfied each partner is and (2) what their alternatives are.

Satisfaction: Our perception of whether our romantic relationship is better or worse than average.

Alternatives: The number and quality of other options we'd have if our current relationship ended.

Derogation of alternatives: The tendency for highly committed people to downgrade possible alternatives, thus avoiding temptation.

Investments: The time, energy, and resources put into a relationship that would be lost if the relationship ended.

Investment model: A statistical model for predicting relationship commitment that includes three factors: satisfaction, alternatives, and investments.

FIGURE 12.6

Interdependence theory says relationship stability is predicted by commitment and that commitment comes from high satisfaction and low alternatives. The investment model includes everything from interdependence theory but adds a third predictor of commitment called investments.

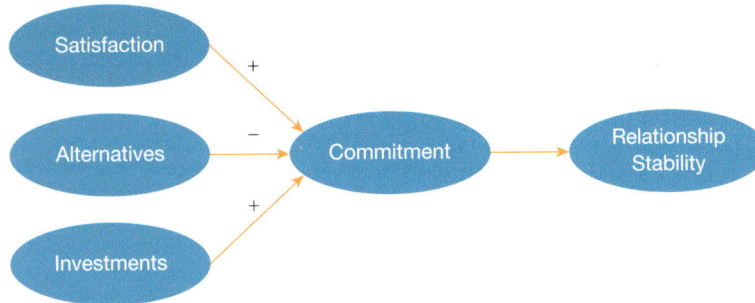

Source: Data from Rusbult (1980).

THE MAIN IDEAS

- Sternberg's triangular theory of love says that relationships are made up of three components: (1) intimacy (the emotional component), (2) passion (the physical component), and (3) commitment (the cognitive component).

- Attachment theory suggests that the way your parents treated you during your early childhood affects your self-esteem and trust in adult, romantic relationships. How you act in these relationships is your attachment "style." Both a three-style and a four-style model have been proposed.

- Interdependence theory suggests that commitment to relationships is based on satisfaction and alternatives. The investment model added a third predictor of commitment called investments; they are the time, effort, and resources we put into relationships that we'd lose if the relationship ended.

CRITICAL THINKING CHALLENGE

- John Bowlby is famous for saying that the attachment style you form as a young child will follow you "from the cradle to the grave," meaning it will be difficult to change over your lifetime. Do you agree or disagree with this belief? Is it possible that happy, secure children can become anxious or avoidant due to negative experiences in young adulthood, such as an abusive relationship? Alternatively, can people who had challenging childhoods heal these emotional wounds by finding loving, supportive adult relationship partners?

- Do you prefer the three-category model of attachment styles or the four-category model? Why?

- One criticism of the model shown in Figure 12.6 is that it's very logical and mathematical, like an algebraic equation to explain love. Do you think people really make decisions like this, with lists of pros and cons in our heads? Or, do we more often "go with our gut" and follow our hearts, even if our logical minds tell us we're making a mistake?

HOW DO GENDER AND CULTURE INFLUENCE RELATIONSHIPS?

>> **LO 12.3:** Analyze ways that gender and culture influence relationships.

The theories covered so far have made one important assumption.

The assumption is that most people respond in similar ways to childhood experiences or current situations. But there are more influences on how we think and act. Many social psychologists have studied how gender and culture change our relationships. This section answers the core question "How do gender and culture influence relationships?" by exploring examples of

(1) gender differences in relationships and

(2) cultural differences in relationships.

Relationships and Gender

To start, sex and gender are not necessarily simple ideas.

For example, many psychologists and biologists argue that there are more than two sexes (e.g., Harper, 2007) and that referring to men and women as "opposite sexes" encourages belief in a false dichotomy. A system with only two categories ignores people with "intersex" conditions (i.e., chromosomes neither XX nor XY or people who have atypical exposure or reactions to prenatal hormones), people who are gender queer, transgender individuals, and more.

Similarly, categorizing sexual orientation as only "heterosexual" or "homosexual" excludes several other possibilities, such as asexuality. Even the label *bisexual* indicates there are only two sexes—and that's why many people now prefer the term *pansexual*. Pansexual orientation acknowledges intersex, queer, and transgender people and notes that sexual attraction can occur regardless of someone's social labels. Encouraging a continuum or spectrum perspective instead of a categorical perspective, Kinsey and colleagues (1948) first suggested that sexual orientation could range from two extreme poles (see Figure 12.7), with most people being somewhere in the middle.

Pansexual: Sexual attraction to some individuals regardless of their perceived sex or gender; some people consider it an updated term for *bisexual*.

FIGURE 12.7

Kinsey et al.'s (1948) continuum of sexual orientation.

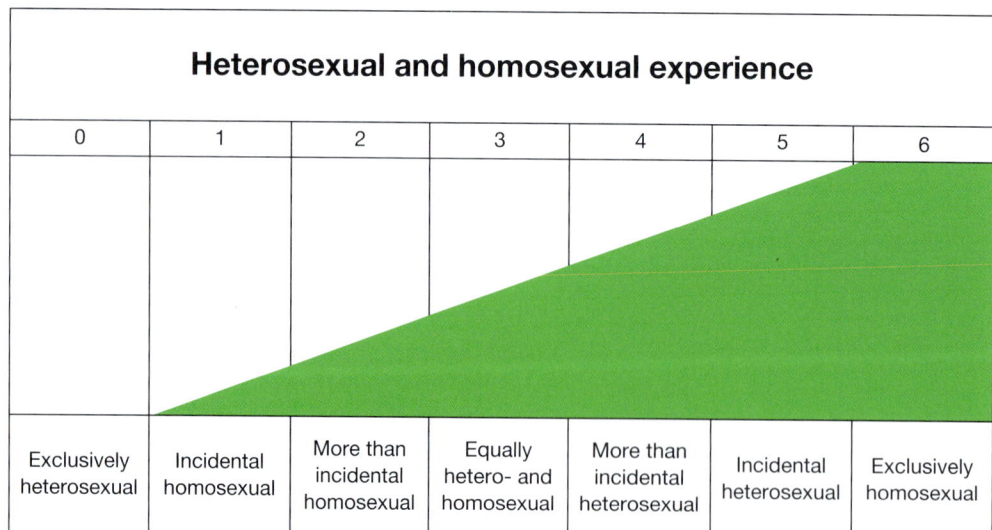

Heterosexual and homosexual experience

0	1	2	3	4	5	6
Exclusively heterosexual	Incidental homosexual	More than incidental homosexual	Equally hetero- and homosexual	More than incidental heterosexual	Incidental heterosexual	Exclusively homosexual

Still, most research has focused on differences between men and women in heterosexual relationships because (1) most people self-identify as fitting into these categories and (2) it's simply easier to conduct research on heterosexual couples. There are more of them available and they are not as concerned with being stigmatized or stereotyped in research studies (a privilege of being the group with more social power).

Patterns from this sample show consistent and cross-cultural differences in relationship choices between men and women. Often, these results are interpreted from an evolutionary point of view because they are tied to sexual interactions and reproduction (just like we saw earlier, with things like attraction to symmetry). While research has uncovered several gender differences in relationships, we'll cover just two examples in depth: jealousy and promiscuity. Then we'll touch on some research findings from same-sex relationships.

Differences in Jealousy

Jealousy can be a powerful emotion.

Do you think men and women are jealous for different reasons? Buss and colleagues (1992) asked participants to consider the following two scenarios and to identify which one would make them more jealous:

> Please think of a serious committed romantic relationship that you have had in the past, that you currently have, or that you would like to have. Imagine that you discover that the person with whom you've been seriously involved became interested in someone else.

> What would distress or upset you more (please pick only one):
>
> (A) Imagining your partner forming a deep emotional attachment to that person.
>
> (B) Imagining your partner enjoying passionate sexual intercourse with that other person.

A full 83% of the women said that emotional infidelity would upset them more (Option A), and 60% of the men in this study said that the sexual infidelity (Option B) would upset them more. This basic result has been replicated in other studies (Brase et al., 2014; Tagler, 2010). Why?

An evolutionary perspective explains these findings by saying that women don't like it when men *love* other people because the men might give them gifts and resources. In an old-fashioned world in which men are the sole family providers with an income, women's fears about access to those resources make sense. On the other hand, evolutionary theory says that men will be particularly jealous when female partners engage in *sexual* infidelity for an entirely different reason.

When a child is born, men have a problem called **paternity uncertainty**: doubt about whether a child is genetically theirs. Even if two people are married and supposedly monogamous, a father could be raising a child that is not genetically his own if his wife had an affair. Note that there's no such thing as "maternity uncertainty"; a woman who is pregnant is 100% sure that the child is genetically her own (unless, of course, surrogacy or in vitro fertilization was involved). Because of paternity uncertainty, this theory makes the prediction that men should be more jealous than women of potential sexual infidelity, which is what this study found.

However, an alternative explanation can be found in cultural expectations of men versus women. In many cultures, it is more socially acceptable for men to be sexually promiscuous than it is for women. Women are trained to be communal—meaning focused on others, putting relationships first, and being nurturing and kind (e.g., Diekman & Eagly, 2000). Thus, women may be more hurt by emotional cheating than by sexual cheating.

Paternity uncertainty: Anxiety from men due to doubt about whether a child is genetically theirs.

On the other hand, cultural expectations guide women to be relatively "chaste" and loyal due to benevolent sexism (see Chen et al., 2009; Glick & Fiske, 1997). Consequently, men may be particularly offended if their wives and girlfriends cheat on them sexually, simply because it is so culturally surprising. As usual, the best explanation relies on how nature (or sex differences) and nurture (or culture) interact in each situation.

Differences in Promiscuity

Who wants to have more sex—men or women?

Evolutionary theory (nature) and cultural explanations (nurture) also offer different perspectives regarding gender differences in **promiscuity**, how many casual sexual partners one has. The stereotype of a heterosexual date in many cultures is that the man will pressure the woman to engage in sexual behaviors. The woman, on the other hand, may demand (or at least expect) some show of commitment before granting sexual favors; she might want him to declare his love, propose marriage . . . or at least go on three dates to show his interest. But does this stereotype reflect reality?

Gender differences in promiscuity were tested in a famous study conducted on a large college campus (Clark & Hatfield, 1989). A social psychology class trained five college women and four college men as *confederates* for the study. (Before the research began, their physical attractiveness was judged to range from slightly unattractive to moderately attractive—but it turned out that their attractiveness didn't affect the results.) All student experimenters were around 22 years old, and they walked around their own college campus looking for people of the "opposite" sex who were sitting by themselves.

When an opportunity arose, the experimenters approached another person and said, "I have been noticing you around campus. I find you to be very attractive." The experimenters then followed up with one of three *randomly assigned* questions: (1) "Would you go out with me tonight?" (2) "Would you come over to my apartment tonight?" or (3) "Would you go to bed with me tonight?" No matter what the innocent other person said, the experimenters were instructed to then explain that this was all part of a psychology experiment.

How would you respond? The percentages in Table 12.2 indicate how many people in each condition said "yes" to the request from the male and female experimenters.

When women in college were approached, about half were willing to go on a date, but only a few agreed to go back to a man's apartment. Not a single woman agreed to go to bed with any of the men. The pattern for men in college was much higher and trended in the opposite direction. About half agreed to a date, almost two thirds agreed to go back to a woman's apartment, and fully three quarters of the men agreed to have casual sex!

An Evolutionary Explanation. Why are men more promiscuous?

Evolutionary theory argues that the main reason for men being more promiscuous is because of a gender difference in **parental investment**, the amount of time, effort, and physical resources needed for someone to produce genetic offspring. Essentially, it's how much work it takes to have a baby. In humans, women clearly have the higher parental investment. After all, from a biological perspective, men

Promiscuity: The number of casual sexual partners one has.

Parental investment: The amount of time, effort, and physical resources needed for an individual to produce and raise genetic offspring.

TABLE 12.2

How Many People Said "Yes" to Three Different Questions From Potential Dates

	TYPE OF QUESTION		
	DATE	APARTMENT	SEX
Female participants	56%	6%	0%
Male participants	50%	69%	75%

Source: Clark and Hatfield (1989).

only need to contribute some sperm and their job is done. Women must contribute an egg, carry the fetus for 9 months, survive childbirth, and provide milk for a baby until it is able to fend for itself.

Men's relatively low parental investment makes it easy for them to have many partners. In fact, being monogamous limits their number of potential children. The male impulse for casual sex (according to this perspective) also provides a genetic benefit: Children with diverse genetic combinations inherit different evolutionary advantages and disadvantages. For example, some offspring may be prone to genetic disorders carried by a particular mother. Having children with a lot of different women thus increases a man's overall genetic strength in the next generation.

However, women's high level of parental investment means that their best strategy is to require a commitment from a potential sexual partner before taking a chance at reproduction. If a woman becomes pregnant, it's quite a commitment to that single child. So women are predicted to be much less promiscuous than men. Women should seek commitment and monogamy from male partners, according to this perspective, so that if they do get pregnant, they will have someone to provide financial and emotional support for her and the child.

A Cultural Explanation. Again, however, there is also a cultural explanation for the same pattern of results.

Many cultures are more accepting of men having more sexual partners and having sex earlier in life, compared to the expectations of women's sexual behaviors. In "Western" cultures, slang terms for men with a lot of sexual experience are generally positive, like "stud," while terms for women are generally negative, like "slut." These double standards indicate that women will be judged much more harshly for exactly the same behaviors; so, some women may not agree to casual sex simply because they don't want to be judged for it (Conley et al., 2012).

Clark and Hatfield (1989) themselves point out three possible explanations for their own findings: (1) parental investment, (2) sexual double standards based on culture, and (3) women's concern about safety and sexual assault, making them more cautious to agree to any of the three scenarios with a stranger. Note that more recent research has also questioned the hypothesis that men are more promiscuous. Two studies point out that these differences seem to disappear when statistical analyses are done differently or when a "bogus pipeline" methodology (see Chapter 6) is used to encourage more honest responding from participants (Alexander & Fisher, 2003; Pedersen et al., 2002; for a full discussion of alternative views, see Conley et al., 2011).

There are other gender differences in sexual behavior. For example, many men prefer younger female partners, and this preference increases the older the man is—but women's preference for men who are slightly older than themselves remains stable over life (Grøntvedt & Kennair, 2013). Men consistently value looks in a partner more than women do, but women are more demanding of partners in most other ways, including things like social status (Li et al., 2013; Schwarz & Hassebrauck, 2012). In a study of over 500 college students, another study found that most men are more comfortable with various sexual behaviors, compared to women, and that men overestimate women's comfort with these behaviors (Reiber & Garcia, 2010).

Technology may also be related to interesting changes in promiscuity patterns. With easily accessible birth control, women are free to engage in casual sex without the pregnancy worries that their ancestors had. In addition, promiscuity is getting easier and easier with cell phones and apps like Tinder, Grindr, and Bumble. As we move into each new decade, more research will always be needed.

Same-Sex Relationships

There are millions of same-sex couples in the world.

Despite this, most research on close relationships is done with heterosexual couples—but more and more studies are focusing on gay and lesbian couples. Many studies have found that the patterns identified in this chapter for heterosexual couples also apply to same-sex couples. That said, there appear to be a few differences.

Some research shows that gay and lesbian couples have a lot in common with heterosexual couples, but more research is needed on same-sex attraction and relationship dynamics.

For example, Lehmiller (2010) discovered that heterosexual men are more likely to feel committed to a relationship based on tangible investments such as jointly shared objects. On the other hand, gay men care more about intangible investments such as sacrifices to be together (see Goodfriend & Agnew, 2008). While similarity was reviewed earlier as a predictor of attraction, this tendency appears to be stronger in heterosexual couples. One study (Kurdek & Schmitt, 1987) found that income and education were *significantly positively correlated* for heterosexual couples living together but not for gay or lesbian couples. Similarity also appears to differ more in other ways; about 21% of married gay and lesbian couples are interracial (compared to about 10% of married heterosexual couples; U.S. Census Bureau, 2010).

There are many possible explanations for these differences. One is that gay and lesbian subcultures emphasize different values and social norms. Another possibility is that fewer gay and lesbian individuals exist in any given town or city, making it harder for them to find happy relationships with similar people due to simply having fewer options. In short, gay men and lesbian women suffer from a smaller **field of eligibles**—a smaller pool of potential dates and mates.

Relationship outcomes may also be different in gay and lesbian couples due to homophobia from others. Same-sex couples may not experience the same freedoms due to prejudice and discrimination, and being forced to live "in the closet" may produce stress and challenges that heterosexual couples can blissfully avoid.

That said, many studies show that gay couples and heterosexual couples have a lot in common. Sutphin (2010) applied interdependence theory to gay couples. For both couple members, satisfaction and commitment went up with being happy about the division of labor in the relationship and with being appreciated for contributions to the home. Relationship violence appears to be a problem in all types of couples, regardless of sexual orientation (e.g., Cruz, 2003; West, 1998). And finally, just as we saw before with gender and jealousy research, lesbian women are more upset with emotional infidelity while gay men are more upset over sexual infidelity in partners. In gay couples, paternity uncertainty doesn't work as an explanation (Frederick & Fales, 2016).

So, while more research is needed, an overarching conclusion might be that in general, same-sex relationships have more similarities than differences with heterosexual relationships. We all want to find loyal, supportive partners.

Relationships and Culture

In Chapter 3, you learned about one of the most-studied cultural differences: individualism versus collectivism.

Hopefully you remember that individualistic cultures (those focused on independence and personal success) differ from collectivistic cultures (those focused on group and family needs) in a variety of ways. That chapter featured the movie *Crazy Rich Asians* as an example of how culture can influence relationships.

In one review of research on this topic (Dion & Dion, 1993), three specific propositions were hypothesized, then supported with evidence from several sources:

1. "Romantic love" is considered more important in individualistic cultures. For example, whether your family approves of your partner matters more in collectivistic cultures (Lee & Stone, 1980), while people from individualistic cultures make decisions like marriage without consulting family members first.

Field of eligibles: The potential dates and mates available for an individual not in a committed romantic relationship, based on that individual's criteria for a romantic partner.

iStockPhoto/ajr_images

2. People from individualistic cultures expect higher levels of emotional intimacy from their romantic partners. For example, in China and in Japan, people often remain emotionally closer to family members than to partners, even after marriage (Hsu, 1985; Roland, 1988). People from Eastern or collectivistic cultures are therefore more likely to prioritize their family of origin over their romantic partner.

3. While individualism fosters expectations of "romance" and "intimacy," it can ultimately lead to problems within relationships. For example, research in Canada found that people who maintained the belief that their own freedom was more important than their partner's happiness were less likely to report high levels of caring or trust toward their partner (Dion & Dion, 1991) and were more open to eventual divorce (Dion & Dion, 1993).

Let's end this chapter with two interesting examples of how culture might affect our views of marriage.

Arranged Marriages

For some cultures, such as China and India, the "traditional" approach to relationships is an **arranged marriage**.

Here, the couple members' families decide two people should get married for pragmatic reasons, such as a good match of socioeconomic status or because the two families have land next to each other (for a review of research on arranged marriages, see Merali, 2012). While people from outside of these cultures often view arranged marriages as lacking in romance, people within the cultures often see them as more "sacramental" or spiritual (Bhopal, 2011). Allowing your family to be involved in marriage decisions is a core example of the values within collectivistic cultures (e.g., Chang & Myers, 1997).

Research on satisfaction in arranged marriages finds inconsistent results (e.g., Blood, 1967; Madathil & Benshoff, 2008). Some studies find that arranged-marriage couples have higher satisfaction, more happiness, and better communication than people who married for love (Yelsma & Athappilly, 1988). Other studies find the opposite, especially for people who have been married for over 20 years (Xiaohe & Whyte, 1990).

While studies are still needed on this topic, one recent suggestion is that it doesn't matter if a marriage is arranged by the family or not as long as the people getting married perceive that they have choice and control over the final decision (Flicker et al., 2019). This ability to choose may be especially important to women. The authors noted that "women with greater influence over their partner selection [even in arranged marriages] reported higher levels of intimacy, passion, commitment and positive marital quality" (p. 1).

Marriage Expectations and Motivations

Finally, whether people choose to get married and what they expect from it varies by culture.

Do people from different cultures feel the same about why they should—or shouldn't—get married? Two studies asked U.S. college students, "If a boy/girl had all the other qualities you desired, would you marry this person if you were not in love with them?" When people were asked in 1967 (Kephart, 1967), 64% of men and 24% of women said no. When the same question was asked of students in 1984 (Simpson et al., 1986), more than 80% of both men and women said no.

It seems that Americans believe love is a necessary component to get married. But this might not be true in other cultures, where other factors may be stressed. One study asked college students from 11 countries—India, Pakistan, Thailand, Mexico, Brazil, Japan, Hong Kong, the Philippines, Australia, England, and the United States—about marriage motives (Levine et al., 2004). In total, they had over 1,000 participants. They started by asking people the same question as the paragraph above, about whether

Arranged marriage: A marriage planned by the couple members' families, often for pragmatic reasons such as similarity or financial benefits.

TABLE 12.3

Answers to Whether You'd Marry Someone Without Love, by Percentage

	NO	YES	UNDECIDED
United States	85.9	3.5	10.6
Brazil	85.7	4.3	10.0
England	83.6	7.3	9.1
Mexico	80.5	10.2	9.3
Australia	80.0	4.8	15.2
Hong Kong	77.6	5.8	16.7
Philippines	63.6	11.4	25.0
Japan	62.0	2.3	35.7
Pakistan	39.1	50.4	10.4
Thailand	33.8	18.8	47.5
India	24.0	49.0	26.9

When college students from 11 different countries were asked if they'd marry someone who had every quality they wanted, but they weren't in love, variance in answer seems to differ a lot based on culture.

Source: Levine et al. (2004).

they'd still get married without love. Their survey also included a self-report scale of collectivism versus individualism.

An initial finding of interest was that within each of the 11 countries, men's and women's answers weren't different. In other words, in this study, country-based culture was more important than gender-based culture. Next, as you can see in Table 12.3, there was a lot of variance in how willing people were to marry someone they don't love. Highest rates of people who said they would refuse a loveless marriage came from the United States, Brazil, England, Mexico, and Australia. England, Australia, and the United States also scored the highest in individualism.

In contrast, people from India, Pakistan, and Thailand were much more willing to marry someone without love, *if* the person had every other desired quality. Importantly, when the self-report scale on cultural values was calculated, Pakistan and Thailand scored highest in collectivism. So in general, the study found that love really is more important in individualistic cultures or for people who value needs of the self, compared to cultures or people who value needs of the family or larger community (collectivistic motives).

Love and relationships do vary around the world, then—but for various reasons. Social psychology is just getting to the point where we can make confident statements about how and why attraction and love occur for most people. But, like the other chapters in this book, more research will always be needed.

THE MAIN IDEAS

- Research has identified different patterns of jealousy and promiscuity between men and women in relationships. The evolutionary perspective explains these differences based on different biological needs and challenges to successful reproduction. However, the same patterns can also be explained by cultural expectations and stereotypes applied to men versus women.

- Many studies show similarities between heterosexual and gay/lesbian relationships, but more research is needed.
- Individualistic versus collectivistic cultures also show different patterns in relationships. For example, collectivistic cultures are more accepting of arranged marriages.

CRITICAL THINKING CHALLENGE

- With more and more advances in birth control, concerns about pregnancy resulting from sexual encounters are decreased. Do you think that these changes have affected the way modern men and women approach potential sexual mates and encounters? Do you think future generations will continue to see any changes?
- For the research on jealousy and promiscuity, both evolutionary (biological) and cultural explanations were offered. Which explanations did you find more persuasive and why?
- List three advantages and three disadvantages to arranged marriages, in comparison to marriages based on love.

CHAPTER SUMMARY

What Causes Attraction?

Three psychological variables have been studied regarding why we are attracted to some people more than others. The first is similarity; the similarity-attraction hypothesis predicts that people form relationships with others who have the same attitudes, interests, and demographics as themselves (such as age or socioeconomic status). A second predictor is mere exposure; we tend to like objects and people more after repeated exposure. This link was tested in the famous Westgate Housing Study. A third predictor is misattribution of arousal, sometimes known as excitation transfer. This hypothesis was tested in the well-known "shaky bridge" study.

Research has also attempted to find patterns of what humans seem to find physically attractive, regardless of culture; three variables have been identified. First, bilateral symmetry in faces (the right half mirrors the left half) appears to be attractive. Second, computer-generated "average" faces are rated as more attractive than individual faces. Third, body type seems to matter. Across cultures, people seem to prefer women who have a 0.7 waist-to-hips ratio and men with a 0.7 to 0.75 waist-to-shoulders ratio. All three of these findings were discussed in terms of an evolutionary perspective to attraction.

How Do We Decide to Commit to a Particular Relationship?

Sternberg's triangular theory of love suggests that all relationships are made up of three components: intimacy (the emotional part), passion (the physical or sexual part), and commitment (the cognitive or logical part). Ideal romantic relationships have high levels of all three components. Another popular theory is attachment theory. Attachment theory suggests that the relationship we had as infants with our primary caregiver (usually our mother) becomes a model for our future relationships. If that initial relationship is secure and built on trust, our later relationships will be healthier. Our pattern of behaviors is called our "attachment style," and both a three-style and a four-style model of attachment have been proposed. Finally, interdependence theory suggests that relationship commitment is based on our level of satisfaction and our alternatives to any given relationship. Later, a third variable was added to this model called investments. Investments are the time, energy, and resources we put into a relationship that we'd lose if the relationship ended. Commitment is predicted by high satisfaction, low alternatives, and high investments.

How Do Gender and Culture Influence Relationships?

Recent ideas suggest that categorizing people into "men versus women" or "heterosexual versus homosexual" promotes false dichotomies and that perhaps sex, gender, and relationships should be viewed from a continuum approach instead. However, most research on relationships uses heterosexual men and women, and this research has found some relatively stable differences based on sex, regardless of culture. Men appear to become more jealous over sexual infidelity, while women appear to be more jealous over emotional infidelity. Men often display patterns of higher rates of promiscuity compared to women. These differences can be explained both from an evolutionary perspective and from the perspective of understanding different norms and expectations for men and women. There are also interesting differences in relationships based on culture. For example, people from individualistic cultures prefer marriages based on love, while people in collectivistic cultures are more comfortable with arranged marriages.

CRITICAL THINKING, ANALYSIS, AND APPLICATION

- Some people believe in "love at first sight" or "soulmates." Others believe that marriage is an outdated concept and that humans aren't meant to commit to only one person for life. What is your opinion on this debate, and what scientific evidence can you use to support your view?

- Some critics of the evolutionary perspective argue that many of the hypotheses are "post hoc," meaning they are only created *after* a trend has already been identified. To be a truly useful perspective, evolutionary psychology should create new, testable hypotheses. Can you identify any additional physical traits that should be correlated with physical attractiveness or any additional gender differences that would make sense from an evolutionary point of view? How would you design a study to test your hypothesis or hypotheses?

- Attachment theory was originally developed in the 1940s and 1950s. As types of family become more diverse, how might early childhood experiences be affected that might influence later relationships? For example, if fathers are the primary caregiver instead of mothers, will it matter? If a child grows up in a family with multiple mothers and fathers, a stepfamily, multiple generations in the same home, and so on, how will that affect attachment?

- When you consider your own experiences in relationships, what major topics are missing from what you've seen in this chapter? Identify a topic and try to find an article on Google Scholar or PsycINFO that provides more information. Then, briefly summarize that article.

iStockPhoto/LoveTheWind

A. Social Psychology and Careers

Core Questions

A.1 Who are you after social psychology?

A.2 Where can a social problem solver work?

Learning Objectives

A.1 Take responsibility for your career by building a career-supporting network.

A.2 Recognize how social problems represent employable opportunities.

"Why do you rob banks?" the interviewer asked.

"Because that's where the money is." It's an old joke, usually attributed to the real bank robber Willie Sutton (1976). For medical students, paying attention to the most obvious answer is sometimes called "Sutton's law." It reminds them to pay attention to the obvious bleeding leg laceration before asking about hair loss (see Mortati et al., 2012).

Willie Sutton perfected his bank-robbing craft for 40 years—in between four imprisonments and three escapes. We are not recommending that you use social psychology to develop a career as a bank robber. Instead, this mini-chapter tells you some of the obvious ways that you can transform what you have learned in social psychology into a satisfying career. Here's an obvious (and less risky) formula for developing your career: Use your undergraduate education—including social psychology—to develop skills that

(a) you value,

(b) few other people have, and

(c) society needs.

If society really needs what you can do—and very few people are doing it—then somebody will have to pay you a great deal of money to apply those skills. The two core questions in this chapter move you forward in your career by asking, "Who are you after social psychology?" and "Where can a social problem solver work?" In other words, first we'll cover social psychological topics that can help you prepare for *any* career. Then, we'll discuss some career options more specifically relevant to social psychology.

WHO ARE YOU AFTER SOCIAL PSYCHOLOGY?

>> **LO A. 1:**   **Take responsibility for your career by building a career-supporting network.**

Social psychology changes you.

After studying social psychology, you (probably) will have the same color hair, prefer the same flavors of ice cream, and have the same quirky sense of humor. But what you believe, worry, and wonder about will be different. Many of those changes will be subtle, perhaps recognized only in hindsight several years later. Other changes may be specific—such as joining a research project—and lead immediately to a distinctive career path. (If you allow each of your 30+ college or university courses to change you just a little, then you will be a very different person by the time you graduate.)

For example, many psychology majors dislike statistics and research designs. Statistics and research designs are not what attracted them to psychology. But that widely shared dislike is one reason that the content of Chapter 2, Research Methods, is so valuable. It is loaded with skill-building, in-demand content that you can use right away. If you let Chapter 2 change you, then you are engaging the realistic formula for a well-paid career: Do something difficult that society needs and that few other people can do.

If you are willing to stretch yourself intellectually, then you will discover a world of useful, exciting, expanding employment opportunities. For example, a partial list of how we [Tom and Wind] have surprised even ourselves by applying our Chapter 2 research skills in our careers includes

- estimating the number of homeless veterans
- describing the number and type of injuries from tractor roll-overs
- applying game design principles to increase rates of college completion
- testing a low-tech persuasion technique to influence how people vote
- documenting the comorbid effects of exposure to chemical warfare
- archiving the "found poetry" of people in nursing homes

- evaluating the effectiveness of distance learning technology
- summarizing reactions of IBM employees to a training session
- exploring public attitudes toward co-generation of electric power
- identifying warning signs of intimate partner violence to educate communities
- connecting psychology to popular culture (*Harry Potter, WestWorld,* etc.).

I [Tom] have had so much fun using research methods that my ninth-grade algebra teacher sent me a note when she saw my name on a book about statistics. "Congratulations," she wrote, and then added, "Of all the students I had over a long career, you are the last one I would have expected to write such a book." Yes, I got a D in Mrs. Jenkins's algebra class. So, what changed? I discovered that math could be a guide to a more interesting, purposeful life—and not as difficult as I had feared once I made up my mind to learn it.

You don't need a graduate degree to do most of the things on our list. But you do need to get very good at something, almost anything, if you want society to deliver a regular paycheck into your bank account. This section helps you develop your employable skills after a course in social psychology by

(1) emphasizing that you—and only you—are responsible for your career,

(2) teaching you social psychological networking skills that advance your career, and

(3) recognizing how social psychology improves your thinking and communication skills.

You Are Responsible for Your Career

There is no "job box" out there with your name on it, just waiting for you to graduate and grab it.

One student in a capstone senior seminar class came from a family of committed and well-connected elementary schoolteachers. It was the career she had been aiming at since she was a little girl "teaching" her dolls. There seemed to be a job box waiting for her. But during her student teaching, she discovered that "I hated it. All I did was wipe noses and look for lost boots."

How do you find a job that's a fit for what you really want to do?

Exercise Your Internal Locus of Control

Here's one way you are changing: locus of control.

Your internal locus of control will become more important as you approach graduation. In Chapter 5, you learned that locus of control is your private assessment of how much you control your own life—and in this case, your career (Spector, 1988). An internal locus of control implies that you believe that you can shape your own career. An external locus of control implies the opposite. You would believe, for example, that something outside of yourself, such as the astrological alignment of the stars or a lucky break, will somehow influence your career and job search.

A research team in Serbia tested the locus of control of their undergraduate psychology students (Ćurić Dražić et al., 2018). They were interested in how their students perceived their own employability. At the time, the Serbian economy was emerging from several years of political instability and the financial collapse at the end of 2015. The unemployment rate among people aged 14 to 24 was 31.9%. So, there were few if any job boxes waiting for these emerging college graduates. The Serbian researchers found that

> both internal locus of control and ambition lead to *proactive* behaviors that are relevant for employability and consequently result in securing a sustainable job. (p. 1)

It sounds like a self-fulfilling prophecy. If you believe that you can influence your job hunt, then you are going to do the things likely to help get you a job—and doing those things actually helps you get a job. This pattern has been replicated among undergraduates in Korea (see Kim et al., 2016), among OTs (occupational therapists) working in combat zones (Smith-Forbes et al., 2016), and in many other societies and work settings. To get a job, you might have to take control of your fate. As the hockey legend Wayne Gretzky famously stated, "You miss 100% of the shots you don't take."

You want to exercise an internal locus of control as you move toward graduation. That may mean joining an academic club, volunteering in a professor's lab, or creating an internship. The specifics of "how" are less important than just getting moving. (Your school's career services department can help.)

Get Started With a Personal SWOT Analysis

A SWOT analysis can help you create a strategic career plan.

The technique of **SWOT analysis** originally was developed as a way for organizations to engage in strategic planning (see Helms & Nixon, 2010; Wang & Wu, 2019). SWOT stands for Strengths, Weaknesses, Opportunities, and Threats. You essentially make a list of each to assess what your best choices are. When used by businesses, employees simply list the organization's internal strengths and weakness and then the external opportunities and threats they can perceive in the environment. You can also use a SWOT analysis to develop a strategic plan for your career.

About 100 of the psychology undergraduates in the Serbian locus of control study mentioned earlier completed a "personal career SWOT analysis." They were asked to list at least three career-related strengths, weaknesses, opportunities, and threats. One of the interesting observations from this exercise was that their undergraduates had difficulty naming even three examples in any of the categories.

Can you do any better? Table A.1 gives you an opportunity to list at least four of what you perceive as your own career-related strengths and weaknesses plus the career-related opportunities and threats you see in the world of work you are about to enter. You can use this as an exercise "for your eyes only." But sharing the results anonymously as a class, with friends, or potentially your academic advisor or career services office may help you add many more items to your personal career SWOT analysis.

TABLE A.1

A SWOT Analysis of Your Career Choices

PERSONAL CAREER STRENGTHS	PERSONAL CAREER WEAKNESSES
1.	1.
2.	2.
3.	3.
4.	4.
CAREER OPPORTUNITIES IN THE ENVIRONMENT	**CAREER THREATS IN THE ENVIRONMENT**
1.	1.
2.	2.
3.	3.
4.	4.

SWOT analysis: Analysis of strengths, weaknesses, opportunities, and threats in decision making.

Networking: How to Go From Nothing to Something

The cynical student will say, "It's not what you know, it's who you know."

They're partially right. Yes, it helps if your mother-in-law happens to be the president of something-or-other. But where's the joy and challenge in that? With just a little training, you also can quickly get to know important people. (Also, working for your in-laws might not be such a great life decision.)

The goal of career networking is to make it easy for other people to help you advance your career. And surprise! People like helping other people. **Networking** is proactively interacting with others in order to exchange information, provide mutual support, and develop future contacts (see Macintosh & Krush, 2017; Taber & Blankemeyer, 2015). You already have overlapping family networks, friendship networks, and probably some online networks based on common interests. A career network is just another network—but you have to build it.

Career networking seems to work. *Longitudinal studies* that follow the same people for a long time period are rare because they can be expensive, and it takes so long to collect meaningful data. But a longitudinal study of career networkers found that their networking predicted the growth rate of salary and job satisfaction (Wolff & Moser, 2009). How do you do it?

Networking Is a Skill

Some people seem to be born networkers; good for them.

However, the rest of us need to learn how to build, maintain, and use our connections. And even "born networkers" can improve their skills because networking requires more than a winning personality. Lee and Chen (2017, p. 70) were particularly interested in the networking skills that were most helpful to college students. After *surveying* almost 600 students, they were able to divide their networking skills into two categories: cultural competency and digital competency.

- *Cultural competency:* Effective networking is a result of "socialization into various cultural genres at an early age. . . . [It] casts a long shadow on networking skills." Translation: Be open to diversity and embrace working with different kinds of people.

- *Digital competency:* Effective networking is a result of "frequent engagement in digital cultural production." Translation: Do what you do best online—and do it a lot. Turn that screen time into payoffs. Warning: In a digital world with the ability to screenshot images, *everything* you post is public. Be careful and thoughtful; what you think might impress your friends might not impress future employers.

Where do you start? When teaching networking skills to an internship class, I [Tom] challenge the group of 15 to 20 students to a game: Get an internship offer in 1 week. Every year, about 75% succeed and about two thirds of the class gets a job offer before the end of their internship. More important, they also know whether they want to accept the job offer, based on their several weeks of experience. There are only three rules to this real-life networking game:

1. Your leads must come only from people you already know or people your classmates know.

2. You can't ask any faculty for help.

3. You may not use email unless someone asks you first.

I added Rule 3 because it is easier to tell someone "no" online than to tell them no in person or on the phone. The purpose of this game is to have students experience "yes."

Networking: Proactively interacting with others to exchange information, provide support, and develop career contacts.

The MNQ: "Who Else Do You Know That Might Be Able to Help Me?"

As scientists, we dislike using the word *magic*.

Of course, it's not really magic, but the effectiveness of the "Magic Networking Question" (MNQ) will surprise you as you start building your career network. For example, one student thought that she might want to become a school psychologist. But she thought she had a problem: No one in the class said that they personally knew any school psychologists. That's ridiculous, of course, because all of these students went to high schools, and many of them have school psychologists. But they needed to figure that out for themselves by applying Sutton's law to their career search: Do the obvious first.

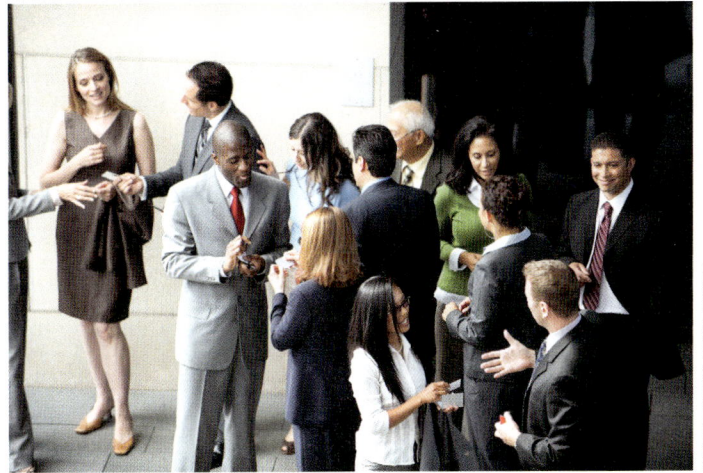

Networking may feel intimidating, but it's an extremely valuable skill.

Eventually someone said, "My uncle is an elementary school teacher." That was a little closer. I asked that student if she would share her uncle's phone number with her classmate. Yes. And her uncle put her in touch with the school psychologist at his school—who passed her name to a friend in another district. And she had her internship. It took two days and three phone calls.

It's the same pattern for all those starry-eyed students who imagine becoming criminal profilers for the FBI. No one in class is likely to know any profilers or anyone in the FBI. But everyone knows how to contact the campus police. The desk officer will have a boss who knows someone in local law enforcement who knows someone at the state level who knows someone who knows someone who is working for the FBI. It may take seven phone calls, but it's better than wasting your life wishing. And if the FBI doesn't work out, you've probably already impressed the local police department and could get an internship there.

If this sounds like work, then you are correct. Fortunately, your networking skills will improve with practice. The first skill is something that hopefully showed up in your career SWOT analysis under Personal Career Strengths: determination. Don't give up when someone says that they cannot help you.

Instead, use the Magic Networking Question (MNQ): "Who else do you know that might be able to help me?" Don't say "*will* help me" or "*can* help me." The person trying to help you senses that their contact might not help you—and that would make them look bad. Make it easier for them to help you by asking for the names of people who *might* be able to help you.

Networking Tips

Even if they did not give you any names:

1. Be polite and say something like, "Thank you for speaking with me."

2. Use the MNQ before you end: "Who else do you know that *might* be able to help me?"

3. Business cards have somehow survived the digital world; ask for theirs and give one.

4. Take notes: name, email, phone plus your observations. They'll be impressed with your conscientiousness.

5. Organize your notes the way a tree branches so you know who recommended whom.

6. When someone gives you a name, ask, "May I use your name when I contact them?" The question is a courtesy that also may flatter them into giving you

more names. When you call the next person, really do use the first person's name—the next person will feel more obligated to help you.

7. A world-class networker will send a few key people a handwritten thank you note. It takes more time and effort than an email, and people notice.

Don't bother feeling embarrassed by needing to network. You will quickly discover that almost everyone in the working world

(a) understands what you are doing, and

(b) will go out of their way to help you.

Networking is how people get jobs, shift careers, explore opportunities, and keep their careers moving forward. The sooner you get good at it, the faster your career can develop.

You Can Think and Communicate Clearly

Social psychology helps you develop two career-enhancing skills: thinking and communicating.

Don't assume that everyone can communicate appropriately. I once witnessed someone being fired for not having an Executive Summary (similar to an Abstract) in a report. Here is how your career benefits whenever your professors insist that you use APA style, rewrite a paper, or present your results in a graph:

- Using APA style trains you to pay attention to details.
  - With practice, paying attention to details will become automatic.
- Rewriting a paper requires you to rethink and then communicate more clearly.
  - Every time you rewrite, your paper gets a little better.
- Creating a visual display of data summarizes complex information.
  - Visual communications have become an in-demand skill in many industries.

Thinking Like a Social Psychologist at Work

Almost all work is social psychological.

Even a lonely poet in an attic is trying to communicate something to somebody. For example, notice all the social psychological ideas (in *italics* below) when a coworker, we'll call her Susan, has suddenly become less productive.

A coworker might say, "Susan is lazy." You, more than your coworkers, will be mindful of the *power of the situation* and that the *fundamental attribution error* directs our attention to Susan's personality and to overlook Susan's circumstances. You also are more likely to think of *confounding variables* because you recognize that "lazy" is not Susan's *baseline behavior* or her general *personality*. Susan may be caring for an aging parent or grandparent, dealing with an unexpected divorce, or rethinking her life after inheriting a large amount of money.

After social psychology, you also recognize the tendency in yourself and others to make *self-serving attributions*. If Susan were in line for a promotion that others also wanted, then someone else's explanation of "lazy" could be self-serving. Once people believe that she might be lazy, the *confirmation bias* will kick in and they'll notice only things that support that idea. The only thing you know for sure is that explaining Susan accurately will *require more data*. The overall effect of your training in social psychology is that you quietly withhold judgment. Your reluctance to judge someone too quickly is something that other people are likely to notice and admire.

Communicating Data More Effectively

When listing your personal career strengths, did you include "Creating visual displays of data?"

Visual data may be the most advantageous communication skill that social psychology has been helping you develop. You have seen several types of visual communications in this textbook (just flip through the book to find a few examples). If you took the time to understand them, then you have been developing a valuable, career-enhancing skill. Like a well-written Executive Summary, business managers with limited time love a well-designed visual display of critical information. You'll get a lot of credit for handing your boss a beautiful graphic that tells an important story about what's happening in your organization.

There are two practical reasons for developing the skill of creating and reading visual displays of social psychological data. First, a well-designed visual display of data (also called an **infographic**) is persuasive because it clarifies a complex data story that can be understood almost at a glance. If you've ever thought, "Wow, the graph makes so much more sense to me than the description with words," then you know how powerful a good infographic can be.

A second reason for learning how to create and read infographics is to protect you from people who are telling you visual lies. Visual data lies are common in advertising—and when it's your money on the line, you want to know if someone is trying to trick you. Figure A.1 demonstrates one of several ways that cunning advertisers can manipulate a graph to lie to you.

FIGURE A.1

These two graphs show the same data, but they deliver very different messages.

Same Data, Different Y-Axis

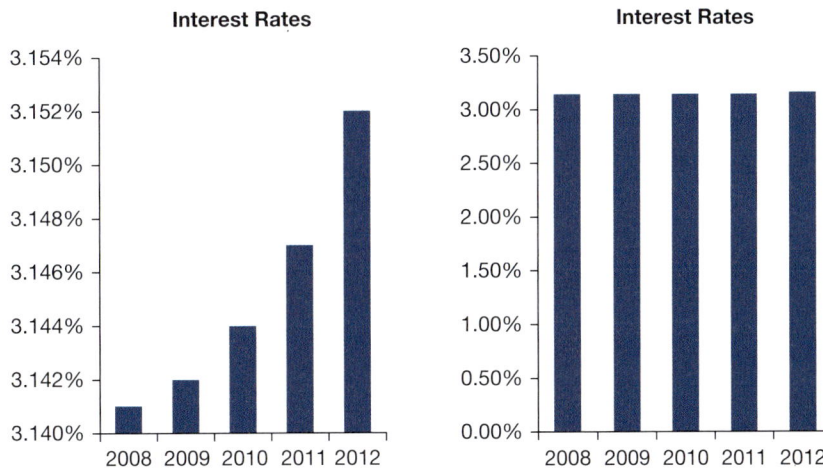

Source: Parekh, R. (April 14, 2014) How to lie with data visualization. Retrieved from https://heap.io/blog/data-stories/how-to-lie-with-data-visualization

The visual trick demonstrated in Figure A.1 is taken from Matt Bishop's (2017) website about deceptive data visualizations. The two bar graphs leave different impressions even though they rely on the exact same data. The only difference is the range on the vertical y-axis. You can learn about more statistical tricks and opportunities for insights in an APA publication edited by Stowell and Addison (2017). If interested, also don't miss Darrell Huff's (1993) classic *How to Lie With Statistics*. Of course, the point of reading the book is to learn how *not* to lie, or to avoid being tricked by others.

THE MAIN IDEAS

- Having an internal locus of control about your career is associated with more success; this may be an example of a self-fulfilling prophecy. One strategy to consider is a SWOT analysis that considers strengths, weaknesses, opportunities, and threats.

Infographic: A well-designed visual display of data.

- Networking is often essential in any career. Persistence pays off, sometimes through the "magical" question, "Who else do you know that might be able to help me?"

- A skill that will help in any career is the ability to create and understand infographics, or well-designed visual displays of data.

CRITICAL THINKING CHALLENGE

- Networking skills include both cultural competency and digital competency. Discuss your own future career goals and explain how each of these skills will be relevant to your daily tasks.

- Find a news story online that makes use of an infographic. First, explain the data displayed in the infographic in your own words. Then, analyze whether the infographic is done without bias.

WHERE CAN A SOCIAL PROBLEM SOLVER WORK?

>> **LO A. 2:** Recognize how social problems represent employable opportunities.

Everything changes when you take responsibility for your own career.

As a student of social psychology, your potential job title is now "social problem solver." That doesn't actually help you get a job, however, because it is too general. You could use the principles of attitudes and persuasion in Chapter 6 to persuade addicts to embrace drug rehab. You could also use those same insights to be a political speech writer, persuade juries to side with your client as a lawyer, or create marketing to persuade consumers to buy a certain brand of ice cream. That single chapter might lead to dozens of job options. So the job title of "social problem solver" doesn't point you to a path that directly leads to a career and a paycheck. We need to organize careers related to social psychology into more specific, meaningful categories. This section answers the core question "Where can a social problem solver work?" by

(1) describing what applied social psychologists do, and

(2) demonstrating how social entrepreneurs are solving social problems.

Apply Social Psychology to Everyday Problems

Applied social psychology has plenty of room for smart, motivated graduates.

For example, the social problem of aggression (Chapter 11) includes working against abuse and neglect of people living in nursing homes, political beliefs that lead to violence, sexual abuse by people with social power, bullying in schools, and much more. Each of those have several job titles attached to them.

- For nursing homes, you might work as a surveyor inspecting institutions, as a recreation therapist inside the home, or as a social worker helping individuals and families make difficult decisions about family members.

- For political beliefs that provoke violence, you may work for a campaign or for a legislator, as a lobbyist, or as a journalist documenting violence.

- Sexual abuse of vulnerable people may put you in an advocacy law office, give you a job training people with prevention workshops, or serving as a community trauma advocate.

- Dealing with school bullies probably places you inside a school or with an educational foundation. The world is full of problems, and social psychology has answers waiting for individuals to apply them (see Steg et al., 2017). But you have to take charge of your career.

Table A.2 summarizes how content from each chapter can lead to a specific career. These careers are just examples of the many, many options relevant to ideas studied in social psychology. Let's take a deep dive into two examples. You will probably recognize the first one: the social psychology of consumer behavior. The second one may surprise you: the social psychology of driving behavior.

TABLE A.2

Examples of Careers Tied to Social Psychology

CHAPTER	EXAMPLE CHAPTER CONTENT	CREATE A CAREER AS A . . .
Chapter 1 Introduction	Social psychology trains you to become a habitual critical thinker.	journalist who uses healthy skepticism when interviewing people in power.
Chapter 2 Research Methods	Co-occurring events do not mean that one event caused the other.	data analyst who understands that correlations do not imply causation.
Chapter 3 The Social Self	Our sense of self includes a personal, group, and cultural identity.	dispute mediator who reduces conflict between people from different groups.
Chapter 4 Social Cognition	We use two thinking systems: (1) fast and intuitive and (2) slow and reasoned.	first responder who also trains others how to make good decisions under stress.
Chapter 5 Person Perception	First impressions create sticky perceptions that lead to biased explanations.	teacher who knows how labeling a student can become a self-fulfilling prophecy.
Chapter 6 Attitudes and Persuasion	Cognitive dissonance is one way to change the strength and content of our beliefs.	marketing specialist who understands how and why attitudes change.
Chapter 7 Social Influence	Social norms influence conformity across cultures and generations.	public health worker who disrupts conformity to increase healthy norms in a community.
Chapter 8 Group Processes	Group living supports evolutionary benefits, leadership, and creativity.	company manager or military leader who knows how to inspire creativity in a cohesive group.
Chapter 9 Stereotyping, Prejudice, and Discrimination	The mental convenience of stereotypes can lead to prejudice and discrimination.	human resource manager who ensures that hiring and promotions are fair.
Chapter 10 Helping and Prosocial Behavior	What looks like altruism can be self-serving and influenced by situations.	community organizer who creates conditions that encourage mutual support and individual responsibility.
Chapter 11 Aggression	Worldwide aggression is declining, but there are still many types of aggression.	athletic coach who can separate fierce competition from interpersonal aggression.
Chapter 12 Intimate Relationships	Interpersonal attraction can be predicted by specific, social influences.	app designer who creates a dating site based on social psychology findings.

Thomas Trutschel / Photothek/Getty Images

The social psychology of products like diamonds is a particularly lucrative career option.

The Social Psychology of Consumer Behavior

When I [Wind] got engaged, I experienced a lot of people trying to persuade me to get a huge solitaire diamond ring.

I didn't want one. I was worried about the ethics of the diamond trade, and I also thought spending that much money on a portable rock was quite a waste of money. In addition, I thought a "traditional" ring was just kind of boring. But the people working in the jewelry stores were experts at persuasion; they tried all kinds of tricks to upsell me. It didn't work. I ended up choosing a unique ring that was only around $700 and was certified as "conflict free" in terms of where the stones came from. The people in the stores were clearly surprised and disappointed—their persuasive tricks usually work, apparently. But I recognized those tricks, as an expert in social psychology.

We often make irrational purchases. That irrationality, however, has a strange characteristic. Dan Ariely (2008) describes much of our economic behavior as "predictably irrational." And our "predictably irrational" consumption behavior creates several opportunities for the graduate who wants to apply social psychology to consumer behavior. The larger discipline that includes consumer behavior is now called behavioral economics; you can learn more in the mini-chapter on money.

Predictably Irrational: The Diamond Ring.   Diamonds are a case study in predictable irrationality.

Buying a diamond ring that (stereotypically) one lover uses to propose marriage to another is profoundly irrational. It was not always done that way. Diamonds cost a great deal of money that many young couples do not have. Slipping a diamond ring on a finger implies a sense of "ownership" to people; the original tradition was that women wore rings, but their husbands didn't.

Diamonds have other problems. They have been called "blood diamonds" because of their known history of being mined by people suffering through brutal circumstances (see Saunders & Nyamunda, 2016). The proceeds from diamond mining are sometimes used to fund terrorism (see Geldenhuys, 2019). Diamonds are only pragmatically useful in industrial settings when extreme hardness is required—and there are now alternatives.

There are many rational arguments for not using diamonds as a symbol of romantic devotion, marital commitment, and undying love. Diamonds do only one thing that humans really seem to like: glitter. Nevertheless, thanks mostly to advertising (see Bergenstock & Maskulka, 2001), diamonds continue to represent a predictably irrational symbol of romantic commitment (Davis, 2018).

Where Are the Careers?   Where are the careers?

The obvious "Sutton's law" opportunity related to diamonds is to work for an advertising agency or jewelry store, persuading people to keep on buying diamonds. But if you have moral objections, then you may want to be part of a nongovernmental organization (NGO) persuasion campaign that seeks to change the predictably irrational attitudes and behavior toward the use of diamonds that promote terrorism. You may want to create some cognitive dissonance, for example, by making people feel uncomfortable about using diamonds to express their love. Or you might want to join organizations undermining the connection between conflict diamonds and terrorism (see Bieri, 2013).

The diamond trade, of course, is only one example of the opportunities that connect social psychology to consumer behavior. Pick your favorite product: You can do some quick research in PsycINFO, GoogleScholar, and trade publications and then shape your job application around that. Your proactive, internal locus of control approach to your career suggests a different approach to job hunting and career development. Your chances of success are higher if you are the only applicant for a job you want but doesn't exist yet than to be one of 100 people applying for a job that exists but you may not want.

The Social Psychology of Driving Behavior

Traffic is a relative term.

There aren't too many traffic jams in Wind's rural hometown of Storm Lake, Iowa. There, "traffic" is getting stuck behind a tractor or combine on the road that's moving from one farming area to another. But traffic jams are expected near Tom's home in northern New Jersey. We don't ask "how far is it?" but "how long will it take?" And yet people keep moving here. Go figure—really, figure out why New Jersey is such a popular state. There are real social psychological jobs related to tourism, traffic management, and correlating driving distances to real estate prices. Someone is already doing these jobs, and the odds are pretty good your training is as good or better than their training. Whatever state you prefer to live in, the social psychology of driving behavior is something that people all over the country live with every day.

Even traffic jams might be better understood through social psychology.

iStockPhoto/Sean Davis

Traffic Jams, Cheaters, and Prosocial Behavior. Imagine, for example, that you're in a traffic jam.

That's not difficult for people in New Jersey, Los Angeles, or other urban areas. You're stuck in the far right-hand lane of a six-lane highway. You look in your right-side mirror and see a "cheater" coming up behind you, passing everyone by driving on the shoulder. It's a great opportunity to connect the social psychology of driving behavior with *prosocial behavior,* or altruism as many people think of it (see Chapter 10). Here are your two choices:

- Choice 1: Do nothing; let the cheater get away with it.
- Choice 2: Pull a little into the right-hand shoulder to stop the cheater.

Choice 1: Do Nothing. Watch your own thoughts.

If you immediately respond with anger after seeing the cheating driver in your mirror, then you have experienced an *automatic, intuitive* response. If you then reason that the cheating driver may have had a good explanation, then you have demonstrated a *slower, reasoned* response. Your *dual-processing* brain is probably reacting just as *social cognition* predicts because you have *two thinking systems.*

Because you have taken social psychology, you also have to consider whether you are committing the *fundamental attribution error* by thinking of the driver as a cheater. What about *situational explanations* such as someone driving a pregnant woman to the hospital? Your negative *attitude* toward the driver is based on a possibly *biased belief* that the cheater is being selfish.

All of this mental activity happens within about 500 milliseconds (half a second).

Choice 2: Pull Into the Right-Hand Lane to Stop the Cheater. But there is even more mental activity during those 500 milliseconds.

You may carry around a *self-concept* that you are a decent person who *believes in a just world.* Your *belief about yourself* leads to a *behavioral intention* that "this cheating driver needs to be taught a lesson." Everyone else is patiently waiting—cheating just isn't fair. As the *theory of planned behavior* predicts, your *intention turns into a behavior* when you swerve into the right-hand lane so that the cheating driver has to stop cheating.

Because you have taken social psychology, you also may imagine hundreds of drivers quietly saying, "Thank you!" as they remain stuck in traffic. Perhaps you have demonstrated *pure altruism* by putting yourself at risk of being the victim of road rage by standing up (or driving sideways, in this case) for fairness. On the other hand, if anyone noticed, they may have thought, "What a fool for taking such a risk." You may have engaged in *impression management* or *self-serving biases* when you were interpreting your motives.

Where Are the Careers? Where are the careers?

The obvious "Sutton's law" opportunity related to driving behavior is to work for the insurance industry. They probably are not interested in the meditations of drivers in traffic jams. But they are interested in many of your other Chapter 2 social psychological research skills. Your ability to communicate visual data stories will be especially powerful. And the basic research side of driving behavior is very interested in what you are thinking about as you drive because driving simulators demonstrate the danger of multitasking (e.g., texting) and other distractions while driving (Brookhuis & De Waard, 2010; Karthaus et al., 2020).

The insurance industry has many other components, and most of them are linked to human social behavior. Cheating insurance companies, for example, is expensive for all of us because we all pay higher premiums. So, understanding human motives and being able to summarize research (hopefully with a sharp-looking infographic) is a nice way to network your way into an industry (see Kareem et al., 2017). Being proactive makes you stand out from all the other applicants.

As a student of social psychology, you will quickly recognize that the social psychology of driving is closely related to public health (see Schreier et al., 2018). A hot topic in the transportation industry related to the public health is driverless trucks. With more and more transportation technology, we might soon see 18-wheelers making long-haul trips with no one in the cab (and no need for rest stops)! Your research skills are in demand here, and showing just a little bit of self-motivated interest can pull you into one of the hot transportation technology firms (see Bakhmutov et al., 2018). You also can work on the surprising social effects as we begin to trust driverless vehicles (Bissell et al., 2020).

Become a Social Entrepreneur

A social entrepreneur creates an enduring business or organization designed to solve specific social problems.

A pair of researchers (Petrovskaya & Mirakyan, 2018) interviewed 78 Russian entrepreneurs hoping to discover what characteristics distinguished conventional entrepreneurs from social entrepreneurs in Russian society. They discovered four "servant leadership" attributes that distinguished the social entrepreneurs: altruism, integrity, trust in others, and empathy. If you think those traits describe you, you might have a huge and positive impact on the world.

Small Beginnings With Big Ideas

In Chapter 8, we introduced you to the social entrepreneur Muhammad Yunus.

Yunus lent small amounts of money called "micro-loans" to 42 hardworking women in Bangladesh so that they could start their own businesses. The project succeeded with a repayment rate of 98% and grew into a bank that collected an average of $1.5 million in *weekly* installments—that it keeps reinvesting in poor people with ambition (Yunus, 2007).

Yunus might be an outlier in an interesting trend: There is a distinct international and female orientation to many social entrepreneurship activities. A study of 601 German college students found that women were more likely to translate the desire to be a social entrepreneur into actually doing it (Dickel & Eckardt, 2020). Indonesian women, some of whom were already active as social entrepreneurs, described three ways that social entrepreneurship benefited Indonesian society: social empowerment, social benefits, and social sustainability (Anggahegari et al., 2018). There's even now a scale to measure someone's tendency toward being a social entrepreneur (Jilinskaya-Pandey & Wade, 2019).

Social entrepreneur: Someone who creates a new business or organization designed to solve a social problem.

Social Entrepreneurship in Asia: The COVID-19 Virus Pandemic

Social psychology thrives on information.

As of writing this book, we have some probable information about where the COVID-19 (novel coronavirus disease 2019) virus probably came from: bats (Rothan & Byrareddy, 2020; Zhou et al., 2020). But it wasn't the bats' fault. A virus just wants some new place to live, and humans had been crowding into the bats' territory.

The virus eventually found a friendly home in crowded "wet markets" where humans bought their food. A **zoonotic spillover** (transmission of a pathogen from animals to humans) occurred when the COVID-19 made its survivalist leap into available *Homo sapiens* (Malta et al., 2020). The virus found many happy homes among close-knit human communities. It started leaping between people, into communities, across regions, then sailed and flew overseas inside their humans until it became the world-wide pandemic of 2020.

Many countries in Asia were the first to be hit hard by COVID-19. Digital social entrepreneurs have been responding. The privacy values in a democracy needed to be reconciled with the threat of massive loss of life. The South Korea democracy made a relatively prompt decision to test hundreds of thousands of people. They used phone data to track the virus among its citizens and combined their data with satellite mapping. A variety of digitally minded social entrepreneurs appear to have helped contain the virus more effectively in South Korea than comparable countries.

Marianne Bray and Beh Lih Yi (2020) reported that social entrepreneurs have been practically minded social problem solvers in other countries as well. In Singapore, a group called Soap Cycling Singapore was collecting, cleaning, and redistributing used hotel soap products to ensure more people could wash their hands. In Hong Kong, the Soap Cycling group also distributed hygiene kits and masks to around 3,000 of the city's 21,000 street cleaners. They already had masks, but their work involves pushing heavy carts that lead to perspiration that makes their masks ineffective.

Also in Hong Kong, the group Sew On Studio sells face mask kits with fabric made by elderly tailors. Residents can assemble the face masks at home. The Hong Kong group Rooftop Republic normally promotes urban farming. During the crisis, they worked with a uniform supplier to design washable, ecofriendly masks that provided added protection in humid conditions. These groups may not be formally trained as applied social psychologists. But they are behaving as if they were. They are just trying to figure out the best way to solve urgent social problems, and they may have saved countless lives. While the COVID-19 brought out scary social reactions in some, it also brought out the best in others. That's the fascinating thing about social psychology; it shows every side of us. And there will always be careers exploring the good and bad aspects of our social world.

THE MAIN IDEAS

- Table A.2 provides several examples of careers relevant to social psychology topics. Two examples are working in consumer behavior and analyzing the psychology of driving behavior.

- Social entrepreneurs create businesses or organizations designed to solve specific social problems. One career path is to create new opportunities for people based on specific social needs of a given area.

CRITICAL THINKING CHALLENGE

- Identify the three examples of careers in Table A.2 that are of the most interest to you. Explain why these careers are appealing and, for each, identify one person you think might help you further explore this interest.

- Look up the social entrepreneur scale mentioned earlier (Jilinskaya-Pandey & Wade, 2019). Take the scale and then make an infographic showing the results.

Zoonotic spillover:
Transmission of a pathogen, or disease, from an animal species to humans.

Time & Life Pictures/The LIFE Picture Collection/Getty Images

B. Social Psychology of Humans and Their Pets

Core Questions

B.1   How do humans think about animals and pets?

B.2   What do pets mean to humans?

Learning Objectives

B.1   Explain how anthrozoology helps explain relationships between humans and animals.

B.2   Articulate how pets influence human personalities, health, and culture.

Walt Disney wasn't satisfied.

One animator on the film *Bambi* had spent 6 months sketching forest scenes in Maine's Baxter Park (see Lutts, 1992). Disney animators even viewed the anatomical dissection of two fawns. Walt Disney wanted precise drawings—but something was wrong: Bambi as a drawn fawn looked real—but he wasn't cute. Hal Herzog (2010) described the Disney solution: "babyfication."

> Disney told the artists to reduce the length of Bambi's muzzle and make Bambi's head bigger. Then they gave Bambi huge eyes with lots of white in them. Bambi was morphed into a human baby. (p. 40)

Bambi's head became almost as large as his body. He had "exceptionally large white eye patches," huge pupils, and enormous eyelashes. To the dismay of many in the sports-hunting community, Bambi became irresistibly cute and sympathetic (see Lutts, 1992). But the widespread positive human reaction to Bambi tells us more about how humans related to other animals than it does to deer, hunting, and forest fires.

The SONY Corporation got the message. The latest version of their artificial intelligence robot pet dog, AIBO, has an even shorter muzzle, huge blinking eyes, and a long sweeping forehead (but no eyelashes). You can see AIBO for yourself on YouTube. More popular in Japan than in the United States, AIBO's head-shaking, leg-stretching, fetching, and cuddling behaviors are remarkably dog-like—and cute.

We will see in this chapter that we humans use imagined pets (stuffed animals), robotic pets, real pets, and even stories about pets to satisfy our own psychological needs. Pets in particular are part of the growing field of **anthrozoology**, the study of the human-animal bond (see Bradshaw, 2017, pp. xi–xii).

HOW DO HUMANS THINK ABOUT ANIMALS AND PETS?

>> **LO B.1:** Explain how anthrozoology helps explain relationships between humans and animals.

The size of the pet industry suggests we spend a lot of time—and money—thinking about pets.

The American Veterinary Medical Association (AVMA, 2018) and the Institute of Insurance Information (III, 2019) estimate that about two thirds of American households are providing shelter for 144.7 million cats, dogs, birds, and horses. Fish contribute another 76 million. Poultry as pets add another 15 million. Reptiles, rabbits, livestock, and ferrets represent another 11.5 million pets (see AVMA, 2018). Estimates from the Insurance Information Institute are higher, especially regarding the number of cats.

Pet-keeping is increasing around the world. The American Pet Products Association (APPA, 2019) estimates annual spending on pets at about $72 billion. Recent trends in the industry indicate that 68% of American households have a pet and 62% of the pet owners belong to one of the post–baby boom generations (see Kestenbaum, 2018). In other words, young people seem to especially like pets. This section answers the core question "How do humans think about animals and pets?" by

(1) recognizing obstacles to clear thinking about pets and animals,

(2) documenting how cuteness and love for our pets bias our thinking, and

(3) describing moral dilemmas that reveal how we think and feel about animals.

How to Think Clearly About Pets and Animals

There is a paradox behind all this money spent on animals.

Keeping pets doesn't make sense. Pet-keeping costs humans significant time, effort, and money (see Serpell & Paul, 2011). So why do most of us do it? We can start

Anthrozoology: The study of human-animal bonds.

thinking clearly about pets by (a) trying to define what a pet is, (b) recognizing our own cognitive biases, (c) acknowledging how cuteness influences affection for animals, and (d) confronting moral dilemmas.

Difficult Definitions: "Pets" and "Owners"

We humans "prefer to believe what we prefer to be true."

That warning from the philosopher Francis Bacon (1561–1626) can help us think more clearly about the animals among us. We think we all know what we mean by "pets." But problems with definitions tell you that the world is more complicated than simple definitions. Hal Herzog (2011, pp. 72–74) summarized those definitional difficulties in a book with an alarming title: *Some We Love, Some We Hate, Some We Eat*. Here are three candidates for defining what a pet is.

- Definition 1. Pets are "animals allowed in the house, given a name, and never eaten" (see Thomas, 1983). But what about pet dogs not allowed in the house and aquarium fish without names?

- Definition 2. Pets live and move with independence within the owner's home but are constrained from leaving voluntarily (see Bradshaw, 2017, p. 8). But then why do we limit their in-home independence with cages?

- Definition 3. Pets are animals we live with that have no obvious function (see Serpell, 1989). However, pets clearly function to meet nonmaterial psychological needs.

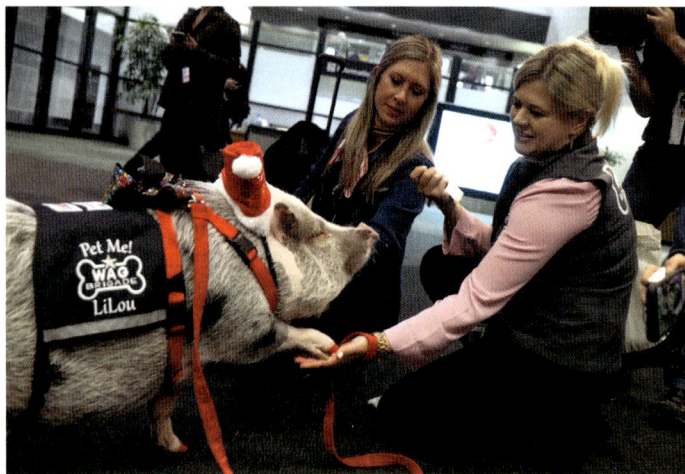

Do emotional support animals really help with problems like flying anxiety?

Bradshaw (2017, p. xiii) reported similar difficulty finding the best term to describe people who "own" pets. Are we "owners," "companions," "guardians," "parents," or "caregivers"? Every term that solves one problem creates another. For example, "caregivers" strikes Bradshaw as "too impersonal and transient, more appropriate for those devoted souls who look after pets in rehoming facilities."

Mental Traps to Clear Thinking

Our tendency to believe what we prefer to be true makes it difficult to think clearly about anything!

For example, a pig-petting air passenger may sincerely claim that "I know pet therapy works because my anxiety always goes away when my therapy pig is with me!" We don't doubt the sincerity of such reports. But we are skeptical that the flying pig caused the benefit. You are already familiar with three explanations for why the passenger might not need a pig to minimize flying anxiety (see also Bradshaw, 2017, pp. 82–83):

1. Confirmation bias. If you expect to feel better being with your pig, then you probably will notice when you feel better carrying your pig and not notice when you feel worse. In other words, it might be a porcine placebo.

2. Self-fulfilling prophecies. The therapist or the patient may be so enthusiastic about pet therapy that their enthusiasm does the trick. Their enthusiasm improves their mood, but they give credit to the pig.

3. The correlation confusion. We tend to perceive a causal relationship whenever two notable events (a pig on board and lower anxiety) occur at the same time. But it could be a third variable, such as distraction. An engaging movie might help even more.

The Cuteness Bias About Pets

Cuteness also makes it difficult for humans to think clearly about pets.

Love and cuteness probably serve the same evolutionary purpose (Lorenz, 1943). A strange phenomenon signals our complicated thinking about cuteness. **Cute aggression** refers to the impulse to bite or squeeze cute things without a desire to cause harm (Stavropolous & Alba, 2018). When my [Tom's] mother was showing off her first grandchild to an old family friend, the friend naturally agreed she was beautiful and then added, "Don't you just want to eat her up?!" It was a disturbing thought for a new parent.

The Universal Power of Cute

The power of "cuteness" reflects a universal standard.

Among humans, cuteness triggers positive maternal impulses and behaviors (see Langlois et al., 1995). It has a similar influence on both men and women (see Parsons et al., 2011) and represents a shared understanding across cultures and ethnicities (Golle et al., 2015). Cuteness triggers positive reactions across multiple brain regions (Luo et al., 2015), and it has huge marketing appeal across cultures (see Granot et al., 2014). The power of cuteness is not reserved for living animals. Stuffed animals also receive significant affection (Barlow et al., 2012). Cute is a source of social power.

John Bradshaw (2017) summarized the benefits of being a cute animal:

> Cute dogs stand the best chance of being adopted, while their not-so-cute kennel mates get euthanized. Most would-be adopters spend less than a minute evaluating each dog, and most use its appearance as their main criterion. Puppies and younger dogs generally find homes more quickly than their less cute peers. People assume cute dogs will be more loving; . . . the less inhibited of us spontaneously break into "baby talk" when we catch sight of a puppy or kitten. (p. 181)

The effects of cuteness appear to be survival-enhancing, care-giving emotions toward the appearance of youth and vulnerability. These infantile features include what Walt Disney and his animators discovered: Cute means a large head, round face, big eyes, high forehead, small nose, and a small mouth (Bradshaw, 2017, pp. 182–183; Glocker et al., 2009). Think Bambi, Mickey Mouse, and AIBO.

Anthropomorphism: Cute Animals Are in the Eye of the Beholder

Cuteness in pets and other animals is at least partly in the eye of the human beholder.

We humans generally find furry critters cute—but woe to the slimy. However, more than a few people think slimy slugs are cute (and easy to care for). They are fascinated by the differences between leopard, banana, and common garden slugs.

Moving from slimy skin to numbers of legs, Marlene Zuk (2011) points out in her book *Sex on Six Legs* that humans are fussy about the number of legs on animals. Two seems normal and four is nice (hence all those kittens on the Internet), but a six-legged pet seems weird. An eight-legged pet sounds creepy, and keeping a centipede as a pet seems downright revolting.

But we humans (in much of the Western world) find it cute to have a needy, tail-wagging, nose-muzzling, bed-hopping creature greet us with ridiculous enthusiasm the moment we get home. We may not feel fully appreciated in our families, at school, or work. But a rustling treat bag will bring your number one fan running and begging for your attention. How cute!

Anthropomorphism occurs when we assign human traits to nonhuman animals and objects. For example, my [Tom's] granddaughter said, "That's a friendly tree," because it had several low, easy-to-climb branches. Herzog (2011, p. 38) recognized the fundraising consequences of anthropomorphic cuteness for the World Wildlife Fund. Their logo uses the furry, large-eyed, round-faced Chinese panda rather than the equally rare but slimy Chinese salamander.

Cute aggression: The impulse to bite or squeeze cute things without wanting to harm them.

Anthropomorphism: The perception that nonhuman objects have human traits.

Parasitic Puppies

But what if cute puppies and mewing kittens are just pet parasites?

Parasitism occurs when organisms survive by feeding off a host. Viruses such as COVID-19 are parasites. You usually hear about parasites as sometimes-dangerous infections feeding off some system in the human body. But parasitism is an effective survival strategy across many species.

It is not unusual, for example, for a brown-headed cowbird to lay its eggs in the nest of an Eastern phoebe. The phoebe does all the nest-building work, feeding and caring for the cowbird until it leaves the family nest. Herzog (2011) suggests that "the phoebe probably gets great emotional satisfaction … not realizing that she has been the victim of a Darwinian sting operation" (pp. 91–92).

The cute, mewing kitten at your back door is a setup for parasitism. So is a dog enjoying daily feedings, comfortable naps, and timely treats right in *your* own home! An alien from Mars observing humans cleaning up after their dogs would likely assume that dogs were the masters, humans the servants (an observation stolen from Jerry Seinfeld).

Moral Dilemmas Reveal Biases About Animals

Some research approaches are elegant.

"Elegant" to an experimenter usually means someone has created a simple yet revealing way to conduct studies. The "trolley problem" presented in Table B.1 is elegant. It creates situational moral dilemmas that can reveal our values and be adapted for many other purposes (see Colman et al., 2019). Consider each; what would you do? And do you like what the answers say about the type of person you are?

TABLE B.1

The "Trolley Problem" and Two Animal-Related Moral Dilemmas

Problem 1	An out-of-control trolley is headed toward a group of the world's last five remaining mountain gorillas. You can throw a switch and send it toward one 25-year-old man instead. Should you?
Problem 2	The trolley is headed toward a man whom you do not know. You can throw a switch and send it hurtling toward your pet dog instead. Should you?

Moral Dilemma 1. Why Did the Nazis Love Their Pets More Than People?

There is no good choice in trolley problems.

So, we are likely to feel a little disgusted with ourselves no matter how we answer (see Haidt, 2001; McManus, 2017). Disgust is a powerful emotion. But the usual decision people make in these Trolley Problem studies is straightforward: Save people over pets (see Herzog, 2010, p. 55; Petrinovich et al., 1993).

However, that type of moral reasoning apparently slipped past the Nazis in the leadup to World War II and the Holocaust. They enacted a wide range of animal protection policies that Hitler signed into law in 1933 (see Arluke & Sax, 1992). It was a revealing social psychological display of values under an authoritarian leader, considering what we all know was going to happen a few years later.

Did disgust for other humans allow the Nazis to officially love their pets more than they loved people?

Moral Dilemma 2. Should Kal-El Have Surgery?

Wind's dog Kal-El was fairly young (only 7 years old) and was one of the happiest dogs she knew.

Parasitism: When an organism survives by feeding off a host.

Except that he had slowly started to feel crippling back pain. Three different pain medications hadn't helped. When the pain kicked in, he would actually scream. It was possible that surgery would help, but it would cost thousands of dollars—and it might not help at all. Should she pay for the surgery or put him to sleep so that his pain was gone? That money could go toward charities like the Humane Society. It was impossible to ask Kal-El what he wanted. If he were a human family member in constant pain, would he have the right to decide when he wanted to go?

Should Kal-El have the surgery?

Moral Dilemma 3. Did Cookie the Crocodile Deserve to Die?

Cookie was a 12-foot, 1,800-pound Nile crocodile.

Herzog (2010, pp. 50–51) described what happened on Labor Day at Miami Serpentarium. Cookie was sunning himself when the father of 6-year-old David X. lifted his son up to the wall for a better look. When he briefly turned his back, David fell, and Cookie did what crocodiles with small brains instinctively do. David's body was retrieved from Cookie's pond several hours later. Later that night, the distraught owner of the park pumped nine shots into Cookie.

Did Cookie deserve to die?

Moral Dilemma 4. Is Animal Abuse More Acceptable for Rich, White People?

Football player Michael Vick was severely punished for his participation in a dog-fighting operation.

But animal abuse appears to be more socially acceptable among rich White people than among poor people and people of color. Kathy Rudy (2007) is a strong animal advocate, active in dog rescues, and despises dog-fighting. But as an ethicist, she also pointed out a social class contradiction in the Michael Vick case.

> Dog fighting is not the only "sport" that abuses animals. Cruelty also occurs in rodeos, horse and dog racing (all of which mistreat animals and often kill them when no longer useful). There are also millions of dogs and cats we put to death in "shelters" . . . and billions of creatures we torture in factory farms for our food. . . . But I see one important difference between these more socially acceptable mistreatments and the anger focused on Vick: Vick is Black, and most of the folks in charge of the other activities are White.

Comedian and actor Chris Rock made a similar point on a late-night comedy show. He described a photograph of vice presidential candidate Sarah Palin posing for a photograph with a dead moose.

> She's holding a dead, bloody moose. And Michael Vick's like, "Why am I in jail?" They let a White lady shoot a moose, but a Black man wants to kill a dog? Now that's a crime.

Is the morality of animal abuse racist?

Moral Dilemma 5. Is Cockfighting Worse Than Eating Chicken Nuggets?

Cockfighting is an 8,000-year-old, internationally popular activity, a sporting event to those who enjoy it.

Cockfighting is especially popular in the southern United States. The roosters are sent into a small pit, their feet enhanced into weapons with steel gaffes. It is a bloody and vicious end to the losing rooster. But Herzog's (2010, pp. 149–173) detailed description reveals that the life of a gamecock is far more pleasant than the chicken that finds its way to a McDonald's restaurant or your own dinner table. The game cock is carefully nourished, even pampered, until the day it is sent into the ring. Its death is sudden and brief. Millions of broiler chickens, by contrast, have a miserable life from beginning to end.

> The chicks will never see sun nor sky. Because they are so top-heavy, broiler chickens spend most of their day lying down.... The broiler houses are humid, the air laced with ammonia produced by the action of microbes on the accumulated urine and the excrement of tens of thousands of birds. The gas burns the lungs, inflames the eyes, and causes chronic respiratory disease.

Herzog asks: "Which you rather be, a gamecock or a broiler?"

Moral Dilemma 6. Should You Recommend Dolphin-Assisted Therapy (DAT)?

Dolphins have not chosen to be therapists; they are captured, wild, intelligent animals.

The main evidence that swimming with dolphins will alleviate your problems are research anecdotes, stories confidently reported as probable facts. Some researchers have concluded that dolphin-assisted therapy (DAT) produces positive outcomes for everything from Down syndrome to AIDS, epilepsy, and chronic back pain (see Herzog, 2010; Nathanson, 1998; Nathanson et al., 1997). But a closer look at DAT research procedures (see Marino & Lilienfeld, 1998, 2007) warned that

> a plethora of serious threats to validity and flawed analytic procedures render the findings uninterpretable and the conclusions unwarranted and premature, ... an explanation in search of a phenomenon.

They are not alone in their criticisms of DAT (see Humphries, 2003; Salgueiro et al., 2012). Psychologists don't enjoy raining on people's happy, hopeful parades. We especially dislike discouraging desperate parents. Many of us are struggling parents, too; we also have children with disabilities and emotional problems. Why not just let them have fun with a good, old-fashioned dolphin-filled placebo experience and keep our mouths shut?

First of all, working with any large marine animal is dangerous. Despite their gentle reputations, dolphins can be aggressive. In addition, DAT tends to

- Be expensive for individual families
- Be profitable for others
- Mislead other desperate families
- Distract attention from more promising therapies
- Take away the dolphins' freedom

Should you recommend dolphin-assisted therapy for a troubled child? Interacting with other species when the power differences almost always favor humans creates moral dilemmas. These moral decisions make it even more difficult to think clearly about pets and other animals.

THE MAIN IDEAS

- Anthrozoology is the study of human-animal bonds. One interesting question within this field is how humans define "pets."

- Humans might not have clear thinking when it comes to pets. One reason may be because of a cuteness bias, when we are drawn to cute things or animals and anthropomorphize them (assume they have human-like tendencies).

- Considering various moral dilemmas about how animals are treated reveals insights into anthrozoology as well.

CRITICAL THINKING CHALLENGE

- By today's standards, things like human slavery and genocide are judged as awful and barbaric. In 200 years, will humans look back on pet ownership and eating meat in the same way? Why or why not?

- Increasingly, colleges and universities are allowing students to live with pets and to have "comfort animals" with them, even in class. What is your opinion about the benefits and drawbacks to this trend, both the students with animals and to other students in their dorms or classrooms?

WHAT DO PETS MEAN TO HUMANS?

>> **LO B.2:** **Articulate how pets influence human personalities, health, and culture.**

It probably won't surprise you that dogs are more popular than cats.

A Gallup poll found that about 70% of people (in the United States) describe themselves as "dog people" compared to the 20% who identify as "cat people" (see Newport et al., 2006). Whether dog, cat, hamster, or fish, about 60% of all pet owners believe that they lead more satisfying lives than non–pet owners. Clearly, many people believe that pets in general—and some pets in particular—are very important.

This section answers the core question "What do pets mean to humans?" by

(1) describing personality patterns of people and pets,

(2) the health consequences of living and working with other species, and

(3) cultural differences in pet-keeping.

Personalities and Appearances

Three questions usually come immediately to mind when most people think about pets:

How do dog people differ from cat people?

Do dogs (and cats) provide unconditional love?

Do owners and pets gradually come to look like each other?

Here's the nice thing about psychological science: We have answers. They aren't always complete answers, and they always raise more questions. But we're working on them, too. Here's what we've got so far.

Dog People and Cat People

It's a popular hypothesis.

People who like pet dogs are different from people who like pet cats. But are there really differences between "dog people" and "cat people"? And if so, *how* are they different? Because this is a textbook, we also describe the methods used to test this hypothesis.

The Big 5 and Pets

The Big Five is a well-established model of personality differences (McCrae & Costa, 1987).

We all share these five dimensions of personality but on a *continuum* indicating varying degrees of each personality dimension. People usually remember

FIGURE B.1

Self-identified "cat people" versus "dog people" and their pet ownership. People are often very aware of whether they feel like a dog person or a cat person, and their pet ownership usually aligns.

If you had to choose—which would you say you are—more of a dog person or more of a cat person?
(Results by pet ownership)

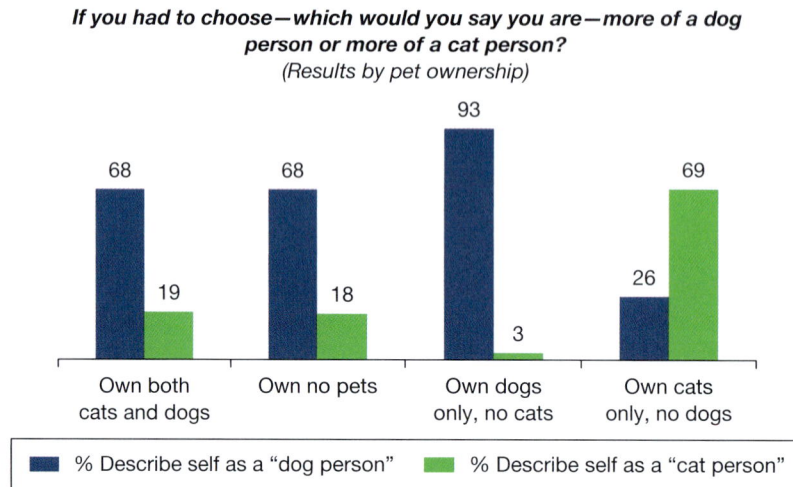

■ % Describe self as a "dog person"   ■ % Describe self as a "cat person"

Source: Gallup poll from 2006.

the five dimensions of personality by the term OCEAN: Openness to Experience, Conscientiousness, Extraversion, Agreeableness, and Neuroticism.

The research methodology for most *self-report* personality studies is straightforward. For example, Gosling et al. (2010) used a publicly accessible website to recruit participants who identified themselves either as dog people or cat people. Then those participants described themselves by completing the Big Five personality inventory. Here's what they found:

- Dog people were higher in Extroversion (specifically assertive, outgoing, articulate, and friendly).

- Dog people were higher in Agreeableness (loyal, humble, kind, and considerate).

- Dog people were higher in Conscientiousness (persistent, self-disciplined, resourceful, and planful).

- Cat people were higher in Neuroticism (awkward, moody, testy, and jealous).

- Cat people were higher in Openness to Experience (imaginative, liking variety, daring, and curious).

You can add gender to personality differences in pet-keeping preferences. Women are more likely to call themselves cat people and men to call themselves dog people (Perrine & Osbourne, 1998). Patterns about personality and gender differences always come with qualifications. The research only indicates tendencies that were computed as averages across many people. The Gosling et al. (2010) study recruited 4,565 people. The patterns are reliable, but describing people as belonging into any two groups is crude and necessarily inaccurate.

The impulse to divide the world into dog people and cat people may tell us more about the simplistic but convenient way that people like to think than it does about pet preferences.

Nature-Nurture Differences Between Dogs and Cats

A backward glance in time will help us understand the dogs and cats we live with today.

The social history of cats as pets ranges from worship (in ancient Egypt) to accusations of witchcraft (in the Middle Ages). Cats are still associated with evil witches in Halloween traditions. Cats were independent, meat-eating hunters who survived by stealth and surprise.

The social history of dogs as pets involves working alongside their humans for hunting and herding. They continued that association as herders, pointers, and by using their sensitive noses to sniff out dangers to their humans—everything from bombs to diseases. Dogs were pack-hunting creatures in their earlier lives who survived by cooperating and working within an established order.

Bradshaw (2017) summarized the end result of the nature-nurture interactions that produced these enduring differences in dogs and cats. He described what happens when a pet owner of a dog or cat moves to a new home:

> Cats, descended from a solitary territorial ancestor, value place above all else. Hence, moving from home is a very different experience, requiring quite different management, for dogs and cats. Dogs are content to go where their owners go, but cats strenuously attempt to return to the place where they used to live.... They can be very persistent in retracing their steps—and may end up living with a former neighbor. (p. 14)

The different traits of dogs and cats map closely to the different traits of the people who prefer dogs and cats. Dogs tend to be outgoing, friendly, loyal, and persistent. Cats tend to be more moody, testy, jealous, and curious. In the world of pets, we humans seem to prefer the kind of animals that we think are similar to ourselves, and we profess to admire those qualities.

Unconditional Love

Here's another popular belief: Pets (especially dogs) love humans unconditionally.

But is it true? Three themes emerged from a survey by Herzog (2010, p. 78) at North Carolina veterinary offices. He asked a simple question: What do you get out of your relationships with your pets? Common answers were "My pets are ..."

(1) members of my family,

(2) my children, and

(3) my friends.

A related study (see Herzog et al., 2003) analyzed comparisons between the benefits of human and animal relationships. The benefits provided by dogs and cats were about the same at reducing loneliness, increasing companionship, and feeling needed. Humans were better than pets when individuals needed someone to talk to. Their pets, however, were better at providing what was experienced or perceived as unconditional love.

Dogs That Look Like Their Humans

The faces of many married people become more similar over time (Zajonc et al., 1987).

It's not a dramatic shift, and it doesn't happen for every couple. But it happened often enough in one research study (Zajonc et al., 1987) that it was statistically significant (probably not due to chance). Does something like that happen between pets and their owners? There are two competing theories. The **convergence theory** proposes that dogs and their owners gradually come to resemble one another over time. The

Convergence theory: For pets, it's the argument that pets and their owners gradually change to look alike.

Is it true that dogs often look like their owners? If so, why?

selection theory proposes that owners select animals that already look like themselves.

Stanley Coren (1999) helped establish the initial observation that dogs and their owners resemble one another. He noticed that women with long hairstyles framed their faces in a manner similar to lop-eared dogs (the English Springer Spaniel and the Beagle), and women with short hairstyles were similar to prick-eared dogs (the Siberian Husky and the Basenji). As predicted by principles of familiarity, liking, and attraction (see Chapter 12), the 261 women in this study tended to prefer the breeds that looked more like themselves. This tended to support the folk wisdom that dogs and their owners looked similar.

But why? That really is the more interesting part of this research story.

Roy and Nicholas (2004) helped explain how that happens by showing observers 45 photographs of dog owners, their dog, and an alternate dog. The observers were better than average at matching dogs and their owners. They also found that length of ownership did not influence their success at matching dogs to owners. But it did help if the dog was a purebred with predictable, identifiable features.

Taken together, these two studies suggest that dogs and their owners tend to look alike but that their appearances do not converge over time. This supports selection theory: The similarity between dogs and their owners probably happens at the moment when owners are selecting which dog they prefer to own—a dog that just happens to look a little bit like themselves.

Health Consequences of Pet-Keeping

People have been living with animals for centuries.

So, it is not surprising that our contacts have produced both health hazards and health benefits for humans. Zoonotic (pronounced zoo-NOT-ic) diseases are infections spread between animals and humans. Zooeyia (pronounced "zoo-AY-uh") outcomes refer to how pets contribute to human health. COVID-19 is a zoonotic disease that came from bats.

Health Hazards From Pet-Keeping

We'll give you bad news first.

Each year, about 90,000 emergency room visits in the United States are caused by trips and falls related to pets. Dogs are the most common cause of these injuries, simply by getting in the way. However, dog leashes are often involved when the leash gets wrapped around someone's legs and ankles as the dog begins a chase (see Hendrick, 2009). Ninety thousand is a big number, and it's just one example of how pet ownership can be dangerous.

Disease Distribution. The Centers for Disease Control and Prevention (CDC, 2019c) list four ways that zoonotic diseases are transmitted from animals to humans:

- **Direct contact:** Coming into contact with the saliva, blood, urine, mucous, feces, or other body fluids of an infected animal. Examples include petting or touching animals and bites or scratches.

- **Indirect contact:** Coming into contact with areas where animals live and roam, or objects or surfaces that have been contaminated with germs. Examples include aquarium tank water, pet habitats, chicken coops, plants, and soil, as well as pet food and water dishes.

Selection theory: For pets, it's the idea that people adopt pets that already look like them.

Zoonotic diseases: Infections spread between animals and humans.

Zooeyia outcomes: Ways in which pets help and harm human health.

Fiona Hanson/PA Images /Getty Images

- **Vector-borne:** Being bitten by a tick or an insect, like a mosquito or a flea.

- **Foodborne:** Each year, one in six Americans get sick from eating contaminated food. Eating or drinking something unsafe (such as unpasteurized milk, undercooked meat or eggs, or raw fruits and vegetables that are contaminated with feces from an infected animal).

Pet Hoarding. Hoarding is now classified as a disorder in the *DSM-5*.

People with **hoarding disorder** are described by the American Psychiatric Association (APA, 2019) as people who "excessively save items that others may view as worthless. They have persistent difficulty getting rid of or parting with possessions, leading to clutter that disrupts their ability to use their living or work spaces." Hoarding can apply to live animals as well as possessions. Its fundamental, emotional mental flaw may be represented by the title of one particular journal article: "My Possessions Need Me: Anthropomorphism and Hoarding" (see Burgess et al., 2018).

The record for hoarding animals may be "The Great Bunny Rescue of 2006." The PRNewsire (2006) reported that a Michigan animal sanctuary had adopted 511 rabbits from a woman in Reno, Nevada. They were only about a third of the estimated 1,600 rabbits on just one acre of land. The woman had started with good intentions of helping. But animal rescue volunteer Carrara (Carrara, 2006) observed that despite these good intentions, it gradually became a

> hoarding type situation [that] began with a few rabbits where breeding was out of control . . . in extremely poor health, malnourished, had injuries so severe that there were abscesses down to the bone and ears and genitals were torn off.

Hoarding is somehow intertwined with poorly understood gender differences. Herzog (2010, p. 308) reported that most animal abusers are men but that three times as many women as men end up hoarding animals. Herzog (2010) described what happened when he went to a home that he heard was for sale:

> "Overpowering" does not quite capture the stench of feces and urine. Cats and clothing were strewn about the living room. A forty-pound bag of dried cat chow lay spilled open in the middle of the floor. There was no place to sit. . . . I counted two dozen cats, but there were probably others roaming the nearby woods. I did not stay long, and we did not buy the house. We could have probably gotten it cheap. (p. 138)

These complicated, intertwining issues somehow related to gender, animal abuse, and animal hoarding need further research—for the sake of the animals and the people hoping to care for them.

Health Benefits From Pet-Keeping

The good news about pet-keeping comes with a qualification.

Pet-keeping appears to provide a variety of psychological and physiological benefits. But those benefits are seldom as grand, quick, or long-lasting as their reputation. The science suggests that something real seems to be going on in animal-assisted therapy—but it's a long way from justifying that therapy pigs should fly on airplanes.

Animal-Assisted Therapy. So, what does the science tell us about animal-assisted therapy?

Animal-assisted therapy (AAT) refers to the use of nonhuman animals to achieve therapeutic outcomes for humans. One of the early *meta-analyses* (a study that finds trends in all the existing studies) was mildly encouraging for AAT (Nimer & Lundhal, 2007, p. 225). Their overall guidance was to "investigate the conditions under which AAT can be most helpful."

And that's what happened. A systematic review of the literature 10 years later added details about who was most likely to benefit from AAT. However, there were relatively

Hoarding disorder: The excessive saving of items or animals leading to the inability to live or work safely.

Animal-assisted therapy: The use of nonhuman animals to achieve therapeutic outcomes for humans.

few studies that controlled for logic problems such as confirmation bias, self-fulfilling prophecies, and correlation confusion. Those experimental studies suggested that

1. The benefits of pet therapy are real, but not dramatic.

2. Those most likely to benefit were people with autism-spectrum symptoms, medical difficulties, and behavioral problems (note: but not anxiety).

3. The help that pets provide may be related to neurochemicals that decrease blood pressure (see Allen, 2003; Odendaal, 2000).

4. The most promising applications of AAT were equine therapies for people with autism and canine therapies for childhood trauma (Hoagwood et al., 2017, p. 1).

Robotic Pet Therapy. Robotic pets: They're not coming; they're here.

The SONY Corporation designed and sold their artificial intelligence robot dog (AIBO) mostly in Japan. The most recent version of AIBO responds to petting by arching its back and performing many other realistic, dog-like movements and behaviors. Humans experience the AIBOs as "living animals, such as having mental states, being a social other, and having moral standing" (Melson et al., 2009). AIBO was piloted as a possible therapy tool with three people with long-term schizophrenia (Narita et al., 2016, p. 245). Their medications did not change over the 8 weeks of the study. At each session, the patients played with the AIBO together for about 20 minutes.

> The AIBO-assisted therapy sessions included greeting, petting, playing ball-games and teaching the AIBO to walk as activities of daily living (ADL), and the patients chose the actions for the AIBO. (Narita et al., 2016, p. 245)

The sessions and patient progress were evaluated in multiple ways, including assessments by multiple members of the staff. The verbal reports from the patients, for example, were all positive:

- Case 1, a 54-year-old woman, 18 years of hospitalization. "The first time, I did not like playing with the robot because I was depressed and anxious. But I feel good while playing with AIBO now. It heals my mind."

- Case 2, a 43-year-old man, 24 years of hospitalization. "I'm looking forward to the next AIBO-assisted therapy session. After I played with AIBO, I felt good. I enjoy it."

- Case 3, a 27-year-old woman, 8 years of hospitalization. "After I played with AIBO, I felt good. I enjoy it with other patients."

All of the numerical shifts in their pretest-posttest design were either stable or in a positive direction. None of the three patients were evaluated as worse after playing with AIBO for 8 weeks. Are you ready to endorse AIBO and lobby legislators for AIBO funding? We all hope that AIBO is an effective treatment option. But first think about what you have learned about expectations (by staff and patients), placebo effects, and that correlations do not imply causation.

Skepticism does not mean that we think that AIBO doesn't work. It only means that we don't know—and that we have to be cautious about our own tendency to "prefer to believe what we prefer to be true."

Attachment Theory: Accepting Pets as Family Members. Several weird but compelling studies come to the same conclusion:

Many people think and treat their pets as family members. For example, a grim but interesting archeological study of burial sites indicates that dogs were often treated in death the same way as human members of the family (Morey, 2006). Another startling study (Cohen, 2002) found that some people would be willing to give a scarce drug to their pet rather than to a person who was not a family member. A more conventional (less weird) survey across 11 states found that 87% of pet owners considered their animals to be members of the family (Cain, 2016).

For the present generation, the data suggest that in the United States, having kids declines as pet ownership increases (Aruah et al., 2019). This international research team from the United States and Nigeria found some practical explanations for the important life decision to delay or forgo childbearing:

> Dog-loving ladies interviewed in the piece claim that dogs bring them as much joy as a baby would, with less work (no baby-sitters, no diaper changes, no need to save for college tuition).

They explained this decision to have pets instead of human babies in terms of social bonding, grounded in Bowlby's (1958) theory of attachment. Aruah et al. (2019) also found that pets are a consistent source of attachment security.

> Although the want for children has reduced, the need to love and have a companionship has not. Human beings still crave for someone to care for and nurture, and so they acquire pets. Pets can clearly provide the emotional attachment bond important in promoting a sense of security and well-being.

The investment model of relationships proposed by Rusbult (1980) appears to apply also to the relationships between humans and their pets (Baker et al., 2016). The model proposes four elements that influence the strength of the relationships, shown in Table B.2.

TABLE B.2

The Investment Model of Pet Ownership

ELEMENT OF RELATIONSHIP	CRITICAL QUESTIONS
Satisfaction	How satisfying is your relationship with your pet?
Investment	How invested have you been in the welfare of your pet?
Comparison with alternatives	How does the relationship with your pet compare to any alternatives, such as a different pet or no pet?
Commitment	How committed are you to the welfare of your pet?

Source: Baker et al. (2016).

Your responses to the four critical questions in Table B.2 will help you evaluate your relationship with your pet, just as it does for your relationships with other humans.

Dogs, Dating, and Decent Behavior. Romantic movies might have the right idea—for Western audiences.

Several U.S. movies use dogs as part of the plot related to romantic attraction: *Must Love Dogs, My Boyfriends' Dogs, Who Gets the Dog?, Dog Park,* and *Rescue Dogs* are just some. In general, having a dog at your side appears to promote positive social interactions. From an experimental perspective, a dog may even help some men get started on romantic relationships (see Guéguen & Ciccotti, 2008). These four *field experiments* always used a *confederate* approaching someone in public, either with or without a dog.

1. A male confederate solicited people for money.

2. A female confederate solicited people for money.

3. A male dropped coins on the ground to see if people would help him pick them up.

4. A male solicited young women for their phone numbers.

In each situation, the presence of the dog increased helping and compliance. Go dogs!

Cultural Differences in Animals and Pet-Keeping

The cuteness of dogs in films—or in different cultures—is not universal.

For example, ominous music starts playing when dogs appear on the screen in the 2017 Nollywood (Nigerian) film *Spirit of Dogs and Men.* The film summary declares that "men are dogs in the realm of the spirit, using their powers to get wealth, not considerate of other people including their family members." The lounging, tough-looking dogs morph through cinematic magic into evil, ruthless humans.

Eating Dogs, Cats, and Cows

It's easy to confuse what is different or unfamiliar with being somehow morally wrong.

For example, if you are a meat eater, do you feel that it is wrong to eat dogs and cats? The answer is "yes" in much of the Western world—but not in South Korea. And some Western influences are trying to get South Koreans to change their ways (see Podberscek, 2009, p. 615). It is going to be a difficult persuasion effort because

> consumption of dogs has a long history in South Korea, while the consumption of cats is more recent. Pet ownership is a more recent phenomenon and is growing steadily. . . . Unlike cat consumption, dog consumption is strongly linked to national identity in South Korea, and it seems that calls from the West to ban the practice are viewed by South Koreans as an attack on their culture.

If you think eating cats and dogs is disgusting and morally wrong, then how do you justify eating cows (if you do)? Beef has been a significant industry in the United States. But that practice is profoundly disturbing to Hindus. Harris (1989) proposed one possible evolutionary explanation for the sacred Hindu taboo on beef consumption.

> During droughts and famines, farmers are severely tempted to kill or sell their livestock. Those who succumb to this temptation seal their doom, even if they survive the drought, for when the rains come, they will be unable to plow their fields.

Much of Indian agriculture has depended on seasonal rains, the monsoon. A taboo against killing cows would need a widely accepted social influence, such as religion, to enforce its cow-preserving requirements (see Agoramoorthy & Hsu, 2012). If not, one farmer or even a few could cheat but still survive—but that would tempt others to slaughter their cattle, too, when times are tough. But if every farmer made the same decision, then none of the fields could be plowed—the entire population would be more likely to perish.

Does it make sense to judge someone else's culture for eating certain animals when you know that people from other cultures are judging you for doing the same thing?

Humans Breastfeeding Their Pets

What about humans breastfeeding monkeys?

If that seems wrong, then what about antelopes, dogs, and piglets? Humans breastfeeding other species has occurred around the world and across a variety of cultures (see Simoons & Baldwin, 1982). It is more likely to occur on behalf of orphaned animals and in the absence of other animals that can give milk. For example, a woman in Colorado suckled her Labrador pup after he refused milk from a bottle. Does that make humans suckling other species a little more acceptable? If we think it's cute when a dog lets a kitten breastfeed, then why is it weird when we do it for another species?

There are four explanations for humans breastfeeding other species (see Herzog, 2019; Simmons & Baldwin, 1982):

- Affectionate breastfeeding: Women nursing baby animals out of "compassion, warmth, love." They were essentially pets treated like human babies. This form of nursing was most common among the hunter-gatherers of the Amazon and the Malay Peninsula.

- Economic breastfeeding: Young animals were nursed primarily for utilitarian purposes, for example, the rearing of a hunting dog. On Polynesian islands where dogs were on the menu, puppies were breastfed in order to improve the flavor of their flesh when they were consumed as adults.

- Ceremonial breastfeeding: This rare form of animal nursing was practiced by the Ainu in Japan who raised bear cubs for sacrificial slaughter.

- Human welfare breastfeeding: Animals were nursed for the benefit of the humans, such as by lactating women to relieve their breast pain. Breastfeeding puppies in Polynesia may even have been used as a form of contraception by extending lactation.

There are many other cultural differences in pet-keeping. Several cultures would be horrified to allow a dog into their home and downright astonished for allowing them to sleep on our beds. Most people in the United States think of horses as admirable companions, but eating horse is common in countries like Japan and Kazakhstan. Our attitudes and behaviors toward pet-keeping appear to be largely influenced by culture.

Humans have complicated relationships with the other animals among us. We love them, we hate them, and we eat them.

THE MAIN IDEAS

- Interesting research has compared the personalities of "dog people" to "cat people." Either way, we tend to think that our pets love us unconditionally.

- Sometimes dogs look like their owners. This appears to be due to selection bias (we adopt pets who already look like us), as opposed to each gradually coming to look alike over time.

- There are both health benefits and health hazards to keeping pets. Hazards include pet hoarding or getting infections. An example benefit is animal-assisted therapy (although research is mixed).

- Views on pet ownership and which animals are acceptable to eat vary widely by culture.

CRITICAL THINKING CHALLENGE

- Choose someone you know who picked out a pet dog. Then, think objectively about whether that dog looks like the person who adopted it. Does this particular case study seem to support selection theory?

- If you traveled to a country where eating horse was considered standard, would you order it at a restaurant? What if you were in a private person's home and didn't want to be rude? Finally, imagine that you eat a meal and later realize that you're not sure what kind of meat it was. Would you want to know or prefer to live in ignorance?

- Does reading this chapter make you reconsider your views on either hunting or being a vegetarian? Why or why not?

AP Photo/Rajanish Kakade

C. Social Psychology and a Sustainable Environment

Core Questions

C.1 What are threshold effects?

C.2 How can social psychologists contribute to a sustainable environment?

Learning Objectives

C.1 Explain the tragedy of the commons and threshold effects, including several examples.

C.2 Explain how social psychologists can respond to environmental threats.

If you're looking for a meaningful life, then you might consider saving the planet.

You won't be able to do it alone, of course—but you can inspire others. In Chapter 7, we introduced you to the 11 million pounds of trash that once filled Versova Beach in Mumbai, India—and to Afroz Shah (Arora, 2017). The young lawyer explained, "I have to protect my environment and it requires ground action." Soon over 1,000 volunteers had joined Shah, including local politicians, Bollywood actors and actresses, and children.

There was a new social norm. It happened both suddenly and slowly. After 2 years, the United Nations labeled Versova Beach the "world's largest beach clean-up project" (Arora, 2017). In 2019, one day after students around the world cut class to demand government action on climate change, thousands more volunteers participated in International Coastal Cleanup. On one day, they collected 8,190 *tons* of trash from coastlines around the world (see Haarr et al., 2019).

Protecting and increasing a **sustainable environment** is the most threatening global problem we face as a species. The rapid rise in global temperatures (i.e., global climate change) is just one of many indicators of the quickly increasing escalation of this danger (see DesJardine et al., 2019; Dominelli, 2012; Stoett, 2019). That's why creating a sustainable environment is part of a larger set of opportunities for psychology students related to **environmental psychology**, the mutual influence between individuals and their surroundings.

The *Titanic* can be used as a metaphor for modern environmental crises.

WHAT ARE THRESHOLD EFFECTS?

>> **LO C.1:** Explain the tragedy of the commons and threshold effects, including several examples.

The *Titanic* was doomed.

An iceberg scraped holes into 6 of its 16 watertight compartments on the starboard (right) side of the ship. The ship was believed to be unsinkable, thanks to modern (at the time) technology. Perhaps the *Titanic* passengers could have survived one or two compromised compartments—but not six. The ship designers were so sure that the *Titanic* was unsinkable that they were short on lifeboats. The massive ship sank in 2 hours.

We are not the first to apply the metaphor of the doomed *Titanic* to environmental crises (Sandler & Studlar, 1999). Our environment is in trouble now, and the effects are escalating. We maybe could survive one or two problems—but what about six massive, global problems all at once? Stoett (2019) argues that the rising generation of college students remains relatively unaware of the urgency of the situation. However, worldwide student protests in 2019 suggest we may have reached a tipping point in terms of public activism—maybe your generation (or the next) will be the solution.

This section answers the core question "What are threshold effects?" by

(1) explaining the tragedy of the commons,

(2) recognizing that Earth is a limited resource, and

(3) describing human limitations regarding some specific examples of current environmental issues.

Sustainable environment: A state in which the resources of the world are not overtaxed, allowing living things (including humans) to survive now and in the future.

Environmental psychology: The psychological study of the interplay between individuals and their surroundings.

The Tragedy of the Commons

"We have met the enemy and he is us."

This caption from the famous Pogo cartoon demonstrates why environmental threats need social psychological solutions (see Gross & De Dreu, 2019). The insight that not I, but *we*, are the problem with the environment is more formally called the **tragedy of the commons**. It's the idea that things would be fine if we all took responsibility and shared in a solution—but if we all act selfishly, we create a bigger problem. The term comes from the idea of a community of farmers who share grazing land (the "commons"). Each individual farmer is tempted to graze more of his cattle on the shared land, depleting the supply of grass at the expense of all the other farmers—and harming the commons (see Hardin, 1968).

In the COVID-19 outbreak, we saw a massive shortage of supplies like toilet paper. A few people hoarded the resources, ensuring their own needs would be met. But the panic led to more people doing the same, until most people were negatively affected. The overall effect of people thinking only of themselves and their own needs is tragedy for all.

The tragedy of the commons is a social psychological problem because what benefits the individual can harm society. So, how can individuals become convinced to give up their own immediate preferences by sacrificing their own comfort for the good of the planet or the future? Versova Beach in India demonstrates that what benefited the community also benefited many individuals . . . eventually. The entire group benefits if its individual members can delay gratification and avoid diffusion of responsibility by keeping the long-term goal in mind.

The tragedy of the commons is *our* tragedy—unless we use our social psychological skills to help millions of individuals "keep in mind" the beauty of a secure, creative environment.

Even the Earth Has Its Limits

Life on Earth has limits.

The planet will continue to calmly rotate in space even without many of its current inhabitants. But many of Earth's "compartments" are in trouble. They have exceeded what Rockström et al. (2009, p. 472) call **thresholds**, a point that marks the maximum level before a certain event occurs. The unpredictable ways Earth's subsystems react to excessive pressures include several thresholds:

> Many subsystems of Earth react in a nonlinear, often abrupt, way, and are particularly sensitive around threshold levels of certain key variables. If these thresholds are crossed, then important subsystems, such as a monsoon system, could shift into a new state, often with deleterious or potentially even disastrous consequences for humans.

We may not know when we have crossed an environmental threshold. But it is plain to see sometime *after* we have crossed it. The consequences of going past environmental limits for stressors such as noise, overcrowding, or pollution are called **threshold effects**—and they damage the individual as well as the group. Table C.1 describes three of those thresholds.

The middle column, called "Preindustrial Value," is what Earth was experiencing before the Industrial Revolution. The next column, "Proposed Threshold," is the point at which Earth entered the estimated danger zone of unpredictability. That unpredictability is magnified when more than one over-the-threshold subsystem has entered its danger zone.

The far-right and final column, "Current Status," reports about where we are now. The cell showing current CO_2 concentrations was reported as "unprecedented over the last 3 million years" (Willeit et al., 2019). Now focus on the bottom row (rate of biodiversity loss).

Tragedy of the commons: The idea that individuals, in their attempt to benefit themselves, will collectively harm society.

Threshold: A point that must be exceeded for a certain effect or consequence to occur.

Threshold effects: Consequences that result from exceeding a certain limit (e.g., passing the Earth's capacity for pollution, overcrowding, etc.).

TABLE C.1

Earth-Systems Processes

EARTH-SYSTEMS PROCESSES	PARAMETERS	PREINDUSTRIAL VALUE	PROPOSED THRESHOLD	CURRENT STATUS
Climate Change 1	Atmospheric carbon dioxide concentration (parts per million)	280	350	Around 400 (Willeit et al., 2019)
Climate Change 2	Change in radiative forcing (watts per meter squared)	.01–1	10	>100
Rate of biodiversity loss	Extinction rate (number of species per million, per year)	0	35	121

Before the Industrial Revolution, the average number of species that went extinct each year was zero. The estimated threshold for species loss is just 35 species per year. A recent estimate is that we are now losing about 121 unique, never-to-be-seen-again species *each year*. Dozens of species enter the danger zone and never come back.

Current rates of extinction appear to be happening so quickly that they are difficult to measure—but also because scientists keep discovering new species (see Boakes et al., 2018; Tapley et al., 2018). Davis et al. (2018, p. 11266) summarized the current, depressing story when they estimated the *millions* of years needed for classes of species to recover from recent losses:

> Extinction is part of evolution, but the unnatural rapidity of current species losses forces us to address whether we are cutting off twigs or whole branches from the tree of life.

Individually, most of us have never seen most of these species, except perhaps on some *National Geographic* documentary or in an exotic zoo. It is easy to think that "the disappearance of these plants and animals doesn't affect my life at all." Is that true? What if some other species were saying that about *us*? What if one of these species holds the secret to curing cancer? We might never know.

Humans Also Have Limits: Noise, Crowding, and Pollution

Humans also have limits.

Noise can be experienced as something beautiful (music), annoying (fingers squeaking on a chalkboard), or damaging (hearing loss). Crowding can encourage civilized, cooperative behavior (millions living together in large cities), frustration (traffic jams), or cruelty (rejection of starving refugees). Pollution is something people in big cities get used to—but it may seem so overwhelming that we give up on trying to decrease it. Let's discuss each threat in turn.

Excessive Noise

Noise is unwanted, annoying sounds.

That means that your perception influences how you experience sounds. If you look forward to the sound of your neighbor's daughter learning to play the trombone, then it's not noise to you. But if you find her trombone playing disruptive and aggravating, then it qualifies as noise. There are both auditory (physiological) and nonauditory (psychological) responses to noise. We focus first on excessive noise because it may not come to mind as quickly as littering, air pollution, or chemical spills and because it's a problem often rooted in social interactions.

PTSD and the Sounds of War: Three features make noise stressful:

- Volume
- Unpredictability
- Perceived lack of control

You can see all three at work in Ellis's (1976, pp. 62–63) accounts of an intense bombardment of World War I soldiers:

> Twenty to thirty shells would be landing in a company sector every minute. . . . [Perceived lack of control]. Suddenly the barrage would lift and then, five minutes later, start up again. [Unpredictability]. As the evening wore on the intervals would get shorter and shorter and the almost continuous noise grow to a crescendo [Volume].

You can also recognize the effects of extreme volume, unpredictability, and lack of control in Captain Greenwell's description of the sounds of battle:

> Modern warfare . . . reduces men to shivering beasts. There isn't a man who can withstand shellfire of the modern kind without getting the blues. . . . [Perceived lack of control]. [Imagine] on some overhead platform ten thousand carters were tipping loads of pointed steel bricks that burst in the air or on the ground [Unpredictability] all with a fiendish devastating ear-splitting roar that shook the nerves of the stoutest [Volume].

AP Photo/Steve Stibbens

Extreme noise has harmful auditory effects through noise-induced hair cell and nerve damage. It also has nonauditory effects such as sleep deprivation that lead to hypertension, cardiovascular disease, and deficits in cognitive performance (Basner et al., 2014). Lieutenant Chandos recorded that "the sensation . . . is not that of a sound. You feel it in your ears more than hear it, unless it is only about one hundred yards away."

For thousands of these World War I soldiers, the physiological effects had lasting emotional consequences. Soldier Henri Barbussed wrote that

> a diabolical uproar surrounds us, . . . a sustained crescendo, an incessant multiplication of the universal frenzy; a hurricane of hoarse and hollow banging, . . . where we are buried up to our necks, and the wind of the shells seems to set it heaving and pitching.

It didn't take long for this kind of noise to affect soldiers. Healthy soldiers were quickly transformed into "shell-shocked" damaged humans. The stress created by the consequences of "shell shock" had lasting effects. The modern clinical term, of course, is posttraumatic stress disorder (PTSD). You can better appreciate the disturbing clinical meaning of that phrase by searching YouTube for "Shell Shock WW I." In World War I, its effects often lingered, even in soldiers who appeared to have recovered (Ellis, 1976, p. 63):

> It is very nice to be home again. Yet am I at home? One sometimes doubts it. There are occasions when I feel like a visitor amongst strangers whose intentions are kindly, but whose modes of thought I neither altogether understand nor altogether approve.

Soundscapes: From Problem to Social Psychological Solutions. Noise-induced stress affects different animals in different ways.

Those effects then circulate throughout the ecosystem. For example, noise pollution increased pollination but decreased seed dispersal of honeybees and birds. This, in turn, influenced patterns of vegetation (Francis & Barber, 2013). The honeybees may have been driven by the stress of noise pollution to load up on food supplies while birds that normally distribute seeds fled noise-polluted environments and did not return.

The effects of noise on humans appear to produce changes in learning capability. Matheson and colleagues found evidence in both field and lab studies of children. "Chronic aircraft noise exposure impairs reading comprehension and long-term memory and may be associated with raised blood pressure" (Matheson et al., 2003, p. 243). Do you have faith that technology will come to the rescue?

Some innovative technological solutions to noise pollution are emerging in Paris. The technique is crowd-sourced scientific observations. French "citizen-scientists" have been equipped with cell phones capable of monitoring the environment and using those data to draw a noise map of Paris (Maisonneuve et al., 2009).

That's interesting in itself, but now others have produced soundscapes of Paris (search for "soundlandscapes blog" online). You can hear the welcome, comforting sounds of everyday life in Paris during a walk through a park, waiting in a train station, and even listening to a xylophone player performing in a Metro (subway) station. There's no predicting where human creativity will take you when you start solving social problems.

Crowding

Your experience of crowding depends on where you live and how much you travel.

One of your authors lives in Storm Lake, Iowa. It's pretty quiet there compared to your other author's home in northern New Jersey, just outside of New York City. But both of us have experienced far greater crowding when traveling to places such as China and India, where the problems of crowding and noise often mix.

Prior to recent noise regulation efforts, some of the three-wheeled taxis in Mumbai, India, had painted "Please beep" signs (in English) on their rear fenders. Their purpose

was to help drivers ahead of them avoid crashing while navigating tight traffic by sound. In some parts of India, you're legally required to honk when you pass another vehicle. The amount of noise and crowding can be overwhelming until you get used to it.

Density and crowding are not the same thing. **Density** is an objective numerical calculation that measures how many people occupy a particular space. **Crowding** is the subjective sense that there are too many people in a given space. Ten people in a village isn't density—but 10 people in a single elevator is probably crowding. In other words, crowding is a psychological perception that comes with wide individual differences. Fear of overcrowding may have been exaggerated by the popular media, however, perhaps due to a lack of good statistical understanding.

Robert Nickelsberg / Archive Photos/Getty Images

Busy subways in India, Los Angeles, or any other major urban area can be good examples of both noise and crowding.

Maybe the most well-known and infamous study about crowding is so disturbing that de Waal et al. (2000) called it a "nightmarish experiment" (see Calhoun, 1962a, 1962b). Calhoun arranged for an expanding population of rats to be crammed into a room. It produced what he called a "behavioral sink" in which rats soon started killing, sexually assaulting, and eventually cannibalizing each other. The popular press ran with this most dramatic element of the research story. "In no time, popularizers were comparing politically motivated street riots to rat packs, inner cities to behavioral sinks, and urban areas to zoos" (de Waal et al., 2000, p. 77).

Consequently, Calhoun is best known for what he did not want to be known for: a dismal view of a human future viciously turning on itself due to overpopulation (see Ramsden & Adams, 2009). In reality, Calhoun simply wanted to explore how we could

Density: An objective calculation of how many people occupy a particular space.

Crowding: The subjective sense that there are too many people in a given space.

design space more effectively. A review of these crowding experiments (Ramsden & Adams, 2009) concluded that

> through the effective design of space, [Calhoun] attempted to develop more collaborative and intelligent rodent communities, capable of withstanding greater degrees of density. For Calhoun, contrary to many interpretations, population growth was not inherently bad and humanity was not destined to destroy itself. (p. 763)

The reality of crowding effects thus might not be quite as dismal as the popular media would have us believe (see Lawrence, 1974). For example, Pinker (2011) makes a statistical argument that human aggression is declining—even in the face of a more densely populated Earth (see Chapter 11).

Even though humans crowded together generally behave better and more creatively than you might expect, there are other crises related to overpopulation—and they are urgent. A research team in India provides a discouragingly long list of the most urgent crises:

> Overpopulation has resulted in a series of catastrophic consequences by causing increased pressure on existing natural resources. Deforestation, welfare, effect on climate change, decline in biocapacity, urban sprawl, food security, increase in energy demand, and effect on marine ecosystems. (Uniyal et al., 2016, p. 1)

The Earth has many more subsystems than the *Titanic* had supposedly watertight compartments. But similar to the *Titanic*, Earth's compartments are interdependent as they approach their thresholds. Failures of one subsystem can cascade through all the others. de Waal et al. (2000) document an insight that also delivers a warning. "We have a natural, underappreciated talent to deal with crowding, but crowding combined with scarcity of resources is something else" (p. 81).

Pollution

The problem was hiding in plain sight.

A study named *Toxic Wastes and Race in the United States* (United Church of Christ, 1987) connected environmental harm to social injustice. The Reverend Benjamin Chavis stated the case bluntly in his foreword to Robert Bullard's (1993) edited collection of case studies and commentary: "People of color bear the brunt of the nation's pollution problem" (Bullard, 1993, p. 3). The unavoidable conclusion was that pollution is a particularly vicious form of social injustice.

Pollution and Social Injustice. How vicious?

The human cruelty of pollution is apparent in a study commissioned by *The Lancet* that concluded, "Pollution is the largest environmental cause of disease and premature death" (Landrigan et al., 2018, p. 1). Deaths from pollution are 15 times more likely than deaths from all wars and other forms of violence—and 3 times more likely than from the combined effects of AIDS, tuberculosis, and malaria. Hang on . . . the story gets worse, especially if you are poor or a minority. That same commission concluded that

> pollution disproportionately kills the poor and the vulnerable. Nearly 92% of pollution-related deaths occur in low-income and middle-income countries and, in countries at every income level, disease caused by pollution is most prevalent among minorities and the marginalised. (p. 1)

Pollution is difficult to control. Air pollution, for example, drifts indiscriminately across regional boundaries. But it also tends to settle over cities. Those who live in cities suffer more health crises such as asthma and rhinitis (see Norbäck et al., 2018;

Sunyer et al., 1997). The negative health consequences of pollution are not limited to those who are socially vulnerable.

> Children are at high risk of pollution related disease and even extremely low-dose exposures to pollutants during windows of vulnerability in utero and in early infancy can result in disease, disability, and death in childhood and across their lifespan. (Landrigan et al., 2018, p. 1)

The Disappearing Luxury of Obliviousness. Pollution is expensive.

Even if you happen to be in a privileged class of society, air pollution will find its way to your lake home, fertilizers will choke out the plant life, and fish species will disappear. There are consequences for exceeding the thresholds for survival. We no longer have the "luxury of obliviousness" (Johnson, 2006, p. 22). In other words, we have to start paying attention. Even the wealthy are paying attention because pollution is expensive and is driving up health care costs. *The Lancet* authors (Landrigan et al., 2018, p. 1) observed that

> pollution-related disease also results in health-care costs that are responsible for up to 7% of health spending in middle-income countries that are heavily polluted and rapidly developing. Welfare losses due to pollution are estimated to amount to US $4.6 trillion per year: 6.2% of global economic output.

Pollution is also expensive because it damages entire ecosystems and encourages global climate change through fuel combustion. Some biologists are already debating how to prioritize which species they should attempt to save (see Urban et al., 2017). It is a complicated debate because approximately 85% of airborne particulates come from fuel combustion in middle- to higher-income countries.

Almost all pollution by oxides related to sulfur and nitrogen are the main drivers of climate change. The sources of damaging carbon dioxide include "electricity-generating plants, chemical manufacturing, mining operations, deforestation, and petroleum-powered vehicles." The chief culprit, what *The Lancet* calls "the world's most polluting fossil fuel," is coal (Landrigan et al., 2018, p. 1).

None of us can escape pollution—and we're all, individually, responsible for doing something about it.

THE MAIN IDEAS

- The "tragedy of the commons" problems occur if individuals only do what is best for them, personally (but these individual actions harm the group).

- Threshold effects occur when the planet passes a kind of point of no return, when consequences begin after resources have been exhausted, pollution has reached a certain limit, species have gone extinct, and so on.

- Three emerging human limits are related to noise, crowding, and pollution. Each problem has subjective, psychological aspects to it and will only be overcome if each of us takes personal responsibility for the solution.

CRITICAL THINKING CHALLENGE

- Can you identify two examples of the tragedy of the commons in your school, town, or region? What are examples of actions that are harming the larger group because individuals are choosing to engage in behaviors that are good for them, personally?

- Analyze whether noise and crowding are problems for your own local campus or town. If so, what might be done to reduce these problems? If they are not problems, what about your environment has prevented noise and crowding, and how could you apply your situation to other people?

HOW CAN SOCIAL PSYCHOLOGISTS CONTRIBUTE TO A SUSTAINABLE ENVIRONMENT?

>> **LO C.2:** Explain how social psychologists can respond to environmental threats.

Survival is a great motivator.

Many countries are experiencing **climate refugees**, people displaced from their home by changes in their environment. This situation is loaded with positive and negative potentials waiting to be influenced by social psychologists. If Kurt Lewin were working today, it is easy to imagine that he might have prioritized the opportunities for humanistic action research represented by climate refugees.

Estimates of populations on the move by midcentury due to climate change—when current millennial college-age students are in their 50s—range from 50 million to 200 million (see Behrman & Kent, 2018). Some estimates of climate migration are significantly higher by factoring in the **threat multiplier effect** in which climate change aggravates other existing social and political tensions that accelerate migration, like military conflict (Causevic, 2017; Hallegate et al., 2015; O'Sullivan, 2015, but see also White, 2016).

An extraordinary level of cooperation will be needed as nations, states, and local communities figure out who will take responsibility for the social changes demanded by mass migration (Ahmed, 2018; Brown, 2016; Zafarullah & Huque, 2018). Around the world, legal systems and economists are preparing for millions of climate refugees (see Antonopoulos, 2019; Jolly & Ahmad, 2019; Pettus, 2019).

For example, the island nation of Kirbati, in the Pacific Ocean, rises only 2 meters (6–7 feet) above average sea levels. The combined equatorial islands of Kirabati have approximately 100,000 residents. If sea levels continue to rise, the people must go somewhere. The president of Kirabati, Anote Tong, told the United Nations that they were preparing for mass migration by training citizens with new skills likely to be appealing to overseas employers (see Byravan & Rajan, 2015).

Social psychologists recognize the many escalating social problems associated with mass migration, including the many triggers for aggression associated with climate change and refugee status. They include ethnic conflict, PTSD-traumatized refugees, temperature, and status vulnerability (see Luiking et al., 2019; Hecker et al., 2015; Park et al., 2017). But social psychologists also see something more.

Displaced people, fleeing for their lives and for the protection of their families, are keenly aware of the benefits of diversity—especially when it provides them with a way to earn a living. Acceptance of cultural diversity also can produce a deep organizational commitment among employees (Newman et al., 2018). For example, Debora MacKenzie (2015) makes an economic opportunity argument for embracing refugees.

For climate refugees, the social psychological expression of our ancient impulse to survive is **resilience**, the ability to consistently respond positively to problems (see Pelling, 2010). Social psychologists have tended to view resilience as a personality trait (Di Fabio & Saklofske, 2018; Roth & Herzberg, 2017) usually associated with positive psychology (see Compton & Hoffman, 2019). But resilience is also recognized as a community characteristic (see Aldrich & Meyer, 2015).

For climate refugees, **translocal social resilience** matters; it's the social practices of vulnerable populations (e.g., cooperation). It recognizes that most people prefer local community coping to mass migration (Sakdapolrak et al., 2016). That local resilience to climate change has been documented in at least one isolated arctic community (see Berkes & Jolly, 2002). However, social resilience to the effects of climate change also has produced effective—and constantly improving—national policies, particularly in European countries, most notably in Dutch and German governments (see Bauer & Steurer, 2015). Translocal social resilience is just one example of how social psychology

Climate refugees: People displaced from their home by changes in the environment.

Threat multiplier effect: Occurs when climate change aggravates other existing social or political problems.

Resilience: The ability to consistently respond positively to problems.

Translocal social resilience: The social practices of vulnerable populations.

is relevant to solving global environmental problems. This section answers the core question "How can social psychologists contribute to a sustainable environment?" by emphasizing the need to

(1) evaluate scientific claims,

(2) collect and analyze data,

(3) persuade others, and

(4) design a better environment.

Evaluate Scientific Claims

There is a familiar formula for evaluating scientific claims: reliability and validity.

Reliability and validity are how we know whether we can trust information. For example, you can be mildly skeptical when only one isolated scientist or lab warns us

The Carolina parakeet, now extinct due to climate change.

that climate change is a real, accelerating problem. However, you have a right to be more trusting when many independent scientists, from different labs, using a variety of research methods, keep coming up with the same findings. There have been many studies of various threshold effects due to climate change. Parmesan (2006) summarized the evidence about 15 to 20 years ago; the situation has grown more desperate since then.

> These observed changes are heavily biased in the directions predicted from global warming and have been linked to local or regional climate change through correlations between climate and biological variation, field and laboratory experiments, and physiological research. (p. 637)

Parmesan emphasized that the evidence for global warming comes from different independent sources: archival analyses, field observations, lab experiments, and physiological studies. Parmesan groups her *Titanic*-like compartments into marine, freshwater, and terrestrial animals. The animals most affected had "restricted ranges"— those that could not escape their environment. For example, "polar and mountaintop species . . . have been the first groups in which entire species have gone extinct due to recent climate change" (p. 637).

The range restriction for the Carolina parakeet, for example, was limited to forest edges and river bottoms where it could find the foods it had adapted to eat for many centuries. Called the most colorful bird in North America, the last Carolina parakeet was killed in Okeechobee County, Florida. It lost its native habitat to logging, farming, and the destruction of wetlands. If you are thinking, "too bad, but it has nothing to do with me," then think about the loss of the Carolina parakeet as raising the water level in an environmental compartment. You're on the same ship as that parakeet was.

Collect and Analyze Data

Researchers are getting more creative every year.

All the sciences make discoveries by inventing new and better methods to collect meaningful data. Social psychologists are much better now at collecting data automatically. Similar to tracking devices worn by threatened species, humans are leaving behind detailed breadcrumb trails of digital data.

Information Trails of Data

How do we know if we are being effective?

To assess changing attitudes toward the environment, a relatively new approach is emerging from game designers (described below). Researchers are now looking at social information through the lens of "information trails" that players leave behind while playing a game (see Loh et al., 2015). What happens with that information?

Answer: we need creative social psychology students (you!) to develop the skills to design the game, collect the data, report the results, summarize the information visually (when possible), and communicate the data to the right audiences. Each one of those skills is part of the training in a social psychology graduate program. They represent distinct career opportunities for psychology students.

Geographic Information Systems

You're probably familiar with mapping software.

Google Maps is just one example of the richer opportunities now called geographic information systems (GIS). Like GPS, GIS has moved beyond merely mapping and guiding users to the next gas station or restaurant. GIS is being used by International Coastal Cleanup to identify what coasts around the world are most in need of recovery efforts (Haarr et al., 2019).

GIS can layer additional kinds of data such as the frequency of diseases related to pollution. The purpose, of course, is to isolate any possible environmental influences such as pesticides (see Brody et al., 2004) on diseases like breast cancer (see Jankowska et al., 2019). GIS can also clarify where resources are available for treating mental illnesses (see Townley et al., 2018). Think of GIS as a set of opportunities that leverage a spatial understanding of the social psychology of public health.

For example, GIS also maps social science data on top of information about social-economic status (Kanaroglou et al., 2019). GIS can help identify and warn at-risk populations during a sudden water pollution emergency, such as a chemical spill (Rui et al., 2015). Layered data sets can also help us understand the activity spaces of homeless youth (Townley et al., 2016). These are exciting opportunities that require significant effort and creativity.

What is your situation? If you love ocean beaches, then use your social psychological skills to start long-lasting antilittering beach cleanups. If you live near a national park, then start collecting data about how people use, misuse, and can be persuaded to improve that park. If you love travel but hate noise pollution, analyze data about how certain communities increase or decrease noise-based stress. Environmental sustainability requires personalities that respond to particular situational crises.

The fundamental relations within the ecosystem that have endured for millions of years are changing. The unpredictability of climate change is why some refer to it as "global weirding" rather than to "global warming." A standard psychology curriculum introduces you to the necessary detective-like skills needed to solve these pressing problems, including proper data collection and analysis.

Persuade Others

Persuasion is an opportunity for social psychologists to strut their stuff!

The topic of persuasion has come up in many forms throughout this (and every other) social psychology textbook. Remember these four approaches to persuasion from earlier (see Chapters 4 and 6):

- Logical, systematic thinking versus automatic, intuitive thinking
- The theory of planned behavior
- The elaboration likelihood model and heuristic-systematic model
- Specific persuasion techniques, such as foot-in-the-door

How might each of these approaches to persuasion influence people to (a) value scientific data about climate change, (b) recognize the urgency of the situation, and (c) adjust their behavior sooner, rather than later? For example, how could you increase people's motivation to consider logical arguments? Why are the social norms around coastal cleanup changing so quickly? And how could you use both logic and intuition (e.g., algorithms and heuristics) to convince people to change small daily habits that collectively damage the environment?

A fifth approach to persuasion is one you haven't seen yet in this book: game design. One example comes from how the theory of game design connects to established principles of psychology (see Heinzen, Gordon et al., 2015). The Volkswagen Corporation refers to this as "fun theory" but it is also known as "serious games" by applied game designers (see Aubert et al., 2018; Schell, 2008). Game design is a rich but relatively uncomplicated idea. In the photo shown here, Volkswagen made the experience of walking up steps fun by reengineering the steps as piano keys (which both light up and make noise as people walk on them).

In this way, people are nudged to exercise and avoid the electricity-burning escalator (see Dianoux et al., 2019). They know it works because they collected data from *naturalistic observations*. Someone unobtrusively counted how many people used the stairs versus the escalator before and after installing the piano steps.

Volkswagen also made it fun to pick up litter in a park and dispose of it. How? They modified the trash barrel. They inserted a motion detector that triggered a falling-down-a-deep-well sound every time trash was tossed into the container. The cartoony sound ended with a distant crash. People were reportedly looking for more litter to throw in the trash bin. This simple, harmless, goofy intervention encouraged positive environmental behavior. This kind of "engaging fun" (see Shipman, 2019) is at the heart of game design, and people's motivation to take part in it is at the heart of social psychology.

Design a Better Environment

Did you assume that all buildings were built with people in mind?

Darius Sollohub (2019) and Valki Durán-Narucki (2008) join architects, designers, and environmental psychologists who believe that we can we do a much better job designing spaces that promote human engagement and environmental sustainability.

Become an Environmental Designer

Take a look around your own school or home.

Many buildings appear to be built with economics in mind and the assumption that whatever works for me must work for others. Self-centered or egocentric design is how we end up with kitchen cabinets, airline storage bins, and grocery store shelves designed by and for tall men. It's also why desks, tools, and office equipment are designed by and for right-handed people.

To combat egocentric design, we need psychologically sophisticated designers (Kopec, 2018). A psychologically sophisticated designer can work with architects to build spaces for people with dementia, for example (see Mansoori et al., 2019). A psychologically trained designer can help create eco-efficient workplaces that people actually enjoy living and working in (see Kuo et al., 2018). We need psychologically informed designers to create pro-environment cityscapes (see Whitburn et al., 2018), schools that promote the joy of learning (see Durán-Narucki, 2008), and a small army of millennial architects and designers sensitive to climate change, crowding, pollution, and the effects of population growth (see Sollohub, 2019).

The social psychological coping skills that help make living in a dense society pleasant are similar to those that help us cope with noise. We cope better if we have perceived control over a crowded situation. Perceived control enables us to wait for

the next elevator, leave a crowded stadium, or excuse ourselves from a too-tight dance floor. We can find ways to assert our **personal space**, the invisible boundary around our bodies that gives us a sense of control over our environment.

If you care about environmental sustainability, the careers are waiting for your creativity.

Become a User Experience Specialist

Here's an emerging job skill for psychology students: **user experience specialist**.

This role requires someone who can focus, for example, on how consumers engage with and experience their everyday environments (see Tullis & Albert, 2013). A user experience specialist is a specific career within the larger field called **human factors**, an academic discipline devoted to designing products, spaces, and systems that maximize human interaction and potential.

Products such as "standing desks" are meant to be used in more productive and comfortable ways by humans. This type of product is developed by user experience specialists.

Many of the skills you are learning as a psychology student apply to measuring and understanding your environment. And once you start looking at your world through the lens of the user's experience, you start seeing all sorts of problems that can be fixed by better design.

For example, Don Norman (2013) has pointed out that many award-winning designs of doors don't really deserve the recognition. Their problem is ambiguity. As you approach, you are made to feel uncertain about whether it is a "push" door or a "pull" door. It may look beautiful in a photograph (hence the awards), but a door should not require instructions. That is why ambiguous doors are known as "Norman doors." Likewise, some stove knobs do not signal which burner they light, and many light switches don't naturally tell us which lights they operate. Buildings are often not designed around the people who will use them.

Personal space: The individual boundary around our body that gives us a sense of control over the environment.

User experience specialist: A career focused on how consumers engage with and experience their everyday environments.

Human factors: An academic discipline within psychology devoted to designing products or systems that best cater to human needs.

Without the labels on these doors, it would be impossible to know whether they are meant to be pulled open or pushed open; this is an example of poor design.

Become an Applied Game Designer

You have probably experienced the dynamics of game design many times.

There are specific principles, often referred to as **game mechanics**, motivating experiences that keep you engaged as a player (see Schell, 2008). Game designers sometimes assert that they don't design games; they design experiences. Then they use games to create that experience.

You will probably recognize some of these game mechanics from your own experience playing anything from a crossword puzzle to a card game to the latest video game:

- Onboarding: creating initial engagement

- Leveling up: maintaining engagement

- Flow zone: sustaining an achievement by increasing difficulty

You can start down the road to a career as a user experience specialist or game designer by combining your skills as a psychology student with the principles you intuitively understand from playing video games, sports, and related activities. The principles of game design can be used to solve hundreds of real-world problems through **gamification**, the application of game-based principles to nongame settings (e.g., Rutledge et al., 2018).

Here's how you can get started. Conduct a survey of the buildings at your school. Look for examples of design that increase or detract from a pleasant, intrinsically engaging environment. Examples of questions you could ask are shown in Table C.2.

TABLE C.2

Example Questions Regarding the Psychology of Your Environment

What message does the architecture of academic buildings send to students?
Do the hallways of your academic buildings have alcoves that encourage conversations and study—or are they straight, narrow, and plain?
Are the classrooms clean and inviting? Are trash cans overflowing?
Do your professors' offices have chairs that encourage conversation?
Are there images of engaged students that you can identify with?
What is the experience of using the restrooms?
What is the proportion of male and female restrooms relative to the people who typically use the space?
Are the restrooms located close to where students gather?
Are the wash basins and hand dryers conveniently located?
Are they clean?
What is it like to use the classrooms?
Do the light switches suggest which lights they will operate?
Are chairs arranged to encourage lectures, discussion, or both?
Are the electronic supports working—and do professors know how to use them?
Are there display cabinets or images that promote the achievements of students, promote curiosity, or encourage further engagement and perseverance?

Game mechanics: Motivating experiences that keep someone engaged as a player.

Gamification: Application of gaming principles to a nongame setting.

Here is a chapter-by-chapter reminder of how you can apply social psychology to environmental sustainability, both personally and professionally. You might be able to change the world based on what you've learned from social psychology.

Chapter 1. An Introduction	Participate in the tradition of social activism highlighted by Kurt Lewin's declaration of "action research."
Chapter 2. Research Methods	Evaluate whether solar panels, electric cars, or recycling is cost-effective or just something that makes us feel virtuous.
Chapter 3. The Social Self	Join or organize an environmental group with a social identity that strengthens your personal identity.
Chapter 4. Social Cognition	Listen to both intuition and logic when deciding whether to believe the science about climate change.
Chapter 5. Person Perception	Consider how to persuade others, knowing how first impressions and halo effects can become self-fulfilling prophecies.
Chapter 6. Attitudes and Persuasion	Work in marketing to strengthen science-based beliefs about climate and climate change.
Chapter 7. Social Influence	Resist conforming to harmful social norms by publicly picking up loose garbage.
Chapter 8. Group Processes	Refer to "groupthink" in a public or organizational meeting, just to remind people of its dangers.
Chapter 9. Stereotyping, Prejudice, and Discrimination	Openly oppose stereotypes, prejudice, and discrimination, knowing others may quietly support you.
Chapter 10. Helping and Prosocial Behavior	Recognize and sustain the prosocial environmental work of others.
Chapter 11. Aggression	Redirect frustrations over a filthy environment that lead to escalating aggression.
Chapter 12. Intimate Relationships	Promote conditions that foster healthy relationships that promote respect.

THE MAIN IDEAS

- Climate refugees are people displaced from their home by changes in the environment. This is just one example of how psychology and the environment affect each other.

- Social psychologists can help environmentalists in many ways, including four important roles to play by (1) evaluating scientific claims made by others, (2) collecting and analyzing relevant data, (3) persuading the general population to believe trends in the data, and (4) designing better environments.

CRITICAL THINKING CHALLENGE

- Spend time going to three websites for charities such as Habitat for Humanity, St. Jude Children's Research Hospital, and so on. Analyze how the websites are designed to persuade people to contribute time or money, and tie these efforts into one specific theory or concept you've learned in this class.

- Identify two products that seem to be designed poorly because they are not equally accessible to everyone (e.g., they are difficult to use by short people, left-handers, people in wheelchairs, etc.) and explain how you might improve on their design.

D. Social Psychology of Law and the Courtroom

Core Questions

D.1   How do psychology and law fit together?

D.2   What do social psychologists know about false confessions and eyewitness testimony?

Learning Objectives

D.1   Apply the goals and methods of psychology to law and courtroom situations.

D.2   Apply the rule of law to explain the Innocence Project, false confessions, and faulty eyewitness testimony.

"It's like public execution, but you stay alive to go at it again and again, day after day."

Kelly Michaels was telling Oprah Winfrey about what happened after the police knocked on her door. The 22-year-old aspiring actress was getting ready for work at the Wee Care Day Nursery. Her name had been mentioned in a case of child sex abuse. The police questioned but then released her. She thought her short nightmare was over.

There was no physical evidence. The prosecution had to rely on anatomically correct dolls to collect testimony from preschool children. Their accusations included playing piano in the nude, "making poopie cakes," and "inserting silverware into the children." She was convicted of 115 counts of abuse and sentenced to 47 years in prison.

Whatever they had majored in during college, the detectives had not developed the habit of critical thinking. They presented the dolls to children and then asked leading questions such as, "Where *could* Miss Kelly have touched you?" For psychology students, this trial demonstrates the importance of scientific reasoning about human behavior.

The accusations were a social illusion.

HOW DO PSYCHOLOGY AND LAW FIT TOGETHER?

>> **LO D.1:** **Apply the goals and methods of psychology to law and courtroom situations.**

Justice delayed is justice denied.

That's the goal: Get it right and get it right now (see Humphreys, 2018; Yasmin & Iqbal, 2019). Unfortunately, that international standard of justice has been especially brutal toward people of color in the United States (see Adewakun, 2018; Bosworth et al., 2018; Franklin, 2018; Lens, 2019). For example, the notorious case of the "Central Park Five" (see Burns, 2012) convicted five Hispanic and Black 14- to 16-year-old boys with rape. The boys grew into men in prison before they were exonerated by another man's confession that also was supported by DNA evidence.

Social psychology is concerned with the case of the Central Park Five because

- the victim of the crime tells a powerful story of recovery through social support,

- the case demonstrates the psychology of false confessions,

- social media promoted negative stereotypes,

- the president of the United States rejected DNA evidence, and

- the psychology of persuasion led to false convictions.

Decades later, the Central Park Five continues to make headlines, as well as inspire books and even a Netflix mini-series (Burns, 2012; Guniss, 2018; Meili, 2003). The Kelly Michaels case and the Central Park Five case are just two examples among thousands. This section answers the core question "How do psychology and law fit together?" by

(1) criticizing the false television-inspired world of forensic psychology,

(2) categorizing real applications of social psychology to the law,

(3) identifying common goals of psychology and law, and

(4) naming social roles that illustrate the everyday work of forensic psychologists.

The False Television World of Forensic Psychology

There is a bad fit between criminal profilers on TV and reality.

Many undergraduates suffer from the **CSI effect** (Crime Scene Investigation effect): unrealistic expectations of forensic science that are created by watching fictional television shows (see Cole & Dioso-Villa, 2006; Scanlan, 2015). One colleague joked, with dark humor, "There just aren't enough serial killers to go around" to employ the many students who want to become criminal profilers.

But there is a bigger question: Does criminal profiling reliably identify criminals?

Most Research Does Not Support Criminal Profiling

It's time to be realistic about your career opportunities.

In reality, people who actually do criminal profiling are seldom trained in psychology, have little understanding of reliability and validity, and have simply declared themselves "experts." Scientific approaches for criminal profiling have not been established or even agreed upon. And the evidence for the accuracy and helpfulness of criminal profiling is so thin that it is seldom admitted in court or considered as expert testimony (see Fulero & Wrightsman, 2008).

Chelsea Van Aken (2015) summarized the information from the FBI's Behavioral Unit (the National Center for the Analysis of Violent Crime, or NCAVC). She described how they "utilize definitions, typographies, and motives to create a criminal profile to investigate serial killings. Ultimately, these profiles are inadequate because they are inconclusive." But she did not stop there. She also pointed out that criminal profiling is worse than ineffective because they "exclude multiple suspects that are potentially dangerous."

She is not the only one to reach this conclusion. A review by Fallon and Snook (2019) asserted that criminal profiling is "a dubious practice and that its use of law enforcement agencies should be prohibited until there is compelling empirical evidence that it works" (p. 8). The titles of many books and articles reveal the deep skepticism about criminal profiling:

- *Criminal Profiling: Granfalloons and Gobbledygook* (Snook et al., 2008)

- *The Criminal Profiling Reality: What Is Behind the Smoke and Mirrors?* (Kocsis, 2013)

- *Questioning the Validity of Criminal Profiling: An Evidence-Based Approach* (Chifflet, 2015)

- *Media Effects and Criminal Profiling: How Fiction Influences Perception and Profile Accuracy* (Bolton, 2019)

A meta-analysis of 40 years and 412 studies of criminal profiling (a.k.a. offender profiling) recognizes that there have been some advances. Nevertheless, Fox and Farrington (2018) conclude that

> despite being applied often in active police investigations, very few evaluations of the profiles' accuracy or effectiveness have taken place. This lack of scientific evidence on the validity and impact of profiling, despite the technique's widespread use, seriously questions its efficacy in real world investigations, as it currently stands. (p. 1248)

Data About the CSI Effect

Fortunately, we also have data about the CSI effect.

One study found that regular viewers of crime dramas would probably make slightly better burglars! That's not good! They were more likely to know, for instance, that using gloves and wearing a hat would prevent certain evidence from being left at the crime scene (Vicary & Zaikman, 2017). Please don't take that as a career recommendation.

CSI effect: Unrealistic expectations of forensic science created by watching fictional television shows.

Not all television crime dramas are alike, and particular episodes, of course, will feature different content. A comparison of three television crime drama franchises included *Law & Order* (1990–2010), *CSI* (2000–2015), and *NCIS* (2003–present; see Hust et al., 2015). The focus of the study was on the degree to which viewers of crime dramas tend to accept myths about rape and their willingness to intervene if they observe sexual assault. When they surveyed 313 first-year college students, their observations added to the importance of the #MeToo movement. They found that

(a) Exposure to the *Law & Order* franchise is associated with decreased rape myth acceptance, increased intentions to adhere to expressions of sexual consent, and increased intentions to stop unwanted sexual activity. That's good.

(b) The *CSI* franchise is associated with decreased intentions to seek consent and decreased intentions to adhere to expressions of sexual consent. That's not good.

(c) Exposure to the *NCIS* franchise is associated with decreased intentions to stop unwanted sexual activity. That's not good.

These observations are not strong patterns of behavior. This particular aspect of the CSI effect appears to be small but real. The CSI effect is a reality check if you are planning on a career in criminal profiling. But don't get discouraged too quickly. The reality of forensic psychology has many more exciting, consequential career paths waiting to be explored.

The Real World of Forensic Psychology

There is a better fit waiting for you in forensic psychology.

It will require thinking like a scientist and allowing your training to change you. And . . . you won't get to play the hero on television. **Forensic psychology** is the application of psychological theory and research to legal processes. The overlap between social psychology and the law is summarized by the six categories shown in Table D.1. Each one represents some version of a career goal for psychology students.

Psychologists usually influence the legal world through an **amicus brief**, a perspective report offered to a trial as a "friend of the court." For example, social psychologists Bruck and Ceci helped Kelly Michaels by submitting an amicus brief that summarized research about using anatomically correct dolls. They pointed out the many violations

Anatomically correct dolls such as these are sometimes used in court or therapy settings to help children communicate about possible sexual abuse.

Bettmann/Bettmann/Getty Images

TABLE D.1

Six Applications of Forensic Psychology

AREA OR CONTEXT	EXAMPLES
Interrogations	Ethics of lying to suspects
	Confessions
	Lie detection
	Torture
Evidence evaluation	Fingerprints
	DNA
	Criminal profiling
	Cognitive errors and bias in police, lawyers, jurors, witnesses, etc.
Person evaluation	Jury selection
	Eyewitness identification
	Competency/sanity of defendants
	Trauma assessment
	Risk assessment
Family law	Child custody
	Dispute mediation
	Sexual abuse
	Relationship violence
Workplace assessment	Harassment
	Discrimination
	Policy compliance
Policy evaluation	Program evaluation
	Prison sentencing
	Rehabilitation
	Death penalty

Forensic psychology: The application of psychological theory and research to legal processes (e.g., suspect interrogations, evaluation of potential jurors).

of reliability and validity as others were collecting data from children: interviewer bias, repeated questioning, peer pressure, and even using the anatomically correct dolls in the first place (see Bruck & Ceci, 1995, 2009; Ceci & Bruck, 1995).

The amicus brief helped; at age 33, Kelly Michaels was released from prison.

You also can see the good fit between psychology and the law in the December 2019 issue of the APA publication *Monitor on Psychology*. In addition to the famous *Brown v. Board of Education* ruling, the *Monitor* described 10 cases in which psychology influenced American law. The three cases in Table D.2 represent rulings directly influenced by social psychological research.

Amicus brief: A report including information or arguments the court might want to consider when making a decision.

TABLE D.2

Three Court Cases Influenced by Social Psychological Research.

CASE	ISSUE	SOCIAL PSYCHOLOGICAL CONCLUSION	RULING
1989 *Price Waterhouse v. Hopkins*	**Gender discrimination at work** Ann Hopkins sued after being denied a promotion because of interpersonal problems such as needing to wear more makeup and walk/talk in a more "feminine" manner.	Stereotyping can create discriminatory personnel practices.	Under Title VII, gender stereotypes are not a legitimate basis for personnel decisions.
2011 *Warney v. State of New York*	**False confessions** Later exonerated by DNA testing, Douglas Warney's intellectual disabilities and AIDS-related dementia influenced his false confession to a murder in the face of pressure tactics by interrogators.	The length of interrogation, lies by interrogators, mental illness, and low IQ can elicit false confessions.	Mr. Warney was entitled to reparations after a long prison sentence because police departments were aware of the risks of a false confession.
2017 *People v. Boone*	**Cross-race identification** A Black man from Brooklyn, New York, Otis Boone was sentenced to 25 years for two robberies based only on the testimony of two White victims.	Eyewitness testimony has even less credibility for cross-race identification.	Mr. Boone was acquitted at retrial; the court decision cited the APA's brief.

Social psychology and law both aim to solve similar social problems related to social self-regulation (see Goldstein, 1968). They both ask the same fundamental question: How can we live and work together in peace? But the relationship between psychology and law is also contentious. Each represents cultural values that are often in conflict. Many of the attitudes, training experiences, and professional values of lawyers and psychologists will never fit together.

Psychology and the Law: Common Goals and Different Methods

Using anatomically correct dolls helped convict an innocent Kelly Michaels.

The goal was to identify whether Kelly Michaels had sexually abused children. But the tests were not reliable—so they could not be valid no matter what Kelly Michaels may or may not have done. The anatomically correct doll test is intuitively appealing, but it has two ways of being wrong.

How Psychologists Worry About Fairness

Like parallel train tracks, reliability and validity work together to help justice arrive at a fair decision.

In this context, a false positive occurs when an interviewer decides that a child has been abused when he or she hasn't. A **false negative** occurs when an interviewer decides that a child has not been abused when he or she has. You will recognize these same ideas in statistics as a Type I error (a false positive) and a **Type II error** (a false negative). Both outcomes are errors and can have disastrous effects.

In addition, the theoretical orientation of the therapist will lead to different interpretations. Refusing to touch the doll could indicate abuse to a Freudian who interprets not touching as repression or denial. However, playing enthusiastically with the doll could also be interpreted as pathological disinhibition and a sign of abuse. Cognitive problems like confirmation bias are bound to occur to even the most well-intentioned therapists. Either way, Kelly Michaels is considered guilty—and that's not fair.

How Lawyers Worry About Fairness

Reliability and validity are also familiar worries to attorneys (Friedemann & Morgan, 1985).

The California Supreme Court decided that it could not determine if using anatomically correct dolls was a *valid* way to assess child sex abuse. So, the Court referred the problem back to the scientific community (see Yates & Terr, 1988, p. 254). The Court ruled that "use of the dolls . . . is admissible in court only if it has been accepted as generally reliable in the scientific community." It was a win for scientific reasoning in the courtroom.

Psychologists and lawyers have other similar goals. In addition to valuing reliability and validity, both want the best for their clients in ways that also promote social justice. However, the points of contention are also fundamental to each discipline.

Different Philosophies: Advocacy Versus Objectivity

Lawyers and psychologists don't think the same way.

What is "right" according to law is generally determined by precedent, what prior authorities have ruled. The psychologist, however, determines what is "right" by empirical observations (in other words, research data). There are other critical differences summarized in Table D.3. Lawyers can only react to and process ongoing events. Psychologists get to choose what to study. The practice of law is based on advocacy. The practice of psychology requires objectivity. Consequently, trying to fit psychology into law has often been difficult—and this tension between psychology and law has been present from their first interactions.

Hugo Münsterberg. The relationship between law and psychology got off to a shaky start.

False negative: Occurs when we think an event or condition is not present when it really is.

Type II error: See *false negative.*

TABLE D.3

Critical Differences Between the Law and Psychology

THE LEGAL APPROACH	THE PSYCHOLOGICAL APPROACH
What is "right" is determined by precedent.	What is "right" is determined by empirical observations.
Lawyers can only process and react to ongoing events.	Psychologists can choose what to study and how to study it.
Law requires advocacy.	Psychology requires objectivity.

When psychologist Hugo Münsterberg published his book *On the Witness Stand* in 1908, he was hoping to influence the legal system to accept psychology in the same way it accepted evidence from other branches of science. He was unsuccessful. Costanzo and Krauss (2015) described the book's "icy reception from legal scholars" (p. 2). One reviewer gave it a "savagely, satirical critique" for Münsterberg's "exaggerated claims for psychology." Even worse, the book was not well received by fellow psychologists.

Louis Brandeis. A later interaction between law and psychology was more promising.

A future Supreme Court justice, Louis Brandeis, understood irrational human psychology better than psychologist Hugo Münsterberg understood the law. Brandeis cited social science as he argued in favor of improving wages and limiting the workday to 10 hours. The case of *Muller v. Oregon* (see Woloch, 1996) involved a woman working long hours in a laundry factory. Brandeis argued from a social science perspective that excessive work hours produced negative social consequences such as infant mortality and children harmed by neglect.

The data were more typical of sociology than psychology, but it introduced empirical social science data to legal reasoning. In these first two examples, the psychologist (Hugo Münsterberg) was trying to push psychology's big ideas through a very small door of legal acceptance. He was ineffective—maybe even counterproductive. But the lawyer (Louis Brandeis) was trying to pull something relatively small (specific social science data) through that same small door of acceptance. Brandeis was more effective—and his small success created bigger opportunities for others.

The famous legal case *Brown v. Board of Education of Topeka* (1954) used psychological research as part of its argument to end school segregation.

Mamie Clark and Kenneth Clark. Mamie and Kenneth Clark were more successful (legally) but still disappointed (psychologically) when they combined law and psychology.

We introduced you to the Clarks in Chapter 1 when we described Mamie Clark's original master's thesis. She originated a series of doll studies that influenced the 1954 Supreme Court case that ended legal school segregation, *Brown v. Board of Education of Topeka*. The consequences of that legal victory demonstrate critical differences in how psychologists and lawyers define success.

The lawyers who prevailed in *Brown v. Board of Education of Topeka* were happy about their legal victory. But the Clarks were, over time, profoundly disappointed because so little changed. The lives of most of the children that they were trying to empower continued to suffer from the kinds of institutional and cultural discrimination we described in Chapter 9. A longer view, if they had lived to see it, might have given the Clarks both more comfort but also accompanied by a deeper disappointment that progress was so slow.

The Working World of Forensic Psychology

Costanzo and Krauss (2015) can help introduce you to the everyday work of forensic psychologists: trial consultants, dispute mediation, evaluation research, and reformers.

Trial Consultants

Trial consultants try to influence the outcome of a trial.

They typically employ three strategies:

(1) helping to select a sympathetic jury,

(2) developing trial strategies such as persuasion techniques, and

(3) assisting in witness preparation.

Trial consultant:
Someone who tries to influence the outcome of a trial by (1) helping to select a sympathetic jury, (2) developing trial strategies, and (3) assisting in witness preparation.

In their book *Stack and Sway,* Neil Kressel (a social psychologist) and Dorite Kressel (a lawyer) described the necessary psychological skills, the corresponding costs, the sociological aspects, and the effectiveness of hiring jury consultants. They also explore the public's perception of unfairness when only the wealthy can afford the luxury of jury consultants (Kressel & Kressel, 2002).

Jury profiling and juror dynamics are among the most enduring television and movie plot devices (e.g., *Bull* [Attanasio et al., 2016], *Runaway Jury* [Fleder et al., 2003], *Twelve Angry Men* [Fonda et al., 1957/1997]). However, it is logically impossible to determine whether jury consultants have been effective, partly because jury deliberations are confidential. Psychological jury consultants and researchers will therefore sometimes create **mock juries** to anticipate how different pieces of evidence might be processed by a real jury.

Understanding the psychological dynamics of a jury is not necessarily reserved for the super-wealthy—but neither is it practical for those with very little money. The more relevant observation is that, on a practical level, very few cases go to trial anyway (Galanter, 2005). Why? Because both sides decide to settle out of court—usually sometime shortly before one or both of the parties spend the last of their money on lawyers.

Dispute Mediation

Jury trials are rare.

Almost everyone settles out of court. That has created another industry that appears to be good for psychologists: dispute mediation. Like other areas of overlap between psychology and law, the practitioners are not necessarily lawyers or psychologists—although that training is likely to help. But there are ways to obtain training and certification in dispute mediation, depending on the nature of the conflict (see Barsky, 2014; Love & Waldman, 2016).

Career tip: It is helpful financially—and for networking—to obtain certifications in subspecialties.

There are as many career opportunities for mediators as there are ways for people to have conflicts with one another. On a large scale, there are dispute mediators between nations to resolve international conflicts (Ascher & Brown, 2014). Many civil disputes involve conflict over land, so particular experience, training, and certifications in agriculture, forestry, real estate, or boundary disputes can help individuals become better mediators for those circumstances (see Dhiaulhaq et al., 2015).

Families, however, also get into conflicts that can be solved before siblings or others start taking one another to court (Eisenberg, 2016). A separate skill in divorce mediation can help families take better care of themselves and of children who are unavoidably drawn into the conflict. In those cases, the skills of a family therapist may also be applicable. Judges frequently become advocates for dispute mediation to prevent unproductive lawsuits from clogging up the court system.

Evaluation Research

You already participate in the world of evaluation research.

At a superficial (but still consequential) level, you participate in evaluation research when you comment on a class, click a Like button, respond to a survey, or join a focus group. However, the world of evaluation research is much more sophisticated when people start assessing the consequences of new public policies, such as whether harsh sentencing guidelines for first-time drug offenders are biased against people of color, by age, or in other ways (Spohn, 2014). Every new law needs to be evaluated—or should be, because there are usually real lives and great amounts of money at stake.

Psychology students may not recognize the monetary value of the practical evaluation skills that they already have. Your knowledge of statistics and—more important—the design of experiments is a great advantage. Your scientific training can be put to excellent use in high-paying evaluation departments. You might even want to

Mock juries: Groups of people paid to act like a jury before a trial, to see how regular people respond to evidence and arguments.

volunteer or shadow someone at your own university's "institutional research" division to get a sense of how important their work is to the quality of students' experiences.

Reformers

It takes courage to be a reformer.

Perhaps the most important role that forensic psychologists have played is to challenge the accepted wisdom of the legal system. Social psychologists have challenged the validity of confessions (see Kassin, 2015; Kassin & Kiechel, 1996), eyewitness testimony (Loftus & Palmer, 1996), repressed memories (Loftus & Ketcham, 1996), children's testimony, and the unreliability of anatomically correct dolls (see Ceci & Bruck, 1995). These courageous forensic psychologists often hold up a scientific stop sign that refuses to let dangerous assumptions go forward without being challenged.

These scholars have devoted much of their academic careers to these injustices. The results are restoring some dignity to individuals falsely accused and imprisoned. Social psychologists Kassin, Fiske, Wrightsman, Ceci, and Loftus (and many others) have played important roles in both conducting the basic research related to forensic psychology and applying it to causes related to social justice.

The case of Kelly Michaels was only one of a large collection of cases of false accusations of child sex abuse in daycare centers. As the media reported one rolling accusation after another, they produced a **moral panic** based on a widespread belief that a particular group was threatening society (see Downes et al., 2013). Moral panic is the scientific term for what you've probably heard called a "witch hunt." It won't make you popular at the time, but social psychologists are often on the front lines of resistance to a developing moral panic against a particular group. After all, there really weren't any witches in Salem during the witch trials.

Social psychology has deep scientific and philosophical roots. It is also a practical discipline full of opportunities for social justice.

THE MAIN IDEAS

- The CSI effect creates unrealistic expectations of forensic science, created by watching fictional television shows. For example, most research does not support the practice known as "criminal profiling."

- Forensic psychology is the application of psychological theory and research to the legal process. One goal is to avoid both Type I errors (also known as false positives) and Type II errors (also known as false negatives).

- Four careers that are possible in forensic psychology are trial consultants, dispute mediators, evaluators, and reformers.

CRITICAL THINKING CHALLENGE

- Why does television or movie portrayal of certain types of careers have such influence over people's expectations, when viewers know and acknowledge that the situations are fictional? Can you think of a time when your views or perceptions of a career or certain situation were misguided, and you believe it was due to media influence?

- Which of the four careers in forensic psychology (trial consultants, dispute mediators, evaluators, and reformers) sounds the most appealing to you, personally, and why?

Moral panic: The widespread belief that a particular group of people pose an urgent threat to society, based on accusations of a moral nature.

WHAT DO SOCIAL PSYCHOLOGISTS KNOW ABOUT FALSE CONFESSIONS AND EYEWITNESS TESTIMONY?

>> LO D.2: **Apply the rule of law to explain the Innocence Project, false confessions, and faulty eyewitness testimony.**

"I was absolutely terrified."

Kelly Michaels explained to Oprah Winfrey that "you're being accused, you're being attacked, you can't do anything except say the words, 'I am innocent.'" She probably could have received a shorter sentence if she had been willing to plead guilty. But she wasn't guilty.

Imagine being in Kelly Michael's moral, legal, and psychological dilemma. She knew that she was innocent. Plea bargaining created an opportunity for her to receive a lower sentence by pleading guilty to a less severe crime. The alternative was to risk a longer prison sentence, roll the dice, and hope that the jury finds you not guilty. The advantage of plea bargaining is that it keeps the clogged-up court system moving faster. The price for such efficiency is putting some innocent people in jail. Kelly Michaels could have made a false confession. Instead, she rolled the dice and went to trial. She lost.

This section answers the core question "What do social psychologists know about false confessions and eyewitness testimony?" by

(1) summarizing the importance of the rule of law,

(2) discussing the psychology of the Innocence Project,

(3) identifying common reasons for false confessions, and

(4) demonstrating the unreliability of eyewitness testimony.

Social Psychology Can Strengthen the Rule of Law

The **rule of law** means that no one, not even a president, is above the law.

Unlike a monarchy or dictatorship, justice in a democratic republic is determined by laws based on principles of both a democracy and a republic. And when those laws are unjust, the representatives of the people being ruled are empowered to change those laws. Even a nation's elected leader, no matter how popular or persuasive, is constrained by the rule of law.

The World Justice Project (see Agrast et al., 2013; World Justice Project, 2019) recognizes four universal principles that represent the rule of law:

- **Accountability** The government as well as private actors are accountable under the law.

- **Just Laws** The laws are clear, publicized, and stable; are applied evenly; and protect fundamental rights, including the security of persons and contract, property, and human rights.

- **Open Government** The processes by which the laws are enacted, administered, and enforced are accessible, fair, and efficient.

- **Accessible and Impartial Dispute Resolution** Justice is delivered timely by competent, ethical, and independent representatives and neutrals who are accessible, have adequate resources, and reflect the makeup of the communities they serve.

Rule of law: The idea that no one is above the law; we all have to follow it, equally.

Some of the saddest and most embarrassing moments in the history of the United States involve Black defendants who only made false confessions after being beaten (Kassin, 1997; Kassin & Wrightsman, 1985; Wrightsman & Kassin, 1993; Wrightsman et al., 1994). This situation persisted until *Brown v. Mississippi* (1936) started to (slowly) alter the legal landscape. In that case, the Supreme Court ruled that a trial "is a mere pretense" if a conviction has been "obtained by violence." The law was strengthened.

The Innocence Project

Your opinion of the legal system probably depends on your personal experience.

Have you been victimized by a wrongful conviction? Do you know someone who has? If you have not, then you probably have some measured faith that the rule of law will deliver justice. But even under the rule of law, wrongful convictions and other forms of injustice are surprisingly common. The frequency of innocent people being imprisoned has led to the **Innocence Project** composed mostly of attorneys committed to fighting for people wrongfully convicted of a crime.

The Innocence Project has grown rapidly. There is a new educational movement that teaches both prelaw and law students about the realities of wrongful convictions (see Carmack & Wallace, 2018; Waters, 2019). And the movement is much larger than modifications in legal education. The frequency of wrongful convictions has produced Innocence Projects in many other countries (see Singh & Majunmdar, 2018). Norris's (2019) book *Exonerated* summarizes the difficult, dramatic history of the Innocence Movement.

The most attention-getting cases usually involve murder convictions when the accusations have been refuted by DNA evidence. But to the individual serving time for a crime that they did not commit, public attention is a temporary luxury or torment that they do not need. In 2011, Perske published a list of false confessions made by 75 people with mental disabilities. There had been 65 exonerations and some posthumous pardons. He reported that "there is a heartening wave of Innocence Project organizations that are springing up around the country" (Perske, 2011, p. 365).

Social psychologists have made significant contributions to Innocence Projects by (a) understanding the psychology of false confessions, (b) empirically demonstrating the unreliability of eyewitness testimony, and (c) bringing attention to the grim reality of wrongful convictions.

The Power of the Situation: Psychologists Are Vulnerable, Too

Terrorism creates a particular kind of social-psychological environment.

Alex Schmid describes the terror situation as "a state of mind, created by a level of fear that so agitates body and mind that those struck by it are not capable of making an objective assessment of risks anymore" (Schmid, 2005). As the Russian communist Vladimir Lenin understood only too well, "The purpose of terrorism is to produce terror." And it is easy to make bad decisions in an atmosphere of terror, uncertainty, and fear.

After 9/11, some leaders of the American Psychological Association (APA) secretly coordinated with the White House, CIA, and the Department of Defense. They created a new ethics policy that justified torturing people into making untrustworthy (false) confessions. These are generally accepted, in hindsight, as bad decisions; they were criticized harshly by the APA membership when they were exposed.

If any group of people should be able to keep thinking clearly in a crisis, you hope that psychologists would be on that list. The lessons learned—and still to be learned—are summarized in many articles (see Ackerman, 2015; Kassin, 1997, 1998; McCormick, 1992; Richardson & Bellanger, 2016; Wrightsman & Kassin, 1993). You may recognize Kurt Lewin's elegant formula in this disturbing chapter of psychology's story: B = f(P, E). These bad decisions were a **f**unction of the interaction between individual **p**ersons making critical decisions in an **e**nvironment of extreme stress and perceived urgency.

What about you? What kind of environment, for example, would induce you into making a **false confession** about a crime that you did not commit?

Innocence Project: A group of lawyers, students, professors, and volunteers fighting for people who may have been falsely convicted of a crime.

False confession: When someone claims to be responsible for a crime they didn't actually commit.

Social Psychologists Understand Why People Make False Confessions

Potential jurors (all of us) are human.

That means that we are all subject to all the biases we have discussed in this textbook. The end result is that we tend to automatically accept confessions as authentic—and are then reluctant to abandon our first impression. Consequently, a false confession tends to be believed (see Kassin & Sukel, 1997; Kassin et al., 1990; Kassin et al., 2012). We cling to confessions even when the confessions

(a) have been discredited,

(b) are ruled inadmissible, and

(c) the judge has instructed jurors to disregard the confession.

Social psychology helps explain two features of false confessions. The first is why people report doing something they didn't really do (see Kassin, 1997, 1998; McCormick, 1992; Wrightsman & Kassin, 1993). The second is why

Even though history has shown us repeatedly that confessions under duress, such as torture, are not reliable, it took quite some time for psychological research to provide scientific evidence of this fact.

jurors tend to believe even discredited false confessions of guilt. Costanzo and Krauss (2015, p. 39) organized the literature about false confessions into the four situations summarized in Table D.4.

TABLE D.4

Four Possible Situations Leading to False Confession

	COERCED (FORCED)	VOLUNTARY (NOT FORCED)
Instrumental (confessor does not believe confession is the truth)	Confesses to end the interrogation (e.g., under conditions of torture)	Confesses to protect someone else or to gain notoriety
Authentic (confessor believes confession is the truth)	Confessor gradually comes to believe she or he is guilty	Confessor is delusional, ill, or under stress

Source: Costanzo and Krauss (2015).

Instrumental, Coerced Confessions

An **instrumental confession** means that the person has a reason for confessing, but they know they didn't really do it. A **coerced confession** means that it is forced.

This is the situation when people being tortured admit to doing something, just to make the pain stop. They'll say anything under this kind of duress. In fact, instrumental, coerced confessions arguably have become the most contentious issue that the American Psychological Association (APA) has faced in several decades because of the controversy over psychologists getting involved in torture. In criminal cases, the instrumental, coerced confession is most common, sometimes because people believe they have to "confess" to a lesser charge as part of a plea bargain.

In either situation (torture or false confessions as part of plea bargains), the truth never comes to light.

Instrumental confession: A false confession when the person knows they are not guilty but are claiming guilt for some other reason.

Coerced confession: A confession as a result of force, such as torture or intense interrogation.

Instrumental, Voluntary Confessions

Instrumental, **voluntary confessions** are given for a reason that is typically known only to the person confessing.

Costanzo and Krauss (2015) provided several examples of purposeful, voluntary confessions. A parent might "take the fall" to protect a child from harm. Someone seeking notoriety might confess to gain attention. The serial killer Henry Lee Lucas falsely confessed to several murders that he did not commit in an effort to secure his name and reputation among the elite killers of all time. "Peculiar" was how Costanzo and Krauss summarized many of the motives for these voluntary false confessions.

Authentic, Coerced False Confessions

Authentic confessions occur when people honestly believe they committed the crime in question—even when they didn't.

For example, Clifton Lawson admitted to a brutal murder on camera. He provided details that could only be known by someone who had been there (Kassin & Wrightsman, 2012). But Lawson had a very low IQ and was anxious. He was worried about getting to choir practice on time. Now he was simply telling his interrogators what he believed they wanted him to say.

But what about the details of the murder? Clifford Lawson had learned those details by listening. He spent long hours sitting in the police station, listening to the officers as they discussed the case. He barely avoided conviction and seemed confused about whether he had actually committed the crime. This confession can be considered coerced because it never would have happened if Lawson had been treated more fairly and with more respect.

Authentic, Voluntary False Confessions

Authentic, voluntary false confessions involve someone with mental illness (such as a delusion) or severe psychological pressure.

Someone really believes that they committed a crime and confesses to something that they didn't do. The (unverified) story of "Himmler's missing pipe" suggests that innocent people being punished may come to believe that they must have done something wrong. The Nazi leader Himmler had lost his favorite pipe during a tour of a concentration camp. Six people confessed to stealing it before he discovered it in his own vehicle.

The main explanation for authentic, voluntary false confessions is related to the just world hypothesis (see Jones & Brimbal, 2017; Jordan & Hartwig, 2013; Kassin, 2015). The authentic false confession is a way to make sense of a disturbing, profoundly unjust world. "I must have done something to deserve this terrible fate."

But you need to be worried about more than false confessions if you ever land on a jury involving eyewitness testimony. What social psychologists have learned about eyewitness testimony will bring your critical thinking to a whole new level.

Social Psychologists Can Demonstrate the Unreliability of Eyewitness Testimony

Memory is constructed in our mind.

That means that our sincere memories can be manipulated, both innocently and deliberately. The **misinformation effect** occurs when exposure to false information or leading questions about an event leads to errors in recall of the original event. We may be sincere, but we are sincerely mistaken.

The now well-supported **construction hypothesis** proposes that memories are not like computer files, waiting to be accessed. Instead, they are constructed as needed at the time we're asked to use them. Consequently, our memories are subject to momentary influences, bias, stereotypes, moods, and wishes (Loftus, 1975; Loftus & Zanni, 1975).

Voluntary confession: For false confessions, these occur when the confessor either mistakenly believes they are guilty or confesses to gain some benefit, such as protecting another person or getting famous.

Authentic confession: When people honestly believe they committed a crime (even if they didn't).

Misinformation effect: Occurs when exposure to false information or leading questions about an event leads to errors in our ability to recall the original event.

Construction hypothesis: The idea that memories are constructed as needed at any given time, making them subject to bias.

Presuppositions: Does "a" Versus "the" Really Matter?

Our mental biases are powerful because they are automatic—and subtle.

Elizabeth Loftus (1975) had participants view a 1-minute film of a multicar accident. The crash itself lasted only 4 seconds. Then she asked participants a series of questions about the accident they had just witnessed. Some participants were asked, "Did you see a broken headlight?" and other participants, "Did you see the broken headlight?"

The word *the* in the second version is a **presupposition**, wording that assumes something. Participants could automatically infer that there was a broken headlight. In reality, there was not a broken headlight in the video—but participants who received the presupposition version of the question were significantly more likely to say "yes," there was a broken headlight. This simple change of a single word changed their memories. Think about that the next time you consider how witnesses are asked questions by the police, by their friends, and by lawyers during a trial.

Elizabeth Loftus is one of the most well-known psychologists to devote a career to conducting research that can apply to courtrooms. Her studies investigate how easily memory for events can be manipulated.

Leading Questions: Don't Think About Broken Glass

Loftus didn't stop with "a" versus "the."

In other versions of this experiment, Loftus (1975) focused on leading questions that subtly direct the perceptions of the person answering the question. For example, early on in the survey participants received after witnessing a car accident, Loftus asked people either:

1. How fast was Car A going when it ran the stop sign?

2. How fast was Car A going when it turned right?

The critical question was not how fast the car was going but whether or not they believed that they had witnessed seeing a stop sign. Later in the survey, everyone was asked whether they saw a stop sign. Importantly, no stop sign existed in the actual event. But when people had been subtly introduced to the idea of a stop sign in an earlier question, 55% now said yes, they had seen a stop sign.

In contrast, only 35% of people who had been asked about the car turning right reported seeing a stop sign. People now remembered false things about what they had witnessed. The only available explanation was being asked leading questions.

The most famous version of this experiment was included in a 1974 report by Loftus and Palmer. They showed people a car accident and then asked half of the participants each of these questions:

1. About how fast were the cars going when they smashed into each other?

2. About how fast were the cars going when they bumped into each other?

Everyone saw the same accident, but the word *smashed* elicited higher speed estimates. Even more interesting was that 1 week later, everyone was asked whether they had witnessed broken glass. There was no broken glass. But broken glass seemed plausible as a result of a car accident—and especially plausible with "smashing" cars. People who had received that question a week earlier were now more likely to invent a memory of broken glass.

These "eyewitnesses" had no idea that their memories had been altered. They thought they were honestly remembering what they saw—their answers were sincere. Consider again how real-life eyewitnesses might change their memories based on

Presupposition: Wording that assumes a certain condition exists.

questions they receive from the police, from lawyers, or even from their own family members. These participants, acting as witnesses, had constructed plausible memories and then convinced themselves that they were telling "the truth, the whole truth, and nothing but the truth." But they were wrong.

The search for justice demands humility about the reliability of our memories.

THE MAIN IDEAS

- The rule of law is the idea that no one is "above" the law, meaning everyone has to follow it, equally. The Innocence Project helps people who have been falsely convicted of crimes become exonerated.
- One example of a modern application of psychology to law is in research on false confessions. For example, a typology by Costanzo and Krauss (2015) identifies four different reasons people might give false confessions.
- Another application of psychology to law is research on eyewitness testimony and the misinformation effect, which occurs when memories are changed based on exposure to postevent incorrect information or leading questions.

CRITICAL THINKING CHALLENGE

- Why do you think it took a relatively long period of time for lawyers, judges, and juries to make use of psychological research that is relevant to various aspects criminal justice procedures? Alternatively, why did it take psychology so long to devote research to everything psychological that occurs before, during, and after a crime?

- Which of the four reasons to provide a false confession do you think is most common—and which do you think would be most likely to lead to a false confession from you, personally?

- Now that you know about research on the misinformation effect, how confident are you that your own memories are really accurate? Can you identify any specific examples of how your own memories might have been manipulated or changed based on things that happened after the event in question?

Bettmann/Bettmann/Getty Images

iStockPhoto/fizkes

E. Social Psychology of Stress and Health

Core Questions

E.1 How do environmental stressors influence health?

E.2 How can social psychology improve medical adherence?

Learning Objectives

E.1 Explain the techniques and benefits of stress management.

E.2 Apply persuasion tactics to increase compliance in a health setting.

You are complicated; we all are.

Our complicated biology, psychology, and surrounding environments are why we can apply Kurt Lewin's interactionist perspective to the social psychology of health. Our health outcomes are a function of both the environment *and* how each individual interprets their particular circumstances. It took many years for medicine to take advantage of Kurt Lewin's insight. Psychiatrist George Engel's (1977) landmark article in *Science* argued that a model of health and sickness based only on biology neglected to consider how psychological factors and sociological factors come into play.

While there are now entire textbooks on the quickly expanding world of health psychology, this application mini-chapter will discuss just two important questions relevant to how social psychology can contribute to our understanding of stress, health, and medical behaviors.

HOW DO ENVIRONMENTAL STRESSORS INFLUENCE HEALTH?

>> **LO E.1:** **Explain the techniques and benefits of stress management.**

Environmental stress is relative.

Syrian refugees, for example, experience many health-harming stressors (Yayan et al., 2019). So do people living in high-crime areas (Weisburd et al., 2018). But smaller, daily stressors and new events also create harmful stress for many people. Early childhood teachers are at risk (Jeon et al., 2018), and so is anyone who has become pregnant (Ertekin et al., 2018). Stress-related depression and posttraumatic stress disorder (PTSD) can accelerate a downward spiral into unhealthy habits (Tice & Baumeister, 2018).

Fortunately, most of us are not passive victims of the stressors that life throws at us. We all have things that help us de-stress, like sleeping in on the weekend, listening to music, or playing a video game. Self-care is important. That said, don't deceive yourself by thinking you have complete control over your stress level or how it might affect you.

For example, the American Cancer Society emphasizes that there is no established relationship between getting or recovering from cancer and having a crabby attitude versus maintaining a positive outlook on life (American Cancer Society, 2019). However, a positive attitude may help you ask better questions, comply with medical advice, enlist social support, and improve your coping strategies (Gallagher et al., 2019).

This section answers the core question "How do environmental stressors influence health?" by

(1) summarizing two theoretical models that describe stress and our reactions to it (interactionism and general adaptation),

(2) using the weathering hypothesis to explain some stress-related health problems such as PTSD, and

(3) describing how stress is being measured and managed.

The Interactionist Perspective: Multiple, Interacting Stressors

The interactionist perspective applied to medicine is called the **biopsychosocial model** (see Figure E.1).

Engel proposed that health is the combined product of interacting biological, psychological, and social forces. At the time, it was a significant departure from its predecessor model, which focused only on biological factors. The biopsychosocial model is a

Biopsychosocial model: The idea that human health is the combined product of biological, psychological, and social forces.

FIGURE E.1

The biopsychosocial model of health (Engel, 1977) considers a wide variety of contributing factors to people's wellness behaviors.

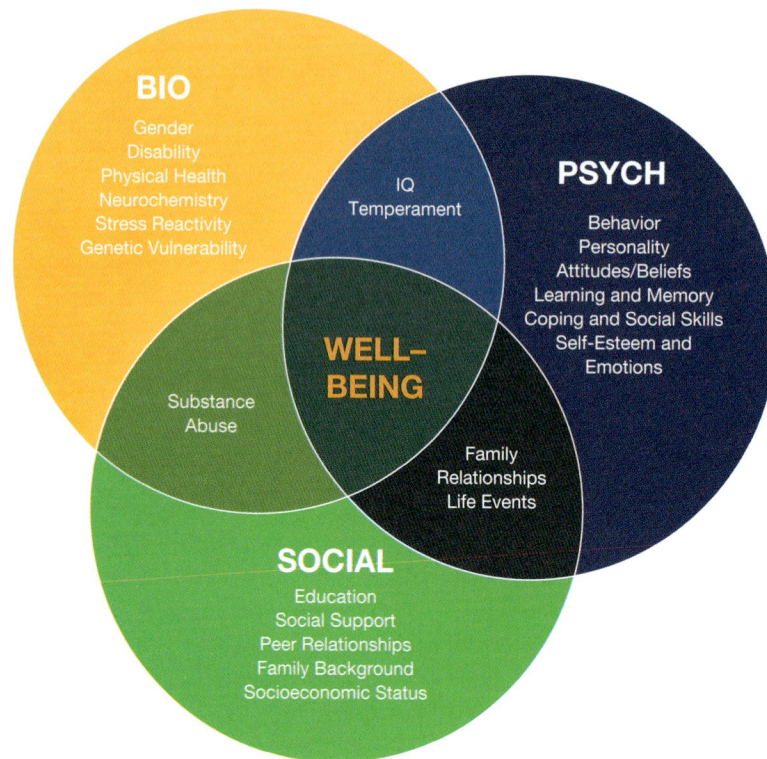

comprehensive approach that has been gaining acceptance for more than 40 years (but see also Ghaemi, 2009). In 1977, Engel wrote that

> the dominant model of disease today [in 1977] is biomedical, and it leaves no room within its framework for the social, psychological, and behavioural dimensions of illness. A biopsychosocial model . . . provides a blueprint for research, a framework for teaching, and a design for action in the real world of health care. (p. 135)

The biopsychosocial model makes room for an important factor in our health: stress. **Stress** occurs when an individual's assessment of the current environment exceeds their coping abilities or resources and therefore threatens their well-being (see Lazarus & Folkman, 1984). The key word in that definition is "exceeds" because stress is not necessarily a bad thing.

The **Yerkes-Dodson law** predicts that *moderate* amounts of stress are associated with optimal performance (see Belavkin, 2001; Teigen, 1994). You might relate to this in terms of getting homework done. No stress might mean you lack motivation to do it, and high levels of stress probably distract you. Like Goldilocks, we want our level of stress to be "just right." In fact, small amounts of environmental stress can actually help initiate biological adaptations that benefit problems like heart disease (Arnold et al., 2007). However, there is a dark side to the relationship between stress and health.

Hans Selye (1973) was an endocrinologist who proposed a three-stage theory of how organisms respond to stress. His theory, called **general adaptation syndrome**, described how the body reacts to persistent stress in ways that make us vulnerable to disease. Figure E.2 and Table E.1 suggest the pattern of responses: After an initial alarm

Stress: When someone's assessment of the current environment exceeds their coping abilities or resources and therefore threatens their well-being.

Yerkes-Dodson law: Predicts that moderate amounts of stress are associated with optimal performance.

General adaptation syndrome: A three-stage theory proposing we respond to stress with (1) an initial alarm phase, (2) resistance, and (3) eventual exhaustion if the stress continues.

FIGURE E.2

Selye's (1973) general adaptation syndrome model suggests that reactions and resistance to stress come in three phases.

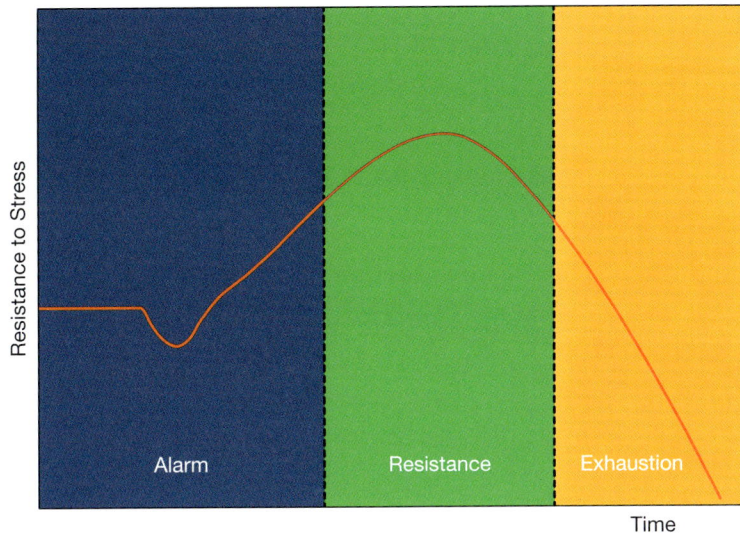

phase, the body tries to settle down and readjust if possible. However, we become more vulnerable to diseases if the stressors persist over time and exhaust our resources.

Stress-Related Health Problems

Flu, sore throats, headaches, and backaches; it's not a happy list.

But those are the stress-related illnesses that were found in a study of 75 married couples (DeLongis et al., 1988). It gets worse. Another team investigated stress during pregnancy and found that stress was associated with earlier births and lower birthweights (Lobel et al., 2008). Stress is among a reliable constellation of variables related to heart disease: acute and chronic life stressors, anxiety and depression, personality traits such as anger and hostility, reactive behavioral coping strategies, and the absence of social support (Carney & Freedland, 2007).

TABLE E.1

Hans Selye's General Adaptation Syndrome

STAGE	DESCRIPTION
Stage 1. Alarm	The body is briefly stunned but then reacts with preparation for "fight or flight" as the sympathetic nervous system responds to the stressor.
Stage 2. Resistance	The parasympathetic system returns the body toward its normal state, but we remain vigilant.
Stage 3. Exhaustion	If stressors persist beyond the body's capacity, resources are depleted and we become vulnerable to diseases.

Source: Adapted from Selye (1973).

Ageism and the Weathering Hypothesis

We are all likely to experience more health-related stress as we age.

One of the psychological stress-related risk factors for disease is **ageism**. These are recurrent experiences of age-related negative stereotypes and discrimination experienced by many older individuals, only due to their age. The theory of weathering (often called the "weathering hypothesis"; see Geronimus, 1992) is similar to Selye's general adaptation syndrome.

Weathering proposes that the cumulative effects of chronic stressors and high-effort coping predispose individuals to physical deterioration, premature aging, and chronic diseases. Weathering also can be experienced, for example, as chronic exposure to economic and social disadvantages. Weathering appears to explain some systematic differences in health outcomes (Forde et al., 2019).

There is an ironic twist to ageism for people who spent their working and social lives as part of the dominant culture. Now they too may get to experience being the victim of prejudice and discrimination. Older people are subject to persistent discrimination that other minorities and disenfranchised people have experienced routinely for their entire lives (see Chapter 9 and Carr et al., 2003; Geronimus, 1992).

War-Related Posttraumatic Stress Disorder

Stress can lead to PTSD.

PTSD has its own curious history, beginning with what was called in various wars "shell shock," "war trauma," and "battle fatigue." We recommend viewing, even if only for a few minutes, some film clips from World War I (search YouTube for "shell shock"). What you will see is so disturbing that you may not want to watch for very long, but it will help you understand the origins, severity, and devastation associated with PTSD.

In 2017, the U.S. Department of Veterans Affairs (2017) described four types of PTSD symptoms, some of which you can see plainly in those early war films:

(1) Reliving the trauma
   (a) Nightmares
   (b) Flashbacks
   (c) Triggers that lead to flashbacks

(2) Avoiding situations that remind you of the trauma
   (a) Avoiding crowds
   (b) Avoiding driving, especially if your trauma involved a vehicle
   (c) Keeping busy and avoiding therapy so that you do not have to confront the traumatic experience

(3) Negative changes in beliefs and feelings
   (a) Avoiding positive, loving relationships
   (b) Forgetting parts of the traumatic event
   (c) Refusing to talk about the traumatic event
   (d) Believing that no one can be trusted in a dangerous world

(4) Hyperarousal
   (a) Difficulty sleeping
   (b) Difficulty concentrating
   (c) Deeply startled by loud noises or surprises
   (d) Positioning yourself in rooms so that you can keep an eye on everyone

The Expanding Recognition of PTSD

The modern diagnosis of PTSD has expanded well beyond the boundaries of war trauma.

Ageism: Negative stereotypes and discrimination experienced by older individuals, which often leads to stress.

Weathering: The idea that chronic stressors and high-effort coping predispose some people to physical deterioration, premature aging, and chronic diseases.

PTSD now includes individuals who have experienced varying degrees of trauma from other life events. A brief description of life traumas comes from research by Kubany and colleagues (2000). Respondents indicated how often they experienced 22 potentially traumatic events (e.g., physical abuse, sexual assault, natural disaster; see Table E.2); the different types of trauma show that PTSD can come from a wide variety of negative experiences that go well beyond the scope of war.

There is an emotional logic to PTSD that defies common sense. In one study, the most enduring PTSD-related symptoms among 157 victims of a violent crime were anger and shame—and shame lasted even longer than anger (Andrews et al. 2000). They were victims, not perpetrators, yet they somehow experienced a long-lasting shame over something that was done to them (perhaps due to victim-blaming stigmas placed on them by others).

In another study (Clohessy & Ehlers, 1999), 56 ambulance service workers first described the most distressing aspects of their work and were then screened for PTSD symptoms. The procedure meant that they were deliberately triggered (or primed) as the researchers probed for symptoms. Of the 56 participants, 21% met the criteria for PTSD and 22% more indicated a need for further screening for psychiatric symptoms. In other words, almost half of the people in this sample of first responders showed signs of severe stress.

How common is PTSD in the general population? The answer lies in your understanding of the "D" in PTSD. We have all endured something unpleasant, even if it is "only" witnessing a bad traffic accident or one of the experiences in Table E.2. So, we all have some measure of PTS—but most of us can still get through our days without having to experience flashbacks or other symptoms. For those who are suffering from more severe traumas and/or more severe posttrauma symptoms, however, PTSD is a serious problem.

Measuring and Managing Stress

The task of measuring stress began with the now-famous Holmes and Rahe (1967) scale in Table E.3.

TABLE E.2

Traumatic Event Exposure

TRAUMA TYPE	N	%
Physical violence/assault	93	28.9
Sexual violence/assault	66	20.5
Loved one survived a life-threatening accident or illness	62	19.3
Other serious accident	19	5.9
Motor vehicle accident	17	5.3
Natural disaster	16	5.0
Abortion or miscarriage	14	4.3
Other traumatic event not listed	14	4.3
Being stalked	13	4.0
Life-threatening illness	6	1.9
Combat	2	.6

Source: Kubany et al. (2000).

TABLE E.3

The Holmes-Rahe Life Stress Inventory

INSTRUCTIONS: Mark down the point value of each of these life events that has happened to you during the previous year. Then, find the total of these associated points.

LIFE EVENT	VALUE	LIFE EVENT	VALUE
Death of spouse	100	Son or daughter leaving home	29
Divorce	73	In-law troubles	29
Marital separation from mate	65	Outstanding personal achievement	28
Detention in jail or other institution	63	Spouse/partner beginning or ceasing work outside the home	26
Death of a close family member	63	Beginning or ceasing formal schooling	26
Major personal illness or injury	53	Major change in living condition	25
Marriage	50	Revision of personal habits (dress, manners, quitting smoking, etc.)	24
Being fired from work	47	Trouble with the boss	23
Retirement from work	45	Major changes in working hours or conditions	20
Major change in the health or behavior of a family member	44	Change in residence	20
Pregnancy	40	Change to a new school	20
Sexual difficulties	39	Major change in usual type and/or amount of recreation	19
Gaining a new family member (birth, adoption, etc.)	39	Major change in church activity (e.g., a lot more or less)	19
Major business readjustment	39	Major change in social activity (clubs, movies, visiting, etc.)	18
Major change in financial state (better or worse)	38	Taking on a loan (car, TV, furniture, etc.)	17
Death of a close friend	37	Major change in sleeping habits (e.g., a lot more or less)	16
Changing to a different line of work	36	Major change in number of family get-togethers	15
Major change in number of arguments with spouse/partner	35	Major change in eating habits (e.g., a lot more or less, different meal hours or surroundings)	15
Taking on a mortgage	31	Vacation	13
Foreclosure on mortgage or loan	30	Major holidays	12
Major change in responsibility at work (promotion, demotion, etc.)	29	Minor violations of the law (traffic tickets, etc.)	11

Estimate your stress level by adding up all your points:

- 150 points or fewer implies a relatively low amount of life change and a low susceptibility to stress-induced health breakdown.
- 150 to 300 points implies about a 50% chance of a major health breakdown in the next 2 years.
- 300 points or more raises the odds to about 80%, according to the Holmes-Rahe statistical prediction model.

Source: Holmes and Rahe (1967).

Their strategy for measuring stress was to identify events that participants had experienced within 3 years (or some other time frame) and give them points, depending on how stressful they are to most people. Importantly (as you can see in Table E.3), these events could be negative (a death in the family) or positive (an outstanding achievement). Negative stressors are called **distress**, while positive events are called **eustress**. Even positive events, such as a wedding or a promotion at work, cause stress due to the required changes, pressure to succeed, and so on.

Scales That Measure Stress

The Holmes and Rahe (1967) stress scale got the research community started. Later researchers created additional stress scales (and similar checklists) for specific purposes, populations, cultures, and situations. For example, Boals and Schuler (2017) are working to help establish the scientific foundation for positive psychology by developing a revised version of a posttraumatic growth scale.

The possibility of growth by successfully coping with stress is one of positive psychology's contributions to stress management. (There is more about positive psychology in another mini-chapter.) The rest of this section examines different variables and approaches to managing stress. Which seems like it would work best for you?

The Mindfulness Approach to Stress Management

There's a new popular trend in the world of counseling and stress management: mindfulness.

Mindfulness is a meditative focus on the present. In practice, mindfulness therapies represent a constellation of related practices (see Crane et al., 2019) most often focused on addressing chronic health concerns (both physical and mental health). Mindfulness-based stress reduction programs using meditation appear to offer some health benefits (e.g., Grossman et al., 2004).

Mindfulness meditation interventions appeared to produce significant benefits for medical students experiencing the stress of their medical education (Shapiro et al., 1998). Mindfulness also seems to be effective as a stress management approach for generally healthy people (Chiesa & Serretti, 2009). A review of the effectiveness of mindfulness on managing chronic lower back pain suggests that there is a modest benefit to the practice of mindfulness (see Hilton et al., 2016). However, some studies indicate that cognitive-behavioral techniques for stress reduction appear to be more effective, at least when the goal is to reduce work-related stress (van der Klink et al., 2001). Other studies suggest the effects of mindfulness meditation are little to none in terms of decreasing typical levels of depression and anxiety in adolescents (Sinclair & Goodfriend, 2013).

Mindfulness is extremely popular right now—although the research remains skeptical.

Healthy Skepticism About Mindfulness. The business of mindfulness has grown dramatically (see Berthon & Pitt, 2019).

However, research so far indicates that the benefits of mindfulness are pretty modest (Schumer et al., 2018). Research without comparison groups leaves open the possibility that mindfulness is nothing more than a distraction (see Koukounas et al., 2019; Shires et al., 2019). Mindfulness could be a **placebo** that produces therapeutic benefits based solely on expectations that the treatment will work.

When comparison groups *have* been used, the supposedly dramatic effects of mindfulness sometimes disappear or have minimal effects that could be due to chance. That was the story when researchers used both qualitative and quantitative measures testing the therapeutic benefits of mindfulness among older people (Fiocco et al., 2019).

Simple Solutions to Complex Problems. Psychological science is fighting several battles—over you.

Distress: Stress due to negative events, such as a death in an individual's family.

Eustress: Stress due to positive events, such as a wedding or a promotion at work.

Mindfulness: A meditative focus on the present; often used in therapeutic or stress management settings.

Placebo: An intervention that produces positive results not because it's effective in and of itself but because people *believe* it's effective.

The battle lines pit popular myths about psychology against established scientific findings (see Lilienfeld et al., 2011). It would be nice to stumble onto relatively simple solutions to complex problems. But that approach is seldom effective in the long run—and sometimes embarrassing.

For example, simple solutions to complex problems limited the effectiveness of public health campaigns trying to improve oral health (Baker, 2019). Researchers also discovered surprising complexity in getting people to take their medications (Wurmbach et al., 2018). The Brexit debate in England demonstrated the dangers of seeking simple solutions to complex problems (Glencross, 2018). There are many more examples of these social behavioral problems.

As you learn more about mindfulness, practice healthy skepticism. The scientific goal is to extract only what is real from the popularity and profits that mindfulness is creating.

Meta-Analyses About Mindfulness. Scientific evidence is accumulating and refining our understanding of mindfulness.

One *meta-analysis* of existing studies found moderate effects for mindfulness. Those effects were equivalent to standard therapies, but that is still a moderately encouraging finding (Khoury et al., 2013). Another meta-analysis found stronger but perhaps "partly inflated" effects for nonclinical populations (Eberth & Sedlmeier, 2012). A third found modest effectiveness at reducing stress, depression, and anxiety, and distress (Khoury et al., 2015). A fourth meta-analysis looking at psychiatric disorders was also cautiously optimistic but still unclear about what might make mindfulness effective (Goldberg et al., 2018).

Big picture: Mindfulness-based stress reduction programs using meditation appear to offer small health benefits (Grossman et al., 2004). It would be nice to know *why* mindfulness appears to reduce stress. The literature may be moving toward the possibility of placebo effects (see Rutherford, 2018), at least in terms of stress and pain management (Zeidan et al., 2019). Of course, if you are under extreme stress or experiencing acute pain, you don't care if mindfulness is a placebo or working because it's a welcome distraction—you just want relief. But if you are a social psychologist, it is your job to figure out *why* something works or doesn't work.

Social Support and Stress Management

Social support is the degree to which you are embedded in a network of people who can provide various kinds of assistance.

For example, one study found that the effects of stress among new immigrant Hispanic families were not as damaging as feared. Why? Other environmental factors were at work: strong families and social support (Perreira et al., 2019). Resilience is the human capacity to positively adapt to significant adversity (see Luther et al., 2000). We will explore resilience as a personality trait in the next section (see Oshio et al., 2018).

Community Resilience. Community resilience is connected, but different, from personality resilience.

Community resilience relies on social cooperation to adapt to a changing environment. We introduce community resilience now because it is the product of social support. The health consequences of resilience often rely on communities of people. Climate change, for example, is an acute environmental stressor that requires resilience for people living in the middle of the rising Pacific Ocean (Ebi & Boyer, 2019). No amount of personality resilience will change the reality of climate change or delay the rising ocean levels in the Pacific.

However, community planning for survival is a practical form of shared resilience. A similar planning strategy is evolving (see Meerow & Newell, 2019) to promote **urban resilience**. Urban resilience takes the form of healthy infrastructure responses to rapid changes in densely populated areas (see Huck & Monstadt, 2019; Leitner et al., 2018).

Social support: The degree to which we're surrounded by people who can assist us in times of need.

Community resilience: Social cooperation in a certain area that produces healthy responses to environmental stressors.

Urban resilience: Healthy infrastructure responses to environmental changes and stressors in densely populated areas.

Types of Social Support. There are different kinds of social support.

One succinct definition of social support is whether you have someone you know you can call on if you need $100 right away. Money, for example, would be considered a "tangible" form of social support. Uchino (2004) and others have articulated four types of social support (see Table E.4).

The link between social support and better health is well established. But the psychological mechanisms that make that connection work are not yet well understood (Uchino et al., 2012). One explanation is the **buffering hypothesis** (see Farmer & Sundberg, 2010). This proposes that social support provides critical resources needed to overcome environmental stressors. Just knowing that we have support in place and can rely on it if needed helps us manage our stress.

People experiencing stress probably don't care about the psychological mechanisms anyway. They only know that their lives are a little better off, more manageable, and more secure when they have the necessary social supports when they need them.

Personality Types and Stress Management

You may have noticed that people react to stress in different ways.

Some grow calmer; others become more dramatic. Two personality types that cope effectively with stress are hardiness and resiliency. The **hardy personality** is resistant to stress-related diseases because their thinking style keeps their physiology calm (Allred & Smith, 1989). The **resilient personality** copes positively with adversity (Skodol, 2010) and bounces back from defeats. The two personality types are similar in that they both deal with stress effectively.

On the other hand, the "**Type A personality**" was originally developed by cardiologists Friedman and Rosenman (1974). They noticed that certain personalities appeared to be more prone to heart disease. They used a particular kind of interview technique called a *structured interview* that standardized the questions and order of presentation when they spoke with their patients.

Their approach included a *behavioral interview* that included observing their patients' nonverbal behaviors such as time-checking, speaking quickly, interrupting, and general restlessness. People high in a Type A personality are impatient. They don't seem to manage stress well because they internalize it, leading to poor heart health. They also experience hostility when things don't go the way they want. Subsequent

iStockPhoto/VanderWolf-Images

Buffering hypothesis: The idea that social support provides critical resources needed to overcome environmental stressors.

Hardy personality: A personality type where people cope effectively with stress because their thinking style keeps their physiology calm.

Resilient personality: A personality type where people react appropriately to stress because they are able to cope positively with adversity.

Type A personality: A personality type characterized by competitiveness, impatience, and hostility. Type A people do not manage stress well and experience poor health.

TABLE E.4

Four Types of Social Support, According to Uchino (2004)

TYPES OF SOCIAL SUPPORT	DEFINITION AND EXAMPLE
Emotional support . . .	provides warmth and nurturing through empathy and expressions of concern.
Tangible (or instrumental) support . . .	provides material needs such as loaning someone money or a car.
Informational support . . .	provides problem-solving information or advice such as the best way to travel to a foreign country.
Companionship (or belonging) support . . .	provides a sense of belonging by engaging in shared activities.

research has focused on the central emotional experience of stress-induced hostility as the predictor of heart disease (Everson-Rose & Lewis, 2005).

The Big Stressor: An Unhealthy Environment

Climate instability is creating alarming levels of stress for all living things.

For example, Wells et al. (2016) have accumulated evidence about the negative health effects of damaged environments such as disrupted housing, crowding, noise, chaos, and technological as well as natural disasters. Researchers no longer have to look very far into the future to predict outbreaks of infectious disease due to climate change. COVID-19 may have gained a foothold in the human population when weakened environmental safeguards did not protect people from a bat virus (Shereen et al., 2020).

Some researchers (e.g., Swaminathan et al., 2017) predict a continuing increase in the distribution, transmission, and survival of microbes due to climate change. This change is facilitated because changing climates require microbes, whose only interest is in surviving. These microbes are naturally trying to find new vectors of transmission and new hosts to increase the distribution of disease. A changing climate encourages the transmission and spread of diseases.

We are very good at dealing with stress, but wouldn't it be nice if we could devote more energy to lowering the human-created strains on the environment rather than becoming better at coping with them? That is why another entire mini-chapter explores social psychology and the environment—and some of the career opportunities the pairing creates.

THE MAIN IDEAS

- The interactionist perspective is that stress results from both the environment and our individual interpretation of that environment. The theory called the general adaptation syndrome suggests that we experience stress in three phases: alarm, resistance, and exhaustion.

- When stress leads to severe symptoms, people may suffer from posttraumatic stress disorder (PTSD). Various methods and scales have been created to measure stress.

- Several variables have also been investigated in terms of managing stress. Various techniques or ideas include mindfulness, social support, personality types, and promoting a healthier environment.

CRITICAL THINKING CHALLENGE

- One population of people who are more likely to suffer from posttraumatic stress disorder are military veterans. What is the government's responsibility to care for the psychological well-being of veterans? How can the care provided to this important population be improved?

- Imagine you've just experienced a personal crisis. When you consider the types of social support listed in Table E.4, which do you think will be the most important? Rank-order them by importance based on the type of stress you think you're most likely to experience at this stage in life.

HOW CAN SOCIAL PSYCHOLOGY IMPROVE MEDICAL ADHERENCE?

>> **LO E. 2:**   **Apply persuasion tactics to increase compliance in a health setting.**

You have probably heard some version of this prayer: "Grant me the serenity to accept what I cannot change, the courage to change what I can, and the wisdom to know the difference." It is used in many addiction treatment programs, such as Alcoholics Anonymous. But the social psychology of health asks a more specific question: Why don't people who "know the difference" still not change their behaviors?

Why won't people change habits when they know they are at risk for diabetes, heart disease, or lung cancer? Why do people refuse vaccines despite mounds of evidence showing that they are necessary? These are all questions of compliance, also called **medical adherence**: following the advice of qualified health care providers.

This section answers the core question "How can social psychology improve medical adherence?" by

(1) recognizing the size of the problem and

(2) applying social psychological techniques to improve the problem.

Nonadherence Is a Big Problem

How big?

Epidemiology is the statistical analysis of patterns of disease. As you probably suspected, statistical rates of nonadherence depend on many factors. For example, a physician may recommend anything from drinking more water to a dramatic drug intervention to exercising three times per week. Those are very different recommendations and likely to produce individual differences. A relatively easy way to get started is to assess medication adherence.

Many people with schizophrenia require tightly managed medical adherence. Failure to take antipsychotic medications can aggravate the illness. A review of 10 reports of medication usage among people with schizophrenia found an average nonadherence rate of 41.2% (Lacro et al., 2002). Why so high?

Compare that to this: You would expect people with memory-related cognitive impairment (CI) to have higher rates of nonadherence. They forget to take their meds. However, when Smith and her colleagues (2017) reviewed 15 studies of medication adherence among people with CI, they found that the range of nonadherence was from 10% to 38%. Why was that a little lower than the nonadherence rate of people with schizophrenia?

The studies they reviewed surveyed patients with and without caregiver supports—people who could encourage adherence. Their findings suggest that (a) social support is critical to adherence, and (b) there is more to nonadherence than forgetting to take your pills. So having loving, supportive friends and family around who remind you to take your pills helps avoid nonadherence. But there's more.

Social Psychologists Can Help Change Health Behaviors

Think of nonadherence as a behavior problem.

Nonadherence is high for behavioral interventions such as losing weight or exercising (see DiMatteo, 2004). Becoming effective persuaders is therefore important to people in the medical field. Haynes and colleagues (2008) estimated that "effective ways to help people follow medical treatments could have far larger effects on health than any treatment itself" (p. 20). Table E.5 summarizes reasons patients give for not adhering to medical advice (see Brannon et al., 2013).

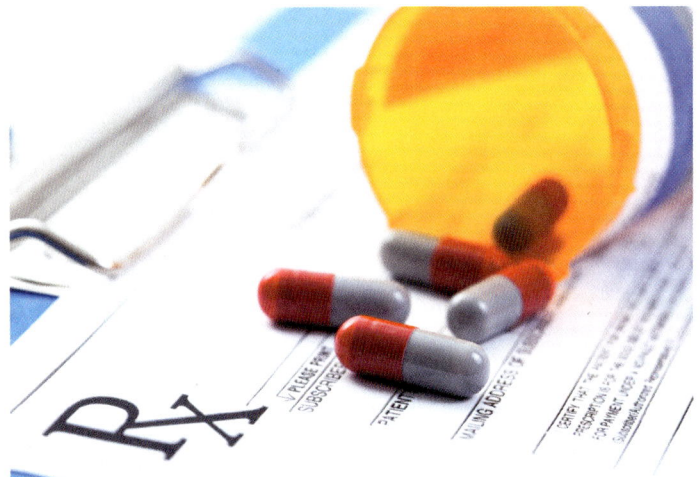

© istockphoto.com/GMVozd

Medical adherence: Following the advice of a qualified health care provider.

Epidemiology: The statistical analysis of the patterns of a disease (like incidence and spread).

TABLE E.5

Reasons Patients Give for Not Following a Doctor's Orders

IT'S TOO MUCH TROUBLE.	I GAVE SOME OF MY PILLS TO MY HUSBAND SO HE WON'T GET SICK.
I just didn't get the prescription filled.	The doctor doesn't know as much as my other doctor.
The medication was too expensive, so I took fewer pills to make them last.	The medication makes me sick.
The medication didn't work very well. I was still sick, so I stopped taking it.	I don't like the way that doctor treats me, and I'm not going back.
The medication worked after only 1 week, so I stopped taking it.	I feel fine. I don't see any reason to take something to prevent illness.
I have too many pills to take.	I don't like my doctor. He looks down on people without insurance.
I won't get sick. God will save me.	I didn't understand my doctor's instructions and was too embarrassed to ask her to repeat them.
I forgot.	I don't like the taste of nicotine chewing gum.
I don't want to become addicted to pills.	I didn't understand the directions on the label.

Source: Brannon et al. (2013).

Create Cognitive Dissonance: Practice Applying One Principle of Persuasion

Physicians probably prefer to think of themselves as healers rather than salespeople.

But physicians often find themselves in the persuasion business. Fortunately, you now have some understanding of persuasion strategies. They include attitude change, social influence tactics, the power of social norms, and the theory of planned behavior (described in Chapter 6). Public health (an excellent career path for psychology majors) needs people who can learn how to apply scientifically developed principles of persuasion.

Give this case study a try.

Case Study: A Family With Unhealthy Habits. You are playing the role of psychological consultant to a medical clinic. Your job is to apply principles of persuasion to the medical problems in the fictional situation described below.

Physician: **Dr. S.** is a board-certified family practice physician. She has asked for your help with a family that is demonstrating a variety of unhealthy behaviors.

The family:

Father: **Carl** is 41 years old, 5'11", and weighs 255 pounds. Carl is a warehouse manager whose job also occasionally requires some physical labor. Dr. S. has told him that he is "prediabetic" and needs to lose weight. He experiences a lot of stress on the job and likes to relax when he comes home by having several alcoholic drinks. He almost never exercises and usually has fast food for lunch. His hours are more predictable than his wife's so he does most of the school pickups, after-school activities, doctor's appointments, and so forth.

Mother:	**Linda** is 39 years old, 5'2", and weighs 186 pounds. Linda works for a car insurance company and spends much of her workday online and making phone calls. She smokes cigarettes almost constantly. She has recently starting to show early signs of hoarding; she keeps things that the rest of the family considers garbage. A month ago, she decided to adopt an entire family of kittens that she found in the yard, but she doesn't keep up with cleaning the litter box.
Son:	**Ray** is 13 years old, 5'6", and weighs 169 pounds. Ray is big for his age; he is already being recruited by the J.V. football coach even though he is not especially active or interested in athletics. He has recently been in trouble at school for bullying younger students. Ray has also been vaping after school with his friends and isn't worried about that because he thinks vaping is a healthy alternative to cigarettes.
Daughter:	**Melody** is 10 years old, 5'1", and weighs 74 pounds. Melody is very thin but doesn't think she is developing a problem—she says she just isn't hungry. When she does eat, it's usually just celery, carrots, or lettuce. She has also started responding to her mother's hoarding tendencies by doing things like washing her hands over and over with extremely hot water, to the point at which her hands are starting to bleed.

Use Cognitive Dissonance as a Persuasion Tool. In Chapter 6, you learned about some sorority sisters who made progression in their battles with eating disorders (Becker et al., 2008).

Their symptoms lessened after they were recruited to give talks to incoming first-year students about the dangers of eating disorders. To resolve the dissonance between the advice they gave to first-year students and their own behavior, they changed their own behavior. They began (and continued) to eat a more normal, healthy diet.

Devise activities for each family member, based on cognitive dissonance, that they are likely to engage in. Keep in mind a teenager's concerns about avoiding social embarrassment as you create activities that have a chance of success.

1. How could you create cognitive dissonance that might lead to healthy behaviors for each family member?

2. What could go wrong with this plan?

3. Should you try to influence the entire family together or try different approaches for each individual in the family?

4. Dr. S is not being paid for anything except office visits. Does she have any responsibility to try to play the role of social psychologist—or does the responsibility for health management rest solely with the family?

5. How will you know whether your intervention has been successful? In other words, what does success look like? How will you measure it?

Explore Alternative Persuasion Tactics. Cognitive dissonance is only one of many social psychological persuasion tactics. Select or combine the tactics listed here to create an intervention that might help the family overall, or apply different techniques to each person. How can these ideas apply to health psychology?

1. Which type of persuasive communication (see Chapter 4) is more likely to succeed: intuition and emotion or logic and reason?

2. The theory of planned behavior (see Chapter 6):
   a. Attitudes → Evaluations and judgments toward relevant objects and behaviors

b. Subjective norms → Beliefs about what others are doing

c. Perceived control → Beliefs about the degree of control one has over behaviors or the situation

3. Common persuasion tactics (see Chapter 6):

1. Foot-in-the-door → People are more likely to comply with a large request if they first agree to a small request.

2. Reciprocity → People feel obliged to give back to others who have first given to them ("return the favor"), such as the door-in-the-face technique.

3. Liking → People prefer to say yes to other people whom they like.

4. Consensus → People tend to behave according to how they believe others are behaving.

5. Authority → People trust those who are credited with superior knowledge or wisdom.

Assessment: Know What Success Looks Like. "The surgery was successful, but the patient died."

It's an old but grim joke about a boastful surgeon who had the wrong criteria for assessing the outcome of a surgery. Assessment is important. As a consultant, you want to know whether your great ideas actually worked.

Formative assessments provide meaningful feedback that will help you get better. **Summative assessments** evaluate whether your particular intervention was successful (see Dunn et al., 2013). Formative assessments are the ungraded feedback and suggestions you get on a rough draft of a paper. Summative assessments are your grade on the final version.

For managing stress and health, specify ahead of time what success looks like. Making assessment part of your original design from the very beginning offers many advantages. It ensures that you and your client

1. agree on the goals of your consultancy,

2. know what success (and failure) look like,

3. can discover new ways to use your services,

4. learn how to create a better intervention next time, and

5. do not dispute whether you have earned your fee.

Assessment is a critical part of all biopsychosocial health care interventions. Assessment also represents a career path that psychology students are already on. As you develop the habit of critical thinking, you will create assessment designs that make it easier for you to get better for your next consultancy job (see Heinzen, Landrum, et al., 2015).

Formative assessments: Evaluations designed to give meaningful feedback to help someone learn how to improve.

Summative assessments: Evaluations designed to know whether an intervention was successful.

THE MAIN IDEAS

- Medical adherence is following the advice of a health care provider. Several persuasion techniques from social psychology might be applied to increase patients' likelihood to follow medical advice.

- Assessment of medical interventions requires operationalization of success in advance.

CRITICAL THINKING CHALLENGE

- If you were consciously aware that a medical practitioner was attempting to persuade you using psychological techniques, would that make you less likely to be persuaded? Why or why not?

- How can medical schools better prepare future health practitioners for the social psychological aspects of their careers? Give three specific suggestions.

F. Social Psychology and Happiness

Positive Psychology

Core Questions

F.1   What is positive psychology?

F.2   How is positive psychology changing?

Learning Objectives

F.1   Describe positive psychology's distinctive approach to exploring human behavior.

F.2   Compare early research in positive psychology with current trends.

Juanita stood in my [Tom's] open office doorway.

"I got in," she told me. "And they offered me a scholarship." She wasn't crying, but she was close.

Born in the United States, Juanita [not her real name] experienced an uncertain back-and-forth childhood between the United States and Mexico. When she was 12, her family surprised her by staying in the United States. They enrolled her in a high school with only one other Spanish-speaking student. It was an awkward transition for a teenager who did not speak English.

Juanita was lost in a school full of formal rules and informal expectations that she did not understand. But a school psychologist helped her design achievable goals and get the tutoring help she needed to achieve them. With that support, she accomplished what her parents had been hoping for: She graduated from high school. That same school psychologist guided Juanita first to a community college and later to my university. And now she was saying goodbye once again. She was going to graduate school to become a school psychologist.

Like other first-generation college students, Juanita faced challenges that people more familiar with the U.S. higher education system take in stride. For example, experienced people and families understand that the Free Application for Federal Student Aid (FAFSA) is the open doorway to money for education. But for an immigrant family of a first-ever college student, the FAFSA looks like a request for private information that might be used against them or their family.

Too many first-generation college students do not get across the finish line of graduation. Juanita, however, was among those who persisted and was now planning to attend graduate school. She understood that she was starting a tradition of higher . . . and higher . . . education that would load the achievement dice for her siblings, cousins, and generations to come. How many 22-year-olds can look so far into their futures and with such purpose? Such students are much smarter than their standardized test scores might suggest. Juanita's story is full of positive psychology.

WHAT IS POSITIVE PSYCHOLOGY?

>> LO F. 1: **Describe positive psychology's distinctive approach to exploring human behavior.**

Positive psychologists try to understand people like Juanita, the school psychologist who guided her, and the institutions that supported her.

Positive psychologists are more interested, for example, in how students succeed than why they fail. Positive psychology is the scientific study of what ordinary humans keep doing extraordinarily well, including achievement, happiness, and more (see Compton, 2005; Seligman & Csikszentmihalyi, 2000). Positive psychology and social psychology are not the same thing. But they often share similar ambitions to help people thrive and reach their full potential. Let's look at three important concepts of positive psychology: positive subjective experiences, positive individual traits, and positive institutions.

This section answers the core question "What is positive psychology?" by

(1) describing the three pillars of positive psychology,

(2) explaining how positive psychology enlarges what psychologists study, and

(3) demonstrating how a scientific approach (PERMA) can distinguish positive psychology from "pop" psychology.

Three Pillars of Positive Psychology

They are called the "three pillars of positive psychology":

1. positive subjective experiences,

2. positive individual traits, and

3. positive institutions (Seligman & Csikszentmihalyi, 2000).

FIGURE F.1

The three pillars of positive psychology.

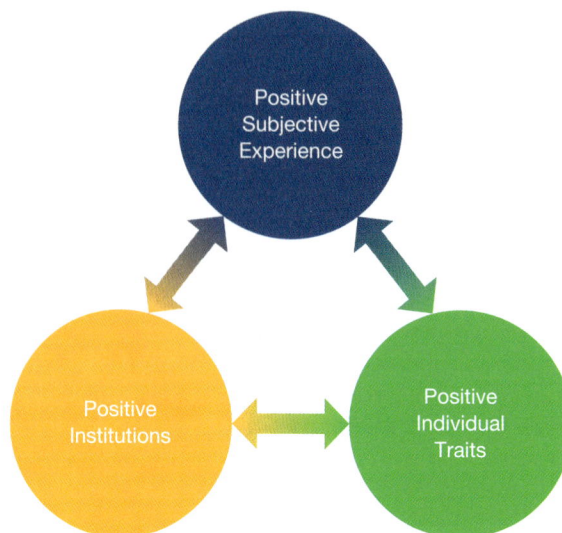

Source: Adapted from Seligman & Csikszentmihalyi (2000).

Juanita, of course, did not experience her life within these neat categories—but they were all operational in her life. Positive psychology exerts its greatest influence when these three pillars are aligned so that they create the kind of cycle displayed in Figure F.1. Each pillar strengthens the others.

Positive Subjective Experiences

Subjective experiences can be interpreted in a variety of ways.

Juanita's subjective experience could have been profoundly negative. It is difficult to imagine what it must have felt like for a 12-year-old to arrive in a strange classroom full of different-looking people who spoke a new language. Seligman and Csikszentmihalyi (2000) described this pillar in their seminal article in *American Psychologist:*

> The field of positive psychology at the subjective level is about valued subjective experiences: well-being, contentment, and satisfaction (in the past); hope and optimism (for the future); and flow and happiness (in the present). (p. 5)

Did Juanita "value" these kinds of subjective experiences? Probably. She looked at her past as a series of obstacles she had to overcome and family satisfactions that, despite many difficulties, she still treasured. She certainly expressed hope and optimism about her future as a graduate student and school psychologist. And she was definitely happy about her present, having just heard about being accepted into graduate school and receiving a scholarship.

Positive Individual Traits

Here is how Seligman and Csikszentmihalyi (2000) described the second pillar of positive psychology: positive individual traits.

> At the individual level, [positive psychology] is about positive individual traits: the capacity for love and vocation, courage, interpersonal skill, aesthetic sensibility, perseverance, forgiveness, originality, future mindedness, spirituality, high talent, and wisdom. (p. 5)

Subjective experiences:
The way people mentally experience and perceive events in their life.

Juanita also displayed distinctive positive individual traits. Her desire to become a school psychologist was much more than an intellectual choice or an accidental career opportunity. It was a vocation born of gratitude for how another school psychologist had intervened in her life. And getting to this point had required a quality of perseverance that is difficult for others to appreciate if they have grown up in settled homes and secure communities.

Positive Institutions

The third pillar of positive psychology is positive institutions.

People must be surrounded by organizations and institutions that provide respect and opportunity. Seligman and Csikszentmihalyi (2000) emphasize that positive psychology

> is about the civic virtues and the institutions that move individuals toward better citizenship: responsibility, nurturance, altruism, civility, moderation, tolerance, and work ethic. (p. 5)

There are five insights between the lines of Juanita's story that demonstrate the importance of positive institutions:

1. A school psychologist was present and aware of her needs.

2. The school psychologist had the time to devote to a student with particular needs.

3. Publicly funded higher education had developed her skills.

4. Some anonymous donors had given money to funds that provided her—and many others—with the money to pursue her chosen career.

5. Juanita had strong emotional support from her family.

Juanita's family may not have understood the potential risks and rewards of the decisions their daughter was making. But they decided to support her anyway. In Juanita's case, the three pillars of positive psychology describe a social psychological formula for academic success. It is also a formula for the kind of meaningful, constructive life and career that positive psychologists hope all of us can achieve.

Subjective Well-Being: Shifting From Negative to Positive Psychology

We all have a personal back story; so does the story of positive psychology.

The medically based disease model shaped psychology's approach to clinical problems. The **disease model** assesses and treats deficits in functioning. The implicit goal is to bring the person back to a state of neutrality or "normalcy."

The disease model has many benefits, and it was desperately needed after World War II when so many people around the world needed to heal from physical and mental wounds. It is also profitable (see Seligman, 2002). Clinical practitioners have clients. Funding agencies support researchers. The pharmaceutical industry investigates drug interventions. And we are all better off understanding the causes and cures related to specific forms of human suffering.

By contrast, positive psychology emphasizes human strengths and virtues. Positive psychology aims to fill out the positive or right side of the normal, bell-shaped curve of human experience (see Figure F.2). The starting point is called **subjective well-being**, what people perceive and feel about their lives and psychological health.

After World War II, the Hungarian psychologist Csikszentmihalyi (pronounced "Cheek-sent-me-ha-li"; Seligman & Csikszentmihalyi, 2000, p. 9) glimpsed the importance of positive psychology when he noticed two things. First, many of the war's

Disease model:
A medical model toward health that assesses and treats deficits, bringing someone back to neutrality.

Subjective well-being:
People's perceptions and feelings about their lives and psychological health (see *PERMA approach*).

FIGURE F.2

Psychology usually pays attention to the left side of the curve: mental illness, prejudice, ostracism, aggression, and so on. However, positive psychology focuses on the right side of the curve, helping people thrive and grow.

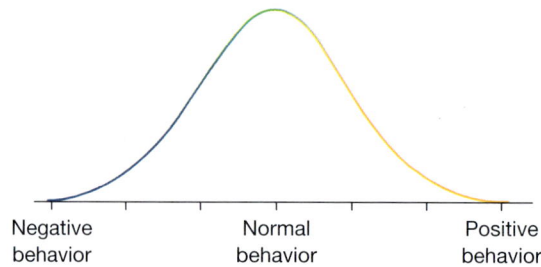

Negative behavior   Normal behavior   Positive behavior

survivors were struggling emotionally. "Without jobs, money, or status, they were reduced to empty shells." Second, there were exceptions. "Yet there were a few who kept their integrity and purpose despite the surrounding chaos. Their serenity was a beacon that kept others from losing hope." These are the people whom positive psychologists want to know better.

Social psychology was likewise caught up in the focus on the negative—and with good reason. The urgent postwar demand to social psychologists was to somehow "fix"—or at least start to understand—a world that was skilled at creating new weapons of mass destruction but awkward at resolving social conflicts. Positive psychology had to overcome decades of attention given to the negative in order to gain traction in the psychology community.

In 1998, Martin Seligman, then serving as president of the American Psychological Association, issued a formal call for psychologists to turn their attention to the sources of well-being. He urged psychologists to explore positive, adaptive thoughts, feelings, and behaviors. The result was that psychology suddenly had many new (or newly emphasized) research questions. They included, "What kinds of families result in children who flourish, what work settings support the greatest satisfaction among workers, what policies result in the strongest civic engagement, and how people's lives can be most worth living" (Seligman & Csikszentmihalyi, 2000, p. 5).

The general approach has been to start asking questions related to the three pillars described earlier. Experimental social psychologists Gable and Haidt describe the change represented by positive psychology as an expansion rather than a replacement. A great deal of previous psychological research had focused on "how to bring people up from negative eight to zero." Its mission under positive psychology was to understand "how people rise from zero to positive eight" (Gable & Haidt, 2005, p. 103).

Positive Psychology Is Not "Pop Psychology"

Don't confuse positive psychology with pop psychology.

Pop psychology refers to vague, superficial applications of untested, temporarily popular, and sometimes exotic ideas. Pop psychology promises simple cures for complex problems, and these cures sometimes take on a "fad" feeling. Want to improve your memory? Rub these essential oils on your forehead. Feeling blue? Wave some crystals around. Want to relax your soul? Try reiki massage, which doesn't actually involve touch but instead moves around your body's "energy" as someone else waves their hands around your body. An alarming number of popular beliefs about psychology are myths, placebo effects, superstitions, and self-deceptions (see Lilienfeld et al., 2011).

Pop psychology:
The vague and superficial application of untested, temporarily popular, and sometimes exotic ideas to everyday life.

Placebo Effects

Pop psychology today is what "patent medicines" were in the 1920s.

Patent medicines were homemade concoctions that circulated freely through an unregulated society. You may have heard of the famous example "snake oil," originally marketed as a cure for arthritis. No matter what they claimed to cure, many patent medicines contained just enough alcohol (or other drugs, such as cocaine) to make you feel good. Pop psychology promises similar "cures" such as remembering "past lives" to explain your problems, relieve your depression, calm your nerves, or improve your mood.

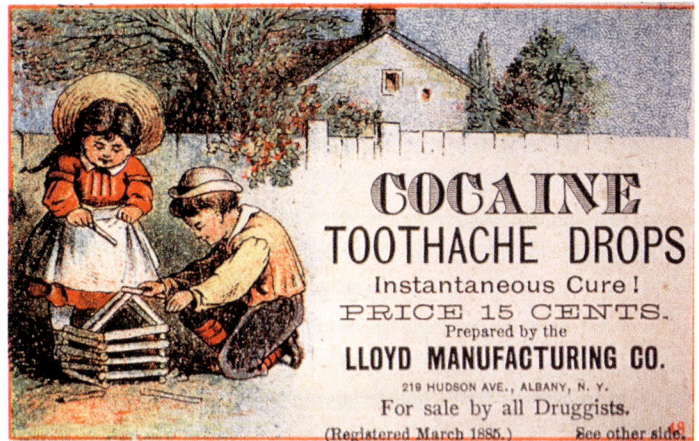

COCAINE
TOOTHACHE DROPS
Instantaneous Cure!
PRICE 15 CENTS.
Prepared by the
LLOYD MANUFACTURING CO.
219 HUDSON AVE., ALBANY, N. Y.
For sale by all Druggists.
(Registered March 1885.)   See other side.

Pop psychology is full of placebo effects that occur when the strength of your belief leads you to experience the expected benefits of a medical or psychological treatment. The placebo itself has no independent effect on you. Anything can be a placebo: a nasty-tasting drink, a colorful rock, a pleasant aroma, or even an accidental gesture that is perceived to have meaning. They all require one thing: your belief. They all are merely potential *confounding variables,* alternative explanations that briefly can make you feel better—but only if you believe in them.

Pop psychology refers to fads that claim to make your life better without any scientific evidence, just like these "medical treatments" claimed to do for problems like rheumatism and toothaches.

The Peer Review Process

The scientific community relies on the **peer review process** to distinguish between positive and popular psychology.

Peer review is not a perfect system, but for now it is the best that we can do. Peer review relies on multiple, independent experts to decide whether a journal should publish a paper. The goal is to ensure publications are of high quality. If someone wants to publish research findings, the article is first reviewed by several other, well-respected people in the field (the "peers") before it sees the light of day. They ask important questions regarding the reliability and validity of the claimed conclusions.

But in the case of positive psychology, there was so much enthusiasm for its possibilities that the peer review process was very slow at catching some obvious errors (Brown et al., 2014; Fredrickson, 2013; Fredrickson & Losada, 2005). This led to some unfortunate crossover between positive and pop psychology at the beginning of positive psychology's growth. A modern example might even be counseling's current excitement about "mindfulness," which appears to have very small lasting effects (for more, see Mini-Chapter E. on stress and health). As we warned you, peer review is not a perfect system.

However we accomplish it, positive psychology needs a scientific approach to distinguish between placebos and the real thing. Thus, the conscious intention of positive psychology is now to avoid pop psychology by systematically testing hypotheses and building a scientific foundation one study at a time. A scientific foundation, especially one based on peer review, is guaranteed to slow things down.

For example, science requires measuring the underlying *constructs*—and that means testing every new measure for *reliability* and *validity*. Seligman and Csikszentmihalyi (2000) wanted to put positive psychology on a scientific as well as a conceptual foundation. They wanted to move past a "self-help" or "do-it-yourself" mentality to an authentic scientific approach. They proposed the PERMA approach to measure the concepts of positive psychology.

Peer review process: How the scientific community uses experts to decide whether a journal should publish a paper, to ensure publications are of high quality.

PERMA approach: An approach to measuring subjective well-being that considers an individual's positive emotions, engagement, relationship to others, meaning and purpose, and achievement.

The PERMA Approach

Positive psychology is not a new idea.

Jung and Maslow had proposed similar concepts decades earlier. However, the **PERMA approach** organizes positive psychology into testable ideas—and that is relatively new. It represented positive psychology's first efforts to measure, or *operationalize*, the central concepts of positive psychology summarized by the phrase "subjective well-being." PERMA refers to Positive emotions, Engagement, Relationship to others, Meaning and purpose, and Achievement. The evolving strategy for measuring PERMA is slightly different for every component.

- Positive emotions (happiness): Measured by a language assessment of the ratio of positive to negative words someone (or a group) uses when interacting with others.

- Engagement (or "flow," meaning truly experiencing events): Identifying and measuring our signature strengths and challenges.

- Relationship to others (social interactions): Measured by how we habitually respond to good news. Our response tendencies are summarized in Table F.1, which isolates the response of positive psychology as both constructive and active. Imagine, for example, all the different things that a person might say in response to learning that their spouse received a job promotion to be the head of research.

- Meaning and purpose: Measured by the degree of commitment to some long-lasting cause to something meaningful that is bigger than yourself (e.g., joining the military to support your country, donating time or money to Habitat for Humanity, providing scholarship support for students).

- Achievement: Measured by our level of determination and tenacity; sometimes referred to as "grit." High levels of achievement also require significant self-discipline and the ability to delay gratification.

TABLE F.1

Four Possible Responses to Good News From a Spouse

	CONSTRUCTIVE RESPONSES	DESTRUCTIVE RESPONSES
Active responses	"Congratulations and well done! I bet it was your last data analysis that convinced them. It was a clear, thoughtful presentation."	"Well, you certainly got lucky. There were several more deserving candidates. When will I see a bump in your paycheck?"
Passive responses	"That's great."	"Now you can buy better food at the grocery store, so maybe your cooking will improve."

Note: Positive psychology says that responses to good news from someone in our social world should be both constructive and active.

THE MAIN IDEAS

- Positive psychology is the scientific study of what ordinary humans keep doing extraordinarily well, such as happiness and achievement. Three "pillars" of positive psychology are positive subjective experiences, positive individual traits, and positive institutions.

- While much of psychology (at least, in the past) focused on moving people from having mental illnesses or problems to a state of neutrality, positive psychology attempts to move people from a state of neutrality to achieving happiness and their full potential.

- Pop psychology is the vague and superficial application of untested, temporarily popular, and sometimes exotic ideas to improve everyday life. Positive psychology is not pop psychology because it uses scientific methods and evidence to back up claims.

- One approach to positive psychology is called PERMA, which stands for the measurement of Positive emotions, Engagement, Relationship to others, Meaning and purpose, and Achievement.

> ### CRITICAL THINKING CHALLENGE
>
> - Think about the idea that much of psychology (such as clinical and counseling) hopes to move people from negative to neutral, while positive psychology hopes to move people from neutral to positive. When subjective well-being is placed on a normal bell curve which "half" of the curve do you think is more important? Should research and focus in psychology stick to the "negative" half, attempting to help people avoid depression and low self-esteem, or should it help people move up on the "positive" half? Certainly, both are important—but which is *more* important?
>
> - Imagine that you see a news article claiming that a new pill increases happiness. How can you investigate this claim to see if it comes from pop psychology versus scientific, positive psychology? What will you look for in the fine print? How will you operationalize "happiness"?

HOW IS POSITIVE PSYCHOLOGY CHANGING?

>> **LO F.2:** **Compare early research in positive psychology with current trends.**

Humans love fads.

From patent medicines to pet rocks to selfies with "duck lips," we humans repeatedly latch on to engaging, gossipy items and events. Popular psychology has also been full of fads. People have been drawn to horses that can do higher math, believed that head bumps communicated character, released repressed memories through primal scream therapy, and used magical crystals to move their emotions.

Is positive psychology just another fad?

Publication history (*archival data*) is one way to see the dramatic growth of positive psychology. The starting period (1999) co-occurs with Seligman's call for more attention to positive psychology. From the years 2000 to 2010, the term *positive psychology* appeared in only 2,252 articles listed in the PsycINFO database. In the following decade (2011–2019), the number more than doubled to 5,264. The growth is so dramatic that it sparks the worry that positive psychology is just another intellectual fad (see Ellickson & Brown, 1990).

However, the history of positive psychology is much longer than these numbers suggest. In previous generations, the three pillars (positive subjective experiences, positive individual traits, and positive institutions) were often defined by different terms such as self-actualization, need for achievement, and peak experiences. Searching for articles with these and other relevant terms gets you many, many more hits. This section answers the core question "How is positive psychology changing?" by

(1) reviewing the early history of positive psychology, and

(2) peeking into the possible future of positive psychology.

The Early History of Positive Psychology

Seligman and Csikszentmihalyi (2000) knew that they were rediscovering early themes in psychology (see Froh, 2004).

They recognized, for example, that "William James, Carl Jung, Gordon Allport, and Abraham Maslow were interested in exploring spiritual ecstasy, play, creativity, and peak experiences" (p. 10). The long history of creativity research also testifies to psychologists' desire to understand what kinds of people and circumstances seemed to encourage, support, and inspire innovation, group creativity, and original thinking (see Albert & Runco, 1999; Compton, 2005).

Sport Psychology: The First Positive Psychology Experiment

The distinguishing characteristic of the modern positive psychology movement is the development of its scientific foundations.

> We well recognize that positive psychology is not a new idea. It has many distinguished ancestors, and we make no claim of originality. However, these ancestors somehow failed to attract a cumulative, empirical body of research to ground their ideas. (Seligman & Csikszentmihalyi, 2000, p. 13)

The scientific foundation of positive psychology began quietly, as a sport psychology experiment. We introduced you to Norm Triplett (1898) in Chapter 8 when we reviewed his bicycle studies on social facilitation. Triplett might be surprised by the mark he left on history, including the still developing history of positive psychology.

Peak Performance and Slumping Athletes. Triplett was just trying to answer a question about peak athletic performance.

He wanted to know why bicycle racers performed better in the presence of others—he wanted a scientific explanation for peak performance. And that experiment made him the world's first scientific social psychologist, the first empirically minded positive psychologist, and the first sport psychologist (see Strube, 2005).

Triplett himself might reject those honorary titles because his own article referenced a previous study by E. B. Turner. Turner had used a similar (probably archival) approach to analyze the same question about bicycle racing. (Turner's general concerns were more about the effects of cycling on health than they were about social or positive psychology.) Triplett's work is the basis for the study of peak performance, a goal at the very heart of positive psychology.

Modern **sport psychology** focuses on what the American Psychological Association (APA, 2017) describes as the scientific study of how psychology influences both participant and performance of sports, exercise, and any type of physical activity. Sport psychologists already focus on many of the positive aspects of sports. They gravitate to topics such as peak achievement, team building, and learning how to win and lose with grace. The APA presents a positive, forward-looking, achievement-oriented agenda for sport psychologists—a good fit for positive psychologists.

Ethical Issues for Performance Psychologists. As a professional psychologist, unless you have a very good reason, you will want to stay out of trouble.

Gable and Haidt (2005) emphasize that "positive psychology's aim is not the denial of the distressing, unpleasant, or negative aspects of life, nor is it an effort to see them through rose-colored glasses" (p. 105). Likewise, the values of the Association for Applied Sport Psychology (AASP, 2017) assert that members' first responsibility is to promote ethics, not peak performance. The modern sport industry offers a long list of opportunities to address ethics issues that correspond to the three pillars of positive psychology:

- Positive subjective experience: Reducing fan expressions of race prejudice will improve the subjective experience of targeted players.

- Positive individual traits: Reducing the use of performance-enhancing drugs will create fairness for players who kept their integrity by not using them.

- Positive institutions: Correcting how colleges and universities profit from athletics will promote institutional integrity and respect from students.

de Benutzer Hase, CC BY-SA 3.0

Lance Armstrong eventually admitted that he had used performance-enhancing drugs to help him win the Tour de France seven times. A positive sport psychologist would be interested in comparing his subjective experience to athletes who preserved their integrity by resisting the temptation to use this kind of drug.

Sport psychology: The scientific study of how athletic performance is influenced by psychological concepts.

For sport psychologists, that means avoiding ethical violations that can cost you your license, damage your reputation, and embarrass you and everyone associated with you. One recurring, difficult-to-avoid ethical concern involves dual relationships that occur when a professional takes on incompatible roles with a client.

For example, a professor should not serve as a student's therapist (there are exceptions, but they are rare). In the same way, it is inappropriate for a sport psychologist to also serve as coach (Ellickson & Brown, 1990). A mature, positive institution will not allow dual relationships to develop that might encourage ethical compromises.

The Future of Positive Social Psychology

We have yet to meet a social psychologist who does not want to use science to produce a positive social impact.

That is not surprising; we are the intellectual offspring of Kurt Lewin. Like sport psychology, positive psychology and social psychology have always been aligned with applied psychology. Just a few of the career opportunities (and challenges) for future positive psychologists are related to clinical psychology, military training, game-based assessments, controversial "life coaches," and health.

Positive Psychology Aims to Build Resilience

Thinking scientifically challenges assumptions.

For example, a scientific foundation for positive psychology may require some clinicians to think differently about their own successes and failures. Seligman and Csikszentmihalyi (2000) emphasize that health practitioners need to focus on amplifying strengths, not just repairing weaknesses. Positive psychology has brought particular attention to personal resilience.

Hope and Family Build Resilience. Resilience requires social support.

Juanita, the woman described at the beginning of this mini-chapter, would probably agree with findings from an example study related to resilience and positive psychology. It examined the beliefs of 131 Mexican American college students (Vela et al., 2017). They found that two predictors stood out when trying to understand what helped teenagers maintain resilience as they pushed forward in their education: hope and family.

Hope and family were more important (they were *statistically significant*) than competing variables that included subjective happiness, meaning in life, and a college self-efficacy scale. Hope and family kept Juanita persevering when she could not understand any of the words spoken in her new school. Hope and family helped her persevere along the path toward graduate school.

Resilience Training in the Military. Resilience also affects soldiers.

One research team helped create an assessment tool for the army to measure resilience training (Vie et al., 2016). The impetus, unfortunately, was once again related to war. There has been a sharp increase in depression, posttraumatic stress disorder (PTSD), alcohol use, and suicide among soldiers returning from battles in Iraq and Afghanistan (see Berge, 2019; Havemen-Gould & Newman, 2018).

Thus, many health initiatives have been inspired or influenced by positive psychology (see Bergmann et al., 2019). The treatment focus on depression, for example, adds more attention on building positive coping skills that lead to subjective well-being. Therapy is about increasing strengths that can make therapeutic gains permanent. For example, positive psychology has clarified the value of physical exercise for depressed individuals (Lambert et al., 2016).

Positive Psychology Encourages Failing Forward

Human-computer interactions (HCIs) are also contributing to positive psychology.

Another expression of positive psychology is emerging from the world of assessment, especially from HCIs. There are many types of assessments but, like a multiple-choice exam, they often focus on what a student has done wrong rather than right. You may have been frustrated by taking something like a multiple-choice exam that asked you specific questions leading to a poor grade when you felt that you had not gotten the opportunity to truly display what you had learned.

Bellotti and colleagues (2013) and several others are pioneering ways to capture authentic strengths and weaknesses through more creative ways to assess learning (see Jans-Beken et al., 2019). People provide such information as they engage in designed activities, including playing games that encourage peak performance (see Shute & Ventura, 2013).

Their general recognition is that we have been systematically missing much of the most important data when we focus on what participants have *not* done well instead of measuring what they have done well. An important element of that, to a game designer, is the game mechanic referred to as "failing forward" that recognizes the importance of learning through failure. The notion that failing forward is a positive experience is being recognized across multiple disciplines, including college teaching (Ocasio, 2019), economic policy (Nicoli, 2019), and political science (see Giralt et al., 2019).

The Controversy Over Life Coaches

It sounds positive—but what's the deal with all these life coaches?

One of the emerging careers that belong more or less under the umbrella of positive psychology is that of the life coach. A **life coach** works with individuals as they make career and personal decisions, giving advice and inspiring them. Unfortunately, often people in this career do not have formal education or credentials related to counseling. The range of descriptions sometimes used to describe a life coach suggests both its role and criticisms of its role: "Friend for hire" is at the positive end and "a fraud counselor working without a license" at the negative end.

Meanwhile, a more formal discussion of the work and the popularity of life coaching as a career has led to richer discussions about if and how to legitimatize life coaching (George, 2013). For now, this career is very controversial. Many professional psychologists believe that life coaches are not particularly well trained to offer advice or guidance to people struggling, compared to licensed practitioners who have advanced degrees.

Health Benefits of Positive Psychology

Positive psychology claims positive health benefits.

Long before Seligman's appeal for a positive psychology, its principles were already being applied to health promotion. For example, Aspinwall and Tedeschi (2010) have documented early empirical work on optimism and posttraumatic growth. They also expressed concerns about the damaging effects of popular psychology weakening the scientific base of positive psychology.

Others have focused on heart disease and the opportunities for positive psychology to encourage better health habits (Huffman et al., 2016). The specific mechanisms that promote health remain unclear—which means that science just doesn't know yet whether we are dealing with placebo effects. This is, therefore, an area where more people and more research are needed.

If everyone in the field is successful in their goal of making humans happy, healthy, and successful, then positive psychologists put themselves out of business. If this happens, Gable and Haidt (2005) bluntly assert that "the future of positive psychology is just plain psychology" (p. 108). Positive psychology is a corrective measure, a returning to our roots, and a way to expand the range of topics and possibilities within psychology. If the positive psychology movement is successful, then it will disappear.

Life coach: Someone who provides support and inspiration for others who are making career and personal decisions. Controversial because often they lack professional credentials.

THE MAIN IDEAS

- Positive psychology is not new in the field; topics were simply studied under different terms or subfields. An example is Triplett's research on peak performance in cyclists that was covered in Chapter 8.

- One area that has a lot of overlap with positive psychology is sport psychology. Other areas where positive psychology crosses over to influence research are clinical psychology, military training, game-based assessments, controversial life coaches, and health.

CRITICAL THINKING CHALLENGE

- What do you think about the career path known as "life coaching"? Do you think you or your friends would benefit from a paid life coach? Should people in this career have certain educational requirements, licenses, background checks, and so on?

- What other areas of psychology do you think would benefit from having more overlap with positive psychology? Explain your answer.

- Do you think that positive psychology will continue to grow in popularity? Will there ever be a point when positive psychology is no longer needed, because people in the field have successfully elevated humanity to the point of great happiness and achievement?

G. Social Psychology and Money

Core Questions

G.1 What is behavioral economics?

G.2 How can I apply behavioral economics to my personal finances?

Learning Objectives

G.1 Compare the standard economic model (SEM) with the behavioral economic model (BEM).

G.2 Describe how subjective ownership, mental accounting, and reference points influence your personal finances.

Choose Y for "yes" or N for "no":

- **Y N** If you were eating at a restaurant in a strange city, and you knew you would never return to this location, would you leave a tip for your waiter?

- **Y N** Does a five-dollar pill somehow cure your headache faster than a five-cent pill?

- **Y N** Would you be unhappy about a surprise 10% raise in salary if you also found out that your coworker received a surprise 15% raise?

- **Y N** Do you spend more money shopping with a credit card than when shopping with cash?

- **Y N** Would you be happier winning two lottery tickets worth $50 and $25 each, compared to winning one lottery ticket worth $75 and one worth nothing?

Did you answer "yes" to even one question?

If you did, then you are familiar with the invisible psychological boundary between rational and irrational economic thinking. Retailers and advertisers are aware of your movements back and forth across this boundary. And behavioral economics explores much more than your tipping habits or whether you buy lottery tickets. It asks why you chose your major and how you study, what you wish for in marriage and in a marriage partner, what you value in life and why you value it, and more.

Behavioral economics is about you: the daily decision maker.

WHAT IS BEHAVIORAL ECONOMICS?

>> LO G.1: **Compare the standard economic model (SEM) with the behavioral economic model (BEM).**

"I hate losing more than I love winning."

Tennis legend Jimmy Conners expressed an emotion shared by many athletes. The psychological phrase that captures Jimmy Conners's dislike of losing comes from Kahneman and Tversky (1979): "Losses loom larger than gains" (p. 279). Economists and psychologists refer to Conners's attitude as **loss aversion**, our greater sensitivity to losses than to gains.

Conners wasn't the only athlete to feel this way. Loss aversion also had practical consequences for professional golfers, according to data from the U.S. Open golf championships (at Pebble Beach Golf Links and the Oakmont Country Club; see Elmore & Urbaczewski, 2019). Loss aversion is only one of many insights that unite economics and psychology in the discipline now called **behavioral economics**, the psychological factors that influence how, why, and what we value (see Ariely, 2008; deCremer et al., 2006; Harmon-Jones, 2007; Politser, 2008; Schwartz, 2008).

This section answers the core question "What is behavioral economics?" by

(1) comparing the histories of economics and psychology, and

(2) describing the boundary between rational and irrational economic behavior.

Comparative Histories: Economics and Psychology

An invisible guiding hand?! Sounds a bit creepy.

This theory sounds more like the myth about tooth fairies than a respectable academic theory. But don't laugh too long or too loud. This bizarre-sounding idea came from Adam Smith, the Scottish founder of economic philosophy. And the invisible guiding hand theory continues to be taught in almost every introductory course in economics.

Loss aversion: The tendency for potential losses to be more psychologically influential than potential gains.

Behavioral economics: The study of how economic decisions are influenced by psychological factors.

The Invisible Guiding Hand Theory

Here's the theory:

An "invisible guiding hand" (IGH) relies on the laws of supply and demand to direct economic behavior in ways that, in the long term, benefit society. He argues that eventually, the economy sorts itself out to benefit almost everyone. Smith described his views of human economic behavior in his book *The Theory of Moral Sentiments* (Smith, 1759) and again in his more famous book *The Wealth of Nations* (Smith, 1776). Bizarre sounding? Yes. But the theory is based on reasonable assumptions about human behavior.

Defenders of the invisible guiding hand theory encourage doubters just to wait; the guiding hand will take care of things *in the long run*. Unfortunately, in the long run, we're all dead. And the theory isn't particularly comforting to people who are currently, desperately poor. That's why doing nothing in the face of climate change, for example, is a powerful argument against—or at least a modification to—the IGH theory (see Storm, 2017).

The IGH theory reminds us that the histories of economics and psychology share a common goal: understanding human behavior. It assumes that humans are **rational economic thinkers**, that we will make logical decisions based on the strict rules of supply and demand—that we will always go for the best deal. By contrast, **irrational economic thinkers** are influenced by all those mental shortcuts, misperceptions, and emotional biases you learned about in Chapter 4 (Social Cognition). It recognizes that humans often ignore the rules of supply and demand, make rash decisions, and justify impulse purchases.

Loss Aversion: A Shared Understanding

Jimmy Conners didn't like losing—and you probably don't either.

For loss aversion research, it's not the actual winning or losing that matters; it's *anticipating* winning or losing that shapes our behavior. The psychological explanations for loss aversion include a neurological component (Higgins & Liberman, 2018). Norepinephrine, for example, appears to be associated with anticipating losses and dopamine with risk taking for rewards (see Sokal-Hessner & Rutledge, 2019). Wilkinson (2008) summarized the deeper evolutionary explanation for why losses loom larger than gains:

> An extra gallon of water can make us feel more comfortable crossing a desert; a loss of a gallon of water may have fatal consequences. (p. 106)

Loss aversion is a psychological response with predictable (but sometimes subtle) economic consequences (Mrkva et al., 2019; see also Gal & Rucker, 2018). For example, a common way to monetize a free online game starts by giving away a lower-grade version, hoping to entice the user to upgrade. Loss aversion involves how we perceive and process the threat of losing the superior benefits of the upgraded version (see Mishra et al., 2018).

Loss aversion also clarifies the complicated economic decisions related to managing an investment portfolio as an individual nears retirement (see Benartzi & Thaler, 1995). When you're young, your long-term horizon allows you to endure the ups and downs of a volatile market. But as you grow older, the threat of losses becomes more powerful because you have less time to recover from those losses.

Loss aversion can also help address a far more serious health (and economic) problem: medical nonadherence. Thousands of lives are lost because individuals do not follow "doctors' orders" or get screened for diseases. A review of this literature suggested that "loss-based messages may be more effective at encouraging screening behaviors, such as mammography screening" (Matjasko et al., 2016, p. S15; see also Schneider et al., 2001). For more about the psychology of health decisions, check out Mini-Chapter E in this book.

Rational economic thinking: The idea that consumers will act rationally according to the strict rules of supply and demand.

Irrational economic thinking: The idea that consumers' decisions are often irrational, influenced by mental shortcuts, misperceptions, and emotional biases.

The Tragedy of Separate Histories

Economics and psychology have always shared the same goal: understanding human behavior.

However, despite their meant-to-be-together beginnings, the two disciplines took different paths for many decades—and they only started "dating" again in the last half of the 20th century. A moment of intellectual separation came during one of the most critical moments in human history. The Great War, soon to be called World War I, ended in 1918 at 11 a.m. on the 11th day of the 11th month.

Forgiveness: An Economic Policy. This window of opportunity opened immediately after silence fell across the battlefields around the world.

It stayed open for more than 7 months. But it slammed shut when the unforgiving Treaty of Versailles was signed on June 28, 1919. After 16 million deaths, the victors, who gathered at Versailles, were in no mood to forgive Germany.

Yet one economist, John Maynard Keynes, urged the victors to forgive Germany its many debts. It was an economic argument for psychological forgiveness. Keynes warned that the bitterly *un*forgiving economic terms under consideration at the Treaty of Versailles would inspire a "vengeance ... before which the horrors of the late German war will fade into nothing" (Keynes, 1920, p. 268). The victorious allies ignored his advice—they wanted Germany to pay dearly for all the blood they had spilled.

The Wisdom of Forgiveness. The victors in World War I were not convinced.

When Keynes could not convince his peers about the self-interested wisdom of forgiveness, he resigned his position as custodian of Great Britain's treasury and his title as Chancellor of the Exchequer. He then published a book bluntly titled *The Economic Consequences of the Peace*. Keynes could see the small cloud of World War II forming in the dark ink of the punishing economic "peace" treaty.

Sadly, Keynes's unhappy predictions started becoming the world's history during Germany's hyperinflation in 1923. A frustrated painter-turned-politician named Adolph Hitler kept reminding the German people of the unforgiving terms of the Treaty of Versailles. Keynes understood that humiliation, vengeance, and embarrassment are social psychological passions with predictable economic consequences. Germany's experience after World War I led to the horrors of World War II (around 60 million deaths).

When World War II finally ended, American foreign policy went in a different direction. They instituted the Marshall Plan that helped the defeated nations rebuild their economies—and their lives. Leffler (2018) described its many consequences within the recognition that

> the Marshall Plan was the most successful U.S. foreign policy program of the Cold War, and arguably the most successful in all of U.S. history. In France, Italy, the United Kingdom, West Germany, and beyond, the plan's $13 billion in aid expedited economic recovery, buoyed morale, and eroded the appeal of communism. (p. 170)

Effective public policies require the united wisdom of both psychology *and* economics: behavioral economics.

Watercolor of St. Charles Church in Vienna, painted by Adolf Hitler (signed in the lower left-hand corner).

Behrouz Mehri/AFP/Getty Images

The Boundary Between Rational and Irrational Behavior

Psychology and economics went their separate ways after World War II.

For about 50 years, economists focused on the implications of rational principles of "supply and demand." Psychologists, on the other hand, focused on cognitive science, new treatments for mental illness, and the rapidly growing discipline of social psychology. But economics and psychology were still meant for each other.

For example, according to the rational law of supply and demand, no one should leave a tip for a meal in a strange city. It's throwing away money that won't result in any kind of benefit for the person who's tipping. You'll never see this server again—why not keep your money? Yet most people (in a tipping culture) will leave a tip anyway. Here are some of the psychological reasons why most people will leave some money on the table. Tipping is

- A habit, an automatic behavior
- Conforming to a social norm
- Feeling sympathy for the server
- Performing a good deed for an imaginary audience
- Trying to make the world a little more just
- A way to avoid imagined social embarrassment
- Validating your self-image as a good or generous person

The rest of this section covers the strange balance between rational and irrational behavior we all have in making money decisions.

Psychology and the Nobel Prize in Economics

Economics and psychology got back together when the 1978 Nobel Prize in Economics was awarded to Herbert Simon.

Simon developed the theory of **bounded rationality** that proposed cognitive limitations on our ability to make rational economic decisions (see Jones, 1999). He was establishing that, despite previous economic models, we don't always make rational economic decisions. And this boundary only could be understood by reuniting economics and psychology.

In 2002, psychologist Daniel Kahneman also won the Nobel Prize in Economics. Kahneman and his longtime collaborator Amos Tversky developed Simon's theory into **prospect theory**, the idea that people make predictable kinds of mistakes when trying to weigh outcomes and probabilities. Kahneman and Tversky (2000) were mapping the boundary areas where rational decision making slipped into the kind of irrational decisions that Herbert Simon had first discovered. You already read about some of these mistakes in Chapter 4 when we talked about mental heuristics.

For example, imagine that you need a car and you have found what looks like a great buy: an expensive, fancy-looking car at an unusually low price. However, the National Highway Traffic Safety Administration (NHTSA, 2020) warns that

> hurricanes have produced record-breaking and devastating rain and floodwaters in recent years, and destroyed homes—and cars. . . . You need to protect yourself from being sold a flood-damaged vehicle.

Bounded rationality: The idea that there is a natural cognitive limit on our ability to make rational economic decisions.

Prospect theory: The idea that we make predictable mistakes when trying to weigh outcomes and probabilities.

Despite that warning, this particular car *looks* great and . . . it has a sunroof and a superior sound system. You *want* it—but will you buy it? Your rational decision-making warning system is flashing red: "This is a lemon. Do not buy!" But your irrational desire for a sunroof and a sound system is flashing green. Even if it doesn't run great, it *looks* great and might impress people. If you go back and forth trying to decide, then you're straddling Simon's boundary between rational and irrational economic decision making.

Psychology Guides the Behavioral Economic Model

The separation of psychology and economics was always awkward.

Psychological variables didn't fit easily into the traditional economic approach called the **standard economic model (SEM)**. The SEM describes how people should behave *if* they were making rational decisions, *if* they always pursued the best financial deal, *if* they were not influenced by the strange cognitive biases, and *if* they were not influenced by a variety of social passions. It's how robots or computers might use money.

Psychologists, on the other hand, recognize that many of our decisions are *not* rational and sometimes leave us muttering, "What in the world was I thinking?" The psychological description of *irrational* (but maybe more realistic) economic decision making is called the **behavioral economic model (BEM)**. The BEM recognizes that we are often sloppy thinkers who, as we learned in Chapter 4, rely on mental shortcuts, perceptual biases, and heuristic problem solving. The BEM recognizes that many of our automatic economic decisions are not the best deal.

The SEM and the BEM are not necessarily in conflict. Wilkinson (2008) argues that psychology's focus on cognitive processes during the 1980s (De Cremer et al., 2006, p. 5) put economic theory on "more realistic psychological foundations" (Camerer & Lowenstein, 2004, p. 3). For a side-by-side comparison of the SEM and BEM, see Table G.1. There have already been two Nobel Prizes in Economics given out to psychologists. If you're interested in behavioral economics, who knows how far you might go?

TABLE G.1

Some Assumptions of the Standard Economic Model (SEM) and the Behavioral Economic Model (BEM)

STANDARD ECONOMIC MODEL (SEM) PEOPLE ARE . . .	BEHAVIORAL ECONOMIC MODEL (BEM) PEOPLE ARE . . .
Always rational	Frequently irrational
Motivated to maximize gains and limit losses	More influenced by losses than by gains
Governed by narrow self-interests	Influenced by inarticulate social self-interests

---

THE MAIN IDEAS

- Behavioral economics studies how economic decisions are influenced by psychological factors that indicate what we value and how much we value it. For example, loss aversion is the idea that we're more motivated to avoid losses than to achieve gains.

- The link between economics and psychology has a long history and provides interesting insights into political decisions, such as the aftermath of World War I and the buildup before World War II.

- The standard economic model (SEM) is based on the assumption that people make logical, rational decisions. The behavioral economic model (BEM), studied by psychologists, extends the SEM by including predictably irrational decision making.

CRITICAL THINKING CHALLENGE

- Form an argument about why, if we already have disciplines of psychology and economics, we should develop a field that blends the two disciplines. What would the combination offer that two separate fields couldn't?

- Think of four things you buy frequently. Try to identify two items you believe you choose based on the standard economic model (you follow the most logical route) and two items you believe you choose based on the behavioral economic model (perhaps your choices aren't the most rational in the world).

Standard economic model (SEM): A model for understanding economic behavior that describes how people behave if they always make sound, rational decisions.

Behavioral economic model (BEM): A model for understanding economic behavior that describes how psychology influences irrational economic decision making.

HOW CAN I APPLY BEHAVIORAL ECONOMICS TO MY PERSONAL FINANCES?

>> **LO G.2:** **Describe how subjective ownership, mental accounting, and reference points influence your personal finances.**

Sean Harkin / Alamy Stock Photo

Auction fever, like a gambling addiction, can be harmful to your finances.

The supporters of a Chicago-based charity event called "the cow parade" started bidding against each other for the life-sized, fiberglass cows in different poses, painted with colorful designs. The bidding rose higher. And higher. And higher again as people influenced each other to keep on bidding due to feelings of competition and the desire to avoid getting "beat" by someone else. Loss aversion was feeding on itself.

The bidders were not all super-wealthy. So, it is easy to imagine someone coming home and mentioning to their spouse, "Oh, by the way, darling. I just spent $25,000 [the average bid] on a very large fiberglass cow. It will be arriving on Tuesday. Where do you suggest we put it?" Behavioral economics can help protect you from **auction fever**, the tendency to overbid the value of an item in a socially competitive environment (see Ku et al., 2005). This section answers the core question "How can I apply behavioral economics to my personal finances?" by

(1) illustrating how subjective ownership influences decisions,

(2) describing features of mental accounting, and

(3) explaining how reference points influence our behaviors.

The Subjective Ownership Effect

You made a small bid on a particular cow, but you don't own it . . . yet.

However, merely imagining owning it creates a sense of ownership called **subjective ownership**. This sense of perceived ownership is also called **mere ownership** and the **endowment effect** depending on the context. Subjective ownership is experienced within virtual reality (Van Dam & Stephens, 2018), as a marketing tool (Pallant et al., 2020), and when describing body parts that do not really exist (see Ehrsson, 2020) such as phantom limb (Pazzaglia et al., 2019). A classic example of subjective ownership is what car salespeople hope you experience with a "test drive." Within social psychology, subjective ownership usually refers to the tendency to evaluate objects more favorably just because they are perceived to be owned. Now, you *want* it.

Subjective ownership begins quietly. But then, someone else starts bidding on *your* cow. You up your bid just a little more—and then so does someone else. You can't let them have *your* cow!

The Neural Circuitry of Rewards

The excitement is in the anticipation.

In auction fever experiments, anticipating the possible thrill of victory and the possible agony of defeat *both* trigger neural activity associated with overbidding. As the anticipation of winning your fiberglass cow increases (I'll name her Bessie!), so does the fear of losing your cow to someone else (not my Bessie!). Like buying a lottery ticket, the excitement is in the anticipation. But now it is a two-sided anticipation: the

Auction fever: The tendency to overbid on an item being sold in a socially competitive environment.

Subjective ownership: The feeling that you own something just by imagining owning it; this feeling leads to irrational behaviors such as paying too much for it.

Mere ownership: See *subjective ownership.*

Endowment effect: See *subjective ownership.*

excitement of winning *plus* the even greater fear of losing (loss aversion).

Knutson et al. (2007) found that anticipation of gains activates the pleasure-related nucleus accumbens (NAcc). Laboratory rats loved neural self-stimulation of the NAcc so much that they would "tune out" the rest of the world, to the point of exhaustion (Olds & Forbes, 1981). They preferred this form of neural self-stimulation to eating, drinking, sex, and sleep—a sad but familiar state of affairs for anyone who has tried to live with an addict.

The Neural Circuitry of Addiction

"The only thing that will make me feel better . . . is another drink."

Fortunately, I [Tom] only had that thought once, after a long weekend and a doghair-like hangover. The thought alone made me feel better—and that scared me even more. I've been a successful social drinker ever since.

But understanding how anticipation activates the neural circuitry of reward helps explain why addicts can get stoned on a memory triggered by merely looking at their drug paraphernalia (Rosen et al., 2015; Robbins & Everitt, 2002). The anticipation (of a loss or a reward) activates different neural circuits. Specifically, Knutson & Gibbs (2007) found that anticipation of losses activates the insula and *de*activates the medial prefrontal cortex. That deactivated brain region is associated with memory and decision making (Euston et al., 2012).

The combination sounds like trouble, right? You've got a pleasure-seeking brain with relatively *de*activated memory function and decision-making skills. Perhaps that helps explain how drug addicts persist even when they know they are harming themselves and disappointing those who love them. As they prepare to inject themselves, their memories become more selective as their decision-making skills deteriorate (Sugam et al., 2012).

Those deactivated decision-making skills are the very thing that would come in handy when someone is in the grip of auction fever. Oh, no! Someone else has started bidding on *your* cow. In Delgado and colleagues' (2008) auction fever experiment, the contemplation of loss led to more overbidding than did the anticipation of a gain (see Knutson et al., 2007; Kuhnen & Knutson, 2005).

Some extreme cases of loss aversion lead to **compulsive hoarding syndrome**, an inner demand to save things in order to reduce anxiety (Leckman & Bloch, 2008). There might even be a life-size, fiberglass cow grazing contentedly somewhere in that mess.

Mental Accounting

You can improve your finances by becoming a better mental accountant.

Mental accounting refers to how we mentally manipulate money when making economic decisions (Wilkinson, 2008). Thaler and Sunstein (2008) tell a story about two famous actors early in their careers: Dustin Hoffman and Gene Hackman. Hoffman asked fellow starving artist Gene Hackman for a loan. Hackman initially agreed, but when he visited Hoffman's apartment, he noticed jars full of money labeled "Rent" and "Utilities." Hackman asked why Hoffman needed a loan if he had all this money lying around, and Hoffman pointed toward an empty jar labeled "Food."

Fungibility

Banks offer the same services as Dustin Hoffman's money jars.

Bank accounts dedicated to a "college fund," a "holiday account," "retirement money," and "vacation savings" are not really necessary. A dollar has the same value

Lots of people have collections . . . but when does the pleasure of gathering things switch to the misery and anxiety of hoarding?

Compulsive hoarding syndrome: A disorder caused by the psychological need to save things to reduce anxiety and/or depression.

Mental accounting: How we mentally think about money and its uses when making economic decisions.

Do you find it helpful to separate money into piles or accounts based on how you plan to spend it?

whether it's designated for rent, utilities, food, spring break, or retirement.

Fungibility is interchangeability. Money is fungible because one unit is readily interchangeable with another. You can use money to hire a plumber, pay the rent, buy a doughnut, or earn interest. You *might* be able to pay the plumber with a brand-new pipe wrench, but you would probably not be able to buy doughnuts with a pipe wrench. A pipe wrench is far less fungible (interchangeable) than money.

Business and household budgets are fungible because you easily can correct your overspending on beer by reducing your spending on clothing or entertainment. When I [Wind] needed to buy a new car, I had to use the $4,000 I had saved up for a trip to Thailand. That was temporarily disappointing but probably a much more logical use of the money. Because money is fungible, it was easy to simply reallocate that amount toward a down payment on a car and go to my local Thai restaurant for some comfort food.

Dustin Hoffman probably organized his money into designated jars because he recognized that he had a problem with self-control (Wilkinson, 2008). We pretend (to ourselves) that our money is not fungible—that the rent money could never be used to pay the electric bill. We engage in this self-deception because we worry about our own lack of self-control. And when it comes to personal finance, self-control matters . . . a lot.

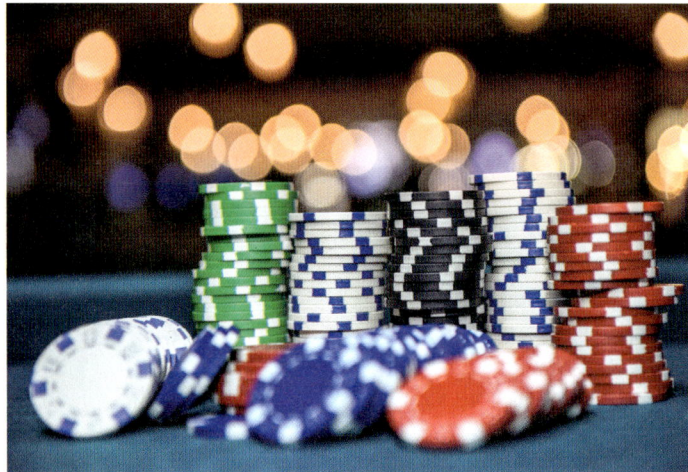

The invention of poker chips was a huge win for casinos, as people spend more money in chip form compared to actual coins or cash.

Payment Coupling: Explaining Credit Card Behavior

Credit cards are the crossroads where self-control meets fungibility (see Gross & Souleles, 2002).

Credit cards are a serious problem for many college students (Wang & Xiao, 2009; Zhu, 2019). It can be a long and personally painful way to learn about the importance of credit, the plague of high interest rates, and the necessity of financial maturity. However, we all seem to be susceptible to the convenience of credits cards.

For example, Prelec and Simester (2001) auctioned off tickets to a sold-out basketball game between the Boston Celtics and the Miami Heat (a game with playoff implications). They secretly assigned people either to pay by cash or by credit card. The use of a credit card increased students' willingness to buy the ticket by 113%. Logical thinking and the standard economic model don't explain greater spending with a credit card. Neither does basic financial awareness, because the people demonstrating their financial immaturity were first-year MBA students at the Massachusetts Institute of Technology.

There is a simpler explanation. Payment decoupling is a type of mental accounting that separates payment from consumption, something that credit cards accomplish by allowing a time interval between consumption and payment (see Thaler, 1999; Wilkinson, 2008): Consume now, pay later—it's immediate gratification.

Payment decoupling may explain why some students are happy when they arrive at class and see a sign saying: "Class Canceled." They get unexpected "free time." They should feel cheated because they already have paid for the class and have potentially lost the knowledge they would have gotten in class, but many don't *feel* cheated because they (or their parents) paid for the class so long ago. Casinos create payment decoupling in a different way. They arrange for people to gamble with chips or plastic

Fungibility: For money, the idea that its use is interchangeable (you can use it for rent, food, or anything else).

Payment decoupling: Psychologically separating payment from actually getting or using a product, such as paying later via a credit card or loan.

cards instead of actual coins or cash. Either way, the psychological separation leads to irrational perceptions and decisions.

Opportunity Costs

This section may discourage or motivate you to work harder at your studies.

Our mental accounting system also often ignores **opportunity costs**, the cost of not pursuing alternative opportunities. If you spend your spring break going to Florida, it means you can't use it to visit anywhere else, earn some extra money, or start working on final projects in your classes. Another example is the decision of whether to attend college. When we ask students to estimate the cost of their education, they usually identify costs similar to those in Table G.2.

That's a lot of money—but the actual cost is even higher. That's because of opportunity cost: If you weren't using that year to attend college, you could have been working a full-time job. So really, the cost of college is the amount of bills you have *plus* the lost wages you could have been earning instead. Note that we're not arguing for you to drop out of college! We're just making the point that you should really value the opportunity you have in front of you.

TABLE G.2	
Student Costs While Going to College	
Tuition	$20,000
Books	$2,000
Fees	$4,000
Dormitory/rent	$12,000
Food	$5,000
Total	**$43,000**

Reference Points Influence Our Decisions

If you need a conversation starter at a party, ask people, "What was the worst job you ever had?"

Their unpleasant work experience is a **reference point** that enables their mental accounting system to estimate values and make meaningful comparisons (Tversky & Kahneman, 2004). My worst job [Wind] was de-tasseling corn. Each summer, starting when I was 12 years old, I went into the hot Iowa cornfields to rip the tops off the plants so the farmers could create corn hybrids. It was sweaty, hard work, and it made me appreciate the value of earned money. This reference point serves as a reminder when I think about the type of career I want—and the type I don't want.

Reference Points and Default Decisions

One commonly used reference point is the **default decision**, the decision that gets made if we do nothing.

The website at Tom's bank has a default that kicks me out of their website if I have not interacted with it after a certain amount of time. The bank never asked for my opinion—their default kicked me out. My lawn mower has a default lever that stops the blade when I take my hands off the handle. The manufacturer never asked what I wanted—the default decision stopped the blade. The default on your grades is that you will fail your classes if you do nothing to prevent that from happening. You have to do things to earn points; they don't just appear.

Reference Points and Social Consequences. Some default reference points can save thousands of lives.

For example, if you should die in a tragic car accident, then your body has life-saving value to several of the more than 100,000 people (in the United States) who are hoping for an organ transplant of your kidneys, liver, heart, or other organs (you can sign up at http://optn.transplant.hrsa.gov/data/). Yes, it is a grim idea—unless you are the one waiting for a transplant. But it is a default decision that needs to be made before the first responders arrive at the scene of your accident. In the United States, the default is that you are not an organ donor.

Take a close look at Figure G.1. Why are the rates of organ donation so different in these particular countries? It seems like a mystery because Germany (12%) and Austria

Opportunity cost: The "cost" of not pursuing other, alternative opportunities.

Reference point: A psychological starting place used for comparisons when we estimate the value of something.

Default decision: The outcome that will inevitably happen if no action is made.

(99.98%) have similar cultures, overlapping histories, and share a border. Yet their rates of formal consent to organ donation are dramatically different. Is there some deep difference in the national personality of Germans and Austrians or between Danes and Swedes?

FIGURE G.1

The likelihood that people will be organ donors varies quite a bit from country to country. This might be because of the default reference point.

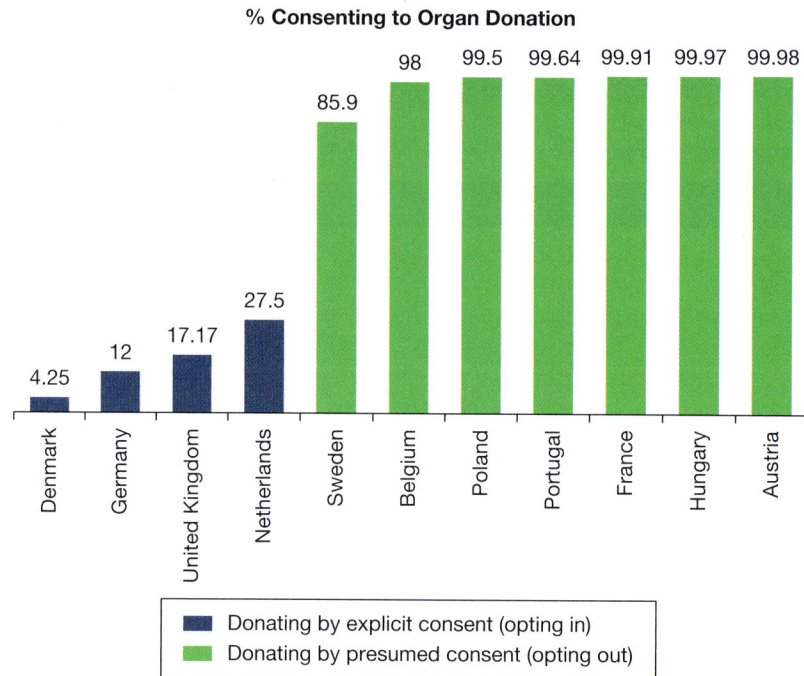

% Consenting to Organ Donation

Country	%
Denmark	4.25
Germany	12
United Kingdom	17.17
Netherlands	27.5
Sweden	85.9
Belgium	98
Poland	99.5
Portugal	99.64
France	99.91
Hungary	99.97
Austria	99.98

■ Donating by explicit consent (opting in)
■ Donating by presumed consent (opting out)

Would you feel better buying shirts that have a $50 price tag and are "on sale" for $35, compared to shirts with a $20 price tag and no sale? Probably—because even though you're spending more on the $35 shirts, you feel like you've scored a deal.

This comparison study by Johnson and Goldstein (2003) suggests that the dramatic difference in rates of organ donation are due to default decisions that require people either to "opt in" or "opt out" of organ donations. In the countries to the left in Figure G.1 (Denmark, Germany, the United Kingdom, and the Netherlands), the automatic default reference point is that no, you do not want to be an organ donor. You must sign some paperwork in order to opt in to be an organ donor.

In the countries to the right (like Sweden), the default reference point (a different, automatic default decision) is that yes, you do want to be an organ donor. You must sign some paperwork to opt out and not be an organ donor. Most people make this critical, life-saving decision automatically, based on the default reference point.

Price Tags Are a Reference Point. The department store entrepreneur John Wanamaker invented the price tag.

Wanamaker was a devoutly religious man. He believed that people should be treated equally in terms of price, just as they should be treated equally in every aspect of their lives (Lovett & Miranda, 2014). Before the invention of the price tag in 1861, every customer bargained with an individual clerk.

However, the price tag also established a reference price for the "original" cost. A discount only has meaning if there is a reference price to begin with. An easy way to offer a dramatic discount is to inflate the initial reference price in order to create what Ellen Shell (2009) calls "full prices dressed up in discount drag" (p. 100).

Discounts encourage customers to stock up on merchandise, and that is exactly how a merchandiser wants you to behave. Even if it shrinks their profit margin for each item, Wansink et al. (1998) explain that stocking up on a product benefits the retailer by

Buying in bulk amounts might be cheaper—but how much of any product do you really need?

- preventing discretionary purchases from another store or manufacturer,
- generating an immediate increase in revenue,
- creating a product habit,
- encouraging consumers to switch stores or brands,
- reducing the holding costs and risks to inventory,
- encouraging accelerated consumption, and
- promoting new uses of the product.

Reference Points and Selling Soup. Let's discuss soup—and how to sell it.

Wansink et al. (1998) rotated three different signs with different reference points. Shoppers bought the most soup when the reference point in the sign suggested, "Limit of 12." They bought fewer cans of soup with "Limit of 4," and even fewer when no specific number was suggested. In the "Limit of 4" condition, no one bought *more* than four cans of soup. In the "No limit" condition (which you probably recognize as the *control condition*), only about 25% of the shoppers bought four or more cans of soup.

But the marketing bonanza was in the "Limit of 12" condition: Nobody purchased *only* one or two cans of soup—and about 7% of the shoppers purchased the so-called limit of 12 cans of soup. You might recognize that the anchoring and adjustment heuristic (see Chapter 4) predicts this shopping pattern.

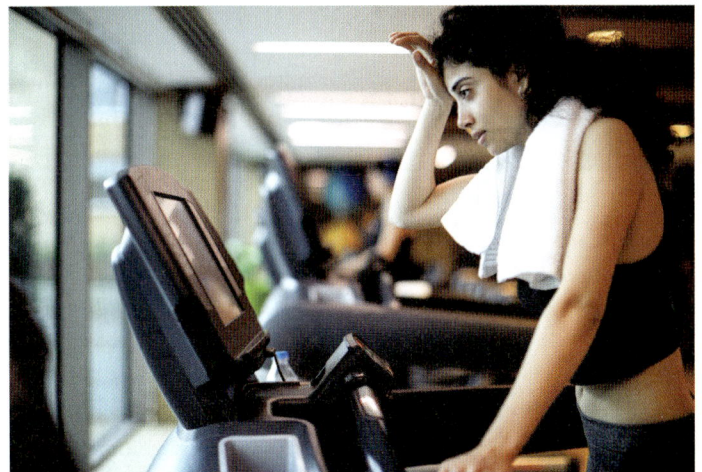

Sometimes happiness operates like a treadmill. Despite time and ground passing under our feet, we never seem to go anywhere—our happiness stays in the same place.

Human Happiness Requires Reference Points

Many of our life decisions are based on automatic reference points.

For example, when we see a sign declaring "70% OFF!" our automatic brain may light up and tell us to buy-buy-buy before the discount disappears. But economists and psychologists also are interested in the deeper question that you probably also ask yourself: Does all that buying make us happy?

Affective Forecasting: Getting off the Hedonic Treadmill. This is only a thought experiment; it didn't really happen.

Remember this story from Chapter 5: Imagine a mischievous grandchild quietly spreading some stinky cheese on a snoring grandparent's mustache. The grandparent wakes up and says, "This room stinks." He leaves the room and declares, "This whole house stinks." Finally, he walks outside and tells everyone, "The whole world stinks!"

The problem in this little story is that the grandfather didn't realize that his point of reference never shifted; it was right under his nose the entire time. Psychology research shows that, perhaps surprisingly, most of us are fairly bad at shifting our perceptions to reflect our current circumstances. This is sometimes called the hedonic treadmill. It's a metaphor that describes how people's happiness, despite a changing reference point, somehow remains approximately the same. (We keep running, but we don't move.)

The hedonic treadmill offers one common answer to the question of whether more money buys us happiness—and the answer is that it doesn't. Our level of happiness can *temporarily* shift because of changes in our financial situation, but they will eventually go back to where they started. In short, happy people are probably going to stay happy (and sad people are probably going to stay sad). The correlations between financial wealth, owning a lot of stuff, and happiness are surprisingly low (Csikszentmihalyi, 1999).

That said, some negative life events can push us right off the hedonic treadmill: Widowhood, being an accident victim, and unemployment (Diener et al., 2009) are some examples. People who experience these traumas are able to adapt to these dramatic, new changes in their reference point but not always completely (Diener & Oishi, 2005). Others have argued that it's possible to step off the hedonic treadmill completely (e.g., Mochon et al., 2008). But perhaps the relevant point here is that there may be wisdom to the old saying, "Happiness isn't getting what you want—it's wanting what you already have."

THE MAIN IDEAS

- Subjective ownership is the experience of feeling like we own something before we actually do, which can lead to irrational decisions (such as auction fever, or paying too much for something).
- Mental accounting is how we psychologically manipulate money and its uses. For example, we sometimes forget that money is fungible, or equally used for any purchase, if we feel that we've "saved" it for a special reason.
- Reference points are mental starting points we use for comparisons. This can affect our buying behavior (e.g., if a price tag shows a "discount" that has been created to manipulate us).

CRITICAL THINKING CHALLENGE

- Imagine you are the owner of a clothing store. Explain how you would use two of the ideas from this mini-chapter to get your customers to buy more items in your store.

- Now that you know about the hedonic treadmill, are you more or less motivated to achieve your long-term goals? Do you think that achieving them will really change your overall happiness in any real, tangible way? On the other hand, will finally owning that product you've been coveting change your level of happiness? Identify an example and discuss.

H. Social Psychology and Relationship Violence

Core Questions

H.1 What does relationship violence look like?

H.2 How can survivors heal and move forward?

Learning Objectives

H.1 Describe forms of relationship violence, then analyze types of abusers and the psychology of victims.

H.2 Outline factors that help survivors escape, explain narrative therapy, and describe the process of posttraumatic growth.

Relationship violence may be the greatest contradiction in human psychology. Intimate, committed relationship partners can be—and often are—loving, supportive, and a source of joy. So, something has gone terribly wrong when relationships turn abusive—and it happens more often than you might imagine.

About 1 in 4 women and 1 in 10 men in the United States have been the victim of sexual violence, stalking, and/or physical abuse by an intimate partner (CDC, 2019b). Of these people, 11 million women and 5 million men report that the violence occurred before they were 18 years old. And relationship violence doesn't have to be just physical; over 40 million women and almost 40 million men report that their partners have been psychologically or emotionally abusive (CDC, 2019b). In fact, some research shows that psychological abuse can be even more harmful (Follingstad et al., 1990).

The topic of relationship violence is a harsh, depressing one. But it is a problem that doesn't seem to be going away, and ignoring it doesn't help anyone. Fortunately, social psychologists have been a source of information, understanding, and activism regarding relationship violence.

WHAT DOES RELATIONSHIP VIOLENCE LOOK LIKE?

>> **LO H.1:** **Describe forms of relationship violence, then analyze types of abusers and the psychology of victims.**

This research story begins with an argument over terminology.

What do we call people who have endured these crimes? Some argue that the word *victim* should never be used because it connotes "helplessness and pity" (Helloflo.com, 2017; Kirkwood, 1993). Many people with this perspective believe that the term *survivor* should be used to refer to all targets of violence because *survivor* implies someone with the strength to get past the violence—a more empowering idea. For the purpose of this chapter, both terms will be used from a pragmatic view. *Victim* will be used when referring to someone who is still experiencing a violent relationship, while *survivor* will refer to someone who has successfully escaped the violence. It's not a perfect way to resolve the problem, but it gets us started.

Scholarly understanding of relationship violence is a relatively new endeavor, simply because for years, researchers thought it would be too hard to get a real, honest view of the problem. One challenge is social desirability (a term described first in Chapter 2), the idea that participants in studies aren't always honest or authentic if that would make them look bad. A second challenge is the very nature of relationship violence: It's an extremely personal, emotional issue. People might not be lining up to tell strangers all the intimate details on a questionnaire.

One of the first questions that researchers tried to answer was simply, "What does relationship violence look like?" In other words, how common is it? What kinds of people are abusers, and what are their specific actions? Is relationship violence usually physical, emotional, sexual—or all of the above? It turns out that we get a very different answer to these questions, depending on the methodology used.

Two Forms of Relationship Violence

In Chapter 2, we discussed two very different options for collecting data.

One option asked people to complete *self-report surveys*. A second option involved gathering information from *archival data* (sources of data originally created for another purpose). The definition and understanding of relationship violence also began as a highly charged controversy simply because different people chose each option—and these different sources each told a very different story (see Johnson, 1995, 2007).

Early attempts to study this phenomenon used *archival data* such as police reports, domestic violence shelter surveys, information from hospital emergency rooms, and divorce court records (Johnson, 2007). Patterns from these sources painted a certain picture of relationship abuse: (1) Women were almost always the victims of male perpetrators; (2) violence escalated over time, sometimes reaching deadly levels; (3) perpetrators often had other criminal behaviors, such as public intoxication or violence outside of the home; and (4) violence was physical, emotional, sexual, and psychological. This conclusion fit many people's stereotypes of "domestic abuse" or "wife battery."

But results from other sources, including *self-report surveys* and *interviews*, resulted in a very different view. The first large-scale, national, anonymous survey that collected data on relationship violence was the National Family Violence Survey (NFVS), which included responses from 2,143 people in 1975 and from 6,002 people in 1985 (NFVS, 1975, 1985; as cited in Johnson, 1995). The results were controversial for two reasons.

First, they claimed that relationship violence was much more common than previously thought; about 16% of participants said they had experienced abuse. That said, the severity didn't seem particularly high; people reported slapping and shoving but not much worse. A second controversy was that *both* men and women admitted to being perpetrators and victims of relationship violence. Claims that husbands were frequent victims of relationship violence were met with heated skepticism (see Dobash & Dobash, 1992). Both results violated stereotypes about relationship abuse. So, which version was true?

There's a surprise in the answer: both. In two groundbreaking articles that helped settle the debate about the picture of relationship violence, Johnson (1995, 2007) laid out a framework for two separate forms or types of violence. By acknowledging that both types of violence exist, both researchers and community members gain insight into how abuse can vary from one relationship to the next (Leone et al., 2007). Let's take a closer look at the two types.

Type 1: Intimate Terrorism

Most people have stereotypical images of domestic violence in their head.

The stereotypical "wife battery" form of relationship violence seen in police files, domestic violence shelters, and emergency rooms is what Johnson (1995, 2007) calls **intimate terrorism**. In his original article, Johnson called this form "patriarchal terrorism" because it is more common to be perpetrated by men against women instead of vice versa or in same-sex couples. Later he changed the name to intimate terrorism, partially to acknowledge that it is possible to have this phenomenon occur regardless of the sex or gender of the couple members involved.

Intimate terrorism includes severe forms of physical violence that may require police or medical intervention, but it also includes psychological, emotional, and sexual violence. Johnson notes that intimate terrorism often includes dynamics suggested in the "power and control wheel" first suggested by Pence and Paymar (1993), shown in Figure H.1. Thus, this type of relationship violence includes economic abuse (such as disallowing someone access to money), intimidation, threats, and more. A second version of the power and control wheel designed for college relationships can be seen in Figure H.2.

The violence in intimate terrorism typically escalates over time in terms of both frequency and severity, and victims often feel completely powerless. Leone and colleagues (2007) note that this form of relationship violence is more likely to appear in shelter and court records because it leads to dramatic outcomes that often require intervention—and that it's less likely to appear in *self-report surveys* because victims fear that honest answers will result in retaliation from their abuser.

Type 2: Situational Couple Violence

On the other hand, the survey responses are also *valid* representations of relationship violence; they show a very different type of experience.

Situational couple violence is defined by Johnson (1995, 2007) as occasions when couple members argue, but neither attempts to take general control and the incidents are relatively minor (although still unhealthy). Here, fights escalate out of everyday

Intimate terrorism: Relationship violence in which one couple member controls the other through severe physical violence as well as psychological, emotional, and sexual violence.

Situational couple violence: Relationship violence in which both couple members argue violently, but neither attempts to take general control and incidents are relatively minor, although still unhealthy.

FIGURE H.1

Power and control wheel.

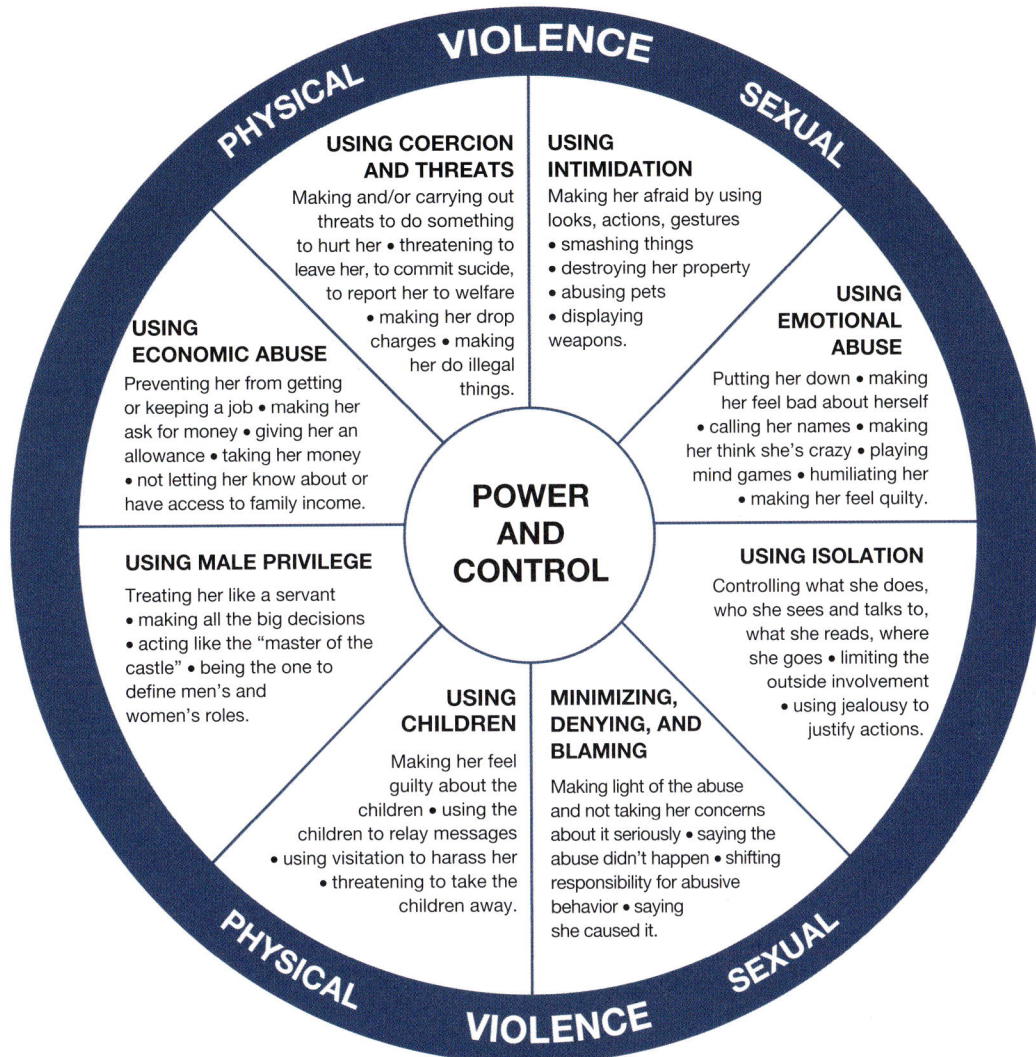

VIOLENCE

PHYSICAL · **SEXUAL**

USING COERCION AND THREATS
Making and/or carrying out threats to do something to hurt her • threatening to leave her, to commit sucide, to report her to welfare • making her drop charges • making her do illegal things.

USING INTIMIDATION
Making her afraid by using looks, actions, gestures • smashing things • destroying her property • abusing pets • displaying weapons.

USING ECONOMIC ABUSE
Preventing her from getting or keeping a job • making her ask for money • giving her an allowance • taking her money • not letting her know about or have access to family income.

USING EMOTIONAL ABUSE
Putting her down • making her feel bad about herself • calling her names • making her think she's crazy • playing mind games • humiliating her • making her feel guilty.

POWER AND CONTROL

USING MALE PRIVILEGE
Treating her like a servant • making all the big decisions • acting like the "master of the castle" • being the one to define men's and women's roles.

USING ISOLATION
Controlling what she does, who she sees and talks to, what she reads, where she goes • limiting the outside involvement • using jealousy to justify actions.

USING CHILDREN
Making her feel guilty about the children • using the children to relay messages • using visitation to harass her • threatening to take the children away.

MINIMIZING, DENYING, AND BLAMING
Making light of the abuse and not taking her concerns about it seriously • saying the abuse didn't happen • shifting responsibility for abusive behavior • saying she caused it.

PHYSICAL · **SEXUAL**

VIOLENCE

conflicts about specific situations, and *both* couple members reciprocate in perpetrating violence. However, situational couple violence usually does not include psychological or emotional abuse, and physical abuse is typically restricted to actions that do not lead to lasting injury. Johnson (2007) believes that this form of relationship violence is much more common than intimate terrorism.

In a study that directly compared couples experiencing each type of violence (Leone et al., 2007), results showed that compared to situational couple violence:

- Victims of intimate terrorism were older, in longer relationships, and less likely to be employed.

- Violence in intimate terrorism was significantly more severe (physically), more likely to increase in both frequency and severity over time, more likely to result in injury, and more likely to lead to depression and posttraumatic stress disorder symptoms in victims.

- Victims of intimate terrorism were twice as likely to call the police and four times as likely to seek medical help after a violent incident.

FIGURE H.2

College power and control.

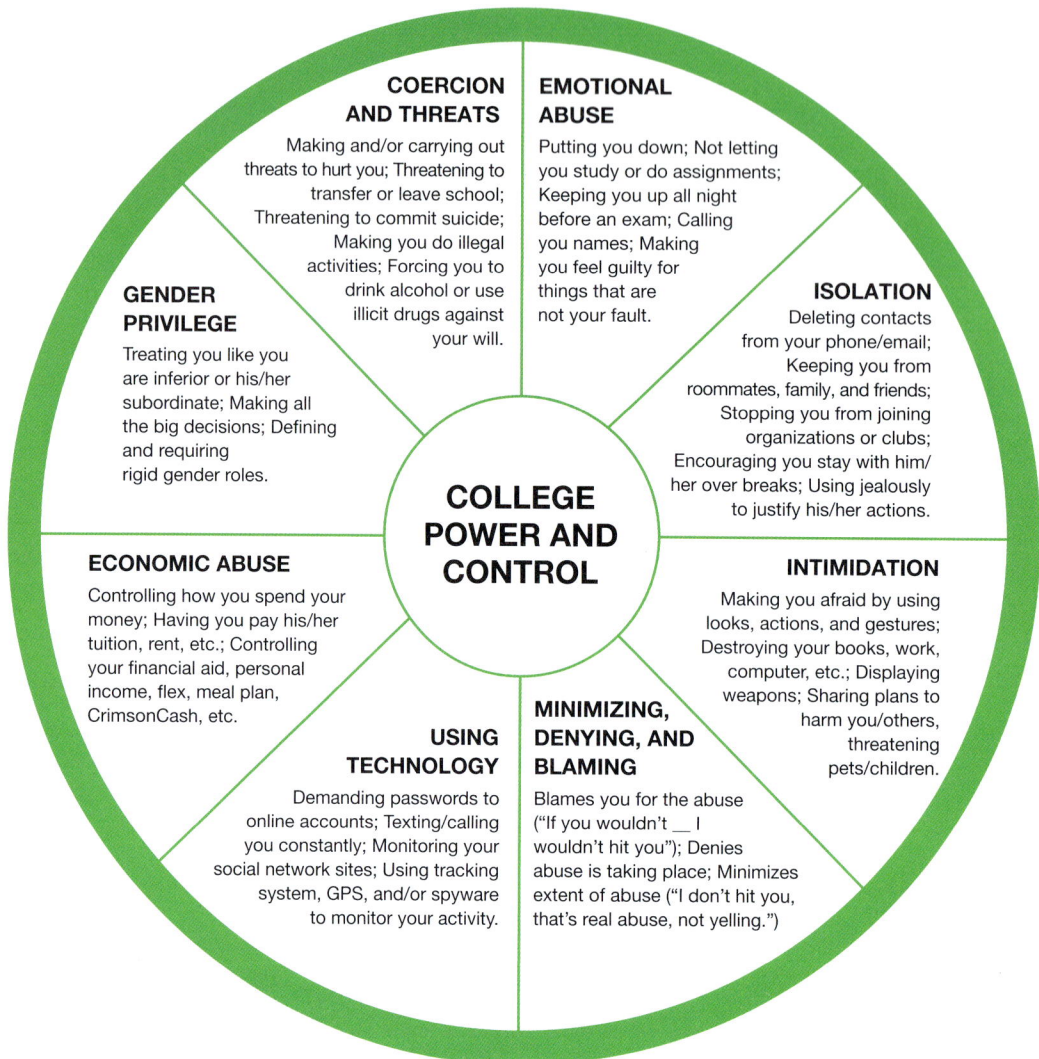

Insight Into Perpetrators

What kinds of people become perpetrators of relationship violence? There are hundreds of important studies that provide one piece of that puzzle. Let's cover just a few here.

The I³ Model

For example, the **I³ model** (pronounced "I-cubed") breaks down situational couple violence by offering cues for when it's more or less likely to occur (Finkel, 2008, 2014; Finkel et al., 2009; Finkel & Hall, 2018).

The I³ model says three factors predict violence: instigation, impellance, and inhibition. *Instigation* is the immediate aspects of a conflict that lead either or both couple members to become angry, frustrated, and aggressive. Examples are jealousy or when the other person "started it" with emotional or physical violence, and that violence is reciprocated. Instigation is the feeling that you've been provoked.

I³ model: An attempt to predict the likelihood of relationship violence based on aspects of the situation and couple members.

Impellance is parts of people's past or their personality that predispose them to violence. These might be growing up in a violent family or having a narcissistic personality. It could also be parts of the immediate situation that are external to the couple but still have an influence, such as heat or noise in the environment. It's background factors that influence the couple member's perceptions and reactions.

Finally, the third "I" in the I³ model is *inhibition,* or aspects of the conflict that actually *decrease* aggressive urges. Inhibiting influences might be cultural norms against violence, self-discipline or self-control and being happy and satisfied in the relationship in general. While the first two Is (instigation and impellance) are positively correlated with violence, the third one (inhibition) is negatively correlated with violence.

In summary, violence is more likely to result from conflict when instigating triggers and impelling influences are strong, but it's less likely to occur if inhibiting influences are also strong. The I³ model is one way to recognize that the forces at work on any given couple are simply complicated. This model has been supported in several studies, including those that specifically find that relationship violence is most likely to happen when the perpetrator feels they have just been provoked (instigation), have a highly aggressive personality (impellance), and have a low ability to control their impulses (a lack of inhibition; Chester & DeWall, 2018; Finkel, 2014; Finkel et al., 2012). Actions are influenced by personality, culture, people's childhood, and much more—so any aspect of intimate relationships, especially one like intimate aggression, is going to take a lot of attention to understand and ameliorate.

Pit Bulls and Cobras

In Chapter 11 (Aggression), you read about another insight.

The Spotlight on Research Methods described research on the surprising relationship between physiological arousal and perpetrators of relationship violence. Recall that researchers Jacobson and Gottman (1998) recruited abusive couples and brought them into the lab. Once there, the couple got into an argument while the men's physiological arousal was measured through heart rate monitors and galvanic skin response (sweaty palms). (Note that all of the couples studied in their lab were heterosexual with a male perpetrator and female victim.)

Results showed that for 80% of the men, arousal and conflict were positively correlated. As the argument escalated, their arousal increased. That was what they were expecting. Jacobson and Gottman call these men **pit bulls**, because their increasing anger and aggression were obvious. They would yell, their faces would become red, and their posture leaned forward and clearly expressed anger. The surprise, however, was that about 20% of men showed the *opposite* pattern. For these abusers, as conflicts with their wives or girlfriends progressed, their physiological responses got calmer and more peaceful.

Here's something else that might be a surprise: The calmer, lower-heart-rate men were the *most* abusive. Jacobson and Gottman labeled these men **cobras**, because they sit back calmly, waiting to strike. Their calm demeanor masked more extreme violent tendencies, a pattern also found in psychopaths and people with antisocial personality disorder (Holtzworth-Munroe & Meehan, 2004; Holtzworth-Munroe et al., 2000; Holtzworth-Munroe & Stuart, 1994). Cobra men also showed more consistent psychological and emotional manipulation, compared to pit bulls. Wives of "cobras" were less successful in leaving their abusive partners. Perhaps they understood how scary their partners could become and just how dangerous their situations were.

Insight Into Victims

"Why don't they just leave?" is an unfortunate question and a classic example of victim blaming (see Barnett et al., 1997; Cruz, 2003; Goetting, 1999; Jones, 2000).

Victims of relationship violence don't enjoy abuse and don't deserve to be treated disrespectfully. Being involved in violence is complicated, as we've already discussed,

Pit bulls: Perpetrators of relationship violence who get physiologically aroused (e.g., increased heart rate) as conflict increases.

Cobras: Perpetrators of relationship violence who get physiologically calm as conflict increases but are still extremely violent and manipulative.

Does the *Beauty and the Beast* fairytale encourage women to fall in love with men who treat them badly?

and the process of escape can take time. Researchers want to understand the psychological perspective of people while they are still victims—before they become survivors. This will increase other people's empathy and enable communities to provide practical help for the needs of each individual enduring relationship violence. Several lines of research have thus explored the perceptions of relationship violence victims. Here's a sampling of some interesting findings, although much more research exists on this topic.

The Cycle of Violence

Early research attempting to understand the psychology of people experiencing relationship violence produced a theory called the **cycle of violence** (Walker, 1979, 1984).

The cycle theoretically has three phases: (1) tension building, in which an abuser becomes increasingly upset; (2) explosion, in which abuse occurs; and (3) contrition, in which the abuser apologizes and makes promises to stop their behavior. Other researchers have supported the idea of a cycle in violent relationships (e.g., Dutton, 1998) and suggested that victims sincerely hope and believe their partner's promises in the contrition phase. It is only after going through the full cycle multiple times that some victims realize that their partner's behaviors probably will not change—at least not anytime soon. Even if physically violent behaviors decrease in older adulthood (e.g., after retirement), emotional and psychological abuse will likely remain.

Romantic Myths

Are Disney fairytales bad for us?

Rosen (1996) *interviewed* 22 women who had experienced (or were still experiencing) violence to see how they were initially attracted to and pulled into violent relationships, what she calls "processes of seduction." In her interviews, several of the women discussed **romantic myths**, or cultural messages regarding what romance is "supposed" to look like in traditional gendered ideas or social roles. Other research has defined romantic myths as "forms of popular culture [that] provide young girls with 'texts of meaning' of femininity and heterosexuality" regarding what to expect in relationships (Jackson, 2001, p. 306; see Davies, 1989; Jackson, 1993).

Rosen identified two specific romantic myths that encouraged "seduction" in violent relationships. The first is what she calls the **Cinderella fantasy**; this is the idea that a man who is a relative stranger can enter a woman's life and transform it by removing fears and saving her from problems (Rosen, 1996). Rosen points out that this myth encourages patriarchal power dynamics in which "Prince Charming" controls his wife's life and she is defined by him. The second romantic myth identified by Rosen is the **Beauty and the Beast fantasy**, in which women are told that patient, self-sacrificing love can turn a "beast" who is troubled and violent into a loving and sensitive partner. Unfortunately, Rosen notes that too often, beasts remain beasts.

Cognitive Dissonance and Minimization

Earlier in this book (see Chapter 6), we introduced the theory of cognitive dissonance.

Cognitive dissonance is the idea that it makes us anxious or uncomfortable to maintain two conflicting beliefs or to behave in a way that conflicts with our values or self-concept. Victims of relationship violence mostly likely do not believe that abuse in relationships is acceptable. Simultaneously, however, they may not be able to leave at a certain time due to financial dependency, fear, a motivation to protect children, and so on. This may cause dissonance.

Some research suggests that one way current victims can decrease dissonance is to perceive the abusive behaviors as non-abusive. In other words, victims may minimize

Cycle of violence: States that relationship violence occurs in three cyclic phases: (1) tension building, (2) explosion, and (3) contrition.

Romantic myths: Cultural messages regarding what romance is supposed to look like that support traditional gendered ideas and can encourage seduction into violent relationships.

Cinderella fantasy: A romantic myth in which a man who is a relative stranger enters a woman's life and transforms it by saving her from problems (see *romantic myths*).

Beauty and the Beast fantasy: A romantic myth in which women are told that patient, self-sacrificing love can turn a violent "beast" into a loving and sensitive partner (see *romantic myths*).

their partner's behaviors by denying it occurred, downplaying the significance or severity of what occurred, or providing some kind of justification for the behaviors. Dunham and Senn (2000) found that women who experienced relationship violence often omit information about it when discussing their relationship with others—and that omission occurred more as the severity of abuse increased (a *positive correlation*).

One intriguing study found that victims might acknowledge the specific behaviors that occurred but interpret them in ways that avoid labeling them as "abusive" or "violent." Arriaga (2002) discovered that when victims were given the opportunity to say that a partner's physically violent actions were "just a joke," many of them agreed with this interpretation—even when the behaviors were as severe as being kicked, beat up, or struck with a weapon.

Follow-up research that *interviewed* women at a domestic violence shelter asked women to recall a particularly violent incident, then explain why it happened (Goodfriend et al., 2017). When the women were still highly committed to their partners and planned to return to the relationship, cognitive dissonance would prevent them from blaming their abuser. Instead, the women blamed themselves, claimed their partner had an uncontrollable problem such as alcoholism, or said that violence was so common that leaving would be pointless.

Faulty Affective Forecasting

A fourth explanation to understand some victim's hesitancy to immediately leave a violent relationship is a lack of accurate **affective forecasting**.

Affective forecasting (sometimes called **hedonic forecasting**; see Figure H.3) is when someone tries to predict how they will feel in the future—and several studies have shown that we are not particularly good at it (Buehler & McFarland, 2001; Gilbert et al., 1998; Hoerger et al., 2010). This appears to be true of victims of relationship violence as well.

Arriaga and her colleagues (2013) conducted a *longitudinal study* in which they first asked victims to predict how happy they would be if their relationship ended. Several months later, about one fourth of the relationships had ended. Once the relationship (and abuse) was over, people who were now survivors were significantly happier than they had predicted they would be. The study concluded that "expecting doom without

Affective forecasting: When someone tries to predict how they'll feel in the future; most of us aren't able to do so effectively.

Hedonic forecasting: see *affective forecasting*.

FIGURE H.3

Research on "affective forecasting" finds that people are not very good at predicting their own future emotions.

a partner functions to maintain a relationship, even when life without an aggressive partner turns out to be better than expected" (p. 681).

Understanding Male Victims

Most researchers of relationship violence agree that the type of violence described as intimate terrorism is more likely to be perpetrated by men toward women than in any other form.

Some articles don't even acknowledge the possibility of male victims, or they quickly discount violence against men as being minimally important or harmful (Campbell, 2002; Johnson, 2007; Kilpatrick, 2004; Klein et al., 1997). However, consider again the sources of information about intimate terrorism: police records, hospitals, and domestic violence shelters. For all three sources, male victims are significantly less likely to seek help after being victimized by a relationship partner, due in part to social stigmatization (Arnocky & Vaillancourt, 2014).

A study focusing on this problem (Arnocky & Vaillancourt, 2014) asked participants to complete a social stigma scale regarding stereotypes and victim blaming within relationship violence scenarios (see Table H.1 for the items used). Participants were randomly assigned to answer the questions in terms of either male or female victims (so sex of the victim was the independent variable). Average scores on the stigma scale were the dependent variable.

TABLE H.1

Partner Violence Stigma Scale

Men/women who are abused by their romantic partners should be ashamed of themselves.
Men/women who are abused by their romantic partners are weak.
Men/women who stay with abusive partners deserve what they get.
Men/women who are abused by their romantic partners probably cannot attract anyone better.
Men/women who are abused by their romantic partners are not men/women I want to be friends with.
Many men/women who say they are abused by their romantic partners are probably lying or exaggerating.
When a woman/man hits her/his partner, it is most likely self-defense.
When a woman/man hits her/his partner, it was most likely provoked.

Participants responded to each item on a 1–7 scale, with 1 indicating "I strongly disagree" and 7 indicating "I strongly agree."

Source: Arnocky and Vaillancourt (2014).

Results showed that male victims were judged significantly more negatively than female victims—and this was true even for participants who had experienced relationship violence themselves. In addition, follow-up surveys revealed that male participants said they were much less likely to seek help or to admit to violence if it happened to them.

Despite the stereotypes and stigmas, we know that men do suffer as victims of relationship violence. According to the National Intimate Partner and Sexual Violence Survey (2010), severe physical violence by an intimate partner was experienced by about 22% of women and 14% of men. Other studies estimate the rates of male victims of relationship violence to be even higher, around 23% (e.g., Coker et al., 2000). Abuse toward male partners can begin early, with 10% of male college students reporting that their partners are violent or extremely controlling of them (Association of American Universities, 2019). *Both* men and women have multiple negative outcomes of such violence, including poor mental and physical health, substance abuse, and long-term injury or scars (Coker et al., 2002; Coker et al., 2005).

Stigmatization and lack of understanding are compounded when a man is a victim of violence within a gay relationship and thus might already be struggling with stereotyping, harassment, and discrimination (West, 1998). Gay victims may also fear that reporting violence will further enforce negative views of gay couples from outsiders as unhealthy or dysfunctional (Elliot, 1996; Hart, 1986). Still, violence in same-sex couples is prevalent; one classic study reported the highest rates of violence within lesbian couples (48%), then gay male couples (38%), then heterosexual couples (28%; Straus, 1979).

Interviews with 25 gay men who had been in violent relationships (Cruz, 2003) found that the top three reasons men reported temporarily staying in the relationship (after it had become violent) were (1) financial dependence on their partner, (2) inexperience with same-sex couple dynamics, and (3) feelings of love despite the violence. Another study focused on forms of abuse within same-sex couples that do not appear in heterosexual couples (West, 1998), such as "homophobic control," or threatening to "out" a partner without their consent. Like all topics regarding gay, lesbian, transgender, and queer individuals, more research attention is needed—and more research acknowledging male victims in general (including within heterosexual relationships) is warranted as well.

MAIN IDEAS

- Two forms of relationship violence are (1) intimate terrorism, in which one person manipulates and controls the other through physical, sexual, and psychological violence and (2) situational couple violence, in which both couple members argue violently.

- Two ways to categorize and predict perpetration of relationship violence are summarized. The first, the I³ model, suggests that instigation, impellance, and inhibition predict whether violence will occur. The second model distinguishes between "pit bulls," whose physiological arousal is positively correlated with conflict, and "cobras," who show the opposite pattern but are still violent.

- Several studies trying to understand the psychology of victims have explored the cycle of violence, the influence of romantic myths, cognitive dissonance, and faulty affective forecasting. Finally, male victims should not be forgotten or further stigmatized by the larger culture.

CRITICAL THINKING

- Consider the forms of psychological abuse shown in the two power and control wheels shown in Figures H.1 and H.2. Which two forms of abuse do you think are the most damaging to a typical victim and why?

- If romantic myths contribute to the perpetuation of violence, how can children—both boys and girls—be taught to appreciate these fairytales for their positive aspects but warned against learning the types of lessons that may lead to acceptance of relationship violence?

HOW CAN SURVIVORS HEAL AND MOVE FORWARD?

>> **LO H.2:** Outline factors that help survivors escape, explain narrative therapy, and describe the process of posttraumatic growth.

Ideally, researchers would be able to understand relationship violence enough to prevent it from happening in the first place.

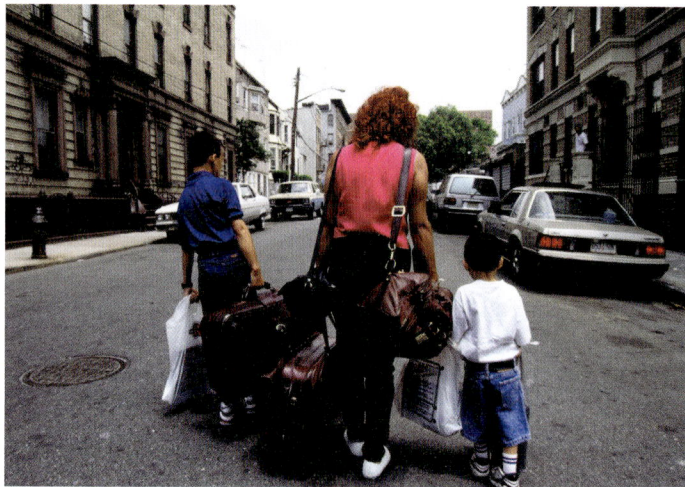

Viviane Moos/Corbis Historical/Getty Images

When people working on this problem consider prevention efforts, they are typically broken up into three types of intervention (Cathey & Goodfriend, 2012). **Primary prevention** reaches people to stop violence before it begins on an individual level; again, this is the ideal. Primary prevention occurs through education and empowerment; for example, a program might teach middle schoolers what potential warning signs of violence might be within their own relationships. However, the reality of the current world is that millions of people experience relationship violence every day. Thus, two additional types of intervention are also needed.

Secondary prevention intervenes after relationship violence has begun and provides victims with resources and knowledge to prevent it from happening again. Finally, **tertiary prevention** involves educating the larger community, such as a college or university campus or a given town, regarding dynamics of relationship violence to increase empathy and understanding (Cathey & Goodfriend, 2012). Most research on response to relationship violence occurs at the secondary level. How can victims escape and become survivors instead?

Escape: From Victims to Survivors

How do people get out?

In her book *Leaving Abusive Partners*, Kirkwood (1993) *interviewed* a diverse group of 30 women who had successfully escaped violent relationships. These survivors noted that there were several obstacles that each needed to be overcome in order for them to successfully escape; these included the following:

- Finding housing and economic resources
- Obtaining medical aid for both short-term and long-term needs
- Obtaining safety and protection from their ex-partners
- Dealing with a dramatic change of circumstances

Another study interviewed 22 survivors (Rosen & Stith, 1997) and identified the "disentanglement process" (p. 174) many of them went through to get out of the relationship. In this study, there were five distinct steps the victims took in order to leave:

- *Step 1: Seeds of Doubt.* Victims were no longer able to deny or minimize what was happening to them to the same level as before. They started to acknowledge what was happening to them and that it wasn't okay.

- *Step 2: Turning Points.* This was a small cognitive or psychological shift in how they interpreted behaviors from their partner.

- *Step 3: Objective Reappraisals.* This step involved seeing what was happening from a more objective view. Here, victims reevaluated themselves and their partners and realized that (1) they were in real danger, (2) their partners did not truly love them, (3) the violence was not going to stop, and/or (4) they had options to escape.

- *Step 4: Self-Reclaiming Actions.* Next, victims sought counseling or built up a supportive network of friends.

- *Step 5: Last Straw Events.* Finally, an event occurred that was so bad or severe, the victims took the steps to leave permanently.

Primary prevention: Prevention of relationship violence before it begins through education and empowerment.

Secondary prevention: Interventions that occur after relationship violence has begun, to stop it from happening again.

Tertiary prevention: Educating the larger community regarding dynamics of relationship violence to increase empathy and understanding.

Treatment: Healing and Moving Forward

Once victims become survivors, it still can be difficult to psychologically move forward.

Some survivors—especially those subjected to severe intimate terrorism—have both physical and emotional scars. Treatment programs for survivors vary widely, and there are many approaches to helping people deal with trauma. In fact, jobs in what is now known as **trauma psychology** are growing; this field helps people recover from any severely stressful event that impairs long-term psychological functioning (see, e.g., the description on psychologyschoolguide.net, which also lists schools that offer relevant master's degree programs).

Consider two examples of research on how survivors can find closure and heal.

Narrative Therapy

Healing from the trauma of violence is important.

One option for individuals who want to heal from the trauma of relationship violence is called **narrative therapy**, which is the process of writing down autobiographical events in a therapeutic setting (Cathey & Goodfriend, 2012). Traditionally, the narratives are chronological stories, like a typical autobiography, but they could also come in the form of poems, drawings, or anything else useful to the survivor.

A series of studies by Pennebaker (see Pennebaker, 1997, for a review) showed that when people who have survived a trauma write about it, there are both psychological and physical benefits. In a review of 13 studies on narrative therapy, Smyth (1998) found that people who wrote about traumas showed significant improvements in mental health, physical health, and general functioning (such as academic grades and work absenteeism). In a summary of the benefits of narrative therapy, Cathey and Goodfriend (2012) noted that it helps survivors feel closure, helps them process what happened in manageable pieces, and provides an avenue for self-expression.

In my [Wind's] book with colleague Pamela Cathey (Cathey & Goodfriend, 2012), we worked with 10 relationship violence survivors who wrote their stories in both individual and group therapy sessions over about a year. Those stories are published in the book and represent a wide variety of experiences, including childhood sexual trauma, college dating violence, and domestic violence. In addition, three of the stories are from male survivors. The book, titled *Voices of Hope*, has also been condensed into a 1-hour theatrical performance that can be performed as a fundraiser and educational intervention for communities or universities. The play is available free of charge and has already been performed at several universities around the country.

Posttraumatic Growth

Many victims of severe trauma experience posttraumatic stress disorder (PTSD; e.g., Street & Arias, 2001).

However, other research has attempted to discover whether survivors of trauma such as relationship violence can heal to the point of becoming even stronger than they were before the abusive relationship started (Tedeschi & Calhoun, 1996). In this way, survivors can feel that even though what they experienced was inexcusable, they have grown past it and the violence no longer defines who they are (see Table H.2).

One attempt to capture this empowering attitude is the development of a scale to measure **posttraumatic growth**, or feelings of positive psychological change and resilience as a result of trauma and adversity. The idea of posttraumatic growth is that after a trauma, individuals should not hope to return to the same level of self-esteem or empowerment they had beforehand; instead, they should strive to become even stronger. You can see some of the items from the scale developed by Tedeschi and Calhoun (1996, 2004) to measure posttraumatic growth.

Every year, thousands of people create new lives by moving from victim to survivor to personal growth (Boals & Schuler, 2017). For researchers, therapists, and individuals, social psychology might be able to help survivors escape from their violent

Trauma psychology: A field of psychology focused on helping people recover from any severely stressful event that impairs long-term psychological functioning.

Narrative therapy: The process of writing down autobiographical events in a therapeutic setting.

Posttraumatic growth: Feelings of positive psychological change and resilience as a result of trauma and adversity.

TABLE H.2

Selected Items From the Posttraumatic Growth Inventory

I changed my priorities about what is important in life.
I have a greater appreciation for the value of my own life.
I developed new interests.
I have a greater feeling of self-reliance.
I have a better understanding of spiritual matters.
I more clearly see that I can count on people in times of trouble.
I established a new path for my life.
I have a greater sense of closeness with others.
I am more willing to express my emotions.
I know better that I can handle difficulties.

Source: Adapted from Tedeschi and Calhoun (1996); full scale is 21 items.

relationships safely, heal from their physical and psychological wounds, and become empowered.

Perhaps because of the hopeful nature of posttraumatic growth, research on this topic has growth quickly in just two decades, with hundreds of studies now published. In one review of 16 studies (Elderton et al., 2017), the authors concluded that growth occurs in 71% of relationship violence survivors. One reason this growth might occur is because it leads survivors to question assumptions they previously held about themselves and the world (Valdez & Lilly, 2015). Posttraumatic growth is more likely when survivors have spiritual and social support for their new lives (Anderson et al., 2012), or when they have a role model of another survivor to show them the way through (Cobb et al., 2006).

Let's end this mini-chapter with a qualitative study that highlights the stories of survivors from their own voice (Taylor, 2004). Here, 21 survivors (they all happened to be African American, heterosexual women) were interviewed about their resiliency and recovery. The researcher found six themes; each is defined below and illustrated with a quotation from the article.

1. *Shattering silences:* revealing information about the relationship to others. "Black folks don't want to show their dirty laundry. . . . Keep the closet door closed because there's so much negative stuff about us in the press. I think that's hurtful. I think it keeps a problem under cover that should have the covers thrown off and be shown for what it is" (p. 39).

2. *Reclaiming the self:* defining the self as beyond the abuse. "I'm really clear on what I want out of a relationship. . . . Nothing you can say or do will make me believe that I deserve to be devalued, misused [or] treated like I'm nothing" (p. 40).

3. *Renewing the spirit:* nurturing the self and restoring well-being. "I have to do it the right way and God's way. It's a lot of praying involved. A lot of humbling myself. A lot of quiet time, meditation has to be there for me to have my serenity. I handle situations that I wasn't able to handle before. So that's basically spirituality for me" (p. 41).

4. *Self-healing through forgiveness:* forgiving the previous partner for the abuse. "I had to learn how to forgive him because I didn't want to walk through my

life with that kind of hate and never being able to move on through that. And I learned how to move on" (p. 41).

5. *Finding inspiration in the future:* being optimistic about the future. "I have to start looking towards the whole purpose in life and [my] ultimate goals. What is my purpose in life? To see something really change for the better. . . . My ultimate goal is to be a happy woman, respected, and a good role model for my daughter" (p. 42).

6. *Engaging in social activism:* participating in community service or positive parenting to promote societal change. "I gave my daughter the messages that, 'Don't do something because a man wants you to do it. Don't use that for reasoning,' and for my son it's like, 'Women are your equal. Treat them as your equal. Don't be disrespectful to them just because she's female.' So for me it helped with parenting. Don't allow a man to claim you as a piece of property because you are more than a piece of property. I talk to them about being independent, being able to earn their own money, being able to think for yourself, and not accepting someone who treats you with disrespect" (p. 43).

MAIN IDEAS

- Prevention of relationship violence can come in three levels: primary, which tries to stop violence before it begins; secondary, which attempts to prevent further violence after it starts; and tertiary, which involves educating the larger community.

- Research on escape from violent relationships shows that it occurs over several steps, such as cognitive reappraisals and self-empowerment actions.

- Research on healing from the trauma of relationship violence shows that healing can occur through interventions such as narrative therapy (writing one's story) and that this type of effort can eventually lead to posttraumatic growth.

CRITICAL THINKING QUESTIONS

- Some people will be able to heal from the trauma of relationship violence more quickly or more effectively than others. Identify two variables that you think might be associated with an individual's ability to experience posttraumatic growth, then explain how you might scientifically test your hypothesis. What would be the procedure of your study? How would you operationalize your variables? What statistical tests would you need to use to analyze your data?

- Most schools engage in prevention and education programs focused on relationship violence. Identity three programs, offices, staff, faculty, training opportunities, talks, performances, or anything else your college or university offers regarding education and prevention of relationship violence, then explain where each of these three people, programs, or offices fall on the framework of primary, secondary, and tertiary prevention.

REFERENCES

Abel, S. M., Krever, E. M., & Alberti, P. W. (1990). Auditory detection, discrimination and speech processing in ageing, noise-sensitive and hearing-impaired listeners. *Scandinavian Audiology, 19*(1), 43–54.

Abrams, M., & Bartlett, M. L. (2019). #SportToo: Implications of and best practice for the #MeToo movement in sport. *Journal of Clinical Sport Psychology, 13*(2), 243–258.

Ackerman, J. (2015). Persuasion by proxy: Vicarious self-control use increases decision compliance. In K. Diehl & C. Yoon (Eds.), *ACR North American advances* (pp. 68–73). Duluth, MN: Association for Consumer Research.

Adewakun, T. (2018). Hanging on to justice: Why the display of a hangman's noose in the workplace gives rise to a racially hostile work environment. *Rutgers Race & Law Review, 20*, 13–38.

Adhikary, A. K. (1984a). Hunters and gatherers in India: A preliminary appraisal of their structure and transformation. *Journal of the Indian Anthropological Society, 19*(1), 8–16.

Adhikary, A. K. (1984b). *Society and world view of the Birhor: A nomadic hunting and gathering community of Orissa.* Calcutta: Anthropological Survey of India.

Adler, A. (1930). Individual psychology. In C. Murchison (Ed.), *Psychologies of 1930* (pp. 395–405). Worcester, MA: Clark University Press.

Adorjan, M., Christensen, T., Kelly, B., & Pawluch, D. (2012). Stockholm syndrome as vernacular resource. *The Sociological Quarterly, 53*(3), 454–474.

Adorno, T. W., Frenkel-Brunswik, D. J., Levinson, D. J., & Sanford, R. N. (1950). *The authoritarian personality.* New York, NY: Harper & Row.

Aggarwal, P., & O'Brien, C. L. (2008). Social loafing on group projects: Structural antecedents and effect on student satisfaction. *Journal of Marketing Education, 30*(3), 255–264.

Aghababaei, N., Mohammadtabar, S., & Saffarinia, M. (2014). Dirty Dozen vs. the H factor: Comparison of the dark triad and honesty–humility in prosociality, religiosity, and happiness. *Personality and Individual Differences, 67*, 6–10.

Agnew, C. R., Loving. T. J., Le, B., & Goodfriend, W. (2004). Thinking close: Measuring relational closeness as perceived self-other inclusion. In D. Mashek & A. Aron (Eds.), *Handbook of closeness and intimacy* (pp. 103–115). Mahwah, NJ: Lawrence Erlbaum.

Agnew, C. R., Van Lange, P. M., Rusbult, C. E., & Langston, C. A. (1998). Cognitive interdependence: Commitment and the mental representation of close relationships. *Journal of Personality and Social Psychology, 74*(4), 939–954.

Agoramoorthy, G., & Hsu, M. J. (2012). The significance of cows in Indian society between sacredness and economy. *Anthropological Notebooks, 18*(3), 5–12.

Agrast, M. D., Bučar, B., Galič, A., Kerševan, E., Knez, R., Kraljić, S., . . . Tičar, L. (2013). *The world justice project rule of law index: 2012–2013.* Maribor, Slovenia: Univerza v Mariboru.

Agthe, M., Spörrle, M., & Maner, J. K. (2010). Don't hate me because I'm beautiful: Anti-attractiveness bias in organizational evaluation and decision making. *Journal of Experimental Social Psychology, 46*(6), 1151–1154.

Agthe, M., Spörrle, M., & Maner, J. K. (2011). Does being attractive always help? Positive and negative effects of attractiveness on social decision making. *Personality and Social Psychology Bulletin, 37*(8), 1042–1054.

Aguinis, H., Pierce, C. A., & Quigley, B. M. (1995). Enhancing the validity of self-reported alcohol and marijuana consumption using a bogus pipeline procedure: A meta-analytic review. *Basic and Applied Social Psychology, 16*(4), 515–527.

Ahonen, L., & Loeber, R. (2016). Dating violence in teenage girls: Parental emotion regulation and racial differences. *Criminal Behaviour and Mental Health, 26*(4), 240–250.

Ainsworth, M. S. (1979). Infant–mother attachment. *American Psychologist, 34*(10), 932–937.

Ajzen, I. (1991). The theory of planned behavior. *Organizational Behavior and Human Decision Processes, 50*(2), 179–211.

Ajzen, I., & Fishbein, M. (1980). *Understanding attitudes and predicting social behavior.* Upper Saddle River, NJ: Prentice Hall.

Akgunduz, Y., & Eryilmaz, G. (2018). Does turnover intention mediate the effects of job insecurity and co-worker support on social loafing? *International Journal of Hospitality Management, 68*, 41–49.

Aksu, H., Babun, L., Conti, M., Tolomei, G., & Uluagac, A. S. (2018). Advertising in the IoT era: Vision and challenges. *IEEE Communications Magazine, 56*(11), 138–144.

Akcaoglu, M., & Lee, E. (2016). Increasing social presence in online learning through small group discussions. *The International Review of Research in Open and Distributed Learning, 17*(3), [online].

Alain, C., McDonald, K. L., Ostroff, J. M., & Schneider, B. (2004). Aging: A switch from automatic to controlled processing of sounds? *Psychology and Aging, 19*(1), 125–133.

Albert, R. S., & Runco, M. A. (1999). A history of research on creativity. *Handbook of Creativity, 2*, 16–31.

Aldrich, D. P., & Meyer, M. A. (2015). Social capital and community resilience. *American Behavioral Scientist, 59*(2), 254–269.

Alexander, M. G., & Fisher, T. D. (2003). Truth and consequences: Using the bogus pipeline to examine sex differences in self-reported sexuality. *Journal of Sex Research, 40*(1), 27–35.

Alharthi, S., Levy, Y., Wang, L., & Hur, I. (2019, March 25). Employees' mobile cyberslacking and their commitment to the organization. *Journal of Computer Information Systems*, pp. 1–13.

Alicke, M. D., LoSchiavo, F. M., Zerbst, J., & Zhang, S. (1997). The person who out performs me is a genius: Maintaining perceived competence in upward social comparison. *Journal of Personality and Social Psychology, 73*(4), 781–789.

Al-khatib, B. A. (2012). The effect of using brainstorming strategy in developing creative problem solving skills among female students in Princess Alia University College. *American International Journal of Contemporary Research, 2*(10), 29–38.

Allee, W. C. (1938). *The social life of animals.* New York, NY: Norton.

Allee, W. C., Collias, N. E., & Lutherman, C. Z. (1939). Modification of the social order in flocks of hens by the injection of testosterone propionate. *Physiological Zoology, 12*(4), 412–440.

Allen, J. J., & Anderson, C. A. (2017). General aggression model. In P. Rossler (Ed.), *The International encyclopedia of media effects* (pp. 1–15). Hoboken, NJ: Wiley-Blackwell.

Allen, K. (2003). Are pets a healthy pleasure? The influence of pets on blood pressure. *Current Directions in Psychological Science, 12*(6), 236–239.

Allport, F. H. (1920). The influence of the group upon association and thought. *Journal of Experimental Psychology, 3*(3), 159–182.

Allport, G. W. (1935). Attitudes. In C. Murchison (Ed.), *Handbook of social psychology* (Vol. 2, pp. 798–844). Worcester, MA: Clark University Press.

Allport, G. W. (1937). *Personality: A psychological interpretation.* New York, NY: Holt.

Allport, G. W. (1954). *The nature of prejudice*. New York, NY: Addison.

Allport, G. W. (1966). Traits revisited. *American Psychologist*, *21*(1), 1–10.

Allport, G. W. (1979). *The nature of prejudice*. New York, NY: Basic Books.

Allport, G. W., & Ross, J. M. (1967). Personal religious orientation and prejudice. *Journal of Personality and Social Psychology*, *5*(4), 432–443.

Allport, G. W., & Vernon, P. E. (1933). *Studies in expressive movement*. New York, NY: Haffner.

Allred, K. D., & Smith, T. W. (1989). The hardy personality: Cognitive and physiological responses to evaluative threat. *Journal of Personality and Social Psychology*, *56*(2), 257–266.

Altemeyer, B. (1981). *Right-wing authoritarianism*. Winnipeg, Canada: University of Manitoba Press.

Altemeyer, B. (1990). Altemeyer replies. *Canadian Psychology*, *31*(4), 393–396.

Altemeyer, B. (1994). Reducing prejudice in right-wing authoritarians. In M. P. Zanna & J. M. Olson (Eds.), *The psychology of prejudice: The Ontario symposium* (Vol. 7, pp. 131–148). Hillsdale, NJ: Lawrence Erlbaum.

Altemeyer, B., & Hunsberger, B. (1992). Authoritarianism, religious fundamentalism, quest, and prejudice. *International Journal for the Psychology of Religion*, *2*, 113–333.

Altemeyer, B., & Hunsberger, B. (2004). A revised religious fundamentalism scale: The short and sweet of it. *International Journal for the Psychology of Religion*, *14*, 47–54.

Alter, A. L., Oppenheimer, D. M., Epley, N., & Eyre, R. N. (2007). Overcoming intuition: Metacognitive difficulty activates analytic reasoning. *Journal of Experimental Psychology*, *136*(4), 569–576.

Alter, A. L., Oppenheimer, D. M., & Zemla, J. C. (2010). Missing the trees for the forest: A construal level account of the illusion of explanatory depth. *Journal of Personality and Social Psychology*, *99*(3), 436–451.

Amato, P. R. (1983). Helping behavior in urban and rural environments: Field studies based on a taxonomic organization of helping episodes. *Journal of Personality and Social Psychology*, *45*(3), 571–586.

Ambady, N., Hallahan, M., & Conner, B. (1999). Accuracy of judgments of sexual orientation from thin slices of behavior. *Journal of Personality and Social Psychology*, *77*(3), 538–547.

Ambady, N., & Rosenthal, R. (1993). Half a minute: Predicting teacher evaluations from thin slices of nonverbal behavior and physical attractiveness. *Journal of Personality and Social Psychology*, *64*(3), 431–441.

American Cancer Society (2019). *Attitudes and cancer*. Retrieved March 27, 2020, from https://www.cancer.org/cancer/cancer-basics/attitudes-and-cancer.html

American Psychological Association. (2017). *Sport psychology*. http://www.apa.org/ed/graduate/specialize/sports.aspx

Amir, T. (1984). The Asch conformity effect: A study in Kuwait. *Social Behavior and Personality*, *12*(2), 187–190.

Amir, Y. (1976). The role of intergroup contact in change of prejudice and race relations. In P. A. Katz (Ed.), *Towards the elimination of racism* (pp. 245–280). New York, NY: Pergamon.

Anderson, C. A. (1987). Temperature and aggression: Effects on quarterly, yearly, and city rates of violent and nonviolent crime. *Journal of Personality and Social Psychology*, *52*(6), 1161–1173.

Anderson, C. A. (1989). Temperature and aggression: Ubiquitous effects of heat on occurrence of human violence. *Psychological Bulletin*, *106*(1), 74–96.

Anderson, C. A., & Bushman, B. J. (2002). Human aggression. *Annual Review of Psychology*, *53*, 27–51.

Anderson, C. A., & Bushman, B. J. (2018). Media violence and the general aggression model. *Journal of Social Issues*, *74*(2), 386–413.

Anderson, C. A., & Carnagey, N. L. (2004). Violent evil and the general aggression model. In A. G. Miller (Ed.), *The social psychology of good and evil* (pp. 168–192). New York, NY: Guilford Press.

Anderson, C. A., Shibuya, A., Ihori, N., Swing, E. L., Bushman, B. J., Sakamoto, A., Rothstein, H. R., & Saleem, M. (2010). Violent video game effects on aggression, empathy, and prosocial behavior in Eastern and Western countries: A meta-analytic review. *Psychological Bulletin*, *136*(2), 151–173.

Anderson, J. R. (1984). The development of self-recognition: A review. *Developmental Psychobiology*, *17*(1), 35–49.

Anderson, J. R., Myowa–Yamakoshi, M., & Matsuzawa, T. (2004). Contagious yawning in chimpanzees. *Proceedings of the Royal Society of London, Series B: Biological Sciences*, *271*, S468–S470.

Anderson, K. B., Cooper, H., & Okamura, L. (1997). Individual differences and attitudes toward rape: A meta-analytic review. *Personality and Social Psychology Bulletin*, *23*(3), 295–315.

Anderson, K. M., Renner, L. M., & Danis, F. S. (2012). Recovery: Resilience and growth in the aftermath of domestic violence. *Violence Against Women*, *18*(11), 1279–1299.

Anderson, S. M., Lepper, M. R., & Ross, L. (1980). Perseverance of social theories: The role of explanation in the persistence of discredited information. *Journal of Personality and Social Psychology*, *39*(6), 1037–1049.

Andrews, B., Brewin, C. R., Rose, S., & Kirk, M. (2000). Predicting PTSD symptoms in victims of violent crime: The role of shame, anger, and childhood abuse. *Journal of Abnormal Psychology*, *109*(1), 69–73.

Andrews, E. (2016, June 28). Stanford researchers develop new statistical test that shows racial profiling in police traffic stops. *Stanford News*. Retrieved December 23, 2019, from https://news.stanford.edu/2016/06/28/stanford-researchers-develop-new-statistical-test-shows-racial-profiling-police-traffic-stops/

Angell, J. R. (1909). The influence of Darwin on psychology. *Psychological Review*, *16*(3), 152–169.

Anggahegari, P., Yudoko, G., & Rudito, B. (2018). Female social entrepreneur movement in Indonesia. *International Journal of Entrepreneurship*, *22*(Suppl).

Antoniadou, N., Kokkinos, C. M., & Markos, A. (2019). Psychopathic traits and social anxiety in cyber-space: A context-dependent theoretical framework explaining online disinhibition. *Computers in Human Behavior*, *99*, 228–234.

Antonopoulos, I. (2019). *Climate induced displacement*. Springer Nature.

APA. (2019). What is hoarding disorder? *Psychiatry.org*. Retrieved December 15, 2019, from https://www.psychiatry.org/patients-families/hoarding-disorder/what-is-hoarding-disorder

APPA. (2019). *Americans are spending more on pets than ever before*. Retrieved February 1, 2020, from https://www.americanpetproducts.org/press_releasedetail.asp?id=191

Arad, A., Tolmach, M., & Ziskin, L. (Producers), & Webb, M. (Director). (2012). *The amazing Spider-Man* [Motion picture]. United States: Marvel Entertainment.

Archer, J. (2004). Sex differences in aggression in real-world settings: A meta-analytic review. *Review of General Psychology*, *8*(4), 291–322.

Archer, J. (2006). Cross-cultural differences in physical aggression between partners: A social-role analysis. *Personality and Social Psychology Review*, *10*(2), 133–153.

Archer, J., & Birring, S. S., & Wu, F. C. (1998). The association between testosterone and aggression among young men: Empirical findings and a meta-analysis. *Aggressive Behavior*, *24*(6), 411–420.

Ariely, D. (2008). *Predictably irrational: The hidden forces that shape our decisions*. New York, NY: HarperCollins.

Arluke, A., & Sax, B. (1992). Understanding Nazi animal protection and the Holocaust. *Anthrozoös*, *5*(1), 6–31.

Armstrong, K. (2000). *The battle for God: Fundamentalism in Judaism, Christianity, and Islam*. New York, NY: Knopf.

Arnocky, S., & Vaillancourt, T. (2014). Sex differences in response to victimization by an intimate partner: More stigmatization and less help-seeking among males. *Journal of Aggression, Maltreatment & Trauma, 23*(7), 705–724.

Arnold, D. L., Jackson, R. W., Waterfield, N. R., & Mansfield, J. W. (2007). Evolution of microbial virulence: The benefits of stress. *TRENDS in Genetics, 23*(6), 293–300.

Aron, A., Aron, E. N., & Norman, C. (2001). Self-expansion model of motivation and cognition in close relationships and beyond. In G. Fletcher & M. Clark (Eds.), *Blackwell handbook of social psychology: Interpersonal processes* (pp. 478–501). Hoboken, NJ: Blackwell.

Aron, A., Aron, E. N., & Smollan, D. (1992). Inclusion of Other in the Self Scale and the structure of interpersonal closeness. *Journal of Personality and Social Psychology, 63*(4), 596–612.

Aron, E. N., & Aron, A. (1996). Love and the expansion of the self: The state of the model. *Personal Relationships, 3*(1), 45–58.

Aronson, E. (1999). Dissonance, hypocrisy, and the self-concept. In E. Harmon-Jones & J. Mills (Eds.), *Cognitive dissonance: Progress on a pivotal theory in social psychology* (pp. 103–126). Washington, DC: American Psychological Association.

Aronson, E., Blaney, N., Stephan, C., Sikes, J., & Snapp, M. (1978). *The jigsaw classroom*. Beverly Hills, CA: Sage.

Aronson, E., & Mills, J. (1959). The effect of severity of initiation on liking for a group. *Journal of Abnormal and Social Psychology, 59*(2), 177–181.

Arora, M. (2017, May 22). From filthy to fabulous: Mumbai beach undergoes dramatic makeover. *CNN*. http://www.cnn.com/2017/05/22/asia/mumbai-beach-dramatic-makeover/index.html

Arriaga, X. B. (2002). Joking violence among highly committed individuals. *Journal of Interpersonal Violence, 17*(6), 591–610.

Arriaga, X. B., Capezza, N. M., Goodfriend, W., Rayl, E. S., & Sands, K. J. (2013). Individual well-being and relationship maintenance at odds: The unexpected perils of maintaining a relationship with an aggressive partner. *Social Psychological and Personality Science, 4*(6), 676–684.

Arthur, N., & Lee, C. (2008). Young Australian women's aspirations for work, marriage and family: 'I guess I am just another person who wants it all'. *Journal of Health Psychology, 13*(5), 589–596.

Aruah, D. E., Ezeh, V. O., & Tom, C. I. (2019). Relationship between pet ownership, pet attachment and decision to have children among single people in the United States: A need for flexible child care facilities in the United States. *Open Journal of Social Sciences, 7*(9), 15–30.

Asch, S. E. (1946). Forming impressions of personality. *Journal of Abnormal and Social Psychology, 41*(3), 258–290.

Asch, S. E. (1951). Effects of group pressure upon the modification and distortion of judgments. In H. Guetzkow (Ed.), *Groups, leadership and men: Research in human relations* (pp. 177–190). Oxford, UK: Carnegie Press.

Asch, S. E. (1952). Effects of group pressure on the modification and distortion of judgments. In G. E. Swanson, T. M. Newcomb, & E. L. Hartley (Eds.), *Readings in social psychology* (2nd ed.). New York, NY: Holt.

Asch, S. E. (1955). Opinions and social pressure. *Scientific American, 193*(5), 31–35.

Asch, S. E. (1956). Studies of independence and conformity: I. A minority of one against a unanimous majority. *Psychological Monographs: General and Applied, 70*(9, Whole No. 416), 1–70.

Ascher, W., & Brown, S. R. (2014). Technologies of mediation: An assessment of methods for the mediation of international conflicts. *Contributions of Technology to International Conflict Resolution, 1987*, 95–103.

Aspinwall, L. G., & Tedeschi, R. G. (2010). The value of positive psychology for health psychology: Progress and pitfalls in examining the relation of positive phenomena to health. *Annals of Behavioral Medicine, 39*(1), 4–15.

Association for Applied Sport Psychology. (2017). *Home*. http://www.appliedsportpsych.org/

Association of American Universities. (2019, October 15). *AAU campus climate survey*. https://www.aau.edu/key-issues/campus-climate-and-safety/aau-campus-climate-survey-2019

Attanasio, P., McGraw, P., McGraw, J., Falvey, J., Frank, D., Goffman, M., . . . Garcia, R. (Producers). (2016). *Bull* [Television series]. United States: CBS Television Distribution.

Atwood, M. (1986). *The handmaid's tale*. Boston, MA: Houghton Mifflin Harcourt.

Aubert, A. H., Bauer, R., & Lienert, J. (2018). A review of water-related serious games to specify use in environmental multi-criteria decision analysis. *Environmental Modelling & Software, 105*, 64–78.

AVMA. (2018). *US pet ownership statistics*. Retrieved December 9, 2019, from https://www.avma.org/resources-tools/reports-statistics/us-pet-ownership-statistics

Avnet, J., & Kerner, J. (Producers), & Herek, S. (Director). (1992). *The mighty ducks* [Motion picture]. USA: Walt Disney Pictures, Avent-Kerner Productions, The Kerner Entertainment Company, & Buena Vista Pictures.

Babad, E., Avni-Babad, D., & Rosenthal, R. (2004). Prediction of students' evaluations from brief instances of professors' nonverbal behavior in defined instructional situations. *Social Psychology of Education, 7*(1), 3–33.

Bachman, J. G., & O'Malley, P. M. (1986). Self-concepts, self-esteem, and educational experiences: The frog pond revisited (again). *Journal of Personality and Social Psychology, 50*(1), 35–46.

Bagley, C., van Huizen, A., & Young, L. (2019). 20 Multi-ethnic marriage and interculturalism in Britain and the Netherlands. In D. Woodrow, G. K. Verma, M. B. Rocha-Trindade, G. Compani, & C. Bagley (Eds.), *Intercultural education: Theories, policies and practices* (pp. 317–328). Surrey, UK: Ashgate.

Bakan, D. (1966). *The duality of human existence: An essay on psychology and religion*. Oxford, UK: Rand McNally.

Baker, P. (2018). 1 in 10: The diabetes crisis in men. *Trends in Urology & Men's Health, 9*(2), 25–28.

Baker, S. R. (2019). "No simple solutions, no single ingredient": Systems-orientated approaches for addressing Wicked Problems in population oral health. *Community Dental Health, 36*, 3–4.

Baker, Z. G., Petit, W. E., & Brown, C. M. (2016). An investigation of the Rusbult Investment Model of commitment in relationships with pets. *Anthrozoös, 29*(2), 193–204.

Bakhmutov, S., Saykin, A., Endachev, D., Evgrafov, V., Shagurin, A., Kulikov, I., & Fedoseev, K. (2018, February). Prospects of development of land driverless trucks. In *IOP Conference Series: Materials Science and Engineering* (Vol. *315*, No. 1, p. 012001). Bristol, UK: IOP Publishing.

Bandura, A. (1977). *Social learning theory*. Oxford, UK: Prentice-Hall.

Bandura, A. (1986). *Social foundations of thought and action: A social cognitive theory*. Englewood Cliffs, NY: Prentice-Hall.

Bandura, A., Ross, D., & Ross, S. A. (1961). Transmission of aggression through imitation of aggressive models. *Journal of Abnormal and Social Psychology, 63*(3), 575–582.

Bandura, A., Ross, D., & Ross, S. A. (1963a). Imitation of film-mediated aggressive models. *Journal of Abnormal and Social Psychology, 66*(1), 3–11.

Bandura, A., Ross, D., & Ross, S. A. (1963b). Vicarious reinforcement and imitative learning. *Journal of Abnormal and Social Psychology, 67*(6), 601–607.

Barbaranelli, C., Farnese, M. L., Tramontano, C., Fida, R., Ghezzi, V., Paciello, M., & Long, P. (2018). Machiavellian ways to academic cheating: A mediational and interactional model. *Frontiers in Psychology, 9*, 695.

Bargh, J. A. (1997). The automaticity of everyday life. In R. S. Wyer Jr. (Ed.), *Advances in social cognition* (Vol. *10*, pp. 1–61). Mahwah, NJ: Lawrence Erlbaum.

Bargh, J. A. (2018). It was social consistency that mattered all along. *Psychological Inquiry, 29*(2), 60–62.

Bargh, J. A., & Chartrand, T. L. (1999). The unbearable automaticity of being. *American Psychologist, 54*(7), 462–479.

Bargh, J. A., Chen, M., & Burrows, L. (1996). Automaticity of social behavior: Direct effect of trait construct and stereotype activation. *Journal of Personality and Social Psychology, 71*(2), 230–244.

Bargh, J. A., & McKenna, K. Y. A. (2004). The Internet and social life. *Annual Review of Psychology, 55*, 573–590.

Bargh, J. A., & Williams, E. L. (2006). The automaticity of social life. *Current Directions in Psychological Science, 15*(1), 1–4.

"Barkley is arrested after Orlando bar fight." (1997, October 27). *The Washington Post*. https://www.washingtonpost.com/archive/sports/1997/10/27/barkley-is-arrested-after-orlando-bar-fight/27787d5d-d345-4641-b019-f8e7952a75f8/?utm_term=.88be893efcce

Barlow, F. K. (2019). Nature vs. nurture is nonsense: On the necessity of an integrated genetic, social, developmental, and personality psychology. *Australian Journal of Psychology, 71*(1), 68–79.

Barlow, M. R., Hutchinson, C. A., Newton, K., Grover, T., & Ward, L. (2012). Childhood neglect, attachment to companion animals, and stuffed animals as attachment objects in women and men. *Anthrozoös, 25*(1), 111–119.

Barnes, C. D., Brown, R. P., & Osterman, L. L. (2012). Don't tread on me: Masculine honor ideology in the U.S. and militant responses to terrorism. *Personality and Social Psychology Bulletin, 38*(8), 1018–1029.

Barnett, J., & Coulson, M. (2010). Virtually real: A psychological perspective on massively multiplayer online games. *Review of General Psychology, 14*(2), 167–179.

Barnett, O. W., Miller-Perrin, C. L., & Perrin, R. D. (1997). *Family violence across the lifespan: An introduction*. Thousand Oaks, CA: Sage.

Baron, R. A. (1972). Aggression as a function of ambient temperature and prior anger arousal. *Journal of Personality and Social Psychology, 21*(2), 183–189.

Baroni, C., & Orombelli, G. (1996). The Alpine "Iceman" and Holocene climactic change. *Quaternary Research, 46*(1), 78–83.

Barr, J., Malbran, P., Berko, A., Lockett, A., & Kostura, J. (2012). Hazing trend involves horrifying violation of young athletes. *ESPN*. http://www.espn.com/espn/feature/story/_/id/17507010/otl-investigation-trend-sodomy-hazing

Barrett, D. W., Wosinska, W., Butner, J., Petrova, P., Gornik-Durose, M., & Cialdini, R. B. (2004). Individual differences in the motivation to comply across cultures: The impact of social obligation. *Personality and Individual Differences, 37*(1), 19–31.

Barsky, A. (2014). Response to article on 'Abused mothers' safety concerns and court mediators' custody recommendations. *Journal of Family Violence, 29*(4), 357–358.

Bartels, J. (2019). Revisiting the Stanford prison experiment, again: Examining demand characteristics in the guard orientation. *Journal of Social Psychology, 159*, 780–790.

Bartels, J. M., Milovich, M. M., & Moussier, S. (2016). Coverage of the Stanford prison experiment in introductory psychology courses: A survey of introductory psychology instructors. *Teaching of Psychology, 43*(2), 136–141.

Bartholomew, K., & Horowitz, L. M. (1991). Attachment styles among young adults: A test of a four-category model. *Journal of Personality and Social Psychology, 61*(2), 226–244.

Bartholow, B. D., & Heinz, A. (2006). Alcohol and aggression without consumption: Alcohol cues, aggressive thoughts, and hostile perception bias. *Psychological Science, 17*(1), 30–37.

Bartlett, F. C. (1932). *Remembering*. Cambridge, UK: Cambridge University Press.

Basner, M., Babisch, W., Davis, A., Brink, M., Clark, C., Janssen, S., & Stansfeld, S. (2014). Auditory and non-auditory effects of noise on health. *The Lancet, 383*(9925), 1325–1332.

Bass, B. M. (1998). *Transformational leadership: Industrial, military, and educational impact*. Mahwah, NJ: Lawrence Erlbaum.

Bassili, J. N. (2003). The minority slowness effect: Subtle inhibitions in the expression of views not shared by others. *Journal of Personality and Social Psychology, 84*(2), 261–276.

Basu, B. S., & Pooja, A. (2017). Cyberloafing: The disguised digital way of loafing on the job. *IUP Journal of Organizational Behavior, 6*(1), 19–37.

Batool, S., & Malik, N. I. (2010). Role of attitude similarity and proximity in interpersonal attraction among friends. *International Journal of Innovation, Management and Technology, 1*(2), 142–146.

Batson, C. D. (1987). Prosocial motivation: Is it ever truly altruistic? *Advances in Experimental Social Psychology, 20*, 65–122.

Batson, C. D. (1990). How social an animal? The human capacity for caring. *American Psychologist, 45*(3), 336–346.

Batson, C. D. (1991). *The altruism question: Toward a social-psychological answer*. Hillsdale, NJ: Lawrence Erlbaum.

Batson, C. D. (1998). Altruism and prosocial behavior. In D. T. Gilbert, S. T. Fiske, & G. Lindzey (Eds.), *The handbook of social psychology* (Vols. *1–2*, 4th ed., pp. 282–316). New York, NY: McGraw-Hill.

Batson, C. D. (2012). A history of prosocial behavior research. In A. W. Kruglanski & W. Stroebe (Eds.), *Handbook of the history of social psychology* (pp. 243–264). New York, NY: Psychology Press.

Batson, C. D., Bolen, M. H., Cross, J. A., & Neuringer-Benefiel, H. E. (1986). Where is the altruism in the altruistic personality? *Journal of Personality and Social Psychology, 50*(1), 212–220.

Batson, C. D., Duncan, B. D., Ackerman, P., Buckley, T., & Birch, K. (1981). Is empathic emotion a source of altruistic motivation? *Journal of Personality and Social Psychology, 40*(2), 290–302.

Batson, C. D., & Gray, R. A. (1981). Religious orientation and helping behavior: Responding to one's own or the victim's needs? *Journal of Personality and Social Psychology, 40*(3), 511–520.

Batson, C. D., Naifeh, S. J., & Pete, S. (1978). Social desirability, religious orientation, and racial prejudice. *Journal for the Scientific Study of Religion, 17*(1), 31–41.

Batson, C. D., Schoenrade, P., & Ventis, W. L. (1993). *Religion and the individual: A social-psychological perspective*. New York, NY: Oxford University Press.

Bauer, A., & Steurer, R. (2015). National adaptation strategies, what else? Comparing adaptation mainstreaming in German and Dutch water management. *Regional Environmental Change, 15*(2), 341–352.

Baumeister, R. F. (1998). The self. In D. T. Gilbert, S. T. Fiske, & G. Lindzey (Eds.), *Handbook of social psychology* (Vol. *2*, 4th ed., pp. 680–740). New York, NY: McGraw-Hill.

Baumeister, R. F., Campbell, J. D., Krueger, J. I., & Vohs, K. D. (2003). Does high self-esteem cause better performance, interpersonal success, happiness, or healthier lifestyles? *Psychological Science in the Public Interest, 4*(1), 1–44.

Baumeister, R. F., & Hutton, D. G. (1987) Self-presentation theory: Self-construction and audience pleasing. In B. Mullen & G. R. Goethals (Eds.), *Theories of group behavior* (pp. 71–87). New York, NY: Springer.

Baumeister, R. F., & Leary, M. R. (1995). The need to belong: Desire for interpersonal attachments as a fundamental human motivation. *Psychological Bulletin, 117*(3), 497–529.

Baumeister, R. F., Smart, L., & Boden, J. M. (1996). Relation of threatened egotism to violence and aggression: The dark side of high self-esteem. *Psychological Review*, *103*(1), 5–33.

Baumrind, D. (1964). Some thoughts on ethics of research: After reading Milgram's "behavioral study of obedience." *American Psychologist*, *19*(6), 421–423.

Baxter, L. A., & West, L. (2003). Couple perceptions of their similarities and differences: A dialectical perspective. *Journal of Social and Personal Relationships*, *20*(4), 491–514.

BBC News. (2008). Hindus opposing EU swastika ban. *BBC News*, International version. http://news.bbc.co.uk/2/hi/europe/6269627.stm

Beck, L., & Madresh, E. A. (2008). Romantic partners and four-legged friends: An extension of attachment theory to relationships with pets. *Anthrozoös*, *21*(1), 43–56.

Becker, E. (1973). *The denial of death*. New York, NY: Academic Press.

Beckerman, S., & Feitschans, B. (Producers), & Milius, J. (Director). (1984). *Red dawn* [Motion picture]. USA: United Artists, Valkyrie Films, & MGM/UA Entertainment Company.

Bedeian, A. G. (2016). A note on the aphorism "there is nothing as practical as a good theory." *Journal of Management History*, *22*(2), 236–242.

Begany, J. J., & Milburn, M. A. (2002). Psychological predictors of sexual harassment: Authoritarianism, hostile sexism, and rape myths. *Psychology of Men & Masculinity*, *3*(2), 119–126.

Begue, L. (2005). Self-esteem regulation in threatening social comparison: The roles of belief in a just world and self-efficacy. *Social Behavior and Personality*, *33*(1), 69–76.

Behrman, S., & Kent, A. (Eds.). (2018). *Climate refugees: Beyond the legal impasse?* New York, NY: Routledge.

Belavkin, R. V. (2001). The role of emotion in problem solving. In *Proceedings of the AISB'01: Symposium on emotion, cognition and affective computing* (pp. 49–57). Heslington, UK: AISB Press.

Bellotti, F., Kapralos, B., Lee, K., Moreno-Ger, P., & Berta, R. (2013). Assessment in and of serious games: An overview. *Advances in Human-Computer Interaction*, *2013*(2), 1–11.

Belo, J. (1935). The Balinese temper. *Journal of Personality*, *4*(2), 120–146.

Belz, M., Pyritz, L. W., & Boos, M. (2013). Spontaneous flocking in human groups. *Behavioural Processes*, *92*, 6–14.

Bem, D. J. (1967). Self-perception: An alternative interpretation of cognitive dissonance phenomena. *Psychological Review*, *74*(3), 183–200.

Bem, D. J., & McConnell, H. K. (1970). Testing the self-perception explanation of dissonance phenomena: On the salience of premanipulation attitudes. *Journal of Personality and Social Psychology*, *14*(1), 23–31.

Benartzi, S., & Thaler, R. H. (1995). Myopic loss aversion and the equity premium puzzle. *The Quarterly Journal of Economics*, *110*(1), 73–92.

Benjamin, A. J., Jr., Kepes, S., & Bushman, B. J. (2018). Effects of weapons on aggressive thoughts, angry feelings, hostile appraisals, and aggressive behavior: A meta-analytic review of the weapons effect literature. *Personality and Social Psychology Review*, *22*(4), 347–377.

Benjamin, L. T., & Crouse, E. M. (2002). The American Psychological Association's response to *Brown v. Board of Education:* The case of Kenneth B. Clark. *American Psychologist*, *57*(1), 38–50.

Bennett, J. C. (1991). The irrationality of the catharsis theory of aggression as justification for educators' support of interscholastic football. *Perceptual and Motor Skills*, *72*(2), 415–418.

Bennett, J. W. (1967). *Hutterian brethren: The agricultural economy and social organization of a communal people*. Stanford, CA: Stanford University Press.

Berge, E. E. (2019). *PTSD relapse in veterans of Iraq and Afghanistan: A systematic review* (Master's thesis). NTNU, Trondheim, Norway. http://hdl.handle.net/11250/2590060

Bergenstock, D. J., & Maskulka, J. M. (2001). The De Beers story: Are diamonds forever? *Business Horizons*, *44*(3), 37–44.

Bergmann, J. S., Renshaw, K. D., & Paige, L. (2019). Psychological well-being in Iraq and Afghanistan veterans: Risk and protective factors. *Psychological Trauma: Theory, Research, Practice, and Policy*, *11*(4), 434–441.

Berkes, F., & Jolly, D. (2002). Adapting to climate change: social-ecological resilience in a Canadian western Arctic community. *Conservation Ecology*, *5*(2), [online].

Berkowitz, L. T. (1989). Frustration-aggression hypothesis: Examination and reformulation. *Psychological Bulletin*, *106*(1), 59–73.

Berkowitz, L. T., Cochran, S. T., & Embree, M. C. (1981). Physical pain and the goal of aversively stimulated aggression. *Journal of Personality and Social Psychology*, *40*(4), 687–700.

Berkowitz, L. T., & LePage, A. (1967). Weapons as aggression-eliciting stimuli. *Journal of Personality and Social Psychology*, *7*(2), 202–207.

Bernstein, D. M., Erdfelder, E., Meltzoff, A. N., Peria, W., & Loftus, G. R. (2011). Hindsight bias from 3 to 95 years of age. *Journal of Experimental Psychology: Learning, Memory, and Cognition*, *37*(2), 378–391.

Bernstein, M. J., Sacco, D. F., Brown, C. M., Young, S. G., & Claypool, H. M. (2010). A preference for genuine smiles following social exclusion. *Journal of Experimental Social Psychology*, *46*(1), 196–199.

Berry, D. S., Jones, G. M., & Kuczaj, S. A. (2000). Differing states of mind: Regional affiliation, personality judgement, and self-view. *Basic and Applied Social Psychology*, *22*(1), 43–56.

Berry, J. W. (1967). Independence and conformity in subsistence-level societies. *Journal of Personality and Social Psychology*, *7*(4, Pt. 1), 415–418.

Berthon, P. R., & Pitt, L. F. (2019). Types of mindfulness in an age of digital distraction. *Business Horizons, 62*(2), 131–137.

Berscheid, E., & Regan, P. C. (2005). *The psychology of interpersonal relationships*. Upper Saddle River, NJ: Pearson Prentice Hall.

Bessenoff, G. R. (2006). Can the media affect us? Social comparison, self-discrepancy, and the thin ideal. *Psychology of Women Quarterly*, *30*(3), 239–251.

Betsch, C., Bohm, R., & Korn, L. (2013). Inviting free-riders or appealing to prosocial behavior? Game-theoretical reflections on communicating herd immunity in vaccine advocacy. *Health Psychology*, *32*(9), 978–985.

Bettelheim, B. (1943). Individual and mass behavior in extreme situations. *Journal of Abnormal and Social Psychology*, *38*(4), 417–452.

Bhatia, S., Carrion, M., Cohn, E., Cori, A., Nouvellet, P., Lassmann, B., . . . Brownstein, J. (2019). Big brother is watching: Using digital disease surveillance tools for near real-time forecasting. *International Journal of Infectious Diseases*. Advance online publication.

Bhattacharyya, A. (1953). An account of the Birhor of Palamau. *Bulletin of the Department of Anthropology (India)*, *2*, 1–16.

Bhogal, M. S., Bartlett, J. E., & Farrelly, D. (2019). The influence of mate choice motivation on non-financial altruism. *Current Psychology*, *38*(4), 959–964.

Bianchi, A., & Phillips, J. G. (2005). Psychological predictors of problem mobile phone use. *CyberPsychology & Behavior*, *8*(1), 39–51.

Bieri, F. (2013). *From blood diamonds to the Kimberley Process: How NGOs cleaned up the global diamond industry*. Burlington, VT: Ashgate.

Billig, M., & Tajfel, H. (1973). Social categorization and similarity in intergroup behavior. *European Journal of Social Psychology, 3*(1), 27–52.

Binder, J., Zagefka, H., Brown, R., Funke, F., Kessler, T., Mummendey, A., . . . Leyens, J. (2009). Does contact reduce prejudice or does prejudice reduce contact? A longitudinal test of the contact hypothesis among majority and minority groups in three European countries. *Journal of Personality and Social Psychology, 96*(4), 843–856.

The biology of beauty. (1996, June 2). http://www.newsweek.com/biology-beauty-178836

Bishop, M. (2017, December 6). *Visual lies: Usability in deceptive data visualizations.* http://ixd.prattsi.org/2017/12/visual-lies-usability-in-deceptive-data-visualizations/

Bissell, D., Birtchnell, T., Elliott, A., & Hsu, E. L. (2020). Autonomous automobilities: The social impacts of driverless vehicles. *Current Sociology, 68*(1), 116–134.

Bizumic, B., & Duckitt, J. (2018). Investigating right wing authoritarianism with a very short authoritarianism scale. *Journal of Social and Political Psychology, 6*(1), 129–150.

Björkqvist, K. (2018). Gender differences in aggression. *Current Opinion in Psychology, 19*, 39–42.

Blair, K. L. (2016, November 10). A "basket of deplorables"? *A new study finds that Trump supporters are more likely to be Islamaphobic, racist, transphobic and homophobic.* http://blogs.lse.ac.uk/usappblog/2016/10/10/a-basket-of-deplorables-a-new-study-finds-that-trump-supporters-are-more-likely-to-be-islamophobic-racist-transphobic-and-homophobic

Blanc, A. K. (2001). The effect of power in sexual relationships on sexual and reproductive health: An examination of the evidence. *Studies in Family Planning, 32*(3), 189–213.

Blanck, P. D., Rosenthal, R., Hart, A. J., & Bernieri, F. (1990). The measure of the judge: An empirically-based framework for exploring trial judges' behavior. *Iowa Law Review, 75*, 653–684.

Blaney, N. T., Stephan, C., Rosenfield, D., Aronson, E., & Sikes, J. (1977). Interdependence in the classroom: A field study. *Journal of Educational Psychology, 69*, 121–128.

Blanton, H., Jaccard, J., Klick, J., Mellers, B., Mitchell, G., & Tetlock, P. E. (2009). Strong claims and weak evidence: Reassessing the predictive validity of the IAT. *Journal of Applied Psychology, 94*(3), 567–582.

Blass, T. (2004). *The man who shocked the world.* New York, NY: Basic Books.

Block, C. J., Cruz, M., Bairley, M., Harel-Marian, T., & Roberson, L. (2019). Inside the prism of an invisible threat: Shining a light on the hidden work of contending with systemic stereotype threat in STEM fields. *Journal of Vocational Behavior, 113*, 33–50.

Blood, R. J. (1967). *Love match and arranged marriage: A Tokyo-Detroit comparison.* New York, NY: Free Press.

Boakes, E. H., Isaac, N. J., Fuller, R. A., Mace, G. M., & McGowan, P. J. (2018). Examining the relationship between local extinction risk and position in range. *Conservation Biology, 32*(1), 229–239.

Boals, A., & Schuler, K. L. (2017). Reducing reports of illusory posttraumatic growth: A revised version of the Stress-Related Growth Scale (SRGS-R). *Psychological Trauma: Theory, Research, Practice, and Policy.* Advance online publication.

Boehler, M. L., Rogers, D. A., Schwind, C. J., Mayforth, R., Quin, J., Williams, R. G., & Dunnington, G. (2006). An investigation of medical student reactions to feedback: A randomised controlled trial. *Medical Education, 40*(8), 746–749.

Bolton, A. (2019). *Media effects and criminal profiling: How fiction influences perception and profile accuracy.* Broward County, FL: Nova Southeastern University Theses and Dissertations.

Bond, C. F., & Titus, L. J. (1983). Social facilitation: A meta-analysis of 241 studies. *Psychological Bulletin, 94*(2), 265–292.

Bond, R., & Smith, P. B. (1996). Culture and conformity: A meta-analysis of studies using Asch's (1952b, 1956) line judgment task. *Psychological Bulletin, 119*(1), 111–137.

Boninger, D. S., Gleicher, F., & Strathman, A. (1994). Counterfactual thinking: From what might have been to what may be. *Journal of Personality and Social Psychology, 67*(2), 297–307.

Bonn, S. A. (2010). *Mass deception: Moral panic and the US war on Iraq.* New Brunswick, NJ: Rutgers University Press.

Bonta, B. D. (1997). Cooperation and competition in peaceful societies. *Psychological Bulletin, 121*(2), 299–320.

Bontempo, R., Lobel, S., & Triandis, H. (1990). Compliance and value internalization in Brazil and the U.S.: Effects of allocentrism and anonymity. *Journal of Cross-Cultural Psychology, 21*(2), 200–213.

Book, A. S., Starzyk, K. B., & Quinsey, V. L. (2001). The relationship between testosterone and aggression: A meta-analysis. *Aggression and Violent Behavior, 6*(6), 579–599.

Bosson, J. K., Swann, W. B. Jr., & Pennebaker, J. W. (2000). Stalking the perfect measure of implicit self-esteem: The blind men and the elephant revisited? *Journal of Personality and Social Psychology, 79*(4), 631–643.

Bosworth, M., Parmar, A., & Vázquez, Y. (Eds.). (2018). *Race, criminal justice, and migration control: Enforcing the boundaries of belonging.* Oxford, UK: Oxford University Press.

Boulette, T. R., & Andersen, S. M. (1986). "Mind control" and the battering of women. *Cultic Studies Journal, 3*(1), 25–35.

Bouts, P., Spears, R., & van der Pligt, J. (1992). Counterfactual processing and the correspondence between events and outcomes: Normality versus value. *European Journal of Social Psychology, 22*(4), 387–396.

Bovet, J., & Raymond, M. (2015). Preferred women's waist-to-hip ratio variation over the last 2,500 years. *PLoS One, 10*(4), e0123284.

Bowers, S. (2018). *Investigating contagious behaviors in Canis familiaris* (Unpublished doctoral dissertation). Yale University, New Haven, CT.

Bowlby, J. (1958). The nature of the child's tie to his mother. *International Journal of Psychoanalysis, 39*, 350–373.

Bowlby, J. (1988). Defensive processes in response to stressful separation in early life. In E. J. Anthony & C. Chiland (Eds.), *The child in his family: Vol. 8. Perilous development: Child raising and identity formation under stress* (pp. 23–30). Oxford, UK: John Wiley.

Bradshaw, J. (2017). *The animals among us: How pets make us human.* Basic Books.

Brandstätter, E. (2000). Comparison based satisfaction: Contrast and empathy. *European Journal of Social Psychology, 30*(5), 673–703.

Brandt, M. J., & Reyna, C. (2014). To love or hate thy neighbor: The role of authoritarianism and traditionalism in explaining the link between fundamentalism and racial prejudice. *Political Psychology, 35*, 207–223.

Brannen, J. (1995). *Mixing methods: Qualitative and quantitative research.* Milton Park, UK: Routledge.

Brannigan, A. (2013). Stanley Milgram's obedience experiments: A report card 50 years later. *Society, 50*(6), 623–628.

Brannigan, A., Nicholson, I. A. M., & Cherry, F. (2015). Introduction to the special issue: Unplugging the Milgram machine. *Theory & Psychology, 25*(5), 551–563.

Brannon, L., Feist, J., & Updegraff, J. A. (2013). *Health psychology: An introduction to behavior and health.* Boston, MA: Cengage Learning.

Brans, K., & Verduyn, P. (2014). Intensity and duration of negative emotions: Comparing the role of appraisals and regulation strategies. *PLoS One, 9*(3), e92410.

Brase, G. L., Adair, L., & Monk, K. (2014). Explaining sex differences in reactions to relationship infidelities: Comparisons of the roles of sex, gender, beliefs, attachment, and sociosexual orientation. *Evolutionary Psychology*, *12*(1), 73–96.

Bratt, C. (2008). The Jigsaw classroom under test: No effect on intergroup relations evident. *Journal of Community & Applied Social Psychology*, *18*, 403–419.

Braun, M. F., & Bryan, A. (2006). Female waist-to-hip and male waist-to-shoulder ratios as determinants of romantic partner desirability. *Journal of Social and Personal Relationships*, *23*(5), 805–819.

Bray, M., & Yi, B.-L. (2020). How Hong Kong's social enterprises are tackling the coronavirus. *Thomson Reuters Foundation News*. Retrieved March 18, 2020, from https://news.trust.org/item/20200227161518-whueu

Brennan, K. A., Clark, C. L., & Shaver, P. R. (1998). Self-report measurement of adult attachment: An integrative overview. In J. A. Simpson & W. S. Rholes (Eds.), *Attachment theory and close relationships* (pp. 46–76). New York, NY: Guilford.

Breuer, J., & Freud, S. (1955). *Studies on hysteria* (Standard ed., Vol. *II*). London, UK: Hogarth. (Original work published 1893–1895)

Brewer, M. B. (1991). The social self: On being the same and different at the same time. *Personality and Social Psychology Bulletin*, *17*(5), 475–482.

Bridges, A. D., & Chittka, L. (2019). Animal behaviour: Conformity and the beginnings of culture in an insect. *Current Biology*, *29*(5), R167–R169.

Briggs, J. L. (1994). "Why don't you kill your baby brother?" The dynamics of peace in Canadian Inuit camps. In L. E. Sponsel & T. Gregor (Eds.), *The anthropology of peace and nonviolence* (pp. 155–181). Boulder, CO: Lynne Rienner.

Brink, A., Eller, C. K., & Gan, H. (2015). Reporting fraud: An examination of the bystander effect and evidence strength. In D. B. Schmitt (Eds.), *Advances in accounting behavioral research* (pp. 125–154). Bingley, UK: Emerald Group.

Brockner, J. (1984). Low self-esteem and behavioral plasticity: Some implications for personality and social psychology. In L. Wheeler (Ed.), *Review of personality and social psychology* (Vol. *4*, pp. 237–271). Beverly Hills, CA: Sage.

Brody, J. G., Aschengrau, A., McKelvey, W., Rudel, R. A., Swartz, C. H., & Kennedy, T. (2004). Breast cancer risk and historical exposure to pesticides from wide-area applications assessed with GIS. *Environmental Health Perspectives*, *112*(8), 889–897.

Brookhuis, K. A., & De Waard, D. (2010). Monitoring drivers' mental workload in driving simulators using physiological measures. *Accident Analysis & Prevention*, *42*(3), 898–903.

Brooks, A. S., Luyt, R., Zawisza, M., & McDermott, D. T. (2019). Ambivalent homoprejudice towards gay men: Conceptual development and theory validation. *Journal of Homosexuality*. Advance online publication. doi:10.1080/00918369.2019.1585729

Brown, B. B. (1982). The extent and effects of peer pressure among high school students: A retrospective analysis. *Journal of Youth and Adolescence*, *11*(2), 121–133.

Brown, D. A. (2016). Climate change refugees: Law, human rights and ethics. In L. Westra & S. Juss (Eds.), *Towards a refugee oriented right of asylum* (pp. 55–74). Milton Park, UK: Taylor & Francis.

Brown, N. L., Sokal, A. D., & Friedman, H. L. (2014). Positive psychology and romantic scientism. *American Psychologist*, *69*(6), 636–637.

Brown, R. (1965). *Social psychology*. Oxford, UK: Free Press of Glencoe.

Brown v. Board of Education of Topeka, 347 U.S. 483 (1954).

Brown v. Mississippi, 297 U.S. 278, 56 S. Ct. 461, 80 L. Ed. 682, 1936 U.S. LEXIS 527 (U.S. Feb. 17, 1936).

Bruck, M., & Ceci, S. J. (1995). Amicus brief for the case of State of New Jersey v. Michaels presented by Committee of Concerned Social Scientists. *Psychology, Public Policy, and Law*, *1*(2), 272–322.

Bruck, M., & Ceci, S. J. (2009). Reliability of child witnesses' reports. In J. L. Skeem & S. O. Lilienfeld (Eds.), *Psychological science in the courtroom: Consensus and controversy* (pp. 149–171). New York, NY: Guilford.

Brummett, B. R., Wade, J. C., Ponterotto, J. G., Thombs, B., & Lewis, C. (2007). Psychosocial well-being and a multicultural personality disposition. *Journal of Counseling & Development*, *85*(1), 73–81.

Bruner, J. S., & Tagiuri, R. (1954). The perception of people. In G. Lindzey (Ed.), *Handbook of social psychology* (Vol. *2*). Cambridge, MA: Addison Wesley.

Bruza, B., Welsh, M., Navarro, D., & Begg, S. (2011). Does anchoring cause overconfidence only in experts? chrome-extension://oemmndcbldboiebfnladdacbdfmadadm/http://csjarchive.cogsci.rpi.edu/proceedings/2011/papers/0443/paper0443.pdf

Bucchianeri, M. M., & Corning, A. F. (2012). An experimental test of women's body dissatisfaction reduction through self-affirmation. *Applied Psychology: Health and Well-Being*, *4*(2), 188–201.

Buchner, E. F. (1910). Psychological progress since 1909. *Psychological Bulletin*, *7*(1), 1–16.

Buck, R. (1980). Nonverbal behavior and the theory of emotion: The facial feedback hypothesis. *Journal of Personality and Social Psychology*, *38*(5), 811–824.

Buckley-Zistel, S. (2009). Nation, narration, unification? The politics of history teaching after the Rwandan genocide. *Journal of Genocide Research*, *11*(1), 31–53.

Buehler, R., Griffin, D., & Ross, M. (1994). Exploring the "planning fallacy": Why people underestimate their task completion times. *Journal of Personality and Social Psychology*, *67*(3), 366–381.

Buehler, R., & McFarland, C. (2001). Intensity bias in affective forecasting: The role of temporal focus. *Personality and Social Psychology Bulletin*, *27*(11), 1480–1493.

Buisine, S., & Guegan, J. (2019). Proteus vs. social identity effects on virtual brainstorming. *Behaviour & Information Technology*. Advance online publication.

Bullard, R. D. (Ed.). (1993). *Confronting environmental racism: Voices from the grassroots*. New York, NY: South End Press.

Burgess, A. M., Graves, L. M., & Frost, R. O. (2018). My possessions need me: Anthropomorphism and hoarding. *Scandinavian Journal of Psychology*, *59*(3), 340–348.

Burleson, K., Leach, C. W., & Harrington, D. M. (2005). Upward social comparison and self-concept: Inspiration and inferiority among art students in an advanced programme. *British Journal of Social Psychology*, *44*(1), 109–123.

Burns, S. (2012). *The Central Park Five: The untold story behind one of New York City's most infamous crimes*. New York, NY: Vintage.

Burnstein, E., Crandall, C., & Kitayama, S. (1994). Some neo-Darwinian decision rules for altruism: Weighing cues for inclusive fitness as a function of the biological importance of the decision. *Journal of Personality and Social Psychology*, *67*(5), 773–789.

Bushman, B. J. (2002). Does venting anger feed or extinguish the flame? Catharsis, rumination, distraction, anger, and aggressive responding. *Personality and Social Psychology Bulletin*, *28*(6), 724–731.

Bushman, B. J. (2018). Teaching students about violent media effects. *Teaching of Psychology*, *45*(2), 200–206.

Bushman, B. J., & Anderson, C. A. (2001a). Is it time to pull the plug on hostile versus instrumental aggression dichotomy? *Psychological Review*, *108*(1), 273–279.

Bushman, B. J., & Anderson, C. A. (2001b). Media violence and the American public: Scientific facts versus media misinformation. *American Psychologist*, *56*(6–7), 477–489.

Bushman, B. J., Baumeister, R. F., & Phillips, C. M. (2001). Do people aggress to improve their mood? Catharsis beliefs, affect regulation opportunity, and aggressive responding. *Journal of Personality and Social Psychology*, *81*(1), 17–32.

Bushman, B. J., Baumeister, R. F., & Stack, A. D. (1999). Catharsis, aggression, and persuasive influence: Self-fulfilling or self-defeating prophecies? *Journal of Personality and Social Psychology*, *76*(3), 367–376.

Bushman, B. J., & Whitaker, J. L. (2010). Like a magnet: Catharsis beliefs attract angry people to violent video games. *Psychological Science*, *21*(6), 790–792.

Buss, A. H. (1961). *The psychology of aggression*. New York, NY: John Wiley.

Buss, D. M. (1985). Human mate selection. *American Scientist*, *73*(1), 47–51.

Buss, D. M. (1989). Sex differences in human mate preferences: Evolutionary hypotheses tested in 37 cultures. *Behavioral and Brain Sciences*, *12*(1), 1–49.

Buss, D. M. (1994). *The evolution of desire: Strategies of human mating*. New York, NY: Basic Books.

Buss, D. M. (2005). *The murderer next door: Why the mind is designed to kill*. New York, NY: Penguin.

Buss, D. M., & Duntley, J. D. (2006). The evolution of aggression. In M. Schaller, J. A. Simpson, & D. T. Kenrick (Eds.), *Evolution and social psychology* (pp. 263–285). New York, NY: Psychology Press.

Buss, D. M., & Kenrick, D. T. (1998). Evolutionary social psychology. In D. T. Gilbert, S. T. Fiske, & G. Lindzey (Eds.), *The handbook of social psychology* (Vols. 1–2, 4th ed., pp. 982–1026). New York, NY: McGraw-Hill.

Buss, D. M., Larsen, R. J., Westen, D., & Semmelroth, J. (1992). Sex differences in jealousy: Evolution, physiology, and psychology. *Psychological Science*, *3*(4), 251–255.

Butera, P. C., Wojcik, D. M., & Clough, S. J. (2010). Effects of estradiol on food intake and meal patterns for diets that differ in flavor and fat content. *Physiology & Behavior*, *99*(1), 142–145.

Butz, D. A., & Yogeeswaran, K. (2011). A new threat in the air: Macroeconomic threat increases prejudice against Asian Americans. *Journal of Experimental Social Psychology*, *47*(1), 22–27.

Byravan, S., & Rajan, S. C. (2015). Sea level rise and climate change exiles: A possible solution. *Bulletin of the Atomic Scientists*, *71*(2), 21–28.

Byrne, S., & Pease, K. (2003). Crime reduction and community safety. In T. Newburn (Ed.), *Handbook of policing* (pp. 286–310). Portland, OR: Willan Publishing.

Cacioppo, J. T., Petty, R. E., Feinstein, J., & Jarvis, W. B. G. (1996). Dispositional differences in cognitive motivation: The life and times of individuals varying in need for cognition. *Psychological Bulletin*, *119*(2), 197–253.

Cacioppo, J. T., Petty, R. E., & Kao, C. F. (1984). The efficient assessment of need for cognition. *Journal of Personality Assessment*, *48*(3), 306–307.

Cain, A. O. (2016). Pets as family members. In M. B. Sussman (Ed.), *Pets and the family* (pp. 5–10). New York, NY: Routledge.

Calhoun, J. B. (1962a). A behavioral sink. In E. Bliss (Ed.), *Roots of behavior*. New York, NY: Harper.

Calhoun, J. B. (1962b). Population density and social pathology. *Scientific American*, *206*(2), 139–150.

Camerer, C. F., & Lowenstein, G. (2004). Behavioral economics: Past, present, future. In C. F. Camerer, G. Lownstein, & M. Rabin (Eds.), *Advances in behavioral economics* (pp. 3–51). New York, NY: Russell Sage Foundation.

Cameron, C. D., Brown-Iannuzzi, J. L., & Payne, B. K. (2012). Sequential priming measures of implicit social cognition: A meta-analysis of associations with behavior and explicit attitudes. *Personality and Social Psychology Review*, *16*(4), 330–350.

Campbell, D., & Stanley, J. (1966). *Experimental and quasi-experimental designs for research* (N. Gage, Ed.). Chicago, IL: Rand McNally.

Campbell, J. C. (2002). Health consequences of intimate partner violence. *The Lancet*, *359*(9314), 1331–1336.

Campbell, M. W., & De Waal, F. B. (2011). Ingroup-outgroup bias in contagious yawning by chimpanzees supports link to empathy. *PLoS One*, *6*(4), e18283.

Cardona, G. B., & Napierski-Prancl, M. (2019). Examining the bystander effect and sexual violence: Do middle school prevention programs work? [Russell Sage College]. *Journal of Student Research*.

Carey, B. (2009, July 27). In battle, hunches prove to be valuable. *New York Times*.

Carlo, G., Koller, S. H., Eisenberg, N., Da Silva, M. S., & Frohlich, C. B. (1996). A cross-national study on the relations among prosocial moral reasoning, gender role orientations, and prosocial behaviors. *Developmental Psychology*, *32*(2), 231–240.

Carlsmith, K. M., Wilson, T. D., & Gilbert, D. T. (2008). The paradoxical consequences of revenge. *Journal of Personality and Social Psychology*, *95*(6), 1316–1324.

Carmack, B., & Wallace, D. (2018). Teaching an innocence case review course to undergraduate students. *Journal of Criminal Justice Education*, *29*(4), 577–596.

Carney, R. M., & Freedland, K. E. (2007). Depression and coronary heart disease: More pieces of the puzzle. *American Journal of Psychiatry*, *164*(9), 1307–1309.

Carr, P. L., Szalacha, L., Barnett, R., Caswell, C., & Inui, T. (2003). A "ton of feathers": Gender discrimination in academic medical careers and how to manage it. *Journal of Women's Health*, *12*(10), 1009–1018.

Carrara, L. (2006). My experience with the great rabbit rescue of 2006. *Dontdumprabbits.org*. Retrieved December 15, 2019, from https://dontdumprabbits.org/reno-rabbit-rescue-tributes/my-experience-with-the-great-rabbit-rescue-of-2006/

Carson, R. C., Butcher, J. N., & Mineka, S. (1996). *Abnormal psychology and modern life* (10th ed.). New York, NY: HarperCollins.

Case closed: Rape and human rights in the Nordic countries. (2010). https://web.archive.org/web/20131020202147/http://www.amnesty.dk/sites/default/files/mediafiles/44/case-closed.pdf

Cashin, R. (n.d.). Scientists have confirmed which famous man has the "most perfect face." *Joe.ie*. Retrieved February 23, 2020, from https://www.joe.ie/life-style/science-confirms-most-handsome-man-596711

Cassese, E. C., & Holman, M. R. (2019). Playing the woman card: Ambivalent sexism in the 2016 US presidential race. *Political Psychology*, *40*(1), 55–74.

Cassidy, B. S., & Krendl, A. C. (2016). Dynamic neural mechanisms underlie race disparities in social cognition. *NeuroImage*, *132*, 238–246.

Cathey, P., & Goodfriend, W. (2012). *Voices of hope: Breaking the silence of relationship violence*. Storm Lake, IA: Institute for the Prevention of Relationship Violence.

Causevic, A. (2017). Facing an unpredictable threat: Is NATO ideally placed to manage climate change as a non-traditional threat multiplier? *Connections*, *16*(2), 59–80.

CDC. (2019a). *Managing anxiety & stress*. Retrieved March 27, 2020, on https://www.cdc.gov/coronavirus/2019-ncov/prepare/managing-stress-anxiety.html

CDC. (2019b). *Preventing intimate partner violence*. Retrieved April 3, 2020, from https://www.cdc.gov/violenceprevention/intimatepartnerviolence/fastfact.html

CDC. (2019c). *Zoonotic diseases*. Retrieved December 14, 2019, from https://www.cdc.gov/onehealth/basics/zoonotic-diseases.html

Cecen, A. F. (2019). Discussing Facebook algorithm and ads in the context of political manipulation and negative campaign. In R. Yilmaz (Ed.), *Handbook of research on narrative advertising* (pp. 238–250). Sumsun, Turkey: IGI Global.

Ceci, S. J., & Bruck, M. (1995). *Jeopardy in the courtroom: A scientific analysis of children's testimony.* Washington, DC: American Psychological Association.

Cervone, D. (2004). The architecture of personality, *Psychological Review, 111*(1), 183–204.

Cervone, D., & Peake, P. K. (1986). Anchoring, efficacy, and action: The influence of judgmental heuristics on self-efficacy judgments and behavior. *Journal of Personality and Social Psychology, 50*(3), 492–501.

Chagnon, N. A. (1983). *Yanomamö: The fierce people* (3rd ed.). New York, NY: Holt, Rinehart, & Winston.

Chaiken, S. (1980). Heuristic versus systematic information processing in the use of source versus message cues in persuasion. *Journal of Personality and Social Psychology, 39*(5), 752–766.

Chance, S. E., Brown, R. T., Dabbs, J. M., & Casey, R. (2000). Testosterone, intelligence and behavior disorders in young boys. *Personality and Individual Differences, 28*(3), 437–445.

Chandra, S. (1973). The effects of group pressure in perception: A cross-cultural conformity study. *International Journal of Psychology, 8*(1), 37–39.

Chang, C. Y., & Myers, J. E. (1997). Understanding and counseling Korean Americans: Implications for training. *Counselor Education and Supervision, 37,* 35–49.

Chapin, J. R., & Coleman, G. (2012). Optimistic bias about dating/relationship violence among teens. *Journal of Youth Studies, 15*(5), 645–655.

Chapman, G. B., & Johnson, E. J. (2002). Incorporating the irrelevant: Anchors in judgments of belief and value. In T. Gilovich, D. Griffin, & D. Kahneman (Eds.), *Heuristics and biases: The psychology of intuitive judgment* (pp. 120–138). Cambridge, UK: Cambridge University Press.

Chen, J. M., Kim, H. S., Mojaverian, T., & Morling, B. (2012). Culture and social support provision: Who gives what and why. *Personality and Social Psychology Bulletin, 38*(1), 3–13.

Chen, S., & Chaiken, S. (1999). The heuristic-systematic model in its broader context. In S. Chaiken & Y. Trope (Eds.), *Dual-process theories in social psychology* (pp. 73–96). New York, NY: Guilford.

Chen, Z., Fiske, S. T., & Lee, T. L. (2009). Ambivalent sexism and power-related gender-role ideology in marriage. *Sex Roles, 60*(11–12), 765–778.

Chester, D. S., & DeWall, C. N. (2018). The roots of intimate partner violence. *Current Opinion in Psychology, 19,* 55–59.

Chick, G., Loy, J. W., & Miracle, A. W. (1997). Combative sport and warfare: A reappraisal of the spillover and catharsis hypotheses. *Cross-Cultural Research, 31*(3), 249–267.

Chiesa, A., & Serretti, A. (2009). Mindfulness-based stress reduction for stress management in healthy people: A review and meta-analysis. *Journal of Alternative and Complementary Medicine, 15*(5), 593–600.

Chifflet, P. (2015). Questioning the validity of criminal profiling: An evidence-based approach. *Australian & New Zealand Journal of Criminology, 48*(2), 238–255.

Chou, H. G., & Edge, N. (2012). "They are happier and having better lives than I am": The impact of using Facebook on perceptions of others' lives. *Cyberpsychology, Behavior, and Social Networking, 15*(2), 117–120.

Chu, J. M. (2018). *Crazy rich Asians* [motion picture]. Warner Bros.

Chuck, E. (2016, March 31). Fact sheet: Who has nuclear weapons, and how many do they have? *NBC News.* http://www.nbcnews.com/news/world/fact-sheet-who-has-nuclear-weapons-how-many-do-they-have-n548481

Chung, H., & Zhao, X. (2003). Humour effect on memory and attitude: Moderating role of product involvement. *International Journal of Advertising, 22*(1), 117–144.

Cialdini, R. B. (2001). *Influence: Science and practice* (4th ed.). Boston, MA: Allyn & Bacon.

Cialdini, R. B. (2007). *Influence: Science and practice* (5th ed.). Boston, MA: Allyn & Bacon.

Cialdini, R. B., Bordern, R. J., Thorne, A., Walker, M. R., Freeman, S., & Sloan, L. R. (1976). Basking in reflected glory: Three (football) field studies. *Journal of Personality and Social Psychology, 34*(3), 366–373.

Cialdini, R. B., Kallgren, C. A., & Reno, R. R. (1991). A focus theory of normative conduct: A theoretical refinement and reevaluation of the role of norms in human behavior. *Advances in Experimental Social Psychology, 24,* 201–234.

Cialdini, R. B., Levy, A., Herman, C. P., Kozlowski, L. T., & Petty R. E. (1976). Elastic shifts of opinion: Determinants of direction and durability. *Journal of Personality and Social Psychology, 34*(4), 633–672.

Cialdini, R. B., & Trost M. R. (1998). Social influence: Social norms, conformity, and compliance. In D. T. Gilbert, S. T. Fiske, & G. Lindzey (Eds.), *The handbook of social psychology* (Vols. 1–2, 4th ed., pp. 151–192). New York, NY: McGraw-Hill.

Cialdini, R. B., Vincent, J. E., Lewis, S. K., Datalan, J., Wheeler, D., & Darby, B. L. (1975). Reciprocal concessions procedure for inducing compliance: The door-in-the-face technique. *Journal of Personality and Social Psychology, 31*(2), 206–215.

Ciucci, E., Caussi, P., Menesini, E., Mattei, A., Petralli, M., & Orlandini, S. (2011). Weather daily variation in winter and its effect on behavior and affective states in day-care children. *International Journal of Biometeorology, 55*(3), 327–337.

Clark, R. D., & Hatfield, E. (1989). Gender differences in receptivity to sexual offers. *Journal of Psychology & Human Sexuality, 2*(1), 39–55.

Clarkson, M. (2010). The long and short of it: Leg length, aggression and the evolution of the human mind. *Australian Archaeology, 70,* 81.

Clauss-Ehlers, C. S., Chiriboga, D. A., Hunter, S. J., Roysircar, G., & Tummala-Narra, P. (2019). APA multicultural guidelines executive summary: Ecological approach to context, identity, and intersectionality. *American Psychologist, 74*(2), 232–244.

Clement, R. W., & Krueger, J. (2002). Social categorization moderates social projection. *Journal of Experimental Social Psychology, 38*(3), 219–231.

Clement, R. W., Sinha, R. R., & Krueger, J. (1997). A computerized demonstration of the false consensus effect. *Teaching of Psychology, 24*(2), 131–135.

Clifford, M. M., & Walster, E. (1973). Research note: The effect of physical attractiveness on teacher expectations. *Sociology of Education, 46*(2), 248–258.

Clohessy, S., & Ehlers, A. (1999). PTSD symptoms, response to intrusive memories and coping in ambulance service workers. *British Journal of Clinical Psychology, 38*(3), 251–265.

Cobb, A. R., Tedeschi, R. G., Calhoun, L. G., & Cann, A. (2006). Correlates of posttraumatic growth in survivors of intimate partner violence. *Journal of Traumatic Stress, 19*(6), 895–903.

Cohen, A. H., & Krueger, J. S. (2016). Rising mercury, rising hostility: How heat affects survey response. *Field Methods, 28*(2), 133–152.

Cohen, D., Nisbett, R. E., Bowdle, B. F., & Schwarz, N. (1996). Insult, aggression, and the Southern culture of honor: An "experimental ethnography." *Journal of Personality and Social Psychology, 70*(5), 945–960.

Cohen, S. P. (2002). Can pets function as family members? *Western Journal of Nursing Research, 24*(6), 621–638.

Coker, A. L., Davis, K. E., Arias, I., Desai, S., Sanderson, M., Brandt, H. M., & Smith, P. H. (2002). Physical and mental health effects of intimate partner violence for men and women. *American Journal of Preventive Medicine, 23*(4), 260–268.

Coker, A. L., Smith, P. H., McKeown, R. E., & King, M. J. (2000). Frequency and correlates of intimate partner violence by type: Physical, sexual, and psychological battering. *American Journal of Public Health, 90*(4), 553–559.

Coker, A. L., Weston, R., Creson, D. L., Justice, B., & Blakeney, P. (2005). PTSD symptoms among men and women survivors of intimate partner violence: The role of risk and protective factors. *Violence and Victims, 20*(6), 625–643.

Coker, J. S., Heiser, E., & Taylor, L. (2018). Student outcomes associated with short-term and semester study abroad programs. *Frontiers: The Interdisciplinary Journal of Study Abroad, 30*(2), 92–105.

Cole, S., & Dioso-Villa, R. (2006). CSI and its effects: Media, juries, and the burden of proof. *New England Law Review, 41*(3), 435–470.

Coles, N. A., Larsen, J. T., & Lench, H. C. (2019). A meta-analysis of the facial feedback literature: Effects of facial feedback on emotional experience are small and variable. *Psychological Bulletin, 145*, 610–651.

Collard, R. (2017). "We have to support these people." *TIME*. Retrieved January 22, 2020, from https://time.com/4854392/malala-yousafzai-iraq-mosul-isis-girl-power/

Collins, S. (2008). *The hunger games*. New York, NY: Scholastic Press.

Collins, S. (2009). *Catching fire*. New York, NY: Scholastic Press.

Collins, S. (2010). *Mockingjay*. New York, NY: Scholastic Press.

Collison, K. L., Vize, C. E., Miller, J. D., & Lynam, D. R. (2018). Development and preliminary validation of a five factor model measure of Machiavellianism. *Psychological Assessment, 30*(10), 1401–1407.

Colman, A. M., Gold, N., & Pulford, B. D. (2019). Comparing hypothetical and real-life trolley problems: Commentary on Bostyn, Sevenhant, and Roets (2018). *Psychological Science, 30*(9), 1386–1388.

Comacho, L. M., & Paulus, P. B. (1995). The role of social anxiousness in group brainstorming. *Journal of Personality and Social Psychology, 68*(6), 1071–1080.

Compton, W. C. (2005). *Introduction to positive psychology*. Belmont, CA: Thomson Wadsworth.

Compton, W. C., & Hoffman, E. (2019). *Positive psychology: The science of happiness and flourishing*. Thousand Oaks, CA: Sage.

Conley, T. D., Moors, A. C., Matsick, J. L., Ziegler, A., & Valentine, B. A. (2011). Women, men, and the bedroom: Methodological and conceptual insights that narrow, reframe, and eliminate gender differences in sexuality. *Current Directions in Psychological Science, 20*(5), 296–300.

Conley, T. D., Moors, A. C., Ziegler, A., & Karathanasis, C. (2012). Unfaithful individuals are less likely to practice safer sex than openly nonmonogamous individuals. *Journal of Sexual Medicine, 9*(6), 1559–1565.

Connolly, T., Routhieaux, R. L., & Schneider, S. K. (1993). On the effectiveness of group brainstorming: Test of an underlying cognitive mechanism. *Small Group Research, 24*(4), 490–503.

Cooper, W. H. (1981). Ubiquitous halo. *Psychological Bulletin, 90*(2), 218–244.

Coren, S. (1999). Do people look like their dogs? *Anthrozoös, 12*(2), 111–114.

Corey, S. (1937). Professed attitudes and actual behavior. *Journal of Educational Psychology, 28*(4), 271–280.

Correll, J., Park, B., Judd, C. M., & Wittenbrink, B. (2002). The police officer's dilemma: Using ethnicity to disambiguate potentially threatening individuals. *Journal of Personality and Social Psychology, 83*(6), 1314–1329.

Cortland, C. I., Shapiro, J. R., Guzman, I. Y., & Ray, L. A. (2019). The ironic effects of stigmatizing smoking: Combining stereotype

threat theory with behavioral pharmacology. *Addiction, 114*(10), 1842–1848.

Cosmides, L., & Tooby, J. (1992). Cognitive adaptations for social exchange. In L. Cosmides & J. Tooby (Eds.), *The adapted mind: Evolutionary psychology and the generation of culture* (pp. 163–228). New York, NY: Oxford University Press.

Costanzo, M., & Krauss, D. (2015). *Forensic and legal psychology*. London, UK: Macmillan.

Cottrell, C. A., & Neuberg, S. L. (2005). Different emotional reactions to different groups: A sociofunctional threat-based approach to prejudice. *Journal of Personality and Social Psychology, 88*(5), 770–789.

Cottrell, N. B., Wack, D. L., Sekerak, G. J., & Rittle, R. H. (1968). Social facilitation of dominant responses by the presence of an audience and the mere presence of others. *Journal of Personality and Social Psychology, 9*(3), 245–250.

Cox, S. S., & Reichel, C. M. (2019). Rats display empathic behavior independent of the opportunity for social interaction. *Neuropsychopharmacology*. Advance online publication.

Craik, F. I., & Lockhart, R. S. (1972). Levels of processing: A framework for memory research. *Journal of Verbal Learning & Verbal Behavior, 11*(6), 671–684.

Crall, P., & Goodfriend, W. (2016). "She asked for it": Statistics and predictors of rape myth acceptance. *Modern Psychological Studies, 22*, 15–27.

Cramer, R. J., Miller, A. K., Amacker, A. M., & Burks, A. C. (2013). Openness right-wing authoritarianism and antigay prejudice in college students: A meditational model. *Journal of Counseling Psychology, 60*(1), 64–71.

Crandall, C. S. (1994). Prejudice against fat people: Ideology and self-interest. *Journal of Personality and Social Psychology, 66*(5), 882–894.

Crane, R., Brewer, J., Feldman, C., Kabat-Zinn, J., Santorellli, S., Williams, J. M. G., & Kuyken, W. (2019). What defines mindfulness-based programs? The warp and the weft. *Psychological Medicine, 47*(6), 990–999.

Crawford, J. T., Brandt, M. J., Inbar, Y., & Mallinas, S. R. (2016). Right-wing authoritarianism predicts prejudice equally toward "gay men and lesbians" and "homosexuals." *Journal of Personality and Social Psychology, 111*(2), 31–45.

Creswell, J. D., Dutcher, J. M., Klein, W. M. P., Harris, P. R., & Levine, J. M. (2013). Self-affirmation improves problem-solving under stress. *PLoS One, 8*(5), e62593.

Creswell, J. D., Welch, W. T., Taylor, S. E., Sherman, D. K., Gruenewald, T. L., & Mann, T. (2005). Affirmation of personal values buffers neuroendocrine and psychological stress responses. *Psychological Science, 16*(11), 846–851.

Crocker, J., & Major, B. (1989). Social stigma and self-esteem: The self-protective properties of stigma. *Psychological Review, 96*(4), 608–630.

Crocker, J., & Major, B. (2003). The self-protective properties of stigma: Evolution of a modern classic. *Psychological Inquiry, 14*(3–4), 232–237.

Crocker, J., & Nuer, N. (2003). The insatiable quest for self-worth. *Psychological Inquiry, 14*(1), 31–34.

Cropley, D. H., Cropley, A. J., Kaufman, J. C., & Runco, M. A. (2010). *The dark side of creativity*. New York, NY: Cambridge University Press.

Crowder, K., & Goodfriend, W. (2012). Good monkey see, good monkey do: Children's imitative prosocial behavior. *Journal of Psychological Inquiry, 17*(2), 7–16.

Crowne, D. P., & Marlowe, D. (1960). A new scale of social desirability independent of psychopathology. *Journal of Consulting Psychology, 24*(4), 349–354.

Cruz, J. M. (2003). "Why doesn't he just leave?": Gay male domestic violence and the reasons victims stay. *Journal of Men's Studies, 11*(3), 309–323.

Csikszentmihalyi, M. (1999). If we are so rich, why aren't we happy? *American Psychologist*, *54*, 821–827.

Cunningham, W. A., Johnson, M. K., Raye, C. L., Gatenby, J. C., Gore, J. C., & Banaji, M. R. (2004). Separable neural components in the processing of black and white faces. *Psychological Science*, *15*(12), 806–813.

Curhan, J. R., & Pentland, A. (2007). Thin slices of negotiation: Predicting outcomes from conversational dynamics within the first 5 minutes. *Journal of Applied Psychology*, *92*(3), 802–811.

Ćurić Dražić, M., Petrović, I. B., & Vukelić, M. (2018). Career ambition as a way of understanding the relation between locus of control and self-perceived employability among psychology students. *Frontiers in Psychology*, *9*, article 1729. https://doi.org/10.3389/fpsyg.2018.01729

The current situation of gender equality in Sweden—country profile. (2013). http://ec.europa.eu/justice/gender-equality/files/epo_campaign/131006_country-profile_sweden.pdf

Dåderman, A. M., & Ragnestål-Impola, C. (2019). Workplace bullies, not their victims, score high on the dark triad and extraversion, and low on agreeableness and honesty-humility. *Heliyon*, *5*(10), e02609.

Damon, W., & Hart, D. (1988). *Self-understanding in childhood and adolescence*. Cambridge, UK: Cambridge University Press.

Dansereau, F., Seitz, S. R., Chiu, C., Shaughnessy, B., & Yammarino, F. J. (2013). What makes leadership, leadership? Using self-expansion theory to integrate traditional and contemporary approaches. *Leadership Quarterly*, *24*(6), 798–821.

Dardis, C. M., Murphy, M. J., Bill, A. C., & Gidycz, C. A. (2016). An investigation of the tenets of social norms theory as they relate to sexually aggressive attitudes and sexual assault perpetration: A comparison of men and their friends. *Psychology of Violence*, *6*(1), 163–171.

Darley, J. M., & Batson, C. D. (1973). 'From Jerusalem to Jericho': A study of situational and dispositional variables in helping behavior. *Journal of Personality and Social Psychology*, *27*(1), 100–108.

Darley, J. M., & Latané, B. (1968). Bystander intervention in emergencies: Diffusion of responsibility. *Journal of Personality and Social Psychology*, *8*(4, Pt. 1), 377–383.

Darwen, P. J., & Yao, X. (2002). Co-evolution in iterated prisoner's dilemma with intermediate levels of cooperation: Application to missile defense. *International Journal of Computational Intelligence and Applications*, *2*(1), 83–107.

Darwin, C. R. (1859). *On the origin of the species by means of natural selection*. London, UK: John Murray. http://darwin-online.org.uk/content/frameset?itemID=F373&viewtype=text&pageseq=1

Darwin, C. R. (1872). *The expression of the emotions in man and animals*. London, UK: John Murray.

Darwin, C. R. (1877). A biographical sketch of an infant. *Mind*, *2*, 85–94.

Davenport, F. G. (1917). *European treaties bearing the history of the United States and its dependencies to 1648* (Vol. *1*). Washington, DC: Carnegie Institution of Washington.

Davidson, A. R., & Jaccard, J. J. (1979). Variables that moderate the attitude-behavior relation: Results of a longitudinal survey. *Journal of Personality and Social Psychology*, *37*(8), 1364–1376.

Davies, B. (1992). Women's subjectivity and feminist stories. In C. Ellis & M. Flaherty, *Investigating subjectivity: Research on lived experience* (pp. 53–76). Newbury Park, CA: Sage.

Davies, M. F. (1982). Self-focused attention and belief perseverance. *Journal of Experimental Social Psychology*, *18*(6), 595–605.

Davis, C. G., & Lehman, D. R. (1995). Counterfactual thinking and coping with traumatic life events. In N. J. Roese & J. M. Olson (Eds.), *What might have been: The social psychology of counterfactual thinking* (pp. 353–374). Hillsdale, NJ: Lawrence Erlbaum.

Davis, C. G., Lehman, D. R., Silver, R. C., Wortman, C. B., & Ellard, J. H. (1996). Self-blame following a traumatic event: The role of perceived avoidability. *Personality and Social Psychology Bulletin*, *22*(6), 557–567.

Davis, C. G., Lehman, D. R., Wortman, C. B., Silver, R. C., & Thompson, S. C. (1995). The undoing of traumatic life events. *Personality and Social Psychology Bulletin*, *21*(2), 109–124.

Davis, C. N., Slutske, W. S., Martin, N. G., Agrawal, A., & Lynskey, M. T. (2018). Genetic and environmental influences on gambling disorder liability: A replication and combined analysis of two twin studies. *Psychological Medicine*. Advance online publication.

Davis, L. (2018). *The diamond elephant in the room: A phenomenological analysis of the meaning couples make of engagement rings* (Unpublished doctoral dissertation). Alliant International University.

Davis, M., Faurby, S., & Svenning, J. C. (2018). Mammal diversity will take millions of years to recover from the current biodiversity crisis. *Proceedings of the National Academy of Sciences*, *115*(44), 11262–11267.

Dawes, R. M. (1989). Statistical criteria for establishing a truly false consensus effect. *Journal of Experimental Social Psychology*, *25*(1), 1–17.

Dawes, R. M., & Mulford, M. (1996). The false consensus effect and overconfidence: Flaws in judgments or flaws in how we study judgment? *Organizational Behavior and Human Decision Processes*, *65*(3), 201–211.

Dawkins, R. (1976). *The selfish gene*. New York, NY: Oxford University Press.

de Castro, J. M. (2000). Eating behavior: Lessons from the real world of humans. *Nutrition*, *16*(10), 800–813.

De Cremer, D., Zeelenberg, M., & Murnighan, J. K. (2006). Social animals and economic beings: On unifying social psychology and economics. In D. De Cramer, M. Zeelenberg, & J. K. Murnighan (Eds.), *Social psychology and economics* (pp. 3–14). Part Drive, UK: Taylor and Francis Ltd.

de Geus, E., Eijzenga, W., Menko, F. H., Sijmons, R. H., de Haes, H. C. J. M., Aalfs, C. M., & Smets, E. M. A. (2016). Design and feasibility of an intervention to support cancer genetic counselees in informing their at-risk relatives. *Journal of Genetic Counseling*, *25*(6), 1179–1187.

De Luca, M., Horovitz, R., & Pitt, B. (Producers), & Miller, B. (Director). (2011). *Moneyball* [Motion picture]. United States: Columbia.

de Waal, F. B., Aureli, F., & Judge, P. G. (2000). Coping with crowding. *Scientific American*, *282*(5), 76–81.

de Wijze, S. (2019). Political evil—warping the moral landscape. In S. Harrosh & R. Crisp (Eds.), *Moral evil and practical ethics* (pp. 165–198). New York, NY: Routledge.

Deets, L. E. (1931). The origins of conflict in the Hutterische communities. *Publications of the American Sociological Society*, *25*, 125–135.

Delfour, F., & Marten, K. (2001). Mirror image processing in three marine mammal species: Killer whales (*Orcinus orca*), false killer whales (*Pseudorca crassidens*) and California sea lions (*Zalophus californianus*). *Behavioural Processes*, *53*(3), 181–190.

DeLongis, A., Folkman, S., & Lazarus, R. S. (1988). The impact of daily stress on health and mood: Psychological and social resources as mediators. *Journal of Personality and Social Psychology*, *54*(3), 486–495.

DeNault, L. K., & McFarlane, D. A. (1995). Reciprocal altruism between male vampire bats, *Desmodus rotundus*. *Animal Behaviour*, *49*(3), 855–856.

DeNeys, W. (2006). Dual processing in reasoning: Two systems but one reasoner. *Psychological Science*, *17*(5), 428–433.

Dennis, I., Newstead, S. E., & Wright, D. E. (1996). A new approach to exploring biases in educational assessment. *British Journal of Psychology, 87*(4), 515–534.

DePaulo, B. M., Kashy, D. A., Kirkendol, S. E., Wyer, M. M., & Epstein, J. A. (1996). Lying in everyday life. *Journal of Personality and Social Psychology, 70*(5), 979–995.

Dereli, E., & Karakuş, Ö. (2011). An examination of attachment styles and social skills of university students. *Electronic Journal of Research in Educational Psychology, 9*(2), 731–744.

DesJardine, M., Bansal, P., & Yang, Y. (2019). Bouncing back: Building resilience through social and environmental practices in the context of the 2008 global financial crisis. *Journal of Management, 45*(4), 1434–1460.

Deutsch, F. M., & Lamberti, D. M. (1986). Does social approval increase helping? *Personality and Social Psychology Bulletin, 12*(2), 149–157.

Deutsch, M., & Gerard, H. B. (1955). A study of normative and informational social influences upon individual judgment. *Journal of Abnormal and Social Psychology, 51*(3), 629–636.

De Vos, J. (2010). From Milgram to Zimbardo: The double birth of postwar psychology/psychologization. *History of the Human Sciences, 23*(5), 156–175.

DeVries, D. L., & Ajzen, I. (1971). The relationship of attitudes and normative beliefs to cheating in college. *Journal of Social Psychology, 83*(2), 199–207.

DeWall, C. N., Anderson, C. A., & Bushman, B. J. (2011). The general aggression model: Theoretical extensions to violence. *Psychology of Violence, 1*(3), 245–258.

Dhiaulhaq, A., De Bruyn, T., & Gritten, D. (2015). The use and effectiveness of mediation in forest and land conflict transformation in Southeast Asia: Case studies from Cambodia, Indonesia and Thailand. *Environmental Science & Policy, 45*, 132–145.

Dianoux, C., Heitz-Spahn, S., Siadou-Martin, B., Thevenot, G., & Yildiz, H. (2019). Nudge: A relevant communication tool adapted for agile innovation. *Journal of Innovation Economics Management, 1*, 7–27.

Dickel, P., & Eckardt, G. (2020). Who wants to be a social entrepreneur? The role of gender and sustainability orientation. *Journal of Small Business Management*. Advance online publication.

Didion, J. (2005). *The year of magical thinking* (Book club kit). New York, NY: Knopf.

Di Fabio, A., & Saklofske, D. H. (2018). The contributions of personality and emotional intelligence to resiliency. *Personality and Individual Differences, 123*, 140–144.

Diekman, A. B., & Eagly, A. H. (2000). Stereotypes as dynamic constructs: Women and men of the past, present, and future. *Personality and Social Psychology Bulletin, 26*(10), 1171–1188.

Diekman, A. B., & Goodfriend, W. (2006). Rolling with the changes: A role congruity perspective on gender norms. *Psychology of Women Quarterly, 30*(4), 369–383.

Diener, E. (1979). Deindividuation, self-awareness, and disinhibition. *Journal of Personality and Social Psychology, 37*(7), 1160–1171.

Diener, E., Fraser, S. C., Beaman, A. L., & Kelem, R. T. (1976). Effects of deindividuation variables on stealing among Halloween trick-or-treaters. *Journal of Personality and Social Psychology, 33*(2), 178–183.

Diener, E., Lucas, R. E., & Scollon, C. N. (2009). Beyond the hedonic treadmill: Revising the adaptation theory of well-being. In E. Diener (Ed.), *The science of well-being* (pp. 103–118). Springer.

Dietrich, D. M., & Berkowitz, L. (1997). Alleviation of dissonance by engaging in prosocial behavior or receiving ego-enhancing feedback. *Journal of Social Behavior & Personality, 12*(2), 557–566.

Dietrich, D. M., & Schuett, J. M. (2013). Culture of honor and attitudes toward intimate partner violence in Latinos. *Sage Open, 3*(2), 1–11.

Dietz, M. G. (1986). Trapping the prince: Machiavelli and the politics of deception. *American Political Science Review, 80*(3), 777–799.

DiMatteo, M. R. (2004). Variations in patients' adherence to medical recommendations: A quantitative review of 50 years of research. *Medical Care, 42*(3), 200–209.

Dion, K., Berscheid, E., & Walster, E. (1972). What is beautiful is good. *Journal of Personality and Social Psychology, 24*(3), 285–290.

Dion, K. K., & Dion, K. L. (1991). Psychological individualism and romantic love. *Journal of Social Behavior and Personality, 6*, 17–33.

Dion, K. K., & Dion, K. L. (1993). Individualistic and collectivistic perspectives on gender and the cultural context of love and intimacy. *Journal of Social Issues, 49*(3), 53–69.

Di Pellegrino, G., Fadiga, L., Fogassi, L., Gallese, V., & Rizzolatti, G. (1992). Understanding motor events: A neurophysiological study. *Experimental Brain Research, 91*(1), 176–180.

Disney, W. (Producer), & Sharpsteen, B., & Luske, H. (Directors). (1940). *Pinocchio* [Motion picture]. United States: Walt Disney Productions.

Dixson, A. F., Halliwell, G., East, R., Wignarajah, P., & Anderson, M. J. (2003). Masculine somatotype and hirsuteness as determinants of sexual attractiveness to women. *Archives of Sexual Behavior, 32*(1), 29–39.

Djeriouat, H., & Trémolière, B. (2014). The dark triad of personality and utilitarian moral judgment: The mediating role of honesty/humility and harm/care. *Personality and Individual Differences, 67*, 11–16.

Dobash, R. E., & Dobash, R. P. (1992). *Women, violence and social change*. New York, NY: Routledge.

Dobuzinskis, A. (2017, May 29). Two men stabbed to death on Oregon train trying to stop anti-Muslim rant. *Reuters*. http://www.reuters.com/article/us-usa-muslims-portland-idUSKBN18N080

Dockery, T. M., & Bedeian, A. G. (1989). "Attitudes versus actions": LaPiere's (1934) classic study revisited. *Social Behavior and Personality, 17*(1), 9–16.

Dodge, K. A., Lochman, J. E., Harnish, J. D., Bates, J. E., & Pettit, G. S. (1997). Reactive and proactive aggression in school children and psychiatrically impaired chronically assaultive youth. *Journal of Abnormal Psychology, 106*(1), 37–51.

Dollard, J., Miller, N. E., Doob, L. W., Mowrer, O. H., & Sears, R. R. (1939). *Frustration and aggression*. New Haven, CT: Yale University Press.

Dominelli, L. (2012). *Green social work: From environmental crises to environmental justice*. Cambridge, UK: Polity.

Donahue, M. J. (1985). Intrinsic and extrinsic religiousness: The empirical research. *Journal for the Scientific Study of Religion, 24*(4), 418–423.

Donnellan, M. B., Trzesniewski, K. H., Robins, R. W., Moffitt, T. E., & Caspi, A. (2005). Low self-esteem is related to aggression, antisocial behavior, and delinquency. *Psychological Science, 16*(4), 328–335.

Donnerstein, E., & Donnerstein, M. (1976). Research in the control of interracial aggression. In R. G. Green & E. C. O'Neal (Eds.), *Perspectives on aggression* (pp. 133–168). New York, NY: Academic Press.

Doosje, B., & Branscombe, N. R. (2003). Attributions for the negative historical actions of a group. *European Journal of Social Psychology, 33*(2), 235–248.

Doosje, B., Branscombe, N. R., Spears, R., & Manstead, S. R. (1998). Guilty by association: When one's group has a negative history. *Journal of Personality and Social Psychology, 75*(4), 872–886.

Dougherty, M. R. P., Gettys, D. F., & Ogden, E. E. (1999). MINERVA-DM: A memory process model of judgments of likelihood. *Psychological Review, 106*(1), 180–209.

Dovidio, J. F., & Morris, W. N. (1975). Effects of stress and commonality of fate on helping behavior. *Journal of Personality and Social Psychology, 31*(1), 145–149.

Dovidio, J. F., & Penner, L. A. (2001). Helping and altruism. In G. J. O. Fletcher & M. S. Clark (Eds.), *Blackwell handbook of social psychology: Interpersonal processes* (pp. 162–195). New York, NY: Blackwell.

Downes, D., Rock, P., Chinkin, C., & Gearty, C. (Eds.). (2013). *Crime, social control and human rights: From moral panics to states of denial, essays in honour of Stanley Cohen*. Abingdon, UK: Routledge.

Downey, G., & Feldman, S. I. (1996). Implications of rejection sensitivity for intimate relationships. *Journal of Personality and Social Psychology, 70*(6), 1327–1343.

Downey, J. L., & Christensen, L. (2006). Belief persistence in impression formation. *North American Journal of Psychology, 8*(3), 479–488.

Dragolov, G., Ignácz, Z. S., Lorenz, J., Delhey, J., Boehnke, K., & Unzicker, K. (2016). *Social cohesion in the Western world*. New York, NY: Springer.

Drouin, M., & Landgraff, C. (2012). Texting, sexting, and attachment in college students' romantic relationships. *Computers in Human Behavior, 28*(2), 444–449.

Dubner, S. J., & Levitt, S. D. (2006, November 5). The way we live now: Freakonomics; the price of climate change. *New York Times*. Retrieved March 7, 2007, from http//:www.nytimes.com

Duckitt, J., & Sibley, C. G. (2010). Right-wing authoritarianism and social dominance orientation differentially moderate intergroup effects on prejudice. *European Journal of Personality, 24*(7), 583–601.

Dugatkin, L. A. (2007). Inclusive fitness theory from Darwin to Hamilton. *Genetics, 176*(3), 1375–1380.

Dugosh, K. L., Paulus, P. B., Roland, E. J., & Yang, H.-C. (2000). Cognitive stimulation in brainstorming. *Journal of Personality and Social Psychology, 79*(5), 722–735.

Dulin, P., Hill, R. D., Anderson, J., & Rasmussen, D. (2001). Altruism as a predictor of life satisfaction in a sample of low-income older adult service providers. *Journal of Mental Health and Aging, 7*(3), 349–360.

Dunbar, R. I. M. (1998). The social brain hypothesis. *Brain, 9*(10), 178–190.

Duncan, L. E., Peterson, B. E., & Winter, D. G. (1997). Authoritarianism and gender roles: Toward a psychological analysis of hegemonic relationships. *Personality and Social Psychology Bulletin, 23*(1), 41–49.

Dunham, K., & Senn, C. Y. (2000). Minimizing negative experiences: Women's disclosure of partner abuse. *Journal of Interpersonal Violence, 15*(3), 251–261.

Dunn, D. (2013). *The psychologically literate citizen: Foundations and global perspectives*. Oxford, UK: Oxford University Press.

Dunn, D. S. (2016). "It's still a prison to me": A new dramatic film portrayal of the Stanford Prison Experiment [Review of the media *The Stanford Prison Experiment*. K. P. Alvarez]. *PsycCRITIQUES, 61*(3).

Dunn, D. S., Baker, S. C., Mehrotra, C. M., Landrum, R. E., & McCarthy, M. A. (2013). An overview of assessment: Demonstrating effective teaching and learning. In *Assessing teaching and learning in psychology: Current and future perspectives* (pp. 1–7). New York, NY: Wadsworth.

Dunn, M., Thomas, J. O., Swift, W., & Burns, L. (2012). Elite athletes' estimates of the prevalence illicit drug use: Evidence for the false consensus effect. *Drug and Alcohol Review, 31*(1), 27–32.

Dunnette, M. D., Campbell, J., & Jaastad, K. (1963). The effect of group participation on brainstorming effectiveness for 2 industrial samples. *Journal of Applied Psychology, 47*(1), 30–37.

Dunning, D., & Madey, S. F. (1995). Comparison processes in counterfactual thought. In N. J. Roese & J. M. Olson (Eds.), *What might have been: The social psychology of counterfactual thinking* (pp. 103–131). Hillsdale, NJ: Lawrence Erlbaum.

Dunning, D., & Parpal, M. (1989). Mental addition and subtraction in counterfactual reasoning: On assessing the impact of actions and life events. *Journal of Personality and Social Psychology, 57*(1), 5–15.

Dunwoody, P. T., & Plane, D. L. (2019). The influence of authoritarianism and outgroup threat on political affiliations and support for antidemocratic policies. *Peace and Conflict: Journal of Peace Psychology, 25*(3), 198–210.

Durán-Narucki, V. (2008). School building condition, school attendance, and academic achievement in New York City public schools: A mediation model. *Journal of Environmental Psychology, 28*(3), 278–286.

Durkheim, E. (1984). *The division of labor in society* (W. D. Halls, Trans.). New York, NY: Free Press. (Original work published 1893)

Dustin, D. L., Wright, B., Harper, J., Lamke, G., Murphy, J., & McDonald, C. (2019). Travel hopefully: The obvious and not so obvious dividends from professional investments. *SCHOLE: A Journal of Leisure Studies and Recreation Education, 34*(1), 62–68.

Dutton, D. G. (1998). *The abusive personality: Violence and control in intimate relationships*. New York, NY: Guilford.

Dutton, D. G., & Aron, A. P. (1974). Some evidence for heightened sexual attraction under conditions of high anxiety. *Journal of Personality and Social Psychology, 30*(4), 510–517.

Dworkin, S. L., & O'Sullivan, L. (2005). Actual versus desired initiation patterns among a sample of college men: Tapping disjunctures within traditional male sexual scripts. *Journal of Sex Research, 42*(2), 150–158.

Dyer, R. (2016). The matter of Whiteness. In P. S. Rothenberg (Ed.), *White privilege* (5th ed.). New York, NY: Worth.

Dys-Steenbergen, O., Wright, S. C., & Aron, A. (2016). Self-expansion motivation improves cross-group interactions and enhances self-growth. *Group Processes & Intergroup Relations, 19*(1), 60–71.

Eagly, A. H. (1987). *Sex differences in social behavior: A social role interpretation*. Hillsdale, NJ: Lawrence Erlbaum.

Eagly, A. H. (2009). The his and hers of prosocial behavior: An examination of the social psychology of gender. *American Psychologist, 64*(8), 644–658.

Eagly, A. H., & Chaiken, S. (1993). *The psychology of attitudes*. Fort Worth, TX: Harcourt Brace Jovanovich.

Eagly, A. H., & Chaiken, S. (2007). The advantages of an inclusive definition of attitude. *Social Cognition, 25*(5), 582–602.

Eagly, A. H., Wood, W., & Chaiken, S. (1978). Causal inferences about communicators and their effect on opinion change. *Journal of Personality and Social Psychology, 36*(4), 424–435.

Eagly, A. H., Wood, W., & Diekman, A. B. (2000). Social role theory of sex differences and similarities: A current appraisal. In T. Ekes & H. M. Trautner (Eds.), *The developmental social psychology of gender* (pp. 123–174). Mahwah, NJ: Lawrence Erlbaum.

Earp, B. D., & Trafimow, D. (2015). Replication, falsification, and the crisis of confidence in social psychology. *Frontiers in Psychology, 6*, 621.

Eberth, J., & Sedlmeier, P. (2012). The effects of mindfulness meditation: A meta-analysis. *Mindfulness, 3*(3), 174–189.

Ebi, K., & Boyer, C. (2019). Building resilience of health systems to climate change in Pacific Least Developed Countries: Implementation science. *The Lancet Planetary Health, 3*, S6.

Eby, L. T., Cader, J., & Noble, C. L. (2003). Why do high self-monitors emerge as leaders in small groups? A comparative analysis of the behaviors of high versus low self-monitors. *Journal of Applied Social Psychology, 33*, 1457–1479.

Echols, L., & Graham, S. (2013). Birds of a different feather: How do cross-ethnic friends flock together? *Merrill-Palmer Quarterly, 59*(4), 461–488.

Eden, D. (1990). *Pygmalion in management: Productivity as a self-fulfilling prophecy.* Lexington, MA: Lexington Books.

Edwards, A. M., Dutton-Challis, L., Cottrell, D., Guy, J. H., & Hettinga, F. J. (2018). Impact of active and passive social facilitation on self-paced endurance and sprint exercise: encouragement augments performance and motivation to exercise. *BMJ Open Sport & Exercise Medicine, 4*(1), e000368.

Edwards, K. M., Gidycz, C. A., & Murphy, M. J. (2015). Leaving an abusive dating relationship: A prospective analysis of the investment model and theory of planned behavior. *Journal of Interpersonal Violence, 30*(16), 2908–2927.

Ehrsson, H. H. (2020). Multisensory processes in body ownership. In K. Sathian & V. S. Ramachandran (Eds.), *Multisensory perception* (pp. 179–200). Cambridge, MA: Academic Press.

Einhorn, H. J., & Hogarth, R. M. (1986). Judging probable cause. *Psychological Bulletin, 99*(1), 3–19.

Eisenberg, N. I., Fabes, R., & Shea, C. (1989). Gender differences in empathy and prosocial moral reasoning: Empirical investigations. In M. M. Brabeck (Ed.), *Who cares? Theory, research, and educational implications of the ethic of care* (pp. 127–143). New York, NY: Praeger.

Eisenberg, R. (2016). Home visiting quality and parent involvement: Examining mediation in home visiting. *Dissertation Abstracts International Section A, 76.* http://preserve.lehigh.edu/etd/2583

Eisenberger, N. I., & Lieberman, M. D. (2005). Why it hurts to be left out: The neurocognitive overlap between physical and social pain. In K. D. Williams, J. P. Forgas, & W. von Hippel (Eds.), *The social outcast: Ostracism, social exclusion, rejection, and bullying* (pp. 109–130). New York, NY: Psychology Press.

Eisenberger, N. I., Lieberman, M. D., & Williams, K. D. (2003). Does rejection hurt? An fMRI study of social exclusion. *Science, 302*(5643), 290–292.

Ekman, P. (2006). *Darwin and facial expression: A century of research in review.* Cambridge, MA: Malor Books.

Ekman, P., & Frank, M. G. (1993). Lies that fail. In M. Lewis & C. Saarni (Eds.), *Lying and deception in everyday life* (pp. 184–200). New York, NY: Guilford.

Ekman, P., & Friesen, W. V. (1969). Nonverbal leakage and clues to deception. *Psychiatry, 32*(1), 88–97.

Ekman, P., & Friesen, W. V. (1971). Constants across cultures in the face and emotion. *Journal of Personality and Social Psychology, 17*(2), 124–129.

Ekman, P., & Friesen, W. V. (1974). Detecting deception from body or face. *Journal of Personality and Social Psychology, 29*(3), 288–298.

Ekman, P., & O'Sullivan, M. (2006). From flawed self-assessment to blatant whoppers: The utility of voluntary and involuntary behavior in detecting deception. *Behavioral Sciences & the Law, 24*(5), 673–686.

Ekman, P., O'Sullivan, M., & Frank, M. G. (1999). A few can catch a liar. *Psychological Science, 10*(3), 263–266.

Ekman, P., O'Sullivan, M., & Matsumoto, D. (1991). Confusions about context in the judgment of facial expression: A reply to 'The contempt expression and the relativity thesis'. *Motivation and Emotion, 15*(2), 169–176.

Elderton, A., Berry, A., & Chan, C. (2017). A systematic review of posttraumatic growth in survivors of interpersonal violence in adulthood. *Trauma, Violence, & Abuse, 18*(2), 223–236.

Ellerby, K. (2017, July 10). *What the Handmaid's Tale reminds us about gender equality.* From The Square. Retrieved December 20, 2019, from https://www.fromthesquare.org/what-the-handmaids-tale-reminds-us-about-gender-equality/#.Xf0sx-hKg2w

Ellickson, K. A., & Brown, D. R. (1990). Ethical considerations in dual relationships: The sport psychologist-coach. *Journal of Applied Sport Psychology, 2*(2), 186–190.

Elliot, P. (1996). Shattering illusions: Same-sex domestic violence. *Journal of Gay & Lesbian Social Services, 4*(1), 1–8.

Ellis, J. (1976). *Eye-deep in Hell: Trench warfare in WW I.* Baltimore, MD: Johns Hopkins University Press.

Ellison, N. B., Steinfield, C., & Lampe, C. (2007). The benefits of Facebook "friends": Social capital and college students' use of online social network sites. *Journal of Computer-Mediated Communication, 12*(4), 1143–1168.

Elmore, R., & Urbaczewski, A. (2019). Loss aversion in professional golf. http://dx.doi.org/10.2139/ssrn.3311649

Emmerich, K., & Masuch, M. (2018, April). Watch me play: Does social facilitation apply to digital games? In *Proceedings of the 2018 CHI Conference on Human Factors in Computing Systems* (p. 100). New York, NY: ACM.

Emswiller, T., Deaux, K., & Willits, J. E. (1971). Similarity, sex, and requests for small favors. *Journal of Applied Social Psychology, 1*(3), 284–291.

Engel, G. L. (1977). The need for a new medical model: A challenge for biomedicine. *Science, 196*(4286), 129–136.

Epley, N. (2004). A tale of tuned decks? Anchoring as accessibility and anchoring as adjustment. In D. J. Koehler & N. Harvey (Eds.), *Blackwell handbook of judgment and decision making* (pp. 240–257). Malden, MA: Blackwell.

Epley, N., Boaz, K., & Van Boven, L. (2004). Perspective taking as egocentric anchoring and adjustment. *Journal of Personality and Social Psychology, 87,* 447–460.

Epley, N., & Gilovich, T. (2001). Putting adjustment back in the anchoring and adjustment heuristic: Differential processing of self-generated and experimenter-provided anchors. *Psychological Science, 12,* 391–396.

Epley, N., & Gilovich, T. (2004). Are adjustments insufficient? *Personality and Social Psychology Bulletin, 30*(4), 447–460.

Epley, N., & Gilovich, T. (2006). The anchoring-and-adjustment heuristic: Why the adjustments are insufficient. *Psychological Science, 17*(4), 311–318.

Epley, N., Keysar, B., Van Boven, L., & Gilovich, T. (2004). Perspective taking as egocentric anchoring and adjustment. *Journal of Personality and Social Psychology, 87*(3), 327–339.

Epstein, J., Noel, J., Finnegan, M., & Watkins, K. (2016). Bacon brains: Video games for teaching the science of addiction. *Journal of Child & Adolescent Substance Abuse, 25*(6), 504–515.

Ertekin P. S., Duran Aksoy, O., Daglar, G., Yurtsal, Z. B., & Cesur, B. (2018). Effect of stress management training on depression, stress and coping strategies in pregnant women: A randomised controlled trial. *Journal of Psychosomatic Obstetrics & Gynecology, 39*(3), 203–210.

Essock-Vitale, S. M., & McGuire, M. T. (1985). Women's lives viewed from an evolutionary perspective: II. Patterns of helping. *Ethology and Sociobiology, 6*(3), 155–173.

Euston, D. R., Gruber, A. J., & McNaughton, B. L. (2012). The role of medial prefrontal cortex in memory and decision making. *Neuron, 76*(6), 1057–1070.

Everson-Rose, S. A., & Lewis, T. T. (2005). Psychosocial factors and cardiovascular diseases. *Annual Review of Public Health, 26,* 469–500.

Falicov, C. J. (1995). Cross-cultural marriages. In N. S. Jacobson & A. S. Gurman (Eds.), *Clinical handbook of couple therapy* (pp. 231–246). New York, NY: Guilford.

Fallon, L., & Snook, B. (2019). Criminal Profiling. *Psychological Science and the Law, 7.*

Farmer, R. F., & Sundberg, N. D. (2010). Buffering hypothesis. In *Corsini encyclopedia of psychology.* New York, NY: John Wiley.

Farr, R. M. (1996). *The roots of modern social psychology, 1872–1954.* Cambridge, MA: Blackwell.

Farrelly, D., & King, L. (2019). Mutual mate choice drives the desirability of altruism in relationships. *Current Psychology, 38*(4), 977–981.

Feely, T. H. (2002). Evidence of halo effects in student evaluations of communication instruction. *Communication Education, 51*(3), 225–236.

Feige, K. (Producer), & Johnston, J. (Director). (2011). *Captain America. The first avenger* [Motion picture]. United States: Marvel Studios.

Feinberg, M., & Willer, R. (2011). Apocalypse soon? Dire messages reduce belief in global warming by contradicting just-world beliefs. *Psychological Science, 22*(1), 34–38.

Feingold, A. (1992). Good-looking people are not what we think. *Psychological Bulletin, 111*(2), 304–341.

Fernan, C., Schuldt, J. P., & Niederdeppe, J. (2018). Health halo effects from product titles and nutrient content claims in the context of "protein" bars. *Health Communication, 33*(12), 1425–1433.

Feshbach, S. (1964). The function of aggression and the regulation of aggressive drive. *Psychological Review, 71*(4), 257–272.

Festinger, L. (1954). A theory of social comparison processes. *Human Relations, 7*(2), 117–140.

Festinger, L. (1957). *A theory of cognitive dissonance.* Stanford, CA: Stanford University Press.

Festinger, L., & Carlsmith, J. M. (1959). Cognitive consequences of forced compliance. *Journal of Abnormal and Social Psychology, 58*(2), 203–210.

Festinger, L., & Maccoby, N. (1964). On resistance to persuasive communication. *Journal of Abnormal and Social Psychology, 68*(4), 359–366.

Festinger, L., Riecken, H. W., & Schachter, S. (2008). *When prophecy fails: A social and psychological study of a modern group that predicted the destruction of the world.* Minneapolis: University of Minnesota Press. (Original work published 1956)

Festinger, L., Schachter, S., & Back, K. W. (1950). *Social pressures in informal groups: A study of human factors in housing.* New York, NY: Harper & Bros.

Feyereisen, P. (2006). Review of nonverbal communication across disciplines. Volume 1: Culture, sensory interaction, speech, conversation. Volume 2: Paralanguage, kinesics, silence, personal and environmental interaction. Volume 3: Narrative literature, theater, cinema, translation. *Gesture, 6*(2), 273–282.

Fiedler, F. E. (1967). *A theory of leadership effectiveness.* New York, NY: McGraw Hill.

Fiedler, F. E. (1996). Research on leadership selection and training: One view of the future. *Administrative Science Quarterly, 41*(2), 241–250.

Fiedler, K., Freytag, P., & Meiser, T. (2009). Pseudocontingencies: An integrative account of an intriguing cognitive illusion. *Psychological Review, 116*(1), 187–206.

Filindra, A., & Pearson-Merkowitz, S. (2013). Together in good times and bad? How economic triggers condition the effects of intergroup threat. *Social Science Quarterly, 94*(5), 1328–1345.

Findlay, L. C., & Coplan, R. J. (2008). Come out and play: Shyness in childhood and organized sports participation. *Canadian Journal of Behavioural Science, 40*(3), 153–161.

Finkel, E. J. (2008). Intimate partner violence perpetration: Insights from the science of self-regulation. In J. P. Forgas & J. Fitness (Eds.), *Social relationships: Cognitive, affective, and motivational processes* (pp. 271–288). New York, NY: Psychology Press.

Finkel, E. J. (2014). The I³ model: Metatheory, theory, and evidence. *Advances in Experimental Social Psychology, 49*, 1–104.

Finkel, E. J., DeWall, C. N., Slotter, E. B., McNulty, J. K., Pond, R. S., Jr., & Atkins, D. C. (2012). Using I³ theory to clarify when dispositional aggressiveness predicts intimate partner violence perpetration. *Journal of Personality and Social Psychology, 102*(3), 533–549.

Finkel, E. J., DeWall, C. N., Slotter, E. B., Oaten, M., & Foshee, V. A. (2009). Self-regulatory failure and intimate partner violence perpetration. *Journal of Personality and Social Psychology, 97*(3), 483–499.

Finkel, E. J., & Hall, A. N. (2018). The I³ model: A metatheoretical framework for understanding aggression. *Current Opinion in Psychology, 19*, 125–130.

Finkel, N. J. (2000). But it's not fair! Commonsense notions of unfairness. *Psychology, Public Policy, and Law, 6*(4), 898–952.

Finley, L., & Esposito, L. (2019). The immigrant as bogeyman: Examining Donald Trump and the right's anti-immigrant, anti-PC rhetoric. *Humanity & Society.* Advance online publication. doi:0160597619832627

Fiocco, A. J., Mallya, S., Farzaneh, M., & Koszycki, D. (2019). Exploring the benefits of mindfulness training in healthy community-dwelling older adults: A randomized controlled study using a mixed methods approach. *Mindfulness, 10*(4), 737–748.

Firestone, I. J., Kaplan, K. J., & Russell, J. C. (1973). Anxiety, fear, and affiliation with similar-state versus dissimilar-state others: Misery sometimes loves nonmiserable company. *Journal of Personality and Social Psychology, 26*(3), 409–414.

Fischer, P., & Greitemeyer, T. (2013). The positive bystander effect: Passive bystanders increase helping in situations with high expected negative consequences for the helper. *Journal of Social Psychology, 153*(1), 1–5.

Fischhoff, B. (1975). Hindsight is not equal to foresight: The effect of outcome knowledge on judgment under uncertainty. *Journal of Experimental Psychology: Human Perception and Performance, 1*(3), 288–299.

Fischhoff, B. (2002). For those condemned to study the past: Heuristics and biases in hindsight. In D. J. Levitin (Ed.), *Foundations of cognitive psychology: Core readings* (pp. 621–636). Cambridge, MA: MIT Press.

Fischhoff, B. (2007). An early history of hindsight research. *Social Cognition, 25*(1), 10–13.

Fish, J., & Syed, M. (2019). The multiple levels of racism, discrimination, and prejudice. In S. Hupp & J. Jewell (Eds.), *Encyclopedia of child and adolescent development.* San Francisco, CA: Wiley-Blackwell.

Fishbein, M., & Cappella, J. N. (2006). The role theory in developing effective health communications. *Journal of Communication, 56*(1), S1–S17.

Fisher, T. D., & Brunell, A. B. (2014). A bogus pipeline approach to studying gender differences in cheating behavior. *Personality and Individual Differences, 61–62*, 91–96.

Fiske, S. T., Cuddy, A. J., Glick, P., & Xu, J. (2002). A model of (often mixed) stereotype content: Competence and warmth respectively follow from perceived status and competition. *Journal of Personality and Social Psychology, 82*(6), 878–902.

Fiske, S. T., Kenny, D. A., & Taylor, S. E. (1982). Structural models for the mediation of salience effects on attribution. *Journal of Experimental Social Psychology, 18*(2), 105–127.

Fleder, G., Kankiewicz, C., & Milchan, A. (Producers), & Fleder, G. (Director). (2003). *Runaway jury* [Motion picture]. United States: 20th Century Fox.

Flicker, S. M., Sancier-Barbosa, F., Afroz, F., Saif, S. N., & Mohsin, F. (2019). Marital quality in arranged and couple-initiated marriages: The role of perceived influence over partner selection. *International Journal of Psychology.* Advance online publication. https://onlinelibrary.wiley.com/doi/pdf/10.1002/ijop.12622

Flynn, F. J., Reagans, R. E., Amanatullah, E. T., & Ames, D. R. (2006). Helping one's way to the top: Self-monitors achieve status by helping others and knowing who helps whom. *Journal of Personality and Social Psychology, 91,* 1123– 1137.

Flyvbjerg, B., Buzelius, N., and Rothengatter, W. (2003). *Megaprojects and risk: An anatomy of ambition.* Cambridge, UK: Cambridge University Press.

Flyvbjerg, B., & Sunstein, C. R. (2016). The principle of the malevolent hiding hand; or, the planning fallacy writ large. *Social Research: An International Quarterly, 83*(4), 979–1004.

Fogelson, A. (Producer), & Gottlieb, L. (Director). (1985). *Just one of the guys* [Motion picture]. USA: Colombia Pictures, Summa Entertainment Group, & Triton.

Follingstad, D. R., Rutledge, L. L., Berg, B. J., Hause, E. S., & Polek, D. S. (1990). The role of emotional abuse in physically abusive relationships. *Journal of Family Violence, 5*(2), 107–120.

Fonda, H., Rose, R., & Donnelly, T. A. (Producers), & Lumet, S., & Friedkin, W. (Directors). (1997). *12 angry men* [Motion picture]. United States: Orion-Nova Productions and MGM Television. (Original work published 1957)

Fontana, D. (1993). *The secret language of symbols: A visual key to symbols and their meanings.* San Francisco, CA: Chronicle Books.

Ford, T. E., Ferguson, M. A., Brooks, J. L., & Hagadone, K. M. (2004). Coping sense of humor reduces effects of stereotype threat on women's math performance. *Personality and Social Psychology Bulletin, 30*(5), 643–653.

Forgas, J. P. (1998). On being happy and mistaken: Mood effects on the fundamental attribution error. *Journal of Personality and Social Psychology, 75*(2), 318–331.

Forsyth, D. R., Lawrence, N. K., Burnette, J. L., & Baumeister, R. F. (2007). Attempting to improve the academic performance of struggling college students by bolstering their self-esteem: An intervention that backfired. *Journal of Social and Clinical Psychology, 26*(4), 447–459.

Fox, B., & Farrington, D. P. (2018). What have we learned from offender profiling? A systematic review and meta-analysis of 40 years of research. *Psychological Bulletin, 144*(12), 1247–1274.

Fox, N. A., & Davidson, R. J. (1988). Patterns of brain electrical activity during facial signs of emotion in 10-month-old infants. *Developmental Psychology, 24*(2), 230–236.

Francis, C., & Barber, J. (2013). A framework for understanding noise impacts on wildlife: An urgent conservation priority. *Frontiers in Ecology and the Environment, 11*(6), 305–313.

Frank, M. G., & Gilovich, T. (1988). The dark side of self- and social perception: Black uniforms and aggression in professional sports. *Journal of Personality and Social Psychology, 54*(1), 74–85.

Franklin, T. W. (2018). The state of race and punishment in America: Is justice really blind? *Journal of Criminal Justice, 59,* 18–28.

Franzen, A., Mader, S., & Winter, F. (2018). Contagious yawning, empathy, and their relation to prosocial behavior. *Journal of Experimental Psychology: General, 147*(12), 1950–1958.

Frederick, D., & Fales, M. (2016). Upset over sexual versus emotional infidelity among gay, lesbian, bisexual, and heterosexual adults. *Archives of Sexual Behavior: The Official Publication of the International Academy of Sex Research, 45*(1), 175–191.

Fredrickson, B. L. (2013). Updated thinking on positivity ratios. *American Psychologist, 68*(9), 814–822.

Fredrickson, B. L., & Losada, M. F. (2005). Positive affect and the complex dynamics of human flourishing. *American Psychologist, 60*(7), 678–686.

Freedman, J. L., & Fraser, S. C. (1966). Compliance without pressure: The foot-in-the-door technique. *Journal of Personality and Social Psychology, 4*(2), 195–202.

Fridlund, A. J. (1994). *Human facial expression.* San Diego, CA: Academic Press.

Friedemann, V. M., & Morgan, M. K. (1985). *Interviewing sexual abuse victims using anatomical dolls: The professional's guidebook.* Eugene, OR: Shamrock Press.

Friedman, M., & Rosenman, R. (1974). *Type A behavior and your heart.* New York, NY: Knopf.

Friedman, S. T. (1964). Parental child-rearing attitudes and social behavior of children. *Dissertation Abstracts, 24*(8), 3415.

Friend, R., Rafferty, Y., & Bramel, D. (1990). A puzzling misinterpretation of the Asch 'conformity' study. *European Journal of Social Psychology, 20*(1), 29–44.

Frieze, I. H., Olson, J. E., & Russell, J. (1991). Attractiveness and income for men and women in management. *Journal of Applied Social Psychology, 21*(13), 1039–1057.

Froh, J. J. (2004). The history of positive psychology: Truth be told. *NYS Psychologist, 16*(3), 18–20.

Fulero, S. M., & Wrightsman, L. S. (2008). *Forensic psychology.* Boston, MA: Cengage Learning.

Fultz, J., Schaller, M., & Cialdini, R. B. (1988). Empathy, sadness, and distress: Three related but distinct vicarious affective responses to another's suffering. *Personality and Social Psychology Bulletin, 14*(2), 312–325.

Furley, P., Schweizer, G., & Bertrams, A. (2015). The two modes of an athlete: Dual-process theories in the field of sport. *International Review of Sport and Exercise Psychology, 8*(1), 106–124.

Furnham, A. (1995). The just world, charitable giving and attitudes to disability. *Personality and Individual Differences, 19*(4), 577–583.

Furnham, A. (2003). Belief in a just world: Research progress over the past decade. *Personality and Individual Differences, 34*(5), 795–817.

Furnham, A., & Dowsett, T. (1993). Sex differences in social comparison and uniqueness bias. *Personality and Individual Differences, 15*(2), 175–183.

Furnham, A., & Gunter, B. (1984). Just world beliefs and attitudes towards the poor. *British Journal of Social Psychology, 23*(3), 265–269.

Gable, S. L., & Haidt, J. (2005). What (and why) is positive psychology? *Review of General Psychology, 9*(2), 103–110.

Gagnon, J. H., & Simon, W. (1987). The sexual scripting of oral genital contacts. *Archives of Sexual Behavior, 16*(1), 1–25.

Gakhal, B., & Senior, C. (2008). Examining the influence of fame in the presence of beauty: An electrodermal 'neuromarketing' study. *Journal of Consumer Behavior, 7*(4–5), 331–341.

Gal, D., & Rucker, D. D. (2018). The loss of loss aversion: Will it loom larger than its gain? *Journal of Consumer Psychology, 28*(3), 497–516.

Galanter, M. (2005). The hundred-year decline of trials and the thirty years war. *Stanford Law Review, 57*(5), 1255–1274.

Gallagher, M. W., Long, L. J., Richardson, A., & D'Souza, J. M. (2019). Resilience and coping in cancer survivors: The unique effects of optimism and mastery. *Cognitive Therapy and Research, 43*(1), 32–44.

Gallo, A., & DeRobertis, J. (2019, February 15). LSU admins on leave amid questions over handling of DKE abuse; ex-student affairs president left in January. *The Advocate.* Retrieved December 17, 2019, from https://www.theadvocate.com/baton_rouge/news/article_01050f1e-3156-11e9-9c6d-27571fb9c610.html

Gallup, A. C., Vasilyev, D., Anderson, N., & Kingstone, A. (2019). Contagious yawning in virtual reality is affected by actual, but not simulated, social presence. *Scientific Reports, 9*(1), 294–303.

Gallup, G. J. (1968). Mirror-image stimulation. *Psychological Bulletin, 70*(6, Pt. 1), 782–793.

Gamble, J. L., & Hess, J. J. (2012). Temperature and violent crime in Dallas, Texas: Relationships and implications of climate change. *Western Journal of Emergency Medicine, 13*(3), 239–246.

Gana, K., Alaphilippe, D., & Bailly, N. (2004). Positive illusions and mental and physical health in later life. *Aging & Mental Health, 8*(1), 58–64.

Gangestad, S. W., Thornhill, R., & Yeo, R. A. (1994). Facial attractiveness, developmental stability, and fluctuating asymmetry. *Ethology & Sociobiology, 15*(2), 73–85.

Gannon, T. A., Keown, K., & Polaschek, D. L. (2007). Increasing honest responding on cognitive distortions in child molesters: The bogus pipeline revisited. *Sexual Abuse: Journal of Research and Treatment, 19*(1), 5–22.

Gansberg, M. (1964, March 27). 37 who saw murder didn't call the police. *New York Times*.

Garrett-Bakelman, F. E., Darshi, M., Green, S. J., Gur, R. C., Lin, L., Macias, B. R., McKenna, M. J., Meydan, T., Nasrini, J., Piening, B. D., Rizzardi, L. F., Sharma, K., Siamwala, J. H., Taylor, L., Hotz Vitaterna, M., Afkarian, M., Afshinnekoo, E., Ahada, S., Ambati, A., . . . & Turek, F. W. (2019). The NASA twins study: A multidimensional analysis of a year-long human spaceflight. *Science, 364*(6436), [onlinel].

Geen, R. G. (1989). Alternative conceptions of social facilitation. In P. B. Paulus (Ed.), *Psychology of group influence* (2nd ed., pp. 15–51). Hillsdale, NJ: Lawrence Erlbaum.

Gelb, B. D., & Zinkhan, G. M. (1986). Humor and advertising effectiveness after repeated exposures to a radio commercial. *Journal of Advertising, 15*(2), 15–34.

Geldenhuys, K. (2019). Diamonds—tools to launder money and fund terrorism. *Servamus Community-based Safety and Security Magazine, 112*(6), 20–24.

Gendron, M., Roberson, D., van der Vyver, J. M., & Barrett, L. F. (2014). Cultural relativity in perceiving emotion from vocalizations. *Psychological Science, 25*(4), 911–920.

George, J., & Wallio, S. (2017). Organizational justice and millennial turnover in public accounting. *Employee Relations, 39*(1), 112–126.

George, K. M., & Basavarajappa. (2016). Impact of brainstorming on creativity among middle school children. *Journal of the Indian Academy of Applied Psychology, 42*(2), 320–327.

George, M. (2013). Seeking legitimacy: The professionalization of life coaching. *Sociological Inquiry, 83*(2), 179–208.

Gerber, A. S., Huber, G. A., Doherty, D., Dowling, C. M., & Panagopoulos, C. (2013). Big five personality traits and responses to persuasive appeals: Results from voter turnout experiments. *Political Behavior, 35*(4), 687–728.

Gergen, K. J., Gergen, M. M., & Barton, W. H. (1973). Deviance in the dark. *Psychology Today, 7*(5), 129–130.

Geronimus, A. T. (1992). The weathering hypothesis and the health of African-American women and infants: Evidence and speculations. *Ethnicity & Disease, 2*(3), 207–221.

Gettleman, J. (2011, December 28). For Somali women, pain of being a spoil of war. *New York Times*, p. A1.

Ghaemi, S. N. (2009). The rise and fall of the biopsychosocial model. *The British Journal of Psychiatry, 195*(1), 3–4.

Gibbons, F. X., & Buunk, B. P. (1999). Individual differences in social comparison: Development of a scale of social comparison orientation. *Journal of Personality and Social Psychology, 76*(1), 129–142.

Gibbons, F. X., Lane, D. J., Gerrard, M., Reis-Bergan, M., Lautrup, C. L., Pexa, N. A., & Blanton, H. (2002). Comparison-level preferences after performance: Is downward comparison theory still useful? *Journal of Personality and Social Psychology, 83*(4), 865–880.

Giesen, A., & Echterhoff, G. (2018). Do I really feel your pain? Comparing the effects of observed and personal ostracism. *Personality and Social Psychology Bulletin, 44*(4), 550–561.

Gilbert, D. T. (1991). How mental systems believe. *American Psychologist, 46*(2), 107–119.

Gilbert, D. T., Giesler, R. B., & Morris, K. A. (1995). When comparisons arise. *Journal of Personality and Social Psychology, 69*(2), 227–236.

Gilbert, D. T., & Gill, M. J. (2000). The momentary realist. *Psychological Science, 11*(5), 394–398.

Gilbert, D. T., & Hixon, J. G. (1991). The trouble of thinking: Activation and application of stereotypic beliefs. *Journal of Personality and Social Psychology, 60*(4), 509–517.

Gilbert, D. T., & Malone, P. S. (1995). The correspondence bias. *Psychological Bulletin, 117*(1), 21–38.

Gilbert, D. T., Pinel, E. C., Wilson, T. D., Blumberg, S. J., & Wheatley, T. P. (1998). Immune neglect: A source of durability bias in affective forecasting. *Journal of Personality and Social Psychology, 75*(3), 617–638.

Gillath, O., Adams, G., & Kunkel, A. (2012). *Relationship science: Integrating evolutionary, neuroscience, and sociocultural approaches*. Washington, DC: American Psychological Association.

Gilovich, T. (1983). Biased evaluation and persistence in gambling. *Journal of Personality and Social Psychology, 44*(6), 1110–1126.

Gilovich, T., Kerr, M., & Medvec, V. H. (1993). Effect of temporal perspective on subjective confidence. *Journal of Personality and Social Psychology, 64*(4), 552–560.

Giralt, M., Murray, L., & Benini, S. (2019, August). *VE, warts and all: 'Catastrophes', 'disasters' and failing better*. Paper presented at the EUROCALL Conference 2019, Louvain-la-Neuve, Belgium.

Glanz, K., Rimer, B. K., & Viswanath, K. (Eds.). (2008). *Health behavior and health education: Theory, research, and practice*. Hoboken, NJ: John Wiley.

Gleick, E. (1997, February 10). Marine blood sports. *Time*, p. 30.

Glencross, A. (2018). *Cameron's European legacy: How Brexit demonstrates the flawed politics of simple solutions*. In U. Staiger & B. Martill (Eds.), *Brexit and beyond: Rethinking the futures of Europe*. London, UK: UCL Press.

Glick, P., & Fiske, S. T. (1996). The ambivalent sexism inventory: Differentiating hostile and benevolent sexism. *Journal of Personality and Social Psychology, 70*(3), 491–512.

Glick, P., & Fiske, S. T. (1997). Hostile and benevolent sexism: Measuring ambivalent sexist attitudes toward women. *Psychology of Women Quarterly, 21*(1), 119–135.

Glick, P., & Fiske, S. T. (2001). An ambivalent alliance: Hostile and benevolent sexism as complementary justifications for gender inequality. *American Psychologist, 56*(2), 109–118.

Glick, P., Sakalli-Ugurlu, N., Ferreira, M. C., & de Souza, M. A. (2002). Ambivalent sexism and attitudes toward wife abuse in Turkey and Brazil. *Psychology of Women Quarterly, 26*(4), 292–297.

Glikson, E., Cheshin, A., & Kleef, G. A. V. (2018). The dark side of a smiley: Effects of smiling emoticons on virtual first impressions. *Social Psychological and Personality Science, 9*(5), 614–625.

Glocker, M. L., Langleben, D. D., Ruparel, K., Loughead, J. W., Valdez, J. N., Griffin, M. D., . . . Gur, R. C. (2009). Baby schema modulates the brain reward system in nulliparous women. *Proceedings of the National Academy of Sciences, 106*(22), 9115–9119.

Glover, D., Pallais, A., & Pariente, W. (2017). Discrimination as a self-fulfilling prophecy: Evidence from French grocery stores. *The Quarterly Journal of Economics, 132*(3), 1219–1260.

Goethals, G. R., Messick, D. M., & Allison, S. T. (1991). The uniqueness bias: Studies of constructive social comparison. In J. Suls & T. A. Wills (Eds.), *Social comparison: Contemporary theory and research* (pp. 149–176). New York, NY: Lawrence Erlbaum.

Goetting, A. (1999). *Getting out: Life stories of women who left abusive men*. New York, NY: Columbia University Press.

Goff, P. A., Jackson, M. C., Di Leone, B. A. L., Culotta, C. M., & DiTomasso, N. A. (2014). The essence of innocence: Consequences of dehumanizing Black children. *Journal of Personality and Social Psychology, 106*(4), 526–545.

Goffman, E. (1959). *The presentation of self in everyday life.* Oxford, UK: Doubleday.

Goffman, E. (1963). *Stigma: Notes on the management of spoiled identity.* Englewood Cliffs, NJ: Prentice Hall.

Goldberg, S. B., Tucker, R. P., Greene, P. A., Davidson, R. J., Wampold, B. E., Kearney, D. J., & Simpson, T. L. (2018). Mindfulness-based interventions for psychiatric disorders: a systematic review and meta-analysis. *Clinical Psychology Review, 59,* 52–60.

Golding, W. (1954). *Lord of the flies.* London, UK: Faber and Faber.

Goldstein, A. L., Wall, A. M., Wekerle, C., & Krank, M. (2013). The impact of perceived reinforcement form alcohol and involvement in leisure activities on adolescent alcohol use. *Journal of Child & Adolescent Substance Abuse, 22*(4), 340–363.

Goldstein, J. (1968). Psychoanalysis and jurisprudence: On the relevance of psychoanalytic theory to law. *The Psychoanalytic Study of the Child, 23*(1), 459–479.

Goldstein, J. H., Davis, R. W., & Herman, D. (1975). Escalation of aggression: Experimental studies. *Journal of Personality and Social Psychology, 31*(1), 162–170.

Golle, J., Probst, F., Mast, F. W., & Lobmaier, J. S. (2015). Preference for cute infants does not depend on their ethnicity or species: Evidence from hypothetical adoption and donation paradigms. *PLoS One, 10*(4), e0121554.

Gonsalkorale, K., & Williams, K. D. (2007). The KKK won't let me play: Ostracism even by a despised outgroup hurts. *European Journal of Social Psychology, 37*(6), 1176–1186.

Goodfriend, W. (2005). Partner-esteem: Romantic partners in the eyes of biased beholders. *Dissertation Abstracts International.* ProQuest #3150766.

Goodfriend, W. (2009). Proximity and attraction. In H. T. Reis & S. Sprecher (Eds.), *Encyclopedia of human relationships* (pp. 1297–1299). Thousand Oaks, CA: Sage.

Goodfriend, W. (2012). Sexual script or sexual improv? Nontraditional sexual paths. In M. Paludi (Ed.), *The psychology of love* (Vol. 1, pp. 59–71). Santa Barbara, CA: Praeger.

Goodfriend, W., & Agnew, C. R. (2008). Sunken costs and desired plans: Examining different types of investments in close relationships. *Personality and Social Psychology Bulletin, 34*(12), 1639–1652.

Goodfriend, W., Agnew, C. R., & Cathey, P. (2017). Understanding commitment and partner-serving biases in close relationships. In J. Fitzgerald (Ed.), *Foundations for couples' therapy: Research for the real world* (pp. 51–60). New York, NY: Routledge.

Goodfriend, W., & Formichella-Elsden, A. (2017). Multiple identities, multiple selves? Diana Prince's actual, ideal, & ought selves. In T. Langley & M. Wood (Eds.), *Wonder Woman psychology: Lassoing the truth* (pp. 139–149). New York, NY: Sterling.

Gordon, A. K., & Kaplar, M. E. (2002). A new technique for demonstrating the actor-observer bias. *Teaching of Psychology, 29*(4), 301–303.

Gordon, D. S., & Platek, S. M. (2009). Trustworthy? The brain knows: Implicit neural responses to faces that vary in dark triad personality characteristics and trustworthiness. *Journal of Social, Evolutionary, and Cultural Psychology, 3*(3), 182.

Gordon, R. A. (1996). Impact of ingratiation on judgments and evaluations: A meta-analytic investigation. *Journal of Personality and Social Psychology, 71*(1), 54–70.

Gorn, G. J., & Goldberg, M. E. (1980). Children's responses to repetitive television commercials. *Journal of Consumer Research, 6*(4), 421–424.

Gosling, S. D., Ko, S. J., Mannarelli, T., & Morris, M. E. (2002). A room with a cue: Personality judgments based on offices and bedrooms. *Journal of Personality and Social Psychology, 82*(3), 379–398.

Gosling, S. D., Sandy, C. J., & Potter, J. (2010). Personalities of self-identified "dog people" and "cat people." *Anthrozoös, 23*(3), 213–222.

Grammer, K., & Thornhill, R. (1994). Human (Homo sapiens) facial attractiveness and sexual selection: The role of symmetry and averageness. *Journal of Comparative Psychology, 108*(3), 233–242.

Granot, E., Alejandro, T. B., & Russell, L. T. M. (2014). A socio-marketing analysis of the concept of cute and its consumer culture implications. *Journal of Consumer Culture, 14*(1), 66–87.

Grasten, R., Grasten, T., Hussain, A., Schwartzman, Y., & Vorhies, A. J. (Producers), & Grasten, P. (Director). (2016). *37* [Motion Picture]. United States: Regner Grasten Film.

Graves, N. B., & Graves, T. D. (1985). Creating a cooperative learning environment. In R. Slavin (Ed.), *Learning to cooperate, cooperating to learn* (pp. 403–436). New York, NY: Plenum.

Greenwald, A. G. (1975). Does the Good Samaritan parable increase helping? A comment on Darley and Batson's no-effect conclusion. *Journal of Personality and Social Psychology, 32*(4), 578–583.

Greenwald, A. G., Banaji, M. R., Rudman, L. A., Farnham, S. D., Nosek, B. A., & Mellott, D. S. (2002). A unified theory of implicit attitudes, stereotypes, self-esteem, and self-concept. *Psychological Review, 109*(1), 3–25.

Greenwald, A. G., & Farnham, S. D. (2000). Using the Implicit Association Test to measure self-esteem and self-concept. *Journal of Personality and Social Psychology, 79*(6), 1022–1038.

Greitemeyer, T., & Mügge, D. O. (2013). Rational bystanders. *British Journal of Social Psychology, 52*(4), 773–780.

Greitemeyer, T., & Mügge, D. O. (2015). 'Video games do affect social outcomes: A meta-analytic review of the effects of violent and prosocial video game play': Corrigendum. *Personality and Social Psychology Bulletin, 41*(8), 1164.

Griffit, W., & Veitch, R. (1971). Hot and crowded: Influence of population density and temperature on interpersonal affective behavior. *Journal of Personality and Social Psychology, 17*(1), 92–98.

Griskevicius, V., Tybur, J. M., Gangestad, S. W., Perea, E. F., Shapiro, J. R., & Kenrick, D. T. (2009). Aggress to impress: Hostility as an evolved context-dependent strategy. *Journal of Personality and Social Psychology, 96*(5), 980–994.

Grobman, A., Landes, D., & Milton, S. (1983). *Genocide, critical issues of the Holocaust: A companion volume to the film,* Genocide. Springfield, NJ: Behrman House, Inc.

Grøntvedt, T. V., & Kennair, L. O. (2013). Age preferences in a gender egalitarian society. *Journal of Social, Evolutionary, and Cultural Psychology, 7*(3), 239–249.

Gross, D. B., & Souleles, N. S. (2002). Do liquidity constraints and interest rates matter for consumer behavior? Evidence from credit card data. *The Quarterly Journal of Economics, 117*(1), 149–185.

Gross, J., & De Dreu, C. K. (2019). Individual solutions to shared problems create a modern tragedy of the commons. *Science Advances, 5*(4), eaau7296.

Grossman, P., Niemann, L., Schmidt, S., & Walach, H. (2004). Mindfulness-based stress reduction and health benefits: A meta-analysis. *Journal of Psychosomatic Research, 57*(1), 35–43.

Gruber-Baldini, A. L., Schaie, K. W., & Willis, S. L. (1995). Similarity in married couples: A longitudinal study of mental abilities and rigidity-flexibility. *Journal of Personality and Social Psychology, 69*(1), 191–203.

Gruter, M., & Masters, R. D. (1986). Ostracism as a social and biological phenomenon: An introduction. *Ethology and Sociobiology, 7*(3–4), 149–158.

Guéguen, N., & Ciccotti, S. (2008). Domestic dogs as facilitators in social interaction: An evaluation of helping and courtship behaviors. *Anthrozoös, 21*(4), 339–349.

Guenther, C. L., & Alicke, M. D. (2008). Self-enhancement and belief perseverance. *Journal of Experimental Social Psychology, 44*(3), 706–712.

Guerin, B. (2001). Replacing catharsis and uncertainty reduction theories with descriptions of historical and social context. *Review of General Psychology, 5*(1), 44–61.

Guild, P. D., Strickland, L. H., & Barefoot, J. C. (1977). Dissonance theory, self-perception and the bogus pipeline. *European Journal of Social Psychology, 7*(4), 465–476.

Guimond, S., Branscombe, N. R., Brunot, S., Buunk, A. P., Chatard, A., Désert, M., . . . Yzerbyt, V. (2007). Culture, gender, and the self: Variations and impact of social comparison processes. *Journal of Personality and Social Psychology, 92*(6), 1118–1134.

Gulati, R., & Puranam, P. (2009). Renewal through reorganization: The value of inconsistencies between formal and informal organizations. *Organization Science, 20*(2), 422–440.

Guniss, C. (2018). The hell that Black people live: Trump's reports to journalists on urban conditions. In R. E. Gutsche Jr. (Ed.), *The Trump presidency, journalism, and democracy* (pp. 140–155). New York, NY: Routledge.

Gunnell, J. J., & Ceci, S. J. (2010). When emotionality trumps reason: A study of individual processing style and juror bias. *Behavioral Sciences & the Law, 28*(6), 850–877.

Guo, F., Ye, G., Hudders, L., Lv, W., Li, M., & Duffy, V. G. (2019). Product placement in mass media: A review and bibliometric analysis. *Journal of Advertising, 48*, 1–17.

Guthrie, R. (2004). *Even the rat was white: A historical view of psychology*. New York, NY: Harper & Row. (Original work published 1976)

Haarr, M. L., Westerveld, L., Fabres, J., Iversen, K. R., & Busch, K. E. T. (2019). A novel GIS-based tool for predicting coastal litter accumulation and optimising coastal cleanup actions. *Marine Pollution Bulletin, 139*, 117–126.

Habashi, M. M., Graziano, W. G., & Hoover, A. E. (2016). Searching for the prosocial personality: A big five approach to linking personality and prosocial behavior. *Personality and Social Psychology Bulletin, 42*(9), 1177–1192.

Hafer, C. L., Begue, L., Choma, B. L., & Dempsey, J. L. (2005). Belief in a just world and commitment to long-term deserved outcomes. *Social Justice Research, 18*(4), 429–444.

Hafer, C. L., & Rubel, A. N. (2015). The why and how of defending belief in a just world. *Advances in Experimental Social Psychology, 51*, 41–96.

Haidt, J. (2001). The emotional dog and its rational tail: A social intuitionist approach to moral judgment. *Psychological Review, 108*(4), 814–834.

Hair, M., Renaud, K. V., & Ramsay, J. (2007). The influence of self-esteem and locus of control on perceived email-related stress. *Computers in Human Behavior, 23*(6), 2791–2803.

Hajir, B. (2019). Between idealism and realism: Critical peace education in divided post-conflict contexts. *Cambridge Open-Review Educational Research e-Journal (CORERJ), 6*(1), 80–96.

Halfmann, E., Bredehoft, J., & Hausser, J. A. (2020). Replicating roaches: A preregistered direct replication of Zajonc, Heingartner, and Herman's (1969) social-facilitation study. *Psychological Science*. Advance online publication.

Hallegatte, S., Bangalore, M., Bonzanigo, L., Fay, M., Kane, T., Narloch, U., Rozenberg, J., Treguer, D., & Vogt-Schilb, A. (2015). *Shock waves: Managing the impacts of climate change on poverty*. The World Bank.

Halperin, C. J. (1984). The ideology of silence: Prejudice and pragmatism on the medieval religious frontier. *Comparative Studies in Society and History, 26*(3), 442–466.

Halsey, L. G., Huber, J. W., Bufton, R. J., & Little, A. C. (2010). An explanation for enhanced perceptions of attractiveness after alcohol consumption. *Alcohol, 44*(4), 307–313.

Hammerton, G., Heron, J., Mahedy, L., Maughan, B., Hickman, M., & Murray, J. (2018). Low resting heart rate, sensation seeking and the course of antisocial behaviour across adolescence and young adulthood. *Psychological Medicine, 48*(13), 2194–2201.

Hancock, J. (2007). Digital deception: When, where, and how people lie online. In K. McKenna, T. Postmes, U. Reips, & A. Joinson (Eds.), *Oxford handbook of Internet psychology* (pp. 287–301). Oxford, UK: Oxford University Press.

Hancock, J. T., Thom-Santelli, J., & Ritchie, T. (2004). Deception and design: The impact of communication technologies on lying behavior. *Proceedings, Conference on Computer Human Interaction, 6*, 130–136.

Haney, C., Banks, W., & Zimbardo, P. (1973). Interpersonal dynamics in a simulated prison. *International Journal of Criminology and Penology, 1*(1), 69–97.

Hansen, C. H., & Hansen, R. D. (1988). Finding the face in the crowd: An angry superiority effect. *Journal of Personality and Social Psychology, 54*(6), 917–924.

Hansen, D. E., Vandenberg, B., & Patterson, M. L. (1995). The effects of religious orientation on spontaneous and nonspontaneous helping behaviors. *Personality and Individual Differences, 19*(1), 101–104.

Hansen, R. D. (1980). Commonsense attribution. *Journal of Personality and Social Psychology, 39*(6), 996–1009.

Harari, Y. N. (2014). *Sapiens: A brief history of humankind*. New York, NY: Harper Perennial.

Hardin, G. (1968). The tragedy of the commons. *Science, 162*, 1243–1248.

Hardy, C. J., & Latane, B. (1988). Social loafing in cheerleaders: Effects of team membership and competition. *Journal of Sport and Exercise Psychology, 10*(1), 109–114.

Harmon-Jones, E. (2007). Asymmetrical frontal cortical activity, affective valence, and motivational direction. In E. Harmon-Jones & P. Winkielman (Eds.), *Social neuroscience: Integrating biological and psychological explanations of social behavior* (pp. 137–156). New York, NY: Guilford.

Harmon-Jones, E., Harmon-Jones, C., & Levy, N. (2015). An action-based model of cognitive-dissonance processes. *Current Directions in Psychological Science, 24*(3), 184–189.

Harper, C. (2007). *Intersex*. Oxford, UK: Berg.

Harris, J. L., Haraghey, K. S., Lodolce, M., & Semenza, N. L. (2018). Teaching children about good health? Halo effects in child-directed advertisements for unhealthy food. *Pediatric Obesity, 13*(4), 256–264.

Harris, L. T., & Fiske, S. T. (2018). Dehumanizing the lowest of the low: Neuroimaging responses to extreme out-groups. *Psychological Science, 17*(10), 847-853.

Harris, M. (1989). *Cows, pigs, wars, & witches: The riddles of culture*. New York, NY: Vintage.

Harrison, A., Summers, J., & Mennecke, B. (2018). The effects of the dark triad on unethical behavior. *Journal of Business Ethics, 153*(1), 53–77.

Hart, B. (1986). Lesbian battering: An examination. In K. Lobel (Ed.), *Naming the violence: Speaking out about lesbian battering* (pp. 173–189). Seattle, WA: Seal Press.

Hart, P. (2010). *The Somme: The darkest hour on the Western Front*. New York, NY: Pegasus Books.

Harvey, J. H., & McGlynn, R. P. (1982). Matching words to phenomena: The case of the fundamental attribution error. *Journal of Personality and Social Psychology, 43*(2), 345–346.

Harvey, J. H., Town, J. P., & Yarkin, K. L. (1981). How fundamental is the fundamental attribution error? *Journal of Personality and Social Psychology, 40*(2), 346–349.

Haselton, M. G., & Funder, D. C. (2006). The evolution of accuracy and bias in social judgment. In M. Schaller, J. A. Simpson, & D. T. Kenrick (Eds.), *Evolution and social psychology* (pp. 15–37). Madison, CT: Psychosocial Press.

Haslam, S. A., Reicher, S. D., & McDermott, M. R. (2015). Studying harm—doing without doing harm: The case of the BBC prison study, the Stanford prison experiment, and the role-conformity model of tyranny. In R. J. Sternberg & S. T. Fiske (Eds.), *Ethical challenges in the behavioral and brain sciences* (pp. 134–144). Cambridge, UK: Cambridge University Press.

Haslam, S. A., Reicher, S. D., Millard, K., & McDonald, R. (2015). "Happy to have been of service": The Yale archive as a window into the engaged followership of participants in Milgram's "obedience" experiments. *British Journal of Social Psychology*, *54*(1), 55–83.

Hassan, N., Mandal, M. K., Bhuiyan, M., Moitra, A., & Ahmed, S. I. (2019, January). Nonparticipation of Bangladeshi women in #MeToo movement. *In Proceedings of the Tenth International Conference on Information and Communication Technologies and Development* (p. 29). New York, NY: ACM.

Haveman-Gould, B., & Newman, C. (2018). Post-traumatic stress disorder in veterans: Treatments and risk factors for nonadherence. *Journal of the American Academy of PAs*, *31*(11), 21–24.

Hawdon, J. E. (2001). The role of presidential rhetoric in the creation of a moral panic: Reagan, Bush, and the war on drugs. *Deviant Behavior*, *22*(5), 419–445.

Haynes, R. B., Ackloo, E., Sahota, N., McDonald, H. P., & Yao, X. (2008). Interventions for enhancing medication adherence. *Cochrane Database of Systematic Reviews*, *2*, CD000011.

Hazan, C., & Shaver, P. (1987). Romantic love conceptualized as an attachment process. *Journal of Personality and Social Psychology*, *52*(3), 511–524.

Hearst, P. C., & Moscow, A. (1988). *Patty Hearst: Her own story*. New York, NY: Avon Books.

Hecker, T., Fetz, S., Ainamani, H., & Elbert, T. (2015). The cycle of violence: Associations between exposure to violence, trauma-related symptoms and aggression—Findings from Congolese refugees in Uganda. *Journal of Traumatic Stress*, *28*(5), 448–455.

Heider, F. (1958). *The psychology of interpersonal relations*. Hoboken, NJ: John Wiley.

Heinzen, T. E. (1995). Commentary: The ethical evaluation bias. *Creativity Research Journal*, *8*(4), 417–422.

Heinzen, T. E., Gordon, M. S., Landrum, R. E., Gurung, R. A. R., Dunn, D. S., & Richman, S. (2015). A parallel universe: Psychological science in the language of game design. In T. Reiners & L. C. Wood (Eds.), *Gamification in education and business* (pp. 133–149). New York, NY: Springer.

Heinzen, T. E., Landrum, R. E., Gurung, R. A., & Dunn, D. S. (2015). Game-based assessment: The mash-up we've been waiting for. In T. Reiners & L. C. Wood (Eds.), *Gamification in education and business* (pp. 201–217). Cham, Switzerland: Springer International.

Helloflo.com. (2017). *Home*. http://helloflo.com/

Helms, M. M., & Nixon, J. (2010). Exploring SWOT analysis–where are we now? *Journal of Strategy and Management*, *3*(3), 215–251.

Henchy, T., & Glass, D. C. (1968). Evaluation apprehension and the social facilitation of dominant and subordinate responses. *Journal of Personality and Social Psychology*, *10*(4), 446–454.

Hendrick, B. (2009). Pets cause thousands of injuries. *WebMD*. Retrieved December 14, 2019, from https://pets.webmd.com/news/20090326/pets-cause-thousands-injuries

Hennessy, D. A., & Wiesenthal, D. L. (2001). Gender, driver aggression, and driver violence: An applied evaluation. *Sex Roles*, *44*(11–12), 661–676.

Henriksen, D., & Dayton, E. (2006). Organizational silence and hidden threats to patient safety. *Health Services Research*, *41*(4, Pt. 2), 1539–1554.

Herek, G. M. (1987). Religious orientation and prejudice: A comparison of racial and sexual attitudes. *Personality and Social Psychology Bulletin*, *13*(1), 34–44.

Heron, K. E., & Smyth, J. M. (2013). Body image discrepancy and negative affect in women's everyday lives: An ecological momentary assessment evaluation of self discrepancy theory. *Journal of Social and Clinical Psychology*, *32*(3), 276–295.

Herzog, H. (2010). *Some we love, some we hate, some we eat*. New York, NY: Harper Perennial.

Herzog, H. (2011). The impact of pets on human health and psychological well-being: Fact, fiction, or hypothesis? *Current Directions in Psychological Science*, *20*(4), 236–239. doi:10.1177/096372 1411415220

Herzog, H. (2019). Did breast-feeding play a role in the evolution of pets? *Humane Society Institute for Science and Policy Animal Studies Repository*. Retrieved February 1, 2020, from https://animalstudiesrepository.org/cgi/viewcontent.cgi?article=1088&context=aniubpos

Herzog, H., Kowalski, R., Burgner, M., & Dunegon, C. (2003, May). Are pets really friends? Perceived benefits of relationships with companion animals. Paper presented at the meeting of the American Psychological Society, Atlanta, GA.

Hewitt, P. L., & Genest, M. (1990). The ideal self: Schematic processing of perfectionistic content in dysphoric university students. *Journal of Personality and Social Psychology*, *59*(4), 802–808.

Higgins, C. A., Judge, T. A., & Ferris, G. R. (2003). Influence tactics and work outcomes: A meta-analysis. *Journal of Organizational Behavior*, *24*(1), 89–106.

Higgins, E. T. (1987). Self-discrepancy: A theory relating self and affect. *Psychological Review*, *94*(3), 319–340.

Higgins, E. T. (2002). How self-regulation creates distinct values: The case of promotion and prevention decision making. *Journal of Consumer Psychology*, *12*(3), 177–191.

Higgins, E. T., & Liberman, N. (2018). The loss of loss aversion: Paying attention to reference points. *Journal of Consumer Psychology*, *28*(3), 523–532.

Hill, D. M., Cheesbrough, M., Gorczynski, P., & Matthews, N. (2019). The consequences of choking in sport: A constructive or destructive experience? *Sport Psychologist*, *33*(1), [online].

Hill, D. M., Hanton, S., Fleming, S., & Matthews, N. (2009). A re-examination of choking in sport. *European Journal of Sport Science*, *9*, 203–212.

Hilton, A., Potvin, L., & Sachdev, I. (1989). Ethnic relations in rental housing: A social psychological approach. *Canadian Journal of Behavioral Science*, *21*(2), 121–131.

Hilton, L., Hempel, S., Ewing, B. A., Apaydin, E., Xenakis, L., Newberry, S., . . . Maglione, M. A. (2016). Mindfulness meditation for chronic pain: Systematic review and meta-analysis. *Annals of Behavioral Medicine*, *51*(2), 199–213.

Hirschberger, G. (2006). Terror management and attributions of blame to innocent victims: Reconciling compassionate and defensive responses. *Journal of Personality and Social Psychology*, *91*(5), 832–844.

Hirschberger, G., Florian, V., & Mikuliner, M. (2005). Fear and compassion: A terror management analysis of emotional reactions to physical disability. *Rehabilitation Psychology*, *50*(3), 246–257.

Hirschman, A. O. (1967). *Development projects observed*. Washington, DC: Brookings Institution.

Hirschman, A. O. (2015). *Development projects observed* (3rd ed.). Washington, DC: Brookings Institution.

Ho, H. C., & Yeung, D. Y. (2019). Effects of social identity salience on motivational orientation and conflict strategies in intergenerational conflict. *International Journal of Psychology*, *54*(1), 108–116.

Hoagwood, K. E., Acri, M., Morrissey, M., & Peth-Pierce, R. (2017). Animal-assisted therapies for youth with or at risk for mental health problems: A systematic review. *Applied Developmental Science*, *21*(1), 1–13.

Hoch, S. J. (1987). Perceived consensus and predictive accuracy: The pros and cons of projection. *Journal of Personality and Social Psychology, 53*(2), 221–234.

Hochschild, A. (2011). *To end all wars: A story of loyalty and rebellion, 1914–1918*. New York, NY: Houghton Mifflin Harcourt.

Hoerger, M., Quirk, S. W., Lucas, R. E., & Carr, T. H. (2010). Cognitive determinants of affective forecasting errors. *Judgment and Decision Making, 5*(5), 365–373.

Hoesey, G. R., Wood, M., Thompson, R. J., & Druck, P. L. (1985). Social facilitation in a 'non-social' animal, the centipede *Lithobius forficatus*. *Behavioural Processes, 10*, 123–130.

Hofmann, E., Fiagbenu, M. E., Ozgümüs, A., Tahamtan, A. M., & Regner, T. (2018). My peers are watching me: Audience and peer effects in a pay-what-you-want context. *Jena Economic Research Papers*. Advance online publication.

Hogg, M. A. (2016). Social identity theory. In S. McKeown, R. Haji, & N. Ferguson (Eds.), *Understanding peace and conflict through social identity theory: Contemporary global perspectives* (pp. 3–17). New York, NY: Springer.

Holmes, D. S. (1968). Dimensions of projection. *Psychological Bulletin, 69*(4), 248–268.

Holmes, D. S. (1978). Projection as a defense mechanism. *Psychological Bulletin, 85*(4), 677–688.

Holmes, T. H., & Rahe, R. H. (1967). The social readjustment rating scale. *Journal of Psychosomatic Research, 11*(2), 213–218.

Holtzworth-Munroe, A., & Meehan, J. C. (2004). Typologies of men who are maritally violent: Scientific and clinical implications. *Journal of Interpersonal Violence, 19*(12), 1369–1389.

Holtzworth-Munroe, A., Meehan, J. C., Herron, K., Rehman, U., & Stuart, G. L. (2000). Testing the Holtzworth-Munroe and Stuart (1994) batterer typology. *Journal of Consulting and Clinical Psychology, 68*(6), 1000–1019.

Holtzworth-Munroe, A., & Stuart, G. L. (1994). Typologies of male batterers: Three subtypes and the differences among them. *Psychological Bulletin, 116*(3), 476–497.

Hopper, E. K. (2017). Trauma-informed psychological assessment of human trafficking survivors. *Women & Therapy, 40*(1/2), 12–30.

Hornberger, R. H. (1959). The differential reduction of aggressive responses as a function of interpolated activities. *American Psychologist, 14*(7), 354.

Horvit, B., Cortés-Martinez, C. A., & Kelling, K. (2018). Journalism, war, and peace. In T. P. Vos (Ed.), *Journalism*. Berlin, Germany: Deutsche Nationalbibliothek.

Hosoda, M., Stone-Romero, E. F., & Coats, G. (2003). The effects of physical attractiveness on job-related outcomes: A meta-analysis of experimental studies. *Personnel Psychology, 56*(2), 431–462.

Hou, L., Wang, Y., Wu, W., Diao, H., & Zhong, J. (2019). Abusive supervision, humility and social loafing: A moderated mediation model. *Academy of Management Proceedings, 2019*(1), 19139.

Hovland, C. I., Janis, I. L., & Kelley, H. H. (1953). *Communication and persuasion: Psychological studies of opinion change*. New Haven, CT: Yale University Press.

Hovland, C. I., Lumsdaine, A. A., & Sheffield, F. D. (1949). *Experiments on mass communication* (Vol. 3). Princeton, NJ: Princeton University Press.

Hovland, C. I., & Sears, R. R. (1940). Minor studies in aggression: VI. Correlation of lynchings with economic indices. *Journal of Psychology, 9*(2), 301–310.

Howe, L. E. A. (1989). Hierarchy and equality: Variations in Balinese social organization. *Bijdragen tot de Taal, Land-en Volkenkunde, 145*(1), 47–71.

Howell, S. (1984). *Society and cosmos: Chewong of peninsular Malaysia*. Oxford, UK: Oxford University Press.

Hsu, F. L. K. (1985). The self in cross-cultural perspective. In A. J. Marsella, G. DeVos, & F. U. K. Hsu (Eds.), *Culture and self: Asian and Western perspectives* (pp. 24–55). London, UK: Tavistock.

Hua, M., & Tan, A. (2012). Media reports of Olympic success by Chinese and American gold medalists: Cultural differences in causal attribution. *Mass Communication & Society, 15*(4), 546–558.

Huck, A., & Monstadt, J. (2019). Urban and infrastructure resilience: Diverging concepts and the need for cross-boundary learning. *Environmental Science & Policy, 100*, 211–220.

Huff, D. (1993). *How to lie with statistics*. New York, NY: Norton.

Huffman, J. C., Millstein, R. A., Mastromauro, C. A., Moore, S. V., Celano, C. M., Bedoya, C. A., . . . Januzzi, J. L. (2016). A positive psychology intervention for patients with an acute coronary syndrome: Treatment development and proof-of-concept trial. *Journal of Happiness Studies, 17*(5), 1985–2006.

Hughes, M., & Louw, J. (2013). Playing games: The salience of social cues and group norms in eliciting aggressive behaviour. *South African Journal of Psychology, 43*(2), 252–262.

Hugo, V. (1831). *The hunchback of Notre-Dame*. Paris, France: Gosselin.

Hui, C. H., & Triandis, H. C. (1986). Individualism-collectivism: A study of cross-cultural researchers. *Journal of Cross-Cultural Psychology, 17*(2), 225–248.

Humphreys, R. (2018). Enhancing our justice system. *Studies: An Irish Quarterly Review, 107*(425), 52–56.

Humphries, T. L. (2003). Effectiveness of dolphin-assisted therapy as a behavioral intervention for young children with disabilities. *Bridges, 1*(6), 1–9.

Hunsberger, B. (1995). Religion and prejudice: The role of religious fundamentalism, quest, and right-wing authoritarianism. *Journal of Social Issues, 51*(2), 113–129.

Huntley, M., & Goodfriend, W. (2019). Feminism in the Legend of Zelda. In A. Bean (Ed.), *Psychology of Zelda* (pp. 219–243). Dallas, TX: BenBella Books.

Hust, S. T., Marett, E. G., Lei, M., Ren, C., & Ran, W. (2015). *Law & Order, CSI*, and *NCIS*: The association between exposure to crime drama franchises, rape myth acceptance, and sexual consent negotiation among college students. *Journal of Health Communication, 20*(12), 1369–1381.

Hutz, C. S., De Conti, L., & Vargas, S. (1994). Rules used by Brazilian students in systematic and nonsystematic reward allocation. *Journal of Social Psychology, 134*(3), 331–338.

Ian, D. (2007). Halo effects in grading student projects. *Journal of Applied Psychology, 92*(4), 1169–1176.

Iedema, J., & Poppe, M. (1999). Expectations of others' social value orientations in specific and general populations. *Personality and Social Psychology Bulletin, 25*(12), 1443–1450.

III. (2019). Insurance Information Institute. Retrieved December 9, 2019, from https://www.iii.org/fact-statistic/facts-statistics-pet-statistics

Ingham, A. G., Levinger, G., Graves, J., & Peckham, V. (1974). The Ringelmann effect: Studies of group size and group performance. *Journal of Experimental Social Psychology, 10*(4), 371–384.

Insko, C. A., Turnbull, W., & Yandell, B. (1974). Facilitative and inhibiting effects of distraction on attitude change. *Sociometry, 37*(4), 508–528.

Isaacson, W. (2011). *Steve Jobs*. New York, NY: Simon & Schuster.

Isaacson, W. (2014). *The innovators: How a group of hackers, geniuses, and geeks created the digital revolution*. New York, NY: Simon & Schuster.

Isenberg, D. (1986). Group polarization: A critical review and meta-analysis. *Journal of Personality and Social Psychology, 50*(6), 1141–1151.

Iyengar, S., & Westwood, S. J. (2015). Fear and loathing across party lines: New evidence on group polarization. *American Journal of Political Science, 59*(3), 690–707.

Izard, E. C. (1990). Facial expressions and the regulation of emotions. *Journal of Personality and Social Psychology, 58*(3), 487–498.

Izuma, K., Saito, D. N., & Sadato, N. (2010). Processing of the incentive for social approval in the ventral striatum during charitable donation. *Journal of Cognitive Neuroscience, 22*(4), 621–631.

Jack, R. E., Garrod, O. B., Yu, H., Caldara, R., & Schyns, P. G. (2012). Facial expressions of emotion are not culturally universal. *Proceedings of the National Academy of Sciences of the United States of America, 109*(19), 7241–7244.

Jackson, J. M., & Williams, K. D. (1985). Social loafing on difficult tasks: Working collectively can improve performance. *Journal of Personality and Social Psychology, 49*(4), 937–942.

Jackson, M., & Grace, D. (2018). *Machiavelliana*. Leiden, Netherlands: Brill Rodopi.

Jackson, S. (1993). Women and the family. In D. Richardson & V. Robinson (Eds.), *Thinking feminist: Key concepts in women's studies* (pp. 177–200). New York, NY: Guilford.

Jackson, S. (2001). Happily never after: Young women's stories of abuse in heterosexual love relationships. *Feminism & Psychology, 11*(3), 305–321.

Jacobs, R. C., & Campbell, D. T. (1961). The perpetuation of an arbitrary tradition through several generations of a laboratory microculture. *Journal of Abnormal and Social Psychology, 62*(3), 649–658.

Jacobson, N. S., & Gottman, J. M. (1998). *When men batter women: New insights into ending abusive relationships*. New York, NY: Simon & Schuster.

James, W. (1890). *The principles of psychology*. New York, NY: Henry Holt.

James, W. (1983). *Talks to teachers on psychology and to students on some of life's ideals* (Vol. 12). New York, NY: Henry Holt. (Original work published 1899)

Janes, L. M., & Olson, J. M. (2000). Jeer pressures: The behavioral effects of observing ridicule of others. *Personality and Social Psychology Bulletin, 26*(4), 474–485.

Janis, I. L. (1972). *Victims of groupthink: A psychological study of foreign-policy decisions and fiascoes*. Boston, MA: Houghton Mifflin.

Jankowska, M. M., Yang, J. A., & Kerr, J. (2019). Physical activity and exposure in breast cancer survivors using GPS, GIS and accelerometry. In D. Barrigan, & N. H. Berger (Eds.), *Geospatial approaches to energy balance and breast cancer* (pp. 81–98). New York, NY: Springer.

Jans-Beken, L., Jacobs, N., Janssens, M., Peeters, S., Reijnders, J., Lechner, L., & Lataster, J. (2019). Reciprocal relationships between state gratitude and high- and low-arousal positive affects in daily life: A time-lagged ecological assessment study. *Journal of Positive Psychology, 14*(4), 512–527.

Jansma, J. M., Ramsey, N. F., Slagter, H. A., & Kahn, R. S. (2001). Functional anatomical correlates of controlled and automatic processing. *Journal of Cognitive Neuroscience, 13*(6), 730–743.

Jensen, B., Valeriano, B., & Maness, R. (2019). Fancy bears and digital trolls: Cyber strategy with a Russian twist. *Journal of Strategic Studies, 42*(2), 212–234.

Jeon, L., Buettner, C. K., & Grant, A. A. (2018). Early childhood teachers' psychological well-being: Exploring potential predictors of depression, stress, and emotional exhaustion. *Early Education and Development, 29*(1), 53–69.

Jhally, S., Ericsson, S., & Talreja, S. (Producers), & Jhally, S. (Director). (1999). *Tough guise: Violence, media, and the crisis in masculinity* [Motion picture]. United States: Media Education Foundation.

Jiang, H., Chen, G., & Wang, T. (2017). Relationship between belief in a just world and Internet altruistic behavior in a sample of Chinese undergraduates: Multiple mediating roles of gratitude and self-esteem. *Personality and Individual Differences, 104*, 493–498.

Jilinskaya-Pandey, M., & Wade, J. (2019). Social entrepreneur quotient: An international perspective on social entrepreneur personalities. *Journal of Social Entrepreneurship, 10*(3), 265–287.

John, O. P., & Srivastava, S. (1999). The big five trait taxonomy: History, measurement, and theoretical perspectives. In L. A. Pervin & O. P. John (Eds.), *Handbook of personality: Theory and research* (2nd ed., pp. 102–138). New York, NY: Guilford.

Johns, A., & Peters, L. (2012). Self-discrepancies and the situational domains of social phobia. *Behaviour Change, 29*(2), 109–125.

Johnson, A. G. (2006). *Privilege, power and difference* (2nd ed.). New York, NY: McGraw Hill.

Johnson, B. T., & Eagly, A. H. (1989). Effects of involvement on persuasion: A meta-analysis. *Psychological Bulletin, 106*(2), 290–314.

Johnson, D. J., & Rusbult, C. E. (1989). Resisting temptation: Devaluation of alternative partners as a means of maintaining commitment in close relationships. *Journal of Personality and Social Psychology, 57*(6), 967–980.

Johnson, E. J., & Goldstein, D. (2003). "Do Defaults Save Lives?" *Science*, 1338–39.

Johnson, J., Guerrero, M. D., Holman, M., Chin, J. W., & Signer-Kroeker, M. (2018). An examination of hazing in Canadian intercollegiate sports. *Journal of Clinical Sport Psychology, 12*(2), 144–159.

Johnson, J. M., & Pettigrew, T. F. (2005). Kenneth B. Clark (1914–2005). *American Psychologist, 60*(6), 649–651.

Johnson, M. P. (1995). Patriarchal terrorism and common couple violence: Two forms of violence against women. *Journal of Marriage and the Family, 57*(2), 283–294.

Johnson, M. P. (2007). The intersection of gender and control. In L. O'Toole, J. R. Schiffman, & M. L. K. Edwards (Eds.), *Gender violence: Interdisciplinary perspectives* (2nd ed., pp. 257–268). New York: New York University Press.

Johnson, R. D., & Downing, L. L. (1979). Deindividuation and valence of cues: Effects on prosocial and antisocial behavior. *Journal of Personality and Social Psychology, 37*(9), 1532–1538.

Johnston, E. (2001). The repeated reproduction of Bartlett's Remembering. *History of Psychology, 4*(4), 341–366.

Johnston, L. (2002). Behavioral mimicry and stigmatization. *Social Cognition, 20*(1), 18–35.

Johnston, R. (2005). *Analytic culture in the U.S. intelligence community: An ethnographic study*. Washington, DC: Government Printing Office.

Jolly, S., & Ahmad, N. (2019). Climate change displacement and refugees: 'Normative debate'. In S. Jolly & N. Ahmad (Eds.), *Climate refugees in South Asia* (pp. 47–78). New York, NY: Springer.

Joly, D. (Ed.). (2016). *Scapegoats and social actors: The exclusion and integration of minorities in Western and Eastern Europe*. Basingstoke, UK: Macmillan.

Jonas, E., Martens, A., Niesta Kayser, D., Fritsche, I., Sullivan, D., & Greenberg, J. (2008). Focus theory of normative conduct and terror-management theory: The interactive impact of mortality salience and norm salience on social judgment. *Journal of Personality and Social Psychology, 95*(6), 1239–1251.

Jonason, P. K., & Webster, G. D. (2010). The dirty dozen: A concise measure of the dark triad. *Psychological Assessment, 22*(2), 420–432.

Jones, A. (2000). *Next time, she'll be dead: Battering and how to stop it*. Boston, MA: Beacon.

Jones, A. M., & Brimbal, L. (2017). Lay perceptions of interrogation techniques: Identifying the role of belief in a just world and right wing authoritarianism. *Journal of Investigative Psychology and Offender Profiling*, *14*(3), 260–280.

Jones, B. D. (1999). Bounded rationality. *Annual Review of Political Science*, *2*(1), 297–321.

Jones, E. E. (1979). The rocky road from acts to dispositions. *American Psychologist*, *34*(2), 107–117.

Jones, E. E., & Harris, V. A. (1967). The attribution of attitudes. *Journal of Experimental Social Psychology*, *3*(1), 1–24.

Jones, E. E., & Pittman, T. S. (1982). Toward a general theory of strategic self-presentation. In J. Suls (Ed.), *Psychological perspectives on the self* (Vol. *1*, pp. 231–262). Hillsdale, NJ: Lawrence Erlbaum.

Jones, T. F., Craig, A. S., Hoy, D., Gunter, E. W., Ashley, D. L., Barr, D. B., . . . Schaffner, W. (2000). Mass psychogenic illness attributed to toxic exposure at a high school. *New England Journal of Medicine*, *342*(2), 96–100.

Jordan, C. H., Spencer, S. J., & Zanna, M. P. (2005). Types of high self-esteem and prejudice: How implicit self-esteem relates to ethnic discrimination among high explicit self-esteem individuals. *Personality and Social Psychology Bulletin*, *31*(5), 693–702.

Jordan, S., & Hartwig, M. (2013). On the phenomenology of innocence: The role of belief in a just world. *Psychiatry, Psychology and Law*, *20*(5), 749–760.

Jussim, L., & Harber, K. D. (2005). Teacher expectations and self-fulfilling prophecies: Knowns and unknowns, resolved and unresolved controversies. *Personality and Social Psychology Review*, *9*(2), 131–155.

Kahneman, D. (2003). A perspective on judgment and choice: Mapping bounded rationality. *American Psychologist*, *58*(9), 697–720.

Kahneman, D. (2011). *Thinking, fast and slow*. New York, NY: Farrar, Straus and Giroux.

Kahneman, D., & Frederick, S. (2005). A model of heuristic judgment. In K. J. Holyoak & R. G. Morrison (Eds.), *The Cambridge handbook of thinking and reasoning* (pp. 267–293). Cambridge, UK: Cambridge University Press.

Kahneman, D., & Tversky, A. (1979). On the interpretation of intuitive probability: A reply to Jonathan Cohen. *Cognition*, *7*(4), 409–411.

Kahneman, D., & Tversky, A. (1982). The simulation heuristic. In D. Kahneman, P. Slovic, & A. Tversky (Eds.), *Judgment under uncertainty: Heuristics and biases* (pp. 201–208). Cambridge, UK: Cambridge University Press.

Kahneman, D., & Tversky, A. (2000). *Choices, values, and frames*. New York, NY: Cambridge University Press.

Kamat, S. S., & Kanekar, S. (1990). Prediction of and recommendation for honest behavior. *Journal of Social Psychology*, *130*(5), 597–607.

Kanaroglou, P., Eyles, J., Finkelstein, N., Giovis, C., & Brook, J. R. (2019). A GIS-environmental justice analysis of particulate air pollution in Hamilton, Canada. *Spatial Aspects of Environmental Policy*. Advance online publication.

Kandel, E. R. (2006). *In search of memory: The emergence of a new science of mind*. New York, NY: Norton.

Kandler, C., Bleidorn, W., & Riemann, R. (2012). Left or right? Sources of political orientation: The roles of genetic factors, cultural transmission, assortative mating, and personality. *Journal of Personality and Social Psychology*, *102*(3), 633–645.

Kaplan, G. (2019). Mirror neurons and humanity's dark side. *Animal Sentience*, *3*(23), 24–28.

Kaplan, J. T., & Iacoboni, M. (2006). Getting a grip on other minds: Mirror neurons, intention understanding, and cognitive empathy. *Social Neuroscience*, *1*(3–4), 175–183.

Karatzias, A., Power, K. G., & Swanson, V. (2002). Bullying and victimisation in Scottish secondary schools: Same or separate entities? *Aggressive Behavior*, *28*(1), 45–61.

Karau, S. J., & Williams, K. D. (1993). Social loafing: A meta-analytic review and theoretical integration. *Journal of Personality and Social Psychology*, *65*(4), 681–706.

Kareem, S., Ahmad, R. B., & Sarlan, A. B. (2017, November). Framework for the identification of fraudulent health insurance claims using association rule mining. In *2017 IEEE Conference on Big Data and Analytics (ICBDA)* (pp. 99–104). Kuching, Malaysia: IEEE.

Karthaus, M., Wascher, E., Falkenstein, M., & Getzmann, S. (2020). The ability of young, middle-aged and older drivers to inhibit visual and auditory distraction in a driving simulator task. *Transportation Research Part F: Traffic Psychology and Behaviour*, *68*, 272–284.

Kärtner, J., Keller, H., & Chaudhary, N. (2010). Cognitive and social influences on early prosocial behavior in two sociocultural contexts. *Developmental Psychology*, *46*(4), 905–914.

Kassin, S. M. (1997). The psychology of confession evidence. *American Psychologist*, *52*(3), 221.

Kassin, S. M. (1998). Eyewitness identification procedures: The fifth rule. *Law and Human Behavior*, *22*(6), 649–653.

Kassin, S. M. (2015). The social psychology of false confessions. *Social Issues and Policy Review*, *9*(1), 25–51.

Kassin, S. M., Bogart, D., & Kerner, J. (2012). Confessions that corrupt: Evidence from the DNA exoneration case files. *Psychological Science*, *23*(1), 41–45.

Kassin, S. M., & Kiechel, K. L. (1996). The social psychology of false confessions: Compliance, internalization, and confabulation. *Psychological Science*, *7*(3), 125–128.

Kassin, S. M., & Sukel, H. (1997). Coerced confessions and the jury: An experimental test of the "harmless error" rule. *Law and Human Behavior*, *21*(1), 27–46.

Kassin, S. M., Williams, L. N., & Saunders, C. L. (1990). Dirty tricks of cross-examination: The influence of conjectural evidence on the jury. *Law and Human Behavior*, *14*(4), 373–384.

Kassin, S. M., & Wrightsman, L. S. (Eds.). (1985). *The psychology of evidence and trial procedure*. SAGE.

Kassin, S. M., & Wrightsman, L. S. (1988). *The American jury on trial: Psychological perspectives*. New York, NY: Taylor & Francis.

Katz, D., Allport, F. H., & Jenness, M. B. (1931). *Students' attitudes; A report of the Syracuse University reaction study*. Oxford, UK: Craftsman Press.

Kay, A. C., Gaucher, D., McGregor, I., & Nash, K. (2010). Religious belief as compensatory control. *Personality and Social Psychology Review*, *14*(1), 37–48.

Keating, C. F., Pomerantz, J., Pommer, S. D., Ritt, S. J., Miller, L. M., & McCormick, J. (2005). Going to college and unpacking hazing: A functional approach to decrypting initiation practices among undergraduates. *Group Dynamics: Theory, Research, Practice*, *9*(2), 104–126.

Keating, J., Van Boven, L., & Judd, C. M. (2016). Partisan underestimation of the polarizing influence of group discussion. *Journal of Experimental Social Psychology*, *65*, 52–58.

Kee, Y. H., Li, C., Wang, J. C., & Kailani, M. I. B. (2018). Motivations for volunteering and its associations with time perspectives and life satisfaction: A latent profile approach. *Psychological Reports*, *121*(5), 932–951.

Kelley, H. H. (1950). The warm-cold variable in first impressions of persons. *Journal of Personality*, *18*(4), 431–439.

Kelley, H. H. (1955). Salience of membership and resistance to change of group-centered attitudes. *Human Relations*, *8*(3), 275–289.

Kelley, H. H. (1967). Attribution theory in social psychology. *Nebraska Symposium on Motivation*, *15*, 192–238.

Kelley, H. H. (1973). The processes of causal attribution. *American Psychologist*, *28*(2), 107–128.

Keltner, D., & Shiota, M. N. (2003). New displays and new emotions: A commentary on Rozin and Cohen (2003). *Emotion, 3*(1), 86–91.

Kemmelmeier, M., Jambor, E. E., & Letner, J. (2006). Individualism and good works: Cultural variation in giving and volunteering across the United States. *Journal of Cross-Cultural Psychology, 37*(3), 327–344.

Kennedy, D. M. (1970). *Birth control in America: the career of Margaret Sanger* (Vol. 18). New Haven, CT: Yale University Press.

Kephart, W. M. (1967). Some correlates of romantic love. *Journal of Marriage and the Family, 49*(3), 470–474.

Kerr, N. L., & Bruun, S. E. (1981). Ringelmann revisited: Alternative explanations for the social loafing effect. *Personality and Social Psychology Bulletin, 7*(2), 224–231.

Kestenbaum, R. (2018, November 27). *The biggest trends in the pet industry*. Retrieved Dec. 14, 2019, from https://www.forbes.com/sites/richardkestenbaum/2018/11/27/the-biggest-trends-in-the-pet-industry/#32d0caedf099

Keynes, J. (1920). *The economic consequences of the peace*. New York, NY: Harcourt, Brace and Howe.

Khansa, L., Kuem, J., Siponen, M., & Kim, S. S. (2017), To cyberloaf or not to cyberloaf: The impact of the announcement of formal organizational controls. *Journal of Management Information Systems, 34*(1), 141–176.

Khoury, B., Lecomte, T., Fortin, G., Masse, M., Therien, P., Bouchard, V., . . . Hofmann, S. G. (2013). Mindfulness-based therapy: A comprehensive meta-analysis. *Clinical Psychology Review, 33*(6), 763–771.

Khoury, B., Sharma, M., Rush, S. E., & Fournier, C. (2015). Mindfulness-based stress reduction for healthy individuals: A meta-analysis. *Journal of Psychosomatic Research, 78*(6), 519–528.

Kidwell, M. C., Lazarević, L. B., Baranski, E., Hardwicke, T. E., Piechowski, S., Falkenberg, L. S., . . . Errington, T. M. (2016). Badges to acknowledge open practices: A simple, low-cost, effective method for increasing transparency. *PLoS Biology, 14*(5), e1002456.

Kiesler, S. B., & Mathog, R. B. (1968). Distraction hypothesis in attitude change: Effects of effectiveness. *Psychological Reports, 23*(3), 1123–1133.

Kilduff, M., & Day, D. V. (1994). Do chameleons get ahead? The effects of self-monitoring on managerial careers. *Academy of Management Journal, 37*, 1047– 1060.

Kilpatrick, D. G. (2004). What is violence against women? Defining and measuring the problem. *Journal of Interpersonal Violence, 19*(11), 1209–1234.

Kim, H., & Markus, H. R. (1999). Deviance or uniqueness, harmony or conformity? A cultural analysis. *Journal of Personality and Social Psychology, 77*(4), 785–800.

Kim, K., Triana, M., Chung, K., & Oh, N. (2016). When do employees cyberloaf? An interactionist perspective examining personality, justice, and empowerment. *Human Resource Management, 55*(6), 1041–1058.

Kim, Y. J., & Na, J. H. (2007). Effects of celebrity athlete endorsement on attitude towards the product: The role of credibility, attractiveness and the concept of congruence. *International Journal of Sports Marketing and Sponsorship, 8*(4), 23–33.

King, E. B., Shapiro, J. R., Hebl, M. R., Singletary, S. L., & Turner, S. (2006). The stigma of obesity in customer service: A mechanism for remediation and bottom-line consequences of interpersonal discrimination. *Journal of Applied Psychology, 91*(3), 579–593.

Kinsey, A. C., Pomeroy, W. B., & Martin, C. E. (1948). *Sexual behavior in the human male*. Oxford, UK: Saunders.

Kirby, R., & Kirby, M. (2019). The perils of toxic masculinity: Four case studies. *Trends in Urology & Men's Health, 10*(5), 18–20.

Kirkwood, C. (1993). *Leaving abusive partners: From the scars of survival to the wisdom for change*. Thousand Oaks, CA: Sage.

Kitayama, S., Snibbe, A. C., Markus, H. R., & Suzuki, T. (2004). Is there any "free" choice? Self and dissonance in two cultures. *Psychological Science, 15*(8), 527–533.

Kite, M. E., Deaux, K., & Haines, E. L. (2007). Gender stereotypes. In F. L. Denmark & M. A. Paludi (Eds.), *Psychology of women: A handbook of issues and theories* (2nd ed., pp. 205–236). Westport, CT: Praeger/Greenwood.

Klein, E., Campbell, J., Soler, E., & Ghez, M. (1997). *Ending domestic violence: Changing public perceptions/halting the epidemic*. Thousand Oaks, CA: Sage.

Kleinbaum, A. M., Jordan, A. H., & Audia, P. G. (2015). An altercentric perspective on the origins of brokerage in social networks: How perceived empathy moderates the self-monitoring effect. *Organization Science, 26*, 1–17.

Kleinke, C. L., & Meyer, C. (1990). Evaluation of rape victim by men and women with high and low belief in a just world. *Psychology of Women Quarterly, 14*(3), 343–353.

Klimmt, C., Hefner, D., & Vorderer, P. (2009). The video game experience as "true" identification: A theory of enjoyable alterations of players' self-perception. *Communication Theory, 19*(4), 351–373.

Klopfer, P. H. (1958). Influence of social interaction on learning rates in birds. *Science, 128*, 903–904.

Klump, K. L., Keel, P. K., Sisk, C., & Burt, S. A. (2010). Preliminary evidence that estradiol moderates genetic influences on disordered eating attitudes and behaviors during puberty. *Psychological Medicine, 40*(10), 1745–1753.

Klump, K. L., McGue, M., & Iacono, W. G. (2003). Differential heritability of eating attitudes and behaviors in prepubertal versus pubertal twins. *International Journal of Eating Disorders, 33*(3), 287–292.

Knickmeyer, R., & Baron-Cohen, S. (2006). Topical review: Fetal testosterone and sex differences in typical social development and in autism. *Journal of Child Neurology, 21*(10), 825–845.

Knutson, B., & Gibbs, S. E. (2007). Linking nucleus accumbens dopamine and blood oxygenation. *Psychopharmacology, 191*(3), 813–822.

Knutson, B., Rick, S., Wimmer, G. E., Prelec, D., & Loewenstein, G. (2007). Neural predictors of purchases. *Neuron, 53*(1), 147–156.

Kocsis, R. N. (2013). The criminal profiling reality: What is actually behind the smoke and mirrors? *Journal of Forensic Psychology Practice, 13*(2), 79–91.

Koehler, D. J., & Poon, C. S. K. (2006). Self-predictions overweight strength of current intentions. *Journal of Experimental Social Psychology, 42*(4), 517–524.

Kontos, A. P., Elbin, R. J., Fazio-Sumrock, V. C., Burkhart, S., Swindell, H., Maroon, J., & Collins, M. W. (2013). Incidence of sports-related concussion among youth football players aged 8–12 years. *The Journal of Pediatrics, 163*(3), 717–720.

Koocher, G. P. (1977). Bathroom behavior and human dignity. *Journal of Personality and Social Psychology, 35*(2), 120–121.

Kopec, D. A. (2018). *Environmental psychology for design*. New York, NY: Bloomsbury.

Korde, R., & Paulus, P. B. (2017). Alternating individual and group idea generation: Finding the elusive synergy. *Journal of Experimental Social Psychology, 70*, 177–190.

Kosloff, S., Irish, S., Perreault, L., Anderson, G., & Nottbohm, A. (2017). Assessing relationships between conformity and meta-traits in an Asch-like paradigm. *Social Influence, 12*(2–3), 90–100.

Koukounas, E., Kambouropoulos, N., & Staiger, P. (2019). The effect of cognitive distraction on the processing of alcohol cues. *Journal of Substance Use, 24*(6), 1–4.

Kraut, R. E., & Johnson, R. E. (1979). Social and emotional messages of smiling: An ethological approach. *Journal of Personality and Social Psychology, 37*(9), 1539–1553.

Kravitz, D. A., & Martin, B. (1986). Ringelmann rediscovered: The original article. *Journal of Personality and Social Psychology, 50*(5), 936–941.

Kressel, N. J., & Kressel, D. (2002). *Stack and sway: The new science of jury consulting.* Boulder, CO: Westview.

Kretschmar, J. M., & Flannery, D. J. (2007). Substance abuse and violent behavior. In D. J. Flannery, A. T. Vazsonyi, & I. D. Waldman (Eds.), *The Cambridge handbook of violent behavior and aggression* (pp. 647–663). Cambridge, UK: Cambridge University Press.

Kroshus, E. (2018). College athletes, pluralistic ignorance and bystander behaviors to prevent sexual assault. *Journal of Clinical Sport Psychology, 2,* 330–344.

Krosnick, J. A., & Petty, R. E. (1995). Attitude strength: An overview. In R. E. Petty & J. A. Krosnick (Eds.), *Attitude strength: Antecedents and consequences* (pp. 1–24). Mahwah, NJ: Lawrence Erlbaum.

Krueger, J. I., & Clement, R. W. (1994). The truly false consensus effect: An ineradicable and egocentric bias in social perception. *Journal of Personality and Social Psychology, 67*(4), 596–610.

Krueger, J. I., & Zeiger, J. S. (1993). Social categorization and the truly false consensus effect. *Journal of Personality and Social Psychology, 65*(4), 670–680.

Krueger, R. F., Hicks, B. M., & McGue, M. (2001). Altruism and antisocial behavior: Independent tendencies, unique personality correlates, distinct etiologies. *Psychological Science, 12*(5), 397–402.

Kruger, D. J., Falbo, M., Blanchard, S., Cole, E., Gazoul, C., Nader, N., & Murphy, S. (2018). University sports rivalries provide insights on coalitional psychology. *Human Nature, 29*(3), 337–352.

Kruger, J., Chan, S., & Roese, N. (2009). (Not so) positive illusions. *Behavioral Brain Science, 32,* 526–527.

Kruse, H., Smith, S., van Tubergen, F., & Maas, I. (2016). From neighbors to school friends? How adolescents' place of residence relates to same-ethnic school friendships. *Social Networks, 44,* 130–142.

Kteily, N. S., Sidanius, J., & Levin, S. (2011). Social dominance orientation: Cause or 'mere effect'? Evidence for SDO as a causal predictor of prejudice and discrimination against ethnic and racial outgroups. *Journal of Experimental Social Psychology, 47*(1), 208–214.

Kubany, E. S., Leisen, M. B., Kaplan, A. S., & Kelly, M. P. (2000). Validation of a brief measure of posttraumatic stress disorder: The Distressing Event Questionnaire (DEQ). *Psychological Assessment, 12*(2), 197–209.

Kubota, J. T., Banaji, M. R., & Phelps, E. A. (2012). The neuroscience of race. *Nature Neuroscience, 15*(7), 940–948.

Kuhnen, C. M., & Knutson, B. (2005). The neural basis of financial risk taking. *Neuron, 47*(5), 763–770.

Kumru, A., Carlo, G., Mestre, M. V., & Samper, P. (2012). Prosocial moral reasoning and prosocial behavior among Turkish and Spanish adolescents. *Social Behavior and Personality, 40*(2), 205–214.

Kuo, T. C., Tseng, M. L., Lin, C. H., Wang, R. W., & Lee, C. H. (2018). Identifying sustainable behavior of energy consumers as a driver of design solutions: The missing link in eco-design. *Journal of Cleaner Production, 192,* 486–495.

Kurdek, L. A., & Schmitt, J. P. (1987). Partner homogamy in married, heterosexual cohabiting, gay, and lesbian couples. *Journal of Sex Research, 23*(2), 212–232.

Kwan, K. (2013). *Crazy rich Asians.* Anchor Books.

Lac, A., Crano, W. D., Berger, D. E., & Alvaro, E. M. (2013). Attachment theory and theory of planned behavior: An integrative model predicting underage drinking. *Developmental Psychology, 49*(8), 1579–1590.

Lacro, J. P., Dunn, L. B., Dolder, C. R., Leckband, S. G., & Jeste, D. V. (2002). Prevalence of and risk factors for medication nonadherence in patients with schizophrenia: A comprehensive review of recent literature. *Journal of Clinical Psychiatry, 63*(10), 892–909.

LaForge, I., & Goodfriend, W. (2012). Developing a new device for measuring preferred body shapes. *Journal of Psychological Inquiry, 17,* 45–49.

LaFrance, M., & Woodzicka, J. A. (1998). No laughing matter: Women's verbal and nonverbal reactions to sexist humor. In J. K. Swim & C. Stangor (Eds.), *Prejudice: The target's perspective* (pp. 61–80). San Diego, CA: Academic Press.

Lageard, V., & Paternotte, C. (2018, November 29). Trolls, bans and reverts: Simulating Wikipedia. *Synthese,* pp. 1–20.

Lake, B. M., Ullman, T. D., Tenenbaum, J. B., & Gershman, S. J. (2016). Building machines that learn and think like people. *Behavioral and Brain Sciences, 40,* e253. https://arxiv.org/pdf/1604.00289.pdf

Lamb, C. S., & Crano, W. D. (2014). Parents' beliefs and children's marijuana use: Evidence for a self-fulfilling prophecy effect. *Addictive Behaviors, 39*(1), 127–132.

Lambert, L., D'Cruz, A., Schlatter, M., & Barron, F. (2016). Using physical activity to tackle depression: The neglected positive psychology intervention. *Middle East Journal of Positive Psychology, 2*(1), 42–60.

Landrigan, P. J., Fuller, R., Acosta, N. J., Adeyi, O., Arnold, R., Baldé, A. B., . . . Chiles, T. (2018). The Lancet Commission on pollution and health. *The Lancet, 391*(10119), 462–512.

Langer, E. J., & Rodin, J. (1976). The effects of choice and enhanced personal responsibility for the aged: A field experiment in an institutional setting. *Journal of Personality and Social Psychology, 34*(2), 191–198.

Langlois, J. H., Ritter, J. M., Casey, R. J., & Sawin, D. B. (1995). Infant attractiveness predicts maternal behaviors and attitudes. *Developmental Psychology, 31*(3), 464–472.

Langlois, J. H., & Roggman, L. A. (1990). Attractive faces are only average. *Psychological Science, 1*(2), 115–121.

Langlois, J. H., Roggman, L. A., & Musselman, L. (1994). What is average and what is not average about attractive faces? *Psychological Science, 5*(4), 214–220.

LaPiere, R. T. (1934). Attitudes vs. actions. *Social Forces, 13*(2), 230–237.

Larrick, R. P., Timmerman, T. A., Carton, A. M., & Abrevaya, J. (2011). Temper, temperature, and temptation: Heat-related retaliation in baseball. *Psychological Science, 22*(4), 423–428.

Larsen, K. S. (1974). Conformity in the Asch experiment. *Journal of Social Psychology, 94*(2), 303–304.

Larsen, K. S. (1982). Cultural conditions and conformity: The Asch effect. *Bulletin of the British Psychological Society, 35,* 347.

Larsen, K. S. (1990). The Asch conformity experiment: Replications and transhistorical comparisons. *Social Behavior and Personality, 5*(4), 163–168.

Latané, B., & Darley, J. (1970). *The unresponsive bystander why doesn't he help?* New York, NY: Appleton-Century Crofts.

Lau, A., Schwarz, J., & Stoll, O. (2019). Influence of social facilitation on learning development using a Wii Balanceboard™. *German Journal of Exercise and Sport Research, 49*(1), 97–102.

Laumann, E. O., Gagnon, J. H., Michael, R. T., & Michaels, S. (1994). *The social organization of sexuality: Sexual practices in the United States.* Chicago, IL: University of Chicago Press.

Lawrence, J. E. (1974). Science and sentiment: Overview of research on crowding and human behavior. *Psychological Bulletin, 81*(10), 712–720.

Lazarus, R., & Folkman, S. (1984). *Stress, appraisal, and coping.* New York, NY: Springer.

Le, B., & Agnew, C. R. (2003). Commitment and its theorized determinants: A meta-analysis of the investment model. *Personal Relationships, 10*(1), 37–57.

Le, B., Dove, N. L., Agnew, C. R., Korn, M. S., & Mutso, A. A. (2010). Predicting nonmarital romantic relationship dissolution: A meta-analytic synthesis. *Personal Relationships, 17*(3), 377–390.

Leach, J. K., & Patall, E. A. (2013). Maximizing and counterfactual thinking in academic major decision making. *Journal of Career Assessment, 21*(3), 414–429.

Learman, L. A., Avorn, J., Everitt, D. E., & Rosenthal, R. (1990). Pygmalion in the nursing home: The effects of caregiver expectations on patient outcomes. *Journal of the American Geriatrics Society, 38*(7), 797–803.

Leary, M. R., Tate, E. B., Adams, C. E., Batts Allen, A., & Hancock, J. (2007). Self-compassion and reactions to unpleasant self-relevant events: The implications of treating oneself kindly. *Journal of Personality and Social Psychology, 92*(5), 887–904.

Leckman, J. F., & Bloch, M. H. (2008). A developmental and evolutionary perspective on obsessive-compulsive disorder: Whence and whither compulsive hoarding? *American Journal of Psychiatry*, [online].

Lee, E., Sitze, G., & Logan, J. R. (2003). Social support to parents-in-law: The interplay of gender and kin hierarchies. *Journal of Marriage and Family, 65*(2), 396–403.

Lee, G. R., & Stone, L. H. (1980). Mate-selection systems and criteria: Variation according to family structure. *Journal of Marriage and the Family, 42*, 319–326.

Lee, J. G., & Thorson, E. (2008). The impact of celebrity-product incongruence on the effectiveness of product endorsement. *Journal of Advertising Research, 48*(3), 433–449.

Lee, K. S., Brittain, H., & Vaillancourt, T. (2018). Predicting dating behavior from aggression and self-perceived social status in adolescence. *Aggressive Behavior, 44*(4), 372–381.

Lee, K. S., & Chen, W. (2017). A long shadow: Cultural capital, techno-capital and networking skills of college students. *Computers in Human Behavior, 70*, 67–73.

Lee, S., Bai, B., & Busser, J. A. (2019). Pop star fan tourists: An application of self-expansion theory. *Tourism Management, 72*, 270–280.

Lee, Y. H., & Mason, C. (1999). Responses to information incongruency in advertising: The role of expectancy, relevancy, and humor. *Journal of Consumer Research, 26*(2), 156–169.

Lee, Y. T., & Ottati, V. (1995). Perceived in-group homogeneity as a function of group membership salience and stereotype threat. *Personality and Social Psychology Bulletin, 21*(6), 610–619.

Leffler, M. P. (2018). Divide and invest: Why the Marshall Plan worked. *Foreign Affairs, 97*, 170–175.

Legaspi, A. (2017). Jay-Z talks infidelity, music as therapy in new interview. *Rolling Stone*. Retrieved February 23, 2020, from https://www.rollingstone.com/music/music-news/jay-z-talks-infidelity-music-as-therapy-in-new-interview-124267/

Le Hénaff, B., Michinov, N., Le Bohec, O., & Delaval, M. (2015). Social gaming is inSIDE: Impact of anonymity and group identity on performance in a team game-based learning environment. *Computers & Education, 82*, 84–95.

Lehmiller, J. J. (2010). Differences in relationship investments between gay and heterosexual men. *Personal Relationships, 17*(1), 81–96.

Leippe, M. R., & Elkin, R. A. (1987). When motives clash: Issue involvement and response involvement as determinant of persuasion. *Journal of Personality and Social Psychology, 52*(2), 269–278.

Leitner, H., Sheppard, E., Webber, S., & Colven, E. (2018). Globalizing urban resilience. *Urban Geography, 39*(8), 1276–1284.

Lens, V. (2019). Judging the other: The intersection of race, gender, and class in family court. *Family Court Review, 57*(1), 72–87.

Leone, J. M., Johnson, M. P., & Cohan, C. L. (2007). Victim help seeking: Differences between intimate terrorism and situational couple violence. *Family Relations: An Interdisciplinary Journal of Applied Family Studies, 56*(5), 427–439.

Lerner, M. J. (1965). Evaluation of performance as a function of performer's reward and attractiveness. *Journal of Personality and Social Psychology, 1*(4), 355–360.

Lerner, M. J. (1980). *The belief in a just world: A fundamental delusion.* New York, NY: Plenum.

Lerner, M. J., & Miller, D. T. (1978). Just world research and the attribution process: Looking back and ahead. *Psychological Bulletin, 85*(5), 1030–1051.

Lerner, M. J., & Simmons, C. H. (1966). The observer's reaction to the "innocent victim": Compassion or rejection? *Journal of Personality and Social Psychology, 4*(2), 203–210.

Levenson, H., Burford, B., Bonno, B., & Davis, L. (1975). Are women still prejudiced against women? A replication and extension of Goldberg's study. *Journal of Psychology, 89*(1), 67–71.

Levine, M., Prosser, A., Evans, D., & Reicher, S. (2005). Identity and emergency intervention: How social group membership and inclusiveness of group boundaries shape helping behavior. *Personality and Social Psychology Bulletin, 31*(4), 443–453.

Levine, R., Sato, S., Hashimoto, T., & Verma, J. (2004). Love and marriage in eleven cultures. In H. T. Reis & C. E. Rusbult (Eds.), *Close relationships: Key readings* (pp. 229–238). Psychology Press.

Levinson, C. A., & Rodebaugh, T. L. (2013). Anxiety, self-discrepancy, and regulatory focus theory: Acculturation matters. *Anxiety, Stress & Coping: An International Journal, 26*(2), 171–186.

Levy, R. I. (1973). *Tahitians: Mind and experience in the Society Islands.* Chicago, IL: University of Chicago Press.

Levy, R. I. (1978). Tahitian gentleness and redundant controls. In A. Montagu (Ed.), *Learning non-aggression: The experience of non-literate societies* (pp. 222–235). Oxford, UK: Oxford University Press.

Lewin, K. (1936). *Principles of topological psychology.* New York: McGraw-Hill.

Lewin, K. (1948). *Resolving social conflicts.* New York, NY: Harper & Row.

Lewin, K. (1951). *Field theory in social science: Selected theoretical papers* (D. Cartwright, Ed.). Oxford, UK: Harpers.

Li, N. P., Yong, J. C., Tov, W., Sng, O., Fletcher, G. O., Valentine, K. A., . . . Balliet, D. (2013). Mate preferences do predict attraction and choices in the early stages of mate selection. *Journal of Personality and Social Psychology, 105*(5), 757–776.

Liden, R. C., Wayne, S. J., Jaworski, R. A., & Bennett, N. (2004). Social loafing: A field investigation. *Journal of Management, 30*(2), 285–304.

Lieberman, M. D. (2000). Intuition: A social cognitive neuroscience approach. *Psychological Bulletin, 126*(1), 109–137.

Lightdale, J. R., & Prentice, D. A. (1994). Rethinking sex differences in aggression: Aggressive behavior in the absence of social roles. *Personality and Social Psychology Bulletin, 20*(1), 34–44.

Lilienfeld, S. O. (2007). Psychological treatments that cause harm. *Perspectives on Psychological Science, 2*, 53–70.

Lilienfeld, S. O. (2017). Microaggressions: Strong claims, inadequate evidence. *Perspectives on Psychological Science, 12*, 138–169.

Lilienfeld, S. O., Lynn, S. J., Ruscio, J., & Beyerstein, B. L. (2011). *50 Great myths of popular psychology: Shattering widespread misconceptions about human behavior.* Hoboken, NJ: John Wiley.

Lim, V., Teo, T., & Zheng, X. (2018). Sleep deprived and lonely: The moderating effect of social exclusion on insomnia and cyberloafing. *Sleep.* Advance online publication.

Lim, V. K., & Chen, D. J. (2012). Cyberloafing at the workplace: Gain or drain on work? *Behaviour & Information Technology, 31*(4), 343–353.

Lindstrom, M. (2011). *Brandwashed: Tricks companies use to manipulate our minds and persuade us to buy.* New York, NY: Crown Business.

Lipsitz, G. (2016). The possessive investment in Whiteness. In P. S. Rothenberg (Ed.), *White privilege* (5th ed). New York, NY: Worth.

Lobel, M., Cannella, D. L., Graham, J. E., DeVincent, C., Schneider, J., & Meyer, B. A. (2008). Pregnancy-specific stress, prenatal health behaviors, and birth outcomes. *Health Psychology, 27*(5), 604–615.

Loftus, E. F. (1975). Leading questions and the eyewitness report. *Cognitive Psychology, 7*(4), 560–572.

Loftus, E. F., & Ketcham, K. (1996). *The myth of repressed memory: False memories and allegations of sexual abuse.* New York, NY: St. Martin's Griffin.

Loftus, E. F., & Palmer, J. C. (1974). Reconstruction of automobile destruction: An example of the interaction between language and memory. *Journal of Verbal Learning and Verbal Behavior, 13*(5), 585–589.

Loftus, E. F., & Palmer, J. C. (1996). Reconstruction of automobile destruction: An example of the interaction between language and memory. In S. Fein & S. Spencer (Eds.), *Readings in social psychology: The art and science of research* (pp. 143–147). Boston, MA: Houghton Mifflin.

Loftus, E. F., & Zanni, G. (1975). Eyewitness testimony: The influence of the wording of a question. *Bulletin of the Psychonomic Society, 5*(1), 86–88.

Loh, C. S., Sheng, Y., & Ifenthaler, D. (2015). Serious games analytics: Theoretical framework. In C. S. Loh, Y. Sheng, & D. Ifenthaler (Eds.), *Serious games analytics* (pp. 3–29). New York, NY: Springer.

Lopes, B., & Yu, H. (2017). Who do you troll and Why: An investigation into the relationship between the Dark Triad Personalities and online trolling behaviours towards popular and less popular Facebook profiles. *Computers in Human Behavior, 77,* 69–76.

Lorenz, K. (1943). The innate forms of potential experience. *Zeitschrift für Tierpsychologie, 5,* 235–409.

Lough, J. W. H. (2006). *Weber and the persistence of religion: Social theory, capitalism, and the sublime.* New York, NY: Routledge.

Lovallo, D., & Kahneman, D. (2003). Delusions of success: How optimism undermines executives' decisions. *Harvard Business Review, 81,* 56–63.

Lovett, M., & Miranda, G. A. (2014). Who killed John Wanamaker?. *Journal of Management and Marketing Research, 16,* [online].

Love, L., & Waldman, E. (2016). The hopes and fears of all the years: 30 years behind and the road ahead for the widespread use of mediation. *Ohio St. Journal on Dispute Resolution, 31,* 123.

Luiking, M. L., Heckemann, B., Ali, P., Dekker-van Doorn, C., Ghosh, S., Kydd, A., Watson, R., & Patel, H. (2019). Migrants' healthcare experience: A meta-ethnography review of the literature. *Journal of Nursing Scholarship, 51*(1), 58–67.

Luo, L., Ma, X., Zheng, X., Zhao, W., Xu, L., Becker, B., & Kendrick, K. M. F. (2015). Neural systems and hormones mediating attraction to infant and child faces. *Frontiers in Psychology, 6,* article 970.

Luther, S. S., Cicchetti, D., & Becker, B. (2000). The construct of resilience: A critical evaluation and guidelines for work. *Child Development, 71,* 543–562.

Lutts, R. H. (1992). The trouble with Bambi: Walt Disney's Bambi and the American vision of nature. *Forest and Conservation History, 36,* 160–171.

MacBeth, A., & Gumley, A. (2012). Exploring compassion: A meta-analysis of the association between self-compassion and psychopathology. *Clinical Psychology Review, 32*(6), 545–552.

MacDonald, G., Zanna, M. P., & Holmes, J. G. (2000). An experimental test of the role of alcohol in relationship conflict. *Journal of Experimental Social Psychology, 36*(2), 182–193.

Macintosh, G., & Krush, M. (2017). Networking behavior and sales performance: Examining potential gender differences. *Journal of Marketing Theory and Practice, 25*(2), 160–170.

MacKenzie, D. (2015). Refugees welcome: The numbers add up. *New Scientist, 277*(3038), 10–12.

Madathil, J., & Benshoff, J. M. (2008). Importance of marital characteristics and marital satisfaction: A comparison of Asian Indians in arranged marriages and Americans in marriages of choice. *The Family Journal, 16*(3), 222–230.

Maisonneuve, N., Stevens, M., Niessen, M. E., & Steels, L. (2009). NoiseTube: Measuring and mapping noise pollution with mobile phones. In I. N. Athanasiadis, P. A. Mitkas, A. E. Rizzoli, & J. Marx Gómez (Eds.), *Information technologies in environmental engineering* (pp. 215–228). Berlin, Germany: Springer.

Major, B., Sciacchitano, A. M., & Crocker, J. (1993). In-group versus out-group comparisons and self-esteem. *Personality and Social Psychology Bulletin, 19*(6), 711–721.

Malta, M., Rimoin, A. W., & Strathdee, S. A. (2020). The coronavirus 2019-nCoV epidemic: Is hindsight 20/20? *EClinicalMedicine.* Advance online publication.

Mankiewicz, R. (2000). *The story of mathematics.* Princeton, NJ: Princeton University Press.

Manning, R., Levine, M., & Collins, A. (2007). The Kitty Genovese murder and the social psychology of helping: The parable of the 38 witnesses. *American Psychologist, 62*(6), 555–562.

Mansoori, S., Mozaffar, F., Noroozian, M., Faizi, M., & Ashayeri, H. (2019). Relationship between neuropsychological and physical environmental perception in patients with dementia and Alzheimer Disease. *Iranian Journal of Psychiatry and Clinical Psychology, 24*(4), 426–443.

Marino, L. (2002). Convergence of complex cognitive abilities in cetaceans and primates. *Brain, Behavior and Evolution, 59*(1–2), 21–32.

Marino, L., & Lilienfeld, S. O. (1998). Dolphin-assisted therapy: Flawed data, flawed conclusions. *Anthrozoös, 11*(4), 194–200.

Marino, L., & Lilienfeld, S. O. (2007). Dolphin-assisted therapy: More flawed data and more flawed conclusions. *Anthrozoös, 20*(3), 239–249.

Marks, G. (1984). Thinking one's abilities are unique and one's opinions are common. *Personality and Social Psychology Bulletin, 10*(2), 203–208.

Markus, H. R. (1977). Self-schemata and processing information about the self. *Journal of Personality and Social Psychology, 35*(2), 63–78.

Markus, H. R., & Kitayama, S. (1991). Culture and the self: Implications for cognition, emotion, and motivation. *Psychological Review, 98*(2), 224–253.

Markus, H. R., & Kitayama, S. (1994). A collective fear of the collective: Implications for selves and theories of selves. *Personality and Social Psychology Bulletin, 20*(5), 568–579.

Marrow, A. (1969). *The practical theorist: The life and work of Kurt Lewin.* New York, NY: Basic Books.

Marrow, J. (2002). Demonstrating the anchoring-adjustment heuristic and the power of the situation. *Teaching of Psychology, 29*(2), 129–132.

Marsh, H. A., Malik, F., Shapiro, E., Omer, S. B., & Frew, P. M. (2014). Message framing strategies to increase influenza immunization uptake among pregnant African American women. *Maternal and Child Health Journal, 18*(7), 1639–1647.

Marsh, H. W., Köller, O., & Baumert, J. (2001). Reunification of East and West German school systems: Longitudinal multilevel modeling study of the big-fish-little-pond effect on academic self-concept. *American Educational Research Journal, 38*(2), 321–350.

Marshall, T. C., Bejanyan, K., Di Castro, G., & Lee, R. A. (2013). Attachment styles as predictors of Facebook-related jealousy and surveillance in romantic relationships. *Personal Relationships, 20*(1), 1–22.

Martijn, C., Sheeran, P., Wesseldijk, L. W., Merrick, H., Webb, T. L., Roefs, A., & Jansen, A. (2013). Evaluative conditioning makes slim models less desirable as standards for comparison and increases body satisfaction. *Health Psychology*, *32*(4), 433–438.

Martini, M. (1994). Peer interactions in Polynesia: A view from the Marquesas. In J. Roopnarine, J. E. Johnson, & F. H. Hooper (Eds.), *Children's play in diverse cultures* (pp. 74–122). Albany: State University of New York Press.

Masser, B. M., & Abrams, D. (2004). Reinforcing the glass ceiling: The consequences of hostile sexism for female managerial candidates. *Sex Roles*, *51*(9), 609–615.

Masters, N. T., Casey, E., Wells, E. A., & Morrison, D. M. (2013). Sexual scripts among young heterosexually active men and women: Continuity and change. *Journal of Sex Research*, *50*(5), 409–420.

Matheny, D., & Miller, K. (2000, January 4). A magical land where all the pets are above average. *Minneapolis Star-Tribune*, p. E1.

Matheson, M. P., Stansfeld, S. A., & Haines, M. M. (2003). The effects of chronic aircraft noise exposure on children's cognition and health: 3 field studies. *Noise and Health*, *5*(19), 31–40.

Matjasko, J. L., Cawley, J. H., Baker-Goering, M. M., & Yokum, D. V. (2016). Applying behavioral economics to public health policy: Illustrative examples and promising directions. *American Journal of Preventive Medicine*, *50*(5), S13–S19.

Matsumoto, D. (2009). Culture and emotional expression. In R. S. Wyer, C. Chiu, & Y. Hong (Eds.), *Understanding culture: Theory, research, and application* (pp. 271–287). New York, NY: Psychology Press.

Matz, D. C., Hofstedt, P. M., & Wood, W. (2008). Extraversion as a moderator of the cognitive dissonance associated with disagreement. *Personality and Individual Differences*, *45*(5), 401–405.

McCall, M., & Nattrass, K. (2001). Carding for the purchase of alcohol: I'm tougher than other clerks are! *Journal of Applied Social Psychology*, *31*(10), 2184–2194.

McConahay, J. B. (1983). Modern racism and modern discrimination: The effects of race, racial attitudes, and context on simulated hiring decisions. *Personality and Social Psychology Bulletin*, *9*(4), 551–558.

McConahay, J. B. (1986). Modern racism, ambivalence, and the modern racism scale. In J. F. Dovidio & S. L. Gaertner (Eds.), *Prejudice discrimination, and racism* (pp. 91–125). San Diego, CA: Academic Press.

McCormick, C. T. (1992). *Handbook of the law of evidence* (4th ed.). St. Paul, MN: West.

McCrae, R. R., & Costa, P. T. (1987). Validation of the five-factor model of personality across instruments and observers. *Journal of Personality and Social Psychology*, *52*(1), 81–90.

McDermott, R. C., & Lopez, F. G. (2013). College men's intimate partner violence attitudes: Contributions of adult attachment and gender role stress. *Journal of Counseling Psychology*, *60*(1), 127–136.

McFarland, S. G. (1989). Religious orientations and the targets of discrimination. *Journal for the Scientific Study of Religion*, *28*(3), 324–336.

McGovern, D. J. (2011). *Eliza undermined: The romanticism of Shaw's Pygmalion*. Retrieved September 26, 2011, from http://mro.massey.ac.nz/bitstream/handle/10179/2414/02_whole.pdf?sequence=1

McGuire, W. J. (1985). Attitudes and attitude change. In G. Lindzey & E. Aronson (Eds.), *Handbook of social psychology* (Vol. 2, 3rd ed., pp. 233–346). New York, NY: Random House.

McIntosh, P. (2011). *White privilege* (4th ed). Worth.

McIntyre, K., & Sobel, M. (2018). Reconstructing Rwanda: How Rwandan reporters use constructive journalism to promote peace. *Journalism Studies*, *19*(14), 2126–2147.

McManus, J. J. (2017). Emotions & ethical decision making at work: How the rational tail wags the emotional dog. *Academy of Management Proceedings*, *2017*(1), 17152.

McMillen, D. L., & Austin, J. B. (1971). Effect of positive feedback on compliance following transgression. *Psychonomic Science*, *24*(2), 59–61.

Mealy, M., Stephan, W., & Urrutia, I. C. (2007). The acceptability of lies: A comparison of Ecuadorians and Euro-Americans. *International Journal of Intercultural Relations*, *31*(6), 689–702.

Mecca, A. M., Smelser, N. J., & Vasconcellos, J. (1989). *The social importance of self-esteem*. Berkeley: University of California Press.

Meerow, S., & Newell, J. P. (2019). Urban resilience for whom, what, when, where, and why? *Urban Geography*, *40*(3), 309–329.

Mehrabian, A., & Stefl, C. A. (1995). Basic temperament components of loneliness, shyness, and conformity. *Social Behavior and Personality*, *23*(3), 253–263.

Mehrotra, A., Zaslavsky, A. M., & Ayanian, J. Z. (2007). Preventive health examinations and preventive gynecological examinations in the United States. *Archives of Internal Medicine*, *167*, 1876–1883.

Mehu, M., Little, A. C., & Dunbar, R. I. M. (2008). Sex differences in the effect of smiling on social judgments: An evolutionary approach. *Journal of Social, Evolutionary, and Cultural Psychology*, *2*(3), 103–121.

Meili, T. (2003). *I am the Central Park jogger: A story of hope and possibility*. New York, NY: Simon & Schuster.

Melson, G. F., Kahn, Jr, P. H., Beck, A., & Friedman, B. (2009). Robotic pets in human lives: Implications for the human-animal bond and for human relationships with personified technologies. *Journal of Social Issues*, *65*(3), 545–567.

Meltzoff, A. N., & Moore, M. K. (1977). Imitation of facial and manual gestures by human neonates. *Science*, *198*(4312), 75–78.

Meltzoff, A. N., & Moore, M. K. (1989). Imitation in newborn infants: Exploring the range of gestures imitated and the underlying mechanisms. *Developmental Psychology*, *25*(6), 954–962.

Melzer, A. (2019). Of princesses, paladins, and player motivations: Gender stereotypes and gendered perceptions in video games. In D. Pietschmann, B. Liebold, B. Lange, & J. Breuer (Eds.), *Evolutionary psychology and digital games: Digital hunter-gatherers* (pp. 205–220). London, UK: Routledge.

Mendel, R., Traut-Mattausch, E., Jonas, E., Leucht, S., Kane, J. M., Maino, K., . . . Hamann, J. (2011). Confirmation bias: Why psychiatrists stick to wrong preliminary diagnoses. *Psychological Medicine*, *41*(12), 2651–2659.

Merali, N. (2012). Arranged and forced marriage. In M. A. Paludi (Ed.), *The psychology of love* (pp. 143–168). Santa Barbara, CA: Praeger/ABC-CLIO.

Merton, R. K. (1948). The self-fulfilling prophecy. *Antioch Review*, *8*(2), 193–210.

Merton, R. K. (1994). Durkheim's division of labor in society. *Sociological Forum*, *9*(1), 17–25.

Mesagno, C., Harvey, J. T., & Janelle, C. M. (2012). Choking under pressure: The role of fear of negative evaluation. *Psychology of Sport and Exercise*, *13*(1), 60–68.

Messner, M. A. (1988). Sports and male domination: The female athlete as contested ideological terrain. *Sociology of Sport Journal*, *5*(3), 197–211.

Michaels, L. (Producer), & Waters, M. (Director). (2004). *Mean girls* [Motion picture]. USA: M. G. Films, Broadway Video, & Paramount Pictures.

Michinov, N. (2007). Social comparison and affect: A study among elderly women. *Journal of Social Psychology*, *147*(2), 175–189.

Middeldorp, N., & Le Billon, P. (2019). Deadly environmental governance: Authoritarianism, eco-populism, and the repression of environmental and land defenders. *Annals of the American Association of Geographers*, *109*(2), 324–337.

Middlemist, R. D., Knowles, E. S., & Matter, C. F. (1976). Personal space invasions in the lavatory: Suggestive evidence for arousal. *Journal of Personality and Social Psychology, 33*(5), 541–546.

Middlemist, R. D., Knowles, E. S., & Matter, C. F. (1977). What to do and what to report: A reply to Koocher. *Journal of Personality and Social Psychology, 35*(2), 122–124.

Middleton, J. S., Gattis, M. N., Frey, L. M., & Roe-Sepowitz, D. (2018). Youth Experiences Survey (YES): Exploring the scope and complexity of sex trafficking in a sample of youth experiencing homelessness. *Journal of Social Service Research, 44*(2), 141–157.

Mifune, N., Inamasu, K., Kohama, S., Ohtsubo, Y., & Tago, A. (2019). Social dominance orientation as an obstacle to intergroup apology. *PLoS One, 14*(1), e0211379.

Mihelič, K. K., & Culiberg, B. (2018). Reaping the fruits of another's labor: The role of moral meaningfulness, mindfulness, and motivation in social loafing. *Journal of Business Ethics, 160*, 713–727.

Milgram, S. (1963). Behavioral study of obedience. *Journal of Abnormal and Social Psychology, 67*(4), 371–378.

Milgram, S. (1970). The experience of living in cities. *Science, 167*(3924), 1461–1468.

Milgram, S. (1974). *Obedience to authority: An experimental view*. New York, NY: Harper & Row.

Milgram, S., Bickman, L., & Berkowitz, L. (1969). Note on the drawing power of crowds of different size. *Journal of Personality and Social Psychology, 13*(2), 79–82.

Milgram, S., & Sabini, J. (1978). On maintaining urban norms: A field experiment in the subway. In A. Baum & J. E. Singer (Eds.), *Advances in environmental psychology* (Vol. *1*, pp. 31–40). Mahwah, NJ: Lawrence Erlbaum.

Miller, D. T., & Ross, M. (1975). Self-serving biases in the attribution of causality: Fact or fiction? *Psychological Bulletin, 82*, 213–225.

Mills, C. W. (2016). Global White supremacy. In P. S. Rothenberg (Ed.), *White privilege* (5th ed). New York, NY: Worth.

Miranda, J. P., & Kanekar, S. (1993). Estimated willingness to help as a function of help-seeking contexts, cost of helping, and subject's sex and involvement. *Revue Internationale de Psychologie Sociale, 6*, 105–120.

Miscenko, D., Guenter, H., & Day, D. V. (2017). Am I a leader? Examining leader identity development over time. *The Leadership Quarterly, 28*(5), 605–620.

Mishra, N., Najafi, S., Najafi Asadolahi, S., & Tsay, A. (2018). *How freemium gets consumers to pay a premium: The role of loss-aversion*. http://dx.doi.org/10.2139/ssrn.2961548

Mita, T. H., Dermer, M., & Knight, J. (1977). Reversed facial images and the mere-exposure hypothesis. *Journal of Personality and Social Psychology, 35*(8), 597–601.

Mitchell, W. E. (1990). Why Wape men don't beat their wives. *Pacific Studies, 13*, 141–150.

Mixon, D. (1972). Instead of deception. *Journal for the Theory of Social Behavior, 2*(2), 145–177.

Mochon, D., Norton, M. I., & Ariely, D. (2008). Getting off the hedonic treadmill, one step at a time: The impact of regular religious practice and exercise on well-being. *Journal of Economic Psychology, 29*(5), 632–642.

Monahan, J. L., Murphy, S. T., & Zajonc, R. B. (2000). Subliminal mere exposure: Specific, general, and diffuse effects. *Psychological Science, 11*(6), 462–466.

Monin, B., & Norton, M. I. (2003). Perceptions of a fluid consensus: Uniqueness bias, false consensus, false polarization and pluralistic ignorance in a water conservation crisis. *Personality and Social Psychology Bulletin, 29*(5), 559–567.

Monroe, B. M., & Read, S. J. (2008). A general connectionist model of attitude structure and change: The ACS (attitude as constraint satisfaction) model. *Psychological Review, 115*(3), 733–759.

Mooradian, T. A., Davis, M., & Matzler, K. (2011). Dispositional empathy and the hierarchical structure of personality. *The American Journal of Psychology, 124*(1), 99–109.

Morey, D. F. (2006). Burying key evidence: The social bond between dogs and people. *Journal of Archaeological Science, 33*(2), 158–175.

Morgan, S. E., Movius, L., & Cody, M. J. (2009). The power of narratives: The effect of entertainment television organ donation storylines on the attitudes, knowledge, and behaviors of donors and nondonors. *Journal of Communication, 59*(1), 135–151.

Morling, B. (2015). *Research methods in psychology: Evaluating a world of information* (2nd ed.). New York, NY: Norton.

Morris, M. W., & Peng, K. (1994). Culture and cause: American and Chinese attributions for social and physical events. *Journal of Personality and Social Psychology, 67*(6), 949–971.

Morrison, K. R., & Miller, D. T. (2008). Distinguishing between silent and vocal minorities: Not all deviants feel marginal. *Journal of Personality and Social Psychology, 94*(5), 871–882.

Morry, M. M. (2005). Relationship satisfaction as a predictor of similarity ratings: A test of the attraction-similarity hypothesis. *Journal of Social and Personal Relationships, 22*(4), 561–584.

Morry, M. M. (2007). The attraction-similarity hypothesis among cross-sex friends: Relationship satisfaction, perceived similarities, and self-serving perceptions. *Journal of Social and Personal Relationships, 24*(1), 117–138.

Mortati, K. A., Arnedo, V., Post, N., Jimenez, E., & Grant, A. C. (2012). Sutton's law in epilepsy: Because that is where the lesion is. *Epilepsy & Behavior, 24*(2), 279–282.

Moscovici, S., & Zavalloni, M. (1969). The group as a polarizer of attitudes. *Journal of Personality and Social Psychology, 12*(2), 125–135.

Moskowitz, D. A., Turrubiates, J., Lozano, H., & Hajek, C. (2013). Physical, behavioral, and psychological traits of gay men identifying as Bears. *Archives of Sexual Behavior, 42*(5), 775–784.

Moskowitz, J. M., Malvin, J. H., Schaeffer, G. A., & Schaps, E. (1983). Evaluation of a cooperative learning strategy. *American Educational Research Journal, 20*, 687–696.

Moskowitz, J. M., Malvin, J. H., Schaeffer, G. A., & Schaps, E. (1985). Evaluation of jigsaw, a cooperative learning technique. *Contemporary Educational Psychology, 10*, 104–112.

Moulton-Tetlock, E. E., Ahn, J. N., Haines, E. L., & Mason, M. F. (2019). Women's work: Remembering communal goals. *Motivation Science, 5*(2), 157–178.

Mrkva, K., Johnson, E. J., Gächter, S., & Herrmann, A. (2019). Moderating loss aversion: Loss aversion Has moderators, but reports of its death are greatly exaggerated. *Journal of Consumer Psychology*. Advance online publication.

Mukherjee, K., & Upadhyay, D. (2019). Effect of mental construals on cooperative and competitive conflict management styles. *International Journal of Conflict Management, 30*(2), 202–226.

Mullen, B., Johnson, C., & Salas, E. (1991). Productivity loss in brainstorming groups: A meta-analytic integration. *Basic and Applied Social Psychology, 12*(1), 3–23.

Mundy, L. (2017). *Code girls: The untold story of the American women code breakers of World War II*. New York, NY: Hachette Books.

Münsterberg, H. (1908). *On the witness stand: Essays on psychology and crime*. New York, NY: McClure.

Murphy, C. M., & O'Farrell, T. J. (1996). Marital violence among alcoholics. *Current Directions in Psychological Science, 5*(6), 183–186.

Murphy, D., DeSanto, T., di Bonaventura, L., Bryce, I., & Spielberg, S. (Producers), & Bay, M. (Director). (2007). *Transformers* [Motion picture]. USA: Di Bonaventura Pictures, DreamWorks Pictures, & Paramount Pictures.

Murphy, Y., & Murphy, R. (1974). *Women of the forest*. New York, NY: Columbia University Press.

Murray, A. A., Wood, J. M., & Lilienfeld, S. O. (2012). Psychopathic personality traits and cognitive dissonance: Individual differences in attitude change. *Journal of Research in Personality*, *46*(5), 525–536.

Murray, J. D., Spadafore, J. A., & McIntosh, W. D. (2005). Belief in a just world and social perception: Evidence for automatic activation. *Journal of Social Psychology*, *145*(1), 35–47.

Murray, S. L., Holmes, J. G., & Griffin, D. W. (1996a). The benefits of positive illusions: Idealization and the construction of satisfaction in close relationships. *Journal of Personality and Social Psychology*, *70*(1), 79–98.

Murray, S. L., Holmes, J. G., & Griffin, D. W. (1996b). The self-fulfilling nature of positive illusions in romantic relationships: Love is not blind, but prescient. *Journal of Personality and Social Psychology*, *71*(6), 1155–1180.

Mussweiler, T., & Strack, F. (2001). "Considering the impossible": Explaining the effects of implausible anchors. *Social Cognition*, *19*, 145–160.

Myers, D. G. (1975). Discussion-induced attitude polarization. *Human Relations*, *28*(8), 699–714.

Myers, D. G., & Diener, E. (1995). Who is happy? *Psychological Science*, *6*(1), 10–19.

Nandedkar, A., & Midha, V. (2012). It won't happen to me: An assessment of optimism bias in music piracy. *Computers in Human Behavior*, *28*(1), 41–48.

Naquin, C. E., Kurtzberg, T. R., & Belkin, L. Y. (2010). The finer points of lying online: E-mail versus pen and paper. *Journal of Applied Psychology*, *95*(2), 387–394.

Nario-Redmond, M. R., Kemerling, A. A., & Silverman, A. (2019). Hostile, benevolent, and ambivalent ableism: Contemporary manifestations. *Journal of Social Issues*. Advance online publication. doi:10.1111/josi.12337

Narita, S., Ohtani, N., Waga, C., Ohta, M., Ishigooka, J., & Iwahashi, K. (2016). A pet-type robot AIBO-assisted therapy as a day care program for chronic schizophrenia patients: A pilot study. *Australasian Medical Journal*, *9*(7), 244–248.

Nathanson, D. E. (1998). Long-term effectiveness of dolphin-assisted therapy for children with severe disabilities. *Anthrozoös*, *11*(1), 22–32.

Nathanson, D. E., de Castro, D., Friend, H., & McMahon, M. (1997). Effectiveness of short-term dolphin-assisted therapy for children with severe disabilities. *Anthrozoös*, *10*(2–3), 90–100.

Nathanson, D. E., de Castro, D., Friend, H., & McMahon, M. (1997). Effectiveness of short-term dolphin-assisted therapy for children with severe disabilities. *Anthrozoös*, *10*(2–3), 90–100.

National Highway Traffic Safety Administration (2020, September 22). Hurricane damaged vehicles. https://www.nhtsa.gov/es/hurricane-damaged-vehicles

Neff, K. D. (2011). Self-compassion, self-esteem, and well-being. *Social and Personality Psychology Compass*, *5*(1), 1–12.

Neff, K. D., & McGehee, P. (2010). Self-compassion and psychological resilience among adolescents and young adults. *Self and Identity*, *9*(3), 225–240.

Neff, K., & Vonk, R. (2009). Self-compassion versus global self-esteem: Two different ways of relating to oneself. *Journal of Personality*, *77*(1), 23–50.

Nenkov, G. Y., Morrin, M., Ward, A., Schwartz, B., & Hulland, J. (2008). A short form of the maximization scale: Factor structure, reliability and validity studies. *Judgment and Decision Making*, *3*(5), 371–388.

Nesse, R. M. (2001). *Evolution and the capacity for commitment*. New York, NY: Russell Sage Foundation.

Neta, M., & Tong, T. T. (2016). Don't like what you see? Give it time: Longer reaction times associated with increased positive affect. *Emotion*, *16*(5), 730–739.

Neufeld, S. D., & Schmitt, M. T. (2019). Solidarity not homogeneity: Constructing a superordinate Aboriginal identity that protects subgroup identities. *Political Psychology*, *40*(3), 599–616.

Neuman, J. H., & Baron, R. A. (2011). Social antecedents of bullying: A social interactionist perspective. In S. Einarsen, H. Hoel, D. Zapf, & C. Cooper (Eds.), *Bullying and harassment in the workplace: Developments in theory, research, and practice* (pp. 201–225). Boca Raton, FL: CRC Press.

Neumann, D. L., Moffitt, R. L., Thomas, P. R., Loveday, K., Watling, D. P., Lombard, C. L., . . . Tremeer, M. A. (2018). A systematic review of the application of interactive virtual reality to sport. *Virtual Reality*, *22*(3), 183–198.

Newman, A., Nielsen, I., Smyth, R., Hirst, G., & Kennedy, S. (2018). The effects of diversity climate on the work attitudes of refugee employees: The mediating role of psychological capital and moderating role of ethnic identity. *Journal of Vocational Behavior*, *105*, 147–158.

Newman, D. M. (2007). *Identities and inequalities: Exploring the intersections of race, class, gender, and sexuality*. Boston, MA: McGraw-Hill.

Newport, F., Jones, J. M., Saad, L., & Carroll, J. (2006). Americans and their pets. *Gallup Poll*. Retrieved December 13, 2019, from https://news.gallup.com/poll/25969/americans-their-pets.aspx

Newton, N. A., Khanna, C., & Thompson, J. (2008). Workplace failure: Mastering the last taboo. *Consulting Psychology Journal: Practice and Research*, *60*(3), 227–245.

Nichol, F. D. (1944). *The midnight cry: A defense of William Miller and the Millerites*. Washington, DC: Review and Herald.

Nicholson, I. A. M. (2011). "Torture at Yale": Experimental subjects, laboratory torment and the "rehabilitation" of Milgram's "obedience to authority". *Theory & Psychology*, *21*(6), 737–761.

Nicholson, I. A. M. (2015). The normalization of torment: Producing and managing anguish in Milgram's 'Obedience' laboratory. *Theory & Psychology*, *25*(5), 639–656.

Nicholson, I. R. (2011). New technology, old issues: Demonstrating the relevance of the Canadian Code of Ethics for Psychologists to the ever-sharper cutting edge of technology. *Canadian Psychology/Psychologie Canadienne*, *52*(3), 215–224.

Nickerson, R. S. (1998). Confirmation bias: A ubiquitous phenomenon in many guises. *Review of General Psychology*, *2*(2), 175–220.

Nicoli, F. (2019). Crises, path dependency, and the five trilemmas of European integration: Seventy years of 'failing forward' from the common market to the European fiscal union. *The Amsterdam Centre for European SSRN Research Paper*, (2019/05).

Nier, J. A. (2004). Why does the 'above average effect' exist? Demonstrating idiosyncratic trait definition. *Teaching of Psychology*, *31*(1), 53–54.

Nier, J. A., Bajaj, P., McLean, M. C., & Schwartz, E. (2013). Group status, perceptions of agency, and the correspondence bias: Attributional processes in the formation of stereotypes about high and low status groups. *Group Processes & Intergroup Relations*, *16*(4), 476–487.

Nimer, J., & Lundahl, B. (2007). Animal-assisted therapy: A meta-analysis. *Anthrozoös*, *20*(3), 225–238.

Nisbett, R. E., Caputo, C., Legant, P., & Marecek, J. (1973). Behavior as seen by the actor and as seen by the observer. *Journal of Personality and Social Psychology*, *27*(2), 154–164.

Nisbett, R. E., Krantz, D. H., Jepson, C., & Kunda, Z. (1983). The use of statistical heuristics in everyday inductive reasoning. *Psychological Review*, *90*(4), 339–363.

Nisbett, R. E., & Kunda, Z. (1985). Perception of social distributions. *Journal of Personality and Social Psychology*, *48*(2), 297–311.

Nisbett, R. E., & Ross, L. (1980). *Human inference: Strategies and shortcomings of social judgment*. Englewood Cliffs, NJ: Prentice Hall.

Nisbett, R. E., & Wilson, T. D. (1977). Telling more than we can know: Verbal reports on mental processing. *Psychological Review*, *84*, 231–259.

Noelle-Neumann, E. (1993). *Spiral of silence*. Chicago, IL: University of Chicago Press.

Noelle-Neumann, E. (1974). The spiral of silence: A theory of public opinion. Journal of Communication, 24, 43–51.

Norbäck, D., Lu, C., Wang, J., Zhang, Y., Li, B., Zhao, Z., . . . Sundell, J. (2018). Asthma and rhinitis among Chinese children—indoor and outdoor air pollution and indicators of socioeconomic status (SES). *Environment International*, *115*, 1–8.

Nordstrom, A. H. (2015). The voices project: Reducing white students' racism in introduction to psychology. *Teaching of Psychology*, *42*(1), 43–50.

Norenzayan, A., & Nisbett, R. E. (2000). Culture and causal cognition. *Current Directions in Psychological Science*, *9*(4), 132–135.

Norman, D. (2013). *The design of everyday things: Revised and expanded edition*. New York, NY: Basic Books.

Norris, R. J. (2019). *Exonerated: A history of the innocence movement*. New York, NY: NYU Press.

Nosek, B. A., Ebersole, C. R., DeHaven, A. C., & Mellor, D. T. (2017, June 16). *The preregistration revolution*. https://doi.org/10.1073/pnas.1708274114

Nucci, C., & Young-Shim, K. (2005). Improving socialization through sport: An analytic review of literature on aggression and sportsmanship. *Physical Educator*, *62*(3), 123–129.

Nye, J. (2008). *The powers to lead*. New York, NY: Oxford University Press.

Obermaier, M., Fawzi, N., & Koch, T. (2016). Bystanding or standing by? How the number of bystanders affects the intention to intervene in cyberbullying. *New Media & Society*, *18*(8), 1491–1507.

O'Brien, B. (2009). Prime suspect: An examination of factors that aggravate and counteract confirmation bias in criminal investigations. *Psychology, Public Policy, and Law*, *15*(4), 315–334.

Ocasio, A. A. (2019). *The pedagogy of failing forward and emancipatory rhetoric in nonfiction literature, freshman composition, and writing center theory* (Unpublished doctoral dissertation). Saint Louis University, St. Louis, MO.

Odendaal, J. S. (2000). Animal-assisted therapy—magic or medicine? *Journal of Psychosomatic Research*, *49*(4), 275–280.

Odintsova, V. V., Willemsen, G., Dolan, C. V., Hottenga, J. J., Martin, N. G., Slagboom, P. E., . . . Boomsma, D. I. (2018). Establishing a twin register: An invaluable resource for (behavior) genetic, epidemiological, biomarker, and 'omics' studies. *Twin Research and Human Genetics*, *21*(3), 239–252.

Ogunfowora, B., Bourdage, J. S., & Nguyen, B. (2013). An exploration of the dishonest side of self-monitoring: Links to moral disengagement and unethical business decision making. *European Journal of Personality*, *27*, 532–544.

Oh, D., Dotsch, R., Porter, J., & Todorov, A. (2019). Gender biases in impressions from faces: Empirical studies and computational models. *Journal of Experimental Psychology: General*, *149*, 323–342.

Öhman, A., & Mineka, S. (2001). Fears, phobias, and preparedness: Toward an evolved module of fear and fear learning. *Psychological Review*, *108*(3), 483–522.

Olčar, D., Rijavec, M., & Golub, T. L. (2019). Primary school teachers' life satisfaction: The role of life goals, basic psychological needs and flow at work. *Current Psychology, 38*(2), 320–329.

Olds, M. E., & Forbes, J. L. (1981). The central basis of motivation: Intracranial self-stimulation studies. *Annual Review of Psychology, 32*(1), 523–574.

O'Neil, A., Sojo, V., Fileborn, B., Scovelle, A. J., & Milner, A. (2018). The #MeToo movement: An opportunity in public health? *The Lancet, 391*(10140), 2587–2589.

Ortiz, J., & Raine, A. (2004). Heart rate level and antisocial behavior in children and adolescents: A meta-analysis. *Journal of the American Academy of Child & Adolescent Psychiatry, 43*(2), 154–162.

Osborn, A. F. (1957). *Applied imagination: Principles and procedures of creative problem solving* (3rd ed.). New York, NY: Scribner.

Oshio, A., Taku, K., Hirano, M., & Saeed, G. (2018). Resilience and Big Five personality traits: A meta-analysis. *Personality and Individual Differences, 127*, 54–60.

Ost, J., Granhag, P., & Udell, J. (2008). Familiarity breeds distortion: The effects of media exposure on false reports concerning media coverage of the terrorist attacks in London on 7 July 2005. *Memory, 16*(1), 76–85.

O'Sullivan, T. M. (2015). Environmental security is homeland security: Climate disruption as the ultimate disaster risk multiplier. *Risk, Hazards & Crisis in Public Policy, 6*(2), 183–222.

Overing, J. (1986). Images of cannibalism, death and domination in a "non-violent" society. In D. Riches (Ed.), *The anthropology of violence* (pp. 86–101). Oxford, UK: Blackwell.

Overing, J. (1989). The aesthetics of production: The sense of community among the Cubeo and Piaroa. *Dialectical Anthropology, 14*(3), 159–175.

Pallant, J., Sands, S., & Karpen, I. (2020). Product customization: A profile of consumer demand. *Journal of Retailing and Consumer Services, 54*, 102030.

Parent, M. C., Gobble, T. D., & Rochlen, A. (2019). Social media behavior, toxic masculinity, and depression. *Psychology of Men & Masculinities, 20*(3), 277–287.

Park, J. W., & Hastak, M. (1994). Memory based product judgments: Effect of involvement at encoding and retrieval. *Journal of Consumer Research, 21*(3), 534–547.

Park, S., Lee, M., & Jeon, J. (2017). Factors affecting depressive symptoms among North Korean adolescent refugees residing in South Korea. *International Journal of Environmental Research and Public Health, 14*(8), 912.

Parker, C. S., & Towler, C. C. (2019). Race and authoritarianism in American politics. *Annual Review of Political Science, 22*, 503–519.

Parker, S. T. (1991). A developmental approach to the origins of self-recognition in great apes. *Human Evolution, 6*(5–6), 435–449.

Parlamis, J. D., Allred, K. G., & Block, C. (2010). Letting off steam or just steaming? The influence of venting target and offender status on attributions and anger. *International Journal of Conflict Management, 21*(3), 260–280.

Parmesan, C. (2006). Ecological and evolutionary responses to recent climate change. *Annual Review of Ecology, Evolution, and Systematics, 37*(1), 637–669.

Parnes, S. J., & Meadow, A. (1959). Effects of "brainstorming" instructions on creative problem solving by trained and untrained subjects. *Journal of Educational Psychology, 50*(4), 171–176.

Parsons, C. E., Young, K. S., Kumari, N., Stein, A., & Kringelbach, M. L. (2011). The motivational salience of infant faces is similar for men and women. *PLoS One, 6*(5), e20632.

Pathak, G., & Nichter, M. (2019). The anthropology of plastics: An agenda for local studies of a global matter of concern. *Medical Anthropology Quarterly, 33*(3), 307–326.

Patrick, C. J., & Verona, E. (2007). The psychophysiology of aggression: Autonomic, electrocortical, and neuro-imaging findings. In D. J. Flannery, A. T. Vazsonyi, & I. D. Waldman (Eds.), *The Cambridge handbook of violent behavior and aggression* (pp. 111–150). Cambridge, UK: Cambridge University Press.

Patulny, R., Bellocchi, A., Mills, K. A., McKenzie, J., & Olson, R. (2019). Happy, stressed, and angry: A national study of teachers' emotions and their management. *Emotions: History, Culture, Society, 3*, 223–244.

Paulhus, D. L., & Williams, K. M. (2002). The dark triad of personality: Narcissism, Machiavellianism and psychopathy. *Journal of Research in Personality, 36*(6), 556–563.

Paulus, P. B., Nakui, T., Putman, V. L., & Brown, V. R. (2006). Effects of task instructions and brief breaks on brainstorming. *Group Dynamics: Theory, Research, and Practice*, *10*(3), 206–219.

Payscale.com. (2019). *The state of the gender pay gap in 2019*. Retrieved December 23, 2019, from https://www.payscale.com/data/gender-pay-gap

Pazzaglia, M., Scivoletto, G., Giannini, A. M., & Leemhuis, E. (2019). My hand in my ear: A phantom limb re-induced by the illusion of body ownership in a patient with a brachial plexus lesion. *Psychological Research*, *83*(1), 196–204.

Pedersen, W. C., Miller, L. C., Putcha-Bhagavatula, A. D., & Yang, Y. (2002). Evolved sex differences in the number of partners desired? The long and short of it. *Psychological Science*, *13*(2), 157–161.

Peetz, J., & Kammrath, L. (2011). Only because I love you: Why people make and why they break promises in romantic relationships. *Journal of Personality and Social Psychology*, *100*(5), 887–904.

Pelling, M. (2010). *Adaptation to climate change: from resilience to transformation*. New York, NY: Routledge.

Pence, E., & Paymar, M. (1993). *Education groups for men who batter: The Duluth model*. New York, NY: Springer.

Penkal, J. L., & Kurdek, L. A. (2007). Gender and race differences in young adults' body dissatisfaction. *Personality and Individual Differences*, *43*(8), 2270–2281.

Pennebaker, J. W. (1997). Writing about emotional experiences as a therapeutic process. *Psychological Science*, *8*(3), 162–166.

Perloff, R. M., & Brock, T. C. (1980). And thinking makes it so: Cognitive responses to persuasion. In M. Roloff & G. Miller (Eds.), *Persuasion: New directions in theory and research* (pp. 67–100). Beverly Hills, CA: Sage.

Perreira, K. M., Marchante, A. N., Schwartz, S. J., Isasi, C. R., Carnethon, M. R., Corliss, H. L., . . . Delamater, A. M. (2019). Stress and resilience: Key correlates of mental health and substance use in the Hispanic Community Health Study of Latino Youth. *Journal of Immigrant and Minority Health*, *21*(1), 4–13.

Perrett, D. I., May, K. A., & Yoshikawa, S. (1994). Facial shape and judgements of female attractiveness. *Nature*, *368*(6468), 239–242.

Perrin, S., & Spencer, C. P. (1981). Independence or conformity in the Asch experiment as a reflection of cultural and situational factors. *British Journal of Social Psychology*, *20*(3), 205–210.

Perrine, R. M., & Osbourne, H. L. (1998). Personality characteristics of dog and cat persons. *Anthrozoös*, *11*(1), 33–40.

Perry, D. G., & Bussey, K. (1979). The social learning theory of sex differences: Imitation is alive and well. *Journal of Personality and Social Psychology*, *37*(10), 1699–1712.

Perry, G. (2013). *Behind the shock machine: The untold story of the notorious Milgram psychology experiments*. New York, NY: New Press.

Perske, R. (2011). Perske's list: False confessions from 75 persons with intellectual disability. *Intellectual and Developmental Disabilities*, *49*(5), 365–373.

Pesciarelli, F., Scorolli, C., & Cacciari, C. (2019). Neural correlates of the implicit processing of grammatical and stereotypical gender violations: A masked and unmasked priming study. *Biological Psychology*, *146*, 107714.

Pessin, J. (1933). The comparative effects of social and mechanical stimulation on memorizing. *The American Journal of Psychology*, *45*(2), 263–270.

Petrinovich, L., O'Neill, P., & Jorgensen, M. (1993). An empirical study of moral intuitions: Toward an evolutionary ethics. *Journal of Personality and Social Psychology*, *64*(3), 467–478.

Petrovskaya, I., & Mirakyan, A. (2018). A mission of service: Social entrepreneur as a servant leader. *International Journal of Entrepreneurial Behavior & Research*. Advance online publication.

Pettigrew, T. F. (2016). In pursuit of three theories: authoritarianism, relative deprivation, and intergroup contact. *Annual Review of Psychology*, *67*, 1–21.

Pettus, K. (2019). The first American climate refugees and the need for proactive relocation. *George Washington Law Review*, *87*, 172–206.

Petty, R. E., & Cacioppo, J. T. (1979). Effects of forewarning of persuasive intent and involvement on cognitive responses. *Personality and Social Psychology Bulletin*, *5*(2), 173–176.

Petty, R. E., & Cacioppo, J. T. (1996). *Attitudes and persuasion: Classic and contemporary approaches*. Boulder, CO: Westview.

Petty, R. E., Cacioppo, J. T., & Haugtvedt, C. P. (1992). Ego-involvement and persuasion: An appreciative look at the Sherifs' contribution to the study of self-relevance an attitude change. In D. Granberg & G. Sarup (Eds.), *Social judgment and intergroup relations: Essays in honor of Muzifer Sherif* (pp. 147–175). New York, NY: Springer-Verlag.

Petty, R. E., Harkins, S. G., Williams, K., & Latane, B. (1977). The effects of group size on cognitive effort and evaluation. *Personality and Social Psychology Bulletin*, *3*(4), 579–582.

Petty, R. E., & Wegener, D. T. (1998). Attitude change: Multiple roles for persuasion variables. In D. T. Gilbert, S. T. Fiske, & G. Lindzey (Eds.), *The handbook of social psychology* (Vol. *1*, 4th ed., pp. 323–390). New York, NY: McGraw-Hill.

Pham, N., Morrin, M., & Bublitz, M. G. (2019). Flavor halos and consumer perceptions of food healthfulness. *European Journal of Marketing*, *53*(4), 685–707.

Phillips, J. G., Butt, S., & Blaszczynski, A. (2006). Personality and self-reported use of mobile phones for games. *Cyberpsychology & Behavior*, *9*(6), 753–758.

Pieters, R., Warlop, L., & Wedel, M. (2002). Breaking through the clutter: Benefits of advertisement originality and familiarity for brand attention and memory. *Management Science*, *48*(6), 765–781.

Pillow, D. R., Hale, W. J., Jr., Crabtree, M. A., & Hinojosa, T. L. (2017). Exploring the relations between self-monitoring, authenticity, and well-being. *Personality and Individual Differences*, *116*, 393–398.

Pinker, S. (2002). *The blank slate: The modern denial of human nature*. New York, NY: Viking.

Pinker, S. (2011). *The better angels of our nature: Why violence has declined*. New York, NY: Viking.

Pittinsky, T. L. (2010). A two-dimensional model of intergroup leadership: The case of national diversity. *American Psychologist*, *65*(3), 194–200.

Plötner, M., Over, H., Carpenter, M., & Tomasello, M. (2015). The effects of collaboration and minimal-group membership on children's prosocial behavior, liking, affiliation, and trust. *Journal of Experimental Child Psychology*, *139*, 161–173.

Plotnik, J. M., de Waal, F. B., & Reiss, D. (2006). Self-recognition in an Asian elephant. *Proceedings of the National Academy of Sciences of the United States of America*, *103*(45), 17053–17057.

Podberscek, A. L. (2009). Good to pet and eat: The keeping and consuming of dogs and cats in South Korea. *Journal of Social Issues*, *65*(3), 615–632.

Podnar, O. (2007, July 25). The day Yugoslav soccer died: Croats celebrate the 15th anniversary of the beginning of the Patriotic War . . . on the soccer field! *Soccerphile*. http://www.soccerphile.com/soccerphile/news/balkans-soccer/football-war.html

Politser, P. (2008). *Neuroeconomics: A guide to the new science of making choices*. New York, NY: Oxford University Press.

Polman, E. (2010). Why are maximizers less happy than satisficers? Because they maximize positive and negative outcomes. *Journal of Behavioral Decision Making*, *23*(2), 179–190.

Porter, E. S. (Producer & Director). (1903). *The great train robbery* [Motion picture]. United States: Warner Bros.

Porter, S., ten Brinke, L., & Wallace, B. (2012). Secrets and lies: Involuntary leakage in deceptive facial expressions as a function of emotional intensity. *Journal of Nonverbal Behavior, 36*(1), 23–37.

Poyatos, F. (2002a). *Nonverbal communication across disciplines: Vol. 1. Culture, sensory interaction, speech, conversation*. Amsterdam, Netherlands: John Benjamins.

Poyatos, F. (2002b). The nature, morphology and functions of gestures, manners and postures as documented by creative literature. *Gesture, 2*(1), 99–117.

Pratto, F., Sidanius, J., Stallworth, L. M., & Malle, B. F. (1994). Social dominance orientation: A personality variable predicting social and political attitudes. *Journal of Personality and Social Psychology, 67*(4), 741–763.

Praxmarer, S. (2011). How a presenter's perceived attractiveness affects persuasion for attractiveness-unrelated products. *International Journal of Advertising, 30*(5), 839–865.

Prelec, D. & Simester, D. (2001). Always leave home without it: A further investigation of the credit-card effect on willingness to pay. *Marketing Letters, 12*(1), 5–12.

Prentice-Dunn, S., & Rogers, R. W. (1982). Effects of public and private self-awareness on deindividuation and aggression. *Journal of Personality and Social Psychology, 43*(3), 503–513.

Priester, J. R., & Petty, R. E. (1996). The gradual threshold model of ambivalence: Relating the positive and negative bases of attitudes to subjective ambivalence. *Journal of Personality and Social Psychology, 71*(3), 431–449.

Prior, H., Schwarz, A., & Güntürkün, O. (2008). Mirror-induced behavior in the magpie (Pica pica): Evidence of self-recognition. *PLoS Biology, 6*(8), e202.

PRNewswire. (2006). Michigan animal sanctuary adopts 511 rabbits of "The Great Bunny Rescue of 2006." *Multivu*. Retrieved December 15, 2019, from http://multivu.prnewswire.com/broadcast/25470/consumer.shtml

Provine, R. (1992). Contagious laughter: Laughter is sufficient stimulus for laughs and smiles. *Bulletin of the Psychonomic Society, 30*(1), 1–4.

Provine, R. (1996). Laughter. *American Scientist, 84*(1), 38–47.

Pruysers, S., Blais, J., & Chen, P. G. (2019). Who makes a good citizen? The role of personality. *Personality and Individual Differences, 146*, 99–104.

Pryor, J. H., Hurtado, S., DeAngelo, L. E., Blake, L. P., & Tran, S. (2010). *The American freshman: National norms fall 2009*. Berkeley: University of California Press.

Przybylski, A. K., Murayama, K., DeHaan, C. R., & Gladwell, V. (2013). Motivational, emotional, and behavioral correlates of fear of missing out. *Computers in Human Behavior, 29*(4), 1841–1848.

Puckett, J. M., Petty, R. E., Cacioppo, J. T., & Fisher, D. L. (1983). The relative impact of age and attractiveness stereotypes on persuasion. *Journal of Gerontology, 38*(3), 340–343.

Pyszczynski, T., Greenberg, J., & Holt, K. (1985). Maintaining consistency between self-serving beliefs and available data: A bias in information evaluation. *Personality and Social Psychology Bulletin, 11*(2), 179–190.

Pyszczynski, T., Greenberg, J., Solomon, S., Arndt, J., & Schimel, J. (2004). Converging toward an integrated theory of self-esteem: Reply to Crocker and Nuer (2004), Ryan and Deci (2004), and Leary (2004). *Psychological Bulletin, 130*(3), 483–488.

Qiongjing, H., Xi, L., & Zhixue, Z. (2018). Self-monitoring in group context: Its indirect benefits for individual status attainment and group task performance. *Acta Psychologica Sinica, 50*(10), 1169–1179.

Ramsden, E., & Adams, J. (2008). Escaping the laboratory: The rodent experiments of John B. Calhoun & their cultural influence. *Journal of Social History, 42*(3), 761–792.

Ray, J. J. (1990). Comment on "right-wing authoritarianism." *Canadian Psychology, 31*(4), 392–393.

Reeder, G. D. (1982). Let's give the fundamental attribution error another chance. *Journal of Personality and Social Psychology, 43*(2), 341–344.

Reiber, C., & Garcia, J. R. (2010). Hooking up: Gender differences, evolution, and pluralistic ignorance. *Evolutionary Psychology, 8*(3), 390–404.

Reichert, T. (Ed.). (2019). *Investigating the use of sex in media promotion and advertising*. New York, NY: Routledge.

Reis, H. T. (2019). A brief history of social psychology. In E. J. Finkel & R. F. Baumeister (Eds.), *Advanced social psychology: The state of the science* (pp. 9–38). New York, NY: Oxford University Press.

Reis, H. T., Maniaci, M. R., Caprariello, P. A., Eastwick, P. W., & Finkel, E. J. (2011). Familiarity does indeed promote attraction in live interaction. *Journal of Personality and Social Psychology, 101*(3), 557–570.

Reis, J. C., Correia, A., Murai, F., Veloso, A., Benevenuto, F., & Cambria, E. (2019). Supervised learning for fake news detection. *IEEE Intelligent Systems, 34*(2), 76–81.

Remarque, E. M. (2013). *Three comrades: A novel*. New York, NY: Random House.

Remmers, H. H. (1934). Reliability and halo effect of high school and college students' judgments of their teachers. *Journal of Applied Psychology, 18*(5), 619–630.

Reppert, S. M., & de Roode, J. C. (2018). Demystifying monarch butterfly migration. *Current Biology, 28*(17), R1009–R1022.

Reynolds-Milon, F. (2019). *A qualitative study of new nurse graduates and experienced nurses' perception of incivility in the workplace*. Unpublished manuscript available from PsycINFO.

Rhodes, N., & Ellithorpe, M. E. (2016). Laughing at risk: Sitcom laugh tracks communicate norms for behavior. *Media Psychology, 19*(3), 359–380.

Rhodes, N., & Wood, W. (1992). Self-esteem and intelligence affect influenceability: The mediating role of message reception. *Psychological Bulletin, 111*(1), 156–171.

Richardson, J. T., & Bellanger, F. (Eds.). (2016). *Legal cases, new religious movements, and minority faiths*. Abingdon, UK: Routledge.

Ringelmann, M. (1913). Recherches sur les moteurs animes: Travail de l'homme [Research on animate sources of power: The work of man]. *Annales de l'Institut National Agronomique, 12*(1), 1–40.

Riniolo, T. C., Johnson, K. C., Sherman, T. R., & Misso, J. A. (2006). Hot or not: Do professors perceived as physically attractive receive higher student evaluations? *Journal of General Psychology, 133*(1), 19–35.

Rivenburgh, N. K. (2000). Social identity theory and news portrayals of citizens involved in international affairs. *Media Psychology, 2*(4), 303–329.

Rizzolatti, G., & Craighero, L. (2005). Mirror neuron: A neurological approach to empathy. In J.-P. P. Changeux, A. Damasio, W. Singer, & Y. Christen (Eds.), *Neurobiology of human values* (pp. 107–123). Berlin, Germany: Springer.

Rizzolatti, G., Fadiga, L., Fogassi, L., & Gallese, V. (1996). Premotor cortex and the recognition of motor actions. *Cognitive Brain Research, 3*, 131–141.

Roberts, L. J., Jackson, M. S., & Grundy, I. H. (2019). Choking under pressure: Illuminating the role of distraction and self-focus. *International Review of Sport and Exercise Psychology, 12*(1), 49–69.

Roberts, R., Rotherham, M., Maynard, I., Thomas, O., & Woodman, T. (2013). Perfectionism and the 'yips': An initial investigation. *The Sport Psychologist, 27*, 53–61.

Robbins, T. W., & Everitt, B. J. (2002). Limbic-striatal memory systems and drug addiction. *Neurobiology of learning and memory, 78*(3), 625–636.

Roch, S. G., Shannon, C. E., Martin, J. J., Swiderski, D., Agosta, J. P., & Shanock, L. R. (2019). Role of employee felt obligation and endorsement of the just world hypothesis: A social exchange theory investigation in an organizational justice context. *Journal of Applied Social Psychology, 49*(4), 213–225.

Rockström, J., Steffen, W., Noone, K., Persson, A., Chapin, F. S., III, Lambin, E. F., . . . Foley, J. A. (2009). A safe operating space for humanity. *Nature, 461*, 472–475.

Rodin, J., & Langer, E. J. (1977a). Long-term effects of a control-relevant intervention with the institutionalized aged. *Journal of Personality and Social Psychology, 35*(12), 897–902.

Rodin, J., & Langer, E. J. (1977b). Erratum to Rodin and Langer. *Journal of Personality and Social Psychology, 36*(5), 462.

Roese, N. J. (1997). Counterfactual thinking. *Psychological Bulletin, 121*(1), 133–148.

Roland, A. (1988). *In search of self in India and Japan.* Princeton, NJ: Princeton University Press.

Roland, E., & Munthe, E. (Eds.). (1989/2017). *Bullying (1989): An international perspective.* New York, NY: Routledge.

Rolls, G. (2013). *Classic case studies in psychology.* Milton Park, UK: Routledge.

Romero, D. (2019, December 28). Guardian Angels to patrol Jewish neighborhoods in New York City after recent attacks. *NBC News.* Retrieved January 21, 2020, from https://www.nbcnews.com/news/us-news/guardian-angels-patrol-jewish-neighborhoods-new-york-city-after-recent-n1108251?fbclid=IwAR16v0RLEkjvzcJWnen29v-zmyTfwqs2j3YgxugsqWPbPR3vbN-m1sV9fow

Rosen, K. H. (1996). The ties that bind women to violent premarital relationships: Processes of seduction and entrapment. In D. D. Cahn & S. A. Lloyd (Eds.), *Family violence from a communication perspective* (pp. 151–176). Thousand Oaks, CA: Sage.

Rosen, K. H., & Stith, S. M. (1997). Surviving abusive dating relationships: Processes of leaving, healing and moving on. In G. Kantor & J. Jasinski (Eds.), *Out of the darkness: Contemporary perspectives on family violence* (pp. 170–182). Thousand Oaks, CA: Sage.

Rosen, L. G., Sun, N., Rushlow, W., & Laviolette, S. R. (2015). Molecular and neuronal plasticity mechanisms in the amygdala-prefrontal cortical circuit: Implications for opiate addiction memory formation. *Frontiers in Neuroscience, 9*, article 399.

Rosenberg, M. (1965). Rosenberg self-esteem scale (RSE). *Acceptance and Commitment Therapy: Measures Package, 61*, 52.

Rosenthal, R. (1994). Interpersonal expectancy effects: A 30-year perspective. *Current Directions in Psychological Science, 3*(6), 176–179.

Rosenthal, R. (2002). Covert communication in classrooms, clinics, courtrooms, and cubicles. *American Psychologist, 57*(11), 839–849.

Rosenthal, R., & Fode, K. (1963). The effect of experimenter bias on the performance of the albino rat. *Behavioral Science, 8*(3), 183–189.

Rosenthal, R., & Jacobsen, L. (1968). *Pygmalion in the classroom: Self-fulfilling prophecies and teacher expectations.* New York, NY: Holt, Rhinehart, and Winston.

Roser, M. (2017). Homicides. *Our World in Data.* https://ourworldindata.org/homicides/

Roseth, C. J., Lee, Y. K., & Saltarelli, W. A. (2019). Reconsidering jigsaw social psychology: Longitudinal effects on social interdependence, sociocognitive conflict regulation, motivation, and achievement. *Journal of Educational Psychology, 111*(1), 149–169.

Ross, L. D. (1977). The intuitive psychologist and his shortcomings: Distortions in the attribution process. In L. Berkowitz (Ed.), *Advances in experimental social psychology* (Vol. 10, pp. 173–220). San Diego, CA: Academic Press.

Ross, L. D., & Nisbett, R. E. (1991). *The person and the situation: Perspectives of social psychology.* New York, NY: McGraw-Hill.

Roth, M., & Herzberg, P. Y. (2017). The resilient personality prototype. *Journal of Individual Differences, 38*(1), 1–11.

Rothan, H. A., & Byrareddy, S. N. (2020). The epidemiology and pathogenesis of coronavirus disease (COVID-19) outbreak. *Journal of Autoimmunity, 109*, 102433.

Rothman, A. J., & Hardin, C. D. (1997). Differential use of the availability heuristic in social judgment. *Personality and Social Psychology Bulletin, 23*(2), 123–138.

Rotter, J. B. (1954). *Social learning and clinical psychology.* Englewood Cliffs, NJ: Prentice-Hall.

Rotter, J. B. (1990). Internal versus external control of reinforcement: A case history of a variable. *American Psychologist, 45*(4), 489–493.

Rotton, J., Frey, J., Barry, T., Milligan, M., & Fitzpatrick, M. (1979). The air pollution experience and physical aggression. *Journal of Applied Social Psychology, 9*(5), 397–412.

Rowatt, W. C., & Franklin, L. M. (2004). Christian orthodoxy, religious fundamentalism, and right-wing authoritarianism as predictors of implicit racial prejudice. *The International Journal for the Psychology of Religion, 14*(2), 125–138.

Rowhani-Farid, A., Allen, M., & Barnett, A. G. (2017). What incentives increase data sharing in health and medical research? A systematic review. *Research Integrity and Peer Review, 2*, 1–10.

Rowling, J. K. (1997). *Harry Potter and the sorcerer's stone.* New York, NY: Scholastic.

Rowling, J. K. (1998). *Harry Potter and the chamber of secrets.* New York, NY: Scholastic.

Rowling, J. K. (1999). *Harry Potter and the prisoner of Azkaban.* New York, NY: Scholastic.

Rowling, J. K. (2000). *Harry Potter and the goblet of fire.* New York, NY: Scholastic.

Rowling, J. K. (2003). *Harry Potter and the order of the phoenix.* New York, NY: Scholastic.

Rowling, J. K. (2005). *Harry Potter and the half-blood prince.* New York, NY: Scholastic.

Rowling, J. K. (2007). *Harry Potter and the deathly hallows.* New York, NY: Scholastic.

Roy, M. M., & Nicholas, J. C. (2004). Do dogs resemble their owners? *Psychological Science, 15*(5), 361–363.

Royet, J. P., Plailly, J., Delon-Martin, C., Kareken, D. A., & Segebarth, C. (2003). fMRI of emotional responses to odors: Influence of hedonic valence and judgment, handedness, and gender. *Neuroimage, 20*(2), 713–728.

Rubin, Z., & Peplau, L. A. (1975). Who believes in a just world? *Journal of Social Issues, 31*(3), 65–89.

Ruddock, H. K., Brunstrom, J. M., Vartanian, L. R., & Higgs, S. (2019). A systematic review and meta-analysis of the social facilitation of eating. *The American Journal of Clinical Nutrition, 110*(4), 842–861.

Rudman, L. A. (1998). Self-promotion as a risk factor for women: The costs and benefits of counterstereotypical impression management. *Journal of Personality and Social Psychology, 74*(3), 629–645.

Rudy, K. (2007). Michael Vick, dogfighting and race. *Duke Today.* Retrieved February 1, 2020, from https://today.duke.edu/2007/08/vick_oped.html

Rui, Y., Shen, D., Khalid, S., Yang, Z., & Wang, J. (2015). GIS-based emergency response system for sudden water pollution accidents. *Physics and Chemistry of the Earth, Parts A/B/C, 79*, 115–121.

Rule, N. O., Ambady, N., Adams, R. B., Jr., Ozono, H., Nakashima, S., Yoshikawa, S., & Watabe, M. (2010). Polling the face: Prediction and consensus across cultures. *Journal of Personality and Social Psychology, 98*(1), 1–15.

Rusbult, C. E. (1980). Commitment and satisfaction in romantic associations: A test of the investment model. *Journal of Experimental Social Psychology, 16*(2), 172–186.

Rusbult, C. E., & Buunk, B. P. (1993). Commitment processes in close relationships: An interdependence analysis. *Journal of Social and Personal Relationships, 10*(2), 175–204.

Russell, B. L., & Trigg, K. Y. (2004). Tolerance of sexual harassment: An examination of gender differences, ambivalent sexism, social dominance, and gender roles. *Sex Roles, 50*(7), 565–573.

Russell, G. (2008). *Aggression in the sports world: A social psychological perspective.* New York, NY: Oxford University Press.

Russo, A. (Producer), & Landis, J. (Director). (1983). *Trading places* [Motion picture]. United States: Paramount Pictures.

Rutherford, M. D. (2018). *Panacea or placebo? A comparison of a brief mindfulness-based intervention and an active control intervention on neurogenic inflammatory response* (Doctoral dissertation). Texas A&M University Libraries.

Rutledge, C., Walsh, C. M., Swinger, N., Auerbach, M., Castro, D., Dewan, M., . . . & Maa, T. (2018). Gamification in action: theoretical and practical considerations for medical educators. *Academic Medicine, 93*(7), 1014–1020.

Sa, B., Ojeh, N., Majumder, M. A. A., Nunes, P., Williams, S., Rao, S. R., & Youssef, F. F. (2019). The relationship between self-esteem, emotional intelligence, and empathy among students from six health professional programs. *Teaching and Learning in Medicine, 31*(5), 536–543.

Saijo, T., Okano, Y., & Yamakawa, T. (2015). *The approval mechanism solves the prisoner's dilemma theoretically and experimentally.* Working Papers SDES-2015-12, Kochi University of Technology, School of Economics and Management.

Sakdapolrak, P., Naruchaikusol, S., Ober, K., Peth, S., Porst, L., Rockenbauch, T., & Tolo, V. (2016). Migration in a changing climate. Towards a translocal social resilience approach. *DIE ERDE–Journal of the Geographical Society of Berlin, 147*(2), 81–94.

Salancik, G. R., & Conway, M. (1975). Attitude inferences from salient and relevant cognitive content about behavior. *Journal of Personality and Social Psychology, 32*(5), 829–840.

Salgueiro, E., Nunes, L., Barros, A., Maroco, J., Salgueiro, A. I., & dos Santos, M. E. (2012). Effects of a dolphin interaction program on children with autism spectrum disorders - an exploratory research. *BMC Research Notes, 5*(1), article 199.

Sampson, E. E. (1988). The debate on individualism. *American Psychologist, 43*(1), 15–22.

Sanchez, R. V., Speck, P. M., & Patrician, P. A. (2019). A concept analysis of trauma coercive bonding in the commercial sexual exploitation of children. *Journal of Pediatric Nursing, 46*, 48–54.

Sande, G. N., Goethals, G. R., & Radloff, C. E. (1988). Perceiving one's own traits and others': The multifaceted self. *Journal of Personality and Social Psychology, 54*, 13–20.

Sandler, K., & Studlar, G. (1999). *Titanic: Anatomy of a blockbuster.* New Brunswick, NJ: Rutgers University Press.

Sanna, L. J. (1992). Self-efficacy theory: Implications for social facilitation and social loafing. *Journal of Personality and Social Psychology, 62*(5), 774–786.

Sapolsky, R. (2017). *Behave: The biology of humans at our best and worst.* New York, NY: Penguin.

Sarnoff, I., & Zimbardo, P. G. (1961). Anxiety, fear, and social isolation. *Journal of Abnormal and Social Psychology, 62*(2), 356–363.

Saucier, D. A., Stanford, A. J., Miller, S. S., Martens, A. L., Miller, A. K., Jones, T. L., . . . Burns, M. D. (2016). Masculine honor beliefs: Measurement and correlates. *Personality and Individual Differences, 94*, 7–15.

Saucier, D. A., Till, D. F., Miller, S. S., O'Dea, C. J., & Andres, E. (2015). Slurs against masculinity: Masculine honor beliefs and men's reactions to slurs. *Language Sciences, 52*, 108–120.

Saunders, R., & Nyamunda, T. (Eds.). (2016). *Facets of power: Politics, profits and people in the making of Zimbabwe's blood diamonds.* Harare, Zimbabwe: Weaver Press.

Scanlan, T. P. (2015). *Influences of CSI effect, Daubert ruling, and NAS report on forensic science practices* (Unpublished doctoral dissertation). Walden University, Minneapolis, MN.

Schachter, S. (1959). *The psychology of affiliation: Experimental studies of the sources of gregariousness.* Stanford, CA: Stanford University Press.

Schaller, M., & Cialdini, R. B. (1988). The economics of empathic helping: Support for a mood management motive. *Journal of Experimental Social Psychology, 24*(2), 163–181.

Schaller, M., & Cialdini, R. B. (1990). Happiness, sadness, and helping: A motivational integration. In E. T. Higgins & R. M. Sorrentino (Eds.), *Handbook of motivation and cognition: Foundations of social behavior* (Vol. 2, pp. 265–296). New York, NY: Guilford.

Scheff, T. J. (2007). Catharsis and other heresies: A theory of emotion. *Journal of Social, Evolutionary, and Cultural Psychology, 1*(3), 98–113.

Schell, J. (2008). *The art of game design: A book of lenses.* Burlington, MA: Elsevier.

Schilling, M. A. (2018). *Quirky.* New York, NY: PublicAffairs.

Schippers, M. C. (2014). Social loafing tendencies and team performance: The compensating effect of agreeableness and conscientiousness. *Academy of Management Learning & Education, 13*(1), 62–81.

Schmale, A., & Iker, H. (1966). The psychological setting of uterine cervical cancer. *Annals of the New York Academy of Sciences, 125*(1), 807–813.

Schmid, A. (2005). Terrorism as psychological warfare. *Democracy and Security, 1*(2), 137–146.

Schnall, S., & Laird, J. D. (2003). Keep smiling: Enduring effects of facial expressions and postures on emotional experience and memory. *Cognition and Emotion, 17*(5), 787–797.

Schneider, B. A., & Pichora-Fuller, M. K. (2001). Age-related changes in temporal processing: Implications for speech perception. *Seminars in Hearing, 22*(3), 227–240.

Schneider, D. (1973). Implicit personality theory: A review. *Psychological Bulletin, 79*(5), 294–309.

Schneider, T. R., Salovey, P., Apanovitch, A. M., Pizarro, J., McCarthy, D., Zullo, J., & Rothman, A. J. (2001). The effects of message framing and ethnic targeting on mammography use among low-income women. *Health Psychology, 20*(4), 256–266.

Schneider, W., & Shiffrin, R. M. (1977). Controlled and automatic human information processing: I. Detection, search, and attention. *Psychological Review, 84*(1), 1–66.

Schreier, D. R., Banks, C., & Mathis, J. (2018). Driving simulators in the clinical assessment of fitness to drive in sleepy individuals: A systematic review. *Sleep Medicine Reviews, 38*, 86–100.

Schumer, M. C., Lindsay, E. K., & Creswell, J. D. (2018). Brief mindfulness training for negative affectivity: A systematic review and meta-analysis. *Journal of Consulting and Clinical Psychology, 86*(7), 569–583.

Schwartz, B., Ward, A., Monterosso, J., Lyubormirsky, S., White, K., & Lehman, D. R. (2002). Maximizing versus satisficing: Happiness is a matter of choice. *Journal of Personality and Social Psychology, 83*(5), 1178–1197.

Schwartz, H. H. (2008). *A guide to behavioral economics.* Reston, VA: Higher Education Publications.

Schwarz, N. (1998). Accessible content and accessibility experiences: The interplay of declarative and experiential information in judgment. *Personality and Social Psychology Review, 2*(2), 87–99.

Schwarz, S., & Hassebrauck, M. (2012). Sex and age differences in mate-selection preferences. *Human Nature, 23*(4), 447–466.

Schweingruber, D., Cast, A. D., & Anahita, S. (2008). "A story and a ring": Audience judgments about engagement proposals. *Sex Roles, 58*(3–4), 165–178.

Seager, M. (2019). From stereotypes to archetypes: An evolutionary perspective on male help-seeking and suicide. In J. A. Barry, R. Kingerlee, M. Seager, & L. Sullivan (Eds.), *The Palgrave handbook of male psychology and mental health* (pp. 227–248). London, UK: Palgrave Macmillan.

Sears, D. O., & Henry, P. J. (2005). Over thirty years later: A contemporary look at symbolic racism. In M. P. Zanna (Ed.), *Advances in experimental social psychology* (Vol. 37, pp. 95–150). San Diego, CA: Academic Press.

Sedikides, C., & Skowronski, J. J. (1997). The symbolic self in evolutionary context. *Personality and Social Psychology Review, 1*(1), 80–102.

Selengut, C. (2017). *Sacred fury: Understanding religious violence.* New York, NY: Rowman & Littlefield.

Seligman, M. E. P. (1975). *Helplessness.* San Francisco, CA: Freeman.

Seligman, M. E. P. (1998). Treatment becomes prevention & treatment. *Prevention & Treatment, 1*(2), 1e.

Seligman, M. E. P. (2002). Positive psychology, positive prevention, and positive therapy. In C. R. Snyder & S. J. Lopez (Eds.), *Handbook of positive psychology* (pp. 3–9). New York, NY: Oxford University Press.

Seligman, M. E. P., & Csikszentmihalyi, M. (2000). Positive psychology: An introduction. *American Psychologist, 55*(1), 5–14.

Selye, H. (1973). The evolution of the stress concept: The originator of the concept traces its development from the discovery in 1936 of the alarm reaction to modern therapeutic applications of syntoxic and catatoxic hormones. *American Scientist, 61*(6), 692–699.

Sergent, J., Aspergren, E., Lawrence, E., & Sanchez, O. (2019, July 17). Chilling first-hand reports of migrant detention centers highlight smell of "urine," "feces," overcrowded conditions. *USA Today.* Retrieved August 1, 2019, from https://www.usatoday.com

Serpell, J. (1989). Pet-keeping and animal domestication: A reappraisal. In J. Clutton-Brock (Ed.), *The walking larder: Patterns of domestication, pastoralism, and predation* (pp. 10–21). London, UK: Unwin Hyman.

Serpell, J. A., & Paul, E. S. (2011). Pets in the family: An evolutionary perspective. In C. Salmon & T. K. Shackelford (Eds.), *The Oxford handbook of evolutionary family psychology* (pp. 297–309). New York, NY: Oxford University Press.

Shaheen, J. G. (2003). Reel bad Arabs: How Hollywood vilifies a people. *The Annals of the American Academy of Political and Social Science, 588*(1), 171–193.

Shapiro, S. L., Schwartz, G. E., & Bonner, G. (1998). Effects of mindfulness-based stress reduction on medical and premedical students. *Journal of Behavioral Medicine, 21*(6), 581–599.

Sharabi, L. L., & Caughlin, J. P. (2019). Deception in online dating: Significance and implications for the first offline date. *New Media & Society, 21*(1), 229–247.

Shariff, M., Rahim, A., Javed, S., Salimin, N., & Abdul Majid, N. (2017). Aggression in the sporting: Catharsis and social support. *Science International, 29*(1), 259–263.

Sharma, S., & Agarwala, S. (2014). Self-esteem and collective self-esteem as predictors of depression. *Journal of Behavioural Sciences, 24*(1), 21–28.

Sharp, F. C. (1928). *Ethics.* New York, NY: Century Company.

Sharp, L. A., & Whaley, B. (2018). Wikis as online collaborative learning experiences: "A different kind of brainstorming." *Adult Learning, 29*(3), 83–93.

Shedler, J., & Manis, M. (1986). Can the availability heuristic explain vividness effects? *Journal of Personality and Social Psychology, 51*(1), 26–36.

Sheldon, K. M., King, L. A., Houser-Marko, L., Osbaldiston, R., & Gunz, A. (2007). Comparing IAT and TAT measures of power versus intimacy motivation. *European Journal of Personality, 21*(3), 263–280.

Sheppard, L. D., & Johnson, S. K. (2019). The femme fatale effect: Attractiveness is a liability for businesswomen's perceived truthfulness, trust, and deservingness of termination. *Sex Roles: A Journal of Research, 81*(11–12), 779–796.

Shepperd, J. A., & Koch, E. J. (2005). Pitfalls in teaching judgment heuristics. *Teaching of Psychology, 32*(1), 43–46.

Sherif, C. W., Sherif, M., & Nebergall, R. E. (1965). *Attitude and attitude change: The social judgment-involvement approach.* Philadelphia, PA: Saunders.

Sherif, M. (1935). A study of some social factors in perception. *Archives of Psychology, 187,* 60.

Sherif, M. (1936). *The psychology of social norms.* Oxford, UK: Harper.

Sherif, M. (1956). Experiments in group conflict. *Scientific American, 195,* 54–58.

Sherif, M. (1966a). *Group conflict and cooperation: Their social psychology.* London, UK: Routledge & Kegan Paul.

Sherif, M. (1966b). *In common predicament: Social psychology of intergroup conflict and cooperation.* Boston, MA: Houghton Mifflin.

Sherif, M., Harvey, O. J., White, B. J., Hood, W. R., & Sherif, C. W. (1961). *The Robbers Cave experiment: Intergroup conflict and cooperation.* Norman: University of Oklahoma Book Exchange.

Sherif, M., & Sherif, C. W. (1969). Ingroup and intergroup relations: Experimental analysis. In M. Sherif & C. W. Sherif (Eds.), *Social psychology* (pp. 221–266). New York, NY: Harper & Row.

Shereen, M. A., Khan, S., Kazmi, A., Bashir, N., & Siddique, R. (2020). COVID-19 infection: Origin, transmission, and characteristics of human coronaviruses. *Journal of Advanced Research, 24,* 91–98.

Sherman, D. K., & Cohen, G. L. (2002). Accepting threatening information: Self-affirmation and the reduction of defensive biases. *Current Directions in Psychological Science, 11*(4), 118–123.

Sherman, J. W., Gawronski, B., & Trope, Y. (2014). *Dual-process theories of the social mind.* New York, NY: Guilford.

Sherman, S. J., Chassin, L., Presson, C. C., & Agostinelli, G. (1984). The role of the evaluation and similarity principles in the false consensus effect. *Journal of Personality and Social Psychology, 47*(6), 1244–1262.

Sherman-Palladino, A. (Director). (2017–). *Marvelous Mrs. Maisel* [Television series]. Culver City, CA: Amazon Studios.

Shipman, H. (2019). Smart art for smart cities. In M. Mateev & P. Poutziouris (Eds.), *Creative business and social innovations for a sustainable future* (pp. 251–253). New York, NY: Springer.

Shires, A., Sharpe, L., & Newton John, T. R. (2019). The relative efficacy of mindfulness versus distraction: The moderating role of attentional bias. *European Journal of Pain, 23*(4), 727–738.

Shute, V., & Ventura, M. (2013). *Stealth assessment: Measuring and supporting learning in video games.* Cambridge, MA: MIT Press.

Silva, Y. N., Hall, D. L., & Rich, C. (2018). BullyBlocker: Toward an interdisciplinary approach to identify cyberbullying. *Social Network Analysis and Mining, 8*(1), 18.

Silveira, J. M., & Hudson, M. W. (2015). Hazing in the college marching band. *Journal of Research in Music Education, 63*(1), 5–27.

Silverstein, M., Gans, D., & Yang, F. M. (2006). Intergenerational support to aging parents: The role of norms and needs. *Journal of Family Issues, 27*(8), 1068–1084.

Silvia, P. J., & Gendolla, G. E. (2001). On introspection and self-perception: Does self-focused attention enable accurate self-knowledge? *Review of General Psychology, 5*(3), 241–269.

Simmons, C. H., & Lerner, M. J. (1968). Altruism as a search for justice. *Journal of Personality and Social Psychology, 9*(3), 216–225.

Simon, H. A. (1955). A behavioral model of rational choice. *Quarterly Journal of Economics, 69*(1), 99–118.

Simon, H. A. (1956). Rational choice and the structure of the environment. *Psychological Review, 63*(2), 129–138.

Simon, J. R. (1990). The effects of an irrelevant directional cue on human information processing. In R. W. Proctor & T. G. Reeve (Eds.), *Stimulus-response compatibility: An integrated perspective* (pp. 31–86). Oxford, UK: North-Holland.

Simon, M., & Devlin, D. (Producers), & Bill, T. (Director). (1980). *My bodyguard* [Motion picture]. USA: Melvin Simon Productions & 20th Century Fox.

Simoons, F. J., & Baldwin, J. A. (1982). Breast-feeding of animals by women: Its socio-cultural context and geographic occurrence. *Anthropos*, 421–448.

Simpson, E. G., Lincoln, C. R., & Ohannessian, C. M. (2020). Does Adolescent Anxiety Moderate the Relationship between Adolescent–Parent Communication and Adolescent Coping?. *Journal of Child and Family Studies, 29*(1), 237–249.

Simpson, J. A., Gangestad, S. W., & Lerma, M. (1990). Perception of physical attractiveness: Mechanisms involved in the maintenance of romantic relationships. *Journal of Personality and Social Psychology, 59*(6), 1192–1201.

Sinclair, C., & Goodfriend, W. (2013). Mindfulness in adolescents: Effects of single-session mindfulness meditation on anxiety and depression. *Journal of Psychological Inquiry, 18*, 37–45.

Singh, D. (1993a). Adaptive significance of female physical attractiveness: Role of waist-to-hip ratio. *Journal of Personality and Social Psychology, 65*(2), 293–307.

Singh, D. (1993b). Body shape and women's attractiveness: The critical role of waist-to-hip ratio. *Human Nature, 4*(3), 297–321.

Singh, D., & Randall, P. K. (2007). Beauty is in the eye of the plastic surgeon: Waist-hip ratio (WHR) and women's attractiveness. *Personality and Individual Differences, 43*(2), 329–340.

Singh, S., & Majumdar, R. (2018). Innocence Project-righting a wrong. *Nirma ULJ, 7*, 11–28.

Siy, J. O., & Cheryan, S. (2016). Prejudice masquerading as praise: The negative echo of positive stereotypes. *Personality and Social Psychology Bulletin, 42*(7), 941–954.

Skodol, A. E. (2010). The resilient personality. In J. W. Reich, A. J. Zautra, & J. S. Hall (Eds.), *Handbook of adult resilience* (pp. 112–125). New York, NY: Guilford.

Slavich, G. M. (2009). On 50 years of giving psychology away: An interview with Philip Zimbardo. *Teaching of Psychology, 36*(4), 278–284.

Sloman, L. (2000). The syndrome of rejection sensitivity: An evolutionary perspective. In P. Gilbert & K. Bailey (Eds.), *Genes on the couch: Explorations in evolutionary psychotherapy* (pp. 257–275). Hove, East Sussex, UK: Brunner-Routledge.

Slusher, M. P., & Anderson, C. A. (1989). Belief perseverance and self-defeating behavior. In R. C. Curtis (Ed.), *Self-defeating behaviors: Experimental research, clinical impressions, and practical implications* (pp. 11–40). New York, NY: Plenum.

Smith, A. (1759). *The theory of moral sentiments*. London, UK: Printed for Andrew Millar, Alexander Kincaid and J. Bell.

Smith, A. (1776). The Wealth of Nations (New York: Modern Library, 1937). *Originally published, 3*.

Smith, C. T., & Nosek, B. A. (2011). Affective focus increases the concordance between implicit and explicit attitudes. *Social Psychology, 42*(4), 300–313.

Smith, D., Lovell, J., Weller, C., Kennedy, B., Winbolt, M., Young, C., . . . Chen, K. (2017). A systematic review of medication non-adherence in persons with dementia or cognitive impairment. *PLoS ONE, 12*(2), e0170651.

Smith, D. N. (2019). Authoritarianism reimagined: The riddle of Trump's base. *The Sociological Quarterly, 60*(2), 210–223.

Smith, P. B., & Bond, M. H. (1993). *Social psychology across cultures: Analysis and perspectives*. Hertfordshire, UK: Harvester Wheatsheaf.

Smith-Forbes, E. V., Quick, C. D., & Brown, K. M. (2016, April–September). Roles of occupational therapists in theater, past and present. *US Army Medical Department Journal*, pp. 66–70.

Smrt, D. L., & Karau, S. J. (2011). Protestant work ethic moderates social loafing. *Group Dynamics: Theory, Research, and Practice, 15*(3), 267–274.

Smyth, J. M. (1998). Written emotional expression: Effect sizes, outcome types, and moderating variables. *Journal of Consulting and Clinical Psychology, 66*(1), 174–184.

Snook, B., Gendreau, P., Bennell, C., & Taylor, P. J. (2008). Criminal profiling: Granfalloons and gobbledygook. *Skeptic (Altadena, CA), 14*(2), 42–48.

Snook, D. W., Williams, M. J., & Horgan, J. G. (2019). Issues in the sociology and psychology of religious conversion. *Pastoral Psychology, 68*(2), 223–240.

Snyder, M. (1974). Self-monitoring of expressive behavior. *Journal of Personality and Social Psychology, 30*, 526– 537.

Snyder, M., & Miene, P. K. (1994). Stereotyping of the elderly: A functional approach. *British Journal of Social Psychology, 33*(1), 63–82.

Sokol-Hessner, P., & Rutledge, R. B. (2019). The psychological and neural basis of loss aversion. *Current Directions in Psychological Science, 28*(1), 20–27.

Sollohub, D. (2019). *Millennials in architecture: Generations, disruption, and the legacy of a profession*. Austin: University of Texas Press.

Solomon, J. D., Genovese, W., Jacobson, M., & Valva, M. (Producers), & Solomon, J. D. (Director). (2016). *The witness* [Motion picture]. United States: FilmRise.

Somech, L. Y., & Sagy, S. (2019). Perceptions of collective narratives and identity strategies as indicators of intergroup relations. *International Journal of Conflict Management*. Advance online publication.

Sommer, J. (2015, March 14). How many mutual funds routinely rout the market? Zero. *New York Times*. http://www.vistawealth.com/assets/files/HowManyMutualFunds.pdf

Son Hing, L. S., Bobocel, D. R., Zanna, M. P., & McBride, M. V. (2007). Authoritarian dynamics and unethical decision making: High social dominance orientation leaders and high right-wing authoritarianism followers. *Journal of Personality and Social Psychology, 92*(1), 67–81.

Soussignan, R. (2002). Duchenne smile, emotional experience, and autonomic reactivity: A test of the facial feedback hypothesis. *Emotion, 2*(1), 52–74.

Souza, M. G. T. C., Roazzi, A., & Souza, B. C. (2011). When killing is a legitimate course of action: A multidimensional investigation into the culture of honor as an explanation for homicides in northeastern Brazil. In Y. Fisher & I. A. Friedman (Eds.), *New horizons for facet theory: Searching for structure in content spaces and measurement* (pp. 85–98). Washington, DC: FTA Publications.

Sparks, E. A., Ehrlinger, J., & Eibach, R. P. (2012). Failing to commit: Maximizers avoid commitment in a way that contributes to reduced satisfaction. *Personality and Individual Differences, 52*(1), 72–77.

Spector, P. E. (1988). Development of the work locus of control scale. *Journal of Occupational Psychology, 61*(4), 335–340.

Spence, J. T., & Buckner, C. E. (2000). Instrumental and expressive traits, trait stereotypes, and sexist attitudes. *Psychology of Women Quarterly, 24*(1), 44–62.

Spencer, S. J., Steele, C. M., & Quinn, D. M. (1999). Stereotype threat and women's math performance. *Journal of Experimental Social Psychology*, 35(1), 4–28.

Spilka, B., Hood, R. W., Hunsberger, B., & Gorsuch, R. (2003). *The psychology of religion: An empirical approach*. New York, NY: Guilford.

Spohn, C. (2014). Twentieth-century sentencing reform movement: Looking backward, moving forward. *Criminology & Public Policy*, 13(4), 535–545.

Stanglin, D., & Gross, E. (1997, March 31). Oprah: A heavenly body. *US News and World Report*, p. 18.

Stanovich, K. E., & West, R. F. (2000). Individual differences in reasoning: Implications for the rationality debate? *Behavioral and Brain Sciences*, 23(5), 645–665.

Stanovich, K. E., & West, R. F. (2002). Individual differences in reasoning: Implications for the rationality debate? In T. Gilovich, D. Griffin, & D. Kahneman (Eds.), *Heuristics and biases: The psychology of intuitive judgment* (pp. 421–440). New York, NY: Cambridge University Press.

Starbuck, W. H. (1963). Level of aspiration. *Psychological Review*, 70(1), 51–60.

Starks, T., Castro, M., Castiblanco, J., & Millar, B. (2016). Modeling interpersonal correlates of condomless anal sex among gay and bisexual men: An application of attachment theory. *Archives of Sexual Behavior: The Official Publication of the International Academy of Sex Research*, 46(4), 1089–1099.

Starr, C. R., Anderson, B. R., & Green, K. A. (2019). "I'm a computer scientist!": Virtual reality experience influences stereotype threat and STEM motivation among undergraduate women. *Journal of Science Education and Technology*, 28(5), 493–507.

Stavropoulos, K. K., & Alba, L. A. (2018). "It's so cute I could crush it!": Understanding neural mechanisms of cute aggression. *Frontiers in Behavioral Neuroscience, 12*, article 300.

Steblay, N. M. (1987). Helping behavior in rural and urban environments: A meta-analysis. *Psychological Bulletin*, 102(3), 346–356.

Steele, C. M. (1988). The psychology of self-affirmation: Sustaining the integrity of the self. In L. Berkowitz (Ed.), *Advances in experimental social psychology* (Vol. 21, pp. 261–302). New York, NY: Academic Press.

Steele, C. M. (1997). A threat in the air: How stereotypes shape intellectual identity and performance. *American Psychologist*, 52(6), 613–629.

Steele, C. M., & Aronson, J. (1995). Stereotype threat and the intellectual performance of African Americans. *Journal of Personality and Social Psychology*, 69(5), 797–811.

Steg, L., Keizer, K., Buunk, A. P., & Rothengatter, T. (Eds.). (2017). *Applied social psychology*. Cambridge, UK: Cambridge University Press.

Steiner, I. D. (1972). *Group process and productivity*. New York, NY: Academic Press.

Steinfeldt, J. A., Foltz, B. D., Kaladow, J. K., Carlson, T. N., Pagano, L. A., Benton, E., & Steinfeldt, M. C. (2010). Racism in the electronic age: Role of online forums in expressing racial attitudes about American Indians. *Cultural Diversity and Ethnic Minority Psychology*, 16(3), 362–371.

Stenico, C., & Greitemeyer, T. (2015). 'The others will help: The presence of multiple video game characters reduces helping after the game is over': Corrigendum. *Journal of Social Psychology*, 155(1), 91.

Sternberg, R. J. (1986). A triangular theory of love. *Psychological Review*, 93(2), 119–135.

Stevens, C. K., & Kristof, A. L. (1995). Making the right impression: A field study of applicant impression management during job interviews. *Journal of Applied Psychology*, 80(5), 587–606.

Stoett, P. J. (2019). *Global ecopolitics: Crisis, governance, and justice*. Toronto, Canada: University of Toronto Press.

Stolier, R. M., & Freeman, J. B. (2016). Neural pattern similarity reveals the inherent intersection of social categories. *Nature Neuroscience*, 19(6), 795–797.

Stone, J., & Cooper, J. (2001). A self-standards model of cognitive dissonance. *Journal of Experimental Social Psychology*, 37(3), 228–243.

Stoner, J. A. F. (1961). *A comparison between individual and group decisions involving risk* (Unpublished master's thesis). Massachusetts Institute of Technology, Cambridge.

Stoner, J. A. F. (1968). Risky and cautious shifts in group decisions: The influence of widely held values. *Journal of Experimental Social Psychology*, 4(4), 442–459.

Storm, S. (2017). How the invisible hand is supposed to adjust the natural thermostat: A guide for the perplexed. *Science and Engineering Ethics*, 23(5), 1307–1331.

Stout, H. A. F. (2011). *Portrayals of relational aggression in popular teen movies: 1980–2009* (Unpublished master's thesis). Brigham Young University, Provo, UT.

Stowell, J. R., & Addison, W. E. (2017). *Activities for teaching statistics and research methods: A guide for psychology instructors* (pp. xi–133). Washington, DC: American Psychological Association.

Strack, F., Martin, L. L., & Stepper, S. (1988). Inhibiting and facilitating conditions of the human smile: A non-obtrusive test of the facial feedback hypothesis. *Journal of Personality and Social Psychology*, 54(5), 768–777.

Strack, F., & Mussweiler, T. (1997). Explaining the enigmatic anchoring effect: Mechanisms of selective accessibility. *Journal of Personality and Social Psychology*, 73(3), 437–446.

Straus, M. A. (1979). Measuring intrafamily conflict and violence: The conflict tactics (CT) scales. *Journal of Marriage and the Family*, 41(1), 75–88.

Straus, S. G., Parker, A. M., & Bruce, J. B. (2011). The group matters: A review of processes and outcomes in intelligence analysis. *Group Dynamics: Theory, Research, and Practice*, 15(2), 128–146.

Street, A. E., & Arias, I. (2001). Psychological abuse and posttraumatic stress disorder in battered women: Examining the roles of shame and guilt. *Violence and Victims*, 16(1), 65–78.

Strick, M., van Baaren, R. B., Holland, R. W., & van Knippenberg, A. (2009). Humor in advertisements enhances product liking by mere association. *Journal of Experimental Psychology: Applied*, 15(1), 35–45.

Strojny, P., Strojny, A., Kałwak, W., & Bańbura, A. (2018). Take your eyes off me: The effect of the presence of witnesses on the conduct of rescue operations. *Bezpieczeństwo i Technika Pożarnicza, 49*, 14–22.

Strömwall, L., Alfredsson, H., & Landström, S. (2013). Blame attributions and rape: Effects of belief in a just world and relationship level. *Legal and Criminological Psychology*, 18(2), 254–261.

Stroud, N. J. (2010). Polarization and partisan selective exposure. *Journal of Communication*, 60(3), 556–576.

Strube, M. J. (2005). What did Triplett really find? A contemporary analysis of the first experiment in social psychology. *The American Journal of Psychology*, 118(2), 271–286.

Subra, B., Muller, D., Bègue, L., Bushman, B. J., & Delmas, F. (2010). Automatic effects of alcohol and aggressive cues on aggressive thoughts and behaviors. *Personality and Social Psychology Bulletin*, 36(8), 1052–1057.

Suddendorf, T., & Butler, D. L. (2013). The nature of visual self-recognition. *Trends in Cognitive Sciences*, 17(3), 121–127.

Sue, D. W. (2003). *Overcoming our racism: The journey to liberation*. San Francisco, CA: Jossey-Bass.

Sue, D. W. (2010). *Microaggressions in everyday life: Race, gender, and sexual orientation*. Hoboken, NJ: John Wiley.

Sue, D. W. (2017). Microaggressions and "evidence": Empirical or experiential reality? *Perspectives on Psychological Science, 12,* 170–172.

Sue, D. W., Capodilupo, C. M., Torino, G. C., Bucceri, J. M., Holder, A. M. B., Nadal, K. L., & Esquilin, M. (2007). Racial microaggressions in everyday life: Implications for clinical practice. *American Psychologist, 62*(4), 271–286.

Sugam, J. A., Day, J. J., Wightman, R. M., & Carelli, R. M. (2012). Phasic nucleus accumbens dopamine encodes risk-based decision-making behavior. *Biological Psychiatry, 71*(3), 199–205.

Suls, J., & Green, P. (2003). Pluralistic ignorance and college student perceptions of gender-specific alcohol norms. *Health Psychology, 22*(5), 479–486.

Suls, J., & Wan, C. K. (1987). In search of the false-uniqueness phenomenon: Fear and estimates of social consensus. *Journal of Personality and Social Psychology, 52*(1), 211–217.

Suls, J., & Wheeler, L. (2000). *Handbook of social comparison: Theory and research.* Dordrecht, Netherlands: Kluwer Academic.

Sundaram, C. S. (2013). Stockholm syndrome. In *Salem press encyclopedia.* Hackensack, NY: Salem Press.

Sundie, J. M., Kenrick, D. T., Griskevicius, V., Tybur, J. M., Vohs, K. D., & Beal, D. J. (2011). Peacocks, Porsches, and Thorstein Veblen: Conspicuous consumption as a sexual signaling system. *Journal of Personality and Social Psychology, 100*(4), 664–680.

Sunstein, C. R. (2019). *Conformity: The power of social influences.* New York: NYU Press.

Sunyer, J., Spix, C., Quenel, P., Ponce-de-Leon, A., Pönka, A., Barumandzadeh, T., . . . Bisanti, L. (1997). Urban air pollution and emergency admissions for asthma in four European cities: The APHEA Project. *Thorax, 52*(9), 760–765.

Sutphin, S. T. (2010). Social exchange theory and the division of household labor in same-sex couples. *Marriage & Family Review, 46*(3), 191–206.

Sutton, W. (1976). *Where the money was.* New York, NY: Viking Press.

Swaminathan, A., Viennet, E., McMichael, A. J., & Harley, D. (2017). Climate change and the geographical distribution of infectious diseases. In E. Petersen, L. H. Chen, & P. Schlagenhauf-Lawlor (Eds.), *Infectious diseases: A geographic guide* (p. 470). Chichester, UK: John Wiley.

Swann, W. J., & Buhrmester, M. D. (2012). Self as functional fiction. *Social Cognition, 30*(4), 415–430.

Swann, W. J., Chang-Schneider, C., & Larsen McClarty, K. (2007). Do people's self-views matter? Self-concept and self-esteem in everyday life. *American Psychologist, 62*(2), 84–94.

Swinkels, A. (2003). An effective exercise for teaching cognitive heuristics. *Teaching of Psychology, 30*(2), 120–122.

Taber, B. J., & Blankemeyer, M. (2015). Future work self and career adaptability in the prediction of proactive career behaviors. *Journal of Vocational Behavior, 86,* 20–27.

Tagler, M. J. (2010). Sex differences in jealousy: Comparing the influence of previous infidelity among college students and adults. *Social Psychological and Personality Science, 1*(4), 353–360.

Tajfel, H. M. (1970). Experiments in intergroup discrimination. *Scientific American, 223*(5), 96–102.

Tajfel, H. M. (1981). *Human groups and social categories: Studies in social psychology.* Cambridge, UK: Cambridge University Press.

Tajfel, H. M. (1982). Social psychology of intergroup relations. *Annual Review of Psychology, 33*(1), 1–39.

Tajfel, H. M., Billig, M. G., Bundy, R. P., & Flament, C. (1971). Social categorization and intergroup behaviour, *European Journal of Social Psychology, 1*(2), 149–178.

Tajfel, H. M., & Turner, J. C. (1979). An integrative theory of intergroup conflict. *The Social Psychology of Intergroup Relations, 33*(47), 33–47.

Tajfel, H. M., & Turner, J. C. (1986). The social identity theory of intergroup behavior. In S. Worchel & W. G. Austin (Eds.), *Psychology of intergroup relations* (pp. 7–24). Chicago, IL: Nelson-Hall.

Tal-Or, N., & Papirman, Y. (2007). The fundamental attribution error in attributing fictional figures' characteristics to the actors. *Media Psychology, 9*(2), 331–345.

Tandy, R. E., & Laflin, J. (1973). Aggression and sport: Two theories. *Journal of Health, Physical Education, Recreation, 44*(6), 19–20.

Tapley, B., Michaels, C. J., Gumbs, R., Böhm, M., Luedtke, J., Pearce-Kelly, P., & Rowley, J. J. (2018). The disparity between species description and conservation assessment: A case study in taxa with high rates of species discovery. *Biological Conservation, 220,* 209–214.

Tatum, B. D. (2017). *Why are all the Black kids sitting together in the cafeteria? And other conversations about race.* New York, NY: Basic Books.

Taubman-Ben-Ari, O., & Findler, L. (2006). Motivation for military service: A terror management perspective. *Military Psychology, 18*(2), 149–159.

Tavris, C., & Aronson, E. (2007). *Mistakes were made (but not by me): Why we justify foolish beliefs, bad decisions, and hurtful acts.* New York, NY: Harcourt.

Taylor, J. Y. (2004). Moving from surviving to thriving: African American women recovering from intimate male partner abuse. *Research and Theory for Nursing Practice, 18*(1), 35–50.

Taylor, S. E. (1981). The interface of cognitive and social psychology. In J. Harvey (Ed.), *Cognition, social behavior, and the environment* (pp. 189–211). Hillsdale, NJ: Lawrence Erlbaum.

Taylor, S. E. (1998). The social being in social psychology. In D. T. Gilbert, S. T. Fiske, & G. Lindzey (Eds.), *The handbook of social psychology* (Vol. 1, 4th ed., pp. 58–95). New York, NY: McGraw Hill.

Taylor, S. E. (2002). *The tending instinct: How nurturing is essential to who we are and how we live.* New York, NY: Henry Holt.

Taylor, S. E., & Brown, J. D. (1988). Illusion and well-being: A social psychological perspective on mental health. *Psychological Bulletin, 103,* 193–210.

Taylor, S. E., & Fiske, S. T. (1978). Salience, attention, and attribution: Top of the head phenomena. In L. Berkowitz (Ed.), *Advances in experimental and social psychology* (Vol. 11, pp. 249–288). New York, NY: Academic Press.

Taylor, S. E., & Gonzaga, G. C. (2006). Evolution, relationships, and health: The social shaping hypothesis. In M. Schaller, J. A. Simpson, & D. T. Kenrick (Eds.), *Evolution and social psychology* (pp. 211–236). New York, NY: Psychology Press.

Taylor, S. E., Kemeny, M. E., Reed, G. M., Bower, J. E., & Gruenewald, T. L. (2000). Psychological resources, positive illusions, and health. *American Psychologist, 55*(1), 99–109.

Taylor, S. E., & Thompson, S. C. (1982). Stalking the elusive "vividness" effect. *Psychological Review, 89*(2), 155–181.

Tedeschi, R. G., & Calhoun, L. G. (1996). The posttraumatic growth inventory: Measuring the positive legacy of trauma. *Journal of Traumatic Stress, 9*(3), 455–471.

Tedeschi, R. G., & Calhoun, L. G. (2004). Posttraumatic growth: Conceptual foundations and empirical evidence. *Psychological Inquiry, 15*(1), 1–18.

Teigen, K. H. (1994). Yerkes-Dodson: A law for all seasons. *Theory & Psychology, 4*(4), 525–547.

Teigen, K. H., & Jensen, T. K. (2011). Unlucky victims or lucky survivors? Spontaneous counterfactual thinking by families exposed to the Tsunami disaster. *European Psychologist, 16*(1), 48–57.

Tello, M. (2017). Racism and discrimination in health care: Providers and patients. *Harvard Health Publishing.* Retrieved December 23, 2019, from https://www.health.harvard.edu/blog/racism-discrimination-health-care-providers-patients-2017011611015 ten Brinke, L., & Porter, S. (2012). Cry me a river: Identifying the behavioral consequences of extremely high-stakes interpersonal deception. *Law and Human Behavior, 36*(6), 469–477.

Teng, C. (2018). Managing gamer relationships to enhance online gamer loyalty: The perspectives of social capital theory and self-perception theory. *Computers in Human Behavior, 79,* 59–67.

Tennen, H., & Herzberger, S. (1987). Depression, self-esteem, and the absence of self-protective attributional biases. *Journal of Personality and Social Psychology, 52*(1), 72–80.

Tesi, A., Aiello, A., Morselli, D., Giannetti, E., Pierro, A., & Pratto, F. (2019). Which people are willing to maintain their subordinated position? Social dominance orientation as antecedent to compliance to harsh power tactics in a higher education setting. *Personality and Individual Differences, 151,* e109390.

Tetlock, P. E. (1992). The impact of accountability on judgment and choice: Toward a social contingency model. In M. P. Zanna (Ed.), *Advances in experimental social psychology* (Vol. 25, pp. 331–376). San Diego, CA: Academic Press.

Thaler, R. H. (1999). Mental accounting matters. *Journal of Behavioral Decision Making, 12*(3), 183–206.

Thaler, R. H., & Sunstein, C. R. (2008). *Nudge: Improving decisions about health, wealth, and happiness.* London, UK: Penguin.

Theoharis, J. (2015). *The rebellious life of Mrs. Rosa Parks.* Boston, MA: Beacon Press.

Thibaut, J. W., & Kelley, H. H. (1959). *The social psychology of groups.* Oxford, UK: John Wiley.

Thomas, B. J., & Meglich, P. (2019). Justifying new employees' trials by fire: Workplace hazing. *Personnel Review, 48*(2), 381–399.

Thomas, K. (1983). *Man and the natural world: A history of modern sensibility.* New York, NY: Pantheon.

Thompson, M. M., Zanna, M. P., & Griffin, D. W. (1995). Let's not be indifferent about (attitudinal) ambivalence. In R. Petty & J. Krosnick (Eds.), *Attitude strength: Antecedents and consequences* (pp. 361–386). Hillsdale, NJ: Lawrence Erlbaum.

Thornberg, R., & Knutsen, S. (2011). Teenagers' explanations of bullying. *Child & Youth Care Forum, 40*(3), 177–192.

Thornhill, R., & Gangestad, S. W. (1994). Human fluctuating asymmetry and sexual behavior. *Psychological Science, 5*(5), 297–302.

Tice, D. M., & Baumeister, R. F. (2018). Longitudinal study of procrastination, performance, stress, and health: The costs and benefits of dawdling. In R. Baumeister (Ed.), *Self-regulation and self-control* (pp. 299–309). New York, NY: Routledge.

Toi, M., & Batson, C. D. (1982). More evidence that empathy is a source of altruistic motivation. *Journal of Personality and Social Psychology, 43*(2), 281–292.

Toma C. L., Bonus, J. A., & Van Swol, L. M. (2019). Lying online: Examining the production, detection, and popular beliefs surrounding interpersonal deception in technologically-mediated environments. In T. Docan-Morgan (Ed.), *The Palgrave handbook of deceptive communication* (pp. 583–601). London, UK: Palgrave Macmillan.

Tottenham, N., Phuong, J., Flannery, J., Gabard-Durnam, L., & Goff, B. (2013). A negativity bias for ambiguous facial-expression valence during childhood: Converging evidence from behavior and facial corrugator muscle responses. *Emotion, 13*(1), 92–103.

Townley, G., Brusilovskiy, E., Snethen, G., & Salzer, M. S. (2018). Using geospatial research methods to examine resource accessibility and availability as it relates to community participation of individuals with serious mental illnesses. *American Journal of Community Psychology, 61*(1–2), 47–61.

Townley, G., Pearson, L., Lehrwyn, J. M., Prophet, N. T., & Trauernicht, M. (2016). Utilizing participatory mapping and GIS to examine the activity spaces of homeless youth. *American Journal of Community Psychology, 57*(3–4), 404–414.

Travis, C. B., Phillippi, R. H., & Tonn, B. E. (1989). Judgment heuristics and medical decisions. *Patient Education and Counseling, 13*(3), 211–220.

Triandis, H. C. (1989). The self and social behavior in differing cultural contexts. *Psychological Review, 96*(3), 506–520.

Triandis, H. C., Hui, C. H., Albert, R. D., Leung, S. M., Lisansky, J., Diaz-Loving, R., . . . Loyola-Cintron, L. (1984). Individual models of social behavior. *Journal of Personality and Social Psychology, 46*(6), 1389–1404.

Triplett, N. (1898). The dynamogenic factors in pacemaking and competition. *American Journal of Psychology, 9*(4), 507–533.

Trope, Y., & Gaunt, R. (2000). Processing alternative explanations of behavior: Correction or integration? *Journal of Personality and Social Psychology, 79*(3), 344–354.

Tufekci, Z., Howard, J., & Greenhalgh, T. (2020, April 22). The real reason to wear a mask. *The Atlantic.* https://www.theatlantic.com/health/archive/2020/04/dont-wear-mask-yourself/610336/

Tullis, T., & Albert, B. (2013). *Measuring the user experience: Collecting, analyzing, and presenting usability metrics.* Amsterdam, Netherlands: Elsevier.

Turner, C. W., Layton, J. F., & Simons, L. S. (1975). Naturalistic studies of aggressive behavior: Aggressive stimuli, victim visibility, and horn honking. *Journal of Personality and Social Psychology, 31*(6), 1098–1107.

Tversky, A., & Kahneman, D. (1973). Availability: A heuristic for judging frequency and probability. *Cognitive Psychology, 5*(2), 207–232.

Tversky, A., & Kahneman, D. (1974). Judgment under uncertainty: Heuristics and biases. *Science, 185*(4157), 1124–1131.

Tversky, A., & Kahneman, D. (2004). Extensional versus intuitive reasoning: The conjunction fallacy in probability judgment. In J. E. Adler & L. J. Rips (Eds). *Reasoning: Studies of human inference and its foundations* (pp. 114–135). Cambridge University Press.

Twenge, J. M. (2006). What is the interface between culture and self-esteem? In M. H. Kernis (Ed.), *Self-esteem issues and answers: A sourcebook of current perspectives* (pp. 389–395). New York, NY: Psychology Press.

Tylka, T. L., & Sabik, N. J. (2010). Integrating social comparison theory and self-esteem within objectification theory to predict women's disordered eating. *Sex Roles, 63*(1–2), 18–31.

Ubbiali, A. Donati, D., Chiorri, C., Bregani, V., Cattaneo, E. Maffei, C., & Visintini, R. (2008). The usefulness of the multidimensional health locus of control form C (MHLC-C) for HIV+ subjects: An Italian study. *AIDS Care, 20*(4), 495–502.

Uchino, B. N. (2004). *Social support and physical health: Understanding the health consequences of relationships.* New Haven, CT: Yale University Press.

Uchino, B. N., Bowen, K., Carlisle, M., & Birmingham, W. (2012). Psychological pathways linking social support to health outcomes: A visit with the 'ghosts' of research past, present, and future. *Social Science & Medicine, 74*(7), 949–957.

Ueda, M. (2017). Developmental risk factors of juvenile sex offenders by victim age: An implication for specialized treatment programs. *Aggression and Violent Behavior, 37,* 122–128.

Uniyal, S., Paliwal, R., Kaphaliya, B., & Sharma, R. K. (2016). Human overpopulation: Impact on environment. *Environmental Issues Surrounding Human Overpopulation, 738*(632), 1–11.

Untied, A. S., & Dulaney, C. L. (2015). College students' perceived risk of sexual victimization and the role of optimistic bias. *Journal of Interpersonal Violence, 30*(8), 1417–1431.

United Church of Christ. (1987). Toxic wastes and race in the United States: A national report on the racial and socio-economic characteristics of communities with hazardous waste sites. *Public Data Access.*

Unzueta, M. M., Everly, B. A., & Gutierrez, A. S. (2014). Social dominance orientation moderates reactions to Black and White discrimination claimants. *Journal of Experimental Social Psychology, 54*(2), 81–88.

Urban, M. C., Zarnetske, P. L., & Skelly, D. K. (2017). Searching for biotic multipliers of climate change. *Integrative and Comparative Biology, 57*(1), 134–147.

U.S. Bureau of Labor Statistics. (2009). https://www.bls.gov/

U.S. Census Bureau. (2010). *2010 Census data.* https://www.census .gov/2010census/data/

U.S. Department of Veterans Affairs. (2017). *PTSD: National center for PTSD.* https://www.ptsd.va.gov/

Vaartstra, M., Dunn, J. G., & Dunn, J. C. (2018). Perfectionism and perceptions of social loafing in competitive youth soccer. *Journal of Sport Behavior, 41*(4), 475–500.

Valdez, C. E., & Lilly, M. M. (2015). Posttraumatic growth in survivors of intimate partner violence: An assumptive world process. *Journal of Interpersonal Violence, 30*(2), 215–231.

Vallacher, R. R., & Solodky, M. (1979). Objective self-awareness, standards of evaluation, and moral behavior. *Journal of Experimental Social Psychology, 15*(3), 254–262.

Valor-Segura, I., Exposito, F., & Moya, M. (2011). Victim blaming and exoneration of the perpetrator in domestic violence: The role of beliefs in a just world and ambivalent sexism. *The Spanish Journal of Psychology, 14*(1), 195–206.

Van Aken, C. (2015). The use of criminal profilers in the prosecution of serial killers. *Themis: Research Journal of Justice Studies and Forensic Science, 3*(1), 127–149.

Van Beest, I., & Williams, K. D. (2006). When inclusion costs and ostracism pays, ostracism still hurts. *Journal of Personality and Social Psychology, 91*(5), 918–928.

van Bommel, M., van Prooijen, J. W., Elffers, H., & Van Lange, P. A. M. (2014). Intervene to be seen: The power of a camera in attenuating the bystander effect. *Social Psychological and Personality Science, 5*(4), 459–466.

van Bommel, M., van Prooijen, J. W., Elffers, H., & Van Lange, P. A. (2016). Booze, bars, and bystander behavior: People who consumed alcohol help faster in the presence of others. *Frontiers in Psychology, 7*, article 128. https://www.researchgate .net/publication/294278434_Booze_Bars_and_Bystander_ Behavior_People_Who_Consumed_Alcohol_Help_Faster_in_ the_Presence_of_Others

Van Dam, L. C., & Stephens, J. R. (2018). Effects of prolonged exposure to feedback delay on the qualitative subjective experience of virtual reality. *PLoS One, 13*(10), e0205145.

Van den Berghe, P. L., & Peter, K. (1988). Hutterites and Kibbutzniks: A tale of nepotistic communism. *Man, 23*(3), 522–539.

van der Klink, J. L., Blonk, R. B., Schene, A. H., & van Dijk, F. H. (2001). The benefits of interventions for work-related stress. *American Journal of Public Health, 91*(2), 270–276.

Van Goozen, S. H. M., Cohen-Kettenis, P. T., Gooren, L. J. G., Frijda, N. H., & Van De Poll, N. E. (1995). Gender differences in behaviour: Activating effects of cross-sex hormones. *Psychoneuroendocrinology, 20*(4), 343–363.

Van Horn, K. R., Arnone, A., Nesbitt, K., Desilets, L., Sears, T., Giffin, M., & Brudi, R. (1997). Physical distance and interpersonal characteristics in college students' romantic relationships. *Personal Relationships, 4*(1), 25–34.

Van Lange, P. A. M., Rusbult, C. E., Semin-Goossens, A., Gorts, C. A., & Stalpers, M. (1999). Being better than others but otherwise perfectly normal: Perceptions of uniqueness and similarity in close relationships. *Personal Relationships, 6*(3), 269–289.

Van Vugt, M., & Van Lange, P. A. M. (2006). The altruism puzzle: Psychological adaptations for prosocial behavior. In M. Schaller,

J. A. Simpson, & D. T. Kenrick (Eds.), *Evolution and social psychology* (pp. 237–261). Madison, CT: Psychosocial Press.

Vandebosch, H., & Van Cleemput, K. (2008). Defining cyberbullying: A qualitative research into the perceptions of youngsters. *CyberPsychology & Behavior, 11*(4), 499–503.

Varnum, M. E., & Grossmann, I. (2017). Pathogen prevalence is associated with cultural changes in gender equality. *Nature Human Behaviour, 1*(1), 0003.

Vartanian, L. R. (2012). Self-discrepancy theory and body image. In T. F. Cash (Ed.), *Encyclopedia of body image and human appearance* (pp. 711–717). San Diego, CA: Elsevier.

Vater, A., Moritz, S., & Roepke, S. (2018). Does a narcissism epidemic exist in modern western societies? Comparing narcissism and self-esteem in East and West Germany. *PLoS ONE, 13*(1), 16.

Vaughan, G., & Guerin, B. (1997). A neglected innovator in sports psychology: Norman Triplett and the early history of competitive performance. *International Journal of the History of Sport, 14*(2), 82–99.

Vela, J. C., Lenz, A. S., Sparrow, G. S., & Gonzalez, S. L. (2017). Using a positive psychology and family framework to understand Mexican American adolescents' college-going beliefs. *Hispanic Journal of Behavioral Sciences, 39*(1), 66–81.

Velanova, K., Lustig, C., Jacoby, L. L., & Buckner, R. L. (2007). Evidence for frontally mediated controlled processing differences in older adults. *Cerebral Cortex, 17*(5), 1033–1046.

Venkatesh, S. A. (1997). The social organization of street gang activity in an urban ghetto. *American Journal of Sociology, 103*(1), 82–111.

Venkatesh, S. A. (2008). *Gang leader for a day: A rogue sociologist takes to the streets.* New York, NY: Penguin.

Verona, E., & Sullivan, E. A. (2008). Emotional catharsis and aggression revisited: Heart rate reduction following aggressive responding. *Emotion, 8*(3), 331–340.

Vicary, A., & Zaikman, Y. (2017). The CSI effect: An investigation into the relationship between watching crime shows and forensic knowledge. *North American Journal of Psychology, 19*(1), 51–64.

Vidyasagar, P., & Mishra, H. (1993). Effect of modeling on aggression. *Indian Journal of Clinical Psychology, 20*(1), 50–52.

Vie, L. L., Scheier, L. M., Lester, P. B., & Seligman, M. P. (2016). Initial validation of the U.S. Army global assessment tool. *Military Psychology, 28*(6), 468–487.

Viki, G. T., & Abrams, D. (2002). But she was unfaithful: Benevolent sexism and reactions to rape victims who violate traditional gender role expectations. *Sex Roles, 47*(5), 289–293.

Violence Policy Center. (2015). *Research, investigation, analysis & advocacy for a safer America.* http://www.vpc.org/

Vohra, N., & Singh, M. (2005). Mental traps to avoid while interpreting feedback: Insights from administering feedback to school principals. *Human Resource Quarterly, 16*(1), 139–147.

von Hippel, C., Kalokerinos, E. K., Haanterä, K., & Zacher, H. (2019). Age-based stereotype threat and work outcomes: Stress appraisals and rumination as mediators. *Psychology and Aging, 34*(1), 68–84.

Vrabel, J. K., Zeigler-Hill, V., & Southard, A. C. (2018). Self-esteem and envy: Is state self-esteem instability associated with the benign and malicious forms of envy? *Personality and Individual Differences, 123*, 100–104.

Wadham, B. (2016). The minister, the commandant and the cadets: Scandal and the mediation of Australian civil–military relations. *Journal of Sociology, 52*(3), 551–568.

Wadsworth, M. E. J. (1976). Delinquency, pulse rates and early emotional deprivation. *British Journal of Criminology, 16*(3), 245–256.

Wagenmakers, E. J., Beek, T., Dijkhoff, L., Gronau, Q. F., Acosta, A., Adams, R. B., Jr., . . . Zwaan, R. A. (2016). Registered replication report: Strack, Martin, & Stepper (1988). *Perspectives on Psychological Science, 11*(6), 917–928.

Wainwright, D. (2015, November 26). Football banning orders fall as figures reveal bad behaviour. *BBC News*. http://www.bbc.com/news/uk-england-34936495

Walker, L. E. (1979). Behind the closed doors of the middle-class wifebeater's family. *Contemporary Psychology, 24*(5), 404–405.

Walker, L. E. (1984). Battered women, psychology, and public policy. *American Psychologist, 39*(10), 1178–1182.

Wallach, M. A., & Kogan, N. (1965). The roles of information, discussion, and consensus in group risk-taking. *Journal of Experimental Social Psychology, 1*(1), 1–19.

Walther, J. B., & Bazarova, N. N. (2007). Misattribution in virtual groups: The effects of member distribution on self-serving bias and partner blame. *Human Communication Research, 33*(1), 1–26.

Wang, F., & Wu, H. B. (2019, August). Current Situation Analysis and Development Strategy Research on Educational Live Broadcasting Technology Based on SWOT Theory in Post-MOOC Era. In *2019 10th International Conference on Information Technology in Medicine and Education (ITME)* (pp. 336–340). IEEE.

Wang, J., Leu, J., & Shoda, Y. (2011). When the seemingly innocuous "stings": Racial microaggressions and their emotional consequences. *Personality and Social Psychology Bulletin, 37*(12), 166–1678.

Wang, J., & Xiao, J. J. (2009). Buying behavior, social support and credit card indebtedness of college students. *International Journal of Consumer Studies, 33*(1), 2–10.

Wang, Q. (2006). Relations of maternal style and child self-concept to autobiographical memories in Chinese, Chinese immigrant, and European American 3-year-olds. *Child Development, 77*(6), 1794–1809.

Wang, Q., Koh, J. K., Song, Q., & Hou, Y. (2015). Knowledge of memory functions in European and Asian American adults and children: The relation to autobiographical memory. *Memory, 23*(1), 25–38.

Wang, S. S., Moon, S., Kwon, K. H., Evans, C. A., & Stefanone, M. A. (2010). Face off: Implications of visual cues on initiating friendship on Facebook. *Computers in Human Behavior, 26*(2), 226–234.

Wann, D. L. (2006). Understanding the positive social psychological benefits of sport team identification: The team identification-social psychological health model. *Group Dynamics: Theory Research, and Practice, 10*(4), 272–296.

Wann, D. L., & James, J. D. (2018). Sport fans: *The psychology and social impact of fandom*. Routledge.

Warner, J. L. (Producer), & Cukor, G. (Director). (1964). *My fair lady* [Motion picture]. United States: Warner Bros.

Wansink, B., Kent, R. J., & Hoch, S. J. (1998). An anchoring and adjustment model of purchase quantity decisions. *Journal of Marketing Research, 35*(1), 71–81.

Waters, B. (2019). Social justice and legal education. *The Law Teacher, 53*(1), 129–131.

Wayne, K., O'Dwyer, A., Barry, D., Dillard, L., Polo-Neil, H., & Warriner, M. (2011). The burden of combat: Cognitive dissonance in Iraq war veterans. In D. C. Kelly, S. Howe-Barksdale, & D. Gitelson (Eds.), *Treating young veterans: Promoting resilience through practice and advocacy* (pp. 33–79). New York, NY: Springer.

Weber, C., Dunaway, J., & Johnson, T. (2012). It's all in the name: Source cue ambiguity and the persuasive appeal of campaign ads. *Political Behavior, 34*(3), 561–584.

Webster, A. (2016, June 2). Review: "The witness," a brother's quest to put Kitty Genovese case to rest [Review of the film *The witness*, by J. Solomon]. *New York Times*. https://www.nytimes.com/2016/06/03/movies/the-witness-review-kitty-genovese.html?mcubz=1&_r=0

Wegener, D. T., & Petty, R. E. (1998). The naive scientist revisited: Naive theories and social judgment. *Social Cognition, 16*(1), 1–7.

Wei, M., Russell, D. W., Mallinckrodt, B., & Vogel, D. L. (2007). The Experiences in Close Relationship Scale (ECR)–short form: Reliability, validity, and factor structure. *Journal of Personality Assessment, 88*(2), 187–204.

Weiner, B. (1974). *Achievement motivation and attribution theory*. Morristown, NJ: General Learning Press.

Weiner, B. (1980). *Human motivation*. New York, NY: Holt, Rinehart & Winston.

Weiner, B. (1986). *An attributional theory of motivation and emotion*. New York, NY: Springer-Verlag.

Weinstein, N. D. (1980). Unrealistic optimism about future life events. *Journal of Personality and Social Psychology, 39*(5), 806–820.

Weisburd, D., Cave, B., Nelson, M., White, C., Haviland, A., Ready, J., . . . Sikkema, K. (2018). Mean streets and mental health: Depression and post-traumatic stress disorder at crime hot spots. *American Journal of Community Psychology, 61*(3–4), 285–295.

Wells, N. M., Evans, G. W., & Cheek, K. A. (2016). Environmental psychology. In H. Franklin (Ed.), *Environmental health: From global to local* (pp. 203–230). San Francisco, CA: John Wiley.

Wertz, J., Belsky, J., Moffitt, T. E., Belsky, D. W., Harrington, H., Avinun, R., . . . Caspi, A. (2019). Genetics of nurture: A test of the hypothesis that parents' genetics predict their observed caregiving. *Developmental Psychology, 55*, 1461–1472.

West, C. M. (1998). Leaving a second closet: Outing partner violence in same-sex couples. In J. L. Jasinski & L. M. Williams (Eds.), *Partner violence: A comprehensive review of 20 years of research* (pp. 163–183). Thousand Oaks, CA: Sage.

West, L. J. (1993). A psychiatric overview of cult-related phenomenon. *Journal of the American Academy of Psychoanalysis, 21*(1), 1–19.

Wharton, J., Khalil, K., Fyfe, C., & Young, A. (2019). Effective practices for fostering empathy towards marine life. In G. Fauville, D. L. Payne, M. E. Marrero, A. Lantz-Andersson, & F. Crouch (Eds.), *Exemplary practices in marine science education* (pp. 157–168). New York, NY: Springer.

Wheeler, S. C., & Petty, R. E. (2001). The effects of stereotype activation on behavior: A review of possible mechanisms. *Psychological Bulletin, 127*(6), 797–826.

Whitburn, J., Linklater, W. L., & Milfont, T. L. (2018). Exposure to urban nature and tree planting are related to pro-environmental behavior via connection to nature, the use of nature for psychological restoration, and environmental attitudes. *Environment and Behavior, 51*(7), 787–810.

White, G. (2016). The specter of climate refugees: Why invoking refugees as a reason to "take climate change seriously" is troubling. *Migration and Citizenship: Newsletter of the American Political Science Association Organized Section on Migration and Citizenship, 4*(2), 1–9.

Whiteley, P., Sy, T., & Johnson, S. K. (2012). Leaders' conceptions of followers: Implications for naturally occurring Pygmalion effects. *The Leadership Quarterly, 23*(5), 822–834.

Whitley, B. E., & Kite, M. E. (2010). *The psychology of prejudice and discrimination*. Belmont, CA: Wadsworth Cengage Learning.

Whitman, M. (1993). Removing a badge of slavery: The record of *Brown v Board of Education*. *Choice Reviews Online, 31*(1), 20.

Wicker, A. W. (1971). An examination of the "other variables" explanation of attitude-behavior inconsistency. *Journal of Personality and Social Psychology, 19*(1), 18–30.

Wieman, C., & Welsh, A. (2016). The connection between teaching methods and attribution errors. *Educational Psychology Review, 28*(3), 645–648.

Wignall, A. E., Heiling, A. M., Cheng, K., & Herberstein, M. E. (2006). Flower symmetry preferences in honeybees and their crab spider predators. *Ethology, 112*(5), 510–518.

Wilkinson, G. S. (1984). Reciprocal food sharing in the vampire bat. *Nature, 308*(5955), 181–184.

Wilkinson, G. S. (1990). Food sharing in vampire bats. *Scientific American, 262*(2), 76–82.

Wilkinson, N. (2008). *An introduction to behavioral economics.* Basingstoke, UK: Palgrave Macmillan.

Willeit, M., Ganopolski, A., Calov, R., & Brovkin, V. (2019). Mid-Pleistocene transition in glacial cycles explained by declining CO_2 and regolith removal. *Science Advances 5*(4), eaav7337.

Williams, D. P., Joseph, N., Hill, L. K., Sollers III, J. J., Vasey, M. W., Way, B. M., . . . Thayer, J. F. (2019). Stereotype threat, trait perseveration, and vagal activity: Evidence for mechanisms underpinning health disparities in Black Americans. *Ethnicity & Health, 24*(8), 909–926.

Williams, K. D. (2002). *Ostracism: The power of silence.* New York, NY: Guilford.

Williams, L. M., Gatt, J. M., Schofield, P. R., Olivieri, G., Peduto, A., & Gordon, E. (2009). 'Negativity bias' in risk for depression and anxiety: Brain-body fear circuitry correlates, 5-HTT-LPR and early life stress. *Neuroimage, 47*(3), 804–814.

Wilson, D. K., Friend, R., Teasley, N., Green, S., Reaves, I. L., & Sica, D. A. (2002). Motivation versus social cognitive interventions for promoting fruit and vegetable intake and physical activity in African American adolescents. *Annals of Behavioral Medicine, 24*(4), 310–319.

Wilson, J. P., Hugenberg, K., & Rule, N. O. (2017). Racial bias in judgments of physical size and formidability: From size to threat. *Journal of Personality and Social Psychology, 113*, 59–80.

Wilson, M. S. (2019). A community-based test of the Dual Process Model of Intergroup Relations: Predicting attitudes towards Christians, Muslims, Hindus, Jews, and Atheists. *New Zealand Journal of Psychology, 48*(1), 163–166.

Wilson, T. D., Houston, C. E., Etling, K. M., & Brekke, N. (1996). A new look at anchoring effects: Basic anchoring and its antecedents. *Journal of Experimental Psychology: General, 125*(4), 387–402.

Wilson, T. D., Lindsey, S., & Schooler, T. Y. (2000). A model of dual attitudes. *Psychological Review, 107*(1), 101–126.

Winslow, D. (1999). Rights of passage and group bonding in the Canadian Airborne. *Armed Forces and Society, 25*(3), 429–457.

Wojcicki, A., Avey, L., Mountain, J. L., Macpherson, J. M., & Tung, J. Y. H. (2013). *U.S. Patent No. 8,543,339.* Washington, DC: U.S. Patent and Trademark Office.

Wolf, S. T., Insko, C. A., Kirchner, J. L., & Wildschut, T. (2008). Interindividual-intergroup discontinuity in the domain of correspondent outcomes: The roles of relativistic concern, perceived categorization, and the doctrine of mutual assured destruction. *Journal of Personality and Social Psychology, 94*(3), 479–494.

Wolff, H. G., & Moser, K. (2009). Effects of networking on career success: A longitudinal study. *Journal of Applied Psychology, 94*(1), 196–206.

Wolke, D., & Lereya, S. T. (2015). Long-term effects of bullying. *Archives of Disease in Childhood, 100*(9), 879–885.

Woloch, N. (1996). *Muller v. Oregon: A brief history with documents (Bedford series in history and culture).* Boston, MA: Bedford Books of St. Martin's Press.

Wong, R. H., Wong, A. K., & Bailes, J. E. (2014). Frequency, magnitude, and distribution of head impacts in Pop Warner football: the cumulative burden. *Clinical neurology and neurosurgery, 118*, 1–4.

Woodzicka, J. A., & LaFrance, M. (2005). The effects of subtle sexual harassment on women's performance in a job interview. *Sex Roles, 53*(1–2), 67–77.

Woosnam, K. M., Draper, J., Jiang, J., Aleshinloye, K. D., & Erul, E. (2018). Applying self-perception theory to explain residents' attitudes about tourism development through travel histories. *Tourism Management, 64*, 357–368.

World Justice Project. (2019). *What is the rule of law?* Retrieved October 3, 2019, from https://worldjusticeproject.org/about-us/overview/what-rule-law

Wright, B. A. (1983). *Physical disability—a psychosocial approach.* New York, NY: HarperCollins.

Wrightsman, L. S., & Kassin, S. (1993). *Confessions in the courtroom.* Thousand Oaks, CA: Sage.

Wrightsman, L. S., Nietzel, M. T., & Fortune, W. H. (1994). *Psychology and the legal system* (3rd ed.). Belmont, CA: Thomson Brooks/Cole.

Wu, C. I. (2001). The genic view of the process of speciation. *Journal of evolutionary biology, 14*(6), 851–865.

Wurmbach, V. S., Lampert, A., Schmidt, S. J., Bernard, S., Thürmann, P. A., Seidling, H. M., & Haefeli, W. E. (2018). Simplifying complex drug therapies: Challenges and solutions. *Bundesgesundheitsblatt, Gesundheitsforschung, Gesundheitsschutz, 61*(9), 1146–1151.

Wyckoff, J. P., Asao, K., & Buss, D. M. (2019). Gossip as an intrasexual competition strategy: Predicting information sharing from potential mate versus competitor mating strategies. *Evolution and Human Behavior, 40*(1), 96–104.

Xiaohe, X., & Whyte, K. J. (1990). Love matches and arranged marriages: A Chinese replication. *Journal of Marriage and the Family, 52*, 709–722.

Yang, J., Yu, K. H. F., & Huang, C. J. (2019). Service employees' concurrent adaptive and unethical behaviors in complex or non-routine tasks: The effects of customer control and self-monitoring personality. *Asia Pacific Journal of Management, 36*(1), 245–273.

Yasmin, A., & Iqbal, R. (2019). Justice delayed is justice denied: The role of justice in Pakistani society, an overview. *Pacific International Journal, 2*(2), 01–06.

Yates, A., & Terr, L. C. (1988). Anatomically correct dolls: Should they be used as the basis for expert testimony? *Journal of the American Academy of Child & Adolescent Psychiatry, 27*(2), 254–257.

Yayan, E. H., Düken, M. E., Özdemir, A. A., & Çelebioğlu, A. (2019). Mental health problems of Syrian refugee children: Post-traumatic stress, depression and anxiety. *Journal of Pediatric Nursing, 51*, e27–e32.

Yelsma, P., & Athappilly, K. (1988). Marriage satisfaction and communication practices: Comparisons among Indian and American couples. *Journal of Comparative Family Studies, 19*, 37–54.

Yi, J. P., Vitaliano, P. P., Smith, R. E., Yi, J. C., & Weinger, K. (2008). The role of resilience on psychological adjustment and physical health in patients with diabetes. *British Journal of Health Psychology, 13*(2), 311–325.

Yildirim, T. M., Kocapınar, G., & Ecevit, Y. A. (2019). Status incongruity and backlash against female legislators: How legislative speechmaking benefits men, but harms women. *Political Research Quarterly.* Advance online publication.

Ying, X., Li, H., Jiang, S., Peng, F., & Lin, Z. (2014). Group laziness: The effect of social loafing on group performance. *Social Behavior and Personality: An International Journal, 42*(3), 465–471.

Yoon, C. (2011). Theory of planned behavior and ethics theory in digital piracy: An integrated model. *Journal of Business Ethics, 100*(3), 405–417.

Yu, R. F., & Wu, X. (2015). Working alone or in the presence of others: Exploring social facilitation in baggage X-ray security screening tasks. *Ergonomics, 58*(6), 857–865.

Yukl, G., & Tracey, J. B. (1992). Consequences of influence tactics used with subordinates, peers, and the boss. *Journal of Applied Psychology, 77*(4), 525–535.

Yunus, M. (2007). *Banker to the poor: Micro-lending and the battle against world poverty.* New York, NY: PublicAffairs.

Zadro, L., Williams, K. D., & Richardson, R. (2004). How long can you go? Ostracism by a computer lowers belonging, control, self-esteem, and meaningful existence. *Journal of Experimental Social Psychology*, *40*(4), 560–567.

Zafarullah, H., & Huque, A. S. (2018). Climate change, regulatory policies and regional cooperation in South Asia. *Public Administration and Policy*, *21*(1), 22–35.

Zajonc, R. B. (1965). Social facilitation. *Science*, *149*(3681), 269–274.

Zajonc, R. B., Adelmann, P. K., Murphy, S. T., & Niedenthal, P. M. (1987). Convergence in the physical appearance of spouses. *Motivation and emotion, 11*(4), 335–346.

Zajonc, R. B., Heingartner, A., & Herman, E. M. (1969). Social enhancement and impairment of performance in the cockroach. *Journal of Personality and Social Psychology*, *13*(2), 83–92.

Zajonc, R. B., & Sales, S. M. (1966). Social facilitation of dominant and subordinate responses. *Journal of Experimental Social Psychology*, *2*(2), 160–168.

Zeidan, F., Baumgartner, J. N., & Coghill, R. C. (2019). The neural mechanisms of mindfulness-based pain relief: A functional magnetic resonance imaging-based review and primer. *Pain Reports*, *4*(4), e759.

Zhao, F., Zhang, Y., Alterman, V., Zhang, B., & Yu, G. (2018). Can math-gender stereotypes be reduced? A theory-based intervention program with adolescent girls. *Current Psychology*, *37*(3), 612–624.

Zhou, D., Zhang, P., Bao, C., Zhang, Y., & Zhu, N. (2020). Emerging understanding of etiology and epidemiology of the novel Coronavirus (COVID-19) infection in Wuhan, China. *Preprints*. Advance online publication. doi:10.20944/preprints202002.0283.v1

Zhu, A. Y. F. (2019). Credit card use of college students: A broad review. *Journal of Personal Finance*, *18*(1), 55–63.

Zillmann, D. (1994). Cognition-excitation interdependencies in the escalation of anger and angry aggression. In M. Potegal & J. F. Knutson (Eds.), *The dynamics of aggression: Biological and social processes in dyads and groups* (pp. 45–71). Hillsdale, NJ: Lawrence Erlbaum.

Zimbardo, P. G. (1960). Involvement and communication discrepancy as determinants of opinion conformity. *Journal of Abnormal and Social Psychology*, *60*(1), 86–94.

Zimbardo, P. G. (1970). The human choice: Individuation, reason and order versus deindividuation, impulse, and chaos. In W. J. Arnold & D. Levine (Eds.), *Nebraska symposium on motivation* (Vol. *18*). Lincoln: University of Nebraska Press.

Zimbardo, P. G. (1973). On the ethics of intervention in human psychological research: With special reference to the Stanford prison experiment. *Cognition*, *2*(2), 243–256.

Zimbardo, P. G. (2007). *The Lucifer effect: Understanding how good people turn evil*. New York, NY: Random House.

Zimbardo, P. G. (2017). On the ethics of intervention in human psychological research: With special reference to the Stanford prison experiment. *Cognition*, *2*(2), 243–256.

Zimmer, C. (2019, April 11). Scott Kelly spent a year in orbit. His body is not quite the same. *New York Times*. Retrieved October 11, 2019, from https://www.nytimes.com/2019/04/11/science/scott-mark-kelly-twins-space-nasa.html

Zinsser, W. (1991). *On writing well*. New York, NY: HarperCollins.

Zois, D. S., Kapodistria, A., Yao, M., & Chelmis, C. (2018, April). Optimal online cyberbullying detection. In *2018 IEEE International Conference on Acoustics, Speech and Signal Processing (ICASSP)*. Calgary, Canada: IEEE.

Zugelder, B. S., Greene, H. C., Warren, L. L., & L'Esperance, M. (2018). Master's students' perceptions toward teacher leadership. *International Journal of Learning, Teaching and Educational Research*, *17*(12), 69–77.

Zuk, M. (2011). *Sex on six legs: Lessons on life, love, and language from the insect world*. New York, NY: Houghton Mifflin Harcourt.

GLOSSARY

Action research: The application of scientific principles to social problem solving in the real world.

Actor-observer bias: Our tendency to think of personality when explaining other people's behavior but remember the circumstances when explaining our own behavior.

Adaptive categorization: The idea that the instinct to group and label other people and things arose because it was a benefit to survival.

Affective forecasting: When someone tries to predict how they'll feel in the future; most of us aren't able to do so effectively.

Ageism: Negative stereotypes and discrimination experienced by older individuals, which often leads to stress.

Agency: A stereotypically male-oriented pattern of behavior that emphasizes being masterful, assertive, competitive, and dominant.

Aggression: Behavior intended to harm others who do not wish to be harmed.

Agreeableness: A personality trait regarding willingness to be flexible, to cooperate, and to try to please others.

Alcohol disinhibition hypothesis: The idea that alcohol interferes with the brain's ability to suppress violent behavior by lowering anxiety and harming the ability to accurately assess a situation.

Algorithm: A systematic, logical, but sometimes slow method of searching for a solution to a problem or question.

Alternatives: The number and quality of other options we'd have if our current relationship ended.

Ambivalent prejudice: A combination of hostile and benevolent prejudice that means some group members are judged very positively while others are judged very negatively, depending on whether they fit our expectations.

American Psychological Association (APA): A large organization of professional psychologists who provide scholarly publications, writing guidelines, and ethical standards for research.

Amicus brief: A report including information or arguments the court might want to consider when making a decision.

Analysis of variance (ANOVA): A statistical test that compares the means and standard deviations of three or more groups, to see if they are different from each other.

Anchoring and adjustment heuristic: Our tendency to be influenced by a starting point when making numerical guesses about something, even if the starting point is unreliable.

Animal-assisted therapy: The use of nonhuman animals to achieve therapeutic outcomes for humans.

Anthropology: The study of culture and human behavior over time.

Anthropomorphism: The perception that nonhuman objects have human traits.

Anthrozoology: The study of human–animal bonds.

Applied science: Research that translates theory into applied problem solving or social action.

Archival data: Stored information that was originally created for some other purpose that can later be used to test hypotheses, such as census or college records.

Arranged marriage: A marriage planned by the couple members' families, often for pragmatic reasons such as similarity or financial benefits.

Assortative mating: The tendency to mate with someone who shares our features and interests (see *similarity-attraction hypothesis*).

Attachment style: Our pattern of trust and self-esteem within relationships; we can be secure (healthy), anxious-ambivalent (insecure), or avoidant-fearful (generally avoiding long-term commitment to others).

Attachment theory: The idea that our early family environment affects our ability to form and maintain healthy adult relationships.

Attitude object: The thing, person, place, or idea we evaluate when we form an attitude.

Attitudes: Inner evaluations or judgments toward something or someone, either positive or negative.

Attribution theory: The idea that we try to understand other people's behavior using commonsense explanations and clues.

Attributions: Our guesses for the cause of other people's actions or events around us.

Auction fever: The tendency to overbid on an item being sold in a socially competitive environment.

Authentic confession: When people honestly believe they committed a crime (even if they didn't).

Authoritarian personality: A personality characterized by submission to authority, discipline toward those who defy authority, and conforming to conventional beliefs.

Autokinetic effect: An optical illusion that occurs when we think a stationary light is moving.

Availability heuristic: Our tendency to overestimate the frequency of something based on how easily it comes to mind.

Averaged face: A computer-generated face created by combining several individual faces. Averaged faces are often perceived as more attractive than individual faces.

Badges: Visual icons that can mark if a study used open science practices.

Basic science: Research that increases understanding and theory within a field like psychology.

Basking in reflected glory (BIRGing): A method of self-enhancement that involves affiliating with an in-group when that group has been successful.

Beauty and the Beast fantasy: A romantic myth in which women are told that patient, self-sacrificing love can turn a violent "beast" into a loving and sensitive partner (see *romantic myths*).

Behavioral economic model (BEM): A model for understanding economic behavior that describes how psychology influences irrational economic decision making.

Behavioral economics: The study of how economic decisions are influenced by psychological factors.

Behavioral genetics: The study of how nature and nurture interact to form our attitudes and behaviors.

Benevolent prejudice: Positive judgments of group members who have traits we value and align with our expectations.

Better than average effect: A form of cognitive bias in which people believe they are better than a typical person, even though statistically it's impossible for everyone to be "better than average."

Big 5 Model: A theory that five fundamental personality traits make us distinct and predict behavior: openness to experience, conscientiousness, extraversion, agreeableness, and neuroticism.

Bilateral symmetry: When left and right halves of a face or body match; symmetry is positively correlated with perceived attractiveness.

Biopsychosocial model: The idea that human health is the combined product of biological, psychological, and social forces.

Bogus pipeline: A fake lie detector machine used to increase honest responses from study participants.

Bounded rationality: The idea that there is a natural cognitive limit on people's ability to make rational economic decisions.

Brainstorming: A group approach to problem solving that emphasizes nonevaluative creative thinking where members don't judge any idea.

Bystander effect: The finding that the likelihood of being helped in an emergency is negatively correlated with the number of people who witness it, probably due to diffusion of responsibility.

Catharsis hypothesis: The idea that purposefully engaging in small aggression will reduce larger aggressive behaviors overall.

Central trait: A major characteristic in a person or object that creates a unified impression about the entire person (a halo effect).

Cinderella fantasy: A romantic myth in which a man who is a relative stranger enters a woman's life and transforms it by saving her from problems (see *romantic myths*).

Classical conditioning: A process when an automatic reaction or attitude to one thing is transferred to another after repeated pairings.

Climate refugees: People displaced from their home by changes in the environment.

Clinical or counseling psychology: A subfield of psychology that helps people who have maladaptive or problematic thoughts and behaviors.

Cobras: Perpetrators of relationship violence who get physiologically calm as conflict increases but are still extremely violent and manipulative.

Coerced confession: A confession as a result of force, such as torture or intense interrogation.

Cognitive dissonance: A state of psychological discomfort that occurs when we experience conflicting beliefs and behaviors.

Cognitive load: The amount of information that an individual's thinking systems can handle at one time.

Cognitive load shifting: When we can smoothly shift back and forth between intuition and logic, as needed.

Cognitive miser: The tendency for humans to take mental shortcuts to minimize cognitive load.

Collective self-esteem: Our evaluation of the worth of our social groups.

Collectivistic: Term for cultures that emphasize the larger social group, interdependence, and family.

Communication-persuasion matrix: Proposes six steps in the persuasion process—attention, comprehension, learning, acceptance, retention, and conclusion—which build on each other.

Communion: A stereotypically female-orientated pattern of behavior that emphasizes being friendly, unselfish, other-oriented, and emotionally expressive.

Community resilience: Social cooperation in a certain area that produces healthy responses to environmental stressors.

Comparative social psychology: Species-level comparisons of social behavior usually used to determine the uniqueness of human behavior.

Compliance: A type of explicit social influence when we behave in response to a direct or indirect request.

Composite face: See *averaged face*.

Compulsive hoarding syndrome: A disorder caused by the psychological need to save things to reduce anxiety and/or depression.

Confirmation bias: Our tendency to notice and remember only evidence that confirms our beliefs and expectations.

Conformity: A type of implicit social influence when we voluntarily change our behavior to imitate those around us.

Confounding variables: Alternative explanations for why results came out as they did, which limit a researcher's ability to claim a causal relationship between variables in a study.

Conscientiousness: A personality trait regarding attention to detail, responsibility, and striving for achievement.

Consensus: The dimension of Kelley's covariation model of attribution that refers to whether other people tend to act the same way toward the target person.

Consistency: The dimension of Kelley's covariation model of attribution that refers to whether the actor in the situation tends to act the same way toward everyone.

Construct validity: The degree to which tests, surveys, and so on chosen for a study really measure what we think they're measuring.

Construction hypothesis: The idea that memories are constructed as needed at any given time, making them subject to bias.

Constructs: Theoretical ideas that cannot be directly observed, such as attitudes, personality, attraction, or how we think.

Contact hypothesis: The idea that prejudice will decrease with exposure to members of a disliked outgroup.

Context variables: Situational aspects of how a message is received, such as repetition.

Contingency theory of leadership: The idea that the "best" leadership style depends on the given group dynamics.

Control group: A group of participants in a true experiment that serves as a neutral or baseline group that receives no treatment.

Convergence theory: For pets, it's the argument that pets and their owners gradually change to look alike.

Coordination loss: When a lack of cooperation and communication weakens a group's effectiveness or increases social loafing.

Correlational analysis: A statistic testing if two continuous variables are systematically associated with each other.

Counterfactual thinking: The tendency to imagine alternative facts or events that would have led to a different future; imagining "what might have been."

Covariation model of attribution: Our attempts to find systematic explanations for why people act how they do.

Critical thinking: The ability to analyze, apply, and explore ideas in new and open-minded ways.

Crowding: The subjective sense that there are too many people in a given space.

CSI effect: Unrealistic expectations of forensic science created by watching fictional television shows.

Culture: A collection of shared beliefs, customs, and social norms passed down from one generation to the next (including stereotypes).

Culture of honor: A culture where individuals, especially men, tend to perceive insults as a threat to their masculinity and often engage in aggression.

Cultureme: Culture-specific symbols that communicate widely shared ideas or social impressions.

Cute aggression: The impulse to bite or squeeze cute things without wanting to harm them.

Cyberbullying: Aggression through electronic outlets, like social media.

Cyber-disinhibition: Lack of social restraints due to the anonymity of the internet, leading to behaviors like trolling or online harassment.

Cyberloafing: When people working in a group reduce their individual level of effort.

Cyberslacking: See *cyberloafing*.

Cycle of violence: States that relationship violence occurs in three cyclic phases: (1) tension building, (2) explosion, and (3) contrition.

Dark triad: A group of three personality traits associated with lack of ethics and need for power: Machiavellianism, narcissism, and psychopathology.

Debriefing: Additional details given to participants after participation in an experiment.

Deception: Hiding the true nature of an experiment from a participant so they act more naturally.

Default decision: The outcome that will inevitably happen if no action is made.

Dehumanize: When a human is perceived as lacking positive human qualities and is seen more like an animal or object.

Deindividuation: When self-awareness is replaced by a social role or group identity, resulting in the loss of individuality.

Density: An objective calculation of how many people occupy a particular space.

Dependent variable: The measured outcome at the end of an experiment that is affected by the independent variable.

Derogation of alternatives: The tendency for highly committed people to downgrade possible alternatives, thus avoiding temptation.

Descriptive designs: Methods of gathering data that define, explain, and clarify patterns that happen without experimenter intervention.

Descriptive norm: Our perception of what most people do in a given situation.

Diffusion of responsibility: When we feel less responsible for an outcome due to the presence of others.

Discrimination: Behaviors toward a people because of their perceived membership in a group.

Disease model: A medical model toward health that assesses and treats deficits, bringing someone back to neutrality.

Disinhibition: Loosening of social restraints when someone feels anonymous or not identifiable.

Distinctiveness: The dimension of Kelley's covariation model of attribution that refers to something unique about this situation that explains the actor's behavior toward a target.

Distress: Stress due to negative events, such as a death in an individual's family.

Door-in-the-face technique: A persuasion technique where people who refuse a large request are then more likely to agree to a later, smaller request.

Double-barreled item: A scale item that includes more than one basic idea, making it difficult for individuals to know how to respond if they agree with one of the ideas but not the other.

Downward counterfactuals: Imagined outcomes that are worse than reality; they can be comforting after things go wrong.

Downward social comparison: When we compare ourselves to someone who is worse than us, often to feel better.

Dual attitudes: When we hold contrasting positive and negative evaluations about a single attitude object.

Dual processing: The ability to process information using both intuition and logic.

Duchenne smile: A genuine, sincere smile.

Duping delight: The facial smirk that appears when people think that they have gotten away with a lie.

Effort justification: See *initiation effect*.

Egoistic altruism: Helping others in exchange for some personal benefit.

Elaboration likelihood model: Proposes two paths to persuasion: a direct, explicit, "central" route and an indirect, implicit, "peripheral" route. Which works better depends on the audience's ability and motivation to pay attention.

Empathy-altruism hypothesis: The idea that feelings of compassion create a purely selfless motivation to help.

Endowment effect: See *subjective ownership*.

Environmental psychology: The psychological study of the interplay between individuals and their surroundings.

Epidemiology: The statistical analysis of the patterns of a disease (like incidence and spread).

Escalation of aggression effect: The tendency for aggression to spiral and increase in a situation.

Eustress: Stress due to positive events, such as a wedding or a promotion at work.

Evaluation apprehension hypothesis: The idea that having other people in the room will affect your task performance because of your anxiety that they are judging you.

Excitation transfer effect: Our tendency to interpret excitement over a situation as excitement about another person (see *misattribution of arousal*).

Explicit attitudes: Controlled, conscious, thoughtful evaluations and judgments we're aware of making.

Explicit expectations: Clearly and formally stated expectations for social behavior.

External attributions: Explanations for someone's behavior that are based on factors outside their control or about the circumstances, such as getting sick, the weather, or luck.

External validity: The extent to which results of any single study could apply to other people or settings (see *generalizability*).

Extrinsic religiosity: Practicing a faith only because of social or practical rewards.

Face validity: When a scale or test obviously appears to measure what it is intended to measure.

Facial feedback hypothesis: The idea that emotions can happen after someone makes a corresponding facial expression.

False confession: When someone claims to be responsible for a crime they didn't actually commit.

False consensus effect: The overestimation of how many other people share our values, perceptions, and beliefs.

False dichotomy: A situation presented as two opposing and mutually exclusive options when there may really be additional options or a compromise.

False negative: Occurs when we think an event or condition is not present when it really is.

False positives: Occurs when we think an event or condition is present when it is not.

False uniqueness bias: The belief that we are more unique than others when it comes to socially desirable traits.

Field of eligibles: The potential dates and mates available for an individual not in a committed romantic relationship, based on that individual's criteria for a romantic partner.

Food accumulation hypothesis: The idea that cultural views of conformity originate from that group's relationship with food.

Foot-in-the-door technique: A persuasion technique where people are more likely to agree to a big request if they've already said yes to a smaller one.

Forensic psychology: The application of psychological theory and research to legal processes (e.g., suspect interrogations, evaluation of potential jurors).

Formative assessments: Evaluations designed to give meaningful feedback to help someone learn how to improve.

Friendship contacts: Individual, positive, personal interactions that reduce prejudice.

Frustration-aggression theory: The idea that our frustrations build until they are released through aggression toward weaker targets we can blame.

Functional distance: How often two people see each other, due to things like architectural design (e.g., who lives next to the stairs in a building).

Fundamental attribution error: Our tendency to overestimate the influence of personality and underestimate the power of the situation when making attributions about other people's behaviors.

Fundamentalism: Belief that one's faith is the only true religion, that teachings should be taken literally, and that evil is all around us.

Fungibility: For money, the idea that its use is interchangeable (you can use it for rent, food, or anything else).

Game mechanics: Motivating experiences that keep someone engaged as a player.

Gamification: Application of gaming principles to a nongame setting.

Gender socialization: The expected patterns of behavior deemed appropriate for men and women.

General adaptation syndrome: A three-stage theory proposing we respond to stress with (1) an initial alarm phase, (2) resistance, and (3) eventual exhaustion if the stress continues.

General Aggression Model (GAM): The theory that aggression is a developmental process including biological responses to the environment, cognitive processing, and decisions about how to behave.

Generalizability: How much the results of a single study can apply to the general population (see *external validity*).

Generational influence: A cultural belief or norm that continues as the people who started it leave and newer members of a group remain.

Genetic determinism: The idea that genetic influence alone determines behavioral outcomes.

Group: When two or more individuals interact with one another or are joined together by a common fate.

Group cohesion: The degree to which members of a group feel connected to one another, work harmoniously, and resist threats.

Group dynamics: The social roles, hierarchies, communication styles, and culture that naturally form when groups interact.

Group norms: See *social norms*.

Group polarization: When a group makes more extreme decisions after a discussion, toward either a more or less risky position.

Groupthink: The tendency for people in cohesive groups to minimize conflict by publicly agreeing with each other, despite any doubts they have.

Halo effect: When an entire social perception of a person is constructed around a single trait.

Hamilton's inequality: A formula that predicts helping will occur when the benefits to ourselves or our genetic relatives outweigh the costs.

Hardy personality: A personality type where people cope effectively with stress because their thinking style keeps their physiology calm.

Hazing: Whenever members of a group establish arbitrary rituals for new members that may cause physical or emotional harm, which can be a type of escalation trap for aspiring members (see *effort justification*).

Hedonic forecasting: See *affective forecasting*.

Herd mentality: The tendency to blindly follow the direction your group is moving toward.

Heuristic: Any mental shortcut that makes it easier to solve difficult problems. While fast, these shortcuts can sometimes lead to mistakes.

Heuristic-systematic model: Proposes two paths to persuasion, called the "heuristic" (indirect) path and the "systematic" (direct) path.

Hindsight bias: Our tendency to believe we could have predicted the outcome of a past event, but only after we already know what happened; the false belief that we "knew it all along."

Hoarding disorder: The excessive saving of items or animals leading to the inability to live or work safely.

Hostile prejudice: Negative judgments of people who do not fit prescribed group stereotypes or push boundaries of what people in their group "should" do.

Hostile-reactive aggression: An impulsive, emotion-based reaction to perceived threats.

Human factors: An academic discipline within psychology devoted to designing products or systems that best cater to human needs.

Hypothesis: A specific statement made by a researcher about the expected outcome of a study.

I³ model: An attempt to predict the likelihood of relationship violence based on aspects of the situation and couple members.

IAT: *See implicit association test.*

Implicit Association Test: An indirect way to measure attitudes or mental associations.

Implicit attitudes: Automatic, unconscious evaluations and judgments that can sometimes be out of our awareness.

Implicit expectations: Unspoken rules enforced by group norms that influence our behavior.

Impression management: Consciously engaging in behaviors we hope will lead to desired outcomes and others liking us.

Inclusion of the Other in the Self (IOS) scale: A scale used to measure psychological inclusion of others in the self-concept with a series of progressively overlapping circles.

Inclusive fitness: The probability that our genetic heritage will be preserved in the offspring of relatives.

Independent self: A self-concept largely based on internal, personal qualities (often found in Western cultures).

Independent variable: A variable that is manipulated at the beginning of an experiment to determine its effect; it's how the groups are different from each other at the start of the study.

Individualistic: Term for cultures that emphasize the self, independence, and personal success.

Infographic: A well-designed visual display of data.

Informational social influence: When we conform to group standards because we want to be "correct."

Informed consent: Participants' right to be told what a study will involve, including potential dangers, before the study starts.

Ingroup: Any group in which you're a member.

Ingroup heterogeneity: The tendency for individuals to see wide diversity within their ingroups.

Initiation effect: We value groups more if they're hard to get into and/or if we had to go through a difficult initiation.

Injunctive norm: Our perception of what we *should* do in a given situation.

Innocence Project: A group of lawyers, students, professors, and volunteers fighting for people who may have been falsely convicted of a crime.

Institutional discrimination: Unfair treatment of individuals or certain groups by society or organizations through unequal selection, opportunity, or oppression.

Institutional review boards (IRBs): Committees of people who consider the ethical implications of any study before giving the researcher approval to begin formal research.

Instrumental confession: A false confession when the person knows they are not guilty but are claiming guilt for some other reason.

Instrumental-proactive aggression: A thoughtful, reason-based decision to harm others to gain resources such as territory, money, self-esteem, or social status.

Interactionist perspective: The idea that our outcomes result from both the environment and individual interpretation of that environment.

Interactions: The combination of several influences on an outcome, such as the influence of both personality and environment on behavior.

Interdependence theory: A model that predicts relationship commitment is based on (1) how satisfied each partner is and (2) what their alternatives are.

Interdependent self: A self-concept largely based on social qualities, group memberships, and relationships with others (often found in Eastern or Asian cultures).

Internal attributions: Explanations for someone's behavior that are about them, like their personality or conscious choices.

Internal validity: The level of confidence researchers have that patterns of data are due to what is being tested, as opposed to flaws in how the experiment was designed.

Intersectionality theory: The study of how multiple identity factors (such as race, gender, and socioeconomic status) combine to form how people are perceived and treated by others.

Intimate terrorism: Relationship violence in which one couple member controls the other through severe physical violence as well as psychological, emotional, and sexual violence.

Intrinsic religiosity: Sincere belief in a faith and attempts to apply those principles to everyday behaviors.

Intuition: The ability to know something quickly and automatically; a "gut feeling" that takes little mental effort.

Investment model: A statistical model for predicting relationship commitment that includes three factors: satisfaction, alternatives, and investments.

Investments: The time, energy, and resources put into a relationship that would be lost if the relationship ended.

Irrational economic thinking: The idea that consumers' decisions are often irrational, influenced by mental shortcuts, misperceptions, and emotional biases.

Jigsaw classroom: A teaching technique in which students are divided into groups that must teach each other class material. Students must rely on each other and work cooperatively to pass tests.

Just world hypothesis: The idea that people need to believe in a fair world where people generally get what they deserve, which can lead to incorrect internal attributions for others' behaviors or outcomes.

Kernel of truth theory: The idea that stereotypes originated with truth for a small group of people at some point in time but are now exaggerated and potentially out of date.

Kinship selection: The evolutionary urge to favor those with closer genetic relatedness.

Life coach: Someone who provides support and inspiration for others who are making career and personal decisions. Controversial because often they lack professional credentials.

Locus of control: Our belief about whether we can control our own future (internal locus) or that our future is up to luck, fate, or a higher power (external locus).

Logic: The ability to use reason, think systematically, and carefully consider evidence when making a decision.

Loss aversion: The tendency for potential losses to be more psychologically influential than potential gains.

Lowball technique: A persuasion technique where people follow through with a decision even after the terms of a "deal" have changed.

Magical thinking: Beliefs or perceptions that do not hold up to reality, such as counterfactual thinking, optimistic bias, and the planning fallacy.

Maltreatment effects: When hazing elicits social dependency, which ironically promotes loyalty to the group.

Mass psychogenic illness: A form of social contagion where symptoms of an illness appear within a group but have no apparent physical cause.

Maximizer: Engaging in high cognitive load when making decisions by exhaustively examining every option

Medical adherence: Following the advice of a qualified health care provider.

Memory structures: Cognitive frameworks that help us organize and interpret social information. They include schemas, scripts, and stereotypes.

Mental accessibility: The ease with which an idea comes to mind.

Mental accounting: How we mentally think about money and its uses when making economic decisions.

Mental structures: See *memory structures*.

Mere exposure: The tendency for us to prefer familiar objects and individuals, especially as exposure to them increases.

Mere ownership: See *subjective ownership*.

Mere presence hypothesis: The idea that just having other people in the room will increase your physiological arousal and affect your task performance, even if they aren't actually watching you.

Message variables: The information provided in a persuasive message and how it is framed.

Message-learning approach: Proposes that there are four elements to the persuasion process: the source (who is doing the persuading), the message (the persuasive information), the recipient (whom they are persuading), and the context (how they are persuading).

Microaggressions: Subtle behaviors or insults that marginalize or negatively stereotype group members. They include microinsults, microassaults, and microinvalidations.

Micro-expression: An involuntary flash of emotional honesty on someone's face.

Mindfulness: A meditative focus on the present; often used in therapeutic or stress management settings.

Minimal group paradigm: An experimental method creating groups based on meaningless categories to study intergroup dynamics.

Mirror neurons: Neurons that respond in parallel when we observe others experience something (e.g., we feel hungry when watching someone eat).

Mirror self-recognition test: A mark is placed on an animal's forehead, and then the animal is placed in front of a mirror. Self-awareness is assumed if the animal touches the mark on its own forehead.

Misattribution of arousal: Our tendency to assume physiological reactions to our environment is really due to sexual attraction to another person (see *excitation transfer effect*).

Misinformation effect: Occurs when exposure to false information or leading questions about an event leads to errors in our ability to recall the original event.

Mock juries: Groups of people paid to act like a jury before a trial, to see how regular people respond to evidence and arguments.

Model of dual attitudes: Proposes that new attitudes override, rather than replace, old attitudes. Both attitudes remain, with one stronger than the other.

Modern-symbolic prejudice: Prejudice from people who think they value equality but oppose any social change that would go away from "tradition" to make equality possible.

Moral hypocrisy: When someone's behavior doesn't match their stated moral and ethical standards.

Moral integrity: When people are motivated to live up to their own stated morals and ethics.

Moral panic: The widespread belief that a particular group of people pose an urgent threat to society, based on accusations of a moral nature.

Mortality salience: When researchers make the idea of death, especially an individual's own unavoidable death, more vivid.

Narcissism: Excessive self-love based on the belief that one is better than others.

Narrative therapy: The process of writing down autobiographical events in a therapeutic setting.

Naturalistic observation: Watching and recording people's behaviors where they would have happened anyway, but for research purposes.

Nature: Influences on our thoughts and behaviors from biology or physiology, such as genetics and hormones.

Negative state relief model: The idea that seeing another person in need causes us emotional distress, and helping decreases those negative emotions.

Negativity bias: Our tendency to notice and remember negative information better than positive information.

Networking: Proactively interacting with others to exchange information, provide support, and develop career contacts.

Neural signatures: Established pathways through regions of the brain.

Nonverbal communication: The many ways we signal information to others through body language, tone of voice, and facial expressions.

Norm of reciprocity: The idea that individuals respond in kind to courtesies and concessions from others, because we like things to be "fair."

Normative social influence: When we conform to group standards to gain social acceptance and fit in.

Nurture: Influences on our thoughts and behaviors from our life circumstances, how we were raised, experiences, and our environment.

Obedience: A type of explicit social influence when we behave in response to an order from someone with power over us.

Old-fashioned prejudice: Obvious, overt prejudice that is considered inappropriate by modern social standards.

Open science: A movement to make science more transparent, cooperative, reproducible, and honest.

Operant conditioning: A process when our attitudes or behaviors are strengthened by previous rewards or weakened by previous punishments.

Opportunity cost: The "cost" of not pursuing other, alternative opportunities.

Optimal distinctiveness theory: The idea that we can simultaneously achieve the goals of being unique and of being in a group through membership in a small and elite group.

Optimal margin theory: Slight distortions of reality can improve psychological well-being.

Optimistic bias: The unrealistic expectation that things will turn out well.

Outgroup: Any group in which you're not a member.

Outgroup homogeneity: The perception that all members of a particular outgroup are identical to each other.

Pansexual: Sexual attraction to some individuals regardless of their perceived sex or gender; some people consider it an updated term for *bisexual*.

Parasitism: When an organism survives by feeding off a host.

Parental investment: The amount of time, effort, and physical resources needed for an individual to produce and raise genetic offspring.

Participant observation: A technique used during naturalistic observation where scientists covertly disguise themselves as people belonging in an environment.

Paternity uncertainty: Anxiety from men due to doubt about whether a child is genetically theirs.

Payment decoupling: Psychologically separating payment from actually getting or using a product, such as paying later via a credit card or loan.

Peace journalism: News reporting focused on ending conflict and its causes, instead of emphasizing aggression and injury.

Peer review process: How the scientific community uses experts to decide whether a journal should publish a paper, to ensure publications are of high quality.

Perceived control: Our perception of whether we're capable of successfully accomplishing a given goal or behavior.

PERMA approach: An approach to measuring subjective well-being that considers an individual's positive emotions, engagement, relationship to others, meaning and purpose, and achievement.

Person perceptions: How we perceive others, based on first impressions and (possibly biased) interpretations of their behavior later.

Personal space: The individual boundary around an individual's body that gives that person a sense of control over his or her environment.

Physical aggression: Intentionally causing harm to someone's body or property.

Physical distance: How far apart two people are from each other.

Pit bulls: Perpetrators of relationship violence who get physiologically aroused (e.g., increased heart rate) as conflict increases.

Placebo: An intervention that produces positive results not because it's effective in and of itself but because people *believe* it's effective.

Planning fallacy: The unjustified confidence that one's own project, unlike similar projects, will proceed as planned.

Pluralistic ignorance: The mistaken belief that we're the only person thinking a certain way in a group.

Pop psychology: The vague and superficial application of untested, temporarily popular, and sometimes exotic ideas to everyday life.

Positive illusions: Unrealistic optimism about the future and an inflated view of one's self-concept.

Positive psychology: The scientific study of human strengths, virtues, positive emotions, and achievements.

Posttraumatic growth: Feelings of positive psychological change and resilience as a result of trauma and adversity.

Preexperiment: A research design in which a single group of people is tested to see whether some kind of treatment has an effect.

Prejudice: Emotion-centered judgments or evaluations about people based on their perceived membership in a group.

Prejudiced personality: The idea that certain traits are linked to a general tendency to dislike all outgroups.

Preregistration: Specifying your hypothesis, procedure, and statistical plan for a study before collecting data.

Presupposition: Wording that assumes a certain condition exists.

Primary prevention: Prevention of relationship violence before it begins through education and empowerment.

Priming: Initial activation of a concept within a semantic network that allows related ideas to come more easily to mind.

Principle of parsimony: The tendency for individuals, especially scientists, to prefer the simplest answer that explains the most evidence.

Procedural artifact: A finding that results from how a researcher conducted the experiment, rather than introduction of the independent variable.

Process loss: Reduction of effort in group settings that comes from a lack of motivation.

Promiscuity: The number of casual sexual partners one has.

Propinquity effect: See *proximity effect*.

Prosocial behavior: Any action performed to help others, either on an individual level or a group level.

Prosocial moral reasoning: Our ability to analyze moral dilemmas in which two or more people's needs conflict with each other and where formal rules are absent.

Prospect theory: The idea that we make predictable mistakes when trying to weigh outcomes and probabilities.

Protestant work ethic: A personality trait valuing discipline, commitment, and hard work.

Proximity effect: The tendency for us to like people who are in close geographic proximity to ourselves, due to the mere exposure effect (see *mere exposure*).

Pure altruism: Helping others purely out of selfless concern for their well-being, with no expectation of a reward.

Quasi-experiment: A research design where outcomes are compared across different groups that occur naturally.

Random assignment: Placing participants into various conditions of a study using a chance method, to eliminate confounding variables by making the groups as equal to each other as possible.

Random sampling: A sampling technique where a researcher randomly chooses people to participate from a larger population of interest.

Rational economic thinking: The idea that consumers will act rationally according to the strict rules of supply and demand.

Reactivity: When people change their behavior because they realize they're being observed.

Realistic conflict theory: The idea that prejudice results from the justifications we create to determine that our ingroup "deserves" limited resources.

Recipient variables: The audience of a persuasive message.

Reciprocal altruism: Altruistic behavior that occurs because we expect to be "paid back" in the future.

Reference point: A psychological starting place used for comparisons when we estimate the value of something.

Rejection sensitivity: The fear of social rejection and ostracism.

Relational aggression: Harming others by damaging their social networks.

Reliability: Consistency of measurement, over time or multiple testing occasions. A study is said to be reliable if similar results are found when the study is repeated.

Religion as quest: A spiritual or philosophical approach to religion that values skepticism and exploration.

Religiosity: The degree to which one is religious and why.

Replication crisis: A recent concern in psychology that the results of some studies aren't found again when scientists try to repeat them.

Representativeness heuristic: Our tendency to make decisions based on what appears to be "typical," even when that goes against statistical likelihood.

Resilience: The capacity to positively adapt to significant adversity or stress.

Resilient personality: A personality type where people react appropriately to stress because they are able to cope positively with adversity.

Results-blind peer review: Asking experts to judge a potential study's value and quality before the data have been collected and analyzed.

Right to withdraw: The right participants have to stop being in a study at any time or to skip questions on a survey.

Risky shift: The tendency of groups to make riskier or more daring decisions after a discussion (see *group polarization*).

Romantic myths: Cultural messages regarding what romance is supposed to look like that support traditional gendered ideas and can encourage seduction into violent relationships.

Rule of law: The idea that no one is above the law; we all have to follow it, equally.

Satisfaction: Our perception of whether our romantic relationship is better or worse than average.

Satisficing: Making "good enough" decisions to avoid cognitive overload.

Scapegoat theory: The idea that prejudice results from blaming an outgroup for our frustrations (see *frustration-aggression theory*).

Schema: A mental structure or framework for organizing the world.

Schema: A cognitive and memory structure for organizing and interpreting the world.

Scientific method: A systematic way of creating knowledge by observing, forming a hypothesis, testing a hypothesis, and interpreting the results.

Script: A memory structure that shapes expectations for how particular social events will occur.

Secondary prevention: Interventions that occur after relationship violence has begun, to stop it from happening again.

Selection theory: For pets, it's the idea that people adopt pets that already look like them.

Self: Individuals' internal narrative about themselves.

Self-affirmation theory: Proposes that we try to impress ourselves to preserve our sense of worth and integrity.

Self-awareness: The understanding that we are a separate entity from other people and objects in our world.

Self-compassion: An orientation to care for yourself in times of failure or suffering.

Self-concept: The personal summary of who we are, including our positive and negative qualities, relationships to others, group memberships, and beliefs.

Self-discrepancy: When a mismatch exists between an individual's actual, ideal, and ought selves.

Self-efficacy: Confidence in your ability to complete a specific task or achieve a particular goal.

Self-esteem: Our subjective, personal evaluation of our self-concept; whether we're happy with who we are.

Self-expansion theory: The idea that we can include close relationships as a way to grow and improve our self-concept.

Self-fulfilling prophecy: Expectations that make themselves come true because they change our own behavior and how others react to us.

Self-justification: The desire to explain our actions in a way that preserves or enhances a positive view of the self.

Self-monitoring: Individuals' ability to strategically notice and adjust their own behavior in different situations.

Self-perception theory: The idea that we form our self-concept by observing our own behaviors and then infer our motivations, attitudes, values, and core traits.

Self-presentation theory: The idea that we present ourselves strategically to make an impression on others.

Self-recognition: See *self-awareness*.

Self-report scale: A survey where participants give information about themselves by responding to several items along the same theme.

Self-schema: A mental structure that summarizes and organizes our perceptions about self-relevant information.

Self-serving cognitive biases: Mental distortions that enhance our self-concept, making us seem better than we really are

Semantic network: A collection of mental concepts that are connected by common characteristics.

Similarity-attraction hypothesis: The tendency to form relationships with others who have similar attitudes, values, interests, and demographics (see *assortative mating*).

Situational couple violence: Relationship violence in which both couple members argue violently, but neither attempts to take general control and incidents are relatively minor, although still unhealthy.

Social agents: People who send messages about cultural beliefs and expectations that help transmit ideas from one generation to the next.

Social cascade: A large social change in response to the beliefs or actions of a few early visionaries.

Social cognition: The study of how we process social information using a combination of logic and intuition.

Social comparison theory: We make assessments about who we are by comparing how we think or act to those around us.

Social contagion: The spontaneous distribution of ideas, attitudes, and behaviors among larger groups of people.

Social desirability: The tendency for participants to provide dishonest responses so that others have positive impressions of them or because they don't want to admit something.

Social dominance orientation: A preference for social hierarchy and having power over outgroups.

Social entrepreneur: Someone who creates a new business or organization designed to solve a social problem.

Social exchange theory: See *interdependence theory*.

Social facilitation: When we work harder in the presence of others than we would by ourselves.

Social identity theory: Our self-concept is composed of two parts: a personal identity and a social identity, made up of our group memberships and culture.

Social influence: When our thoughts, feelings, and behaviors change because of pressure from our social world.

Social leader: A type of leader who focuses on the people involved, building teamwork, and providing emotional support.

Social learning theory: The idea that we copy what we see others do, especially when their behavior is rewarded.

Social loafing: When people working in a group reduce their individual level of effort.

Social norms: Implicit social rules about how people should behave.

Social psychology: The scientific study of how people influence each other's thoughts, feelings, and behaviors.

Social responsibility norm: The idea that we each have a duty to improve the world by helping those in need.

Social role theory: The idea that stereotypes form when we observe what people are doing, assume they are good at that, and then reinforce them to keep doing it.

Social roles: A type of implicit social influence regarding how certain people are supposed to look.

Social support: The degree to which we're surrounded by people who can assist us in times of need.

Sociology: The study of human society and social behavior at the group level.

Source variables: Who creates and gives a persuasive message.

Specificity principle: Proposes that the link between attitudes and behaviors is strong when the attitude and the behavior are measured at the same level of specificity.

Spiral of silence: When fear of rejection leads people to keep silent about a private opinion.

Sport psychology: The scientific study of how athletic performance is influenced by psychological concepts.

Stages of provocation model: Proposes that thoughts, feelings, and behaviors collectively contribute to the escalation of aggression in three stages.

Standard economic model (SEM): A model for understanding economic behavior that describes how people behave if they always make sound, rational decisions.

Stereotype: An oversimplified belief describing all members of a certain group.

Stereotype content model: The idea that two categories of judgment, warmth and competence, interact to form four different types of prejudice and emotional reaction to outgroups.

Stereotype threat: Anxiety about confirming a negative stereotype about our group, which is distracting and ironically leads to poor performance (confirming the negative stereotype).

Sternberg's triangular theory of love: Suggests all intimate relationships are made up of a combination of intimacy, passion, and commitment.

Stockholm syndrome: When hostages develop affection for their captors.

Strange situation: Refers to either the experimental method in which a mother and child are observed in a room as the mother leaves and returns or to the room itself where this occurs.

Stress: When someone's assessment of the current environment exceeds their coping abilities or resources and therefore threatens their well-being.

Subjective age: How old individuals feel, instead of their chronological age.

Subjective experiences: The way people mentally experience and perceive events in their life.

Subjective norms: Our perception of what other people are doing or what we think is "normal" or common in a given situation.

Subjective ownership: The feeling that you own something just by imagining owning it; this feeling leads to irrational behaviors such as paying too much for it.

Subjective well-being: People's perceptions and feelings about their lives and psychological health (see *PERMA approach*).

Summative assessments: Evaluations designed to know whether an intervention was successful.

Superordinate goals: Objectives that cannot be achieved without the cooperation of an outgroup; they often reduce prejudice when the goal is achieved.

Sustainable environment: A state in which the resources of the world are not overtaxed, allowing living things (including humans) to survive now and in the future.

SWOT analysis: Analysis of strengths, weaknesses, opportunities, and threats in decision making.

t-test: A statistical test that compared the mean and standard deviations of two groups, to see if they are different from each other.

Task leader: A type of leader who focuses on completing assignments, achieving goals, and meeting deadlines.

Terror management theory: The idea that when we're reminded of our own eventual death, we embrace comforting beliefs.

Tertiary prevention: Educating the larger community regarding dynamics of relationship violence to increase empathy and understanding.

Theory of informational and normative influence: The idea that there are two ways that social norms cause conformity (see *informational social influence* and *normative social influence*).

Theory of planned behavior: Proposes that behaviors are best predicted by three factors: attitudes, subjective norms, and perceived control.

Threat multiplier effect: Occurs when climate change aggravates other existing social or political problems.

Threshold: A point that must be exceeded for a certain effect or consequence to occur.

Threshold effects: Consequences that result from exceeding a certain limit (e.g., passing the Earth's capacity for pollution, overcrowding, etc.).

Tragedy of the commons: The idea that individuals, in their attempt to benefit themselves, will collectively harm society.

Transactional leader: A type of leader who uses rewards and punishments to motivate group members; these leaders help to maintain the status quo.

Transformational leader: A type of leader who uses inspiration and group cohesion to motivate members; these leaders are useful for challenging established rules or procedures.

Translocal social resilience: The social practices of vulnerable populations.

Trauma psychology: A field of psychology focused on helping people recover from any severely stressful event that impairs long-term psychological functioning.

Trial consultant: Someone who tries to influence the outcome of a trial by (1) helping to select a sympathetic jury, (2) developing trial strategies, and (3) assisting in witness preparation.

True experiment: A research design comparing two or more groups that have been created with random assignment.

Truly false consensus effect: Overestimation that others share our beliefs, even after we have objective statistical information that contradicts that belief.

Type A personality: A personality type characterized by competitiveness, impatience, and hostility. Type A people do not manage stress well and experience poor health.

Type I error: See *false positives*.

Type II error: See *false negative*.

Typologies: Categorical systems that help us organize complex but related events.

Univalenced decision: A decision based on an attitude about an attitude object that is either good or bad but not both.

Universality hypothesis: The idea that nonverbal facial expressions are universal, regardless of culture.

Upward counterfactuals: Imagined outcomes that are better than reality; they can help us learn from mistakes.

Upward social comparison: When we compare ourselves to someone who is better than us, often to improve on a particular skill.

Urban overload hypothesis: The idea that people in cities avoid social interactions like helping strangers because they are overwhelmed by the number of people they encounter each day.

Urban resilience: Healthy infrastructure responses to environmental changes and stressors in densely populated areas.

User experience specialist: A career focused on how consumers engage with and experience their everyday environments.

Verbal aggression: Using communication to cause harm.

Voluntary confession: For false confessions, these occur when the confessor either mistakenly believes they are guilty or confesses to gain some benefit, such as protecting another person or getting famous.

Waist-to-hips ratio: The ratio comparing waist circumference to hips circumference, which often plays a role in determining female body attractiveness.

Waist-to-shoulders ratio: The ratio comparing waist width to shoulder width, which often plays a role in determining male body attractiveness.

Weapons effect: The tendency for the presence of weapons to prime aggressive thoughts, feelings, and behaviors.

Weathering: The idea that chronic stressors and high-effort coping predispose some people to physical deterioration, premature aging, and chronic diseases.

Westgate Housing Study: A research project on how liking increases based on physical proximity and mere exposure to one's neighbors.

What-is-beautiful-is-good effect: When physical attractiveness creates a halo effect such that individuals who are beautiful are also perceived to have several other positive characteristics.

White privilege: The cultural benefits of being White in White-centric societies.

Yerkes-Dodson law: Predicts that moderate amounts of stress are associated with optimal performance.

Zooeyia outcomes: Ways in which pets help and harm human health.

Zoonotic diseases: Infections spread between animals and humans.

Zoonotic spillover: Transmission of a pathogen, or disease, from an animal species to humans.

AUTHOR INDEX

Abel, S. M., 69
Abrams, D., 226
Abrams, M., 264
Ackerman, J., 386
Adams, J., 365, 366
Addison, W. E., 337
Adewakun, T., 377
Adhikary, A. K., 300
Adler, A., 138
Adorjan, M., 190
Adorno, T. W., 230
Agarwala, S., 61
Aggarwal, P., 200
Aghababaei, N., 244
Agnew, C. R., 51, 318, 324
Agoramoorthy, G., 358
Agrast, M. D., 385
Agthe, M., 104, 105
Aguinis, H., 133
Ahmad, N., 368
Ahonen, L., 284
Ainsworth, M. S., 315
Ajzen, I., 129, 138, 139
Akgunduz, Y., 198
Aksu, H., 147
Alain, C., 69
Alba, L. A., 347
Albert, B., 372
Albert, R. S., 415
Aldrich, D. P., 368
Alexander, M. G., 323
Alharthi, S., 201
Alicke, M. D., 44, 132
Al-khatib, B. A., 208
Allee, W. C., 196, 284
Allen, J. J., 274
Allen, K., 356
Allport, F. H., 193
Allport, G. W., 103, 127, 129, 214, 228, 232, 235, 236, 237, 415
Allred, K. D., 401
Altemeyer, B., 231, 232
Alter, A. L., 68, 81, 220
Amato, P. R., 264
Ambady, N., 84, 85
Amir, T., 164
Amir, Y., 235
Anderson, C. A., 132, 274, 275, 276, 294, 295–296, 301
Anderson, J. R., 42, 157
Anderson, K. B., 112
Anderson, K. M., 446
Andrews, B., 397
Andrews, E., 222
Angell, J. R., 101
Anggahegari, P., 342
Antoniadou, N., 169
Arad, A., 79
Archer, J., 284, 287, 303
Arias, I., 445
Ariely, D., 340, 421
Arluke, A., 348
Armstrong, K., 232
Arnocky, S., 442
Arnold, D. L., 394

Aron, A., 50, 51
Aron, A. P., 307
Aron, E. N., 50
Aronson, E., 141, 143, 186, 238
Aronson, J., 219
Arora, M., 361
Arriaga, X. B., 441
Arthur, N., 153
Aruah, D. E., 357
Asch, S. E., 1, 5, 102, 160, 161, 162, 163, 178
Ascher, W., 383
Aspinwall, L. G., 418
Athappilly, K., 325
Attanasio, P., 383
Atwood, M., 223
Aubert, A. H., 371
Austin, J. B., 249
Avey, L., 207
Avnet, J., 295

Babad, E., 84
Bachman, J. G., 43
Bagley, C., 47
Bakan, D., 258
Baker, P., 103
Baker, S. R., 400
Baker, Z. G., 357
Bakhmutov, S., 342
Baldwin, J. A., 358, 359
Banaji, M. R., 7, 8
Bandura, A., 130, 222, 291, 292, 293, 294
Barbaranelli, C., 254
Barber, J., 365
Bargh, J. A., 67, 112, 134, 141, 169
Barlow, F. K., 129
Barlow, M. R., 347
Barnes, C. D., 286
Barnett, J., 169
Barnett, O. W., 439
Baron, R. A., 273, 301
Baron-Cohen, S., 284
Baroni, C., 277
Barr, J., 188
Barrett, D. W., 259
Barsky, A., 383
Bartels, J. M., 168
Bartholomew, K., 317
Bartholow, B. D., 296
Bartlett, F. C., 72
Bartlett, M. L., 264
Basavarajappa, 208
Basner, M., 264
Bass, B. M., 202
Bassili, J. N., 205
Basu, B. S., 201
Batool, S., 307
Batson, C. D., 2, 232, 244, 249, 250, 256, 257
Bauer, A., 368
Baumeister, R. F., 52, 55, 58, 59, 61–62, 64, 81, 190, 393
Baumrind, D., 174
Baxter, L. A., 306
Bazarova, N. N., 122
Beck, L., 357

Gumley, A., 60
Guniss, C., 377
Gunnell, J. J., 104
Gunter, B., 112
Gunz, A., 134
Guo, F., 147
Guthrie, R., 6

Haarr, M. L., 361, 370
Habashi, M. M., 249, 253, 255
Hafer, C. L., 112, 248
Haidt, J., 348, 412, 416, 418
Hair, M., 60
Hajir, B., 228
Halfmann, E., 196
Hall, A. N., 438
Halperin, C. J., 227
Halsey, L. G., 311
Hammerton, G., 282
Hancock, J. T., 99
Haney, C., 167
Hansen, C. H., 92
Hansen, D. E., 256
Hansen, R. D., 76, 92
Harari, Y. N., 244, 251
Harber, K. D., 108
Hardin, C. D., 87
Hardin, G., 362
Hardy, C. J., 198, 199
Harmon-Jones, E., 421
Harper, C., 320
Harrigan, J. A., 98
Harris, L. T., 215
Harris, M., 358
Harris, V. A., 117
Harrison, A., 255
Hart, B., 443
Hart, D., 42
Hart, P., 290
Harvey, J. H., 119
Haselton, M. G., 77
Haslam, S. A., 168, 176
Hassan, N., 265
Hassebrauck, M., 323
Hastak, M., 77
Hatfield, E., 322, 323
Hawdon, J. E., 290
Haynes, R. B., 403
Hazan, C., 315
Hearst, P. C., 189
Hecker, T., 368
Heider, F., 111, 117
Heinz, A., 296
Heinzen, T. E., 172, 295, 371, 406, 418
Helms, M. M., 333
Henchy, T., 196
Hendrick, B., 354
Hennessy, D. A., 170
Henriksen, D., 122
Henry, P. J., 226
Herek, G. M., 232
Heron, K. E., 50
Herzberg, P. Y., 368
Herzberger, S., 55
Herzog, H., 345, 346, 347, 348, 349, 350, 353, 355, 359
Hess, J. J., 297
Hewitt, P. L., 43
Higgins, C. A., 138
Higgins, E. T., 49, 50, 422
Hill, D. M., 220

Hilton, A., 227, 228
Hilton, L., 399
Hirschberger, G., 115
Hirschman, A. O., 81
Hixon, J. G., 112
Ho, H. C., 238
Hoagwood, K. E., 356
Hoch, S. J., 121
Hochschild, A., 290
Hoerger, M., 441
Hoesey, G. R., 196
Hoffman, E., 368
Hofmann, E., 193
Hogarth, R. M., 78
Hogg, M. A., 228
Holman, M. R., 227
Holmes, D. S., 121
Holtzworth-Munroe, A., 439
Hopper, E. K., 190
Hornberger, R. H., 298
Horowitz, L. M., 317
Horvit, B., 300
Hosoda, M., 104
Hou, L., 198
Hovland, C. I., 146, 228
Howe, L. E. A., 300
Howell, S., 300
Hsu, F. L. K., 325
Hsu, M. J., 358
Hua, M., 120
Huck, A., 400
Hudson, M. W., 188
Huff, D., 337
Huffman, J. C., 418
Hughes, M., 170
Hugo, V., 28
Hui, C. H., 46
Humphreys, R., 377
Humphries, T. L., 350
Hunsberger, B., 232
Huntley, M., 222
Huque, A. S., 368
Hust, S. T., 379
Hutton, D. G., 52
Hutz, C. S., 260

Iacoboni, M., 251
Ian, D., 103
Iedema, J., 122
Iker, H., 139
Ingham, A. G., 198
Insko, C. A., 147
Iqbal, R., 377
Isaacson, W., 183, 207
Isenberg, D., 204
Iyengar, S., 204
Izard, E. C., 101
Izuma, K., 193

Jaccard, J. J., 136
Jack, R. E., 98
Jackson, J. M., 198
Jackson, M., 254
Jackson, S., 440
Jacobs, R. C., 158, 159
Jacobsen, L., 106
Jacobson, N. S., 282, 439
James, W., xxii, 41, 415
Janes, L. M., 190
Janis, I. L., 204

Zeidan, F., 400
Zeiger, J. S., 121
Zhao, X., 131
Zhixue, Z., 53
Zhou, D., 343
Zhu, A. Y. F., 428
Zillmann, D., 278

Zimbardo, P. G., 146, 165, 166, 167, 168, 169, 175, 178, 179, 180, 184
Zimmer, C., 243
Zimmermann, D. H., 20
Zinkhan, G. M., 131
Zinsser, W., xxii
Zois, D. S., 273
Zuk, M., 347

SUBJECT INDEX

AAT. *See* Animal-assisted therapy (AAT)
Academic disciplines, 4–5, 372
Academic performance
    optimistic bias, 80
    self-esteem and, 62–64
Action research, 5
Actor-observer bias, 118
"Actual" self, 49
Adaptive categorization, 214–215
Advertisement, 103–104
    sexuality in, 131
Affectionate breastfeeding, 359
Affective forecasting, 441–442
Ageism, 396
Agency, 258
Age, subjective, 56
Aggression, 5, 273
    alcohol consumption and, 283, 296
    ancient, 276–277
    anonymity and, 169–170
    behavioral, 274
    biological influences on, 281–284
    Bobo doll studies, 291–293, 301
    catharsis, 298–301
    content, 274
    cultural influences on, 285–290
    cultures of honor, 285–287
    cultures of peace, 299–300
    cyberbullying, 273, 285
    decline of, 279–280
    definition, 273
    environmental cues, 295–297
    escalation of, 278
    forms of, 274
    frustration-aggression theory, 228
    GAM, 276, 295–296
    gender difference, 284, 287–288
    heart rates and, 282–283 (box)
    heat and, 297–298
    homicide, 279 (figure)
    hostile-reactive, 274
    instrumental-proactive, 274–275
    interactions and, 284
    MAD, 300–301
    management, 298–302
    media violence, 291–292, 293–295, 301
    microaggressions, 275–276
    motivations, 274–275
    in movies, 295 (box)
    persistence of, 276–278
    physical, 274
    relational, 274
    responses to threat, 281
    revenge and, 299
    role models, 291–293
    situational influences on, 290–297
    sports, 288–290
    stages of provocation, 278–279
    testosterone and, 283–284
    typologies, 273–276
    verbal, 274
    violent video games, 294
    war hysteria, 290
    weapons and, 278, 296
    See also Relationship violence

Agitation-related emotions, 50
Agreeableness, 200, 253
AIBO, 356
Alcohol
    and aggression, 283, 296
    disinhibition hypothesis, 283
Algorithm, 85
Alternatives, relationship, 318
Altruism
    egoistic, 245
    empathy-altruism hypothesis, 250–251
    pure, 244
    reciprocal, 247
    sexually attractive, 246
    and social responsibility norm, 248–249
Ambivalent prejudice, 226–227
American Psychological Association (APA), 34
Amicus brief, 379–380
Analysis of variance (ANOVA), 31
Anchoring and adjustment heuristic, 85
Animal(s)
    cultural differences in, 358–359
    moral dilemma, 348–350
    See also Pet(s)
Animal-assisted therapy (AAT), 355–356
Anonymity, 169
    aggression and, 169–170
    intimacy and, 170–171
ANOVA. *See* Analysis of variance (ANOVA)
Anthropology, 4
Anthropomorphism, 347
Anthrozoology, 345
Anxious/ambivalent attachment, 315
APA. *See* American Psychological Association (APA)
Applied game designer, 373
Applied science, 19
Appraisal support, 184 (table)
Archival data, 21
Arranged marriage, 325
Asch, Solomon, 5, 160
    line judgment experiments, 160–163
Assortative mating, 130, 305
Attachment styles, 315–316
Attachment theory, 313–317, 356–357
Attitudes
    ABCs of, 128
    bogus pipeline, 133
    cognitive dissonance and, 140–143
    definition, 127
    direct measurement approach, 133
    dual, 128
    explicit, 128
    IAT, 133–134
    implicit, 128
    impression management, 138
    LaPiere study, 135–136
    measurement, 132–140
    from nature, 130
    from nurture, 130–132
    object, 128
    persuasion and, 144–149
    self-justification and, 140
    self-perception theory, 136–138
    specificity principle, 136
    strength, 147

2E

SOCIAL PSYCHOLOGY

This award-winning text invites students to discover social psychology's relevance to their lives. Authors Thomas Heinzen and Wind Goodfriend capture student interest by weaving stories drawn from their own personal experiences with compelling examples from everyday life, all carefully placed in historical context. Social psychology is presented as an evolving, science-driven conversation; chapters build on core questions central to scientific inquiry, while a methods-in-context approach cultivates psychological literacy. The **Second Edition** has been thoroughly updated with new pop culture examples, additional diversity coverage, more recent critiques of the Zimbardo and Milgram studies, and more than one hundred new citations from the latest research.

SAGE www.sagepublishing.com
Los Angeles | London | New Delhi | Singapore | Washington DC | Melbourne

FSC
www.fsc.org
MIX
Paper from responsible sources
FSC® C011825

Cover Image: © Zoonar GmbH / Alamy

90000>

9 781071 834961